BEYOND THE MYTHS OF CULTURE

Essays in Cultural Materialism

This is a volume in

STUDIES IN ANTHROPOLOGY

Under the consulting editorship of
E. A. Hammel, University of California, Berkeley

A complete list of titles appears at the end of this volume.

BEYOND THE MYTHS OF CULTURE

Essays in Cultural Materialism

Edited by

ERIC B. ROSS

Department of Anthropology
University of Michigan
Ann Arbor, Michigan

ACADEMIC PRESS
A Subsidiary of Harcourt Brace Jovanovich, Publishers
New York London Toronto Sydney San Francisco

Permission has been granted to reprint material from the following:
Tribesmen, by Marshall D. Sahlins, copyright 1968, Prentice-Hall, Englewood Cliffs, N. J.; *The Jivaro*, by Michael J. Harner, copyright 1972, Doubleday, New York; *Highland Peoples of New Guinea*, by Paula Brown, copyright 1978, Cambridge University Press, New York; *Sociology as Social Criticism,* by T. B. Bottomore, copyright 1975, Pantheon, New York; *Culture*, by A .L. Kroeber and Clyde Kluckohn, Papers of the Peabody Museum of Ethnology, Vol. 47, copyright 1952 by the President and Fellows of Harvard College; *Social Anthropology*, by D. F. Pocock, copyright 1961, Sheed and Ward, London; *The End of the Old Order in Europe*, by Jerome Blum, copyright 1978, Princeton University Press, Princeton, N. J.; "A theory of the origin of the state," by R. L. Carneiro, *Science,* Vol. 169, pp. 733–738, 21 August 1970, copyright 1970 by the American Association for the Advancement of Science; *The Kapauku,Papuans of West New Guinea,* by Leopold Pospisil, copyright 1963, Holt, Rinehart & Winston, New York; "Yanomamo social organization and warfare," in *War: The Anthropology of Armed Conflict and Aggression,*edited by Morton Fried, Marvin Harris, and Robert Murphy, copyright 1967 by The American Museum of Natural History, 1968, by Doubleday, New York; *Studying the Yanomamo,* by Napoleon A. Chagnon, copyright 1974, Holt, Rinehart & Winston, New York; "Structuralism and Ecology," Claude Levi-Strauss, copyright 1972, *Barnard Alumnae,* Spring 1972;*Hogmeat and Hoecake: Food Supply in the Old South, 1840–1860*, by Sam Bowers Hilliard, copyright 1972, Southern Illinois University Press, Carbondale, Illinois; *Stone Age Economics,* by Marshall Sahlins, copyright 1972, Aldine, New York; *The Theory of Capitalist Development,* by Paul M. Sweezy, copyright 1942 and 1970, Monthly Review Press, New York; *The Notion of Tribe*, by Morton H. Fried, copyright 1975, Benjamin/Cummings, Menlo Park, California; *Peoples of Africa,* edited by James L. Gibbs, Jr., copyright 1965,Holt, Rinehart & Winston, New York; *Geological Highway Map of Texas,* by Philip Oetking, copyright 1958, Dallas Geological Society.

ACADEMIC PRESS, INC.
111 Fifth Avenue, New York, New York 10003

United Kingdom Edition published by
ACADEMIC PRESS, INC. (LONDON) LTD.
24/28 Oval Road, London NW1 7DX

Library of Congress Cataloging in Publication Data
Main entry under title:

Beyond the myths of culture.

(Studies in anthropology)
Includes bibliographies and index.
1. Ethnology––Addresses, essays, lectures.
2. Culture––Addresses, essays, lectures. 3.
Economic anthropology––Addresses, essays, lectures.
4. Communism and anthropology––Addresses, essays, lectures. I. Ross, Eric B. II. Title: Cultural materialism.
GN357.B48 306 79–6772
ISBN 0–12–598180–5

PRINTED IN THE UNITED STATES OF AMERICA

80 81 82 83 9 8 7 6 5 4 3 2 1

For Sylvia and Julian

Contents

List of Contributors

Numbers in parentheses indicate the pages on which the authors' contributions begin.

WILLIAM S. ABRUZZI (3), Department of Anthropology, State University of New York at Binghamton, Binghamton, New York 13901

JOHN W. COLE (61), Department of Anthropology, University of Massachusetts, Amherst, Massachusetts 01002

FREDERICK C. GAMST (359), Office of Graduate Studies, University of Massachusetts, Boston, Boston, Massachusetts 02125

MARVIN HARRIS (391), Department of Anthropology, University of Florida, Gainesville, Florida 32601

CONRAD PHILLIP KOTTAK (229), Department of Anthropology, University of Michigan, Ann Arbor, Michigan 48104

ANTHONY LEEDS (103), Department of Anthropology, Boston University, Boston, Massachusetts 02215

JOAN P. MENCHER (261), Department of Anthropology, Lehman College and Graduate Center, City University of New York, Bronx, New York 10468

WILLIAM P. MITCHELL (139), Department of Anthropology, Monmouth College, West Long Branch, New Jersey 07740

GERALD F. MURRAY (295), Department of Anthropology, University of Massachusetts, Boston, Massachusetts 02125; and Center for Population Studies, Harvard University, Cambridge, Massachusetts 02138

ROBERT PAYNTER (61), Department of Anthropology, Queens College, Flushing, New York 11367

BARBARA J. PRICE (155), New York, New York

ERIC B. ROSS (181), Department of Anthropology, University of Michigan, Ann Arbor, Michigan 48104

JANE BENNETT ROSS (33), Department of Anthropology, Columbia University, New York, New York 10027

JANE SCHNEIDER (323), Program in Anthropology, Graduate Center, City University of New York, New York, New York 10036

Preface

This book appears at a time when anthropology is retreating from the promise of recent advances in the objective, comparative analysis of cultural similarities and differences which had begun to place the study of human behavior and thought within the province of a general evolutionary paradigm. It comes at a time when there is evidence of a full-fledged revival of the relativistic and idealist sociology of Durkheim and Parsons in which, disarticulated from their material and historical base, "the principal social phenomena, religion, morality, law, economics, and aesthetics, are nothing more than systems of values and hence of ideals"[1] and these ideals—whether denominated as ideals or symbols—become the focus of study, the text or "culture" which supplants behavior as a higher order of human reality. As this occurs, however, an anthropology constructed upon such a fundamentally religious and Platonic epistemology becomes less and less capable of addressing concrete problems of human life except through a metaphysical prism through which the concrete and variable character of human behavior becomes abstract and idealized and invested with a transcendent and arbitrary appearance.

The work assembled here, though it represents a minority voice within anthropology, constitutes a timely dissent with respect to these tendencies, as it questions the idealist construction of culture which seems to place the study of human behavior beyond nature, science, and history. In a series of empirically oriented studies, the contributors demonstrate the methods and theoretical strategy of a school of anthropology which has its intellectual roots in the work of Darwin and Marx and Engels: cultural materialism, as it has come to be called. In their totality, these contributions argue for the merit—the explanatory potential—of developing anthropological analysis within a materialist and evolutionary framework which can explain cultural phenomena in terms other than the tautological and typological ones of culture itself. Through discussions that range from tribal to Euro–American capitalist societies, addressing issues as infamous as

[1]E. Durkheim, *Sociology and Philosophy,* New York: Free Press, 1974.

voodoo and as universal yet puzzling as food preferences, these chapters offer an opportunity for the reader to examine in specific terms a manner of anthropological research that locates the forces that shape human institutions, behaviors, and thoughts, not in enigmatic cells of the human mind or in the transcendent character of culture, but in the real world; and which contends, and demonstrates, that these forces are real, recurrent, and knowable through systematic, empirical, and historical research.

Such research will disaffect those who find in the concept of culture the refuge from objectivity and determinism that past centuries once found in religion. But it is hoped that most readers will find in this volume something of the excitement enjoyed by the authors in unraveling some mysteries of human experience, and that, understanding that none of these chapters pretends to be a total and finished answer to any specific problem, they will come to recognize that it is fully within their own power to explore the remaining questions—and new ones that have been raised—in a similiar vein.

For readers from outside anthropology, this volume is intended to demonstrate an anthropological perspective with which they probably have had little familiarity and which should offer a productive contrast with the kind of anthropology they are likely to have read. To students of the discipline, it was—as should be evident—formulated as a challenge to what they themselves are most apt to encounter in contemporary anthropology: analytical tendencies which, while they have always characterized the field, now are very close to defining cultural phenomena as preeminently ideological or mental, establishing the concept of culture as one which dissociates the study of behavior from any causal processes extrinsic to the human mind and which increasingly tends to isolate cultural anthropologists from productive research in the subdisciplines of archaeology and biological anthropology. Thus, the notion of culture, instead of actually explaining human cross-cultural differences and similarities, which is basically an evolutionary problem, now serves principally to suggest that in the arbitrariness of cultural diversity lies evidence of the ultimate transcendent meaning of human life—a fundamentally religious perspective.

The chapters in this volume have in mind, rather, to explain cultural phenomena in terms of their place and their history in the material circumstances of specific people, and in the productive and reproductive demands of their environment. By focusing on such factors—on the actual life process of real people—the authors seek to clarify certain specific questions of the functions and origins of cultural patterns where previous work has denied adequate attention to the material premises of human existence and often confused the process of anthropological explanation with that of recording native ideology as culture. Implicit in these discussions is an effort both to disambiguate the myths that constitute an essential part of each society's mode of self-explanation and to advance anthropology beyond certain myths that are inherent in the notion of culture itself.

Acknowledgments

As the outgrowth of anthropological and personal convictions of the editor, this book necessarily embodies, if it does not repay, certain intellectual and emotional debts to a few very special individuals: Sylvia and Julian Ross, who first carried me beyond myth; Barrows Dunham, whose wonderful and sadly neglected book, *Man against Myth,* and whose generous gestures of friendship, confirmed my course; Marvin Harris, whose friendship, counsel, and writings have consistently inspired a sense of the importance and potential of anthropology; and Karen Elizabeth Dennis, colleague, comrade, and critic, who is also an important part of this book, in spirit and substance.

I would also especially like to thank the contributors to this book, who always made me feel that it was a necessary and important project. I hope it proves one of which they will always be proud to have been a part.

Empirical observation must in each separate instance bring out empirically, and without any mystification and speculation, the connection of the social and political structure with production. The social structure and the State are continually evolving out of the life-process of definite individuals, but of individuals, not as they may appear in their own or other people's imagination, but as they really *are; i.e., as they operate, produce materially, and hence as they work under definite material limits, presuppositions and conditions independent of their will. . . .*

In direct contrast to [*that*] *philosophy which descends from heaven to earth, here we ascend from earth to heaven. That is to say, we do not set out from what men say, imagine, conceive, nor from men as narrated, thought of, imagined, conceived, in order to arrive at men in the flesh. We set out from real, active men and on the basis of their real life-process we demonstrate the development of the ideological reflexes and echoes of this life-process. The phantoms formed in the human brain are also necessarily sublimates of their material life-process, which is empirically verifiable and bound to material premises.* [*Karl Marx and Frederick Engels,* The German Ideology, *New York: International Publishers, 1970.*]

Introduction

I

It is beyond the scope of these brief introductory remarks to provide a satisfactory review of the development of the idealist orientation of anthropology. The chapter by Harris, which aptly concludes this volume, briefly explores several important aspects of this issue and adds to his previous commentaries of the general subject (Harris 1968, 1980). Various other chapters shed light somewhat more indirectly upon these matters. But, for the moment, it is more appropriate to consider more closely what an idealist definition of culture has pushed beyond the purview of anthropology, at least for those who accept such a definition.

The notion of culture has been consistently employed to bear the burden of anthropology's resistance to the application of an evolutionary, materialist paradigm to questions of the origins and functions of human cultural patterns, both behavioral and mental. It has come to represent a metaphysical boundary which, having appeared somewhere in the hominid past, marks the beginning of being human, after which the pattern of human life has been regarded as increasingly dissociated from material conditions and extrinsic pressures, governed and progressively differentiated by an internal dynamic which Sahlins (1976) for one has called a "thermodynamics of the poetic." Culture, in such a view, defines humans as transcendent above mundane imperatives to adapt to their environments. Rather, as cultural beings, it is argued, humans defy such pressures and live according to the meanings which they impose upon the world through their capacity to symbolize. Since, as proponents of this view maintain, "the symbolic is arbitrary by definition" (Sahlins 1976:207), any anthropological analysis predicated upon such assumptions must assert that differences and similarities in the content of patterns of behavior or thought among different human groups are largely fortuitous and essentially inexplicable in terms of anything objectively knowable. Thus, it is, in fact, becoming increasingly characteristic of anthropology that it suggests that the occurrence of specific cultural patterns is "in no way justifiable by biological, ecological, or economic advantage" (Sahlins 1976:171), that one must be satisfied with the assertion that each "culture" is, in the end, objectively enigmatic but intrinsically meaningful, and that cross-cultural and even intracultural variation serve as evidence of the capacity of the human mind to assert godlike independence over material reality.

Because these themes are so prevalent, they are ones which most of the authors in this volume address. In particular, the chapters by Abruzzi, Price, Mitchell, E. Ross, Mencher, Murray, Schneider, and Gamst explore different sets of material factors—technoeconomic, political economic, demographic—that underlie the emergence both of certain behavioral patterns and of their ideological associations. This is of especial importance for several reasons: first, because these essays should therefore disabuse many readers of the refractory misapprehension that cultural materialists are uninterested in mental phenomena because of their commitment to the strategic priority of material conditions; second, because these papers suggest that even ideological patterns, so often taken as metaphysical in origin, are themselves best explained in terms of adaptational processes examined over historical time (most arguments about the arbitrariness of cultural meaning depend upon a definition of culture which discourages just such a historical approach); third, because, in constructing their explanations, these chapters demonstrate the potential of a culture-free analysis for illuminating the historical and empirical details, for accounting for the variation and process, that are normally obscured beneath the idealized, reified construct of culture, yet are essential for any serious understanding of cultural change.

The idealist concept of culture itself offers little hope of comprehending how cultural systems, as ideological domains, actually evolve. They seem merely to consist of ideas or symbols which somehow have been transformed out of antecedent ideological constructs no less removed from material reality. Cultural evolution is reduced to a metaphysical sequence of combinations of ideas within the minds of succeeding human generations. As Levi-Strauss has written:

> Behind every ideological construct, previous constructs stand out, and they echo each other back in time, not indefinitely but at least back to the fictive stage when, hundreds of thousands [of] years ago and maybe more an incipient mankind[1] thought out and expressed its first ideology [1972:7].

Beyond this, proponents of such an idealist anthropology put forth no coherent explanation of what causes the ideological content of specific populations to transform through time or to differentiate from that of other groups, an important issue if one is going to attribute significant differences in behavior to ideological structures. Yet, despite this, it is commonly maintained in anthropology today that culture—as ideology—outweighs the influence of material conditions to which

[1]It is characteristic of such writing that it continues to speak of *men* and *mankind*. Materialists (since Marx) have made a more deliberate effort in their work to employ language sensitive to human reality, in this instance the existence of two sexes, one of which commonly pretends to speak for both.

humans must adapt, that it represents an intrinsic momentum that shapes behavior in ways that are inexplicable, even irrational, in terms of immediate or recent material circumstances. In this manner, the concept of culture has acquired the deterministic character of the racial theories it once was developed to refute, while similarly diverting serious attention from the material premises upon which daily human experience is constructed. The chapters in this volume all respond in a direct and critical fashion to such thinking. They do so most forcefully by systematic discussion of the historical and ecological contexts in which specific behavioral patterns emerge, in order to demonstrate the degree to which such behavior can be explicated in terms of the full effect of contemporary conditions without the necessity of evoking the force of "culture" even as a provisional explanation.

In this same vein, and most important, most of the chapters address considerable attention to the development of ideology and ideologically infused phenomena. Whether discussing the Aztec origin myth (Price), American meat preferences (E. Ross), caste in India (Mencher), or the difference between "cultural" and "social" anthropology (Harris), they all develop the position that Swanson expressed in his cross-cultural study of the origins of types of beliefs in gods: "Our knowledge about beliefs shows that they do not persist by themselves. An idea or attitude or belief must correspond to current experience with the environment if it is to continue across the generations [1964:5]." It is the character of such experience—and its variation across space and through time—upon which these chapters focus.

Thus, the theoretical perspective of these papers is *processual,* with the authors examining human cultural variability to learn how specific populations respond to temporal and/or spatial differences in demands placed upon productive and reproductive success. This is in marked contrast to the typological perspective that the concept of culture represents, which partitions the world into discrete, relatively autonomous symbolic systems which, as idealized mental configurations, are effectively immunized against processual analysis. This dominant view of cultures as ideologically composed entities resonates with the Platonic vision of nineteenth-century taxonomists who, as Gould observes, envisioned "each species [as] an idea in the mind of God [1978:3]," and it encapsulates the anti-evolutionary bias at the heart of anthropological theory. It removes anthropology even further from the complex, changing world in which human beings move, committing it to a more harmonious and static definition of cultural reality where variability and process no longer seem to intrude on human thought.

The mentalist view of culture has the effect of reducing actual human experience to idealizations and symbolic representations and creating the image of a culture as a moral community, in Durkheim's sense, of shared norms and values (cf. Dolgin, Kemnitzer, and Schneider 1977:3). It thus asserts that, *on a metaphysical level* if not in the *actual* organization of human relations, culture is egalitarian; that worldly hierarchies of power and privilege are less important than moral equality in the kingdom of the mind. Clearly, this bias toward idealized representations and against actual empiricohistorical conditions helps us little to understand how humans actually live and how the patterns of their lives have evolved through time, for it erodes the scientific detachment that is needed to distinguish ideological "truths" from objective ones. Without such distinctions the ethnographic record threatens to become a series of "just-so" stories, as the chapters by Price and Mitchell in particular illustrate.

Yet, it is one of the more conspicuous tendencies today in anthropology to regard a culture not in terms of actual behavior in real historical and material situations, objectively accounted, but "as texts, as imaginative works built out of social materials" (Geertz 1973). It is a perspective through which "a culture" is estranged from its own history and environment and transformed into a wholly cognitive phenomenon that is made to seem prior to the material world rather than something heuristically abstracted from it. In fact, "culture" becomes an internal code for behavior; in an analogy with genetic structure, it is represented as "a template or blueprint for the organization of social and psychological processes" (Geertz 1973:216); but little attention is paid to where such "programs" themselves originate, except for vague allusions to universal mental structures encoded mysteriously in the human brain, that are just a cryptoscientific variation on Platonic idealism. The reader will find several such "structuralist" models specifically and critically reviewed in this book, in the chapters by J. Ross, E. Ross, and Gamst. But, most of the other essays contribute in a general way to a criticism of the mentalist conception of culture by discussing ideology in an evolutionary and ecological framework and demonstrating the processual character of cultural ideas and their relationship to the material conditions out of which they are constructed.

In its persistent dissociation of culture from extrinsic conditions, anthropology generally resists such efforts to penetrate the ideological veneer of society and history, to demonstrate that values and ideas do not always and necessarily form a coherent and harmonious system or are not an adequate representation of actual social life, but rather a functioning part of it; that ideological structures are not above or prior to behavior but formed out of and along with it and, as such, employed strategically. As the chapters by Price, Mitchell, and Mencher suggest, this is especially true in the case of dominant or ruling groups in whose interest it is to obfuscate objective and historical conditions. This, of course, suggests that, rather than elaborating the predominating ideology into a higher-order myth called culture, anthropology ought to examine more attentively the divergence and the functional relationship between such ideology and actual behavior.

The point of pressing beyond the ideological view of culture is well illustrated by the conclusions which the historians Lemon and Nash draw from their study of changes in the distribution of wealth in Chester County, Pennsylvania, through the eighteenth century:

> To be sure, Pennsylvania functioned within a more democratic constitutional [i.e., ideological] framework after 1776 and political participation increased, but neither of these developments . . . stemmed from or led toward a more even distribution of the community's resources. Instead, the political and economic processes were moving in opposite directions. The rhetoric of the revolutionary era may have been strongly egalitarian in tone . . . [but,] the experience of more than a century in Chester County seems

> to suggest that the comparatively open society, operating in a stable pre-industrial economic environment, encumbered with few governmental restraints and subscribing to a liberal ideology . . . led to increasing social stratification, at least measured by the distribution of wealth [1970:187].

Such social and economic differentiation, however, is almost invariably at odds with a dominant ideology which usually bespeaks the justice of the social order; and it is inevitably that ideology which predominates in the idealist construction of culture with its emphasis upon shared values. Thus, the structuralist, Louis Dumont, has written on the subject of social inequality: "A general theory of 'inequality,' if it is deemed necessary, must be centered upon those societies which give it a meaning and not upon those which, while presenting certain forms of it, have chosen to disavow it [1977:86]." The telling phrase, "have chosen to disavow it," conveys the relative helplessness of such a theoretical viewpoint to otherwise account for how ideology is structured. But, the most important point here is that it is not the empirically demonstrable inequalities but the consciousness which denies them that constitutes for Dumont the primary *cultural* reality. It is in this manner repeatedly that the idealist notion of culture enhances social myths—always when it is most necessary to understand their origins and functions and the objective conditions which they obscure—and thus places anthropology in the role of annointing the status quo, by employing the concept of culture so as to diminish the significance of dissent, conflict, and actual history. As the reader will find, the essays here take the opposite approach and thus represent an anthropological framework which is epistemologically congruent with social criticism.

II

This is especially important since the tendency of cultural analysis to inhibit attention to actual behavior in favor of moral and symbolic coherence generally renders anthropology incapable of a critical perspective on the character of human relations in any given society. Aztec ritual sacrifice becomes a "communion" in which victims and ruling class share, and clitoridectomies are described not in terms of painful mutilation which helps to maintain male sexual and economic control over women, but as an expression of cultural values and tradition (cf. Hosken 1976:3). Similarly, by Dumont's criteria, the United States is an egalitarian culture despite the concentration of wealth in a few banks and a relatively few families. Once social realities have been compressed into such *cultural* terms, however, it lends credence to the anthropological position of cultural relativism as an expression of the inherent meaningfulness of every separate culture, even if such "meaningfulness" is only an artifact of an analytical perspective.

Thus, Hoebel and Weaver have recently written: "The concept of cultural relativity states that standards of right and wrong (values) and of usage and effectiveness (adaptive value) are relative to the given culture of which they are a part. In its most extreme form, cultural relativism holds that every custom is valid in terms of its own cultural setting. In practical terms, it means that anthropologists strive to suspend judgments . . . [1979:287].'' Such a viewpoint, however, rests largely upon the assumption that cultures are separate, discrete, homogeneous entities manifesting a kind of preternatural identity, analogous, as Leeds observes, to the concept of *Volk*. In historical perspective, however, few if any such cultural systems actually exist. Just as Weltfish has observed that the ''culture'' of North American Plains Indians was ''a function of the origin, growth and emergence of the American nation as it grew and expanded from the Atlantic westward [1971:203],'' so the chapters by E. Ross, Leeds, Schneider, Kottak, J. Ross, Abruzzi, and Paynter and Cole show how local cultural arrangements have evolved in response to extrinsic forces and events and thus belie the validity of the idealist notion of a world divided into separate, intrinsically determined cultures and world views.

Thus, cultural relativism rests upon a particular idealist metaphysic which does not stand up against a historical inquiry which dispels the view that a culture is merely a configuration of eternal and socially neutral sentiments and values. Only by having reduced culture to that ideological status has it been possible to maintain that ''all cultural systems [are] equally valid as integrated wholes.'' But, through materialist analysis, it becomes evident that what integration exists among a given population is more than likely to emerge, not from moral consensus, but from material force. It is our responsibility to inquire diligently into how such force is exercised.

But, the tradition of cultural relativism imposes a climate of moral neutrality. It does so not simply for the reasons noted above, but also because it does not, paradoxically, cease at the level of culture, but further fragments reality down to the level of the individual mind where any general criteria of reality vanish altogether. In this ultimate expression of a relativistic, cultural reality, the very notion of objectivity is evoked as the paramount threat to individual freedom, since that freedom is viewed as a quality, not of one's relation to extrinsic conditions, but of the mind. Scientific and objective analysis which suggests that material conditions may determine the pattern of human lives and thoughts becomes, in this view, the source of oppression itself. It is a classic example of blaming the bearer of bad news.

This particular attitude toward objective reality, whether it characterizes anthropology or society in general, is not fortuitous, but develops time and again in response to societal crisis, as it becomes increasingly comfortable to think in a less political mode and to dissociate oneself from the wide, momentous world. Such reactions seem invariably to breed the development of psychologistic and idealist theories. Thus, the character of Freudian theory developed against the background of the collapse of the Hapsburg Empire. As Carl Schorske remarks:

> In response to his professional and political frustrations, Freud retreated into social and intellectual withdrawal. . . . The more Freud's life was mired, however, the more winged his ideas became. . . . The brilliant, lonely, painful discovery of psychoanalysis . . . was a counterpolitical triumph of the first magnitude . . . [which] gave his fellow liberals an a-historical theory of man and society that could make bearable a political world spun out of orbit and beyond control [1980:203].

In a similar manner, Freud's contemporary, the philosopher Ludwig Wittgenstein, developed in his most famous work, the *Tractatus,* an approach to ethics that was "ahistorical . . . [and] also entirely apolitical" (Janik and Toulmin 1973:243). (This was in spite of the fact that there was nothing ahistorical in the development of Wittgenstein's own philosophy, as the son of a Viennese steel magnate.)

But, we are talking about a vision of the world that, by reducing reality to a subjective dimension, obviates the need to discuss such strategic realtionships between the self and political economy; it nurtures, rather, a particularly idiosyncratic and antisocial view that sees contemporary events as an inevitable expression of human nature and reduces the hope of salvation to a personal exercise in transcendent will that has little need of a historical empirical sociology.

It rejects, or escapes from, objectivity, history, and nature in favor of a poetic truth which transcends time and place and seems to "represent the testimony of a deeper and more privileged insight—a truth so lofty that, if nature does not conform to it, why then, so much the worse for nature [Medawar 1972:26]."

What may represent an acceptable alternative for the occasional guru is something else for anthropology. For it to detach itself in this fashion from the context of human experience, to maintain that the truth and falsity of explanation is not an issue (cf. Rossi 1974:93), to encourage the development of a theory of culture that does not ultimately rest upon impersonal and operationalizable criteria of verifiability, is not an idiosyncratic act of disengagement, but a trend that is portentously political in its social consequences.

Yet, a mentalist anthropology does, indeed, encourage an "artistic" attitude toward truth, a sense that the objects of the world are less real than the constructs of one's imagination, that the empirical legitimacy of one's statements about the nature of the world and society is not of paramount importance. Thus, Levi-Strauss has declared: "Only those who practice structuralism know by intimate experience the impression of fullness given by its practice, a practice by which mind experiences a true communication with the body [quoted in Rossi 1974:26]." The implication of this statement, that theories are not good to explain, but good to *think,* is the product of a self-indulgent intellect. It characterizes an anthropology that threatens to become, not a source of searching *social* criticism, but a form of *personal* therapy—the reason, perhaps, that these words by Levi-Strauss could probably just as well have been attributed to Werner Erhart. And, in turning its back on social realities, it inevitably expresses antagonism toward any form of objective analysis which does not; which seems to be "arrogating to itself the right of determining the correct segmentation of empirical reality" (Sahlins 1976:220); which suggests that the human condition, to be understood, must be recognized as ultimately mundane, that, as Orwell once observed, "in order that Hitler may march the goosestep, that the Pope may denounce Bolshevism, that the cricket crowds may assemble at Lord's, that the Nancy poets may scratch one another's backs, coal has got to be forthcoming [1937:30]."

The idea, rather, has been to dissociate the "culture" from the coal, individual thought from the constraints and imperatives of material conditions, "truth" from objective reality. Thus, the sociologist, Theodore Roszak, in his book *The Making of a Counter Culture,* argues that the quest for human freedom depends upon a rejection of what he terms "objective consciousness," knowledge based upon "an accumulation of verifiable propositions," and that we must assume instead "the beauty of the fully illuminated personality as our standard of truth . . . of ultimate meaningfulness [1969:237]."

The effect of the presumption that all *ideas* are created equal (even if *social* life is unjust) is to obviate any need for social or political action. If people could only be left to think in peace; if only society could be "placed outside and above history" (Levi-Strauss, quoted in Sontag 1970:196).

That, it often seems, is what anthropology would like when it stresses ideas over behavior, generalities over specifics, emphasizing, as Scholte (1970) says, "the syntax rather than the content of culture," foregoing commentary of a direct and specific kind in order to seek "the permanent structure of the human spirit," an ambition so diffuse that it threatens never to generate statements that have any logical immediacy. Thus, Scholte admits: "If structural investigation is to understand and explicate the implicit workings of [the] unconscious and universal brain . . . it can no longer hope to speak explicitly about the human condition or man's cultural products [1970:149]." Susan Sontag is more blunt: Such an anthropology becomes "a technique of political disengagement " (1970:189).

Objective analysis, on the other hand, provides a basis for informed change, for the development of critical judgment, for engagement of the world rather than retreat, alienation, and solipsism. It is not, as some have hinted, the means through which human life or the human intellect is imprisoned. On the contrary, it is a guardian against the imperialism of personal revelation, a defense against charismatic truths that stake out their claims through demagoguery and coercion, and a fortification against "illuminated personalities" that elevate ideology to the status of supreme reality and rise to positions of brutal power. Thus, Bronowski has truly written:

> It is said that science will dehumanise people and turn them into numbers. That is false, tragically false. Look for yourself . . . [at] the concentration camp and crematorium at Auschwitz. This is where people were turned into numbers. . . . And that was not done by gas. It was done by arrogance. It was done by dogma. It was done by ignorance. When people believe that they have absolute knowledge, with no test in reality, this is how they behave [1973:186].

III

Anthropology is not immune to the intellectual trends shaped by the political and economic condition of its society; many of the themes by which it is now characterized echo trends in other troubled times and must remind us of the responsibilities, perils, and temptations of intellectuals who can always find their own special reasons for creating privately illumined landscapes when political skies darken. Thus, in the 1920s, as Orwell has remarked, writers' eyes were "directed to Rome, to Byzantium, to Montparnasse, to Mexico, to the Etruscans, to the Subconscious . . . to everywhere except the places where things [were] actually happening [1961:136]." Sociological theory experienced a similar contraction, that had an impact on anthropology for decades to follow. As T. B. Bottomore has written:

> During the decade of the Depression and the New Deal, of the revival of intellectual radicalism and left-wing social movements, of the Spanish Civil War and the approaching conflict with the Fascist states, Talcott Parsons . . . turned resolutely aside from any concern with the contemporary economic and political crisis in order to expound the ideas of some earlier European thinkers, and to distill from them a very general and abstract scheme of sociological thought [1974:29].

Such withdrawal, even in the name of culture, has rendered us more vulnerable to the real sources of human immiseration, and prey to political developments that thrive both on the moral neutrality that adheres to relativistic truth and on the political disengagement that is promoted by belief in the human will as a substitute for objective knowledge or as a force superior to historical and material conditions.

Consider the words of Mussolini:

> Fascism is a super-relativistic movement because it has never attempted to clothe its complicated and powerful mental attitude with a definite program but has succeeded by following its every changing individual intuition. Everything I have said and done in these last years is relativism by intuition. . . . If relativism signifies contempt for fixed categories and men who claim to be bearers of an external objective truth . . . then there is nothing more relativistic than Fascist attitudes and activity. . . . From the fact that all ideologies are of equal value, that all ideologies are mere fictions, the modern relativist deduces that everybody is free to create for himself his own ideology and to attempt to carry it out with all possible energy [quoted in Neumann 1944:462–463].

The similarities between these lines and certain tendencies in contemporary anthropology cannot be dismissed as fortuitous or superficial; they indicate how important it is for anthropology to reexamine its theoretical precepts and its role in society, and for students of the discipline to recognize that the strategic alternatives that lie before them must be critically evaluated and chosen among thoughtfully. The differences are not merely personally meaningful but socially consequential. It is hoped that the following chapters will help to clarify the character of these questions by demonstrating the methods and results of an anthropology which, rather than reflecting "an emotional bias toward the world of imagination" (Reichenbach 1951:254), and instead of becoming more esoteric and obscurantist, strives toward "continuous contact with reality" (Marx and Engels 1970:227) and the positive and substantive human change that it may make possible.

References

Bottomore, T. B.
1974 *Sociology as social criticism*. New York: Pantheon.

Bronowski, J.
1973 *The ascent of man*. Boston: Little, Brown.

Dolgin, J., D. Kemnitzer, and D. Schneider (Eds.)
1977 *Symbolic anthropology: A reader in the study of symbols and meanings*. New York: Columbia University Press.

Dumont, Louis
1977 Caste, racism and 'stratification': Reflections of a social anthropologist. In *Symbolic anthropology* (J. Dolgin *et al.*, Eds.). New York: Columbia University Press.

Geertz, C.
1973 *The interpretation of cultures: Selected essays*. New York: Basic Books.

Gould, S.
1978 Heroes in nature. *New York Review of Books,* September 28:31–32.

Harris, M.
1968 *The rise of anthropological theory*. New York: Thomas Crowell.
1980 *Cultural materialism: The struggle for a science of culture*. New York: Random House.

Hoebel, E. A., and T. Weaver
1979 *Anthropology and the human experience*. New York: McGraw-Hill.

Hosken, F.
1976 Genital mutilation of women in Africa. Munger Africana "Library Notes."

Janik, A., and S. Toulmin
1973 *Wittgenstein's Vienna*. New York: Simon and Schuster.

Lemon, J., and G. Nash
1970 The distribution of wealth in eighteenth-century America: A century of change in Chester County, Pennsylvania, 1693–1802. In *Class and society in early America* (G. Nash, Ed.). Englewood Cliffs, N.J. Pp. 166–188.

Levi-Strauss, C.
1972 *Structuralism and ecology. Gildersleeve lecture*. New York: Barnard College.

Marx, K., and F. Engels
1970 *The German ideology*. New York: International Publishers.

Medawar, P.
1972 *The hope of progress*. New York: Anchor.

Neumann, F.
1944 *Behemoth: The structure and practice of national socialism, 1933–1944*. New York: Harper and Row.

Orwell, G.
1937 *The road to Wigan Pier,* London: Penquin.
1961 *Collected essays*. London: Secker and Warburg.

Reichenbach, H.
1951 *The rise of scientific philosophy*. Berkeley: University of California Press.

Rossi, I.
1974 Structuralism as scientific method. In *The unconscious in culture: The structuralism of Claude Lévi-Strauss in perspective* (I. Rossi, Ed.). New York: Dutton. pp. 60–106.

Roszak, T.
1969 *The making of a counter culture*. Garden City: Anchor.

Sahlins, M.
1976 *Culture and practical reason*. Chicago: University of Chicago Press.

Scholte, B.
1970 Lévi-Strauss's unfinished symphony: The analysis of myth. In *Claude Lévi-Strauss: The anthropologist as hero* (E. Hayes and T. Hayes, Eds.). Cambridge: MIT Press. Pp. 145–149.

Schorske, C.
1980 *Fin-de-siecle Vienna: Politics and culture.* New York: Knopf.
Sontag, S.
1970 The anthropologist as hero. In *Claude Lévi-Strauss: The anthropologist as hero* (E. Hayes and T. Hayes, Eds.). Cambridge: MIT Press. Pp. 184–196.
Swanson, G.
1964 *The birth of the gods: The origin of primitive beliefs.* Ann Arbor: The University of Michigan Press.
Weltfish, G.
1971 The Plains Indians: Their continuity and their indian identity. In *North American Indians in historical perspective* (E. Leacock and N. Lurie, Eds.). New York: Random House. Pp. 200–227.

BEYOND THE MYTHS OF CULTURE

Essays in Cultural Materialism

I

PERSPECTIVES ON THE "TRIBE"

1 Flux among the Mbuti Pygmies of the Ituri Forest: An Ecological Interpretation[1]

WILLIAM S. ABRUZZI

Introduction

Several years ago, Colin Turnbull (1968) presented an essay on "The Importance of Flux in Two Hunting Societies." Since publication, the comments made by Turnbull in that paper have largely stood unquestioned. In addition, his article has become adopted into the anthropological literature as a "cautionary tale" against too readily accepting ecological explanations of human social behaviors, even as they relate directly to subsistence activities.

The major criticism here is that Turnbull has made categorical statements claiming that ecological factors are of little, if any, importance in understanding significant regularities associated with Mbuti Pygmy subsistence activities,[2] while at the same time demonstrating a lack of familiarity with ecological concepts and methods. Consequently, he fails to present the necessary data that would substantiate such an unequivocal position, and disregards important information that suggests the operation of ecological processes in Mbuti subsistence activities.

While detailed information on the ecology of the Ituri Forest and on the subsistence activities of the Mbuti is, unfortunately, not available, that which is obtainable suggests conclusions that are distinctly contrary to those pro-

[1] I wish to express my appreciation to Colin Turnbull, Robert Netting, Richard Lee, and Eric Ross for their editorial comments on an earlier draft of this chapter. Acknowledgment is also made to Ruth Blackwell-Rogers for producing the maps.

[2] In Turnbull (1968), he discusses the incidence of flux among both the Mbuti and the Ik. This chapter, however, will concentrate only on the comments made by Turnbull for the Mbuti and will not be concerned with his argument as it relates to the Ik.

BEYOND THE MYTHS OF CULTURE
Essays in Cultural Materialism

ISBN 0-12-598180-5

posed by Turnbull. The specific regularities in Mbuti subsistence behavior to which Turnbull refers may indeed be viewed as effective adaptations of this hunting and gathering population to the material demands of its environment. The argument that follows will show that, contrary to Turnbull, the subsistence behaviors of the Mbuti which were discussed by him are understandable only by a consideration of the specific adaptive requirements imposed upon this population by the material facts of its environment.

Turnbull's Thesis

As the title of his article implies, Turnbull is concerned with the cause of flux among the Mbuti bands. By flux he means "the constant changeover of personnel between local groups, and the frequent shifts of campsites through the seasons [Turnbull 1968:132]." Turnbull is inquiring, therefore, into the reason for the flexibility characteristic of Pygmy bands. Before developing his argument, Turnbull (1968:132) summarizes his conclusion concerning the existence of flux among the Mbuti (and the Ik): "Because neither is under the rigid control a truly marginal economy might impose, each is able to maintain a fluid band composition, a loose form of social structure, and to utilize flux as a highly effective social mechanism."

Turnbull begins his analysis by differentiating the Mbuti into two distinct economic divisions. The first of these is the net-hunters, whose camps are generally large, consisting of between 7 and 30 families, though usually not less than 10 (Turnbull 1965a:99), and whose size is based upon the demands of communal or cooperative hunting. A net hunt, which involves the beating of the underbrush by the women in order to drive small game into the nets attended by the men, "demands cooperation between a minimum of six or seven nuclear families, and allows a maximum of thirty [Turnbull 1968:135]."

The other economic division among the Mbuti consists of the archers, who live in much smaller groups and "hunt individually with bow and arrow [Turnbull 1968:132]." In contrast to the organizational and cooperative demands of the net hunt, "the ideal number of archers for either tracking or ambushing game is three. Five would already be felt as unwieldy [Turnbull 1968:135]." Thus the archer bands usually consist of only two or three nuclear families during most of the year (Turnbull 1968:135).

After introducing these important economic divisions, which exist among the Mbuti, Turnbull turns his attention to a description of their habitat, the Ituri Forest, which he depicts as monotonously uniform throughout.

> Its climate varies scarcely at all throughout the year. . . . Rain falls evenly over the entire area, and is evenly spread throughout the year. Game and vegetable supplies are similarly uniform in distribution, and are abundant throughout the area. There is nothing that makes one part of the forest more or less desirable than any other part at any time of the year [1968:133].

In other words, according to Turnbull, in addition to being spatially uniform, the Ituri Forest is also characterized by a distinct absence of seasonality. This constant uniformity throughout the forest allows the Mbuti to confine their hunting movements, from one year to the next, to within an area of 260 km^2 (100 square miles) (Turnbull 1968:134). The distribution of food, according to Turnbull (1968:134), makes longer distances of travel unnecessary.

Given his view of an invariable forest, Turnbull is forced to conclude that "there is no environmental reason why half [the Mbuti] should be net-hunters and the other half archers [1968:134]". He adds that the net-hunters and archers regard each other as "quaint," and wonder how the other can survive, even though members of each division are knowledgeable of the alternate hunting technique and adopt the appropriate hunting strategy when living among each other (Turnbull 1968:134). Turnbull (1968:135) then reiterates his explanation for the presence of this pervasive economic division among the Mbuti: "The environment is generous enough to allow alternative hunting techniques."

Turnbull then turns to an annual event which recurs among the Mbuti and which he feels sufficiently demonstrates his thesis regarding the role of environmental permissiveness in Mbuti subsistence behavior. This event is the honey season, which lasts for about 2 months in the middle of our calendar year (Turnbull 1965b:286). According to Turnbull, the onset of the honey season is not accompanied by any distinct climate change, but merely represents a period of abundance for this one resource. The seasonal abundance of honey, he feels, does not at all compromise his view of temporal uniformity within the Ituri Forest (Turnbull 1968:136).

It seems, however, that the Mbuti do not concur with Turnbull regarding the stability and uniformity of the forest, but rather recognize distinct seasons associated with periods of scarcity and plenty. But while they view the honey season as a period significantly different from the rest of the year, Turnbull contends that the seasons recognized by the Mbuti are entirely imaginary; "the Mbuti treat their stable environment as though it were unstable, creating imaginary seasons of plenty and scarcity [Turnbull 1968:134]." Furthermore, Turnbull argues that his position on the nonexistence of seasons within the forest is confirmed by the fact that the Mbuti contradict themselves on the matter of seasonality:

> And it is strange indeed that in the same environment and with equally adequate technologies, the net-hunters regard the brief honey season as a time of plenty, while the archers see it as a time of scarcity. Each group takes appropriate measures to meet the perceived situation, the net-hunters splitting into smaller units, and the archers congregating into larger ones [Turnbull 1968:134]!

Having removed any consideration of an ecological basis for Mbuti actions during this period, Turnbull focuses on sociopolitical factors as the cause of these "strange" behaviors. Turnbull views the flux associated with the honey season, as well as the beliefs that attend it, as an institutionalized mechanism to facilitate a regular reorganization of the hunting bands, made possible only by the stability and abundance of the Ituri Forest. At the end of the honey season, when the net-hunter bands reform, there is a careful avoidance of "any lines of fracture that remain unhealed [Turnbull 1968: 134]." Ten months of active cooperation in the hunt and close personal relations, according to Turnbull, lead inevitably to hostilities that must be alleviated before they destroy the "essential unity of the band and consequently ruin the success of the hunt. Thus the honey season is an important safety-valve, allowing for the reconstruction of face-to-face groups [Turnbull 1968:135]."

The archers must also maintain band unity. Their problem, on the other hand, lies in the fact that individual families are scattered throughout the band territory for most of the year. In order to reassert claim to its territory and thus reduce the incidence of trespassing or poaching, Turnbull claims that it is necessary for each band to "draw together all its scattered segments and to act as a band, within its territory, for at least some part of the annual cycle [1968:135]." Consequently, during the honey season,

> the net-hunters spread out into fragmented subbands. . . . At the end of the honey season the band begins to reform. . . . The archers, in exactly the same environment, do precisely the reverse. They hunt in maximal bands *only* during the honey season, and for the rest of the year split up into minor and ultimately minimal segments [1968:135].

The explanation offered by the net-hunters for their behavior during the honey season is that it is a time of plenty, reducing the need for cooperation in the hunt, while the archers insist that this same period is a time of scarcity, requiring increased cooperation among its members. This glaring discrepancy of views among the Mbuti themselves leads Turnbull to conclude that "it all seems to be a rather topsy–turvy world for [the Mbuti] where the things that happen are those that could least reasonably be expected [Turnbull 1968: 136]." He then repeats his concluding theme that since the Mbuti work within their permissive environment, rather than attempting to change it,

> they are unencumbered by the rigid imperatives that would be imposed by a truly harsh environment. Thus they are able to maintain a fluid band composition and a loose social structure; and are able to utilize this flux as a highly effective social mechanism, providing scope for action in all aspects of social life [Turnbull 1968:136–137].

Turnbull's concluding statements consist of functional arguments regarding the mechanisms through which the Mbuti are able to maintain fluid bands, as, for example, through the creation of cross-cutting ties between age mates of different bands in the place of lineage affiliation. He closes by stressing the religious implications of the flux; "by deemphasizing stability in interpersonal relations, the process throws people into closer recognition of the one constant in their lives, the environment and its life-giving qualities [Turnbull 1968:137]."

By characterizing the Ituri Forest as uniform throughout, spatially and temporally, and thus incapable of producing either the pervasive economic division that exists among the Mbuti or the apparently contradictory activities associated with the honey season, Turnbull has attempted to eliminate any basis for proposing ecological arguments to explain these behaviors. Rather, he argues that the flux that occurs during the honey season—including the population movement and the associated changes in subsistence strategy and social organization—must be understood in "sociopolitical" terms. More precisely, he argues that these behaviors must be viewed in terms of the functional role they play in maintaining the "essential unity" of the Mbuti bands, and that the environment is merely a passive agent, permitting a wide latitude of subsistence activities.

Anthropologists for the most part have accepted without question the thesis presented by Turnbull and outlined in the foregoing pages.[3] Bicchieri (1969), for example, completely adheres to Turnbull's central argument; he accepts the thesis of the "permissive environment" and views the distinction between net-hunters and archers in precisely the same terms as does Turnbull, "as the concomitant of a permissive environment that allows for variation in exploitative devices to coexist in the same ecological niche, the Ituri tropical forest [Bicchieri 1969:67]." Bicchieri also accepts Turnbull's account for the existence of flux during the honey season, including their "diametrically opposed socioorganizational response to essentially identical environmental conditions [Bicchieri 1969:68]," concluding that the honey season "allows the net-hunters to relieve the tensions of living together by separating; conversely, the archers are given the opportunity to strengthen ties of friendship and lines of communication [Bicchieri 1969:68]."

In a modular publication, widely employed for pedagogical purposes, Netting (1971:7–8) has also displayed an unquestioning acceptance of the Turnbull thesis, maintaining that the Mbuti provide an example of a population for whom the relaxation of environmental and technological constraints upon work-group composition has permitted the dominance of "social considerations" in band organization. During one of the discussion sections included in the symposium on "Man the Hunter," at which Turnbull's paper on flux was presented, Birdsell appears to have accepted the Turnbull thesis as well. Regarding the constraints imposed upon population growth among hunting and gathering populations he states that "it may well be that we are

[3] Richard Lee is an exception in this regard. Lee (1972) rejects on principle Turnbull's claim that no variation exists within the Ituri Forest, and suggests that Turnbull did not investigate the matter sufficiently.

facing the problem raised by Turnbull's Pygmy examples, where density controls are invisible and social, rather than economic [Lee and DeVore 1968: 245]."

Such blanket acceptance of Turnbull's thesis by several anthropologists is particularly disconcerting as his position is in contradiction to basic ecological assumptions.

No Variation within the Forest

Turnbull's depiction of the Ituri Forest as uniform throughout, a view upon which his thesis of the supremacy of social over ecological considerations is constructed, must be examined first. At least two other authors disagree with Turnbull's position regarding the absence of seasonality within the Ituri Forest. Schebesta (1933) and Putnam (1948) both recognize periods of greater and lesser rainfall within the forest. Putnam, who spent over 20 years living among the Mbuti, clearly distinguishes a "dry season," which he claimed occurs around January and February. Schebesta, on the other hand, described this same period as a wet season. While the two authors do not agree on the timing of climatic variations within the forest, they do agree that they occur. Although no rainfall data are available for the Ituri Forest itself, sufficient information exists for enough locations within geographical proximity to the forest to reconstruct the annual variation in precipitation which occurs there as well. The information available confirms Putnam's position that the months of January and February comprise relatively dry months compared to the rest of the year.

First of all, the continent of Africa experiences alternating wet and dry seasons owing to the vacilating movements of two great air masses, the Tropical Continental and the Equatorial. The former, which produces the dry, dusty conditions so common in the great savanna lands of Africa, is at its furthest southern extension during the months of January and February (Grove 1970:12). This southern penetration of the Tropical Continental air mass is accompanied by the retreat of the moist Equatorial air mass, which provides most of the rain on the continent. In March and April, however, the Equatorial air mass proceeds northward, with the Tropical Continental retreating before it. During June and July when these air masses reach their northernmost location (Grove 1970:12), the African savannas experience their seasonal rains.

Rainfall data from as far west as Bangassou in the Central African Republic–Zaire border area eastward to Arua in the West Nile District of Uganda display identical patterns of annual precipitation (see Figure 1.1). The months of May through October in Bangassou average over 200 mm of rain per month, while those of December through February receive less than 50 mm per month (Grove 1970:Map 5). An average of rainfall for 31 years shows

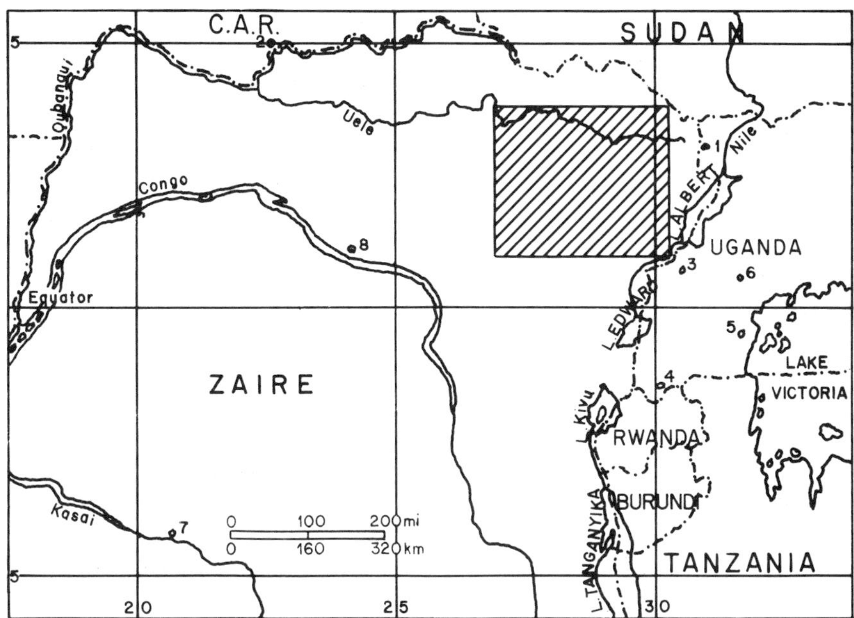

FIGURE 1.1 *Central and Eastern Africa. Towns: (1) Arua (Uganda), (2) Bangassou (Central African Republic), (3) Fort Portal (Uganda), (4) Kabale (Uganda), (5) Masaka (Uganda), (6) Mubuende (Uganda), (7) Port Franqui (Zaire), (8) Yangambi (Zaire). Shaded area: approximate location of the Ituri forest.*

the same pattern in Arua; December thru March are dry months, while April thru November are wet (Parsons 1960c:Fig. 1).[4]

DeSchlippe (1956:152–178) demonstrates that the same rainfall pattern occurs among the Azande in the green belt area near the Sudan–Zaire border. The Azande of the green belt are of particular importance here since they exist in direct proximity to the Mbuti (Turnbull 1965a:19, see Map 2) and should, therefore, display the same climatic fluctuations which affect the Mbuti themselves. DeSchlippe's rainfall data, collected for the entire year of 1950 and for the first 2 months of 1951, clearly demonstrate the existence of distinct wet and dry seasons, which markedly affect the life and diet of the Azande. In accord with the data presented for Bangassou and Arua, no precipitation was recorded from the middle of December to the end of February for either year, yet DeSchlippe registered over 100 mm of rain for each of the months of May through September, with some months receiving as much as 250–300 mm of rain (DeSchlippe 1956:152–178).

To fully appreciate the issue of seasonality within the Ituri Forest, the

[4] Unfortunately, Parsons does not provide specific data on rainfall for Arua, or for Mubende and Kabale referred to later, but rather only graphs the occurrence of seasonality in these three towns on a monthly basis.

problem must be examined within the context of seasonal variation throughout central and eastern Africa. As the Equatorial air system moves north and south, it crosses the equator twice annually. Locations on or near the equator, then, such as Yangambi in Zaire (Phillips 1960:86), and Fort Portal (Parsons 1960c:Map 18) and Mubende (Parsons 1960c:Fig. 1) in Uganda, experience four, not two, alternating wet and dry seasons. Peak periods of precipitation occur in each of these towns around March and April as well as September through November, with dry seasons taking place in January and February and from June through August. The weather pattern for locations south of the equator, naturally, is the reverse of that which occurs in the northern latitudes; peak rains occur in the southern lattitudes usually between December and February, while June and July constitute the middle of the dry season. This pattern has been reported for the Lega (Biebuyck 1973:15) and the Lele (Douglas 1963:22) in southern Zaire, as well as for the towns of Masaka (Parsons 1960a:2) and Kabale (Parsons 1960c:Fig. 1) in Uganda. Rainfall data collected for Port Franqui in southwestern Zaire from 1930–1939, for example, show an average of 17 and 14 mm of rain for the months of June and July, respectively, which is in marked contrast to the 236 mm of rain recorded for December (Douglas 1963:22).

As one moves north and south from the equator, the wet and dry seasons merge into distinct annual rather than semiannual occurrences, and the length of the dry season increases with distance from the equator. In southern Uganda two harvests are possible, whereas the concentration of rainfall into a single season allows only one crop in the north (O'Connor 1971:19)—the location of the West Nile District—where the dry season lasts for 4 months (O'Connor 1971:234). Distances from the equator of only 2° or 3° latitude are sufficient to produce distinct annual wet and dry seasons. Since the Ituri Forest lies approximately between 1° north and 4° north latitude, if the seasonal pattern north of the equator is comparable to that in the south[5]—as the data suggests that it is—then the dry season in the Ituri Forest is likely to last from close to 2 months in the south to perhaps 80 days or more in the north. This is sufficient time to include the months of January and February as suggested by Putnam.

Given the latitude, then, at which the Ituri Forest is situated, in conjunction with the rainfall patterns demonstrated for numerous other localities, both on the periphery of the forest and throughout the region as a whole, the southern extension of the Equatorial and Tropical Continental air masses must certainly produce a period of reduced rainfall in the forest during the months of January and February that warrant the term "dry season." Turn-

[5] Douglas (1963:22) indicates that the length of the dry season in the Kasai River area decreases from about 100 days at 6° south latitude to 80 days at 4° south. An equal decrease of 20 additional days at 2° south latitude would still allow for approximately a 60-day dry season in this area.

bull's failure to provide any data[6] that would substantiate his claim of temporal uniformity within the forest demands that the evidence to the contrary be accepted as a serious challenge to that claim.

In addition to denying any temporal variation within the Ituri Forest, Turnbull claims that the forest is spatially uniform as well. He asserts that "there is nothing that makes one part of the forest more or less desirable than any other part at any time of the year [Turnbull 1968:133]." Again, Putnam contradicts Turnbull's position, maintaining that the forest varies considerably, at least with regard to vegetation. "In some spots there is no underbrush at all, and nothing but leaf molds between boles of the trees; in others there is a wild tangle of bushes, reeds and lianes [Putnam 1948:322]." While Putnam does not indicate just how extensive these distinct areas may be, he does demonstrate that significant variation in the density of vegetation may exist. In fact, Turnbull himself has made the same observation when traveling "above the Lelo River, where the forest was clear of all undergrowth [Turnbull 1961:176]." Neither Putnam nor Turnbull indicate, however, the degree to which the clearing of the undergrowth is natural or man-made.

The most damaging evidence against Turnbull's contention of a spatially uniform forest from the perspective of the Mbuti hunters is his own description of one section of the forest. Turnbull (1965b) states that

> the game supply of the archers is further reduced by the fact that most of them live in areas that have been open to mission and administrative settlements, to economic exploitation by mining, commercial plantations, and tourist centers such as Beni and Mount Hoyo; and finally, to consequent road building. In particular the southeast corner of the forest . . . has been subject to such disturbances, all of which affect both the movement of game and the movement of hunters. Hunting bands in parts of this area are still able to subsist on the forest, but only with great difficulty. Among the archer bands the village is regarded as an absolutely essential source of food, and consequently there is a need for a more stable relationship than that between the net-hunters and the villagers [p. 299].

The southeast corner of the forest is also the area most affected by the activities of agricultural villages which have entered this area from the east.

It seems incredible that Turnbull can acknowledge the existence of such significant disturbances in one general portion of the forest and still claim spatial uniformity for the same forest as regards the subsistence needs of the

---

[6] Turnbull does not provide any rainfall data. In order to support his claim for temporal uniformity within the Ituri Forest, Turnbull (1968:133) only states that temperature varies less than 5°F. throughout the year. However, in a tropical environment, annual variations in temperature are not likely to be a significant limiting factor. Rainfall is usually the most significant variable to consider. Douglas (1963:21), for example, shows that while rainfall varies from less than 20 mm per month in parts of the dry season to over 200 mm per month for several months during the wet season among the Lele of southwestern Zaire, temperature averages between these two seasons vary less than 1°C.

Mbuti. Turnbull's own description of the forest (see also Turnbull 1961: 29; 1965a:95–96) casts serious doubt upon his claim that there is nothing that makes one part of the forest more desirable for hunters and gatherers than any other.

Net-Hunters and Archers

Since the existence of significant variation within the forest is almost certain to have important implications for the adaptive strategies employed by the Mbuti, the presence of such evidence necessitates a consideration of Turnbull's second contention, that there is no environmental reason for the existence of two distinct subsistence strategies employed by the Mbuti. Rather than constituting the fortuitous result of a "permissive environment," a clear ecological basis appears to exist for the division of Mbuti into net-hunters and archers.

Were the net-hunting and archer bands to display a near random distribution throughout the forest, there might be some methodological support for Turnbull's contention that "environmental permissiveness" is operating. But, on the contrary, there appears to be a clear spatial dimension associated with the distribution of these two subsistence strategies (see Figure 1.2). While the net-hunters are found throughout the western half of the forest, the archers are concentrated in its southeast corner (Turnbull 1965b:289) and confined to the eastern third of the forest generally (Turnbull 1965a:317, Map 2). The southeast corner of the forest is precisely the area which Turnbull describes as being modified by the activities of non-Mbuti populations, and the eastern edge of the forest, as will be discussed later, is the area most affected by the encroachment of agricultural populations practicing shifting cultivation. Rather than proposing a "permissive environment" as the cause of this significant division among the Mbuti—which violates the evidence for the operation of nonrandom forces—a more productive explanation is likely to derive from an investigation of the impact that the disturbed conditions have had upon the subsistence activities of the Mbuti.

Turnbull has remarked several times (Turnbull 1965b:290, 301; 1968: 299) that the members of the archer bands are in greater sustained contact with the neighboring agricultural villages than are the members of net-hunting bands. Furthermore, the archers rely more for their subsistence upon the productivity of the agriculturalists' gardens than they do upon the forest (Putnam 1948:333; Turnbull 1965b:301), and subsist solely upon the forest only during the brief honey season (Turnbull 1965b:301; 1968:135). "For most of the year each archer band maintains almost daily contact with the villagers, and the archers' daily diet includes plantains and cassava. Only during the *begbe* [during the honey season], which is a time of plenty, may these Mbuti rely entirely upon the forest [Turnbull, 1965b:301]."

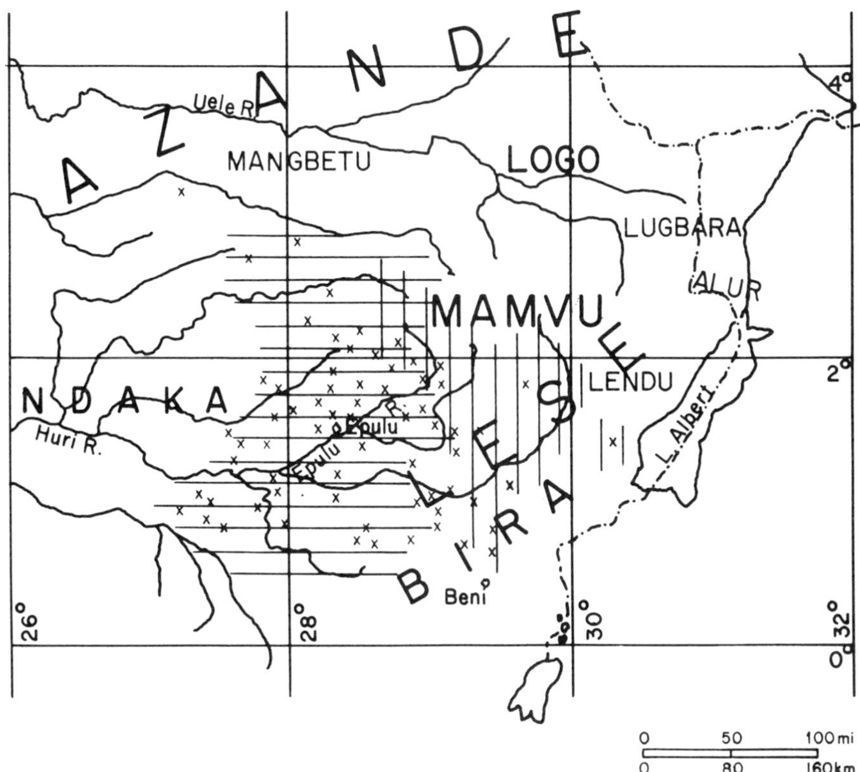

FIGURE 1.2. *Distribution of hunters and cultivators in the Ituri Forest: horizontals, net-hunters; verticals, archers; crosses, approximate location of hunting camps visited by Turnbull; Azande, approximate location of the principal groups of shifting cultivators (information on Mbuti adapted from Turnbull, 1965a:317, Map 2).*

A significant association appears to exist. In the central and more remote sections of the forest, the Mbuti subsist primarily by cooperative and communal net hunting. In the eastern and southeastern section of the forest, on the other hand—that portion of the forest most affected by the impact of intruding populations, particularly the growth of agricultural villages—the Mbuti have fragmented into smaller, independent units.

The reason for the fragmentation of archer bands into smaller, more independent units in the eastern and southeastern section of the forest seems clear. Both Putnam (1948:323) and Turnbull (1965a; 1965b:294) indicate that the socioeconomic relationship between the Mbuti and their agricultural neighbors is based upon a more or less stable exchange betweeen individual families. The Pygmy client protects his Negro patron's garden, particularly from elephants (Putnam 1948:330), and in turn is supported from the produce of that garden. The dependence of the Mbuti, particularly the archers, upon the produce of the agricultural gardens is reflected in the heavy incidence of plantains, cassava, and other domesticated foods in their diet (Putnam 1948:333; Turnbull 1965a:34, 168; 1965b:301; May 1965:111). "From the Pygmy point of view, the village is merely another source of food—acquired by another form of hunting as often as not [Turnbull 1965b:287]." The economic dependence of the archers, unlike that of the net-hunters, is not upon each other; instead, their economic ties are primarily with the external agricultural villages, and not as a group, but rather as individual hunters. Consequently, individual archer families have developed strong socioeconomic relationships with the villagers rather than with each other. This is in contrast to the net-hunters who, being dependent upon each other economically, have organized socially to ensure their survival. The adaptive significance of these distinct subsistence strategies is demonstrated by the persistence they display in spite of a high degree of interchange of personnel (flux) between the two groups.

Thus, it is precisely those groups that are the most dependent upon the gardens of the agricultural villages and have entered into individualized exchange relationships to secure a continued supply from this source, which lack the large, cooperative band organization. In contrast, those groups that exist more autonomous of the agricultural villages and subsist primarily on the produce of the forest have organized into cooperative hunting bands. This dual adaptation is hardly unique among human populations; it should not be surprising. It has been described in the literature before, and for reasons that appear to be similar to the conditions present among the Mbuti (cf. Murphy and Steward 1956).

Imaginary Seasons and Opposite Response

Turnbull has further argued that the Mbuti create "imaginary" seasons where none exist and are able to respond to identical conditions with contradictory behaviors, again because of the permissiveness of their environment. While the net-hunters maintain that the honey season is a time of plenty and the archers insist that it is a period of scarcity, Turnbull contends that the forest experiences no significant change from one part of the year to the next, although he does at times concede a greater productivity within the forest during the honey season (Turnbull 1965b:286; 1968:298). The issue here is whether there is any justification for the divergent views among the Mbuti, or whether Turnbull is correct in claiming the whole affair to be a fantasy on the part of the Mbuti. Although the Mbuti disagree among themselves, the available evidence suggests that their perception of the situation—indeed their very disagreement on the issue—is not only justifiable, but is to be expected.

Information has already been presented that strongly suggests that seasonality occurs within the Ituri Forest. The honey season, which occurs during the months of June and July, would fall within the wetter part of the annual cycle. Since the Mbuti, like most hunters and gatherers, acquire the majority of their caloric intake from vegetable rather than animal sources (Turnbull 1965a:168; Lee 1968:46), an increased abundance of flora produced by the greater rainfall, in conjunction with the seasonal availability of honey, could easily be viewed as a period of plenty. The net-hunters' response during the honey season, then, would appear to be justified. However, if the information on seasonality within the forest supports the behavior of the net-hunters, what justification is there for the apparantly contradictory activities and beliefs of the archers? A review of some of the information already presented should resolve this issue.

As has already been indicated, the archers subsist primarily upon the produce that they receive from the gardens of their agricultural patrons as "the game supply is less adequate" in their portion of the forest (Turnbull 1965b: 289–290). Furthermore, the archers subsist solely upon the forest *only* during the honey season (Turnbull 1965b:301; 1968:135). A complete dependence upon the forest by the archers is indeed a hardship, as has been stressed by Turnbull himself. Owing to the disturbed conditions that prevail in the southeast corner of the forest where the archers are concentrated, "Hunting bands in parts of this area are still able to subsist on the forest but only with great difficulty [Turnbull 1965b:299]."

For the archers, whose habitat has been significantly modified to the point of adversely affecting their ability to subsist solely upon the forest, their attempt to do just that must surely be viewed as a period of hardship for them. Thus, the discordant views of the relative abundance of the honey season among the Mbuti would have some material basis.

But if surviving upon the forest does constitute such a hardship, why do the archers persist upon doing it? Continued year-round subsistence on the gardens of their agricultural patrons would appear to be the more advisable course for them to follow, given the circumstances. Is maintaining band unity that important, or do possibly good material reasons exist for abandoning the agricultural villages at this time? The answer to this question may lie in an understanding of the agricultural cycle in this general area. The Azande farmers of the green belt will serve as the model since they exist in proximity to the Ituri Forest.

In his description of the agricultural cycle of the Azande, DeSchlippe (1956:178–179) distinguishes between the rainy season and the dry season. While he depicts the dry season as a period of general abundance for these farmers, due to the recency of their harvest, he characterizes the rainy season, particularly the period from late April until July, as a period of considerable "nutritional strain." This is a period of planting and preparation for the new agricultural cycle, but it is not yet a time of renewed agricultural productivity.

While increased energy is required for the heavy labor demanded at this time, caloric consumption is at its lowest point in the year, because of the depletion of the supplies gathered during the previous year's harvest.

Assuming that the agricultural cycle in the villages directly contiguous to the Mbuti approximates that of the Azande in the green belt, the honey season, which occurs during June and July, would fall at the very height of the "hungry period." This would be the time when the villages upon which the archers depend would most need sufficient supplies of food, but would be least likely to have them. Providing the Mbuti with food at this time might constitute a considerable additional burden upon their meager resources. June and July may also be a period—after the previous harvest and prior to the growth of the new crops—when the labor of the Pygmies in protection of the gardens is least needed by the villagers, and when the pressure shifts to recruiting them for the heavy agricultural labor, which the Mbuti continually try to avoid (Turnbull 1965a:38–39). Consequently, as the supplies from the gardens begin to dwindle, the archers may be compelled to temporarily switch their dependence to the forest, which is now better able to support them because of the brief honey season. Furthermore, due to the disturbed conditions in their area of the forest and since they hunt communally without the aid of nets, the archers may need to organize into cooperative groups that are larger even then those which are characteristic of net-hunting bands (see, for example, Turnbull 1972:301). With the end of the honey season and the growth of crops in the village gardens, the archers could then return to their dependence upon the villages and resume their role as protectors of the coming year's harvest. Given their different points of origin, the net-hunters and archers could quite reasonably be expected to view the honey season in antithetical terms and respond to it in their characteristic ways.

Further Problems

In addition to the empirical discrepancies just discussed, there are four basic contradictions associated with Turnbull's position. First, as indicated already, Turnbull's claim that flux among the Mbuti, as well as their division into net-hunters and archers, is simply made possible by the existence of a permissive environment is in direct contradiction with his own statements that a significant portion of the forest has been seriously disturbed, and that hunters can subsist in this section of the forest only with great difficulty.

A second inconsistency in Turnbull's argument is his claim that, for the net-hunters, the honey season and all of the "imagined" elements that accompany it serve to facilitate a redistribution of individual Mbuti throughout the forest. The creation of this imaginary season by the Mbuti, according to Turnbull, functions primarily to minimize conflicts that would inevitably destroy the "essential unity of the band and consequently ruin the success of the hunt

[Turnbull 1968:135].'' While population redistribution is important among hunters, Turnbull's thesis is in contradiction with the fact that the Mbuti do not maintain more than 40% continuity from one month to the next (Turnbull 1972:300). The high interband mobility that exists among the Mbuti is illustrated by the following passage (Turnbull 1965a):

> The composition of the band is fluid, to say the least, and does not follow any clear unilineal or cognatic descent system. Throughout the forest, the bands are in a constant state of fragmentation as well as in a constant process of fission and fusion. Members of any band are quite likely at any moment to leave and join another band, temporarily or permanently, for any one of a number of reasons. In-law visiting is common, and permanent attachments to the band are sometimes accomplished this way. But at the same time, with each successive, monthly change of site, the hunting camp also shows another stage in the over-all process of fission and fusion along recognizable lines of structural cleavage [p. 27].

The existence of such a high degree of flux throughout the remainder of the year calls into question Turnbull's position that the Mbuti create such elaborate measures of self-delusion regularly at one time of the year simply to achieve the same goal. Since population redistribution is taking place anyway, other factors are more likely to be responsible for the behaviors associated with the honey season.

The immediate change in material conditions for both the archers and the net-hunters during the honey season is more likely the cause for the events which occur at this time. In addition, for the net-hunters at least, the dispersal of individuals and the reduced dependence upon hunting that occurs during the honey season may function to randomize hunting pressure upon game; the effect that this has upon their movement redistributes these resources more evenly throughout the forest (cf. Moore 1957). As one member of the Epulu (net-hunting) band emphasized, ''The honey season was no time to be bothered with hunting [Turnbull 1961:264].'' The redistribution of game is a long-term adaptation that the anthropologist, spending at the most a year or two in the field, is not likely to observe (Lee 1972:143).

A contradiction also exists in Turnbull's claim that by deemphasizing the stability of interpersonal relations, flux ''throws the people into a closer recognition of the one constant in their lives, the environment and its life-giving qualities [Turnbull 1968:137].'' Two contradictions are present here. First, the Mbuti do *not* recognize their environment as constant; it is Turnbull—not the Mbuti—who attests to the uniformity of the Ituri Forest, and it is this discrepancy that serves as the major theme of his argument. Second, the forest environment is not the primary source of ''life-giving qualities'' for the archers. Rather, their principal source of survival consists of the gardens of the agricultural villages. When the archers have to depend solely upon the ''life-giving qualities'' of the forest in their area, they do not like it because they can do so only with great difficulty.

Turnbull's line of argument leads to still another contradiction. His claim that flux is able to occur among the Mbuti principally because of their "permissive environment" is in opposition to the fact that this same flux has been demonstrated for numerous other populations of hunters and gatherers: Most notably the Bushmen (Lee 1968, 1972a), the Hadza (Woodburn 1968), the Eskimo (Balikci 1968; Damas 1969), the Australian Aborigines (Meggitt 1962), and the Shoshone (Steward 1938, 1955)—none of whom inhabit what Turnbull might label a "permissive environment." His argument, therefore, leads to the inconsistent position that flux occurs among all of these populations because of the "rigor" of their environments, while the very same process occurs among the Mbuti for precisely the opposite reason.

Lee's suggestion that the "worldwide occurrence of this pattern of spatial organization in vastly different kinds of environments indicates the degree to which it was basic to the hunting and gathering adaptation [1972:139]" is considerably more parsimonious. However, flux is perhaps not inherent to a hunting and gathering adaptation, but rather may be typical of such contemporary populations due to the similarities of their present circumstances. Contemporary hunters and gatherers all inhabit a reduced and marginal portion of their former habitats, because of the expansion of competing agricultural and industrial systems. Hunters today, therefore, must all subsist upon a less abundant and stable supply of undomesticated resources.

In addition to containing the above inconsistencies, Turnbull's attempt to explain the cause of flux among the Mbuti is simply inadequate. His explanation, based upon the nebulous and pseudo-ecological concept of a "permissive environment," amounts to no explanation at all. A hunting and gathering population—or any population, for that matter—does not respond to such vague and subjective characterizations as "permissiveness" and "harshness" in its environment; rather, a population adapts to the specific demands presented by its material environment. For hunters and gatherers such as the Mbuti this includes, among other considerations: the specific migratory and herding patterns of the game hunted; the seasonal, annual and long-term variations in climate, particularly those that affect resources; extractive requirements associated with vegetation gathered; and, of course, the impact presented by the presence of other populations of the same species. Unlike harshness or permissiveness, these represent objective features of the environment that can be placed within a spatial and temporal framework, and thus can be specifically related to particular behaviors associated with the population in question.

A functional argument for the role of flux in maintaining the "essential unity" of Mbuti bands suffers from all of the methodological problems inherent in such arguments (Collins 1964; Hempel 1965). Specifically, no attempt has been made by Turnbull to examine, through the deductive application of relevent ecological principles, whether or not the variations in subsistence that occur among the Mbuti may be related to variations which occur spatially or temporally in the value of other, ecologically significant variables.

Instead, the purported result of the flux, the maintenance of band unity, is proposed as the cause of that flux among the population.

Lacking the conditional form inherent to a scientific explanation, Turnbull's explanation of flux among the Mbuti is constructed upon a circular and teleological, functional argument, employing concepts such as a "permissive environment" and "essential unity of the band," which lack any empirical referents. Consequently, his explanation fails to account for the existence of flux among the Mbuti; owing to its qualitative and nonquantified construction, Turnbull's argument is impervious to empirical verification within a spatial and temporal framework. A valid explanation of flux among the Mbuti would have to explain the distinction between the net-hunters and archers, as well as the events that accompany the honey season, with a consistent theoretical model, and within a spatial and temporal framework, which avails itself to objective verification. This is precisely the type of explanation that Turnbull has failed to present and that is proposed in the following section of this chapter.

Ecological Adaptation among the Mbuti

THE ECOLOGICAL NICHE AND ITS APPLICATION TO THE MBUTI

Bicchieri (1969:67) has referred to the Ituri Forest as the ecological niche of the Mbuti. However, as Turnbull (1965a:17) has correctly recognized, the Ituri Forest constitutes the *habitat* of the Mbuti, not their *niche.* The ecological niche comprises more than simply the spatial location of an organism or population[7] under investigation; it is a more comprehensive concept that includes "not only the physical space occupied by an organism [or population], but also its functional role in the community (as, for example, its trophic position) and its position in environmental gradients of temperature, moisture, pH, soil and other conditions of existence [E. Odum 1971:234]." (See Hutchinson 1957; Boughey 1973; Hardesty 1975.) The second, and perhaps most crucial, component of its ecological niche is the role performed by the population in the flow of energy throughout the larger community.[8] While this functional role is often defined in terms of the trophic position occupied by a population within a community food chain (or web), certain nonconsumptive behaviors of one population may affect the niche exploitation of other populations (E. Odum 1971:211–233). Thus, energy flow throughout multi-

[7] The concept of an ecological niche is normally associated with individual organisms or with populations (usually species). Since it is the population that is of concern in evolutionary theory, and thus in this chapter, the niche concept applied here will be associated with the population.

[8] The term *community* in ecology does not necessarily refer to a specific spatial location, but rather denotes one level of analysis (along with the individual organism, the population, and the ecosystem) and is defined as all of the populations within a specified area (cf. Margalef 1968; Whittaker 1975).

species communities is affected by a complex of interspecific relations, including those defined as competition, predation, parasitism, ammensalism, commensalism, and mutualism. Furthermore, the relationship that exists between two species may be variable, rather than absolute, and depend upon the conditions of interaction. Ecological communities containing human populations may have several such populations occupying separate, discrete niches, and exhibiting the same complex of relations at the subspecies level (Barth 1956, 1964, 1969). The third component of the ecological niche comprises any variation in the environment that is significantly associated with the distribution of a particular population.

Given the above definition of the niche, the Mbuti must be viewed as two populations that occupy separate and distinct niches. Regarding the habitat component of the niche, these two populations occupy different areas with apparently little spatial overlap; the archers are located in the eastern and southeastern portion of the forest, while the net-hunters are distributed throughout the remaining area to the west. In addition, the net-hunters and archers diverge with regard to their functional role in the flow of energy through the community. While the net-hunters subsist primarily upon undomesticated resources, the archers live in greater sustained contact with the nearby agricultural villages and employ different technologies and organizational mechanisms to exploit a different range of resources. The methods employed by the archers to acquire these domesticated resources, moreover, are still distinct from those utilized by the villagers themselves, who consume still another unique range of resources.

The significant environmental gradient among the Mbuti is the distribution of non-Mbuti populations, and the disturbed conditions that they have produced within the forest. The intimate association of the archer population with the distribution of agricultural villages qualifies as a distribution along an environmental gradient.

Thus, the Mbuti appear to inhabit at least two distinct ecological niches, with each population located in distinct areas and employing different technologies and social organizations in order to exploit a unique range of resources. The exchange of personnel between these two groups does not alter the fact that ecologically definable populations exist which stand in distinct relations to the other populations within the community (Mayr 1963; Barth 1956, 1964, 1969). This ecological differentiation between the net-hunters and the archers is central to an understanding of the subsistence behaviors of the Mbuti.

POPULATION PRESSURE AND SUBSISTENCE BEHAVIOR AMONG THE MBUTI

Research has amply demonstrated that increases in the size of a population relative to the area that it exploits demands significant changes in the subsistence methods employed by that population if its continued growth, or even maintenance, is to be assured (Carniero 1961, 1967, 1970; Boserup 1965; Clark 1967; Rappaport 1968; Harner 1970; H. Odum 1971; Spooner 1972). The continued growth of a human population within a fixed habitat necessitates an increased intensification in the exploitation of a given unit of land within that territory—in conjunction with a greater cooperation in subsistence activities among the constituent segments of the larger population. Both of these developments are inextricable components of the same adaptive process.

A scale of cooperative organization among the Mbuti may be derived from calculations of the minimal and average size of work teams, as well as the level at which local segments of the population are integrated into effective operational units. Any analysis of the level of social organization involved in subsistence and other maintenance activities must be mindful that variations in organization are likely to occur within the same population. Seasonal variations in organization, associated with fluctuations in the availability and distribution of resources, are quite common, particularly among hunting and gathering populations. Such seasonal variations should be explained in precisely the same terms as the more gradual changes associated with long-term adaptations to population growth, since both variations entail responses to changes in the population–resource ratio.

The implications of this framework for the Mbuti seem clear. As already mentioned, work teams are considerably larger (Turnbull 1968:135), and the level at which decision making and behavioral integration occur is greater among the net-hunters than among the archers. Turnbull (1965b:298) states that in their forest context the net-hunter band "is an egalitarian unit, acting by unanimous accord," whereas among the archers "each section is independent of the others, and cooperates only when called upon to do so by the headman for some purpose related to the village [Turnbull 1965b:300]." The position of headman among the archers, furthermore, is nonhereditary and exists primarily to expedite relations between the Mbuti and their village patrons, with the headman lacking any means of enforcing his orders (Turnbull 1965b:300). It is likewise significant that the individual families assume greater independence among the net-hunters as well when these bands are resident in the village (Turnbull 1965a:85; 1965b:298), while the dominance of the band over individual families occurs among the archers when they are away from the villages and dependent primarily upon the forest during the honey season (Turnbull 1965a:107).

The different levels of integration and cooperation, then, are not specific to each division among the Mbuti; rather they appear only to be typical of each group as a function of its particular place of residence and dependence—village or forest. The large, cooperative bands characterize the net-hunters only because they spend most of their time dependent upon the forest, while the archers, characterized by the prevalence of independent nuclear families, depend primarily upon the village. A more precise understanding of the association between residence–dependence and subordination of the nuclear family would be possible if more quantitative information—instead of qualitative typing—were available on band residence and organization.

As would be expected, the net-hunters, who for the most part subsist in larger, more cooperative units, dependent upon the forest, employ a hunting technology which both demands and facilitates their integration at this level, while the archers, operating in the village for most of the year as independent families, employ a technology that places a premium on small, automomous hunting units. Based on this information, current models of the dynamics between population growth and energy expenditure in subsistence (cf. Boserup 1965; H. Odum 1971) would predict that population pressure[9] is greater among the net-hunters than it is among the archers, and that, consequently, the expenditure of energy in subsistence activities should be greater among the net-hunters as well.

Unfortunately, Turnbull (1961, 1965a, 1965b, 1968, 1972) does not provide any substantial ecological or demographic data from which a conclusive evaluation can be made of the role that variations in population density play in the divergent subsistence strategies employed by the Mbuti. Instead, he only gives a general estimate for the entire Mbuti population at about 40,000 persons inhabiting an area of approximately 50,000 square miles (129,500 km^2) (Turnbull 1972:295)

However, the former distribution of Pygmies in Africa, including the Mbuti, was much greater than it is today (Murdock 1959:48–49), due primarily to the invasion and reduction of the forests by populations of shifting cultivators. Turnbull (1965a:19–20; 1965b:283) lists the groups that are directly contiguous to the Mbuti and acknowledges the impact that this encroachment has had upon the mobility of the Mbuti. The principle invaders of the Ituri Forest are the Azande and Mangbetu to the northwest, and the Mamvu-Mangutu to the north, the Bira to the south, and the Lese to the east. The Ndaka and Mbo may be included to the west. The Alur, Lendu, Logo, and Lugbara may also be added to this list of invaders; while not all of these latter groups have been in direct contact with the Mbuti, each represents a significant factor in the general population explansion into Mbuti territory from the contiguous and more densely settled areas of Uganda to the east and the Sudan to the north. Turnbull (1972:295) estimates the groups that he lists to number 60,000 persons; with the latter groups included, this number would be considerably higher, displaying a sizable population of densely settled shifting cultivators enclosing the Mbuti on the north and east. Baxter and Butt (1953: 20) state that Pygmies were previously located as far north as the Uele River

[9] The claim that population pressure is higher among the net-hunters does not imply that this group has been reduced to near starvation. This statement merely stresses that the ratio of population to explotiable resources is higher among the net-hunters than it is among the archers. Indeed, the thrust of the argument presented here is that the net-hunters, faced with higher population densities, have adopted behaviors which increase the amount of food resources exploited by them, thus minimizing the likelihood of being reduced to a precarious existence.

near the Zaire–Sudan border, an area presently occupied by Azande, while the Alur claim that before they settled in the territory adjacent to Lake Albert on the Zaire–Uganda border, this area was almost exclusively inhabited by bands of Pygmies (Southall 1956:23). The present distribution of Pygmies in the Ituri Forest, then, represents a considerable reduction in area from their previous dispersion. Furthermore, the Mbuti do not enjoy exclusive occupation of the remaining areas of the forest that they inhabit today.

The major thrust of the population invasion into Mbuti territory has been from the east. The present West Nile District of Uganda, north of Lake Albert and containing a diverse population of cultivators and herders, has served as a major staging area for this westward expansion. The population density of the West Nile District is among the highest in Uganda. While the population concentrations in this district do not equal those in the vicinity of Lake Victoria, or in southern Kigezi (on the Rwanda border) where little uncultivated farmland is still available, the average density according to the 1959 census was 74 persons per square mile (1 mi^2 = 2.6 km^2) (Parsons 1960b:49). Many local densities reported were considerably higher; Okoro County (Alur) was estimated at 123 persons per square mile, while Ayiva County (Lugbara) was reported at 324 persons per square mile (Parsons 1960b:49). Southall (1956: 267), meanwhile, estimated the average population density among the Alur at 100 persons per square mile. Even Toro District to the south of Lake Albert registered a population density of 80 persons per square mile (Parsons, 1960a: 7). Even granting a large margin for error in calculation, these figures denote relatively high population densitites for this area relative to other comparable areas in Africa (cf. Stevenson 1968).

The relatively high population density in the West Nile District, and the subsistence pressures that this produces, has been attributed as the principal reason for the replacement of the cereal eulosine by the higher yielding yet less nutritious tuber cassava as the principal food in this area (O'Connor 1971:41–42), and is also likely to be the primary agent making the West Nile District a major source of labor migration into the urban centers of Uganda (O'Connor 1971:42, 261). High population density has also been the major force behind the continuous expansion of peoples from this area into the less densely settled territory of the Mbuti to the West. Climatic factors, combined with the availability of land, made migration westward more attractive than expansion in other directions. This westward expansion has made the eastern portion of Zaire, from Lake Kivu in the south to the Sudan border in the north, one of the most densely settled areas in the country (Trewartha and Zelinsky 1954:70). Population density in northeastern Zaire has been more than double that of the nation as a whole, with local densities reported in 1948 of 75 persons per square mile (Trewartha and Zelinsky 1954:173).

The contemporary picture of population density in northeastern Zaire is in marked contrast to the image presented by the Alur for the period when they first entered the area. Contemporary populations of hunters and gatherers have all experienced a continuous reduction in the size of their habitats as a result of the encroachment of agricultural populations; the Mbuti are no exception. A continual reduction in the size of the Mbuti habitat has occurred as a result of a general population expansion from the east and of Azande expansion and conquest from the north. Recent developments have also had their impact by further reducing the effective size of the Mbuti habitat. Upon returning to Camp Putnam (Epulu) after a 2-year absence, Turnbull (1961:29) describes some of the changes that had taken place during that time. These include the construction of a modern motel, "built by an enterprising Belgian who hoped to attract tourists," the establishment of a "*Station de Chasse* for the capture of forest animals, particularly okapi, and for the training of forest elephants," as well as the building of mud houses for the workers "with a few tiny African stores and an establishment proudly calling itself Hotel de Biere."

The most recent encroachments upon the Mbuti habitat, including those mentioned previously, must be viewed simply as a continuation—albeit dramatic—of a long-standing trend. Meanwhile, Turnbull (1965a:26) maintains that no evidence exists to suggest that a reduction has taken place in the size of the Mbuti population. If this is the case, then it is difficult to accept the contention that these developments have had little impact upon the subsistence methods of the Mbuti, who have been the chief victims of these transgressions.

However, an apparent contradiction exists; of the two divisions among the Mbuti, the archers, located in the eastern and southeastern portions of the forest, those regions most affected by the intrusion of cultivators (and other disruptions), exhibit the behavior and organization which indicate the least affect of population pressure on resources. Unfortunately, the absence of any information on the size of the net-hunter and archer populations specifically, or on the magnitude of their respective territories, precludes any calculation of the relative density of each population. The closest information provided by Turnbull, which might indicate the relative size of the two divisions among the Mbuti, includes the number of huts present in each of several net-hunter and archer camps plus a map of the location of hunting camps in the Ituri Forest visited by him. The number of huts in 6 net-hunter camps were 28, 18, 16, 13, 11, and 8 for an average of 15.66 huts; 7 archer camps contained 25, 11, 10, 9, 6, and 5 huts for an average of 10.85 huts per camp (Turnbull 1965a:99). Turnbull's (1965a:317, Map 2) map indicates that of the total hunting camps visited by him, approximately 50 were net-hunter camps while only about 15 were camps belonging to archers. Although how representative these figures are, unfortunately, cannot be determined, they do at least suggest both a greater size and density of the net-hunter population in the forest relative to that of the archers.

While the density of archers is likely to be less than that for the net-hunters, the overall density of the archer territory should be considerably greater than that of the net-hunter territory, due to the larger concentraton of non-Mbuti populations in this portion of the forest. However, another factor assumes significance, which may account for the absence of behavioral indications of population pressure among the archers relative to the net-hunters. Although neither the archers nor the net-hunters are likely to have maintained the same diet that was common to the Mbuti prior to the invasion of their habitat by agricultural populations—population encroachment, for example, is quite likely to have effected a gradual reduction in the general availability of meat within the forest and in the Mbuti diet—the archers have clearly experienced the greatest dietary transformation. While the net-hunters still subsist mainly upon the forest, the archer diet consists primarily of domesticated foods, particularly cassava and plantains. The archers, then, have experienced more than merely a shift in the relative frequencies of different wild foodstuffs; they have undergone a fundamental change in their trophic position within the forest community, subsisting primarily upon abundant, domesticated resources.

The greater population density made possible by the increased production of edible foodstuffs from the agricultural gardens would provide for a reduction in the pressures of population upon resources among the archers. This is true particularly since the population providing this increased productivity was considerably larger than the archer population and thus could absorb them with little additional stress. The archers appear to have been readily assimilated as daily consumers of the new resources, while at the same time more or less retaining their traditional mode of subsistence; they have not had to become involved in the heavy agricultural labor upon which this new level of productivity is based (Turnbull 1961:172–173; 1965a:39). Rather, the archers operate an important work gate (see H. Odum 1971:43–47.) in the energetics of the agricultural system; by protecting the gardens from destruction by animals, the archers remove a limiting factor that would inhibit the growth and production of crops in those gardens.

Because of their importance in the agricultural system throughout most of the year, the archers may have been able to increase their caloric consumption relative to the labor expended in obtaining those calories. Given the continued encroachment of agricultural populations on at least three sides of the forest, and the reduction that this must have caused in both the size and the natural productivity of the Mbuti habitat, the input–output ratio of energy expended to that received is likely to have proceeded in the reverse direction among the net-hunters, who still subsist primarily upon the undomesticated resources of the forest.

The explanation given here, then, for the distinction between net-hunters and archers may be summarized. As a consequence of a steady intrusion into the forest of populations practicing agriculture—primarily from the east but also from the north—the effective size and natural productivity of the Mbuti habitat suffered a decline relative to the size of the population. The higher population density among the Mbuti, which resulted from this encroachment upon the forest, has demanded more labor and greater cooperation and organization among those groups that still subsist primarily upon the forest if a continued maintenance of the population is to be assured.[10] At the same time, this intrusion of agriculturalists into the forest has created a new niche for some indigenous hunters where the input–output ratio is lower than that which is obtained from traditional subsistence on the forest. This reduced ratio would indeed make the new niche desirable, particularly for hunters living in the most disturbed sections of the forest.

The same considerations can be applied to the temporal variations in subsistence behaviors among the Mbuti as well. The honey season is a period of general abundance in the forest (Turnbull 1965b:286; 1968:298) that follows the resumption of the rains after the brief dry season in January and February. The increased natural productivity of the forest at this time provides a greater variety and amount of food sources for the net-hunters, temporarily reducing the population–resource ratio among them, and facilitating commensurate adjustments in work loads, degree of cooperation, and band organization. The net hunter's beliefs and activities during the honey season are entirely consistent with the predictions for a population experiencing a reduction of population pressure on resources, and the reduced input–output ratio of energy expended to energy received that this affords.

From the same theoretical perspective, the behavior of the archers during the honey season is predictable as well. If the rhythmic productivity of the agricultural cycle produces a period of "nutritional strain" at this time of the year and the archers are unable to rely as usual upon the produce from the gardens of their patrons, then they must band together in order to maintain a subsistence solely upon the most disturbed section of the forest. By doing this, they might also be avoiding pressure to become involved in the heavy agricultural labor required at this time. Because their area of the forest is the most affected by the encroachment of non-Mbuti populations, their subsistence solely upon undomesticated resources represents a shift from a low population–resource ratio for most of the year to a brief period of relatively high population density. Subsistence solely on the natural productivity of the forest in this area demands an appropriate increase in cooperation and work load among the archers. Thus, the *begbe* hunt of the archers during the honey season

> is like the net-hunt in technique, only without the nets, and it similarly demands the cooperation of men, women and children in much larger numbers than could be

[10] Turnbull (1961:94–108) describes the "crime of Cephu," which he refers to as "one of the most heinous crimes in Pygmy eyes, and one that rarely occurs [Turnbull 1961:109]." Cephu was a member of the Epulu net-hunting band who was discovered secretly placing his net ahead of the nets of the other members of the band, thus violating the strict rule of cooperation in the hunt, which is central to the net-hunting band. The seriousness of Cephu's crime in the eyes of the Pygmies, symbolized by the permission given even to children since that event to act disrespectfully towards him, underscores the likelihood that reduction of their habitat has placed pressure upon the net-hunters to cooperate in the hunt.

supplied by any one section of the band. All sections, therefore, gather together at this time and build a single camp [Turnbull 1965b:300].

The behavior of the archers during the honey season, while apparently contradictory to the actions of the net-hunters, is precisely the response expected of a population suddenly forced to depend upon a forest that is unable to provide them with the caloric consumption relative to energy expenditure comparable to that which they receive from the domesticated gardens during the remainder of the year. Given the sudden increase in the population–resource ratio at this time of the year, the response of the archers is quite predictable—increased cooperation and organization and increased per captia expenditure of labor in subsistence activities (archers claim this happens). The greater disruption of the areas of the forest inhabited by the archers would partly account for their formation into larger cooperative bands during this period than those which characterize the net-hunters for the remainder of the year.

Conclusions

This discussion strongly suggests that the Mbuti, like most other populations, respond to spatial and temporal variations in the abundance and distribution of resources within their habitat through ecologically intelligible behavior. As would be expected, the categorical claim that ecological considerations are irrelevant to an explanation of variations in Mbuti subsistence behavior appears to lack foundation; rather than being "strange" (Turnbull 1968:134) or "curious" (Turnbull 1965b:299), the variations that occur in these behaviors are precisely those that would most reasonably be expected (in contrast to Turnbull 1968:136), given the aggregate material context of the Mbuti hunters within the Ituri forest.

The theoretical model employed here suggests that divergent evolution has been occurring among the Mbuti, most likely since the advent of agricultural encroachment upon the forest several centuries ago. The circumscription and invasion of the forest by populations of shifting cultivators has apparently caused the two distinct hunting adaptations. By reducing the total size and natural productivity of the forest, the encroachment of agriculturalists has demanded an increased intensification of subsistence activities among those groups (net-hunters) that still subsist primarily upon the natural productivity of the forest. At the same time, the presence of agricultural villages in the forest has created a new niche for hunters (through their protection of and subsistence upon the village gardens) that has afforded a reduction in the ratio of population to resources compared to that offered by continued subsistence upon the forest. Since these hunters (archers) enjoy a reduced input–output ratio of energy expended to energy received in subsistence, they have sustained a reduction in the intensity of social cooperation and organization among themselves, and have developed greater, individualized socioeconomic ties with the village communities upon which they rely. A seasonal variation in the abundance and distribution of resources within the forest temporarily reverses the relative population–resource ratio among the net-hunters and archers, producing a reversal in the levels of social cooperation, band organization, and work loads associated with these groups.

This explanation for the distinction between net-hunters and archers, as well as for the apparently paradoxical events that accompany the honey season, recognizes the centrality of ecological considerations in subsistence behavior. The ecological explanation of flux among the Mbuti proposed here is not only more consistent with the expectations derived from research on other human populations; it is also more consistent with the aggregate, albeit limited, information available on the spatiotemporal context of the Mbuti hunters than is the opposing claim by Turnbull that environmental considerations are irrelevant to an understanding of variations in Mbuti subsistence behavior

Unfortunately, the conclusions offered here can only remain suggestive; sufficient data for demonstrating the precise operation of ecological processes among the Mbuti are not available.[11] The absence of the necessary supporting data to confirm the explanation proposed is symptomatic of the problems inherent in Turnbull's contention that ecological considerations are irrelevant. While arguing for the primacy of social over ecological considerations in Mbuti subsistence behavior, Turnbull fails to appreciate significant ecological concepts and the kinds of quantitative data they require for their proper evaluation. The lack of a clear ecological or materialist paradigm, with the integral application of a deductive research method to ensure sufficient data collection, precludes any adequate appraisal by Turnbull of the operation of ecological processes among the Mbuti, and makes his claim for the irrelevance of environmental considerations scientifically groundless.

References

Abruzzi, W.
1979 Population pressure and subsistence strategies among the Mbuti Pygmies. *Human Ecology 7:*183–189.

Balikci, A.
1968 The Netsilik Eskimos: Adaptive processes. In *Man the hunter* (R. Lee and I. DeVore, Eds.). Chicago: Aldine. Pp. 78–82.

[11] Additional data on Mbuti ecology became available to the author too late to be incorporated into this chapter. These new data include important quantitative information on Mbuti subsistence and, thus, are of relevance to the thesis proposed here. These data have been discussed in a subsequent article (Abruzzi 1979), and the interested reader is encouraged to consult this later publication.

Barth, F.
1956 Ecological relationships of ethnic groups in Swat, North Pakistan. *American Anthropologist 58:*1079–1089.
1964 Ethnic processes on the Pathan–Baluch boundary. In *Indo-Iranica* (G. Redard, Ed.). Weisbaden: Harrassowitz. Pp. 13–21.
Barth, F. (Ed.)
1969 *Ethnic groups and boundaries: The social organization of culture difference.* Boston: Little, Brown.
Baxter, P., and A. Butt
1953 *The Azande and related peoples of the Anglo–Egyptian Sudan and Belgian Congo.* London: International African Institute.
Bicchieri, M.
1969 The differential use of identical features of physical habitat in connection with exploitative, settlement, and community patterns: The BaMbuti case study. In *Contributions to Anthropology: Ecological Essays* (D. Damas, Ed.). Ottowa: National Museums of Canada, Bulletin No. 230. Pp. 65–72.
Biebuyck, D.
1973 *Lega culture.* Berkeley: University of California Press.
Boserup, E.
1965 *The conditions of agricultural growth: The economics of agrarian change under population pressure.* Chicago: Aldine.
Boughey, A.
1973 *Ecology of populations* (2nd ed.). New York: Macmillan.
Carniero, R.
1961 Slash-and-burn cultivation among the kuikuru and its implications for cultural development in the Amazon basin. *Anthropological Supplement No. 2:*47–67.
1967 On the relationship between size of population and complexity of social organization. *Southwestern Journal of Anthropology 24:*354–374.
1970 A theory of the origin of the state. *Science 169:*733–738.
Clark, C.
1967 *Population growth and land use.* New York: St. Martin's Press.
Collins, P.
1964 The logic of functional analysis in anthropology. Unpublished PhD. Dissertation, Department of Philosophy, Columbia University.
Damas, D.
1969 Environment, history and central Eskimo society. In *Contributions to Anthropology: Ecological Essays* (D. Damas, Ed.). Ottawa: National Museums of Canada, Bulletin No. 230. Pp. 40–64.
DeSchlippe, P.
1956 *Shifting cultivation in Africa: The Zande system of agriculture.* London: Routledge and Kegan Paul.
Douglas, M.
1963 *The Lele of Kasai.* London: Oxford University Press.
Grove, A.
1970 *Africa south of the Sahara* (2nd ed.). London: Oxford University Press.
Hardesty, D.
1975 The Niche concept: Suggestions for its use in human ecology. *Human Ecology 3:*71–85.
Harner, M.
1970 Population and the social evolution of agriculturalists. *Southwestern Journal of Anthropology 26:*67–86.
Hempel, K.
1965 *Aspects of Scientific Explanation.* New York: Free Press.

Hutchinson, G.
1957 Concluding remarks. *Cold Springs Harbor symposium on Quantitative Biology 22*:415–427.
Lee, R.
1968 What hunters do for a living, or, How to make out on scarce resources. In *Man the hunter* (R. Lee and I. DeVore, Eds.). Chicago: Aldine. Pp. 30–48.
1972 !Kung spatial organization: An ecological and historical perspective. *Human Ecology 1*:125–147.
Lee, R., and I. DeVore (Eds.)
1968 *Man the hunter*. Chicago: Aldine.
Margalef, R.
1968 *Perspectives in ecological theory*. Chicago: University of Chicago Press.
May, J.
1965 *The ecology of malnutrition in Middle Africa*. New York: Hafner.
Mayr, E.
1963 *Animal species and evolution*. Cambridge, Mass.: Belknap Press.
Meggitt, M.
1962 *Desert people: A study of the Walbiri aborigines of Central Australia*. Sydney: Angus and Robertson.
Moore, O.
1957 Divination—A new perspective. *American Anthropologist 59*:69–74.
Murdock, G.
1959 *Africa: Its people and their culture history*. New York: McGraw-Hill.
Murphy, R., and J. Steward
1956 Tappers and trappers: Parallel processes in acculturation. *Economic Development and Culture Change 4*:335–353
Netting, R.
1971 *The ecological approach in culture study*. Reading, Mass.: Addison-Wesley.
O'Connor, A.
1971 *An economic geography of East Africa* (2nd ed.). London: G. Bell and Sons
Odum, E.
1971 *Fundamentals of ecology* (3rd ed.). Philadelphia: W. B. Saunders.
Odum, H.
1971 *Environment, power and society*. New York: Wiley.
Parsons, D.
1960a The systems of agriculture practiced in Uganda: The Plantain-Robusta coffee system. *Memoirs of the Research Division, Series 3, No. 2*. Kampala: Uganda Department of Agriculture.
1960b The systems of agriculture practiced in Uganda: The northern systems. *Memoirs of the Research Division, Series 3, No. 2*. Kampala: Uganda Department of Agriculture.
1960c The systems of agriculture practiced in Uganda: Maps. *Memoirs of the Research Division, Series 3, No. 4*. Kampala: Uganda Department of Agriculture.
Phillips, J.
1960 *Agriculture and ecology in Africa*. New York: Praeger.
Putnam, P.
1948 The Pygmies of the Ituri forest In *A reader in general anthropology* (C. Coon, Ed.). New York: Henry Holt. Pp. 322–342.
Rappaport, R.
1968 *Pigs for the ancestors*. New Haven: Yale University Press.
Schebesta, P.
1933 *Among the Congo Pygmies*. London: Hutchinson and Co.
Southall. A.
1956 *Alur society*. Cambridge: W. Heffer.

Spooner, B., (Ed.)
1972 *Population growth: Anthropological implications.* Cambridge, Mass.: M.I.T. Press.

Stevenson, R.
1968 *Population and political systems in tropical Africa.* New York: Columbia University Press.

Steward, J.
1938 Basin-plateau aboriginal socio-political groups. Bureau of American Ethnology, Bulletin 120. Washington, D.C.: U.S. Government Printing Office.
1955 *Theory of culture change.* Urbana: University of Illinois Press.

Trewartha, G., and W. Zelinsky
1954 The population geography of Belgian Africa. *Annals of the Association of American Geographers 44:*163–193.

Turnbull, C.
1961 *Forest people.* New York: Simon and Schuster.
1965a *Wayward servants.* New York: Natural History Press.
1965b The Mbuti Pygmies of the Congo. In *Peoples of Africa* (J. Gibbs, Ed.). New York: Holt, Rinehart and Winston. Pp. 279–317.
1968 The importance of flux in two hunting societies. In *Man the hunter* (R. Lee and I. DeVore, Eds.). Chicago: Aldine. pp. 132–137.
1972 Demography of small-scale societies. In *The structure of human populations* (G. Harrison and A. Boyce, Eds.). Oxford: Clarendon Press, Pp. 283–312.

Whittaker, R.
1975 *Communities and ecosystems* (2nd ed.). New York: Macmillan.

Woodburn, J.
1968 Stability and flexibility in Hadza residential groupings. In *Man the hunter* (R. Lee and I. DeVore, Eds.). Chicago: Aldine. Pp. 103–110.

2 Ecology and the Problem of Tribe: A Critique of the Hobbesian Model of Preindustrial Warfare[1]

JANE BENNETT ROSS

Introduction

Armed conflict in varied forms has been a recurrent feature among many tropical forest horticultural populations, but the conditions that have impelled it and the interrelationship of factors accounting for its persistence and periodicity require greater elucidation. Much of the literature on such behavior among preindustrial societies has tended to emphasize its seemingly irrational, nonmaterial or individualistic aspects, or to focus upon its apparent role in the maintenance of social solidarity and ethnic identity. For Amazonia, in particular, such arguments have been characterized by a lack of serious attention to or even explicit rejection of ecological models developed from ethnographic and historical materials elsewhere. Too little attention, however, has been systematically paid to an ecological viewpoint in which the behavioral components of patterns of aggressive activity are seen in terms of their functions relative to strategic problems of environment utilization.

The purpose of this chapter is to refocus attention on such problems and on their relation to intra- and intergroup hostilities within a delimited ecological and historical context. It offers an analysis of armed conflict at the tribal level, with particular attention to the interrelation of sociopolitical organization, demography, subsistence ecology, colonial impaction, and disease among the Achuarä Jívaro of the northwest Peruvian Amazon.

Throughout this examination, analytical priorities reflect those of the

---

[1] Special thanks are due to Barbara Price, Eric Ross, Robert Paynter, and Marvin Harris for advice and encouragement on earlier versions of this chapter. To Eric Ross, also, my appreciation for the map.

BEYOND THE MYTHS OF CULTURE
Essays in Cultural Materialism

ISBN 0-12-598180-5

cultural materialist research strategy (see Harris 1968:643–687; 1977:31–54). Thus, the behavioral components that comprise the conditions of conflict are viewed in terms of the functions they perform with regard to environment-utilization and the maintenance of crucial population–resource relationships, on the one hand, and additional infrastructural and related structural and superstructural components on the other. This strategy is central to the analysis of armed conflict among the Achuarä Jívaro and to the associated critique of the contrasting Hobbesian approach, which disclaims the relevance of material factors to an explanation of tribal warfare.

Tribal Warfare: The View from Amazonia

Initially, it should be noted that features of Jivaroan armed conflict, including former head-taking expeditions and still-continuing revenge raids, have figured prominently, although with varying emphasis, in the culture history of many Amazonian hunter–horticultural populations (see Biocca 1970; Carneiro 1970a; Chagnon 1966, 1968a,b, 1974; Denevan 1972; Harner 1963, 1972, 1976; Harris 1975; Huxley and Capa 1964; Karsten 1935, 1967; Lathrap 1968, 1970; Metraux 1963; Morey and Marwitt 1975; Murphy 1960; Murphy and Murphy 1974; Siskind 1968, 1973; Up de Graff 1923; Vayda 1961). What we know of their proximate causes and patterning is comparable, moreover, to features of armed conflict among tropical horticulturalists elsewhere. Yet there has been little attempt to draw upon such comparative materials or on the ecological models that have developed in relationship to them.

Napoleon Chagnon, who is perhaps the most explicit advocate of this type of particularism, maintains that models from New Guinea and elsewhere in the ethnographic world simply do not apply to the analysis of warfare in Amazonia; they posit a relationship between warfare, population density, and scarce resources that, he maintains, is conspicuously absent in the South American lowlands (1974:195). There, he writes, the "generally intensive warfare patterns . . . do not correlate well with resource shortages or competition for land or hunting areas [1974:127]." Colleagues who have argued otherwise have been tarred with the brush of mechanical reductionism, accused of assuming "that tribal warfare everywhere is a direct response to population density and resource shortages [Chagnon 1974:xi,195]."

Yet, this interpretation constitutes a systematic misrepresentation of the arguments at issue. It is a response to the relatively recent controversy over faunal protein as a limiting factor to cultural development and population expansion in the Amazon Basin. Proponents of the "protein position" in this dispute (Denevan 1972; Gross 1975; Harris, 1974, 1975, 1977; E. Ross 1976, 1978, 1979a,b; J. B. Ross 1971) simultaneously advocate serious attention to the structural dynamics of general biocultural adaptation in this region. A major emphasis has thus centered upon the relationship between demographic factors and subsistence potential, and behaviors—such as infanticide, abortion, group fission, migration and warfare—that may systematically regulate and/or redistribute population numbers in accordance with techno-environmentally and economically mediated availability of strategic resources. The interpretation of Chagnon's corpus of data from the Yanomamö Indians (Venezuela and Brazil) is an important focus of contention here as is the explanation of tribal warfare among other inland Amerindians such as the Jívaro.

THE HOBBESIAN PERSPECTIVE

Chagnon concedes that from the perspective of general evolution, there is, in his wording, a "legitimate" relationship between warfare, population density and pressure on strategic resources; but in specific cases—the Yanomamö, Jívaro, Tupinamba, and many other tropical forest tribes—he asserts that other factors take explanatory priority, "in particular, the nature of tribal political organization [1974:xi]." He contends that warfare is "the extension of tribal politics in the absence of other means," wedded to "the very nature of the tribal social design [1974:xi]."

Here, he joins Marshall Sahlins (1968, 1972) in advancing the Hobbesian perspective on preindustrial warfare. This is the notion that anarchy and conflict are intrinsic to tribal life in the absence of specialized political institutions capable of adjudicating internal disputes and maintaining supralocal order and integration.

According to Sahlins, tribal society is "the most tenuous of arrangements, without even a semblance of collective organization" [1968:viii]." Internally, in the absence of overarching controls, "individuals and subgroups . . . maintain the certain right and potential inclination to secure by force their safety, gain, and glory [Sahlins 1968:7]." Generalized economic, ritual, and social institutions do, of course, further the interests of preindustrial order, but beneath such "powerful impositions of the cultural system," primitive anarchy is held to prevail. Indeed, for Sahlins, it is the "unconscious of the system" and tribal organization, nothing less than the means to suppress it (1968:7–8).

Anarchy is the equivalent of Hobbes' "Warre," the metaphorical war of "every man against every man" in the absence of political institutions to stop it (Sahlins 1968:7). While this particular circumstance has never actually come to pass, Sahlins considers its potential, for tribal polities, nonetheless compelling—an unruly Pegasus relentlessly chafing against the bit of sociocultural constraints.

This perspective recurs in Chagnon's interpretation of Yanomamö warfare: The Yanomamö persist in such behavior because communities, vis-à-vis each other, "hunger" after sovereignty. Thus, the political stance called "Warre"—the "chronic disposition to do battle, to oppose and dispose of one's sovereign neighbors [Chagnon 1974:77]"—is crucial to the explanation of intervillage hostilities. Chagnon writes that in the absence of supralocal peacemaking institutions, tribal villages are perpetually in a state of "Warre" such that "hostility towards one's neighbors is of the essence of tribal culture [1974:77]" and its actualization in warfare, not the least bit surprising (1974:77).

These assumptions have questionable empirical and logical status. In the first place, Chagnon's essential position on Yanomamö warfare—that "a militant ideology and the warfare it entails function to preserve the sovereignty of independent villages in a milieu of chronic warfare [1968b:112]"—is tautological as an explanation. One cannot maintain that the drive toward sovereignty is intrinsic in the tribal design and, therefore, responsible for tribal warfare, and simultaneously attribute its preservation to the same agonistic patterns *unless* one can support the imputed causal relationships according to canons of scientific proof. At the very least, Chagnon must ground his "explanation" of warfare in a responsible elucidation of the empirical factors that necessitate sovereignty. Then, it is incumbent, given the invocation of the Hobbesian model, to consider why all so-called tribal populations have not historically displayed patterns of armed conflict if it is the case that the truculent preservation of sovereignty is a universal tribal feature. As it now stands, any related attempt to explain the warfare—where we do find such patterns—is rendered quixotic and arbitrary, not to mention opposed to the evidence.

But Sahlins' general overview of tribesmen offers more of the same. He describes their communities as "set apart by [their] own interests from a hostile world [1968:32]," "jealous of their own sovereignty," and recognizing "no greater political cause standing over and against their separate interests [1968:21]." He notes that joint interests may lead them into periodic alliances, but these tend to be limited in duration, evanescing with the accomplishment of whatever purpose gave them life and returning the tribe to its "normal state of disunity [1968:21]."

But it is one thing to speak of documentable evidence of collectivity and disunity and quite another to impute to tribesmen unconscious drives toward jealously guarded autonomy structurally entrenched in a monolithic lifestyle. The lifestyle is simply not monolithic, and we cannot, in any case, explain the variability by recourse to a purported constant.

Variability within and between systems is a given that raises the question of how theory may be expected to handle it. It is an obvious cornerstone of Darwinian theory that without naturally occurring variation, selection would be empirically impossible. But one cannot predict a priori which variations observable within a body of data will be significant in terms of a particular problem and which can safely be ignored. That is, essentially, the province of the paradigm that sets forth the differential importance of whole spheres of behavior and considers some to be codeterminative of others. Variability in a part of the system deemed paradigmatically important must receive close attention. But the spheres under discrimination will differ according to the paradigm of the investigator; and if the latter lacks a paradigm altogether or believes that all facts speak for themselves, the differential importance criterion cannot be used at all.

The Hobbesian approach avoids the confrontation with variability by ignoring it and assuming a homogeneity of response of tribesmen everywhere. Heavy on the metaphor and elegant though it may appear, it offers nothing in the way of predictive value and little more in the way of retrodiction, certainly not in terms of any probabilistic elucidation of the factors responsible for similarities and differences in the warfare patterns and in their frequency among populations with specific evolutionary trajectories.

AMAZONIAN SUBSISTENCE AND SOCIETY: A DARWINIAN PERSPECTIVE

The critical question at the crux of the confrontation between Hobbesian and materialist approaches to Amazonian warfare is that of whether there is a causal relationship between warfare, mode of production, and an ecological limiting factor. The interfluves of Amazonia, where the "least contacted" Amerindians remain, now constitute the major arena for debate. Fundamental to the following discussion is our understanding of carrying capacity and the role of limiting factors—how they articulate with sociocultural behavior, the limitations on our ability to operationalize such articulation, and ways of overcoming such limitations to better comprehend the complex character of warfare in sociocultural life.

A major problem with the Hobbesian approach lies in its categorical distinction between mode of production and warfare, which precludes cognizance of the embeddedness of tribal-level armed conflict in its technoeconomic and demographic context. A biocultural, neo-Darwinian perspective, on the other hand, contends that warfare cannot be isolated from such factors. It operates on the premise that human populations and the cultural repertoires they carry are embedded in the natural world like other animal species and, therefore, subject to the pressures—whether obvious or subtle—of natural selection and adaptive process. Culture, in this view, is as subject to selective pressures as morphology, although the process of transmission across the generations is wholly different. It represents certainly one of the most flexible and powerful of species-specific adaptive strategies, the product of several million years of co-evolution of biology and behavior.

A concept such as natural selection—the differential survival or retention of traits as a result of differential reproductive success under specified conditions—is capable of integrating a behavioral complex, such as warfare, with essentially "biological" phenomena, such as nutrition or disease, as elements of the same system; furthermore, it can do so without reductionism (insofar as it is recognized that the mechanisms of transmission continue to differ). The "specified conditions" of selection pressure are environmental in the broadest sense—more accurately a product of the way a population makes its living and the quantity and distribution of the resources necessary for it to continue doing so. One or another such element, given one or another mode of life, may act as a limiting factor upon the growth or expansion of a given population; clearly, this need not be the same empirical factor at all times and in all places. Availability of water tangibly limits the size and range of desert hunter-gatherers (Lee and Devore 1968). Cultivators may avoid such areas altogether unless their behavioral repertoire includes the technology of irrigation. Water as a limiting factor will act quite differently in these two cases.

What a limiting factor does is to establish the ceiling on the carrying capacity for human populations *until* or *unless* there is a major shift in (*a*) mode of production, or (*b*) natural features of climate, soils, hydrography, vegetation cover, etc. (including biodegradation). To the extent that limiting factors determine demographic ceilings, they act as powerful selective forces, promoting the retention of fundamental features of the human repertoire articulated with continuing natural pressures. When natural pressures are mitigated, and then only so long as cultural systems maintain their mitigation, we may grant that a particular limiting factor no longer sets the ceiling on carrying capacity or does so at a quantitatively different level, or that some other factor may then come into play to limit growth. The concept of limiting factor inevitably invokes the concept of carrying capacity; linkage of the two is obvious in that the former is necessarily used to define the latter.

Allan defines carrying capacity as "the maximum number of people that a given land area will maintain in perpetuity under a given system of usage without land degradation setting in [quoted in Street 1969:104]." But, as Street points out, a given system of land usage assumes unvarying technology and crop patterning as well as qualitatively and quantitatively constant per capita food consumption (1969:104). Then, it has also been assumed that average fallowing practices are such that ultimate impairment of the soil is obviated; Street effectively disabuses us of this notion with specific empirical evidence (1969:104–105).

Additionally, Allan's definition suggests nothing of alternative and supplemental strategies of environmental use by which populations not only maximize per capita caloric return, but secure other necessary elements, e.g., faunal protein among inland Amazonian hunter–horticulturalists. The pan-Amazonian mix of hunting, gathering, fishing, and horticulture is hardly fortuitous in this regard. Indeed, solely on the basis of horticultural productivity, Carneiro (1973) observes that Amerindian staples such as manioc, taro, and yams yield a higher caloric value per unit land sown than cereals and, on this basis, could easily support sedentary villages of 500 persons. Yet, average village size is well below this number (Carneiro 1973) and reflects, as I shall indicate, other constraints, in particular those posed by protein procurement in the Amazonian interfluve.

The limiting factor focus may avert the conceptual and empirical difficulties with carrying capacity in that it admits that a given substantive limiting factor may change in value or be replaced in time and space by some other parameter. Concern is not really with a single factor, as such, but with the host of relationships interdependently limiting on the growth and expansion of village populations (cf. Ross 1978:15). Settlement pattern, socioeconomic organization, and warfare, in effect, take their shape from a complexity of biotic interactions. Agricultural productivity (itself a complex function of technology, environment, and behavior) is one aspect of the total picture, animal biomass and its availability (similarly) are others of a number of interrelated conditions that set limitations on the range of biocultural features characteristic of the human population.

It is curious, then, to consider the basis upon which Sahlins dismisses materialist and ecological perspectives on preindustrial adaptation—largely in reference to the issue of carrying capacity. He has provided an interesting commentary in this regard (1968b:85; 1972:Chap. 2), asserting that such populations usually operate at 20–30% of productive or carrying capacity. Thus, in his opinion, to seek explanations for crucial features of the "cultural" repertoire by recourse to such a measure is certainly injudicious. But he has ignored the question of limiting factor which, in the Amazonian case, effectively lowers the level of carrying capacity as he and others have calculated it. All of the relevant variables must be factored in, such as dietary protein and its relationship to factors of game and fish availability, population densities, technoeconomic strategies—indeed, all aspects of the mode of production and their articulation with an environment—that, *together,* set limits on the growth, stability, and cultural elaboration of Amazonian "tribal" societies.

Warfare cannot, therefore, be understood as separate from features of this sort. It is wedded not to any putative tribal drive toward sovereignty nor to any unconscious state of anarchy in system or in peoples' heads. Rather, it is embedded in the whole mode of production and reproduction, and the product of an opportunistic, but unrelenting process of natural selection.

RESOURCE VARIATION: IMPLICATIONS FOR THEORY

The most striking aspects of variation in Amazonian resource configuration are the following: Its alluvial areas (representing 2% of the Amazon) are abundant in terms of animal biomass concentration but highly restricted spatially; and its nonalluvial regions (comprising some 98%) show game animals dispersed and comparatively scarce (Carneiro 1970b; Denevan 1970; Fittkau 1969; Gross 1975; Lathrap 1968, 1970; Ross 1978). Of immediate relevance, however, is the fact that writers such as Carneiro will acknowledge, with respect to indigenous populations of the Amazonian floodplain, "that we can safely add resource concentration to environmental circumscription as a factor leading to warfare over land [1970a:737]"—with "land" signifying (as it must) all the productive resources of the floodplain: fish, game, and aquatic mammals as well as fertile soils (1970:736)—while they conceive of warfare among hunting-dependent populations of nonalluvial or terra firme zones in an opposite light. Because the terra firme suffers no lack of abundance of "land" (in the strict sense of surface area), it is assumed that the sparse distribution of a major strategic resource—game animals—across the surface is of negligible consequence in the generation of patterns of conflict. Thus, Carneiro has observed of interfluvial warfare, that it "was waged for reasons of revenge, the taking of women, the gaining of personal prestige, and motives of a similar sort. There being no shortage of land, there was, by and large, no warfare over land [1970a:735]." This is largely a red herring, since land is not the limiting resource of the terra firme. Yet, it has been argued from the preceding premises that we should consider factors other than ecological ones and, "in particular, the nature of tribal political organization," for the key to the explanation of patterns of armed conflict (Chagnon 1974:xi). We are, thus, asked to envisage "tribal warfare" as it exists or has existed in the vast Amazonian interfluve as compensatory for the absence of critical "organizational features" of a formal political sort (Chagnon 1974:xi).

Carneiro has alluded, moreover, to the facility with which Amazonian communities fission well before pressing on carrying capacity because of its "ease and frequency . . . for reasons not related to subsistance [1973:104]." This view follows from Leslie White's proposition that, as a rule, "the degree of solidarity [of a society] varies inversely with the size [1973:122n]" and from the assumption that "no great ecological deterrents exist to discourage a faction from splitting off from a parent community [1973:105]."

It is proposed that most Amerindian communities fission because it is easier to divide than to resolve disputes, such disputes being otherwise insoluble chiefly because of the absence of "organizational features" referred to earlier. But this skirts the crucial questions of the sources of such disputes and whether they are associated with issues of the density-related management of a population's resource base. Additionally, it is of special interest how the standard view of the Amazon interfluve has been extended so that one discusses population dispersal and village fissioning in terms of an *absence* of ecological deterrents to such processes, rather than argue that there might in fact be ecological deterrents to permanent, growing settlements.

Specifically, limits on the potential size, stability, and organizational capacity of interfluvial hunter–horticulturalists may be shown to reflect the nature of high quality protein procurement—particularly that derived from terrestrial and arboreal fauna quickly affected by human predation and from fish harvested from small, inland streams. While the limited alluvial zones are relatively rich in such resources, the inland forests tend to be deficient, especially in larger animals; so it is dependence on unstable protein sources, in the absence of domesticated animals or cultigens well supplied with requisite amino acids that, as Lathrap has noted, "largely controls the nature of the social group [1968:24]," including characteristic patterns of organized aggression.

Spatial variation in resource productivity is matched by a temporal variability over much of the Amazon, not only in quantity and distribution, but in security and in the labor demands of procurement. One result of this fluctuation is that both riverine and interriverine populations have regularly aspired to exploit more than one environmental zone. Inland groups are particularly eager to exploit alluvial areas during the dry seasons when fish are easily harvested from land-locked, oxbow lakes and shallow streams and thousands of water turtles lay their eggs on exposed sand beaches (cf. Chrostowski 1972:147; Denevan 1972:171–172). Flornoy, for example, accompanied Achuarä on an excursion with just this purpose in mind in the 1930s (1953:104,110).

By the same token, interzonal resource exploitation was undertaken by groups that were predominantly riverine-dwelling. Productive as the floodplain areas are during the dry season, they are not only highly limited in the Upper Amazon (most floodplain is found downriver of the present Peru–Brazil border), but, during the rainy season, the duration and intensity of which is not entirely uniform from one year to the next (Bates 1962:326–329; Bolian 1971:4), turtles are unavailable in great numbers, fish travel inland with floodwaters, and manioc stores may be under water. Such a situation was observed by the Jesuit missionary, Samuel Fritz, in 1689, when the riverine Jurimaguas Indians had to move inland "in search of dry ground and forest fruits to escape starvation [1922:61]."

Thus, few floodplain populations would not have been periodically pressed during the rainy seasons to avail themselves of resources of the inland forest. In certain cases, this seasonal inland quest was associated with military activity. The Tupían Cocama, who had settled on the floodplain of the lower Ucayali, made annual expeditions up and down the Huallaga and Marañon and into "their creeks and small tributaries to attack the Maina Indians and other tribes of that area [Metraux 1963:688]." With the advent of the dry season, Cocama war parties returned home, laden with booty, captives, and trophy heads (Metraux 1963:688)—for headhunting was an important motivating factor in such raids that removed a fair portion of the population from home communities at a time when seasonal fluctuations proved most taxing.

As Lathrap has pointed out, riverine populations such as the Cocama and Omagua were, at the beginning of the historic era, expanding far up the tributaries of the Amazon (1968:28), establishing colonies along the Napo, Aguarico, and Quebeno Rivers, some of which were located not far to the east of the Jivaroan groups[2] (Metraux 1963:689–690). The general effect was to severely circumscribe the inland populations, restricting their regular access to more productive zones. Certainly, this played a crucial role in isolating the Jivaroans in the region along the tropical forest fringe of the Andean foothills where they were first described in the sixteenth century—an area of generally rugged terrain where game and fish decrease in abundance with elevation.

[2] Even earlier riverine population movements may explain the presence of beautifully crafted and incised ceramic remains in Achuarä territory, along the upper Pastaza in Ecuador and its inland tributary, the Huasaga, in Peru (cf. Porras 1975). These bear no resemblance to contemporary Achuarä pottery; rather, style and radiocarbon dates of approximately 2000 B.C. link them "to a long and eventful sequence of prehistoric occupations [DeBoer, Ross, Ross, and Veale 1977:2]," which may reflect inland colonies that riverine populations established to exploit fish and game in these regions.

Moreover, the western margin of their habitat bordered on the *ceja,* a "rugged, cloud-buried, excessively rainy, precipitous strip between the Puna and . . . lower hills of the Montana [Steward 1963:508; cf. Denevan 1970:74]." Cold, humid, and comparatively devoid of animal life, the ceja was an ecological barrier to westward expansion by a tropical forest subsistance regime. At the same time, this natural limitation was reinforced by periodic pressure from the Inca Empire, seeking to extend its hegemony over the Upper Amazon.

According to the earliest reports—by colonial administrators, missionaries, and travellers—the Jivaroans would seem to be a prime example of the Hobbesian condition of tribal society. Salinas de Loyola, who served as governor of the province of the Santiago around 1580, was among the first to view their seemingly incessant internecine conflicts as a direct consequence of irresolvable differences among local groups lacking chiefly authorities whom all could respect (Stirling 1938:38). Subsequent interpretation, although far more elaborated in form and offering detailed documentation of Jivaroan culture, has nonetheless tended, either directly or by implication, toward much the same perspective: One of the inevitability of anarchy and conflict under conditions where "there is no state, no chiefdom, no corporate kin groups [Harner 1972:170]" to adjudicate internal disputes and enforce decisions. This has a psychological aspect; according to Karsten,

> the Jibaros are by nature impulsive and choleric, qualities which among them frequently give rise to disputes and quarrels which may degenerate into sanguinary feuds. Their unbounded sense of liberty and their desire to be independent . . . is one of the reasons why they do not live in villages but each family separately, for in this way conflicts are more easily avoided [1923:8].

It is with such general descriptions in mind that the historical and ecological circumstances which frame Jivaroan life become especially pertinent. In elaborating upon them, I will emphasize the situation of one particular subgroup, the Achuarä, with whom I worked in 1972–1974.

The Achuarä Jívaro

Currently numbering about 2700 (Instituto Linguistico de Verano 1972:1; Gnerre, personal communication), the Achuarä range over some 13,000 km^2 (5000 square miles) of terra firme forest and, at approximately one person per 2.6 km^2 (= 1.0 square mile), display "one of the highest crude population densities in Amazonia [Mitchell 1971; Ross 1978]." Among the least known and currently more "traditional" of the Jivaroans, they are virtually unique among them as dwellers of low selva. This habitat has significance for understanding the historical and continuing pattern of Achuarä hostilities; furthermore, its difficulty of access to sources of colonization from the highlands and endemic malaria along major bounding rivers (Faura Gaig 1964:188,200, 207) have spared the population the massive changes by government-sponsored and spontaneous movements of *serranos* into the ostensibly land-abundant Andean foothill territory of the Shuarä in Ecuador since the 1950s (Harner 1972:33–34) and the Huambisa and Aguaruna Jivaroans since 1964 in Peru (Varese *et al.* 1970) (see Figure 2.1 for distribution of the Jivaroan groups).

But it would be unreasonable, despite a dearth of historical material, to portray the Achuarä as pristine tribesmen, secreted away in a marginal zone and immune to the centuries of plunder and exploitation which have followed on the Spanish Conquest. Their current situation is intimately linked to the fates of other Jivaroans and of those Amerindians who formerly inhabited the region north of the Marañon (Amazon River, in Peru) into which they have expanded over the last century.

HISTORICAL BACKGROUND

The most persistent pressure on the entire area occupied by the Jivaroans (southeastern Ecuador and adjacent northern Peru) has been along the western frontier of Shuarä territory in Ecuador, in the Upano Valley where the town of Macas is situated. In fact, most of the pressure on the Achuarä seems to have come as a result of events associated with increasing commerical and colonial interest in the western foothill region.

After a hiatus of nearly two and a half centuries during which there is substantially little data on any of the Jivaroan peoples, the Upano population emerges by 1887 suffering a shortage of game as a result of the presence of collectors of cinchona bark (quinine) and other tropical products, who descended into the region from the neighboring Ecuadorian highlands (Vacas Galindo 1895:28–29).[3] Many of the collectors worked primarily out of Macas with its non-Indian residents but occasionally employed the labors of Jívaro inhabitants of the valley in exchange for guns and other trade items (Harner 1972:30). Shuarä who had moved there from more southerly locales (in efforts to establish direct access to Western manufactures at Macas) found, however, that with the stepping up of commercial activity and initiation of cattle ranching, demand was reduced for items they had formerly provided in exchange—deer, pigs, and native salt—although shrunken heads were still a greatly desired commodity (Karsten 1935:36; Harner 1972:29). To sustain their supply of manufactured trade goods, some of the Indians involved themselves directly in cutting pastures for the Macabeos (Harner 1972:29) and others entered the extractive

[3] This was contemporaneous with the development of commercial activities along the upper Marañon and Pastaza, where former Amerindian occupation had been replaced by colonial exploitation, slavery, malaria, and various epidemic diseases; these precluded general access to alluvial areas by inland populations, making the interior forests safer and more hospitable, but clearly delimiting zones of exploitation for the Jivaroan groups.

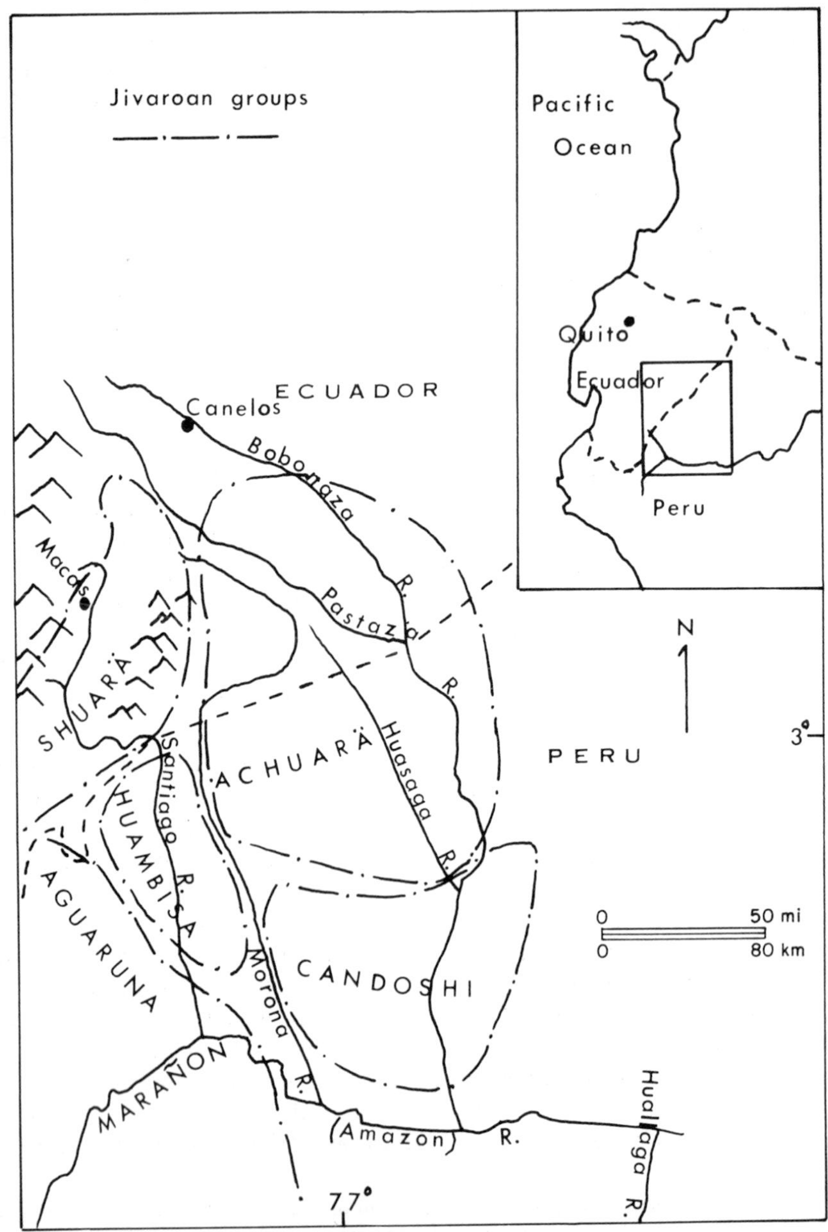

FIGURE 2.1 *The Jivaroan groups of the Upper Amazon.*

industry. The ongoing barter in heads and firearms provided still another avenue of access whose contribution to the escalation of warfare should not be underestimated.[4]

Whatever the nature of Jivaroan warfare during the unreported years of the seventeenth and eighteenth centuries, the apparent reduction in faunal reserves, introduction of contagious diseases, and uneven acquisition of firearms were important elements by the 1800s in the patterning of indigenous hostilities. This was nowhere more evident than in the efforts and success of Upano River Shuarä in displacing militarily less well provisioned Jivaroans from surrounding territories.

Upano Shuarä were noted to have "totally exterminated" the Pindos and Chiguandos residing to their north along the old trail between Macas and Canelos, and to their south, forced Huambisa survivors of their expeditions along the shores of the Morona "to retire to a distant region [Vacas Galindo 1895:163–164; Harner 1972:36]." They similarly drove Candoshi south from settlements in the Morona headwaters and, to the east, across the Sierra de Cutucu, mounted increasingly persistent headtaking raids against the transitional lowland-dwelling Achuarä. The latter, armed only with spears at the time, fled northeast and south from the Chiguasa and Macuma River regions where they were replaced by Shuarä migrants from the Cutucu foothills (Drown and Drown 1961; Harner 1972:36).

Guns were revolutionary in their impact during this period, producing a situation analogous to what Vayda (1970) has reported for the Maori of New Zealand. The same "strenuous efforts" were made by hostile Jivaroan groups to obtain firearms from a limited number of access points. Imbalances in weaponry forced victims, such as the Achuarä, toward alternating strategies of trade and aggression against colonial outposts along the Marañon or upper Pastaza Rivers. Gradual articulation with the frontier economy has been inevitable under such circumstances.

However, the point is not to suggest that indigenous warfare is hopelessly riddled by colonial influences—simply, that historical considerations place the analysis of such behavior in an open system, in which an ecological model must accommodate certain external influences as regular and as effectively comprising an environmental change. If the system is changing, it makes little sense to categorize the components of change as "internal" or "external."

---

[4] The literature is somewhat sparse in this regard, but there is evidence that the competition for firearms encouraged some local groups to ambush their enemies and sell their shrunken heads for guns (Vacas Galindo 1895:173–178). Once certain groups adopted the firearm for warfare, it became imperative for others to follow suit. In the "arms race" that ensued, the exchange in shrunken heads became an important means of keeping up or staying ahead. Karsten certainly considers such barter to have been a major contributing factor to the escalation of warfare among the Aguaruna between 1916 and 1928. Despite the fact that trade of this sort was by then officially prohibited, North American rubber extractors would offer a rifle for each head trophy and the Aguaruna showed no reluctance to take advantage of the opportunity.

ARMED CONFLICT AMONG THE ACHUARÄ

There is little evidence that the Achuarä ever engaged in headtaking on the grand scale reported for upland Jivaroans.[5] However, periodic homicides and escalating revenge feuds continue to embrace a large number of antagonists and exact a heavy mortality from the population. Table 2.1 provides an indication of the magnitude of such mortality in comparison with analogous figures from the Yanomamö Indians.

TABLE 2.1
Deaths by Homicide[a]

	Achuarä	Yanomamö	
	Morona River	Shamatari	Namoweiteri
Adult males	59%	41%	27%
Adult females	27%	5%	8%

[a] Percentages for the Yanomanö include deaths from warfare, duels, and irate husbands (Chagnon 1974:160). Those from the Achuarä are chiefly revenge assassinations motivated by a prior killing or by sorcery accusations following disease-related deaths. To a lesser extent, they are provoked by episodes of wife-stealing or a wife's infidelity.

Mortality is clearly higher in the Achuarä case despite the decidedly less ostentatious format for accomplishing such ends. In tenor Achuarä hostilities resemble the internecine feuding in the back hills of Appalachia (see Jones 1948). Homicides proceed from phase to phase and—by virtue of retaliation—incorporate ever greater numbers of participants. Escalations may proceed to the point, as in 1959–1960, where as many as 80 persons may perish before hostilities can be brought to a halt. In the view of the Achuarä, this constitutes "war," for men, women, and children are subject to assault in contrast to the more selective determination of targets at the earlier stages of confrontation.[6]

However, despite the potential for escalation, revenge feuds seldom rage out of control; certainly, the atomistic picture of individuals from small and isolated communites avenging their grievances—impervious to the concerns of others—is more apparent than real. In fact, the Achuarä operate according to a sure sense of intercommunity (and interpersonal) etiquette that demands that individuals contemplating a homicide seek out, in advance, the counsel of

[5] They seem to have adopted the art from their Shuarä aggressors (Harner 1972:225n.; Achuarä fieldnotes) as a defensive tactic that was, then, directed offensively against more southerly Candoshi Indians against whom they were expanding. The Candoshi, in turn, "learned" it from their Achuarä aggressors (Wallis 1965:37–40) but, in neither case did the headtaking persist.

[6] Twelve percent of children's deaths have resulted from homicides occurring during the course of intercommunity raids.

[7] In those rare cases when such conventions are disregarded, obligations to support are thrown into question and relatives may actually turn against their own when precipitous action forces realignments in loyalty.

respected relatives who would be obligated to provide support if retaliations were to intensify.[7]

Retaliatory raids, furthermore, are only rarely a matter of complete surprise. Word of impending revenge is usually transmitted through communications networks well in advance of any assault. Under the circumstances, the "enemy" has the option of fleeing his settlement or of staying and securing it against the impending attack.

The actual retaliation is often protracted. Its timing depends on many factors, including the status of the person whose death or indiscretion is being avenged and, matter-of-factly, whether there is the possibility or need for immediate action. Such pressures, nonetheless, contribute to the pulsating nature of Achuarä settlement with an apparent pattern of constructing a defensive palisade (*winUk*) and standing one's ground when local resources are worth holding onto, and abandonment and seeking refuge with allies when they are not.

On occasion, the escalation of hostilities leads relatives to "abandon" home communities and unite at a single fortified settlement. Attempts are made to construct separate dwellings, but this (and the development of separate gardens) requires time and great effort. Thus, the stress placed on the facilities and resources available to such communities provides an important impetus to reconcile the difficulties when this is possible.

So, while retaliatory killings may commence in the ostensible interests of one community and be carried out by one or possibly two male avengers, the procedure governing the nature of this activity inevitably draws upon the interests and circumstances of a broader spectrum of communities. It is the members of such a neighborhood cluster who may materially benefit from the protracted routing of "enemy" communities even if resources per se do not constitute the source of contention at any particular stage. Subsequent to a routing, communities have been known to orient hunting and fishing expeditions into such areas and to harvest desirable resources such as ayahuasca from abandoned gardens. Furthermore, settlement histories reveal an amoeba-like expansion of neighborhood clusters in accord with the opening up of new areas by displacement of their former occupants. Thus, a high percentage of Achuarä settlements (in Peru) are established at sites in advanced secondary growth forest in areas formerly occupied by other Achuarä or by Huambisa and Candoshi Indians.

An important consequence of intense hostilities is the recurrent creation of no-man's lands. Such unoccupied zones, frequently about three days' travel in breadth, have been such a common outcome of Jivaroan warfare, at least since the nineteenth century, that special comment is warranted. A similar phenomenon has been analyzed by Hickerson for the southwestern Chippewa of Wisconsin and Minnesota among whom, as I suggest for interfluvial populations of the Amazon, "it was [fundamentally] the supply of furred and large game . . . which determined population size and distribution [1962:15]."

Areas contested by the Chippewa and Dakota Indians became "buffer zones" which, relative to settled areas, were rich in game because of the impracticability of residence in them. While endemic warfare generated and maintained such unoccupied grounds, it did not entirely inhibit hunting in them; however, it did make hunting a military activity.

Hickerson's summary of the contribution made by this facet of warfare to hunting productivity is directly relevant to the Jivaroan case. He observes that

> The very risk involved in hunting on debatable grounds was sufficient to limit the exploitation of game, so that these regions, as long as warfare continued, remained well stocked and attractive to hunters . . . . [However], in those limited areas where peace was brought about . . . hunting grounds were exploited to the point of game exhaustion [1962:27].

Around 1900, Up de Graff described traveling on the lower Santiago River (Jivaroan territory) where "Hunting was good, for the zone through which we were passing is a kind of no-man's land between the Antipas [Aguaruna] and the Huambisas [1923:91]." And, Harner has reported that, while in most of Jívaro territory, hunting productivity has been adversely affected by efficient exploitation "for a long period of time," a profound contrast was provided by the border region between the Shuarä and the Achuarä in southeastern Ecuador; in that zone "which had not been exploited because of the enmity between the two groups, we encountered unprecedented quantities of monkeys and birds [1972:56]." (See Drown and Drown 1961:107.)

Such depopulated stretches also separate the most southerly Achuarä settlements from those of the Candoshi with whom armed conflict has been equally severe (cf. Wallis 1965:23,32–33). However, as I have suggested, buffer zones are not solely a by-product of intertribal war but on a more localized scale are similarly a consequence of escalated revenge feuds among Achuarä subgroups.

In much of the Achuarä range of habitation, faunal refuges are facilitated by the existence of extensive *aguajal* or inundated swamp forest, uninhabitable for horticultural and strategic military reasons, but representing natural reserves for such fauna as the white-lipped peccary, an especially prized protein package. The prominence of such zones in the Achuarä environment not only separates hostile groups but, by limiting areas suitable for habitation and cultivation, tends to promote a relatively high degree of settlement concentration in drier, more elevated, adjacent forest (cf. Denevan 1970:63). This may heighten intercommunity competition in the more circumscribed zones. Indeed, histories of conflict tend to show higher frequencies among neighborhoods occupying continuous "upland" stretches than is the case for those situated on opposite sides of vast aguajal. But, in general, the aguajal exerts a dampening effect on conflict. It affords a supplementary focus for hunting activity while, at the same time, upgrades the availability of migratory fauna in the preferred areas of harvest. This, in combination with the productivity of lowland streams, appears to confer a greater stability on Achuarä settlements than is the case perhaps for Jivaroans residing in the high selva.

Still, armed conflict is an integral aspect of settlement pattern, and the feedback loop between it and population dispersal, emigration/colonization, and the maintenance of game reserves in the face of endemic competition comprises one major aspect of the Achuarä ecosystem. Closely related to it are parameters such as disease and sorcery accusations. The following sections explore the linkages in question and suggest the importance of these interrelations for the explanation of historical and ecological processes of Achuara expansion over the last century.

ECOLOGICAL COVARIATION: DISEASE, SETTLEMENT ORIENTATION, AND SORCERY

Where contact has not drawn them to a major river or stimulated nucleation around a mission, the Achuarä settle in clusters of small, highly dispersed communities overlooking headwater and tributary streams flowing through their territory. Adjacent communities are usually no less than a half-hour's walking distance through the forest; but closely related communities may stretch for many hundreds of miles, requiring a journey of at least several days in any one direction. This pattern of dispersion is seldom altered except on rare occasions when allied communities nucleate in response to intense hostilities. Yet such larger aggregations are not without historical precedent. In some areas, such as the northern zone of contemporary Achuarä habitation, villages commonly ranged up to 150 persons in the mid-nineteenth century (Izaguirre 1929:178).

A principal question, then, centers upon why contemporary Jivaroan settlement is so centrifugal. Among the Achuarä, there are two contrasting movements of some significance in this regard: a related family might change neighborhoods for safety, while, at the same time, another might move into a separate house only several hundred meters across a garden, reducing interhousehold food exchange to a minimum. Settlement histories point to a falling off of game or fish—the latter, sometimes because the principal fishing *quebrada* becomes muddied—as the chief centrifugal factor. Among the upland Shuarä, a similar, although probably more rapid process, occurs; at the higher elevations, that is, 400–1200 meters, the terrain is more rugged and game and fish both less abundant than at lower altitudes. Harner notes that

> Each house, averaging about nine occupants, is usually isolated a half-mile or more from the next; but sometimes two, or rarely three, houses may be located within three hundred yards of one another. Adjacent houses, when they occur, invariably belong to close relatives, usually one being that of a middle-aged man and the other(s) of his son(s)-in-law. Even such limited concentrations are not very permanent, due to such factors as quarreling between the neighboring relatives or the gradual depletion of the local wild game supply [1972:78].

Thus game tends to be a major reason that the population of a single site rarely will exceed 20 persons. But Harner's other observation regarding social tensions may not be unrelated to this factor. The Achuarä, for example, reveal intense male egoism which militates not merely against joint hunts, but sometimes results in actual deception about going off to hunt. Normally, absolute reciprocity governs the sharing of meat- and fish-based meals between households in the community except when poor luck in hunting encourages domestic units to withhold a slim harvest for themselves. Continuation of difficult circumstances may lead to increased reluctance to share the limited resources and to be candid about the plans or results of hunting activity. The grounds for quarreling are seeded by such circumstances, even if the quarrels themselves get triggered by seemingly unrelated events.

Implicated in the whole protein situation is dependence on the shotgun for hunting (and for defense as endemic hostilities lend a certain urgency to reliance on this weapon in both contexts). The shotgun, introduced in the second half of the nineteenth century, has had greater impact on the depletion of local fauna than the traditional blowgun or even the bow and arrow (Ross 1978); and as it has escalated the technology of warfare among the Jivaroans, it may also have reduced the value of larger settlements for protection. Particularly if allies could be assembled anyway from neighborhood sites, a higher dispersal of population might establish a more functional balance between war and game procurement.

However, epidemiological factors exert an equally powerful influence on settlement pattern. The simple fact of the matter is that "epidemics like people": "The higher the population density, the greater the chance that microorganisms will make a successful transfer from host to host [Alland 1969:81]." However, the dispersion, isolation, and small size of contemporary Jivaroan communities have a dampening effect on the spread and potential gravity of epidemic infection. Among the Achuarä, measles and whooping cough have been noted to pass through one neighborhood, but not others, and into some, but not all, communities in any neighborhood cluster. These conditions, as Black points out, will not maintain such pathogens in a stable germ pool; the diseases do not become endemic, and subsequent outbreaks are entirely contingent on reintroductions (1975:517–518).

But, this does not mean that Western infections represent a negligible health hazard for contemporary Jivaroans: actually the reverse is true. Measles, whooping cough, and respiratory infections alone may account for over 50% of Achuarä disease deaths. Sixty percent of the children in the mortality sample succumbed to such ailments; a lower percentage of adult deaths (30.4%)[8] was actually attributed to such causes, but many of the deaths blamed on sorcery for which specific organic cause eluded determination may represent their complications, primarily respiratory tract infections such as pneumonia.

Such conditions have aggravated indigenous hostilities in the past and continue to do so today. Their translation into sorcery accusations linking the incidence of disease mortality to periodic homicides and revenge feuds will now receive consideration.

---

[8] This may be compared with the figure set forth by Chagnon (1968a:20n) for the Yanomamö: 54% of adult deaths resulting from epidemics and malaria. Malaria is endemic to most of Achuarä territory and appears not to take a particularly heavy toll of the population. Periodic contact with outsiders has similarly extended over a longer time span than is true for most Yanomanö; while more pervasive among contemporary Achuarä, the associated disease impact is, again, mitigated to some extent by the small and dispersed settlement pattern.

SHAMANISM AND SORCERY ACCUSATIONS: SCALE OF ESCALATION

The supernatural world is a major focus for ideological elaboration in Jivaroan life. In fact, Harner reports that "the normal waking life is explicitly viewed as 'false' or 'a lie,'" merely an arena for the execution of causal processes emanating from the "real" or "hidden world" (1972:134). This punctuates the importance of the supernatural practitioner. Among the Shuarä, approximately one man in four assumes such a status; among the Achuarä, the figure is not nearly so high, but shamans are nonetheless common to every neighborhood and their access to the supernatural realm equally regarded.[9]

Confidence in their good intentions is of some concern, however, for shamans are generally believed to be of opposite persuasions: Those who consistently use their power to cure and others who just as consistently bewitch (Achuarä fieldnotes; cf. Harner 1972:117–118, 155–156). Individuals who service particular neighborhoods, linked to member communities by cognatic and affinal ties, are consistently acknowledged as curers by their kinsmen. They have demonstrated their character by long-term association and may be trusted with just as much certainty as others may be held in evil disrepute. In essence, the dichotomy between curers and bewitchers lies at the core of shamanistic praxis, providing an essential psychological underpinning for the response to illness and disease-related mortality.

It is, therefore, curious, though by no means contradictory, that evil sorcery, in all likelihood, does not exist in practice. Informants from distant Achuarä neighborhoods consistently name the same individuals in the course of explaining deaths due to sorcery and in free-ranging discussions of shamans with whom they are familiar. Coincidences of this nature are not unexpected; genealogical ties link most Achuarä communities, if only in attenuated form. But, the conflicting assessments of character and behavior of the same individuals from opposite sides of the aguajal are especially striking. This is most evident in reference to acknowledged shamans of considerable reputation.

Another observation deserves consideration in this regard: the remarkable frequency with which shamans, themselves, resort to physical violence in accomplishing their ends. Again, the most powerful shamans take the lead, despite the fact that it is precisely these individuals who are considered most capable of provoking death by supernatural means. Thus, of 29 shamans in the Achuarä sample, the top 6 were named in 32 out of 98 deaths: 8 by sorcery, 24 by homicide. Of the total, 15% of the shamans were blamed for 47% of the sorcery deaths and 85% for the remainder.[10]

---

[9] The acquisition of trade goods in exchange for their services is one attractive feature encouraging entry into such "careers." While the possibility of sorcery accusations and retribution is an ever-present correlate of such activity, the data on Achuarä shamans show the probability of being shot at 40%; it is 59% for adult males in general.

[10] Moreover, all of the shamans interviewed during this study maintained that they had never practiced evil sorcery. In fact, it seems that such attributions are uniformly leveled at enemy shamans but never owned up to by particular individuals nor by their non-shaman kinsmen who depend upon their services and good will.

Localization of these individuals in relation to the communities that leveled the charges shows the most numerous accusations (greater than 3 and less than 11) directed at sorcerers of widespread renown residing at great distances from recriminatory communities. But of the 85% of shamans blamed for fewer deaths, the majority occupied more proximal locations.

These preliminary calculations accord favorably with several other observations. First, it may be noted that deaths are subject to variable interpretation and, hence, to a range of responses and counterresponses. Those of young children tend to be weighed in cumulative fashion, reflecting their greater susceptibility to disease and the complicating synergistic effects of undernutrition (cf. Scrimshaw, Taylor, and Gordon 1968).

A biomedical and nutritional survey of the communities in this study revealed subclinical signs of protein deprivation in all children from infancy to 5 years of age.[11] To some extent this may be correlated with intra-household eating patterns which show little attention to equitable distribution of meat and fish portions—particularly to the youngsters whose access to the communal bowl is substantially contingent on their seizing the initiative. Since most customarily pass their days at play, snacking on foodstuffs high in sugar and carbohydrate content, the likelihood of spoiling the meal is considerable, and adults rarely caution against it.

But the significance of protein undernutrition lies precisely in the vulnerability of this age group to recurrent respiratory infections which themsleves "have the capacity to turn borderline nutritional deficiencies into severe malnutrition [Scrimshaw, Taylor, and Gordon 1968:262]."[12] Associated mortality eventuates in accusations directed at distant, powerful shamans but against whom actual retaliation is of low probability. It is, rather, the supposed supernatural deaths of adult males and females—more costly in terms of labor value lost—that are met by direct action. Here, the likelihood of blaming distant shamans is correspondingly low and the probability of revenge much higher than in the case of children.

Yet, adults display no diagnostic signs of protein undernutrition. The contribution made by faunal protein to the community diet is ample by nutritional standards—84 gm per person per day—although, as I have suggested, this permits adults to get an adequate supply but at the expense of the children. In any case, protein needs in relation to intake *cannot* be reliably assessed by a simple count of number of grams ingested (cf. Chagnon 1979). This measure alone does not adequately describe the diversity of variables that are directly or indirectly involved in achieving nutritional balance, itself by no means a fixed or static condition. Levels of intake that surpass international standards may

[11] Berlin and Markell (1977) report identical results from more extensive surveys among the Aguaruna Jívaro.

[12] Malnutrition is as rare among the Achuarä as seems to be the case elsewhere in the Amazon, but one case each of kwashiorkor and marasmus was observed in infants who had been exposed to viral infections.

merely provide an adequate buffer for adults against a spectrum of stresses that are all too frequently disregarded: threats of sorcery and revenge, pregnancy and lactation, endemic and epidemic disease, including parasite infestation which interferes with normal absorption (Scrimshaw and Young 1976:59; Berlin and Markell 1977; Ross 1978, 1979a:153).

Losses to disease, involving adults and children, are met with accusations of sorcery. When the victim is an adult, a killing follows, which is followed in turn by a retaliatory raid and homicide. Conflict may escalate to involve an entire neighborhood, even region, and as this happens, killings become increasingly less targeted. Communities respond to these developments in either of two ways. They may palisade the settlement and hold out there, or they may move into another neighborhood, to presumably safer terrain. Both strategies involve costs and benefits that may vary at different points in the series of escalating conflicts; these will govern the course of action followed in each case.

But, at any stage of these developments, escalation may be aborted. Retaliatory action is flexible—mediated by the continuing obligation of those contemplating it to consult with close relatives and allies. Therefore, decisions to initiate and perpetuate hostilities are not solely the province of the individual community. They reflect the assessments and concerns of a cluster of communities linked by consanguineal and affinal ties and by residence in a common neighborhood. Allies at the neighborhood level may, as conflict becomes more general, face crosscutting, mutually exclusive loyalties. As they proceed to drop out of the hostilities, the latter de-escalate: new neighborhoods are frequently formed from the process.

A major consequence of intense hostilities is the redistribution of community clusters and the creation of no-man's lands between them. Reoccupation of the no-man's lands often does not occur for several decades; such protracted periods of nonexploitation are important for reestablishing animal numbers, and without them, cropping-induced densities of animal species would not only remain low, but might go below the potential of important species to increase after cessation of hunting.[13] Thus, armed conflict produces conditions that reduce the likelihood of faunal over-predation and increase hunting potential. Moreover, by precipitating premature garden abandonment and increasing the rate at which new gardens must be initiated, it contributes to an increased proportion of secondary to mature forest. In the latter, the activity of herbivorous ungulates—especially the peccary—is more unpredictable, because these animals take erratic and extensive detours through the forest to locate sparsely and unevenly distributed food. In secondary growth sites, sources of food are more concentrated and reduce unpredictability in their movements. It is, therefore, not surprising that Achuarä hunters are commonly

[13] This is more critical in upland Jivaroan environments where natural refuges for animals, such as the aguajal, are lacking and limited fishing reserves place much greater emphasis on hunting in protein procurement strategies.

drawn to these areas and that many of their communities come to occupy them, as well.

In light of the above, it is worth reconsidering the relationship between armed conflict, settlement size, and strategies of protein procurement. Undoubtedly, the Jivaroans of 150 years ago had a different relationship to their resource base than that which characterizes their descendents today. They resided in large communities which, in the Amazonian interfluve, are constrained to pursue the large game species—problematic and risky to hunt, given their nocturnal and solitary occurrence (excepting the peccaries) and with low reproductive efficiencies that render them especially vulnerable to predation. Yet, sizable communities cannot afford the luxury of reliance on the smaller vertebrates (birds, rodents, monkeys), which communities on the order of the Achuarä enjoy. The sheer weight of numbers leaves them no recourse but to

> pursue a *generalist* hunting strategy, exploiting not only smaller game close to home, but also periodically sending groups on long-range expeditions into areas of unusual abundance: the less frequented, uninhabited tracts of forest between the core hunting zones of hostile groups [Ross 1979b:10].

It is the deep-forest hunting of the major, more mobile game species that compels access to fairly extensive territories and which, in turn, institutionalizes intergroup warfare as both a consequence and means by which access may be achieved. Under the circumstances, "precisely because such zones are beyond areas of personal security for solitary hunters . . . sizeable settlements [will] place great stress on communal hunting and cause a convergence of hunting and warring groups [Ross 1978:7]." (See my discussion of Hickerson, above.)

Headhunting may become an important complement to this strategy. Certainly, among the Jivaroans and Munducuru, it became a powerful means of instilling fear in the enemy and a great sense of exhilaration and solidarity at home. It facilitated the routing of enemy settlements from vast tracts of territory, and its relationship to hunting is conspicuous, particularly in the case of the Mundurucu. The Murphys write that the taking of heads on long-distance forays was explicitly identified with the propitiation of game spirits—a means of promoting the fertility of valued species and their vulnerability to native hunters (1974:81); and the most notable "spirit mothers" among the Mundurucu were those of the tapir and peccary (Murphy and Murphy 1974:82), not the lesser vertebrates, as Ross observes, "which are more common, less prone to decimation, and of comparatively less concern to inhabitants of large settlements [1978:8]."

There is also a strong functional relationship between large villages, communal deep-forest hunting, warfare and intervillage feasting, with warfare "not the cause but, rather along with hunting strategy and feasts, a consequence of settlement size [Ross 1978:8]." I am in full agreement with the direction of causality suggested here, although I would point out that once the system is ongoing, the nature of warfare will set a threshold on settlement size below which communities may be especially vulnerable to attack. Chagnon has observed this of Yanomamö villages, which will move in, refrain from splitting, or ally themselves to achieve the requisite size (1968a:39–40). For the Achuarä, as I have noted, small sites do not militate against military strength when necessary, since allies are traditionally summoned and coordinated with relative ease. Such dependence on allies is nonetheless crucial and is a principal factor underlying the reluctance on the part of individual communities to settle too far from the neighborhood cluster.

Still, if warfare sets a lower limit on community size, the nature of community protein procurement sets a critical upper limit; and warfare cannot be seen as an independent factor. It is a necessary and functional correlate of the interriverine hunter–horticultural mode of production which, at a certain level of intensity, has no viable alternative. As interriverine settlements grow larger, they place greater demands on their resource base, especially in nonintensifiable sectors such as hunting when fishing cannot provide a supplementary or alternative means of support (as in the Brazilian Xingú). Competition over women, as among the Yanomamö, may become a major proximate cause of intra- and intergroup contention but, certainly, not without reference to conditions of flagging hunting productivity; these encourage real or imagined marital infidelities within large communities and equally divisive strains between them leading to sorcery accusations and recognition or suspicion of mal-intent. Fission, raiding, and dispersion result and act to shift the demographic load in relationship to fundamental features of the resource base.

One advantage of intervillage alliances between large communities lies in their ability to open up productive hunting zones, particularly when periodic "feasts . . . stimulate groups of hunters to enter more distant areas [Ross 1979b:12]." Chagnon, however, misinterprets this point (1979:912). He notes that competition over unstable protein sources would imply that proximate villages would necessarily be fighting over overlapping territories—not the case for the Yanomamö where "friendly or allied villages are located much closer than are villages whose members are conducting active hostilities [1979:912]." Of course, the nature of such alliances could use some clarification as to duration (they seem rather fragile), frequency of feasting, periodicity, direction, and distances of related hunts, not to mention any association with the patterning and frequency of hostilities with groups in the more distant areas. But, it is not requisite to assume that proximate villages must always compete (cf. Ross 1978:7). Still it is highly interesting, in this regard, that Chagnon reports that they *must* become allies or they will become enemies and that "allies that customarily feast each other do not fight [1968a:117]."

It is simply the case that large villages are forced to exploit more extensive territories to harvest the big game species. Alliances may permit them to peacefully exploit the interstitial zones between member communities or they may equally permit them to enter more distant terrain. However, there is a long-term competitive advantage to the allied contingents, insofar as group hunting trips are coterminus with aggressive displays that may discourage over-predation in vast tracts of forest.

Crucial elements in the pattern described above have been altered among the Jivaroans probably as a consequence of over-predation (cf. Ross 1978:6) and the pressures of colonial intrusion. The introduction of trade, disease, and shotguns and the gradual circumscription of indigenous territory have encouraged a small settlement focus and dependence essentially upon solitary hunting of the smaller game species.

The magnitude of settlement dispersion has shifted also, so that many small communities are now packed into territory which formerly accommodated fewer large ones. Reduced environmental impact from the smaller sites has permitted higher overall population, so that Achuarä density is about 1 per square mile and upland Jívaro about 1.19 (Harner 1972:77). The Yanomamö show densities of .42 and .90 (Chagnon 1974:127), but these reflect the structural entailments of the large village, deep-forest hunting adaptation. Thus, density alone is no clear-cut measure of the intensity of interfluvial warfare (see Chagnon 1974:127), for there is no simple one-to-one correlation between the two parameters. But, this is hardly a reason to dismiss the influence of demographic factors altogether, as the neo-Hobbesian scholars are wont to do. Their articulation with technoenvironmental and economic factors is the very basis of whatever political significance adheres to the practice of warfare in Amazonian tribal societies.

Conclusions

This discussion has treated a number of variables, each distinct but all systemically related and equally essential to the understanding of the Achuarä ecosystem through time. Both the incidence and patterning of warfare are linked to an economic base in which agriculture is necessarily supplemented by hunting and fishing, in an environment where game is scarcer, more costly, and more risky to obtain than agriculture. The result today is one of small settlements, widely distributed, and with great mobility—a pattern that helps to reduce competition between communities. In earlier times, with smaller populations than characterize the area at present, individual villages were larger, rather like those of the Yanomamö today. This pattern implies a necessarily larger sustaining area per community, and is consonant with intense intervillage competition. Given the latter, the advantage of the larger, nucleated village in both attack and defense is obvious, even though subsistence becomes more expensive.

Epidemic diseases—all introduced and therefore more virulent—spread more slowly when settlement is dispersed, especially where the population is growing. Smallpox, measles, and influenza are transmitted by air from person to person; the reservoirs of all of these are the nearby mestizo populations whose immunity levels are higher. Traders form the link between these reservoirs and the Achuarä, traders who supply essential commodities such as steel tools and shotgun shells in exchange for animal skins and lumber, procured in part by using these trade items. Outbreaks of illness and disease-related mortality provoke sorcery accusations and a series of killings, counterkillings, raids, and counterraids, small in scale but escalating in pitch and frequency. In societies where populations are small, mobile, and dispersed, this is the basic pattern of intercommunity warfare.

Subsistence, settlement pattern, warfare, disease, and external contact regularly affect each other; each is explicable only in the context of its interrelations with the others. Warfare takes the form of revenge raiding because villages are small and widely spaced, and neither attacker nor defender can field an army: Both combatants are more or less evenly matched. Community spacing reflects the subsistence complex, and similarly serves to reduce the impact of disease and therefore, again, to reduce warfare. Furthermore, given an expanding population, dispersal—even to the extended family level—serves as an economical way of colonizing new land; warfare, in turn, acts as a means of dispersal, wherein weaker groups are displaced by stronger ones. In the course of colonization, competition with other populations fosters the extension of the warfare pattern as well as the system—in inevitably modified form—of which it is a part.

References

Alland, A.

1969 Ecology and adaptation to parasitic diseases. In *Environment and cultural behavior: Ecological studies in cultural anthropology* (A. P. Vayda, Ed.). New York: Natural History Press. Pp. 80–89.

Bates, H. W.

1962 *The naturalist on the river Amazons.* Berkeley: University of California Press.

Berlin, E. A., and E. K. Markell

1977 An assessment of the nutritional and health status of an Aguaruna Jívaro community, Amazonas, Peru. *Ecology of Food and Nutrition 6*:69–81.

Biocca, E.

1970 *Yanoama: The narrative of a white girl kidnapped by Amazonian Indians* (D. Rhodes, Trans.). New York: E. P. Dutton.

Black, F. L.

1975 Infectious diseases in primitive societies. *Science 187*:515–518.

Bolian, C.

1971 Manioc cultivation in periodically flooded areas. Unpublished manuscript.

Carneiro, R.

1970a A theory of the origin of the state. *Science 169*:733–738.

1970b The transition from hunting to horticulture in the Amazon basin. In *Proceedings, VIIIth International Congress of Anthropological and Ethnological Sciences.* Vol. 3. Tokyo: Science Council of Japan. Pp. 244–248.

1973 Slash-and-burn cultivation among the Kuikuru and its implications for cultural development in the Amazon Basin. In *Peoples and cultures of native South America: An anthropological reader* (D. Gross, Ed.). New York: Natural History Press. Pp. 98–123. (Originally published, 1961.)

Chagnon, N.

1966 Yanomamö warfare, social organization and marriage alliances. Ph.D dissertation, University of Michigan, Ann Arbor.

1968a *Yanomamö: The fierce people.* New York: Holt, Rinehart and Winston.

1968b Yanomamö social organization and warfare. In *War: The anthropology of armed conflict and aggression* (M. Fried, M. Harris, and R. Murphy, Eds.). New York: Natural History Press. Pp. 109–159.

1974 *Studying the Yanomamö.* New York: Holt, Rinehart and Winston.

1979 Protein deficiency and tribal warfare in Amazonia: New data. *Science 203:*910–913.

Chrostowski, M.

1972 The eco-geographical characteristics of the Gran Pajonal and their relationships to some Campa Indian cultural patterns. In *Historia, Etnohistoria y Etnologia de la Selva Sudamericana.* Vol. 4. XXXIX Congreso Internacional de Americanistas. Lima: Instituto de Estudios Peruanos. Pp. 145–160.

DeBoer, W., E. Ross, J. Ross, and M. Veale

1977 Two ceramic collections from the Río Huasaga, northern Peru: Their place in the prehistory of the Upper Amazon. *El Dorado 2*(2):1–12.

Denevan, W.

1970 The aboriginal population of Western Amazonia in relation to habitat and subsistence. *Revista Geografica 72:*61–86.

1972 Campa subsistence in the Gran Pajonal, Eastern Peru. In *Historia, Etnohistoria y Etnologia de la Selva Sudamericana.* Vol. 4. XXXIX Congreso Internacional de Americanistas. Lima: Instituto de Estudios Peruanos. Pp. 161–179.

Drown, F., and M. Drown

1961 *Mission to the head-hunters.* New York: Harper and Brothers.

Faura Gaig, G.

1964 *Los rios de la Amazonia Peruana.* Lima.

Fittkau, E. J.

1969 The fauna of South America. In *Biogeography and ecology in South America* (Vol. 2, E. J. Fittkau *et al.,* Eds.). The Hague: W. Junk. Pp. 624–658.

Flornoy, B.

1953 *Jivaro, among the headshrinkers of the Amazon.* London: Elek Books, Ltd.

Fritz, S.

1922 *Journal of the travels and labours of Father Samuel Fritz in the river of the Amazons between 1686 and 1723* (G. Edmundson, Trans. and Ed.). London: The Hakluyt Society.

Gross, D.

1975 Protein capture and cultural development in the Amazon Basin. *American Anthropologist 77:*526–549.

Harner, M.

1963 Machetes, shotguns, and society: An inquiry into the social impact of technological change among the Jívaro Indians. Ph.D. dissertation, Berkeley.

1972 *The Jívaro: People of the sacred waterfalls.* Garden City: Doubleday/Natural History Press.

1976 The ecological basis for Jívaro warfare. Unpublished manuscript.

Harris, M.

1968 *The rise of anthropological theory: A history of theories of culture.* New York: Thomas Y. Crowell.

1974 *Cows, pigs, wars, and witches: The riddles of culture.* New York: Random House.

1975 *Culture, people, nature: An introduction to general anthropology.* New York: Thomas Y. Crowell.

1977 *Cannibals and kings: The origins of cultures.* New York: Random House.
Hickerson, H.
1962 The southwestern Chippewa: An ethnohistorical study. *The American Anthropological Association Memoir 92.*
Huxley, M., and C. Capa
1964 *Farewell to Eden.* New York: Harper and Row.
Instituto Linguistico de Verano
1972 Informe general correspondiente a los grupos idiomaticos del Peru. Lima.
Izaguirre, B.
1929 Historia de las misiones Franciscanas y narración de los progresos de la geografía en el oriente del Perú. Lima.
Jones, V.
1948 *The Hatfields and the McCoys.* Chapel Hill: University of North Carolina Press.
Karsten, R.
1923 Blood revenge, war, and victory feasts among the Jibaro Indians of eastern Ecuador. *Bureau of American Ethnology Bulletin 79,* Smithsonian Institution. Washington, D.C.: U.S. Government Printing Office.
1935 The head-hunters of western Amazonas: The life and culture of the Jibaro Indians of eastern Ecuador and Peru. *Commentationes Humanarum Litterarum.* Vol. 7 (1). Helsingfors: Societas Scientiarum Fennica.
1967 Blood revenge and war among the Jibaro Indians of eastern Ecuador. In *Law and warfare: Studies in the anthropology of conflict* (P. Bohannon, Ed.). New York: Natural History Press. Pp. 303–325.
Lathrap, D.
1968 The "hunting" economics of the tropical forest zone of South America: An attempt at historical perspective. In *Man, the hunter* (R. Lee and I. DeVore, Eds.). Chicago: Aldine. Pp. 23–29.
1970 *The Upper Amazon.* New York: Praeger.
Lee, R., and I. Devore (Eds.)
1968 *Man the hunter.* Chicago: Aldine.
Meggitt, M.
1977 *Blood is their argument: Warfare among the Mae Enga tribesmen of the New Guinea Highlands.* Palo Alto, California: Mayfield Publishing Company.
Metraux, A.
1963 Tribes of the middle and upper Amazon river. In *Handbook of South American Indians* (Vol. 3, J. H. Steward, Ed.). New York: Cooper Square Publishers. Pp. 687–712. (Originally published, 1948.)
Mitchell, W.
1971 Indices of population pressure and social evolution: An exploratory investigation. M. A. thesis, Columbia University, New York.
Morey, R., and J. Marwitt
1975 Ecology, economy, and warfare in lowland South America. In *War: Its causes and correlates* (M. Nettleship, R. D. Givens, and A. Nettleship, Eds.). The Hague: Mouton. Pp. 439–450.
Murphy, R.
1957 Intergroup hostility and social cohesion. *American Anthropologist 59*:1018–1035.
1959 Social structure and sex antagonism. *Southwestern Journal of Anthropology 15*(1): 89–98.
1960 *Headhunter's heritage.* Berkeley: University of California Press.
Murphy, Y., and R. Murphy
1974 *Women of the forest.* New York: Columbia University Press.
Porras, P.
1975 *Fase Pastaza: El formativo en el oriente ecuatoriano.* Quito: Universidad Católica.

Ross, E.
1976 The Achuarä Jívaro: Cultural adaptation in the Upper Amazon. Ph.D. dissertation, Columbia University, New York.
1978 Food taboos, diet, and hunting strategy: The adaptation to animals in Amazon cultural ecology. *Current Anthropology 19*(1):1–36.
1979a Reply to Lizot. *Current Anthropology 20*(1):151–155.
1979b Hunting, warfare and settlement pattern: A review of the issues. Unpublished manuscript.

Ross, J. B.
1971 Aggression as adaptation: The Yanomamö case. Unpublished manuscript.

Sahlins, M.
1968 *Tribesmen.* Englewood Cliffs, N.J.: Prentice-Hall.
1972 *Stone age economics.* Chicago: Aldine.

Scrimshaw, N., C. Taylor, and J. Gordon
1968 *Interactions of nutrition and infection.* Geneva: World Health Organization.

Scrimshaw, N., and V. Young
1976 The requirements of human nutrition. *Scientific American 235*:51–64.

Siskind, J.
1968 Reluctant hunters. Ph.D. dissertation, Columbia University, New York.
1973 *To hunt in the morning.* New York: Oxford University Press.

Steward, J.
1963 Tribes of the Montaña: An introduction. In *Handbook of South American Indians* (Vol. 3, J. Steward, Ed.). New York: Cooper Square Publishers. Pp. 507–533. (Originally published, 1948.)

Stirling, M.
1938 Historical and ethnographical material on the Jivaro Indians. *Bureau of American Ethnology Bulletin 117,* Smithsonian Institution. Washington, D.C.: U.S. Government Printing Office.

Street, J.
1969 An evaluation of the concept of carrying capacity. *The Professional Geographer XXI* (2):104–107.

Up de Graff, F.
1923 *Head hunters of the Amazon: Seven years of exploration and adventure.* New York: Duffield.

Vacas Galindo, E.
1895 *Nankijukima: Religión, usos y costumbres de los salvajes del oriente del Ecuador.* Ambato: Imprenta de Teodomiro Merino.

Varese, S. *et al.*
1970 *Estudio sondeo de seis comunidades: Aguarunas del Alto Marañon.* Lima: Ministerio de Agricultura.

Vayda, A.
1961 Expansion and warfare among swidden agriculturalists. *American Anthropologist 63*: 346–358.
1970 Maoris and muskets in New Zealand: Disruption of a war system. *Political Science Quarterly 85*:560–584.
1976 *War in ecological perspective: Persistence, change, and adaptive processes in three Oceanian societies.* New York: Plenum Press.

Wallis, E.
1965 *Tariri: My story, from jungle killer to Christian missionary.* New York: Harper and Row.

Zinsser, H.
1963 *Rats, lice and history.* Boston: Little, Brown. (Originally published, 1934.)

3 Ethnographic Overproduction, Tribal Political Economy, and the Kapauku of Irian Jaya[1]

ROBERT PAYNTER AND JOHN W. COLE

It would be easy to quote works of high repute, and with a scientific hall-mark on them, in which wholesale generalizations are laid down before us, and we are not informed at all by what actual experiences the writers have reached their conclusions. . . . [A] *survey . . . ought to be forthcoming, so that at a glance the reader could estimate with precision the degree of the writer's personal acquaintance with the facts which he describes, and form an idea under what conditions information had been obtained from the natives.*
B. Malinowski, *Argonauts of the Western Pacific, 1961, p. 3*

Interpreting the Kapauku Papuans has become a basic exercise for theoreticians of primitive economics. The Kapauku problem, most starkly drawn, has been this: Are these West New Guinea people "primitive capitalists" as suggested by Pospisil, or do they conform to the substantivist model of a big-man political economy? More is at issue than interpreting a particular group living in a small village in the highlands of Irian Jaya[2] (see Figure 3.1). There

[1] Several friends and colleagues have helped us bring this chapter to completion and we want to thank them. Eva Fisch, Debbie Gewertz, Bob Glasse, Art Keene, Mervin Meggitt, Jim Moore, Eric Ross, Jane Schneider, Peter Schneider, Ed Wilmsen, and Martin Wobst have all read and commented on one or another of its drafts. Martin Boksenbaum, Stewart Levenson, and Beth Nooncaster prepared the figures, and Caroline Service typed an early draft as well as the final manuscript.

[2] The names of political entities carry heavy symbolic loads. While a colony of the Netherlands, western New Guinea was known as Dutch New Guinea. It emerged from colonial status as a province of Indonesia and was named Irian Jaya ("Irian Victorious"). Today there is a substantial independence movement there and its supporters refer to their land as West Papua New Guinea. Our use of Irian Jaya in this paper reflects the area's current political status and is not a statement of where our political sympathies lie.

BEYOND THE MYTHS OF CULTURE
Essays in Cultural Materialism

ISBN 0-12-598180-5

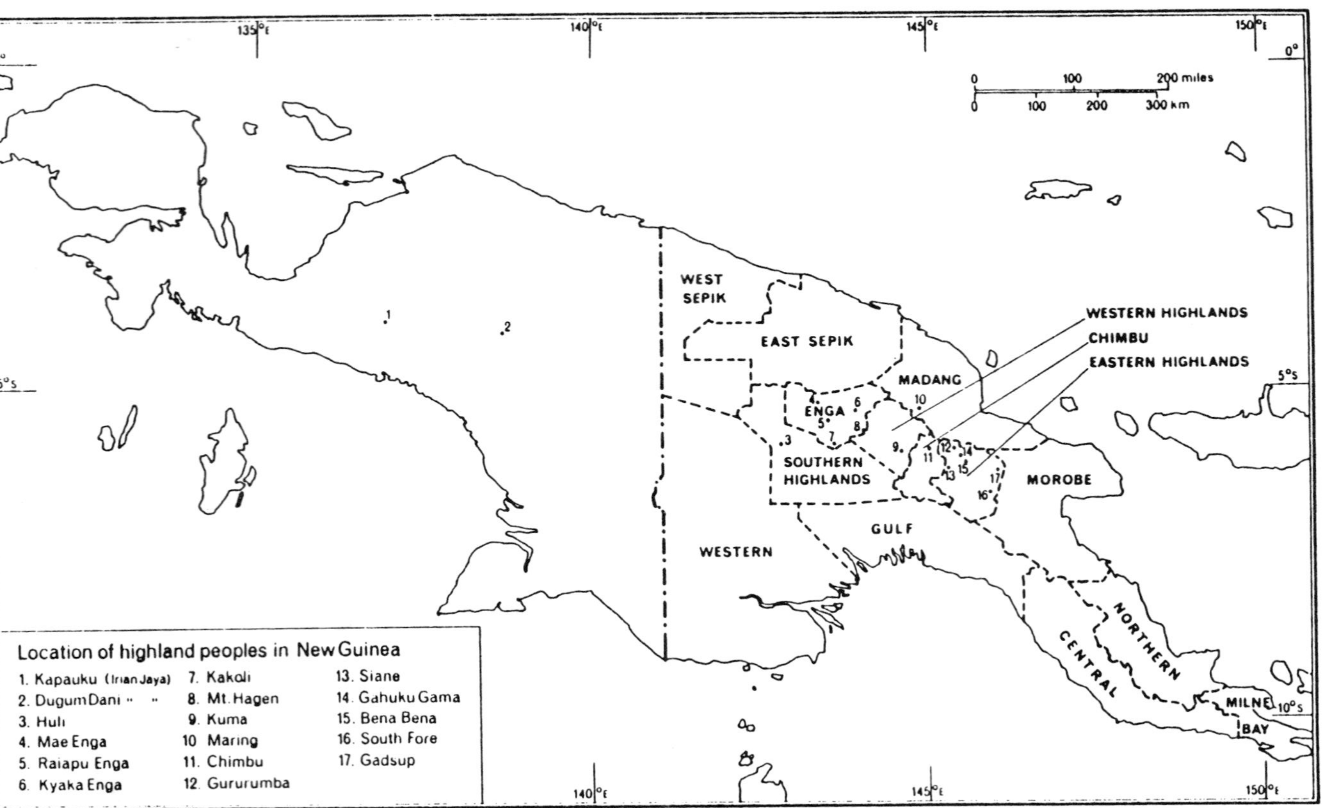

FIGURE 3.1 *New Guinea (Reprinted with permission from Brown 1978).*

has been little disagreement that the Kapauku fall within the broad category of unstratified societies subsisting on domesticates—that stage in cultural evolution known variously as "tribal," "segmentary," or "ranked." One's interpretation of the Kapauku has served as an indicator of one's position in the general debate on the nature of tribal economics. That the Kapauku have achieved this ethnologic renown is due largely to the staggeringly complete ethnography compiled by Leopold Pospisil (1958, 1963a, 1963b).

We will begin with a discussion of these theoretical concerns. Along the way we will sketch the interpretive debate, more closely examine Sahlins' model of the classic Melanesian big-man, and suggest an alternative model derived in the main from Pospisil's information about his own impact on the Kapauku. In the end, these particular analyses lead us beyond the ethnographic to a conclusion that the focus of the Kapauku debate has been misplaced and to a consideration of the nature of tribal economies.

The Kapauku Problem

In his initial interpretation, Pospisil presented the Kapauku as an ethnographic problem for reigning theories of primitive economics. He was particularly concerned with critiquing the primitive–civilized dichotomy of the substantivist school found in the works of Polanyi, Arensberg, Firth, and Malinowski (1963a:399–400). The term "primitive" as Pospisil understood it in the use of these writers, meant specifically a lack of private property, a communistic ethos, a lack of quantitativeness, a concern with nonmaterial wealth, and a political economy organized by status, not contract. In Pospisil's estimation, the supposedly primitive Kapauku lack these patterns and behave in ways characteristic of Western Capitalism.

Pospisil characterizes the Kapauku as: "strictly speaking, profit motivated, [acting in a] true money economy, [having an] obsession with counting, [and possessing a] strong version of individualism, which I daresay, could hardly be surpassed in our capitalistic society [1963a:401–402]." Their strong individualism shatters notions of primitive generosity: "Kapauku individualism permits some natives, especially children from poor homes who are periodically starving, to develop severe symptoms of undernourishment, while individuals from prosperous households are well fed [Pospisil 1963a:403]." These are traits of Western Capitalism, not primitive society; and contemplating this leads Pospisil to say that:

> If I were forced to establish some general types for the economic systems of the world I would not hesitate to put Western Capitalism and Kapauku shell money economy into one category, and distinguish both of these from economic systems such as that of the Trobriand Islands [1961a:400].

Sahlins (1972) and Harris (1975:305–308) have objected to this interpretation. Harris' major point is that too much is obscured by cataloging the relatively egalitarian political economy of the Kapauku with the class structure generated and supported by Western Capitalism. The importance of this distinction is illustrated by the Panai Lake big-man who was killed for trying to limit access by others to his own wealth (Harris 1975:307–308; Pospisil 1958:80). Harris trenchantly sums up his position that a principle other than capitalism underlies the Kapauku: "The truth of the matter is that the Kapauku rich man is an egalitarian redistributor rather than a capitalist. He has capital, but he does not control its disposition: *he cannot afford not to give it away on demand* [1975:307]."

Sahlins has also reinterpreted the Kapauku, both in his use of the Kapauku as the paradigmatic case of the impact of a big-man political economy on the domestic mode of production (DMP) (1972:101–148), and in his notes "On the sociology of primitive exchange." In these notes, Sahlins explicitly calls attention to his differences with Pospisil:

> Described by the ethnographer as sort of upland New Guinea capitalists. The big-man pattern, however, is an ordinary (sweet potato) garden variety. "Loans" and "credit" put out by Kapauku big-men (*tonowi,* generous richman) are not interest bearing in the standard sense . . . they are means of developing status through generosity. . . . The big-man's status sinks if he loses the wherewithal for generosity [1972:59]; . . . if he is excessively demanding he is likely to face an egalitarian rebellion [1972:250]. . . . Wealth is not enough: . . . a selfish individual who hoarded his money and does not lend [sic] it, never sees the time when his word will be taken seriously and his advice and decisions followed, no matter how rich he may become [1972:215].

Thus, the particulars of their behavior and the overall logic of their system fail, in Sahlins' estimation, to support Pospisil's lumping of the Kapauku with Western Captialism.

Harris' and Sahlins' critiques capture the themes of the substantivist responses to Pospisil and present strong alternative interpretations analyzing the Kapauku in terms of egalitarian redistribution. Overall, we agree with Pospisil's critics. Many of Pospisil's behavioral parallels between the Kapauku and Western Capitalism seem strained, and, more importantly, the systemic interrelations are best modeled by a totally different political economy operating under a totally different logic.

However, we do not think that Sahlins' alternative of the classic Melanesian big-man system constitutes the best analysis. In fact, his model exhibits the shortcomings of many models of primitive economies, which will become apparent in a closer examination of the Kapauku. Before beginning this inquiry and presenting our alternative to Sahlins' interpretation, we must attend more closely to his model of the big-man political economy.

The Classic Melanesian Big-Man Political Economy

Sahlins has elaborated and developed his concept of the big-man political economy in many publications (1963, 1968, 1972); we sketch only its salient features here. Of primary importance is that the big-man political economy is embedded within the segmentary tribe. From the outside, the segmentary tribe appears as *hierarchically organized segments,* each segment existing in relative political and economic autonomy from the others—an autonomy enhanced by their spatial segregation (1968:21–22). Intersegment integration is possible, particularly along kinship lines, in the proper contexts. From the perspective of a household the rest of the tribe appears as a set of *concentric sectors.* People from each are further in social space from the close household members as one moves out through the rings (1968:15).

The big-man plays an important role in integrating these atomistic segments and in bridging social distance between sectors (Sahlins 1972:137). The most explicit expression of the integrative effort of the big-man is the public feast that culminates in a giveaway by the big-man of the fruits of his own and his faction's labor. The motive force behind this apparent generosity is the leader's search for renown, which is in direct proportion to his reputation as a feast giver. Rival factions, which are the beneficiaries of the giveaway, are obligated to reciprocate the event at a later date or suffer a diminuation of their own leader's renown. Thus does the competition for renown between big-men lead to a to-and-fro flow of goods that serves to integrate the autonomous tribal segments into higher order sociocultural system:

> In the greater perspective of the society at large, big-men are indispensable means of creating supralocal organization: in tribes normally fragmented into small independent groups, big-men at least temporarily widen the sphere of ceremony, recreation and art, economic collaboration, of war, too [Sahlins 1963:292].

However, a mobilizing effort across segmentary units for these public giveaways is ultimately contradictory. Basically, reciprocity—the big-man's source of leverage within his faction—cannot bear intensification.

> One side of the Melanesian contradiction is the initial reciprocity between a big-man and his people. . . . But, on the other side, a cumulative enlargement of renown forces the big-man to substitute extortion for reciprocity . . . for the final measure of success is to give one's rivals more pigs and food than they can hope to reciprocate. But then, the faction of the triumphant big-man is compelled to "eat the leader's renown" in return for their productive efforts. At this juncture, let the leader beware [Sahlins 1968:90].

As a result of this contradiction, the processes of faction building and exploitation aimed at the quest for renown result in a fairly predictable big-man cycle. During the first stage of a big-man's career, he depends on his own household. Marriage is a strategy for increasing the size and productive potential of his own household so that big-men tend to have more wives than other men. Realization of the household's potential and the judicious distribution of the resulting produce is critical as the basis for building a support faction of other men and their households—the sign of a successful big-man. Loyalty is thus gained through calculated acts of generosity.

The second phase of his career consists of spreading his renown beyond the confines of his own faction through competitive public giveaways. In order to mobilize the goods required for the giveaway he must draw on the fund of good will established by his earlier acts of generosity. To the extent that these demands seem excessive to his followers, he is in danger of disaffection within his faction, which can result in desertion of its members, or even in the big-man's assassination. With no way to compel loyalty except through generosity the big-man is thus restrained in the scope of his activities, either through his own restraint, the loss of his faction, or his life.

In Sahlins' model the processes establishing and limiting the big-man are of the village-scale, small group variety. A big-man may integrate segments, but he can do it only by consolidating a faction within a segment, and then building out:

> Yet always this greater societal organization depends on the lesser factional organization, particularly on the ceilings on economic mobilization set by relations between center-men and followers. The limits and the weaknesses of the political order in general are the limits and weaknesses of the factional in-groups [1963:292].

So, the big-man political economy, as modeled by Sahlins, is a dynamic system driven by a unique logic. The big-man is the incarnation of society, bridging the segmentary households. Initially his leadership is based on the production of his innermost sector—his closest kin. Then through reciprocity, he broadens and deepens his power–production base by adding segments from more distant sectors and driving his followers to efforts of surplus labor. Ultimately this accumulation of social power is checked by the ability of the big-man's support base—the faction—to withdraw support. Thus, the centripetal social tendency of the big-man is checked by the centrifugal tendency of the opposed segments. It is against this framework of the segmentary tribe that Sahlins considers the impact of the big-man political economy on the domestic mode of production (DMP).

CHAYANOV ANALYSIS—PARADIGMATIC BIG-MAN

For Sahlins, the Kapauku are the paradigmatic case of the impact of the big-man political economy on the DMP. Before considering this particular analysis, we need to examine Sahlins' notion of the DMP.

The domestic mode of production (DMP) is a theoretical construct, a particular form of the Marxist concept of the mode of production: "The household is to the tribal economy as the manor to the medieval economy or the corporation to modern capitalism: each is the dominant production-institution of its time [1972:76]." Specifically, the DMP has these qualities:

> The household is as such charged with production, with the deployment and use of labor-power, with the determination of the economic objective. Its own inner relations, as between husband and wife, parent and child, are the principal relations of production in society. . . . How labor is to be expended, the terms and products of its activity, are in the main domestic decisions. And these decisions are taken primarily with a view toward domestic contentment. Production is for the benefit of the producers [1972:76–77].

We have encountered this in a slightly different form before in the segmentary model of the tribe. Thus, the DMP is the abstract model of production congruent with the social model of the segmentary tribe.

A measure of this productive effort is the intensity of labor of each household. The intensity of work is explicitly formulated for the DMP as Chayanov's Rule: "the intensity of labor per worker will increase in direct relation to the domestic ratio of consumers to workers [1972:102]." Social relations beyond the household are an imposition on this mode of production, and thus require greater productive effort to sustain them. This greater productive effort is then observed as deviations from Chayanov's Rule (1972:102).

Sahlins presents a formal method for investigating these deviations that we call *Chayanov Analysis*. Briefly, Chayanov Analysis works as follows. Chayanov's Rule, as interpreted by Sahlins, predicts a linear, positive relation between worker intensity (WI) and a domestic unit's demand. Demand is a function of household size and also of household composition. Quite simply, the household cycle (Goody 1958; Thorner, Kerblay, and Smith 1966) creates differences in household demand based on changing household size and age–sex composition. Thus, the effort of a worker is better understood as being driven by the ratio of consumers to workers (C/W) in a household.

Formally, Chayanov's Rule can be expressed as a linear model—that is WI is positively and linearly related to C/W. Specifically:

$$Y = A + BX \tag{1}$$

where

Y = WI (worker intensity)
X = C/W (consumer–worker ratio)
B = the slope, that is, the number units change in Y for a change in X
A = the Y intercept, that is, the level of WI when C/W is 0.

Theoretically, the value for A is 0; no demand drives no effort. The theoretical value for B can be determined based on culturally defined notions of individual worker reproduction. An expected Chayanov line can then be drawn. Sahlins illustrates these theoretical derivations using both Mazulu and Kapauku data (1972:102–123).

Sahlins uses regression analysis based on the least-squares method to estimate A and B from the observed data. With this method he constructs an observed line relating WI to C/W. Comparison of the line produced by this formula with the expected Chayanov line is the basis for studying the impact of a particular political economy on the DMP. Specifically, Sahlins compares the overall pattern of the expected Chayanov line and the observed line; the impulse to surplus labor (1972:111); the distribution of the impulse to surplus labor (1972:113); and the contribution of surplus labor to the total social product (1972:114).

Sahlins' analysis of the Kapauku (1972:119ff) was duplicated using SPSS Scattergram procedure (Nie and others 1975:292–300) and is presented in Figure 3.2 (data supporting Figure 3.2 are contained in Tables 3.1 and 3.2). The value for B (693.6 kg of sweet potatoes per 8 months)—the daily ration of kilograms per worker times 8 months—was given by Sahlins (1972:117) as developed from Pospisil's data. This is the expected effect on worker intensity of adding one consumer per worker. The formula for the Chayanov expected line was:

$$Y = 693.6X \qquad (2)$$

The observed line formula obtained by the least-squares method was:

$$Y = 52.61 + 959.96X \qquad (3)$$

Sahlins reports that the impulse to surplus labor was that "69 per cent of the Kapauku domestic units, comprising 59 per cent of the labor force, are working at an average of 82 per cent above normal intensity [1972:121]." Our calculations indicate that 56% of the domestic units worked at 78% above normal intensity. Furthermore, we found a slope of 959.96 rather than 1007 reported by Sahlins. These discrepancies are unaccountable and, relatively speaking, minor. We agree that the distribution of the impulse is "slightly to the right of the average household composition [1972:120]," and that "35.37 per cent of the social product is the contribution of surplus domestic labor [1972:121]." The overall interpretation of these measures and graphic patterns is that of a greater intensity of effort above that expected for the DMP.

The reason for performing Chayanov Analysis is *not* to find a good fit to the Chayanov prediction. The atomization of segmentary units characteristic of the tribe is inherent but not usually realized; it is a driving force in Sahlins' analysis that is countered by larger integrating mechanisms if society is to survive (1968:7; 1972:101). Thus, it is the *deviations* from the Chayanov Rule that are of interest as they are due to suprahousehold relations. In this instance, the deviations are due to the effect of big-man political economy.

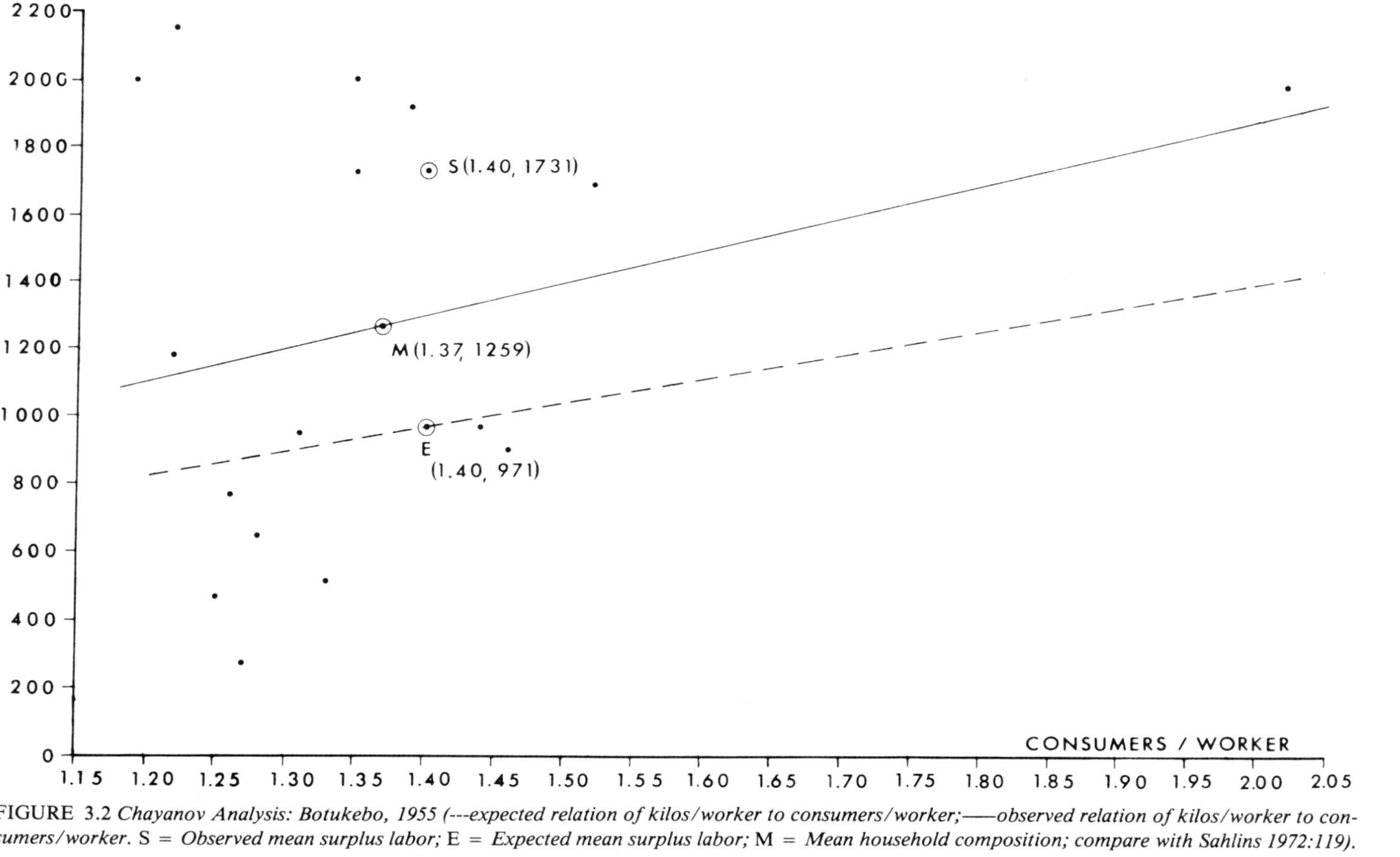

FIGURE 3.2 *Chayanov Analysis: Botukebo, 1955 (---expected relation of kilos/worker to consumers/worker;——observed relation of kilos/worker to consumers/worker.* S = *Observed mean surplus labor;* E = *Expected mean surplus labor;* M = *Mean household composition; compare with Sahlins 1972:119).*

TABLE 3.1
Regression Statistics: Sahlins' Analysis

r = .29294	r^2 = .08581	Standard error of estimate = 641.12590
A = −52.61181		Standard error of A = 1155.26188
B = 959.96290		Standard error of B = 837.39367
N = 16		

The deviations found in the Kapauku analysis are a distinctive pattern—a cluster of nine households fall above the Chayanov expected line while the remaining seven are below. Sahlins interprets this pattern of deviations as being characteristic of the effect of a big-man. Recall that "a big-man is one who can create and use social relations which give him leverage on other's production and the ability to siphon off an excess product—or sometimes he can cut down their consumption in the interest of the siphon [1963:292]." The nine overproducing households are interpreted as being "the big-man or would-be big-men and their followers, whose production they are able to galvanize"; while the remaining seven are "content to praise and live off the ambition of others [1972:117]." Sahlins goes beyond the particulars of the Kapauku analysis and considers the Kapauku exemplary of Melanesian big-men. "The idea seems worth a prediction: that this bifurcate, 'fish-tail' distribution of domestic labor intensity will be found generally in the Melanesian big-man systems [1972:117]." That is, one might expect the pattern in the deviations of a parabola opening toward the left when a big-man political economy is operating.

Thus, Sahlins has presented two formal models. The first is the linear model relating C/W to WI based on Chayanov's Rule. This formal model represents the underlying centrifugal tendency of tribal segments. The second is an empirical curvilinear model based on data from a big-man political economy. The curvilinearity represents the big-man extracting surplus from some—not all—households in a village.

CHAYANOV ANALYSIS—CRITIQUE

Two somewhat technical problems arise in Sahlins' use of linear regression analysis. The first methodological problem lies in trying to study the relationship of C/W to WI on the ground. The basic problem concerns moving from the metaphorical notions of consumption and work intensity to specific measures of these qualities *that do not distort the posited linear relation.* This can be easily illustrated with the notion of a worker. The work capacities of all individuals are not the same, so we cannot expect that households with the same number of members will necessarily have equal work capacities. For example, a household with two adults and three very young children would not have the same work potential as a household made up of five adults, even though both have the same total number of members. If a study did not dis-

TABLE 3.2
Data for Chayanov Analysis: Botukebo, 1955[a]

Household number	Number of consumers	Number of workers	Kilos of sweet potatoes per household	Consumers–workers	Observed kilos of sweet potatoes per household	Expected kilos of sweet potatoes per household	Deviation
4[b]	9.5	8.0	16004	1.19	2000	825	+ 1175
7[b]	11.6	9.5	20462	1.22	2154	846	+ 1308
14[b]	7.9	6.5	7654	1.22	1177	846	+ 331
15	5.6	4.5	2124	1.25	472	867	− 395
6	11.3	9.0	6920	1.26	769	874	− 105
13	9.5	7.5	2069	1.27	276	881	− 605
8	5.1	4.0	2607	1.28	652	888	− 236
1[b]	13.8	10.5	9976	1.31	950	909	+ 41
16	4.0	3.0	1557	1.33	519	922	− 403
3[b]	5.4	4.0	8000	1.35	2000	936	+ 1064
5[b]	7.4	5.5	9482	1.35	1724	936	+ 788
2[b]	14.6	10.5	20049	1.39	1909	964	+ 945
12	10.7	7.5	7267	1.44	969	999	− 30
9	9.5	6.5	5878	1.46	904	1013	− 109
10[b]	3.8	2.5	4224	1.52	1690	1054	+ 636
11[b]	9.1	4.5	8898	2.02	1978	1401	+ 577

[a] Adapted fom Sahlins 1972:116, 120.
[b] Overproducers.

tinguish between these households in estimating workers, we would not be surprised to learn that the expected linear relationship was not observed.

Sahlins presents a straightforward procedure for estimating *C/W* so as not to distort the linear relationship. He starts with estimates of the ability to work and consume for different age and sex classes. Setting an adult male's capacity at one, the other categories are some proportion (1972:115). These proportions are multiplied by the number of individuals in a household in a category to obtain *C/W* ratio for a household. While one may differ with the proportions used (and Sahlins differs with Pospisil on this), as long as the basic demographic data are there, the recalculations are no problem.

Sahlins does not exercise similar care with the other variable in Chayanov's Rule—worker intensity. Collecting information on energy expenditure is usually beyond the capabilities of most ethnographic field workers and is certainly not commonly reported (however, see Thomas 1973). So, Sahlins suggests measuring *WI* with a surrogate based on production. Specifically, Sahlins used kilograms of sweet potato production per worker in the Kapauku instance (acres–producer in the Mazulu example). Minge-Kalman (1977) has quite appropriately pointed out the problem of using only part of a worker's labor in estimating worker intensity and the problem of using surrogate measures of intensity. Our conceptualization is different from hers and not at odds with her critique.

Recall that Chayanov's Rule states a linear relation between intensity of productive effort and demand. By using productive output, Sahlins is suggesting that this, not intensity of effort, is linearly related to demand. Clearly, the functional relationship between work input and production output is not a priori linear. In fact, it is a function of the peculiarity of the local ecology and production technology. At the most general level, the law of diminishing returns (Found 1971:13–15) can be invoked to suggest a more reasonable expectation of some nonlinear relationship (approximated by an exponential)—but even this would be affected by the local situation. Clearly, using the wrong formula (i.e., simple linear) to specify the Chayanov Rule can lead to a rather distorted image of the productive characteristics of a household.

So, while the theory linearly relates *WI* to *C/W*, some surrogate measure of *WI* based on production is not likely to be linearly related to *C/W*. Thus, when *WI* is estimated with a surrogate, it is necessary to specify the new expected Chayanov relationship between the surrogate and *C/W*. That is, one must specify the function that relates a measure of production output to the desired measure of Worker Intensity. Minge-Kalman (1977) in effect specifies this relation in transforming yields into labor inputs: Recasting Chayanov's Rule in a nonparametric form seems a desirable procedure.

The second technical point has to do with the strength of the relationship between *C/W* and *WI*. Sahlins quite appropriately shies away from using regression analysis in this instance as a technique in inferential statistics, in treating it only as an indicator of the "main drift" in variations from the expected (1972:108–109). The vagaries of small sample size and its effect on sample representativeness makes such interpretive conservatism commendable (Evans 1974). However, even using regression analysis for descriptive purposes, it is still possible to evaluate the strength of association between the variables. This can be done with the r^2 statistic also known as the coefficient of determination.

> *The* r^2 *statistic or its complement* (l-r^2) *indicate proportions of variation explained and unexplained, respectively (Nie, Hull, Jenkins, Steinbrenner, and Bent 1975:325; see Snedecor and Cochran 1956: 167–169 on the relationship of the correlation coefficient* r *its square* r^2 *and the regression coefficient* b *for the appropriateness of using* r^2 *to assess the strength of a regression relationship).*

These are descriptive measures, not necessarily inferential, that simply state the amount of variation in kilograms of sweet potatoes attributable to variation in the *C/W* ratio.

In the Kapauku analysis, Sahlins does not report this measure. It can be easily obtained and was part of the output from the SPSS Scattergram procedure. For the Kapauku analysis this value of .08581 means that variation in the *C/W* ratio accounts for only about 9% of the variation in the surrogate measure of *WI*. This certainly fits Sahlins' interpretation that something other than the DMP is operating in this instance. However, methodological problems involved in estimating *C/W* and *WI* may also account for this poor fit, thus vitiating the interpretation in favor of Sahlins' explanation. We are not in a position to sort this out—though the usefulness of reporting the r^2 should be abundantly clear.

One final point concerns fitting mathematical models in general. Sahlins is aware of the methodological problems of using mathematical models in behavioral research, though his very cogent argument and presentation of Chayanov Analysis does invite abuse by others. Specifically, Sahlins notes:

> Clearly the task of research is not finished by the drawing of an intensity profile; it is only thus posed. Before us stretches a work of difficulty and complexity matched only by its promise of anthropological economics, and consisting not merely in the accumulation of production profiles, but of their interpretation [1972:121].

The problem is this: Time and again researchers have found that more than one behavioral model can produce the same mathematical model. This is precisely why arguments based on strong inference (Platt 1964)—that is, rejecting formal models rather than accepting them and using a research strategy incorporating multiple working hypotheses—are used in conjunction with statistical analysis. And just such an alternative interpretation is the subject of the next section.

Ethnographic Overproduction

Our inquiry has become quite narrow: Why were nine households overproducing at Botukebo in Irian Jaya, while the remaining seven were working less hard? Sahlins proposes that this is due to the effect of a classic big-man political economy. Alternatively, we propose that this pattern is due to the presence of a less endogenous factor, the ethnographer.

Our argument begins by considering how Pospisil inserted himself into Kapauku society.

> My first intention was to cross the Kamu Valley and settle in the southwestern part, at that time little known. However, the natives of the first village we entered, Botukebo, were so persuasive that they induced me to change my plans and stay in their territory. They staged a great welcoming party during which they presented me with a pig. Upon the advice of the Dutch officer, I immediately reciprocated with a gift of several steel axes. . . . With the assistance of the natives and the police I started to build myself a house between the villages of Botukebo and Kojogeepa [1963a:19].

Constructing the house was a critical event for Pospisil's study. After four days, the police left.

> I noticed that many young men helped me continuously with my construction. They even built themselves some shelters around my house. All they seemed to want for their help were long Latin personal names. The longer and harder to pronounce they were, the better they liked them. . . . What I did not know at that time was that Kapauku have a laudable custom by which boys and young men can live with wealthy individuals of their society. If the wealthy man likes them, he "adopts" them by giving them names. . . . So, before I realized what I was actually doing I became the "father" of 48 Kapauku boys and 3 girls. Although I was quite content to assume such a role on an honorary basis I became alarmed, after having realized that my Ford Foundation grant would have to feed not just one student of anthropology but 51 additional hungry Kapauku youngsters [1963a:19].

Pospisil's ritual fatherhood proved ultimately profitable for Pospisil and ethnography, as it was through this network of informants that he was able to compile his extraordinarily detailed ethnography.

Pospisil's ritual fatherhood clearly has implications for our problem of overproduction. In his only comment identifying his charges, Pospisil parenthetically discloses that they "did not come from Botukebo [1963a:395]." Clearly, the addition of 52 consumers to a population of 181 (1963a:59) may have driven Botukebo to overproduction.

If Pospisil met his obligations, then he clearly was adding demand for production. The mechanisms by which he fed them are not clear. He only mentions that "the food proved to be inexpensive [1963a:20]." But that he did strive to meet them is abundantly and, to his credit, clearly presented. Included in an accounting of sweet potato and mixed crop production (1963a:395–396) is an entry for "sold to L.P." Pospisil estimates that he bought approximately 10% of Botukebo sweet potato production and between 17 and 18% of their production of other crops during his 8-month study period. Clearly, Pospisil was driving some overproduction at Botukebo.

The following points should be noted regarding these percentages. First, Pospisil evaluated the crops in terms of beads, an exchange medium that he used as his unit of accounting. While the sweet potatoes were reported in both kilograms and beads (13,830 of a total 138,730 kg; 4088 of a total 38,835 beads) the mixed crops were reported in beads only (1200 of a total of 6853 beads of mixed crops). Second, these values are only approximations because of a quirk in the manner of calculation. He arrived at these figures in the following manner. He independently estimated (*a*) the production of sweet potatoes, other crops, and pigs, and (*b*) consumption of these items. He found these independently collected estimates yielded encouragingly similar results for sweet potatoes, especially when added to "the amount of tubers which I ate with my 'sons' [1963a:395]." Discrepancies between the total arrived at through production estimates and independently through consumption estimates were included in the figure sold to him. It is unclear, however, whether the discrepancies should be added or subtracted from these values to obtain a more accurate estimate of his demand on Botukebo production.

The extent of Pospisil's indirect impact can be estimated in one other manner. Sahlins, using Pospisil's estimates, assumes a daily ration of 2.89 kg of sweet potato per adult male (1972:117). Adolescents are evaluated as consuming the same amount as adults, resulting in an estimate of 35,651.04 kg demand created for sweet potatoes by Pospisil and 48 males (i.e., 49 × 693.6) and 3 females (i.e., 3 × .8 × 693.6). This estimate is quite high, yielding a daily intake of 4338.85 cal from sweet potatoes alone for the males (calories per pound of sweet potato is taken from Rappaport 1968:280). Pospisil did not supply the 35,651.04 kg of sweet potatoes to meet this demand (or a lower figure that is more reasonable) but it seems plausible that the supplement was nevertheless the result of local (Botukebo) production. Pospisil may have indirectly driven another 12,000 kg of surplus production. However, we will use the 13,380 kg of sweet potatoes for the estimate of Pospisil's impact. It seems more reasonable in the absence of any report of endemic overweight among the Kapauku and besides, its derivation seems more secure. It is also analytically useful to do so because it tilts the case in favor of least ethnographic impact.

In spite of this tilt, Pospisil's impact appears to be considerable. By his presence, and by adopting 51 sons and daughters, he increased the demand for sweet potatoes by about 10% and for other crops by about 18%. This observation certainly forms the basis for an alternative to Sahlins' model—namely, that Pospisil was driving the overproduction at Botukebo. Evaluating this against Sahlins' model that a big-man political economy was driving the overproduction is considered in the next section.

Model Evaluation

The narrow problem of overproduction is still at issue. Sahlins proposes that the overproduction is driven by the dynamics of a big-man political economy; we have suggested that Leopold Pospisil has driven the overproduction by adopting 51 sons and daughters. They both could reasonably account for the results of the Chayanov Analysis—thus underlining our methodological point about jumping to conclusions when using mathematical models. Resolving this dilemma lies in better identifying who the overproducers are and seeing if implications of these competing propositions are born out by closer consideration.

Two lines of analysis are considered. The first concerns the specific mechanisms driving the overproduction in each proposition. The second is a reanalysis of the Kapauku data with Chayanov Analysis after adjusting for the impact of Pospisil's demand. We analyze the mechanisms of overproduction first.

As in most attempts at post hoc analysis, desirable data are often missing. Specifically, we would expect if Pospisil were driving the overproduction that:

1.1 *Pospisil bought more of his food from the overproducing households than from the others.*
1.2 *The ritual sons and daughters were differentially related to the overproducing households in a manner that led to those households rather than the others looking after their welfare.*

While Pospisil presents good data on the extent of his impact, he does not detail how he obtained the food. Thus, these and other implications concerning Pospisil's articulation cannot be evaluated.

It was possible to evaluate Sahlins' propositions concerning how big-men drive overproduction. The big-man's strategy aims at capturing the labor power of others by capitalizing "on kinship dues and by finessing the relation of reciprocity [1963:291]."

Two test implications follow from a generalized strategy based on both kin and "finance":

2.1 *Big-man households are among the overproducers.*
2.2 *Big-men are "financially" linked to a greater degree to overproduction.*

To carry out these evaluations, it is necessary to identify the big-men of Botukebo (the overproducers are identified in Sahlins' Chayanov Analysis as reported before). In his discussion of Kapauku politics, Pospisil identifies three big-men by referring to them either as *tonowi,* "political and legal authority" (1963a:46), or as rich men, one of the primary characteristics of *tonowi* (1963a:45–46). The sublineage leader and village headman was Awiitigaaj (identified by Pospisil's index number as 6/1) "a wealthy *tonowi*" (1958:107) who however was considered to be a "rather selfish individual" (1958:108). Public popularity lay with Timaajjidainaago (7/1) "a rich man . . . who is generous, popular, and kind. However, the trouble is that this man is too quiet and shy [1958:110]" to challenge Awiitigaaj for leadership. Bunaibomuuma (1/1) was "the only person who opposed Awiitigaaj," unsuccessfully. He was without popular support and his opposition to Awiitigaaj was thus ineffective. In fact, Bunaibomuuma was considered a "notorious criminal" (1958:108).

Table 3.2 (which incorporates Tables 3.4 and 3.5 from Sahlins 1972:116, 120) allows an evaluation of the first implication. The sublineage leader's household is *not* overproducing. Bunaibomuuma's household is just barely overproducing and, given the size of the work force (10.5), this hardly counts as much of an impulse to overproduce. Interestingly, the popular Timaajjidainaago is the *tonowi* who best fits Sahlins' implications with his household consisting of the most intense laborers in the village.

Sahlins was aware of the discrepancy in the behavior of Awiitigaaj's household and suggested that this was because he had amassed enough credits so as not to have to exploit his close kin (1972:117). One would expect that he had managed to tap the labor of other households in the village sector to replace his close kin sector's labor. More generally, this leads to another implication:

2.3 *The big-men who do not have overproducing households should have strong "financial" links to village sector households.*

This and implication 2.2 concerning the links to overproducers can be partially evaluated with "financial" information presented by Pospisil. In January of 1955 he collected information on the debt structure at Botukebo. A few words need to be said about using "financial" data on "debts" in a big-man political economy. We agree with Sahlins (1972:250–251) that these were reciprocal relations rather than "loans" in a Western sense. But, as Pospisil has little place for reciprocal gifts in the Kapauku economy (1963a:334–348) separate from loans, this information should be representative of outstanding obligations. Note in particular that one category is for "debts" owed to members of one's own household. Again, we agree with Sahlins that being in financial debt to members of one's household is better interpreted as reciprocal relations. However, these "loans" are still of interest. Specifically, they are a measure of the potential of a household head to mobilize his immediate kin's labor—the all important first step toward becoming a big-man in Sahlins' model. Thus they are reported as: "Debts between members of the same household." Table 3.3 presents this debt structure, which is based on Table 31 in Pospisil (1963a:448–453).

TABLE 3.3
Total Household Debt (in Glass Beads) to Individual Creditors: Botukebo, 1955 (creditor identification numbers are Pospisil's index numbers)

Creditors (individuals)	Debtors (Households)																		
	1[b]	2[b]	3[b]	4[b]	5[b]	6	7[b]	8	9	10[b]	11[b]	12	13	14[b]	15	16	R[c]	S[d]	Total
1/1 [a]	0	3	0	0	0	0	0	0	0	0	0	0	0	0	0	0	600	0	603
1/6	0	0	0	0	0	0	0	0	0	0	0	0	0	0	0	0	360	0	360
1/9	0	0	0	0	0	0	0	0	0	0	0	0	0	0	0	0	2160	0	2160
2/1	0	0	0	0	0	0	0	0	0	0	0	0	0	0	0	0	0	1830	1830
2/2	0	0	0	0	0	0	0	0	0	0	0	0	0	0	0	0	30	0	30
2/14	0	0	0	0	0	0	0	0	3	0	0	0	6	0	0	0	2765	0	2774
3/1	0	0	0	0	21	0	300	0	0	0	0	0	60	0	0	0	0	0	381
3/2	0	0	0	0	30	0	30	0	0	0	0	0	0	0	0	0	330	0	390
4/1	0	0	0	0	1860	0	30	0	0	0	0	0	0	0	0	0	0	1800	3690
5/1	0	0	0	0	0	0	222	0	0	21	0	0	0	0	0	0	300	0	543
5/2	0	0	0	0	0	0	60	0	0	0	0	0	0	0	0	0	1800	210	2070
5/5	0	0	0	0	0	0	0	0	0	0	0	0	0	0	0	0	0	150	150
6/1 [a]	0	0	0	0	0	6480	30	0	0	0	0	0	3	0	0	0	25200	19020	50733
6/6	0	0	240	0	60	0	279	0	0	0	0	0	0	0	0	0	0	0	579
6/8	0	0	0	0	15	0	0	0	0	0	0	0	0	0	0	0	0	0	15
7/1 [a]	0	0	0	150	600	1800	3540	0	1800	150	0	0	1200	0	0	0	1860	1800	12900
7/7	0	0	0	0	18	0	0	0	0	0	0	0	0	0	0	0	0	0	18
7/14	0	0	0	0	15	0	0	0	0	0	0	0	0	0	0	0	0	0	15
8/1	0	0	0	0	0	0	0	0	60	0	0	0	69	0	0	0	90	600	819
8/4	0	0	0	0	0	0	0	0	0	0	0	0	15	0	0	0	0	0	15

9/1	0	0	0	0	0	0	3	0	0	0	0	0	0	0	0	0	0	0	3
9/2	0	0	0	0	0	0	90	0	0	0	0	0	0	0	0	0	0	0	90
9/8	0	0	0	0	0	0	0	0	0	0	0	0	0	0	0	0	1860	0	1860
9/9	0	0	0	0	0	0	0	0	0	0	0	0	0	0	0	0	0	30	30
10/1	0	2850	0	0	18	0	240	0	0	0	0	0	0	0	0	0	2127	0	5235
10/2	0	0	0	0	0	0	0	0	0	0	0	0	0	0	0	0	0	30	30
11/1	0	3	0	0	0	0	0	0	0	0	0	0	0	30	60	0	330	270	693
11/2	0	0	0	0	0	0	0	0	0	0	0	0	0	0	0	0	3	0	3
11/12	0	0	0	0	0	0	0	0	0	0	0	0	12	0	0	0	30	0	42
12/1	0	0	0	0	0	0	0	0	0	0	0	0	0	240	1800	0	600	0	2640
13/1	300	60	0	180	0	300	240	0	150	0	0	300	0	150	0	0	900	3339	5919
13/3	0	0	0	0	0	0	75	0	0	0	0	0	0	0	0	0	0	60	135
13/5	0	0	0	0	0	0	0	0	0	0	0	0	0	150	0	0	0	0	150
14/3	0	0	0	0	0	0	0	0	0	0	0	0	0	0	0	0	3150	9900	13050
15/1	0	60	0	0	0	0	0	0	0	0	0	0	0	0	0	0	150	0	210
15/2	0	0	0	0	0	0	0	0	2760	0	0	0	0	0	0	0	1800	0	4560
16/1	0	0	0	0	0	0	0	0	0	0	0	0	9	0	0	0	1950	3000	4959
R	2850	0	0	0	660	4380	1495	0	30	1920	1800	0	180	1800	0	1800	0	0	16915
S	1200	30	1800	0	0	420	1890	0	1800	0	0	0	0	0	0	0	0	0	7140
I[e]	405	4380	0	7305	0	420	270	0	39	0	2610	7080	369	3765	0	0	0	0	26643
Total	4755	7386	2040	7635	3297	13800	8794	0	6642	2091	4410	7380	1923	6135	1860	1800	48395	42039	

Source: Pospisil, 1963a:301–305; 351; 411–415; 448–453.

[a] Big-men.
[b] Overproducing households.
[c] *R* = Kin not from Botukebo.
[d] *S* = non-kin not from Botukebo.
[e] *I* = internal household loan.

TABLE 3.4
Social Category of the Leading Creditor for Each Overproducing Household

Social category of creditor	Total number of debtor households
Resident of Botukebo	7: Total
Big-man	1 (household no. 7)
Other resident, from a different household	1 (household no. 5)
Other resident, from the same household	5 (household nos. 2, 4, 7, 11, 14)
Nonresident of Botukebo	3: Total
Kinsman	2
Stranger	1

Awiitigaaj is still anomalous. He is clearly the financial kingpin at Botukebo, but his relations are neither with the overproducers nor even with Botukebo residents. In fact, 99.9% of his credits are with nonresidents, 43% being with nonresident nonkin (strangers). Bunaibomuuma, who is not a very active lender, has made 99.5% of his loans to nonresidents, in this case all relatives. Again, it is the popular Timaajjidainaago who has made loans to Botukebo residents, but even he has 41.1% of his loans going to nonresidents. Moreover, Timaajjidainaago is not strongly linked to the overproducers. Only 20% of his loans are to overproducers, and of this only 9.6% of his loans go outside his own household.

We have been asking if the big-men derive support from the overproducing households. With the exception of Timaajjidainaago, the answer is no, and in his case the answer is only a qualified yes. Even so, it is still possible that the overproducers are stongly and disproportionately in debt to the big-men. Table 3.4 investigates indebtedness from the perspective of the overproducers. It identifies the social category *to which* each overproducer is *most* indebted. Again, the household of Timaajjidainaago (household 7 in Table 3.5)

TABLE 3.5
Overproducer's Debts (Percentage of Total Debts) to Big-Men

Overproducing Household	Bunaibomuuma (1/1)	Awiitigaaj (6/1)	Timaajjidainaago (7/1)
1	8.5	.0	.0
2	>.1	.0	.0
3	.0	.0	.0
4	.0	.0	.0
5	.0	.0	18.2
7	.0	.3	43.3
10	.0	7.2	.0
11	.0	.0	.0
14	.0	.0	.0

best fits Sahlins' model. Its members are in debt to a big-man, namely, Timaajjidainaago (7/1 in Table 3.5), the household head. Strikingly, the other overproducing households are overwhelmingly *not* in debt to big-men. In fact, as shown in Table 3.5, big-men debts are a small percentage of the total debts of overproducing households.

This analysis, based on the "financial" data, is of course potentially fraught with sampling problems—though we think it represents Botukebo relations. First, it was collected only a few months after Pospisil entered the field, so the accuracy might be questioned. However, his overall meticulousness and his eventual "best friend" status with the big-men mitigates this possibility. Second, there may be a cycle in debts so that any one month is biased. Though we cannot demonstrate this, such short-term fluctuations seem unlikely. The role of these debts in creating political factions would tend to make these long-term relations. Supporting this, Pospisil notes that "the creditor's prosperity makes it highly probable that the debt will not have to be repaid [1963a:31]." This does not release the debtor from the power of the creditor for it is exactly this situation that is the basis of factions at Botukebo: "People usually follow decisions of a wealthy man because they are his debtors and are afraid of being asked to return what they owe, or out of gratitude for past financial aid, or because they expect future financial favors [1963a:45]."

To summarize, investigations of Botukebo's "finances" are not consistent with Sahlins' model that the big-men are driving their kin and/or debtors to overproduce. While the data do not conclusively counter Sahlins' model, the explanations making them consistent with his proposition have an ad hoc quality. This is certainly surprising for a supposedly paradigmatic ethnographic example of the big-man political economy.

Our second line of evaluation involves reanalyzing the Kapauku data. We reasoned that if Pospisil were responsible for the overproduction, then by subtracting this amount from the production of the overproducers, a closer approximation to Chayanov should be obtained. Figure 3.3 is the graphic Chayanov Analysis of these adjusted figures and Tables 3.6 and 3.7 supply the supporting data.

It is immediately obvious that the observed intensity *does* more closely approach the Chayanov expected line. This is similarly reflected in the value for the impulse to surplus labor (Sahlins 1972:111), which is reduced from 82% for 59% of the labor force (1972:121) to 57% for 49% of the work force.

TABLE 3.6
Regression Statistics: Adjusted for Pospisil's Effect

$r = .22170$	$r^2 = .04915$	Standard error of estimate = 540.40113
$A = 282.14305$		Standard error of A = 973.76324
$B = 600.44145$		Standard error of B = 705.83405
$N = 16$		

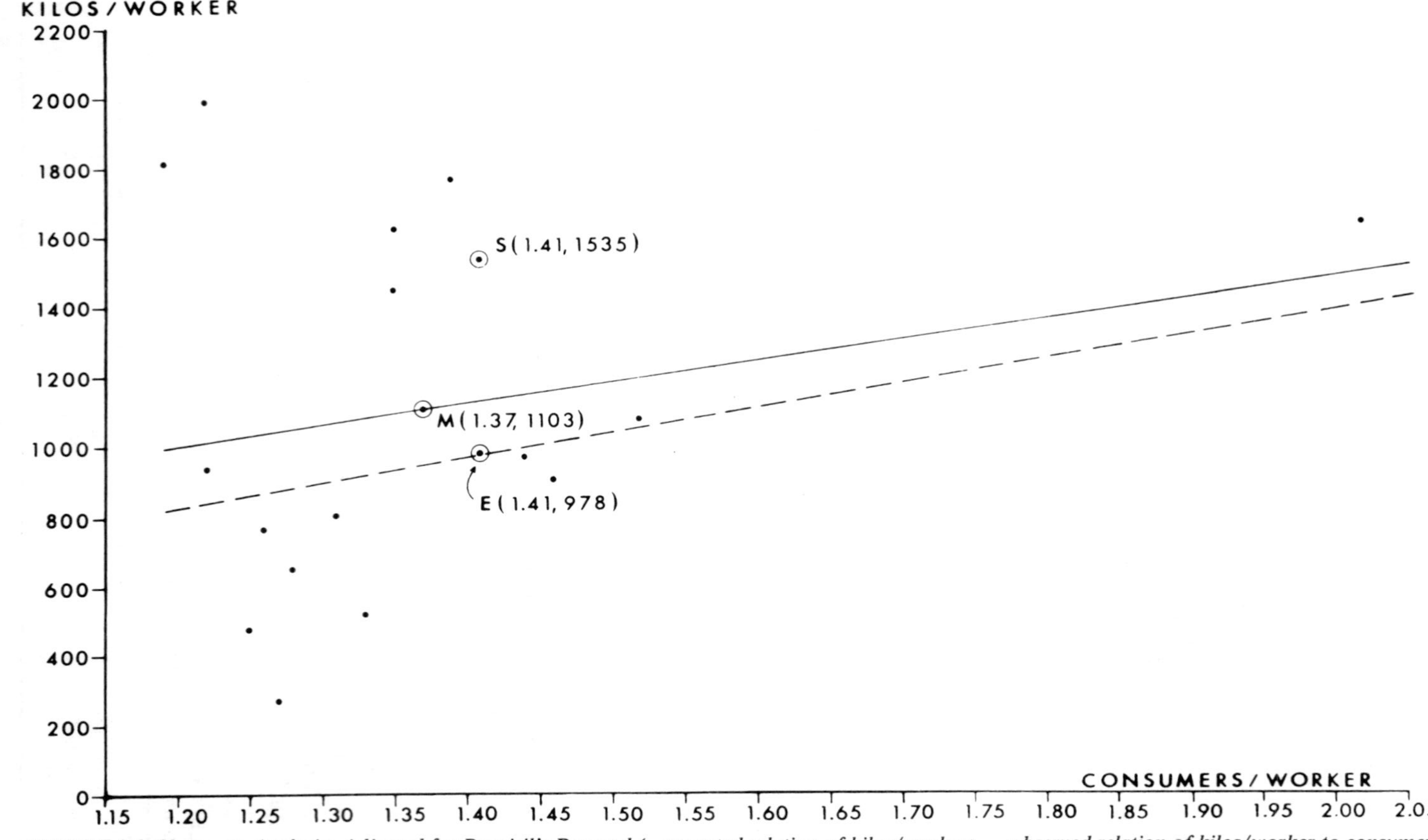

FIGURE 3.3 *Chayanov Analysis: Adjusted for Pospisil's Demand (---expected relation of kilos/worker;——observed relation of kilos/worker to consumer/worker).*

TABLE 3.7

Data for Chayanov Analysis: Adjusted for Pospisil's Demand

Household number	Number of consumers	Number of workers	Kilos of sweet potatoes/household	Consumers/workers	Observed kilos of sweet potatoes/household	Expected kilos of sweet potatoes/household	Deviation
4	9.5	8.0	14463	1.19	1808	825	+ 983
7[a]	11.6	9.5	18925	1.22	1992	846	+ 1146
14[a]	7.9	6.5	6117	1.22	941	846	+ 95
15	5.6	4.5	2124	1.25	472	867	− 395
6	11.3	9.0	6920	1.26	769	874	− 105
13	9.5	7.5	2069	1.27	276	881	− 605
8	5.1	4.0	2607	1.28	652	888	− 236
1	13.8	10.5	8439	1.31	804	909	− 105
16	4.0	3.0	1557	1.33	519	922	− 403
3[a]	5.4	4.0	6963	1.35	1616	936	+ 680
5[a]	7.4	5.5	7945	1.35	1445	936	+ 509
2[a]	14.6	10.5	18512	1.39	1763	964	+ 799
12	10.7	7.5	7267	1.44	969	999	− 30
9	9.5	6.5	5878	1.46	904	1013	− 109
10[a]	3.8	2.5	2687	1.52	1075	1054	+ 21
11[a]	9.1	4.5	7361	2.02	1636	1401	+ 235

[a] Overproducers

Surplus production (1972:114) expectedly drops from 35.37% to 28.82% of the total village product. Also, Bunaibomuuma's household, when corrected for the hypothetical effect of Pospisil's demand, drops below the Chayanov expected line, leaving Timaajjidainaago as the only overproducing big-man household.

Two observations emerge from this reanalysis. First, by adjusting for Pospisil's demand among the overproducing households, a closer approach to the Chayanov expected was obtained. This is consistent with our proposition that Pospisil's demand is driving the overproduction. Second, and just as clearly, Pospisil is not the only force driving overproduction. What is left after Pospisil's demand has been taken into consideration is an intensity profile consistent with Sahlins' model for a big-man political economy. That is, the observed intensity line is above and parallel to the Chayanov expected line and the values about the Chayanov line are fish-tailed in shape. So while the reanalysis is consistent with our proposition, it is also consistent with that of Sahlins.

The overall impression is that neither Sahlins' model nor Pospisil's presence fully accounts for the overproduction at Botukebo. But, just as importantly, neither is inappropriate. Pospisil clearly had an impact on their production efforts and it seems reasonable that he is partially accounting for the deviations from Chayanov expected. Internal household debt is also a key mechanism. It drives both the labor intensity of Timaajjidainaago's household and is the primary form of indebtedness for four other overproducers as well.

The key to building a more appropriate model lies in the other relation of indebtness, which may be driving overproduction. Table 3.5 shows that after Pospisil, indebtedness to *non*-Botukebo individuals is the most important source of credit among the overproducers—not big-men or close sector residents. Similarly, the Botukebo big-men had made considerable portions of their loans to nonresidents of Botukebo. This suggests the importance of regional processes operating in the economy of the Kapauku. And just this perspective helps deal with the anomalous (in Sahlins' model) behavior of Awiitigaaj, and the easy insertion of Pospisil into Kapauku society.

The American Connection

In the previous section, data were presented supporting the notion that a big-man political economy was driving overproduction at Botukebo; but data were also presented that contradict certain implications of Sahlins' model, suggest that something else is going on, and point a finger at Pospisil as an agent of overproduction. The strands of a model that can support these two observations exists in the literature; it is toward a synthesis of these strands that we address the following sections. We begin by inquiring of the status of the ethnographer in a tribal setting. We find that he represents the interaction of two sets of interregional processes: The one located in the highlands, the other articulating the highlands with wider cultural spheres. Each of these itself is capable of driving overproduction, yet neither is an important part of Sahlins' model.

Considering the ethnographer from the vantage point of North America, Pospisil is just one agent of Western penetration. This, in turn, is only one of a number of such penetrations from outside the highlands. Inland populations in New Guinea have long-standing trading relations with coastal populations, and through the overseas trade networks of these communities, to the products of other Melanesian islands (Harding 1967; Hughes 1973). Participation in this trade clearly has had an impact on local level political economy. Less clear is the extent of Indonesian influence in New Guinea prior to the advent of Europeans there.

At this point, however, we wish to take up the question of past contact with agents of European societies and its effect on the nature of Kapauku political economy. There is a substantial literature assaying the nature of culture change in New Guinea following the establishment of direct political control and sustained contact with European institutions. But the central thrust of New Guinea research is on the aboriginal culture. Monographs characteristically begin with a brief narrative of the history of contact with Europeans that stresses how recent sustained contact has been and is designed to assure the reader that the analysis, which is to follow, is of a tribal society untainted by acculturating influences. This approach is consistent with the prevailing ethnographic tactic:

> Anthropologists, except as they become interested in recent cultural changes, rather like to think that the natives still exist in their pristine state—or at least talk about them that way. We adopt the convention of the "ethnographic present," discussing the Iroquois or Hawaiians as they were at the time of European discovery—that is, when they were "really" Iroquois or Hawaiian. . . . for comparative purposes it is necessary to characterize primitive cultures apart from distortions introduced by Europeans [Sahlins 1968:3–4].

Here Pospisil and Sahlins are in accord and in keeping with this anthropological tradition, Pospisil does not include an analysis of the Papuan–European interaction in his monograph. Europeans are not, however, completely invisible, and one passage near the end of *Kapauku Papuan Economy* falls like an ethnographic bombshell.

> How dependent political leadership is on credit can be seen from the effects of the acculturation situation in 1959. At that time the Dutch administration started to build an airport at Moanemoni in the Kamu valley, thus providing the young and ablebodied with an easy income. As a consequence young men were not forced to borrow money from the native *tonowi* and the amount of credits and debts in the region dropped to one fourth of the figure in 1955. This change in economic bal-

> ance had, as a consequence, *a complete loss of influence of the tonowi type of headman and a consequent disintegration of the former headmanship and political structure* [1963a:393, italics added].

In one sense this observation confirms the validity of the strategy of the ethnographic present: Pospisil arrived in time to record the aboriginal political economy before it disintegrated as a result of European influence. But a question nags at us: What if the ethnographer had first arrived at Botukebo in 1959, 1964, or 1974 instead of in 1954 as Pospisil actually did? What then would the ethnographic record show? Perhaps it would show an acculturation situation derived from a recently collapsed big-man system. But it is also possible—given the anthropological penchant to construct a historical analysis based on field observation—that it might show a more egalitarian ethnographic present than Pospisil recorded, one politically more fragmented and without big-men. There is, of course, no way to know, but the question leads us to carefully examine Pospisil's work for information on Papuan–European interaction before and during his stay in Botukebo.

In passing, Pospisil mentions a number of elements in relations between Papuans and Europeans that were approximately coeval with his period of research:

1. Cowrie shell money, originating at the coast and traded overland to eventually arrive in Botukebo, had been augmented by glass beads of European manufacture (1963a:338). In addition, cowrie shell 'blanks' were brought in by air and obtained by the Kapauku directly from the local Dutch government station. Some of the local Kapauku were using these blanks to make counterfeit currency.
2. European-made implements, especially steel axes and machetes, were in common use.
3. Several exotic domesticates, including manioc and the chicken, had been deliberately introduced and promoted by the Dutch and had earned some favor with the Kapauku (1963a:109–110). There is an enigmatic reference to the "distribution" of rice by the Dutch (1963a:363).
4. Some Kapauku women were selling food to the Dutch, earning money that, without these sales, they would not have controlled (1963a:150).
5. There is evidence that the prestige and authority of the Dutch were already considerable. This is apparent in the role of the patrol officer in introducing Pospisil into Botukebo (1963a:19), in the native police officer using his office as the basis on which to farm out a pig to be raised in Botukebo (1963a:217), and in an instance of the Dutch patrol officer adjudicating a "financial" dispute between two Papuans (1963a:221).

It is also clear from Pospisil's work, and from other sources, that the Kapauku had experienced intermittent direct contact with Europeans since the 1920s and indirect contact for an even longer period of time. Steel axes had reached the Kapauku area even before the Europeans did, being traded over existing trade routes between the uplands and the coast. These same trade routes had also carried an increasing flow of cowrie shells and other currencies as a result of European activities on the coast. With Europeans reaching the highlands in the 1920s, these were injected directly into the highlands, greatly expanding the total volume of valuables in circulation there (Dubbeldam 1964).

It is clear from these references that numbers of points of articulation between Kapauku and Europeans had been established well before the time of Pospisil's research. It is certainly possible that, individually and in sum, these had an insignificant impact before 1954–1955. Indeed, Pospisil implies as much in referring to the 1959 situation as an "acculturation" situation, leaving a clear supposition that 1954–1955 was preacculturation. But the kind of detailed analysis that Pospisil brings to economic and legal relations among Papuans is absent in the matter of Kapauku–European relations. Although these contacts may seem minor and insignificant in comparison to the power of the locally derived patterns of interaction that Pospisil does analyze, we may perhaps be excused from raising questions of their significance in view of the fact that the construction of a single airport could cause "a complete loss of influence of the *tonowi* and disintegration of the political structure."

It seems plausible to us that these contacts may well have had a significant impact on the nature of Botukebo political economy. Dubbeldam's (1964) analysis of the role of the inflation in currency in creating 'devaluation' and undermining the authority of the Kapauku *tonowi,* Meggitt's observation of the complex inflationary effect of European goods on the *Te* exchange networks (1971:200–209), and the analyses of Sharp (1953) and Salisbury (1962) on the political impact of the introduction of steel axes in other areas increase our suspicion that even indirect contact with Europeans might have produced radical transformations in political economy. This suspicion is further deepened by Kelly's recent information on Etoro depopulation as a result of casual encounters with Europeans in the 1930s, with its concomitant and lasting impact on their social organization (1977:25–31). The age structure figure for Botukebo presented by Pospisil would be consistent with a similar past population drop for the Kapauku (1963a:60–61; compare Kelly 1977:29).

Two conclusions based on these observations seem permissible. One is that Pospisil's way into Botukebo was paved by the Europeans who had gone before him. The Kapauku were familiar with resident Europeans who exchanged exotic and often useful items for native produce and from the day of Pospisil's arrival, supported by the Dutch, it was clear that he was prepared to play this role. Second, direct and indirect contact with Europeans had clearly been an aspect of Kapauku political economy for more than half a century, yet neither Sahlins nor Pospisil have taken it into account in their analysis.

BOTUKEBO BIG-MAN—A.K.A. LEOPOLD POSPISIL

So, from the perspective of North America, Pospisil is one of a series of agents tying the West New Guinea Highlands to the capitalist West. In what follows we take the perspective of a Papuan and see that, surprisingly,

Pospisil's entry into Botukebo and the role he played there throughout his field study were also prepared by the existing rules of interaction among Kapauku Papuans. Furthermore, these phenomena, particularly Pospisil's adoption practices and the shell inflation, can be seen to have driven overproduction at Botukebo. Clearly, processes such as these are not an integral part of Sahlins' model of tribe. Take note, this is not a particularist critique. As idiosyncratic events, these particular forms of interaction would not likely be of general interest. As examples of interregional processes, however, they point out a serious deficiency in the tribal model. In the following we make a case for the general importance of long-range interactions for understanding any tribal situation.

As in the previous section, we start with the ethnographer, only this time the perspective is internal to a tribal model. What is the social position of the ethnographer in Sahlins' model of the tribe? Recall the sectoral model in which there was a rough correlation between distance in physical space and social space, both inversely correlated with sociability.

> The several sectors of a tribe are graded by sociability. High and positive in the inner sphere of close kinship, sociability declines as the sector of social relations expands, becoming increasingly neutral in distant circles and ultimately, the intertribal field, altogether negative [1968:18].

Pospisil, in this model, is from the furthest circle; he should be the stranger and potential enemy who may and should be cheated in economic dealings. This stands in rather stark opposition to the festive greeting he received which had the effect of changing his research plans. This cannot be easily resolved with Sahlins' model.

Alternatively, Pospisil offers an interpretation of his easy fit into the system: "Since I was a white man with plenty of strange and, in Kapauku eyes, certainly expensive artifacts, I was regarded as particularly wealthy [1963a:19]." He thus accounts for his entourage of sons and daughters.

But more was operating than his strangeness and the expensiveness of his gifts—which is to say his Westernness. Significantly, in giving Latin names, he was also giving access to food. That is, his simple act of taxonomic generosity enmeshed him in a persisting complex set of obligations. Clearly, the sons and daughters were not acting in a social vacuum by attaching themselves to a Westerner. Rather, their behavior is consistent with attaching themselves to a Kapauku big-man.

Pospisil can be seen acting as a Kapauku big-man in a number of social situations. He states that "it is a custom in the Kapauku culture for adolescent boys and young men to come to live for a long period of time with a rich man [1958:4]."

> Besides the debtors a wealthy man has usually several additional ready supporters in his apprentices, who he calls *ani jokaani* "my boys." These young individuals

> usually come from poor families and join the rich man's household in order to obtain from him a good education in business administration and politics, to secure his protection, to share his food and, finally, to be granted a substantial loan for buying a wife. For these favors, in turn, they offer their labor in the gardens and around the house, their support in legal and political disputes, and their lives in case of war [1963b:51].

Thus, in one of Pospisil's first acts, adopting the sons and daughters and indicating he liked them by giving them names, while they were building his house, he indicated that he was like a big-man.

Not only did adolescents perceive him as a big-man, but so eventually did the Kapauku big-men. Pospisil notes that "the second great advance in my relations with the people occurred at the time when three important headmen of the Ijaaj–Pigome Confederacy and a shaman asked me to become their best friend [1963a:20]." Relations between "best friends" are institutionalized in Kapauku society and are characterized by "deep mutual affection, exchange of gifts of high value, and assistance in financial troubles, wars, and legal disputes [1963a:31]." This relationship becomes a very important tool in political dealings, particularly at the interconfederational level: "A shrewd politician is very particular in selecting as his best friends only those individuals who are themselves important and have a lot of followers [1963a:51]." Thus, the inference of Pospisil as big-man seems borne out by the behavior of the Kapauku big-men in asking him to become their best friend.

Pospisil's easy fit into Kapauku society suggests that Kapauku society regularly has big-men integrating regional systems—not simply integrating intravillage segmentary units. In other words, the logic of the Kapauku system appears to operate regularly in a much larger arena than the limited one implicit in Sahlins' model of the tribe.

The importance of such large-scale ties can be found in the literature for other areas of New Guinea. For example, Meggitt identifies extra-parish big-men connections among the Mae Enga. He notes rather striking differences in participation in the *Te* ritual with big-men from different parishes dominating the exchange and doing this at the expense of their local supporters:

> Almost all the Big Men I have known act very much as do Tammany Hall incumbents, keeping the system running tolerably smoothly by paying off these supporters whose aid is essential to them by also retaining for themselves whatever resources they can abstract at the expense of the weaker and poorer members of the group, those whose claims they can safely ignore for a time [1974:190].

This interparish big-man connection takes on the character of "incipient social strata, something approaching two classes of people defined by differential access to particular scarce and valued resources [1974:191]." This big-man relation, Meggitt feels, contributes to the overall adaptation of the Mae Enga at the regional scale. Thus, the theoretical processes driving the behavior of big-men, which are exogenous to the local setting, are at least as important as those endogenous to the village (see also Meggitt 1971:191–200).

Moylan similarly stresses the importance of regional processes when considering the ecological dynamics of New Guinea populations. Specifically with regard to the Kapauku he notes:

> there are indications that the relations within the local system of Botukebo are unstable in the long run and, further the integration of the system seems to exhibit a considerable degree of looseness, such that variation within one or more components of the system might not materially affect relations with other components [1973:67].

After considering other New Guinea cases (Tsembaga Maring and Mae Enga) along with the Kapauku, he concludes that village level demography and ecosystem processes are likely to be misleading.

> Indeed, we ought not to expect that local systems tend toward equilibrium at all, but only that the behavior of local systems contributes in some way to the interactions which compose the regional system tending towards equilibrium [Moylan 1973:68].

While we do not see the necessity for even regional systems to seek equilibrium, we do agree with Moylan's conclusions that little sense is to be made of New Guinea tribes—particularly the Kapauku—from just the intravillage perspective.

An even more extreme statement of the importance of intervillage relations is made by Brookfield and Hart who "regard the very large number of local small communities as local, open systems, all interconnected and aggregated into a wider system that can only notionally be bounded at the edges of Melanesia [1971:77]." This extremely large-scale model is based on their observations of demographic processes in both pre- and post-contact Melanesia. These processes have the effect of spreading population pressure around between the various small but open tribal units found across the Melanesian landscape (1971:92).

Broad-scale models of New Guinea and Melanesian society are certainly consistent with studies of the long-range trade systems for which the area is as famous as it is for its big-man complex (Freedman 1967; Harding 1965, 1967; Hughes 1973; Irwin 1974; Malinowski 1961; Meggitt 1974). These broad-scale studies present both data, which are not easily subsumed under Sahlins' model of tribe, and alternative—though only partially formulated—models of tribe, which stress different processes.

Finally, these broad-scale studies help resolve some of the problems encountered when analyzing the Kapauku with Sahlins' model. First, these processes integrating the extravillage sector allow us to consider Pospisil's easy fit into Kapauku society. Furthermore, Meggitt's ideas about political economy help account for Awiitigaaj's heavy investment in external strangers (possibly other big-men?) and the general negative attitudes of big-men followers. In Sahlins' model, extravillage integration is accomplished by big-men who regularly collect the surplus production of small communities and deploy it outward in their search for renown. Yet it is clear that in Botukebo people were "financially" involved with outsiders at least as often as they were with their fellow villagers, big men included. These outsiders were often "strangers" (Pospisil 1963a:348–356, Tables 30–37, 447–455). These behaviors are less consistent with Sahlins' model where distance makes enemies and power is almost exclusively the result of local faction building. Pospisil's acceptance and Awiitigaaj's behavior make much more sense in a theory of primitive tribal economies, which is areal rather than local in scope.

We would like to make one more point in order to emphasize that the argument for a broader perspective goes beyond the criticism that the New Guinea data—and specifically the supposedly paradigmatic Kapauku—only loosely fit Sahlins' model of tribe. On a theoretical plane, these broader models are more satisfying as a basis for a social theory of tribal society. Let us consider the forces driving Sahlins' model.

Sahlins posits the household–family as a basic theoretical concept. The separation of these segmentary units (households) is essential to his design of the tribe. He implies that they can be pitted against the larger concept of society with a tension between the centripetal forces of society organizing the households and the centrifugal forces of the households shattering society: "The constraints of the household economy are, however, overcome in tribal societies—or else the society is overcome [1968:78]." That is, the reproduction of the DMP is counter to the reproduction of society at large.

This last tension is analytically weak, though central to his argument. A notion of household that could truly create a centrifugal force capable of negating society would not only organize production, but also *reproduce* the conditions for its existence. Production entails bringing labor power together with tools and raw materials to transform the raw material. Thus, we need a notion of household that can transform raw materials with reproducible labor forces and technologies.

Households, as modeled by Sahlins, are capable of reproducing technology and appropriating nature. However, they are not likely to be capable of reproducing the necessary labor power to continue production. Wobst (1974a) has considered the problem of the minimum size of the human-mating network that will reliably reproduce itself under various forms of primitive social organization. Consistent reproduction does not become a reasonable outcome in human-mating networks smaller than about 350 people. Thus, not even the Kapauku village of Botukebo could likely reproduce itself without others.

What this means is that the logic of the household economy *requires* society—it does not, as Sahlins would have it, *contradict* society. True, there are centrifugal forces generated within the household, but there is also the centripetal force of reproducing labor power that implies extrahousehold, and very often, extravillage relations (Wobst 1974a, 1974b). This is consistent with the observations of regional integration for New Guinea societies.

By considering the extravillage character of labor reproduction, a more satisfactory origin for "society" in the tribal model can be developed. At the local scale, as interpreted by Sahlins, society enters as a psychological variable. In Sahlins' design of the tribe the big-man is an important agent of society, integrating the atomistic segmentary units of the households. What, then, is the logical source for the big-man? For Sahlins, the big-man behaves as he does because of ambition: "Any ambitious man who can gather a following can inaugurate a societal career [1968:89]." And similarly by psychological drives, the big-man intensifies production: "Jealous of his increasing reputation, a big-man comes under increasing pressure to extract goods from his followers, to delay reciprocities owing them, and to deflect incoming goods back into external circulation [1968:90]." By considering regional processes one can avoid reducing society to a psychological foundation.

Specifically, the aforementioned New Guinea researchers have suggested that the atomistic segments are socially integrated to control demographic growth and resultant biodegradation. Here, we point out that atomistic households must be socially joined as a precondition for the perpetuation of the domestic economy. Neither of these approaches (which are by no means mutually exclusive) requires psychological drives to account for society in a tribal system.

Lest we be misunderstood, we need to state clearly that we are not advocating throwing out Sahlins' baby with the psychological bathwater. We have found reasonable support for his faction building big-man in some of the activities of Timaajjidainaago, and for his exploitative big-man Awiitigaaji. What is lacking is an explanation for why these men, and especially "notorious criminals" such as Bunaibomuuma, regularly and successfully squander their capital in intervillage relations, and why even "the political boundaries of the confederacy of lineages is no limit whatsoever to business relationships [Pospisil 1963a:356]."

We also agree with Sahlins methodology—a methodology Sweezy calls the "method of 'successive approximations.' " Considering this a bit further indicates a way toward a joint model. The method of successive approximations "consists in moving from the more abstract to the more concrete in a step-by-step fashion, removing simplifying assumptions at successive stages of the investigation so that theory may take account of and explain an ever wider range of actual phenomena [Sweezy 1942:11]." Clearly this is Sahlins' strategy in constructing the DMP—with its abstract, isolated households exerting a centrifugal force, which is only countered by the ambitions of the big-man. Developing this force as a theoretical process requires simplifying assumptions concerning the nature of primitive society. Sweezy goes on to note the criteria by which this method is best judged.

> In each case, the following three questions should be asked about the simplifying assumptions (or abstractions) which give rise to criticism: (1) are they framed with a proper regard for the problem under investigation? (2) do they eliminate the non-essential elements of the problem? (3) do they stop short of eliminating the essential elements [1942:20]?

Our point is not the inappropriateness of Sahlins' method—rather it has to do with criterion 3. Sahlins stopped short of identifying big-man–big-man relations as a regular and necessary feature of both his tribal design and of his model of the DMP. And this is because he drew his system too narrowly. Even considering production, the imports are labor and potential labor—husbands and wives, mothers and fathers.

Thus, we are not advocating disregarding Sahlins' model and processes of big-man political economy. We are trying to integrate these intravillage processes with extravillage processes that seem necessary for a fuller model. This does mean changing some aspects of Sahlins' model. But the exploitation dynamics, limits, and big-man cycle remain. Our point is that these are not the only dynamics or limits.

Here we can only sketch such a synthetic model. The tribal problematic is a lack of stratification associated with an economy based on domesticates. By emphasizing the broader scale, some new perspectives are offered on this problem. The first, suggested in Meggitt's work, is that stratification is a very real impulse in tribal society. Minimally, this is due to the unequal distribution of resources throughout a region—and, hence the potential for socially regulated unequal access to strategic resources. By emphasizing the importance of regional connections as a means of population regulation, Moylan's and Brookfield and Hart's work hints at a mechanism which damps this impulse to stratification. This is accomplished in the short run through Sahlins' limitation on exploitation. In the long run, however, the impulse is damped by redistributing the key limiting resource—labor—over the landscape. The effect is a relatively nonstratified self-damping system of greater size—demographic, spatial, and energetic—and complexity than is usually associated with prestate formations. And certainly this system is of greater dimension than that encompassed by Sahlins' model of tribe.

Conclusions

This began as an inquiry into the Kapauku problem and has gone well beyond that to theoretical issues in economic anthropology. The problems in theories of large-scale processes—both in practice and principle—are provoked by Pospisil's behavior at Botukebo. Understanding this depends on understanding both a neolithic and a capitalist world system.

First, let us consider the neolithic world. We agree with Brookfield and Hart's vision of New Guinea as an open system made up of only semiautonomous villages and tribes. Pospisil's interactions with the Kapauku are further evidence for the existence of such a system. His entourage of sons and daughters from outside of Botukebo and his best friend relations with the big-men of other places replicated the behavior of Kapauku big-man within the indigenous system. Studies for other areas of New Guinea suggest that big-men integrate regional scale systems regularly, and are affected much more by processes operating at this larger level than at the level of the local faction. These are convincing evidence for the existence of a neolithic world system.

There is little place for these relations in Sahlins' model of the tribe. Considering larger-scale interactions contributes not only to understanding the ethnography of New Guinea, but to a theory of primitive economies as well. In Sahlins' model, "society" integrates the atomistic segments of the tribe through the agency of the big-man. But what are the origins of the big-man? Sahlins looks to psychology. However, concern with large-scale processes suggests the culturological nature of these ties as mechanisms relating the population to its environment and damping out incipient stratification.

Working out the structure and organization of a neolithic world system is well beyond the scope of this chapter, yet some tantalizing leads do emerge from considering the Kapauku. The problematic of the neolithic world system is to perpetuate nonstratification on a potentially powerful and diverse energy base. The demographic instability of small populations, demonstrated by Wobst, gives an outward thrust to the DMP. Against Brookfield and Hart's backdrop of open tribal communities, this can regulate population pressure and damp out tendencies toward stratification. By redistributing the population throughout the region, population pressure can be averted. Because labor is the limiting resource in production, stratification is damped. Thus the centralization of the crucial resource of labor power within a big-man's faction, with a concomitant Boserupian impulse towards stratification, is circumvented.

We found that Kapauku integration into a neolithic system was one factor that helped Pospisil to fit into Botukebo. Another was Kapauku participation in the modern world. Pospisil was one in a series of agents and phenomena that have intruded into New Guinea from the developed sectors of the world system. This observation led us to a consideration of the significance of these contacts on Kapauku tribal economy.

Elsewhere than New Guinea, tribal social formations have come to be understood not as survivals from the pristine neolithic past, but as products of the growth of civilization. The classic studies by Secoy (1953) on the Plains Indians and by Leacock (1954) on the Indians of the North American boreal forests demonstrated that crucial elements in these social formations had been forged from early contact with Europeans. Similarly, research on nomadic groups in the Middle East and Central Asia, once seen as a cultural type predating the origins of civilization, have been found to be a by-product of civilization, an ecological and political–economic form that developed among populations expelled by or retreating from the advances of civilization (Lattimore 1962; McNeill 1964; Bates 1971; Irons 1974). It is also now clear that so-called tribes in Africa and Asia were influenced by indigenous state-formation processes long before Europeans arrived on the scene and that some of the apparently most conservative communities in Indonesia and mid-America are the product of European conquest (Wolf 1957).

The accumulation of case studies demonstrating the role played by civilization in creating and perpetuating what we have been calling tribes has been accompanied by attempts to assess their theoretical significance. Service (1962) began by suggesting that certain forms of 'bands' and 'tribes,' which he called *anomalous* and *composite,* were in fact populations of refugees that had come together after a period of depopulation and disorganization resulting from initial contact with Europeans. Later Service (1971) decided that he had not gone far enough and concluded that most so-called primitive societies had been severely altered as a result of such contact. Referring to modern scientific ethnographies he said, "No matter how much confidence we may have in their accuracy, the reports normally describe the cultural remnants that have survived the devastation caused by Euro-American colonial and imperial expansion [1971:152]." (See also Godelier 1977:70–96.) Fried has followed a parallel line of reasoning to the conclusion that, before the arrival of Europeans, primitive cultures in most places had been fundamentally altered by the existence of states. For Fried and Service, pristine tribes are ones that interact only with other tribes. Since they have been articulated with more complex cultures for centuries, all tribes that we know of from anthropological research or historical reference are at least in part the product of civilization. Fried concluded his essay evaluating the concept of tribe with the observation that "tribe is a secondary sociopolitical phenomenon, brought about by the intercession of more complexly ordered societies, states in particular. I call this the "secondary tribe" and I believe that all tribes with which we have experience are of this kind [1975:114]." Certainly these are controversial conclusions, but they are strongly compelling and it is clear that research on so-called tribes will in the future have to assess carefully the history of their relations with other groups and the implications of these relations for internal sociocultural arrangements. The evidence strongly suggests that what anthropologists have in fact been studying is not a collection of autonomous traditional tribes, *but the tribal sector of the world capitalist system.*

Does this conclusion apply equally to New Guinea? The prevailing thrust of ethnographic literature is that it does not. Most ethnographic reports are silent on this question. Where it has been raised, thoughtful scholars have concluded that New Guinea, or at least the highlands, are an exception. Thus:

> In all the world, only inland New Guinea provides an opportunity for understanding an extensive system of neolithic trade in all its complexity–its ecological basis, its physiographic constraints, and the cultural adaptations of those that took part.

> Elsewhere the neolithic traders are dead and have left no records other than a handful of durable artifacts. Most of the area of this study remained prehistoric until the 1930s, some of it until the 1950s [Hughes 1973:97].

However, there is suggestive evidence that sporadic direct contact, or even indirect contact with Europeans through existing trade networks, resulted in cowrie shell inflation, the introduction of steel tools, and possibly even severe depopulation; any one of these could have radically affected indigenous political economy and social organization. Moreover, we do not know the possible impact of complex civilizations such as the Indonesian, on New Guinea, even before Europeans found their way to Melanesia. We therefore conclude that it is problematic whether the Kapauku, as observed by Pospisil, were a contemporary stone age culture, or whether they were a tribal segment of the world capitalist system.

The specific behavior of overproducing households and big-men, whether from Botukebo or New Haven, will be better understood as ethnographic literature expands to include more information on the small, local-scale processes identified by Sahlins, the larger-scale ecological and regional relations suggested by Meggitt, Brookfield and Hart, Moylan, and others, and on the processes incorporating New Guinea into the world capitalist system.

However, our examination of the ethnological treatment of the Kapauku has led us to conclude that the basic problem is not one of insufficient data, but of underdeveloped and misdirected theory. The processes that are organizing a tribal sector of the modern world system are best known by their material results—the trade goods that find their way into remote regions. The political economy and ideology of these relations have been less completely explored. Moreover, the processes organizing past world systems, specifically the neolithic world system, are but dimly perceived.

What the ethnographer actually observes is the remains of neolithic systems transformed by the demands of a succession of state-dominated world systems. We mistrust attempts to read directly from the enthnographic present to the neolithic past. We also mistrust mechanical reconstructions from the scant remains of archaeology, although we recognize that any model of neolithic systems must be consistent with archaeological data. Our claim is that what is most needed now is a theory of neolithic political economy freed from the biases of the "ethnographic present," yet informative for both archaeological and ethnographic data. We have made some suggestions concerning a theory of large-scale tribal systems, but they fall well short of a complete or satisfying development. We expect fuller elaboration to capture our attention in the near future.

References

Brookfield, H. C., and D. Hart
1971 *Melanesia.* London: Methuen.

Bates, Daniel
1971 The role of the state in peasant-nomad mutualism. *Anthropological Quarterly 44:*109-131.

Brown, Paula
1978 New Guinea: Ecology, society, and culture. In *Annual Review of Anthropology* 7:263-291. Palo Alto: Annual Reviews, Inc.

Dubbeldam, L. F. B.
1964 The devaluation of the Kapauku-cowrie as a factor of social disintegration. In *New Guinea: The Central Highlands* (J. B. Watson, Ed.). *American Anthropologist 66*(4,part 2):293-303.

Evans, M.
1974 A note on the measurement of Sahlins' social profile of domestic production. *American Ethnologist 1:*269-279.

Found, W. C.
1971 *A theoretical approach to rural land-use patterns.* New York: St. Martin's Press.

Freedman, M.
1967 *The social and political organization of the Siassi Islands, New Guinea.* Ann Arbor: University Microfilms.

Fried, M. H.
1975 *The notion of tribe.* Menlo Park: Cummings.

Friedman, J.
1975 Tribes, states, and transformations. In *Marxist analysis and social anthropology* (M. Bloch, Ed.). London: Malby Press. Pp. 161-202.

Godelier, M.
1977 *Perspectives in Marxist anthropology.* Cambridge: Cambridge University Press.

Goody, J.
1958 *Development cycle in domestic groups.* Cambridge: Cambridge University Press.

Harding, T. G.
1965 Trade and politics: A comparison of Papuan and New Guinea traders. In *Essays in economic anthropology* (J. Helm, Ed.). Seattle: University of Washington Press. Pp. 46-53.
1967 *Voyagers of the Vitiaz Strait.* Seattle: University of Washington Press.

Harris, M.
1975 *Culture, people and nature* (2nd ed.). New York: T. Y. Crowell.

Hughes, I.
1973 Stone-age trade in the New Guinea inland. In *The Pacific in transition* (H. C. Brookfield, Ed.). London: Edward Arnold. Pp. 97-126.

Irons, W.
1974 Nomadism as a political adaptation: The case of the Yomut Turkmen. *Ethnology 1*(4): 635-658.

Irwin, G.
1974 The emergence of a central place in coastal Papuan prehistory. *Mankind 9:*268-272.

Kelly, R. C.
1977 *Etoro social structures: A study in structural confrontation.* Ann Arbor: University of Michigan Press.

Lattimore, O.
1962 *Inner Asian frontiers of China.* Boston: Beacon.

Leacock, E.
1954 The Montagnais "hunting territory" and the fur trade. *American Anthropological Association* Memoir No. 78. Menasha.

Malinowski, B.
1961 *Argonauts of the western Pacific.* New York: Dutton.

McNeill, W. H.
1964 *Europe's steppe frontier: 1500-1800.* Chicago and London: University of Chicago Press.

Meggitt, M.
1971 From tribesmen to peasants: The case of the Mae Enga of New Guinea. In *Anthropology in Oceania* (L. R. Hiatt and C. Jayawardena, Eds.). Sydney: Angus and Robertson. Pp. 191–209.
1974 Pigs are our hearts. *Oceania 44*:165–203.
Minge-Kalman, W.
1977 On the theory and measurement of domestic labor intensity. *American Ethnologist 4*: 273–284.
Moylan, T.
1973 Disequilibrium in a New Guinea local ecosystem. *Mankind 9*:61–70.
Nie, H. H., C. H. Hull, J. G. Jenkins, K. Steinbrenner, and D. H. Bent
1975 *SPSS: Statistical Package for the Social Sciences* (2nd ed.). New York: McGraw-Hill.
Platt, J. R.
1964 Strong inference. *Science 146*: 347–353.
Pospisil, L.
1958 Kapauku Papuans and their law. *Yale University Publications in Anthropology 54.* New Haven: HRAF Press.
1963a Kapauku Papuan economy. *Yale University Publications in Anthropology 67.* New Haven: HRAF Press.
1963b *The Kapauku Papuans of western New Guinea.* New York: Holt, Rinehart & Winston.
Rappaport, R. A.
1968 *Pigs for the ancestors.* New Haven: Yale University Press.
Sahlins, M.
1963 Poor man, rich man, big-man, chief: Political types in Melanesia and Polynesia. *Comparative Studies in Society and History 5*: 285–303.
1968 *Tribesman.* Englewood Cliffs: Prentice-Hall.
1972 *Stone-age economics.* Chicago: Aldine.
Salisbury, R. F.
1962 *From stone to steel: Economic consequences of a technological change in New Guinea.* London and New York: Cambridge University Press.
Secoy, F. R.
1953 Changing military patterns of the Great Plains. *American Ethnological Society Monographs,* No. XXI, Seattle.
Service, E. R.
1962 *Primitive social organization: An evolutionary perspective.* New York: Random House.
1971 *Cultural evolutionism: Theory in practice.* New York: Holt, Rinehart & Winston.
Sharp, L.
1953 Steel axes for Stone-Age Australians. *Human Organization 11*: 17–22.
Sharp, N.
1977 *The rule of the sword: The story of West Irian.* Victoria: Kibble Books.
Snedecor, G. W., and W. G. Cochran
1956 *Statistical methods* (5th ed.). Ames: Iowa State College Press.
Sweezy, P.
1942 *The theory of capitalist development.* New York: Monthly Review Press.
Thomas, R. B.
1973 Human adaptation to a high Andean energy flow system. *Occasional Papers in Anthropology No. 7,* Department of Anthropology, Pennsylvania State University, University Park.
Thorner, D., B. Kerblay, and R. E. F. Smith (Eds.)
1966 *A. V. Chayanov on the theory of peasant economy.* Homewood: R. D. Irwin.
Wobst, H. M.
1974a Boundary conditions for paleolithic social systems: A simulation approach. *American Antiquity 39*:147–178.

1974b Centripetal tendencies in egalitarian societies. Paper presented at the Annual Meeting of the Society for American Archaeology in the Symposium on Central Place Theory, Washington, D.C.

Wolf, E. R.

1957 Closed corporate communities in Mesoamerica and central Java. *Southwestern Journal of Anthropology 13*(1):1–18.

II

ECOLOGY AND HISTORY

4 System Levels Interaction in the Texas Hill Country Ecosystem: Structure, History, and Evolution

ANTHONY LEEDS

Introduction

This chapter[1] has several purposes. The more immediate is the description of a special type of ecosystem. The broader purpose has to do with the major theoretical issues of the relation between ecological, historical, and evolutionary understandings.

The type of ecosystem to be described is that in which aridity occurs, not as a fixed or periodic attribute of the geographical–climatological area, but aperiodically and unpredictably. It alternates with periods sometimes of "average" and sometimes even of prolonged precipitation or excessive water availability. Even seasonal characteristics may be unreliable in that variability through the years of a given season may be quite extreme so that averages, say of rainfall, are quite misleading from an ecological point of view. Sociotechnical adaptations to, controls over, and even partial restructurings of such environments may be particularly difficult by virtue of the unpredictability. (See Hirschman 1963, chapter on the Northeast of Brazil, for another striking example of the type.) The rather synoptic case study of central Texas which

[1] This chapter grew out of an interest in a proposed world-modeling, which Professor Bassett McGuire, Biology Department, University of Texas, wanted to undertake using the entire Colorado River System as the case material for systems modeling. The funding agency suggested that he do a preliminary trial modeling with a much smaller unit as a feasability study. McGuire chose the highland lakes area because a thermal electric plant was to be installed there but there was great uncertainty as to what its effects would be on the lakes, hence on plant, animal, and human populations, from an expected rise in lake temperatures consequent on the plant's operation. He invited representatives from various disciplines to participate, including persons from the social sciences. Konrad Kelley, Jr., and Victoria Jennings, graduate students in the Department of An-

BEYOND THE MYTHS OF CULTURE
Essays in Cultural Materialism

ISBN 0-12-598180-5

follows traces the history of the cumulation of sociotechnical inputs into the ecosystem, which have increasingly been directed at reshaping the area's water regimen within the limits possible at any given level of technological development.

The larger theoretical concern of this chapter is to link three central interests which have exercised anthropologists and other scientists. One is ecological theory and analysis—mostly, in current practice, a form of structural–processual, in some senses, functional analysis. The second is the "opposition" between historical processes and structural processes, a spurious dichotomy in my view. The third is evolutionary theory. We have not yet successfully brought these three interests together in a single theoretical framework despite great spurts of discussion as in the late 1930s and early 1940s and again, sporadically, in the late 1940s on into the early 1960s.

The cultural and human ecology carried out by anthropologists has focused basically on equilibrium models, thereby virtually automatically excluding both history and evolution, including considerations of sequential transformations, irreversibilities, and the like. In addition, the anthropologists doing both cultural and human ecology have tended to work with quite limited and small-scale societies, almost always explicitly or implicitly asserting them to be more or less self-contained. The ecological–structural models derived from such societies (and the underlying postulates about their closedness as systems) do not lend themselves to treatment of large-scale, multiplex, hierarchiacally organized societies, linked with world markets—such as

---

thropology, were interested in joining me in responding to McGuire's invitation. Empiricists that we anthropologists were, we wanted, unlike some of our social science confrères, to see what the area *looked* like. This started 9 months of field work, mostly on weekends or odd week days, sometimes involving all three or pairs of us, sometimes one of us alone, as well as a 2-weeks' participant observation by Jennings' living in Kingsland. This work was supported in part by a grant made to Kelley and Jennings from the Graduate School at the University of Texas. Our thanks go to that body.

The results of this work were presented in a preliminary form, represented by the draft of this chapter and the papers by Jennings and Kelley, at the annual meeting of the Southwestern Social Science Association in San Antonio, Spring, 1972. All three papers were read and commented on by all three of us. I read a somewhat modified version of this chapter at the Arid Lands Symposium, organized by Nancie Gonzalez and myself for the annual meeting of the American Association for the Advancement of Science in Denver, February 1977. Jennings also did an M.A. thesis on her material.

This chapter in many important respects is a joint work of the three of us. Most particularly, it probably should list Kelley as a coauthor since so much of the data work was done with or by him. Whole sets of his comments have been incorporated into the text, sometimes practically verbatim. As a native Texan of extraordinary insight and fascination with things Texan (and otherwise), he was a monumental fountain of knowledge and information. I grieve to have lost track of him.

I wish to thank Omer Stewart who, listening to the draft version of this chapter read at the AAAS meeting, called my attention to the importance of fire and subsequently sent me copies of a number of his papers. Attention to fire greatly enriched the perspectives of the chapter and my thinking about human control over environment in preagricultural times.

those in which the major part of my field experience has taken place. The Texas Hill Country, of course, represents an instance of such a society or societal segment.

The major contemporary paradigm of cultural evolution, which purportedly contrasts with such equilibrium models, is still grounded in nineteenth-century models, all of whose major shortcomings were clearly set forth by the mid 1930s. The basic model of nineteenth-century evolutionism is grounded on a notion of culture-in-general, not on a conception of different sociocultural systems, each with some sort of boundary conditions delimiting it from some other system or systems. All twentieth-century field anthropology, with its obvious relativism, has postulated such systems and used them as field units. We refer to such a unit as 'a society,' or much more frequently and ambiguously in anthropology, 'a culture.' It is more ambiguous because, especially in a conception of culture based on traits such as was basic to American anthropology from at least the 1880s until about mid-twentieth century, the boundary mechanisms are not set forth, but merely assumed to exist: the mystique of *das Volk.*[2]

The units of nineteenth-century evolutionism were either culture-in-general or the disconnected, decontextualized, monadic or irreducible, practically autonomous culture traits moving through space over time. Given such units, there is no easy transition even from "a culture," localized in time and place and operating as some sort of working sociocultural arrangement, on one hand, and culture-in-general, on the other. (See the attempts in Sahlins and Service [1960] to get around this by talking about 'special' and 'general evolution,' that is respectively, "history" and nineteenth-century evolutionism in new verbal dress.) A transition between such conceptually and analytically tightly bounded systems as those of British social anthropological description and those of cultural and human ecology to culture-in-general as conceived in the nineteenth-century evolutionary paradigm is, because of the paradigm contradictions, virtually impossible. Insofar as "a society" or "a culture" has been the unit of British, French, or American anthropology in this century, they have been, despite much lip service, largely, in fact, nonevolutionary, at least in a processual sense.

---

[2] This emphasis on traits had some interesting implications for American "cultural" anthropology. The objects of description composing the entities to be described—a "people," a "tribe," a *Volk*—were identical to the objects of archaeology, that is, traits. American cultural anthropologists have had no difficulty doing both archaeology and ethnography (e.g., Kroeber, W. D. Strong, and others), and saw them as theoretically isomorphic. Even physical man had traits so that only a very shadowy boundary existed between the cultural and the physical—and people did both physical anthropology and ethnography (e.g., Boas). Further, traits are distributive and diffuse themselves in non-isomorphic distributions. An implication of this is that, de facto, no cultural system is closed or really bounded. I think the fact that men like Kroeber and Boas never wrote "a complete monograph," a "failure" often pointed to in accusatory fashion, is metaphysically entirely consistent with their trait view—if anything, to be applauded for consistency of metaphysics and nonreification of a "tribe."

In a curious way, ecological analysis has exacerbated the nonevolutionary character of the discipline because of its very emphasis on system, closedness, and equilibrium, despite its emphasis on process, because the former emphasis has given renewed life to relativism and has barred us from fruitful, comparative, nomothetic endeavors to construct a new and viable evolutionary theory. Such an evolutionary theory would have concomitantly to cope with (*a*) the *systemic* aspects of human society and culture, which are now well recognized, eschewing the disaggregational and atomizing procedures of nineteenth-century evolutionism; (*b*) the irreversibilities in system histories; and (*c*) lawful, cross-cultural comparison.

A minor evolutionary paradigm, based on a Darwinian model, crops up more or less regularly and as regularly dies, because it is patently inapplicable, at least in all the forms so far put forward (for an example, Ruyle 1973; see Leeds 1974).

This chapter, by means of the case study of a complex societal segment, the Texas Hill Country, seeks to propose a solution to these problems, to link ecological analysis of process and structure, reintroduce history and give a generic model of sociocultural evolution which allows us our relatively bounded systems, but can still talk in a useful fashion about both history and evolution. The metalanguage is that of General Systems Theory and the whole scheme is informed by hierarchy theory in that I try to delimit different hierarchic levels of ecosystem and of other systems, their internal orderings and controls, and their interactions (see Pattee 1973; Whyte, Wilson, and Wilson 1969).

In the present chapter, I deal almost exclusively with the ecosystem narrowly defined to refer to the *interaction* between a given, historically determined technology and its *relevant* environmental variables, excluding for now the broader conception of ecosystem which embraces sociopolitical institutions and ideologies.[3] However, since these are intrinsically involved in certain aspects of technology, some mention of them must indeed be made, especially, as will be seen, in more recent phases of the ecosystem development.

The Texas Hill Country Ecosystem

In the course of examining social and cultural aspects of the Highland Lakes area of the Hill Country of Texas, we found that it was most important to clarify the relationship of those aspects to land use. The more we looked into these, the more we found, also, that these relationships were much more tightly linked to the character of the land and its waters, *given certain technological inputs,* that we had expected. Each such discovery led us to look more into the details of the situation, and this detailing, in turn, made plain to

[3] These were more fully dealt with in the papers by Jennings and Kelly.

us that the interpretation of many of the social aspects required a clarification of the temporal sequence of the ecosystem.

The clarification of the temporal sequence served in part as a methodological control against misinterpretation of the data looked at merely synchronically. It should be noted that this point is a generic methodological one. *All* descriptions of societies and cultures are necessarily interpretations. Contrary to the folk epistemology all too prevalent in anthropology, such descriptions are not inherently True, a view based on naive realism, but only hypothetically true; they are, in fact, complex hypotheses. Insofar as they are based only on synchronic materials, varied past causes producing like results and system trajectories cannot be determined. Further, one cannot determine whether different phenomena in the present came from similar or identical origins, differentiated by some set of impingements not yet identified in the present or no longer operative. Using purely synchronic material, one can only invent putative history, that is to say, putative process, through piling a prioris of reconstruction of an unknown past on top of the a prioris and hypothetical aspects of the interpretation of the present. The substantive material of the past helps specify the range and probability of interpretations in the present.

In view of this methodological stricture, I approach the ecosystem historically and will show that each of several successive ecosystems was disturbed, moved toward a new equilibrium, was disturbed again either by natural causes or unintentional and intentional man-made inputs, moved towards equilibrium again, was disturbed once more, and so on, until the present. As previously remarked, the man-created inputs to be considered here are mainly technological ones, but it is interesting to note from the point of view of the general framework of this chapter that some of these inputs grow out of local institutions, others out of higher-level institutions such as those of state and federal governments. From still another point of view, it is interesting to note that many of these inputs have been ones involving considerable capitalization within the region under consideration, so that the ecological succession is also a succession of increasing capitalization.

THE TEXAS HILL COUNTRY: GEOPHYSICAL ASPECTS

The areas under consideration have been occupied by human beings for thousands of years with a variety of technologies. They are defined geographically and topographically as follows. The largest unit is the watershed of the Texas Colorado River (see Figure 4.1), whose ultimate headwaters are found in easternmost New Mexico and whose mouth is at Matagorda on the Gulf Coast, a distance of about 1100 km (650 miles). The river's course runs, with one exception, through a series of vast sedimentary layers of the earth's surface of varying ages from very recent to Cambrian, the latter lying along the middle course of the stream (see p. 125 and Figure 4.4), the layers getting younger in each direction from it. In the middle of this latter area lies the

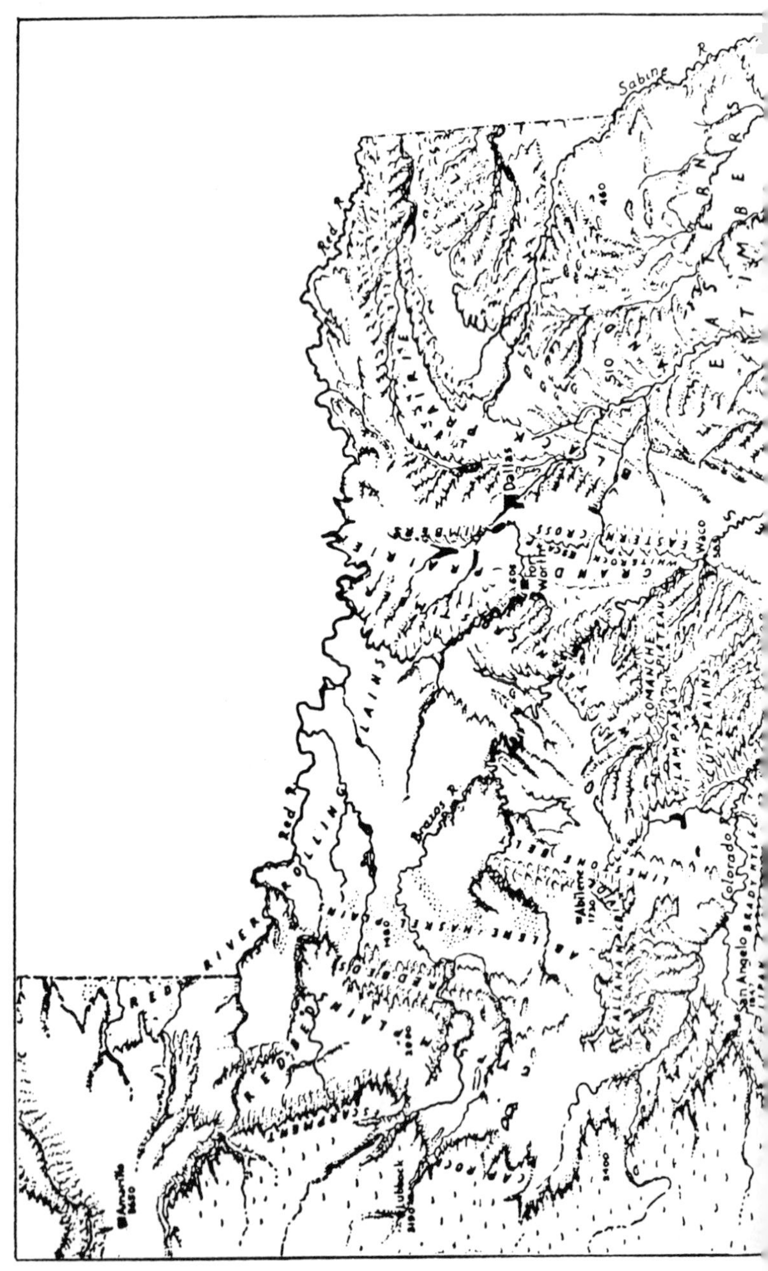

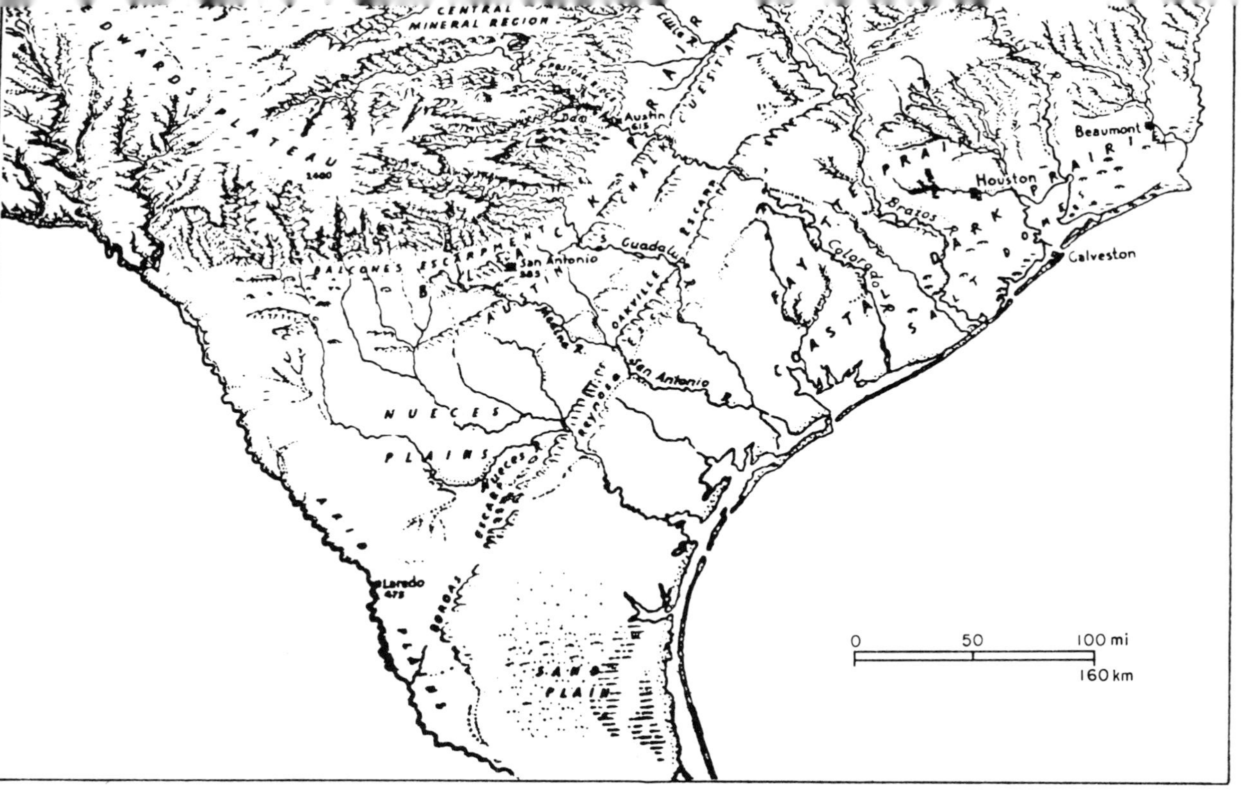

FIGURE 4.1 *Location of the Texal Hill Country, in central part of map (From Oetking 1958).*

FIGURE 4.2 *A Section of the Colorado River in the Texas Hill Country (Courtesy of the USDA, Agricultural Stabilization and Conservation Service).*

Llano uplift of precambrian igneous rocks—granites and schists—which are surrounded by a narrow ring of old sedimentary rocks. These, in turn, for about 300° of a circle, are surrounded by the much younger layers of the Edwards Plateau. The eastern edge of the Edwards Plateau is created by the Balcones Escarpment caused by the Balcones Fault (Figure 4.1), a quite marked feature of the topography and one that sharply sets off and differentiates the geographical area, hence the ecosystem, under consideration. To the east of this escarpment, the land falls away in decreasingly rolling plains, eventually to merge, in intricate inlets, bayous, embayments and bars, with the sea (Figure 4.1). This area to the east is one of the richest agricultural areas of the state today and includes the most important rice production in the United States, under a regime of large-scale irrigation agriculture.

To the west of the escarpment begins what is known as the Hill Country of Texas, a well dissected plateau of limestone with the characteristic features of such terrain, including potholes, canyon-like river course (see Figure 4.2, lower right), marked horizontal outcroppings of harder limestone beds, and the typical mechanics of water flow to be discussed below. The depth of this hill land is about 170 km (100 miles) on the average, its relief probably a maximum of 160 to 200 m (500 or 600 feet) at any given location, and its maximum altitude above sea level on the order of 800 m (2500 feet). Still further to the west (Figure 4.1), one comes successively to the Lipan Flats, near San Angelo, a territory already much flatter with hills or ranges standing out separately and at distances from each other; then, the Callahan Mountains constituting the edge of the next higher layer of Plains, the Gypsum Plains, followed again by the Caprock, behind which lie the renowned High Plains or Llano Estacado running into New Mexico.

Schematically, in sum, we find quite flat country in a great part of the upper course of the river, roughly 600 km (350 miles) wide, with occasional drops at the edges of escarpments such as that of the Caprock. There follows the almost 170 km (100 miles) of hill lands which, in turn, are replaced by the much lower coastal plains (a maximum of about 160 m (500 feet) above sea level) for nearly 330 km (200 miles). Thus, the Hill Lands stand out as a distinctive physiographic province. The distinctiveness pervades every aspect of the ecological system and, in fact, delimits it. I turn to those environmental aspects of this area which are relevant to this study.

In general, the hill lands have very little flat surface, most areas ranging between gentle slope and sharp declivity as in some of the canyon-like passages of the rivers and streams (these features can clearly be seen in the photo of Figure 4.2). The slopes are not due to tilting of beds but to their erosion and to alluviation, producing a striking contoured appearance (Figures 4.2 and 4.3). The horizontality of these beds, which can often be traced for miles by their outcroppings through the countryside, is closely related to the water regimen in that rainfall percolates down through the more permeable layers and then runs out on top of less permeable layers, creating

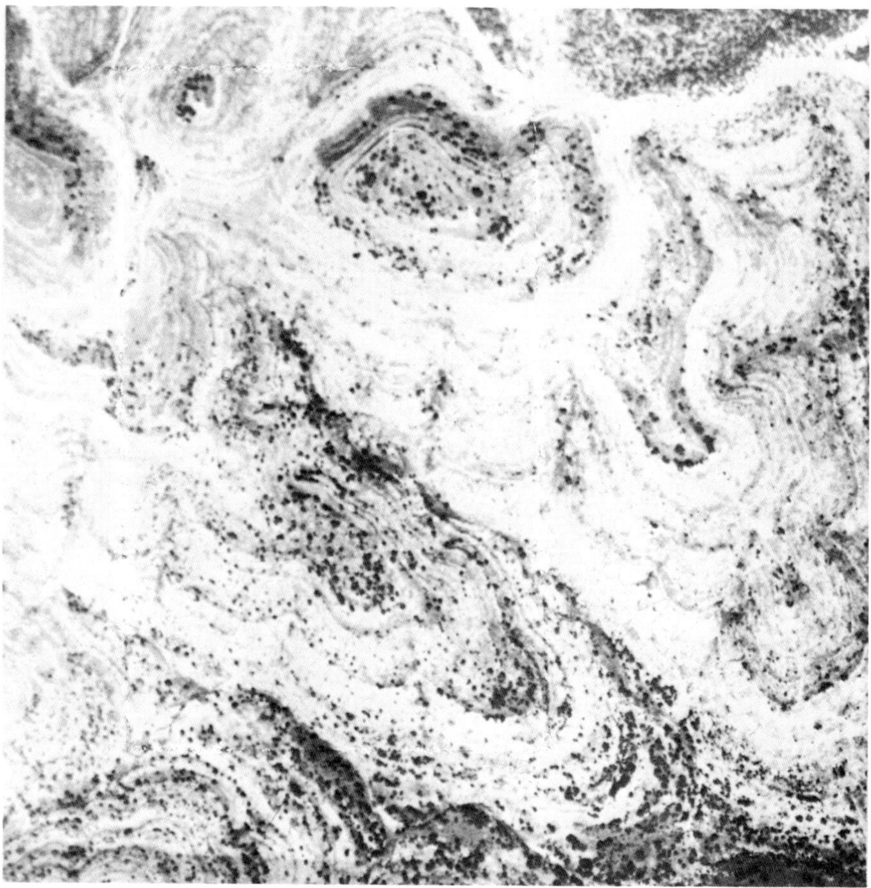

FIGURE 4.3 *The Texas Hill Lands. The photograph shows clearly the contoured outcroppings running for long distances, the marked relief and lack of much level land, the thinness of soil cover (the white areas are exposed limestone), and the dispersed growth of juniper, oaks, and brush.*

springs at the outcropping areas. The consistency of these rocks is such as to hold water for long periods of time, a fact of great importance to the biota given the climatological characteristics, which will be discussed in the following. However, in periods of dry weather or prolonged drought, the water table steadily lowers, the land surface dries, streams literally go underground to ever-deeper levels. In this sort of situation, the longer the dry period, the longer it takes to reestablish water in the aquifers, so that recovery from drought, from the point of view of human users, is a process extended beyond the mere return of the rains after prolonged aridity. This condition is exacerbated by the extreme thinness of topsoil (see Figure 4.3) in the area as a whole, other than in the larger stream beds, a thinness which it is difficult even in an "undisturbed" state to overcome because of the nature of the vegetation.

Before turning to the vegetation, it is necessary briefly to describe the precipitation regimen. At the coast, rain ranges up to over 100 cm (40 in.) a year. By the time one reaches the Balcones Escarpment at Austin, for example, rain averages a little over 75 cm (30 in.) annually. At San Angelo, 580 km (350 miles) inland, it is a little more than 50 cm (20 in.), and by the time one reaches the upper course of the Colorado River in the High Plains, the rain is between 25 and 40 cm (10 and 15 in.) per year, that is technically near-desert. In the hills area, percipitation ranges between about 62.5 and 75 cm (25 and 30 in.) a year.

However, what is striking is the extreme irreularity of the precipitation. A 40-year month-by-month chart of rainfall in Austin at the edge of the hill country indicates enormous variation for *every* month of the year, ranging from almost zero to several inches, such that any pattern at all is difficult to establish, and averages are extremely misleading (see Table 4.1). The reader will note that the data are quite striking if one, for example, compares January, May, September, and December rainfalls for all 40 years. Note such marked differences in total rainfall as those of 1956 and 1957 or even 1963 and 1964.

Although there appear to be two periods of the year (February–April and August–September) which average somewhat more rain than other seasons and one (June–July) that tends to be particularly dry, these are very broad averages, which fundamentally misrepresent the actualities for men, animals, and plants in coping with the water supply at any given time. This variation is of extreme importance when one keeps in mind Liebig's law of the minimum.

Complicating this irregularity and unpredictability are two other features. First, is the long-range, irregular recurrence of severe drought, unusual wetness and "average" rainfall years between (see Table 4.2). The variability is so great that the U.S. Weather Service estimates that a statistical sample of less than 40 years is inadequate to show an "average" or "mean"; 50 years would be better. These oscillations of drought and wet, like drought in the Northeast of Brazil, seem unpredictable (and seem to correlate with the Brazilian periods of drought). Even the length of drought periods varies greatly, sometimes lasting only a few months, others lasting for years as in the disastrous drought of 1950–1957, 3 years of which were accounted "extreme drought" by the National Weather Service (see Table 4.2).

The second feature is the character of many of the rains themselves, most of which come in summer thundershowers or are generated by Gulf hurricanes: their violence in terms of the pelting effect, of the quantity of water that falls at any one time, and sometimes of the form, especially hail, which occurs with some frequency and immense destructiveness. Snowfall forms a negligible part of the total precipitation in most of the area of the middle and lower Colorado river valley.

TOTAL PRECIPITATION

Year	Jan.	Feb.	Mar.	Apr.	May	June	July	Aug.	Sept.	Oct.	Nov.	Dec.	Annual
1931	4.30	5.63	3.35	5.03	0.58	2.63	2.74	1.85	0.02	0.15	1.09	4.24	31.61
1932	6.00	3.03	2.15	2.34	1.11	1.88	1.54	4.97	5.36	0.10	1.26	2.72	32.46
1933	5.10	2.22	1.64	1.30	3.63	0.41	7.16	0.93	3.08	3.05	0.68	1.24	30.44
1934	9.13	2.15	3.82	4.42	1.75	0.20	0.79	0.46	1.07	0.03	5.21	3.72	32.75
1935	1.61	3.86	1.02	1.79	9.21	9.71	1.44	0.24	8.79	1.65	0.85	2.84	43.01
#1936	0.39	1.70	1.52	0.66	8.15	3.30	9.25	2.90	5.22	2.63	2.30	1.88	39.90
1937	2.43	0.12	3.64	0.63	3.67	3.92	0.69	4.26	2.21	4.70	3.62	5.21	35.10
1938	3.93	2.72	1.57	4.96	3.28	3.17	1.34	0.63	2.85	0.24	0.59	1.75	27.03
1939	2.23	1.47	1.04	1.87	3.01	1.00	3.57	1.62	1.64	1.62	2.26	0.80	22.13
1940	0.63	3.73	1.36	5.34	2.12	8.83	0.57	1.77	3.39	4.82	5.07	5.32	42.95
#1941	1.52	3.06	4.66	5.70	3.85	12.60	3.37	0.07	0.72	7.12	1.24	2.25	46.16
#1942	0.07	1.46	0.66	5.56	2.05	2.23	3.69	2.16	8.11	5.14	1.98	1.53	34.64
1943	0.80	0.45	2.54	2.68	5.38	1.27	3.91	0.92	3.31	0.33	1.73	1.42	24.74
1944	5.45	3.89	1.83	0.33	9.25	2.01	0.32	4.47	4.66	0.35	4.55	5.91	42.97
1945	2.83	3.94	4.98	4.11	1.76	5.69	1.61	5.78	2.76	3.00	1.47	2.94	40.87
1946	3.76	2.28	2.77	7.92	6.13	1.34	1.48	3.36	6.00	1.62	7.91	2.71	47.28
1947	3.62	0.43	3.28	2.24	3.55	0.11	2.18	2.12	0.07	0.02	2.07	1.89	21.58
1948	0.92	2.71	1.35	1.68	4.48	1.25	2.29	0.27	1.24	1.78	1.34	1.67	20.98
1949	3.97	2.35	2.24	6.91	0.83	3.52	1.95	2.37	3.77	4.38	0.01	4.04	36.34
1950	0.74	3.79	0.80	7.58	4.19	1.98	0.73	0.59	4.77	0.59	0.03	T	25.79
1951	0.51	2.96	3.73	1.04	3.51	6.19	0.19	2.07	6.45	0.93	1.06	0.34	28.98
1952	0.25	1.73	2.25	5.08	4.06	1.88	0.69	0.00	3.26	T	5.36	3.15	27.71
1953	0.63	1.32	1.73	4.69	1.88	1.59	0.51	2.10	2.98	6.58	0.38	5.29	29.68
1954	1.01	0.28	0.27	1.66	2.86	0.68	0.85	1.14	0.82	0.89	0.35	0.61	11.42
1955	1.87	4.22	0.83	0.75	4.49	2.61	2.02	1.92	1.33	0.09	1.40	1.01	22.54
1956	1.65	1.74	0.26	0.56	3.12	0.94	0.11	1.21	0.09	0.84	2.13	2.76	15.41
1957	0.55	3.14	4.58	9.93	7.38	5.25	1.10	T	6.43	8.79	2.95	1.20	51.30
1958	3.09	6.39	2.55	4.24	3.67	2.89	3.42	0.68	6.89	5.18	0.87	1.15	41.02
1959	0.42	2.30	0.23	4.35	1.66	3.30	3.49	4.80	4.37	5.98	1.95	2.11	34.96
1960	1.03	2.36	1.37	1.01	0.81	4.26	2.41	2.60	1.68	12.31	1.90	4.08	35.82
1961	1.27	4.85	0.67	0.10	1.03	11.43	8.40	0.40	3.68	0.91	2.82	0.91	36.47
1962	0.56	0.63	1.19	4.04	1.06	8.21	0.00	4.58	4.75	4.07	0.92	3.47	33.48
1963	0.59	2.83	0.22	3.51	1.32	2.10	0.58	0.88	1.50	0.78	1.57	1.42	17.30
1964	2.57	1.47	1.95	1.47	1.87	7.54	0.65	2.09	6.29	3.74	2.45	0.88	32.97
1965	4.09	5.06	1.30	1.91	9.98	0.89	0.37	1.32	5.46	3.26	2.65	4.28	40.57
1966	1.58	3.23	0.50	3.74	3.13	1.53	0.47	6.21	3.22	0.60	0.11	0.87	25.19
1967	0.25	1.52	1.09	4.44	3.35	T	1.15	3.71	5.71	4.55	4.36	3.41	33.54
1968	7.94	1.64	2.09	1.87	8.75	3.10	3.11	0.74	3.42	0.60	4.91	0.55	38.72
1969	0.40	4.18	3.26	5.04	3.25	2.66	0.12	5.78	1.17	2.65	0.79	4.29	33.59
1970	1.83	5.70	2.47	1.36	8.18	0.29	0.66	1.00	3.82	5.22	T	0.11	30.64
RECORD MEAN	2.08	2.48	2.25	3.55	4.22	2.82	2.20	2.17	3.65	3.06	2.37	2.52	33.37

AVERAGE TEMPERATURE

Year	Jan.	Feb.	Mar.	Apr.	May	June	July	Aug.	Sept.	Oct.	Nov.	Dec.	Annual
1931	51.4	56.8	55.8	63.2	71.6	82.0	84.0	83.1	83.0	77.0	65.0	53.2	68.8
1932	52.9	60.6	55.4	69.4	74.7	82.5	85.8	84.2	77.3	67.9	55.5	48.5	67.9
1933	58.1	50.5	64.2	69.4	78.8	80.4	84.9	83.8	83.4	74.2	62.4	59.5	70.8
1934	53.0	53.3	58.9	70.1	75.5	84.6	85.7	85.2	79.8	75.4	63.6	54.3	70.0
1935	54.7	54.6	66.5	69.2	72.0	80.0	84.4	85.0	76.4	73.1	58.2	50.4	68.7
#1936	49.4	48.6	65.4	66.6	74.0	83.1	82.2	84.0	79.8	64.8	55.1	53.3	67.2
1937	47.6	53.8	55.7	68.6	76.4	82.0	84.7	86.0	80.1	70.4	55.8	51.5	67.7
1938	52.2	59.2	66.6	65.5	74.4	82.2	84.7	84.8	79.4	72.7	57.0	53.6	69.4
1939	53.1	51.7	63.2	69.0	78.0	82.8	85.1	84.0	81.2	71.5	56.4	55.6	69.3
1940	40.6	52.8	61.8	66.8	74.5	77.7	82.1	83.3	76.7	70.0	56.7	53.6	66.4
1941	53.6	51.0	55.0	66.8	75.0	79.6	83.6	85.1	80.8	74.2	58.2	53.8	68.4
#1942	48.6	51.8	59.8	67.4	74.4	82.8	82.0	82.7	74.6	68.3	62.8	53.5	67.4
1943	49.4	57.6	55.8	70.6	76.0	81.1	83.8	85.6	76.4	68.3	56.7	49.2	67.5
1944	48.4	55.8	58.6	67.6	71.8	81.0	84.4	84.4	77.6	69.3	59.8	48.0	67.2
1945	50.8	54.8	65.8	66.0	74.3	81.4	83.0	83.6	78.8	67.0	63.2	49.8	68.2
1946	48.6	55.0	62.3	69.8	74.6	79.1	83.8	83.8	76.8	70.8	59.1	54.9	68.2
1947	48.0	47.0	54.8	66.1	74.0	82.7	84.0	83.3	79.7	76.2	56.4	52.8	67.1
1948	43.2	50.7	58.0	71.6	76.2	83.7	84.8	85.8	78.4	69.9	58.2	55.4	68.0
1949	45.1	55.3	60.5	63.5	77.6	81.0	83.9	82.5	79.4	69.6	62.6	54.2	68.0
1950	55.7	56.4	59.1	66.0	76.2	80.3	83.8	83.4	78.5	73.6	59.9	52.7	68.8
1951	50.8	54.4	61.8	67.4	74.9	81.8	86.8	87.6	79.2	71.6	56.9	54.0	68.9
1952	59.1	58.1	58.8	64.3	72.8	81.6	83.7	87.1	77.9	65.3	57.3	50.4	68.0
1953	56.2	53.5	66.1	66.4	74.8	84.8	85.1	84.3	78.5	70.9	57.2	48.6	68.9
1954	52.0	59.5	59.4	72.4	73.4	83.5	86.9	86.6	82.4	72.8	59.9	56.5	70.4
1955	51.6	53.8	62.4	72.9	78.0	79.6	84.9	84.5	82.2	71.4	59.2	52.5	69.4
1956	50.8	55.8	61.8	69.1	78.7	84.4	87.0	85.9	81.7	73.7	57.3	56.6	70.2
1957	50.5	60.9	59.5	66.0	73.5	80.9	86.3	86.0	77.0	65.3	55.9	56.3	68.2
1958	45.7	48.8	54.6	66.3	76.0	83.2	85.1	85.8	79.5	67.5	60.7	48.5	67.0
1959	47.7	52.9	59.9	65.1	77.1	82.6	84.2	83.5	80.1	69.5	52.2	53.7	67.4
1960	49.3	47.9	54.3	69.7	73.5	83.4	84.7	83.3	79.3	71.5	60.7	48.5	67.2
#1961	46.0	54.8	63.7	67.5	76.3	79.6	81.6	81.8	78.2	69.8	56.5	52.2	67.3
1962	45.5	60.4	57.9	67.7	76.6	80.3	85.4	86.8	79.7	73.3	59.6	51.0	68.7
1963	43.6	51.6	64.5	72.9	76.9	82.9	86.4	87.5	82.0	75.1	62.6	45.1	69.3
1964	50.3	48.4	60.7	70.8	76.6	81.3	85.2	86.0	77.9	67.6	62.5	52.2	68.5
1965	53.4	49.4	53.4	71.4	74.7	80.7	84.2	84.3	80.5	66.6	64.1	56.0	68.2
1966	45.3	48.9	60.1	69.1	73.9	79.9	84.7	82.2	78.2	68.6	64.2	51.0	67.2
1967	30.9	51.4	67.3	75.9	75.3	83.7	85.2	82.6	75.2	67.7	58.9	49.4	68.6
1968	47.6	47.2	57.3	68.1	74.2	79.5	82.2	84.1	76.0	72.0	55.8	50.4	66.2
1969	53.6	52.6	53.9	69.0	73.7	80.7	86.3	84.9	79.7	68.6	57.9	53.8	67.9
1970	44.0	53.1	55.2	68.7	71.9	79.9	83.8	85.8	79.2	66.7	57.4	58.7	67.1
RECORD MEAN	50.3	53.4	60.3	67.9	74.7	81.6	84.2	84.3	79.1	69.8	59.2	51.7	68.1
MAX	60.6	64.1	71.3	78.4	84.8	91.8	94.8	95.2	89.5	80.9	69.9	61.9	78.6
MIN	40.0	42.7	49.3	57.3	64.6	71.4	73.6	73.4	68.6	58.6	48.5	41.5	57.5

Record mean values above (not adjusted for instrument location changes listed in the Station Location table) are means for the period beginning in 1898 for temperature and 1856 for precipitation.

# Indicates a break in the data sequence during the year, or season, due to a station move or relocation of instruments. See Station Location table.

Source: U.S. Department of Commerce, National Oceanic and Atmospheric Administration, Environmental Data Service, 1970.

TABLE 4.2

Meteorological Drought, High Plains, 1931–1950 and 1951–1970

YEAR	DROUGHT PERIODS												WET PERIODS											
	JAN	FEB	MAR	APR	MAY	JUNE	JULY	AUG	SEP	OCT	NOV	DEC	JAN	FEB	MAR	APR	MAY	JUNE	JULY	AUG	SEP	OCT	NOV	DEC
1931																								
1932																								
1933																								
1934																								
1935																								
1936																								
1937																								
1938																								
1939																								
1940																								
1941																								
1942																								
1943																								
1944																								
1945																								
1946																								
1947																								
1948																								
1949																								
1950																								

Maximum

Maximum

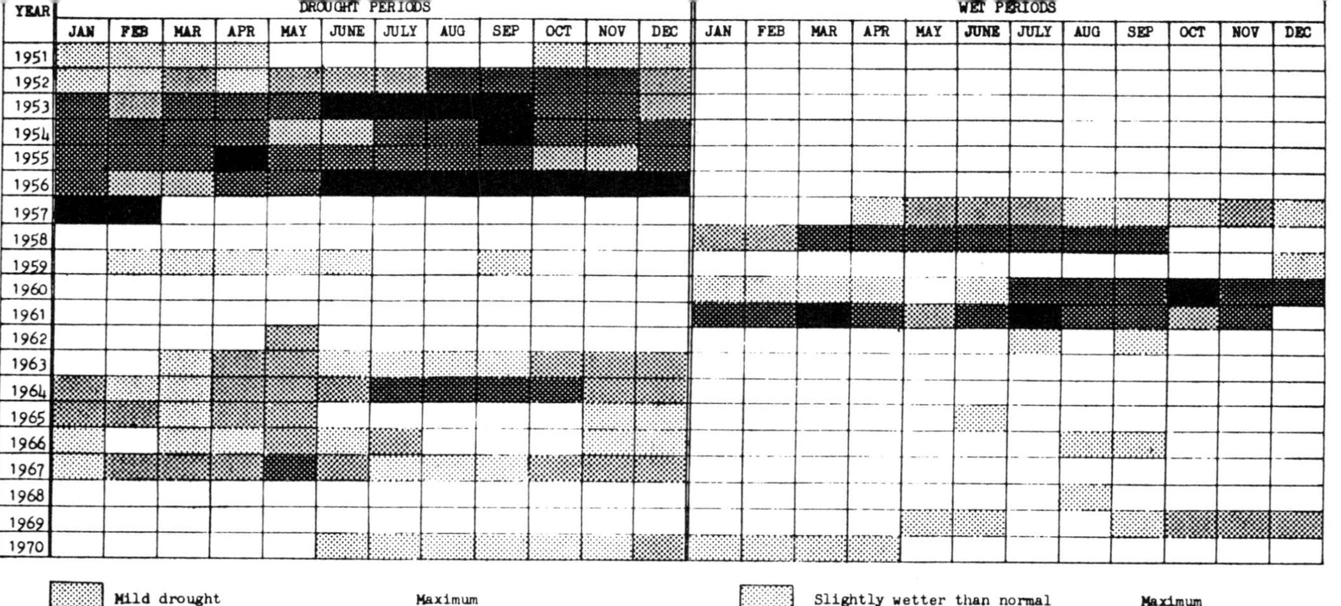

Source: National Weather Service, Austin, Texas.

THE TEXAS HILL COUNTRY: FLORAL AND FAUNAL ASPECTS

To this landscape and climate was adapted a characteristic flora, itself undoubtedly modified by the fauna and by the "prehistoric" aboriginal population of Indians. Apparently this had occurred in such a way that—the archaeological, paleontological, and historical sources substantially agree in this—a relatively stable equilibrium obtained among these variables for any relatively long periods of time such as one or more centuries. A still longer run, such as a millenium, however, suggests a gradual dessication of the entire state and specifically of the inland parts we are now considering, although the evidence is indirect. Meterological records are insufficiently long (systematic recording began in most parts of Texas only in 1931) to determine whether there has been recent dessication or not. The evidence is even contradictory—Llano county claims to have had an average *increase* in rain since the 1890s (see Llano County 1967), though this seems to contradict other records and may be a function of the location of the weather station (see also, p. 127). Thus, even if there has been a long-term decrease in precipitation, the changes in the ecosystem we have observed seem at best indirectly attributable to this, but rather have been directly caused by various interventions, in much shorter runs, by human beings, affecting the relationship among land, water, vegetation, fauna, and themselves—a subject to be dealt with in detail in the following.

The flora of the hill lands is quite characteristic, generally highly adapted to the basic soils of the limestone plateau (as opposed to the generally acidic soils of the coastal plains to the east). The demarcation between these two areas and their soils is clearly marked vegetationally as one passes from one to the other, moving, in the hills, into stands of cedar, various kinds of oak (Spanish, shin, post, live, pin, etc.) and a great many other kinds of trees and shrubs. The typical hardwoods of the coast—elms, white oak, hackberry, etc.—disappear almost at once on crossing the escarpment. On the plateau are found a great range of coarse grasses such as bluestems, buffalo grasses, the gammas, and so on, which are not found on the coastal plain. Today, in addition, one finds vast tracts covered with a variety of cacti such as prickly pear and cholla, an enormous quantity of junipers, and the ubiquitous mesquite. The latter two, in particular, are not native to the area (see below).

In pre-European, pre-Conquest Texas, in the area under consideration, the fauna adapted to this vegetation and, in turn, acting on it appears to have consisted of white-tailed deer, some antelope, a number of smaller mammals, including foxes, the red wolf, rodents of all sorts, various felines, the coyote, a number of poisonous and nonpoisonous snakes, including rattlesnakes and copperheads, and a fairly rich bird-life, including the ever-present hawks and vultures. Of special interest for our purposes are the deer and their apparently aboriginal parasites, especially the screwworm (to which I shall return later).

As herbivorous ungulates go, Texas white-tailed deer are relatively small, perhaps about 100 pounds (the black-tailed deer of the West Texas mountains is much larger). Under aboriginal range conditions, the carrying capacity for deer may have been as high as one deer to 2–5 acres. Given the lifespan of a deer and the fact that a female generally produces one fawn a year, the deer population would have surpassed its carrying capacity very rapidly had it not been controlled by various parasites, particularly the screwworm, and predators such as wolves, coyotes, and humans.

Deer are grazers and browsers. As grazers, however, they are peculiar in that they ordinarily do not eat the grasses, but rather the forbs, or low "weeds" growing among the taller grasses. The shade produced by the latter protects the former to some extent. Deer turn to the grasses themselves in times of stress such as long dry seasons when the incidence of forbs diminishes.

As with the grazing, deer browse selectively. This selectivity accounts for both the stimulation of some plants and the control of others. On some shrubs, the deer ordinarily browse the young, tender leaves, which, like pruning, encourages new leaf formation and controls the size and the spread of the plants over the area. Deer also browse some tree seedlings and large bush seedlings, thus controlling the spread of woody plants, thereby preventing brush invasion of the grasslands and preserving grass stands. Further, they browse lower branches of large woody plants and even eat the bark under conditions of great stress such as long drought or prolonged cold, thus girdling and killing the bushes. Some small trees may suffer the same fate under these conditions. The once plentiful antelope made a slightly different selection and probably consumed more grass than do deer.

The ecological import of these patterns of feeding must be emphasized. Eating forbs leaves undisturbed the tall grasses which were aboriginally characteristic. These grasses typically have quite extensive, twiny root systems that, on one hand, hold the soil together in sod and, if sufficiently developed, in almost a turf and, on the other, provide a degree of shade to their own root systems and to the forbs. Both of these conditions are most important in terms of the water regimen since (*a*) the plant root systems themselves hold water; (*b*) the sods they construct hold water and, if undisturbed over time, tend to build up humus that increases the amount of water held, thin as it is in most of this area; (*c*) the shade provided reduces evaporation from the soil surface and decreases scorching of surface roots and forbs.The effects, then, are to maximize water-retention and to reduce runoff, in turn maximizing plant cover in this harsh environment where uncovered soils can reach 130° or 140°F in the summer sun. It is noteworthy, then, that the aboriginal herbivorous fauna, one of the main food supplies for the human occupants, adapted to its own food supply in such a way as to maximize the conditions of its growth, although there are instances of overfeeding under conditions of environmental stress such as drought. As noted, the browsing tended to control the rate of invasion of large bushes and trees into the grasslands since the plants browsed are destroyed at a fairly regular rate.

HUMANS IN THE HILL COUNTRY ECOSYSTEMS: A BRIEF HISTORY

Human inputs into this complex set of relations among deer, antelope, grazing, browsing, and flora have a history whose origins are lost in the past, whose conditions prior to European invasion are, at least, roughly known, and whose subsequent development is discussed in the following pages. This entire development is, of course, a "history," a historical sequence, characterized by transformations of the ecosystem of an irreversible sort, induced by new inputs into it and perturbations of old relations. It is, therefore, also, a specific evolutional sequence. I shall argue later that certain formal characteristics of this specific sequence are, in fact, examples of generic sociocultural evolution: with respect to these properties, specific histories and generic evolution are isomorphic.

Perhaps the two key human inputs in this area were deer, antelope, and small animal hunting, on one hand, and the use of fire, on the other. The former has been referred to in the preceding. Obviously, human predators on ungulates helped control their population sizes, probably with more or less automatic controls involved. As forage and browse increased in congenial seasons, the deer population increased and success in hunting also undoubtedly increased—and vice versa, while a much less variable human population stayed relatively constant, loosely adapted to an average overall carrying capacity for ungulates.

Nevertheless, hunting and gathering productivity could be increased by technological means over and beyond those we usually consider (such as the bow and arrow, snares, and the like), specifically by the use of fire as a tool. Stewart has repeatedly indicated the importance of the use of fire as a tool by "primitive" (and nonprimitive) populations around the world, throughout the United States, in the Great Plains, and, specifically for our purposes, in Texas (1951, 1953, 1954a,b, 1955a,b, 1956, 1963). He quotes Cabeza de Vaca, exploring southeastern Texas where the Ignaces Indians lived in the year 1528, an area now covered with mesquite:

> [They] go about with a firebrand, setting fire to the plains and timber so as to drive off the mosquitoes, and also to get lizards and similar things which they eat, to come out of the soil. In the same manner they kill deer, encircling them with fires, and they do it also to deprive the animals of pasture, compelling them to go for food where the Indians want [Stewart 1951:317].

Stewart himself remarks

> Aborigines set fires to vegetation for a number of reasons which vary in their importance depending on other geographic conditions. In flat temperate zones with a regular dry period, fires were used to drive game, to improve pasture for wild game, to improve visibility by removing brush and trees, to facilitate travel and approach to game, and to kill insects, rodents, and reptiles for protection and for food [1963:125].

Elsewhere he comments

> Although fire is reported most frequently used to aid hunting—to encircle, to rouse, to stampede—fifteen other reasons for setting fires are given. These were as follows: to improve pasture, improve visibility, collect insects, increase yield of seeds, increase yield of berries, increase other wild vegetable foods, make vegetable food available, remove or thin trees to allow other growth, clear land for planting, stimulate growth of wild tobacco, aid in warfare, facilitate travel, produce a spectacle, and reduce danger from snakes, insects, etc.[1953:43].

Stewart points to a series of effects of continuous fire use that are of singular importance to my theme. More or less sporadic firing of tall grasses reduces tree and brush cover (see also D. Harris 1966), but encourages a lusher growth of grasses and, of course, forbs. This maintains the food resources for deer and antelope. At the same time, it encourages their survival and maximizes the deer-food supply for humans, making it (along with that derived from small animals such as the lizards and rodents already mentioned) more readily available *technologically* in the hunt.

Moreover, the firing reduces pests (e.g., mosquitoes) and dangers lethal to the human population such as the Texas copperheads and rattlesnakes, invisible in tall, or even short, sparser, grasses. It is important to note that the firing is more or less sporadic rather than repeated and systematic in any given locality. The sporadic firing lets tall grasses accumulate sometimes for several seasons so that a density of fuel is achieved sufficient to burn much of the woody brush and tree cover because of the heat of the fire (Stewart 1951:318; 1955a:63). In short, the grass lands perpetuate themselves through human intervention by firing and keep the woody growth limited—an advantage for the human population from the point of view of mobility and food production by hunting.

Thus, the aboriginal ecosystem, before the arrival of the Spanish, can be seen to have been a very delicately balanced system with rather low carrying capacities for plants, animals, and humans. The history of the ecosystem since that time has been one of the introduction of new elements into the system, their degradational effects, efforts to counter these, and resulting reorderings of the ecosystem. Each step of the historical sequence involved expanding linkages of the hill-land ecosystem with larger ecosystems and with the larger geopolitical units of state and nation. It will later be argued that these ever-expanding system linkages, creating not only more extensive systems but also more complex system hierarchies, provide us with a model for a reconceptualized evolutionism.

The first major new input seems to have been the introduction, somewhere in the early seventeenth century, of longhorn cattle by the Spanish. Since we have not yet discovered descriptions of the longhorns at that time, we do not know if they were already grazer–browsers when they came from Spain to the New World or whether that adaptation developed in the Texas environment where cattle, through the last century, tended to become more feral than their European congeners (see Jordan 1972), especially under open-range conditons. The former case may be true since they came from a relatively arid part of Spain. In any case, longhorns, unlike most other cattle, browse as well as graze. Unlike deer, however, they graze on grasses rather than on forbs. The animals are also much larger than deer, perhaps averaging 500 pounds in the early centuries of their presence in Texas. Their food requirements per animal, therefore, were at least 4 or 5 times those of deer. For any one animal, an area about 4 or 5 times as large was needed–perhaps 8 to 20 acres or so under aboriginal conditions.

As, over a long period of time, the numbers of longhorn increased, a slow shift in the vegetation appears to have taken place. The balance between bush and low trees, grasses and forbs appears to have been disturbed by the change of feeding habits represented by the longhorn and by the longhorn's competition with deer for part of the food resources offered in the landscape. Both the increased browsing and the eating of tall grasses began to affect the natural system of water controls on the land surface cumulatively, so that by the middle of the nineteenth century a widespread disappearance of the taller grasses was already notable and some evidence for increased uncontrollability of water, hence some erosion, begins to appear.

The change in grass cover had very significant results. Since the mass of fuel for hot grass fires decreased steadily, the burning of brush and trees became less and less effective with the consequence of ever-increasing invasion of prickly pear and, especially, of mesquite and juniper (respectively, *Prosopis juliflora* and *Juniperus monosperma*) (see p. 120, cf. D. Harris 1966). Both of these, in turn, further reduced and continue to reduce grass cover because their extraordinarily extensive root systems, relatively near the surface, successfully compete with grasses for water (Harris 1966:411, 417) while being quite drought-resistant. Such root systems, on the other hand, do not create sods and turfs as the grasses do. Recent soil and pasture reclamation is very much concerned with technical problems of removal of mesquite trees and brush and of junipers (see *Grassland Restoration* series, Pts. I–VI, especially Vol. II, *Brush Control,* USDA 1964–1970).

Another aspect may also have been important and continues so until today, namely, the ever-increasing effect, as cattle herds get larger, of trampling on the root systems and on their recovery after grazing has taken place. Trampling tends to macerate and destroy roots beyond recovery, thereby reducing water retention and natural controls over wind erosion (dust storms are marked, especially on the western edge of the hill country in the area of the Lipan flats). All of these effects together are usually lumped under the term 'overgrazing.' Increased runoff from such overgrazed areas of course leads to sheet erosion in particular, that is, the removal of soil cover (already quite thin in the area considered), a condition very marked in the sedimentary areas of the hill country.

The spread of juniper and especially of mesquite seems to have been connected with the introduction of longhorns from Mexico into Texas by means of cattle drives, apparently especially in the early part of the last century. Mesquite seeds were carried in by cattle, fertilized by them (increasingly as more cattle come in!), took root in the congenial environment of Texas, and spread rapidly to become a major plant form and, in the view of most human users of the land today, a major pest. In passing, it may be noted that these same human users of land do *not* use the mesquite seed as a food supply in this region, though a number of Indian tribes in North America once did and although it can be a valuable source of food, providing more sustenance than beef in equivalent areas (see Felger 1971 and in press).

The case of the juniper is less clear. There appear to be both native and Spanish-introduced species of juniper. In either case, juniper spread easily under the soil and climatological conditions described; its berries, serving as a prime agent of dispersal, are carried by birds and small and large mammals (D. Harris 1966). In addition, native cedars have also spread as the grass covers decreased. All of these flourish in the hill lands of Texas where they are considered to be major pests from the point of view of cattlemen because they further contribute to killing grasses in the entire area of the root systems, thus reducing forage for cattle and impoverishing the soil surface quality. Junipers and the even greater offender, mesquite, use a large amount of water that, for human purposes, could better go into the maintenance of crops or cattle (at least for those who value beef over mesquite).

The next major phase in the history of the ecosystem of the Colorado River system as a whole, and especially of its hill country and coastal plain segments, was the introduction, systematically and on an ever-increasing scale, of mixed farming. This was done both by Anglo–Saxon immigrants from various parts of the United States and by immigrants from Germany, Moravia, Poland, and elsewhere, beginning during the Republican period of Texas and continuing for about 4 decades into the late 1870s and early 1880s. Mixed farming involved, first, the transference of European styles of farming, adapted to European geographical and climatological conditions and sociopolitical institutions, including land-use patterns, into aboriginal ecosystems or ones partly modified by the introduction of the longhorn, neither suited to the European ones. Second, a combination of raising agricultural crops and milk cattle was introduced in which milk and beef were both consumed and sold.

The effects of these introductions can be gleaned from descriptions in the histories of the area (for example, in the thumbnail sketches of the Soil Conservation Service Work Plans see Hill Country 1967; Llano County 1967) and in novels (e.g., Bogusch's *Hoofbeats along the Llano*). One major effect on the highland area was the virtual elimination of tall grasses. These grasses are described as having been "waist-high" or "up to the belly of a horse," but the new grasses that replaced them do not grow much over a foot, if that. The replacement grasses were also native grasses, filling in, as it were, for the tall grasses now gone. Beneath these middle-height grasses are even shorter grasses that can still be seen today on overgrazed land.

Put another way, the effects of the introductions were several: (*a*) pasturage declined both because of the decrease in the size of the grasses and because of the encroachment of the pest trees—mesquite, juniper, and cedar—as well as various kinds of brush and cactus; (*b*) effective control of the soil decreased because the root systems of grasses deteriorated; (*c*) erosion and runoff of precipitation increased; and (*d*) the relatively marginal productivity of farm lands decreased steadily, except perhaps in the valley bottoms.

With respect to the mesquite and juniper invasion, the introduction of almost exclusively grazing breeds of milk and beef cattle around the middle of the nineteenth century, in addition to the older population of tall-grass grazing and browsing longhorns, led to more and more overgrazing during the nineteenth century and into the twentieth century. Overgrazing reduced grasses and hence any competition for mesquite seedlings. Therefore, mesquite flourished. The increase of cattle was also, of course, paralleled by the increase of the European-derived human population and its crops, livestock, housing, and settlements.

Not only did all of these compete for space with the aboriginal Indian population, but the newcomers wished to protect crops, cattle, housing, and settlements from fire. They therefore went more or less systematically about destroying the aboriginal way of life, including the suppression of grass firing (D. Harris 1966:413)—a destruction completed throughout Texas by about the late 1870s. Suppression of grass burning eliminated the burning out of mesquite and juniper growth by hot grass fires, so that these trees flourished more and more as the nineteenth century wore on, as well as in the twentieth century. Finally, fencing, which began in the later decades of the last century, kept cattle constricted, thus leading both to overgrazing and to greatly increasing concentration of manures, conditions highly favorable to mesquite growth.

The effects described above were intensified in the 1870s and 1880s and beyond by the introduction into the hill country counties of Llano, Burnet, Blanco, western Travis, and others of cotton cultivation, mohair goat raising, and sheep for wool. Sheep and goats crop grasses very closely when they graze and their smaller, sharper hooves trample more destructively than cattle, thereby accelerating overgrazing in conditions such as have been described for this territory. Goats also browse. Under conditions of severe overgrazing, the browsing of the goats may also lead to the destruction of whatever protection brush and trees give to the soil (see p. 119).[4]

[4] However, goats can be used to *restore* pasture. The technical procedures are described at length in *Grassland Restoration* Pt. II:27–28. They are quite complex and require a great deal of control over the animals in order to achieve the desired effect, e.g., controlling when, where, and how long they feed and in what numbers.

Cotton was essentially unsuitable to the area although it was economic for some time until cotton prices began to slip some 40 or 50 years ago. Further, cotton is very hard on soil—exhausting it rather rapidly. With its marginal productivity in the quite reduced agricultural lands of the counties cited, it could not survive and has died out entirely.

Thus, in the last part of the past century and the earlier part of this, the entire natural system of water control deteriorated drastically, with two major consequences: (*a*) massive erosion and removal of top soil throughout the area, and (*b*) increased frequency, scale and uncontrollability of floods (to which I shall return later). In passing, it may be hypothesized that the changes in soil–water relationships on the land may also have had some microclimatological effects, specifically reducing rainfall, a phenomenon frequently alluded to in the literature in referring to small-scale climatic variation.

In short, perturbations introduced from outside into the aboriginal ecosystem increasingly disrupted that delicately balanced equilibrium, with generally destructive long-term effects. As will be shown next, human beings made efforts to reestablish the earlier equilibrium (see U.S. Government, *Grassland Restoration,* series 1964–1970; Hill Country 1967; Llano County 1967; U.S. Government 1961, 1972; Resource Conservation and Development Project 1968; also Soil Conservation Service USDA 1971), but, in order to do so, had to make system linkages which had not previously existed—as the very "authors" of the citations indicate!

HILL COUNTRY ECOSYSTEMS LINKS TO OTHER SYSTEMS—EMERGENT HIERARCHIES

Before moving to more recent times, we must consider the changes in the Hill Country ecosystemic relationships in the context of the larger ecosystem of the Colorado River Valley as a whole. For our purposes, two segments of this valley are of utmost importance— that to the west of the hill country, that is, the Lipan Flats and the Limestone Belt to their north as well as the escarpment of the Callahan Mountains to their west, on the one hand, and on the other, the entire coastal plain to the east. During the latter half of the nineteenth century, the former region became increasingly important as cattle and goat country, with effects on the flora and consequently on water control similar to those previously described. However, the Flats present no natural physical retention systems of the kinds found in the hill lands, such as the gnarled hills broken by stone outcroppings (see Figures 4.2, 4.3) and the water-retentive caliche. Once the soil-protective flora degenerates in the Flats area, runoff, especially in the violent sorts of precipitation characteristic of this country, can swell enormously and sweep over the countryside in devastating fashion (note terms such as "a wash" and the flood gauge signs in stream beds at bridges and fords; the signs are vertical posts marked off in 1-foot measures up to 6–8 feet) with drastic local sheet erosion as a result. Both the runoff and the erosion, however, do not affect only the locality, but the entire downstream area, both hill lands and especially the coastal plain.

These floodwaters moving into the hill lands, sometimes swollen by runoff from the hill lands themselves, encounter watercourses which become more constricted, more funnel-like, as the previous mention of canyons would indicate (see Figure 4.2 lower right corner). Perhaps the longest and deepest such constriction occurs in the last 25 km (15 miles) or so of the bed of the river as it approaches the Balcones Escarpment and debouches all at once into the westernmost side of the coastal plain. This is precisely the point at which the founding fathers of the Nation and State of Texas planted the capital of the state, Austin (see Figure 4.1). As would be expected from this situation, Austin suffered, especially in this century, a number of severe floods which washed parts of the city lying low near the water's edge downstream causing many millions of dollars of damage. There is some evidence that the floods tended to increase in scale although this is difficult to establish with certainty. The amount of dollar damage, however, seems quite certainly to have increased over time.

Meanwhile, in the coastal plain, the small mixed farming gave way in part to larger and larger enterprises dedicated to the irrigated cultivation of rice, a process which began in the early years of this century, coming to flower in the late 1920s and 1930s and continuing as a major agricultural production of the area and state until today. For the rice farmer–enterpreneurs, control of water for irrigation is essential. The same floods that eroded the up-river watersheds of the Lipan Flats and the Limestone Belt, that contributed to the soil degradation of the hill lands, especially the flood plains and bottom lands of the rivers, that severely damaged Austin and other towns at the edge of the escarpment, also raised havoc with rice farmers both in terms of siltation and flooding.

As a consequence of these various effects, there was an increasing pressure from a number of interest and civic groups in various parts of the Colorado River system to devise a *system* of water-control which was to help maintain the previous and then still-extant land-uses and ecosystem. The solution proposed as a response to these pressures consisted of a series of dams in the hill country, two smaller ones just to the east of the escarpment next to the city of Austin, a system of artificial lakes in the Flats area, and, today, a continuing variety of water-control mechanisms, including tanks, terracing, contouring, soil–flora regeneration, and so on (see *Grassland Restoration* series, esp. Pts. III and V; U.S. Government 1961, 1971; Resource Conservation and Development Project 1968, section called "Water Management," pp. 87–97; Hill Country 1967; Llano County 1967).

The earliest of these responses, on the whole, were dams, notably those at Austin and Marble Falls, built by the municipalities. Though these were bold and foresighted undertakings, they were insufficient to control the worst of the floods. At one point, Austin had three city dams, the third destroyed just 2 years after the second—one can still see some of the remains. Larger dams cost more than any municipality could afford, hence it became necessary, given the scale of the river ecosystem as a whole and the hill country ecosystem in particular, to turn to a more inclusive geopolitical unit for the capital inputs that could help maintain and even reestablish the ecosystem as it had been known. In other words, the local system became intertwined with higher-level systems which, in turn, subsume many other local systems—the ever more marked emergence of a complex, multilevel, multiecosystemic, and internally differentiated and specialized hierarchy of systems (see Pattee 1973; Whyte, Wilson, and Wilson 1969).

For our purposes, the significant technological input into the ecosystem in the period under discussion—the late 1930s and 1940s—is the dams, since these were generally restricted to the hill country and all the largest ones are to be found in that area. The four most important dams going from Austin inland—Tom Miller, Mansfield (one of the largest in the United States), Wirtz (formerly Granite Shoals), and Buchanan—were built between 1937 and 1950. It is worthy of note that their use for power had already been anticipated since the late 1880s and for hydroelectric power since their earliest initiation.

In connection with the large dams, it is also interesting to note that the resources required to carry out projects of this magnitude were not available even at the state level. The first enterprise to take an interest in the dam-building was the Ingersoll group of Chicago, which planned to build the Buchanan dam in the early 1930s (LCRA n.d.), but went into bankruptcy before it had much more than begun work on the site. Subsequently, the dam was continued and finished under the aegis of the Federal Government, both in terms of funding of the dams themselves and in terms of supplying labor through the W.P.A. as a major absorber of labor during the national crisis of the Great Depression. The allocation of funds by the Federal Government for water-control purposes of this sort entails certain responsibilities and requirements on the part of the state and also involves certain guarantees with respect to the use of the bodies of water created, specifically recreational and conservational.

The state's responsibility is carried out through a state agency, in this part of Texas, the Lower Colorado River Authority (LCRA), whose very name is a recognition of the ecosystemic character of this part of Texan territory. It has jurisdiction over the water system, its use for electric power, its recreational and conservational uses, and control over water quality (although this falls under the wider jurisdiction of the Texas Water Quality Control Board). Thus, the LCRA and the Texas Water Quality Control Board, both with jurisdictions much wider than the hill country ecosystem itself, have become institutional elements at the state geopolitical level of the ecosystem of the Colorado River Valley and the hill country ecosystem. It should, of course, be remembered that the building of the dams involved an enormous capital input from the highest level geopolitical system, the federal government.

In sum, by 1950, a thoroughgoing change in the water regimen of the last 650 km (400 miles) or so of the Colorado River had been effected by deliberate, technological intervention. In a sense, the coastal plain segment had been partially restored to a prior state of equilibrium—that is, a more or less even water supply for its irrigation farming. The upper segment in the San Angelo area remains in a somewhat ambiguous status because the great water-storage lakes that were to have been created there filled to only one-third of expected level and then dried up shortly after and have not had water since.[5] Swimming signs sticking up out of caked mud warning swimmers of the dangers of diving in shallow water give testimony to the irregularity of rains in the area! The central segment where the high dams are located has gone through major socioecological changes (see Kelley 1972; Jennings 1972; Clark, Willis, and Pieper 1967).

A SUBSYSTEM OF THE HILL COUNTRY ECOSYSTEM: THE LLANO UPLIFT

Before turning to some of the more physical and economic aspects of these socioecological changes, it is necessary to describe in greater detail the hill country along a smaller segment of the Colorado River itself, specifically, the Llano uplift, which topographically forms part of the Hill Country though it is geologically quite different from the surrounding Edwards Plateau and must be discussed in terms of the issues raised in this chapter. Its western boundary is essentially the edge of the Hill Country where it runs into the Lipan Flats (see Figure 4.1, where it is designated ''Central Mineral Region'' and surrounded by the hill country, with the Flats to the west and Figure 4.4, where it is designated ''Llano Basin''). In the preceding pages, I simplified the portrait of the hill country, treating it as if it were homogenous in its geology and topography by omitting discussion of the Llano uplift. This was because the hill country as a whole stands out against other physiographic areas and presents common problems of water flow control.

Lying between the eastern and central Edwards Plateau and the southern Grand Prairie, which are related sedimentary systems of fairly recent times, topographically rather similar and biotically alike, the Llano uplift raises a vast mass of granite and schist almost 125 km (75 miles) across. This mass is surrounded by paleozoic, cambrian, and slightly more recent, but still very ancient rock formations, heavily metamorphosed in part. The soil inventories overlying the central part of the uplife form a separate series from those of the surrounding Edwards Plateau and Grand Prairie, with different potentials for human use in agriculture and animal raising, being even less auspicious for either than the rest of the hill country. The floral cover overlaps with the

[5] As of 1972 when the first draft of this chapter was written. An idea of flood problems in this area can be gotten from photographs in U.S. Government 1961, e.g., p. 9. The source also shows pictures of the shallow-water storage lakes discussed here. It is said that the engineers who built one such lake, a large one near San Angelo, calculated that it would take 7 years to fill it. Shortly after it was finished, one of those incredible thunderstorms and rainfalls described in the text occurred. The lake filled overnight. Thereafter it emptied slowly until it dried out and has not had significant amounts of water in it since.

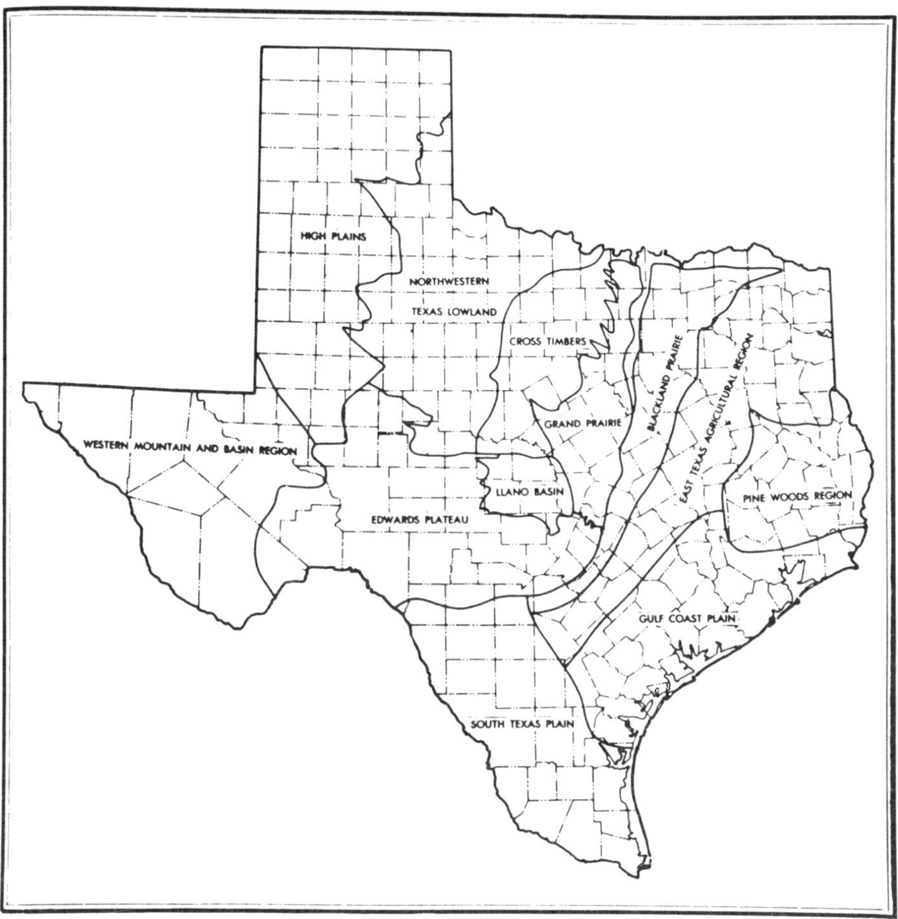

FIGURE 4.4 *Geographic Regions of Texas (From Chambers 1948).*

floral inventory described above for the plateau, but it is also significantly differentiated from it. Finally, the water regimen, from the point of view of the ground-system, is quite different from that of the sedimentary plateau. It is particularly the latter point which is of interest to us here.

The granitic rock mass is very poorly permeable to water and provides no aquifers. It is also virtually impenetrable or penetrable at great cost and with little guarantee in terms of drilling wells for water. Where the granites are overlaid by sedimentary formations, ground water tends to percolate downward until it hits the granite, then to flow laterally over the granite surfaces. Thus, in general, the water availability of the area has been even less secure or less regulated than elsewhere, while the rockiness and soils of the area have not lent themselves to more than a low agricultural productivity, in fact have prevented significant agrarian activity.

It should be pointed out, however, that the granites, various other minerals, some precious stones, talc, marble, various spars, and so on, have themselves proved to be resources to be exploited for markets outside the area. The Llano uplift became, in the late 1880s, a major center within Texas for extractive industries. These industries attracted population to the area and, unlike ranching, were able to support rather sizable numbers of people in rather small areas—the populations of both Burnet and Llano counties grew rapidly at the end of the last century and, in the latter case, reached a peak of about 11,000 people at the turn of the century. With the decline of the industries and of cotton growing and with the elimination of the screwworm plague (see below), labor needs in the area declined sharply and, with them, the population declined also. The population of Llano county declined to only about 5500 people, though, as a consequence of retirement population immigration revolving about the lakes, it has gone up again to about 7000.

Returning to the water-regimen changes after the lakes were put in, one finds a rather surprising situation developing. As the lakes filled, sometimes several hundred feet deep where the river had passed through canyons, their filled water levels were higher than the previous water tables. Water from the lakes has thus tended to move *up* over the granitic underslopes where they are covered by sedimentary layers. On these same layers of limestone or other rock, cattle ranching had been carried on, water being supplied from wells run with windmills, as well as from the unreliable streams. As the lake waters moved back into the underlayers of sedimentary rock in nonconformity with the granites beneath, the wells were recharged with more water than before the existence of the lakes. The effect of this has been a tendency for cattle ranchers to judge carrying capacity for cattle by improved water supply—which they took to be from precipitation—and hence to overstock their lands. This has resulted in still greater overgrazing than before.

At the same time, runoff introduced waters poorly filtered and full of solutes, specifically nitrates degraded into nitrites toxic to animals and humans, into the previously nonexisting lakes and into wells. High enough concentrations tend to produce intestinal symptoms in humans, particularly in children. Severe cases can be fatal to the latter. Animal manure solutes may also be carried by runoff into the lake waters and must be controlled. Some of these solutes and organic compounds may be carried back into the wells by recharging from the lakes. Thus, we have an intensified degradation of the soils and land surfaces from an apparent increase in the regularity and quantity of water resulting from the filling of the lakes.

Federal requirements regarding lake uses must also be regarded as ecosystem inputs, in this case from a nonlocalized higher level system to a localized lower-level system. I shall argue in the conclusion that the increasing frequency of such inputs is a characteristic of sociocultural evolution. Indeed, such inputs have been crucial in the hill country as the development of subdivision after subdivision (with such intriguing names as Camp Pajama,

Curiosity Cave, Paleface Pedernales, etc; Clark, Willis, and Pieper 1967:44–53) and of summer, weekend, vacation, and retirement homes indicates. Connected with this development has been the restocking of the lake with game fish and the replacement of one kind of game fish with another (apparently handled quite ineptly with a considerable mortality of young fish). Needless to say, boating and allied activities are unbiquitous (it is one of those singular areas which, instead of three-car garages, sports three-boat garages).

All of these developments entail, at least in the neighborhood of the lakes, distinctive changes in land-use and orientations towards land as resources and wealth, a subject discussed elsewhere by Kelley (1972). They also entail the emergence of a burgeoning inventory of services in response to the new local "needs" and local capacity to pay. This expansion produces a major change in the labor market and in the structure and functions of the cities in the lakes area in particular, but more broadly in the hill country at large, as such cities provide for needs like governance, distribution, and specialized services. The services include highly technical medical treatment (especially for the very large population of elderly and aged retired people), agricultural extension, technical aid, etc. The expansion and alteration of services is discussed in Jennings (1972).

THE RETURN OF THE DEER SLAYERS: NEW SYSTEM LINKAGES

Before concluding, I wish to return to one important item mentioned above: the screwworm. The screwworm is a most destructive pest which attacks especially cattle and deer. Its ravages can be fatal to both unless immediate care is taken of the animal by treating its infestation. Effective treatment requires virtually daily examination and care of the cattle (see McMurtry's novel, *Leaving Cheyenne*), which may be scattered over hundreds of acres of pasture. The labor requirements for such care were quite great, giving employment to considerable numbers of ranch hands throughout the area. It should be noted, too, that the cattle were at a competitive advantage over the deer in that they were protected and aided by men, while the deer population was constantly being kept in check by the screwworm and hunters. At the same time, the deer constituted a natural repository for the screwworm.

In the 1960s, the U.S. Department of Agriculture devised a means of eradicating or at least markedly controlling the screwworm by controlling the vectors that carry it—a kind of fly.[6] The USDA procedure is, of course, another significant input into the local ecosystem from the more inclusive geopolitical system of the Federal Government. The effects of screwworm control were dramatic and drastic: Labor absorption decreased sharply—and with it the population of the cattle areas of the highland counties, especially

[6] The technique was to sterilize male flies raised in laboratories by radiation, then let them loose at breeding time, thereby drastically reducing reproduction. Apparently, after a number of years, radiation-resistant males began to develop, hence the recrudescence of screwworms.

the younger cohorts for whom work had disappeared. The profitability of cattle-raising increased because of cost-reduction and the reduced mortality of cattle. Of great significance, too, was the decrease in deer mortality, so that the deer population of the hill country area began to increase sharply. Interestingly, and perhaps connected with that increase, it has been reported in the last few years that the screwworm has increased again.[7] This may also be related to the introductions of exotic ungulates for hunting as wild game, a subject to which I shall return.

Despite the initial success in controlling the screwworm, with the accompanying advantages for ranching, several factors led to a situation of increasing difficulties in maintaining ranches of cattle, sheep, and goats: (*a*) the interaction of changing land values in the lakes area; (*b*) the degradation of grazing lands; (*c*) the ever-increasing infestation of pastures with mesquite and brush; and (*d*) declining prices for mohair, wool, and beef—or at least prices which did not rise at rates equivalent to increases in costs of production. At the same time, the recreational and tourist aspects of the area, which have constantly intensified in the last 30 or 40 years, encouraged hunting for sport. The aboriginal natural goal of such hunting was the deer, which, especially after control of the screwworm developed, became a major resource for land owners of the region as well as other enterpreneurs through the development

---

[7] From The Austin American, about May 1, 1977 (reprinted with permission). Weather Conditions Prompt New Screwworm Invasion by CLARK BOLT, Farm Editor. MISSION—The screwworm eradication program, which offically eradicated screwworms from Texas in 1964 is now completely out of hand and likely won't improve any until freezing weather.

Harried officials at the Mission Fly laboratory here said Thursday the count of screwworm infestations in Texas now is running five times higher than a year ago.

More than 2,000 cases have been reported in the state thus far in more than 90 counties. Central Texas counties which have cases include Williamson, Guadalupe, Hays, Coryell, Hill, Hamilton, and it is expected that more counties will become infested.

"A fantastic combination of weather conditions is given as the main reason for the sudden outbreaks. Temperature and moisture conditions all over the Southwest and Mexico have been ideal for the rapid increase of screwworm populations that moved in from Mexico," Dr. M. E. Meadows, director of the Mission screwworm eradication program, said.

Rains throughout South Texas have prevented airplanes from air-dropping screwworms over areas which have infestations.

In at least one case, sterile screwworms have been put out by horseback; other ranchers are using trucks and pickups to do the job.

Capacity of the fly laboratory at Mission has been increased to about 200,000,000 sterile screwworms per week. But this may mean trouble further down the road for the program. Money which would normally be used to operate the program later this year has been diverted to increase production.

A meeting will be held May 23 here among technical personnel to review the situation, Dr. Meadows said. "Some of them will be from Washington, D.C., while most will be specialists connected with the program here. We will look over the situation carefully, evaluate it as best we can, and then make decisions regarding the future of this program," he said.

Dr. Meadows said there is no truth to stories that the screwworms being produced at the Mission plant are losing their effectiveness. "We have changed the strain of our flies from time to time to avoid this situation, and we have had our sterilization equipment checked recently. . . ."

of hunting leases. The deer became so valuable as a resource that many ranchers found they could make more money by leasing hunting rights during the 6-week hunting season—say, to a group of oil executives from New Jersey (as one informant reported to us)—than by raising cattle all year round. To maintain deer herds ready for the hunting season, however, it also became necessary to feed the deer—a situation made difficult by the present inadequacy of the grasses.

A number of major responses to this problem of maintaining the deer ensured. First, land owners began to feed them hay. Obviously, given the depletion of tall grasses, hay had to be imported (from Oklahoma). Second, the deer were given manufactured supplements. Third, they were provided with salt licks and farm ponds for water. Fourth, range and pasture management changed so as to encourage the renewed growth of tall grasses, leaving trees for cover on the uplands and a controlled amount of brush for browse. Fifth, goat populations were reduced.

Obviously, hay imports, pond building, and large-scale pasture improvements require considerable capital outlays. Since hunting and hunting leases have proved so valuable, an even larger capital outlay has been involved, because exotic ungulates have been imported from Africa and India for use as game (see Roe 1972). Here and there, as one drives in Texas, one may see impala (*Grassland Restoration,* Pt. VI:33), Indian blackbuck antelope, wild Corsican rams, African aoudad sheep, axis and silka deer (Texas Highway Department ca. 1972:186), moufflon sheep, and so on. They, like the white-tailed deer, continue to establish themselves and spread. Capital for such innovation has been generally restricted to large-scale ranchers and businessmen–investors from the large cities, especially Houston (whence also substantial investment in the subdivisions, retirement homes, resort developments).

In sum, the ecosystem has changed in such a way that the labor structure, land use, relationship to urban centers, relation to national centers, linkage to other production areas, and even personnel have been transformed pervasively and dramatically. It is interesting to note, however, that these changes tend to be ecologically limited by the geological vectors of the system. Where the Llano uplift meets the Edwards Plateau to the south, there is almost an immediate shift from the patterns of recreational residential development and sport hunting to cattle raising. To the northeast, a similar shift takes place but with a greater admixture of agriculture because of the enclaves of blackland soils characteristic of the western part of the coastal plain.

The highland lakes part of the highland hills, then, tends to have become a highly specialized ecological subsystem of the hill country ecosystem. This subsystem entails a subsystemic interrelationship of the urban centers of the area, and a higher level of system interrelationship with towns outside the area but still in the hill country or, like Austin, just at the edge of it. Certain features, such as the retirement homes, the major resort developments, and the like, bring, as noted above, investment from the major financial centers like Houston, Memphis, and New York. They bring in business and banking interests of varying kinds also from the national city system. Finally they bring in people—retirees—from all over the country, who carry with them their portfolios of stocks, bonds, and other finances which constitute a new source of capitalization in the region, feeding back to generate new services, new agencies, new organizations, and new links with cities at various system levels.

Conclusions

Any ecological analysis describes a "functional" system, that is, one in which the "parts" or, far better, "variables" interact, affect each other, and display mutual causality. These variables can be said to be functions of each other. Critical, however, on one hand, is the time involved in such affectings and causings and, on the other, are the feedback effects. In general, negative feedbacks are understood as system-maintainers—equilibrium mechanisms—although negative feedbacks may maintain systems so rigidly that they break down or change radically and rapidly under perturbations of any degree of significance. Even negative feedback requires time—hence history.

Positive feedbacks are generally understood as system-modifying, even though, as my case history illustrates, they may be directed at system-maintenance—or at least the maintenance of some structure or some of the variables of the system. Positive feedbacks are also, of course, intrinsically time-linked, hence historical. Since they involve the succession comprised of the changes of the system as in the particular case described here, they are also histories or historical in the generally understood meaning of those concepts, including their implications of specific sequences of causality. Positive feedbacks are, of course, also functional in all the senses given above.

Put another way, any *historical* analysis dealing with causes is also a functional analysis. It is true that historians tend not to look at "whole" systems (in my view, a questionable conception with reificatory overtones), but rather at linear sequences of causality of rather specific events and variables. However, these linear sequences are nevertheless effects, even mutual effects. That is, they are functions spread out linearly, temporally. Anthropologists and others have tended to look at "whole" systems, but have rather tended to run from the temporal mapping of "functions." My argument is that the two approaches are not only not mutually exclusive, but, indeed, are not even two approaches. I have tried to illustrate their unity in the treatment of the case history presented in this chapter. It is a unity I call 'structural history' (or, less desirably, 'historical structuralism,' *not* to be confused with Lévi-Straussian Structuralism), an approach much elucidated by General Systems Theory.

Finally, the structural history of the Texas hill country ecosystem presents certain properties of extreme interest. These are the increasing linkage of the local ecosystem with other local ecosystems translocally so as to create a larger, more inclusive system, and with supralocal, ecologically nonlocalized systems such as the state and federal Governments, the banking networks, and the like. Concurrently, localized variables with localized feedback loops become increasingly detached from the loops, hence from the localities, and increasingly hooked into complex chains of linkage going through the translocal and supersystem or supralocal networks, only having feedback inputs into the locality after having been intermediated by many external systems (see my treatment of the income tax in Leeds, in press).

I propose that, in a condensed way, temporally and spatially, this case history presents us with a general paradigm of sociocultural evolution. The pattern of decreasing localization, increasing detachment of variables from local feedback, and greater and greater linkage into trans- and supralocal systems, an ever-increasing intermediation by systems intervening between a system output and its feedback effect is the general pattern of sociocultural evolution. Its presents us with a general approach which permits us to deal with "function" and "history"— or structural history—and evolution in a single conceptual model. It permits us to deal with "holistic" structural approaches and "atomistic" trait approaches, which have, up to now, represented two impermeable paradigms (e.g., Boasians versus British and French structuralists and functionalists; see Harris 1968, Chaps. 10–14 vs. Chaps. 18 and 19; or Sahlins and Service 1960 versus Forde 1934). Traits, with their diffusion and reabsorption in a formerly alien milieu, clearly involve historical sequences. But, one can show their functionality (an idea already explicit in Boas himself) by considering them as novel inputs or, sometimes, as negative feedbacks in a historically functional system. By considering them, like any other variable, in terms of their feedback effects in the system, of the accomodations to them of other variables of the system under consideration, the paradigm allows a synthesis of Boasian historicism and various forms of structural analysis.

Thus, the formal paradigm of evolution proposed here synthesizes with "history" and "function" into a single, unified framework with which to approach any population. Clearly, there are almost staggering implications of this. For example, it really demands a review of all our sacred texts, the "classical" monographs from "the" Nuer to "the" Ndembu to "the" Kung, practically all of which, because of the separation of functional, historical, and evolutionary paradigms, can be shown to be implausible, impossible, or downright false. (See, for example, Johnson 1979, on clear misrepresentation or falsenesses in Evans-Pritchard regarding the Nuer.)

Historical perspectives show that many "functional" interpretations which have been given for various societies are only one of a number of possible hypotheses and quite often clearly inferior ones. Functional perspectives on historical interpretations often show the rather narrow selectivity of lines of connection to be inadequate; more complex causes and contexts must be taken into account. More "holistic" systems are operating. Evolutionary or "general historical" (to use the conception of one of the great founders of modern historiography in the early nineteenth century, von Rancke) perspectives help sort out unique events from general processes, among various hypothetical interpretations of data. The syntheses of the three anterior programs of interpretation leads to a more comprehensive and a much more subtly processual view of the world than we have had. In particular, it leads to a view of evolution as process instead of as result, the standard model until today (see Leeds 1974).

References

Bogusch, E.
1955 *Hoofbeats along the Llano*. San Antonio: Naylor.
Chambers, W.
1948 Geographic regions of Texas. *The Texas Geographic Magazine,* Spring.
Clark, C. T., J. E. Willis, and C. A. Pieper
1967 *The highland lakes of Texas: A study in economic development.* Austin: University of Texas, Bureau of Business Research.
Felger, R. S.
1971 Seri use of mesquite, *Prosopis Glandulosa* Var. *Torreyana. The Kiva 37*(1)53–60.
In press Mesquite in southwestern Indian cultures. In *A tree in perspective: Prosopis in desert shrub ecosystems* (B. Simpson, Ed.). Stroudsburg: Dowden, Hutchinson, and Ross.
Forde, C. D.
1934 *Habitat, economy, and society.* (Reprinted by Dutton, New York, 1963.)
Frye, J. C., and A. B. Leonard
1957 Ecological interpretations of pliocene and pleistocene stratigraphy in the Great Plains region. *American Journal of Science 255*:1–11.
Harris, D. R.
1966 Recent plant invasions in the arid and semi-arid southwest of the United States. *Annals of the Association of American Geographers 56*(3):408–422.
Harris, M.
1968 *The rise of anthropological theory: A history of theories of culture.* New York: Thomas Y. Crowell.
Hill Country (Texas) Board of Supervisors
1967 *Program and plan of work: Hill Country Soil and Water Conservation District No. 534. Lampasas,* Texas.
Hirschman, A. O.
1963 *Journeys towards progress: Studies of economic policy-making in Latin America.* New York: Twentieth Century Fund.
Jennings, V.
1972 Changes in the highland lakes economy: Goods and services for the retired population in

the Kingsland-Marble Falls area. Paper presented at the Southwestern Social Science Association, San Antonio.

Johnson, D.

1979 Colonial policy and prophets: The 'Nuer settlement,' 1929–1930. *Journal of the Anthropological Society of Oxford 10*(1):1–20.

Jordan, T. G.

1972 The origin and distribution of open-range cattle ranching. *Social Science Quarterly 53*(1):105–121.

Kelley, Jr., K.

1972 Rural and urban land values in evolution. "From cow pasture to people pasture." Paper presented at the Southwestern Social Science Association, San Antonio.

Leeds, A.

1974 Darwinian and "Darwinian" evolutionism in the study of society and culture. In *The comparative reception of Darwinism* (T. Glick, Ed.). Austin: University of Texas Press. Pp. 437–485.

1976 "Economics and subsistence" [and] "Technology and subsistence." In *Encyclopedia of Anthropology* (D. E. Hunter and P. Whitten, Eds.). New York: Harper and Row.

In press Towns and villages in society: Hierarchies of order and cause. In *Proceedings of the Southern Anthropological Society,* Annual Meeting, Feb., 1979.

LCRA (Lower Colorado River Authority)

n.d. Lake Lyndon B. Johnson and Alvin Wirtz Dam. Austin: LCRA.

n.d. Lake Inks and Inks Dam. Austin: LCRA.

n.d. Lake Buchanan and Buchanan Dam. Austin: LCRA.

Llano County (Texas) Board of Supervisors

1967 *Program and Work Plan: Llano County Soil and Water Conservation District No. 233.* Llano, Texas.

McMurtry, L.

1963 *Leaving Cheyenne.* New York: Harper and Row.

Oetking, P.

1958 *Geological highway map of Texas.* Dallas: Dallas Geological Society.

Pattee, H. R.

1973 *Hierarchy theory: The challenge of complex systems.* New York: George Braziller, International Library of Systems Theory and Philosophy.

Resource Conservation and Development Project, Board of Directors

1968 *Eastern Hill Country: A plan for development and wise use of our natural resources.* Fort Worth and Temple, Texas: U.S. Department of Agriculture Soil Conservation Service.

Roe, E.

1972 Texotic game: More species of exotic game have been released in Texas than any other place in North America. *Texas Star/Austin American-Statesman* January 2.

Ruyle, E. E.

1973 Genetic-cultural pools: Some suggestions for a unified theory of bio-cultural evolution. *Human Ecology 1*(3):201–215.

Sahlins, M. D., and E. R. Service

1960 *Evolution and culture.* Ann Arbor: University of Michigan Press.

Stewart, O. C.

1951 Burning and natural vegetation in the United States. *The Geographical Review 41*(2):317–320.

1953 Why the Great Plains are treeless. *Colorado Quarterly 2*(1):40–49.

1954a The forgotten side of ethnogeography. In *Method and perspective in anthropology: Papers in honor of Wilson D. Wallis* (R. F. Spencer, Ed.). Minneapolis: University of Minnesota Press. Pp. 221–248; 308–310.

1954b Forest fires with a purpose. *Southwestern Lore 20*(3):42–45.

1955a Why were the prairies treeless? *Southwestern Lore 20*(4):59–64.

1955b Forest and grass burning in the mountain west. *Southwestern Lore 21*(1):5–8.

1956 Fire as the first great force employed by man. In *Man's role in changing the face of the Earth* (W. L. Thomas, Jr., Ed.). Chicago: University of Chicago Press. Pp. 115–133.

1963 Barriers to understanding the influence of use of fire by aborigines on vegetation. *Proceedings of the 2nd Annual Tall Timbers Fire Ecology Conference*. Tallahassee, Florida: Tall Timbers Research Station.

Texas Highway Department

ca.1972 *Texas, Land of Contrasts.* Austin: Texas Highway Department.

United States Government

1961 *Northwest laterals watershed of the middle Colorado River watershed, Coleman and Runnels counties, Texas—work plan.* Temple, Texas: U.S. Department of Agriculture, Soil Conservation Service.

1964a The Texas brush problem. *Grassland restoration,* Part I. Temple: U.S. Department of Agriculture, Soil Conservation Service.

1964b Brush control. *Grassland Restoration,* Part II. Temple: U.S. Department of Agriculture, Soil Conservation Service.

1964c Re-establishing forage plants. *Grassland Restoration,* Part III. Temple: U.S. Department of Agriculture, Soil Conservation Service.

1966 Which side of the fence are you on? *Grassland Restoration,* Part IV. Temple: U.S. Department of Agriculture, Soil Conservation Service.

1967 Effect on water yield and supply. *Grassland Restoration,* Part V. Temple: U.S. Department of Agriculture, Soil Conservation Service.

1970 And its effect on wildlife. *Grassland Restoration,* Part VI. Temple: U.S. Department of Agriculture, Soil Conservation Service.

1971 *Soil and water conservation in Texas.* Temple: U.S. Department of Agriculture, Soil Conservation Service.

Whyte, L. A., A. E. Wilson, and D. Wilson (Eds.)

1969 *Hierarchical structures.* New York: American Elsevier.

5 Local Ecology and the State: Implications of Contemporary Quechua Land Use for the Inca Sequence of Agricultural Work[1]

WILLIAM P. MITCHELL

Introduction

It is frequently assumed that, in the Inca economic organization, the peasantry cultivated agricultural lands in sequence—depending on whether the lands belonged to the religion, the emperor, or to themselves. Although there is some disagreement about the precise order because of disparate accounts in the chronicles written after the Spanish conquest, this notion of an agricultural sequence based on social status pervades the modern literature on the Inca. This chapter will discuss such statements in the light of the agricultural adaptation of Quinua, a contemporary community of highland Peru. Data from the contemporary community demonstrate that the sequences postulated by the post-conquest chroniclers and accepted by many modern authors are much too simplistic to describe the actual sequence of work under the Incas.

In addition to the particular historical problem addressed, this chapter has a broader theoretical perspective: to reaffirm the importance of contemporary ethnography in historical and prehistorical interpretation. Some authors have questioned the relevance of contemporary ethnography—as per-

[1] I wish to thank my 1975 graduate seminar at Monmouth College on Ancient Civilizations of Native America, and especially Diane Shapiro, for their stimulating discussions which led to this chapter. Dean Arnold, Glenn King, Barbara Price, and Eric Ross provided excellent criticisms of an earlier version of the chapter. The field research was undertaken in 1966–1967 and the summers of 1973 and 1974. I am grateful to the Foreign Area Fellowship Program and the Monmouth College Grant-in-Aid Committee for their financial help. The map was prepared by Dennis Lewis. I am especially thankful to my wife Daphna for her ideas and comments. An earlier version of this chapter was presented at the 75th Annual Meeting of the American Anthropological Association.

BEYOND THE MYTHS OF CULTURE
Essays in Cultural Materialism

ISBN 0-12-598180-5

formed by ethnographers—in interpreting the past (Reid, Schiffer, and Rathje 1975; Schiffer 1975, 1976; Gumerman and Phillips 1978; Wobst 1978). It is argued by one author, for example, that ethnographic data have become less useful for prehistorians than in the past because of the particularist and idealist biases of ethnographers (Schiffer 1975). In this view, it is the archaeologist rather than the ethnographer who is assigned the task of studying contemporary material culture.

I argue to the contrary: Isolating ethnography and historical and prehistorical interpretation is methodologically unwise. Each of these areas of anthropology, when guided by a cultural materialist strategy, has much to gain from the other (cf. Harris 1968a, 1968b). The basic assumption underlying this chapter is that if the ecological adaptation of a people has maintained sufficient continuity through time, then statements we make about the ethnohistoric and archaeological past must be consistent with what can be proven as possible in the present. This in no way denies that the ultimate test for any proposition is the archaeological and ethnohistoric material itself. However, the proper use of ethnography adds an additional standard of proof to test the validity of propositions about the past.

The Ethnohistoric Problem

Modern descriptions of the Inca usually include a statement to the effect that the land was divided among the state, the state religion, and the peasantry, and that the peasantry cultivated these lands in sequence. Two different agricultural sequences are given. Although citations are not always given, in those cases where they are, the sequences are usually attributed to the chroniclers Garcilaso de la Vega and Bernabe Cobo.

The agricultural sequence attributed to Garcilaso ([1604]1963:150–152) has achieved the least acceptance by scholars. It is used only by Prescott (1874:53–54), Rivero and Von Tschudi (1854:82–83) and Mead (1935:61–62). In this sequence it is held that the fields were cultivated in this order: (*a*) fields of the religion or sun; (*b*) fields of widows, orphans, the incapacitated, and soldiers on duty; (*c*) fields of the peasantry; (*d*) fields of the local political officials (*curacas*); and finally (*e*) fields of the emperor.

Most scholars use the sequence associated with Bernabe Cobo. Cobo ([1653]1964:120–121) states that the people first cultivated the fields of the gods or religion, then those of the government, and finally the lands of the peasants themselves. Some version of this sequence pervades the modern literature on the Inca and is found in Baudin (1961a:71–72; 1961b:224), Josephy (1968:246), Katz (1972:285), Lanning (1967:161), Martin (1974:14), Mason (1968:181–182), Metraux (1969:99), Rowe (1946:265–266), Steward and Faron (1959:123), and Velasco (1841:52–53). Although modern authors attribute this sequence to Cobo, earlier versions of it were given by the chroniclers Polo ([1571]1916:58–60), Acosta ([1590]1962:300), Murua

([1590]1946:335), and Arriaga ([1621]1968:209). Finally, one popular account of the Inca describes at length an agricultural sequence that does not accord with any of the chroniclers (Von Hagen 1961:64–66).

Discussions of the agricultural sequence by modern authors are usually very terse. Some authors simply mention the sequence, as in Lanning (1967: 161): "the . . . fields [of the state and church] were worked first, after which the farmer was free to plant or harvest his own crops." Other authors describe the sequence at greater length as in the following quote from Mason:

> Like all co-operative labour, [communal agricultural work] must have been a jovial and not an onerous occasion, with plenty of chicha beer, singing, and bantering. The songs, perhaps in honour of the gods when working the church lands, or in praise of the emperor while engaged in the state fields, were appropriate to the occasion. As soon as the fields of the gods were finished, the work was repeated on the government lands, and then the people were free to cultivate their own fields [1968:182].

In general, modern authors have approached the question of an agricultural sequence very uncritically. Most do not say why they chose one agricultural sequence over another and some even seem unaware that there are discrepant accounts in the chronicles. Only a few authors suspend judgment on "The order in which these lands were worked . . . [because] contrary evidence precludes definite judgement . . . [Gibson 1948:44]." (See also Osborne 1952:120–122; Valcarcel 1964:406–407; 421–422; 425–426; 428–429; 487; and 502.)

In the remainder of this chapter contemporary data will be used to assess the statements of the chroniclers regarding the Inca agricultural sequence. It will be demonstrated that the two agricultural sequences given by the chroniclers are at variance with the requirements of contemporary Andean agriculture. Data from Quinua, a village in the central Sierra, indicate that these are the primary determinants of cultivation order: (*a*) the types of crop sown, (*b*) the location of the fields in the vertical series of environmental zones along the mountain slope, and (*c*) the particular agricultural cycle being sown. Any sequence according to social status would interfere with crop productivity. Contemporary evidence suggests that such agricultural adaptations are widespread in highland Peru. Moreover, ethnohistoric evidence suggests that such adaptations were also important in the past. Consequently, the agricultural sequences given by modern authors and the chroniclers are probably in error as statements of behavior. The question then arises as to what the statements in the chronicles mean, a problem which will be dealt with later in this chapter.

Although some chroniclers are ambiguous on this point, Cobo and Garcilaso apply their sequences to both the sowing and harvesting of the crops. In both cases the sequences are inadequate, although this chapter will be concerned primarily with the sowing of the crops.

Contemporary Quechua Land Use: Quinua

LOCATION AND ECOLOGICAL SETTING

Quinua is a district in the central Peruvian Highlands to the northeast of the city of Ayacucho on the western slopes of the range of mountains forming the eastern wall of the Ayacucho Valley (see Figure 5.1). The community is an independent one in which most people own their own lands. Except for a small ruling group of townsmen, and recently educated young people, most of the population of 5348 people consists of Quechua-speaking peasants (*campesinos*) (Mitchell 1974).[2]

The people of Quinua are subsistence farmers. Although everyone sells surplus crops from time to time, only a few townsmen and farmers in the valley bottom produce cash crops in any significant way. Although some Old World cultigens and agricultural techniques such as the plow are utilized, they have been integrated into the aboriginal system of cultivation. The basic productive system is an adaptation to the vertical ecology, an adaptation which is pre-Columbian in origin (cf. Murra 1960, 1968, and 1972).

The planting sequence in Quinua is directly related to altitude. Altitude has a major effect on temperature, sunshine, and moisture: The higher the altitude, the colder the climate. In the Ayacucho region temperature decreases .6°C for every 100 m of altitude (Rivera 1967, 1971). In addition, altitude affects cloud cover and moisture loss. Higher altitudes are cloudier, a frequent phenomenon in mountain environments such as Peru (cf. Bowman 1916:155; Hunt and Hunt 1974:137; Peattie 1936:65–66): The further down the mountain slope, the greater the total amount of sunshine. Both sunshine and high temperature cause greater water loss from soil and plants (evapotranspiration), so that the terrain becomes drier as one moves down the mountain slope (Arnold 1975; Tosi 1960).

The effects of altitude on temperature, moisture, and sunshine, along with the consequent effects on human productive activities, allow us to delineate six major vertical ecological zones in Quinua (Arnold 1975; Mitchell 1976a, 1976b; see Table 5.1). The zones are differentiated not only on the basis of vegetative characteristics, but also on the basis of differential human behavior, especially in agriculture and other extractive activities (see Mayer 1977).[3]

---

[2] These social strata correspond with what elsewhere in the Andes are referred to as *Mestizos* and Indians. These terms are inappropriate for Quinua, so that townsmen and peasants or rural folk are used instead (Mitchell 1974).

[3] My discussion of these zones is based on Arnold's (1975) analysis of Tosi's classification for Peru. The English terms for these zones are derived from Holdridge (1947), which formed the basis of Tosi's work. Mayer (1977:62–64) uses the phrase "production zone" rather than "ecological zone" to emphasize that these zones are not strictly environmental but a result of human productive activities in a particular environmental setting. I prefer the phrase ecological zone, for it properly includes human productive activities within its meaning. However, Mayer is correct in asserting that such zones are not strictly environmental.

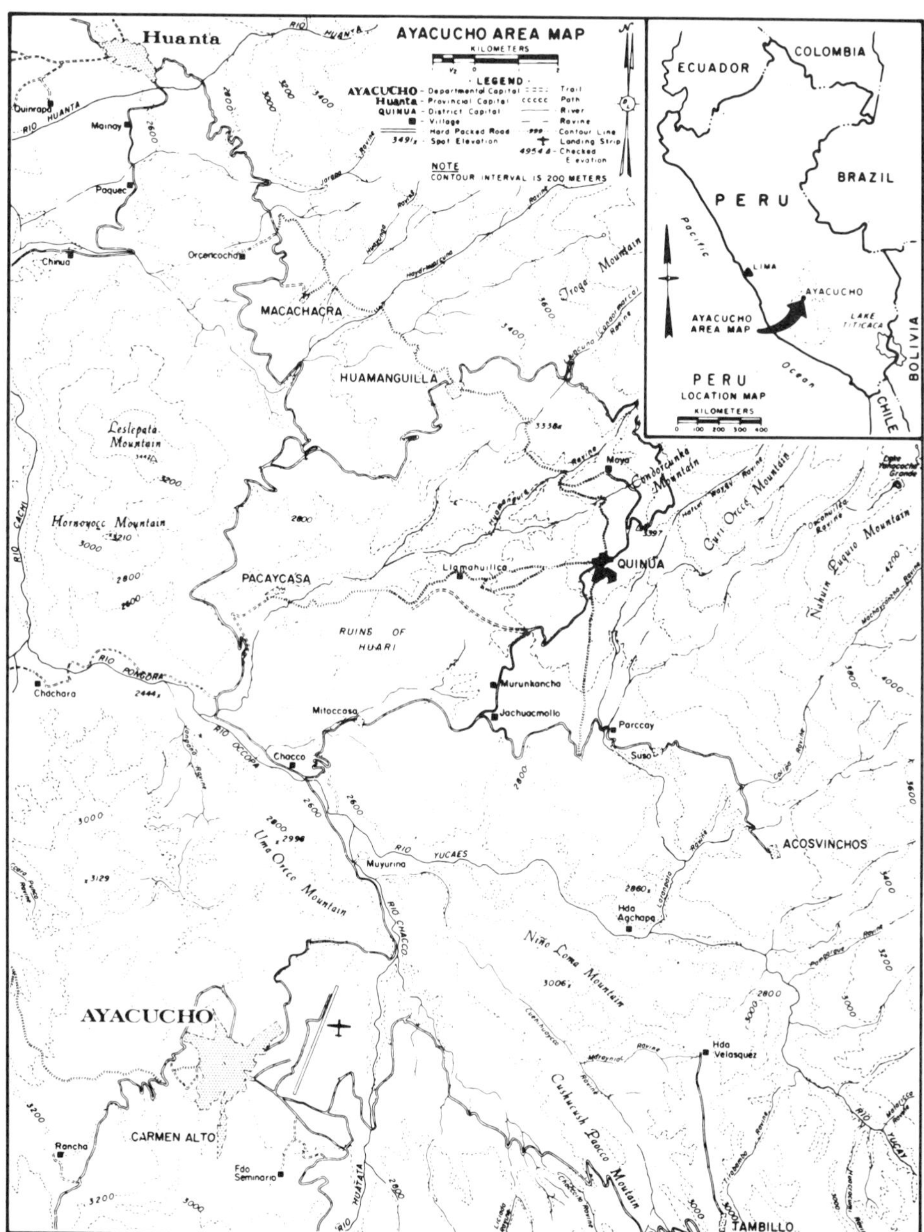

FIGURE 5.1 *The Valley of Ayacucho.*

The highest ecological zone is the alpine rain tundra–subalpine wet paramo (4100 m and above). This zone, usually characterized as the high puna in Peru, is above the level of agriculture, and is very cold, moist, and cloudy. Below it lies the montane prairie (4000–4100 m), which is characterized by

TABLE 5.1
Quinua Ecological Zones

Ecological zone	Elevation	General characteristics
Alpine rain tundra and subalpine wet Paramo	4100 m +	High *puna* grasslands Grazing
Montane prairie	4000–4100 m	Grassland Grazing and nonirrigated potato cultivation
Montane moist forest	3400–4000 m	Dense underbrush of small trees and shrubs Nonirrigated cultivation of tubers and frost resistant, quick maturing crops
Lower Montane savannah	2850–3400 m	Town of Quinua and major population zone Major cultivation zone Zone of irrigated fields
Lower Montane thorn steppe	2500–2850 m	Xerophytic vegetation Nonirrigated cultivation of short growth plants with low water needs
Valley bottom	ca. 2500 m	Xerophytic vegetation Plentiful water from Rio Chacco Irrigated double cropping Truck farming for city of Ayacucho

bunch grass (*Stipa ichu*) and other frost-resistant, small sized vegetation. It is somewhat warmer than the higher zone, so that although it is above the tree line, potatoes can be grown there. Still further down the mountain slope is the moist forest (3400–4000 m), characterized by a dense underbrush of small trees and shrubs. It is warmer than higher zones, so that frost-resistant, quick maturing crops are grown in addition to potatoes.

The lower montane savannah (2850–3400 m) is immediately below the moist forest. The central town is located in the savannah and most of Quinua's population lives here. It is Quinua's major cultivation region, and most of its fields are irrigated. The savannah is divided internally on the basis of irrigation use and altitude into two regions: the upper savannah (3050–3400 m) and lower savannah (2850–3050 m) (Mitchell 1976a, 1977). Immediately below the savannah lies the lower montane thorn steppe (2500–2850 m). This zone is much warmer, sunnier, and drier than the higher ecological zones. It is covered with cactus and in some areas the vegetative cover may be called a cactus forest. The thorn steppe is unirrigated. It is too dry to be maintained with the very limited irrigation water descending from the savannah, so that only plants with low water needs are grown. In the valley bottom, however, plentiful water is obtained from the Rio Chacco. Consequently, the valley bottom is irrigated so that land use differs here from the thorn steppe. It is for this reason that I treat the valley bottom as a separate ecological zone, even though vegetatively it is a part of the thorn steppe.

CULTIVATION SEQUENCE

The sequence in which fields are sown is determined by the type of crop, the agricultural cycle, and location of the field in the series of vertical ecozones. With the exception of maize, the type of crop sown is a minor factor by itself, since it ordinarily means a difference of just a few days or a week. Maize, however, is always the first crop to be sown, since it has the longest growing season and is therefore the one in which timing is of the most importance.

The agricultural cycle is of greater importance to the cultivation sequence than is the type of crop (see Table 5.2). Quinua has two agricultural cycles: a dry season cycle (the *michka*) and a rainy season cycle (*hatun tarpuy*). Different fields are used for each crop cycle. Although the rainy season cycle is found in all ecological zones with agriculture, the dry season cycle is restricted to the valley bottom portion of the thorn steppe and to a small proportion of the fields in the upper savannah. Dry season crops require irrigation and only these zones have sufficient water to plant them.

In the savannah, dry season crops are planted early, usually at the beginning of August. This early planting is sometimes used for double-cropping. Two quick maturing crops are planted in succession. The second crop is planted after the first one is harvested; the time of the second planting depends

TABLE 5.2
Quinua Cultivation Sequence by Ecological Zone.

	Cultivation sequence	
Ecological zone	Dry season planting (*michka*)	Rainy season planting (*hatun tarpuy*)
Alpine rain tundra and subalpine wet Paramo	None	None
Montane prairie	None	November–December
Montane moist forest	None	November–December
Lower montane savannah	August November–April	September–December
Lower Montane thorn steppe	None	December
Valley bottom	As needed	As needed

upon the maturation time of the initial crop. If the early crop is quick maturing, then the second crop is planted in November or December. Sometimes the second crop is planted as late as early April. Generally, however, the land land lies fallow between dry season crops. People usually plant the dry season cycle in the savannah to have an early harvest rather than to double crop.

In the valley bottom, irrigation water is plentiful, so that a dry season planting is the rule rather than the exception. Here the dry season planting is always used for double cropping. Because of the abundance of water and the warm climate, farming in the valley bottom is continuous throughout the year. Unlike other areas of Quinua, there is no established time for sowing the fields. One crop is planted after the harvest of another.

The more important, and more widespread, agricultural cycle is the rainy season planting. It produces most of the district's foodstuff and is present in all the ecological zones that are farmed. In the montane prairie and moist forest, the two highest zones with agriculture, the rainy season crops are planted in November or December with the onset of the rains. In these zones a limited repertoire of frost resistant and quick maturing crops are grown without irrigation (Mitchell 1976a, 1976b).

In the lower montane savannah the sequence for planting the rainy season crops depends upon altitude. In the upper portion of the savannah the crops are usually planted over a period of several months. Planting starts in the highest altitudes of the savannah in September and the sequence of planting descends, field by field, until the final fields are planted with the onset of the rains in December. This order is determined by the physical requirements of agriculture in this zone, rather than by status. Farming in the upper portions of the savannah is made possible by irrigation. Irrigated farming is a widespread and ancient Andean method that permits the cultivation of crops—especially maize—at higher altitudes than would be possible with rainfall alone (Mitchell 1976a, 1977; Murra 1960). The physical requirements of such agriculture (such variables as frost, maturation time of crops, duration of rainy season, and amount of irrigation water) require that higher altitudes be cultivated first (Mitchell 1976a, 1977).

In the lower montane thorn steppe, the time for planting the rainy season cycle is in December with the onset of the rains. In the valley bottom portion of the thorn steppe, however, the rainy season crops are planted whenever the dry season crops are harvested. This is the only area of Quinua in which there is sufficient irrigation water to permit planting without strict considerations of timing.

In sum, the agricultural cycle in Quinua begins in August with the cultivation of the dry season planting (see Table 5.3). It continues with the beginning of the rainy season planting in September in the upper regions of the savannah. The rainy season planting is sown successively as irrigation water moves week by week down the slope in a predetermined sequence. In November and December, the rainy season planting is sown in the montane moist forest and

TABLE 5.3
Quinua Planting Calendar

	Lower Montane Savannah				Lower Montane Thorn Steppe	
Month	Montane prairie	Montane moist forest	Upper savannah	Lower savannah	Upper thorn steppe	Valley bottom
August	–	–	Dry season cycle	–	–	continuous
September	–	–	Rainy season cycle	–	–	continuous
October	–	–	Rainy season cycle	–	–	continuous
November	Rainy season cycle	Rainy season cycle	Rainy season cycle Second crop in dry season cycle	–	–	continuous
December	Rainy season cycle	Rainy season cycle	Rainy season cycle Second crop in dry season cycle	Rainy season cycle	Rainy season cycle	continuous
January–April	–	–	Second crop in dry season cycle	–	–	continuous

montane prairie, the two highest zones with agriculture in Quinua. When the rains come in full force, sometime in December, the remainder of the savannah and the entire thorn steppe are sown with the rainy season crops. In addition, when the dry season planting in the upper savannah is harvested in November or December, or sometimes as late as January through April, a rainy season planting may be sown to replace it. Finally, in the valley bottom section of the thorn steppe, where irrigation water is abundant, planting is continuous throughout the year.

The staggered planting season has a distinct advantage in work organiztion. People ordinarily have fields in several ecozones in order to maximize crop production (Mitchell 1976b). The types of crops grown differ at different altitudes. Moverover, the vagaries of agricultural success frequently differ depending on altitude—so that if crops fail in one zone they may nonetheless do very well in another. In addition, however, the strategy of different fields in different ecozones allows a person to sow his fields in succession, thus staggering the workload.

Discussion

It is apparent from the preceding data that the major determinant of cultivation sequence, aside from consideration of the type of cultigen, is the planting cycle and altitude. The complexity of the planting sequence, as illustrated in Tables 5.2 and 5.3, is required by the nature of the adaptation to Quinua's vertical ecology. If the contemporary adaptation in Quinua is pre-Columbian in origin, it is highly improbable that the agricultural sequences given by the chroniclers could ever have taken precedence over the planting times required by agricultural realities. This is especially true for the rainy-cycle cultivation of irrigated lands in the savannah. Here altitude is the major factor determining the sequence of cultivation.

Higher altitudes are sown first in a rigid sequence in which people speak of not allowing their turn to pass them by. Under such circumstances it is highly improbable that large chunks of land—those of the state and religion—would have been taken out of sequence and cultivated first. It is not only unnecessary, but it would have been very poor agricultural practice. An important element in the altitude sequence is rain. If, for example, lower altitudes were sown before the higher altitudes, the lower altitude seedlings would reach juvenile size before the rains began in December, for maturation is quicker in the warmer and sunnier lower altitudes. Consequently, the probability is great that the crops would be lost for lack of water.[4]

Possibly the fields of the religion, state, and peasants were distributed in

[4] It is true that at the present time certain people are permitted to cultivate their lands out of turn (Mitchell 1976a). However, the difference is usually one of only a week or so. Any significant change in the sequence would threaten the success of the crop.

vertical bands along the mountain slope. In this case, the agricultural sequences given by the chroniclers may have been possible. However, such a distribution of agricultural fields is not very probable since there is no indication of it in the chronicles. Nor would it make ecological sense, for Andean agricultural land cannot be adequately delineated by vertical bands. In Quinua, for example, cultivated land is separated by severely eroded ravines. Any attempt to divide the terrain into three vertical bands would arbitrarily divide topographic units. Such topographic unity is a basic feature in delineating modern hamlet divisions in Quinua and there is no reason to presume that this was not true in the past as well. Moreover, there are two irrigation systems in Quinua and these provide an ecological basis for the division of the community into two barrios (Mitchell 1976a). It is difficult to see how this dual division could have been incorporated into three vertical bands.

My argument thus far rests on the assumptions that the adaptation found in Quinua is (*a*) common throughout the Andes and (*b*) basically pre-Columbian in origin. The evidence for both assumptions is not as complete as I would like. However, the data suggest that my assumptions are not unwarranted. It is apparent, for example, that the exploitation of vertical ecozones is an adaptive strategy found throughout the highlands (cf. Arnold 1975; Brush 1976; Custred 1973; Fonseca 1972; Gade 1975; Mitchell 1976a, 1976b; Rhoades and Thompson 1975; Thomas 1973; Vallee 1971; Webster 1971). Although the data do not allow more precise comparisons, in those cases where agricultural sequences are mentioned, agricultural labor is closely coordinated with crop needs (Brush 1977a, 1977b:99–103; Orlove 1977:112–119). It is true that the ecological adaptation found in Quinua is not present on the coast, so that it is possible that the sequences described by the chroniclers could have been found in this area. This matter can only be resolved through further empirical research into coastal agriculture, although even here I would suggest that crop needs would have taken precedence over any status sequence.

There is also ethnohistorical evidence that the exploitation of vertical ecozones is pre-Columbian, but unfortunately the data lack descriptive detail. Murra (1960, 1968, 1972) has demonstrated that human adaptation to vertical ecozones is a basic Andean pattern that is pre-Columbian in origin. Moreover, he specifically shows that irrigation was used aboriginally to raise the upper limit of maize cultivation (Murra 1960:395). In contemporary Quinua, much of the agricultural sequence is determined by the role of irrigation in raising the upper limit of maize cultivation (Mitchell 1976a, 1977). Consequently, it is very probable that similar sequences occurred in pre-Columbian times wherever irrigation was similarly used.

In sum, I have demonstrated that (*a*) the chroniclers were contradictory on the nature of the agricultural sequences; (*b*) modern authors have generally accepted one or the other sequence uncritically without resolving the historiographic problems raised by the contradictions within the chronicles; (*c*) neither of the sequences given by the chroniclers is in accord with the needs of contemporary agriculture in Quinua; and (*d*) the probability that an agricultural sequence similar to Quinua's was common in pre-Columbian highland Peru.

If my assumption that there is a continuity between present and pre-Columbian agricultural adaptation is correct, then the question remains as to the significance of the sequences given by the chroniclers. It should be kept in mind that there are several problems with the chronicles as factual sources. The chroniclers had their own axes to grind (cf. Gibson 1948:12, 107–115; Means 1928). For example, it is possible that Spanish interest in Indian tribute affected their reporting of Inca labor patterns. It is also possible that native informants were reticent about giving full and accurate information about their labor obligations. For example, Murra (1970:11) reports that in the attempts during the *Visitas* to obtain data on land tenure "the respondents are so aware of the threat to their resources implicit in the inquiry that the words are guarded and the information sketchy." A similar sensitivity is still found in the Andes today. A further problem results from the tendency of chroniclers to borrow from one another without attribution. Many of the statements about the agricultural sequences in the chronicles are so similar that it is very probable that they were borrowed. However, these and similar problems must be left to the ethnohistorian to resolve.

Nonetheless, there are two explanations of the agricultural sequences in the chronicles which can be dealt with here. First, it is possible that the sequences were "all other things being equal" statements. If the requirements of crop cultivation were met, then the status sequences applied. I believe this to be very unlikely, at least for the Sierra. The etic agricultural sequence has so many environmental constraints that the sequences given by the chroniclers would have been of very minor importance in organizing agricultural labor. Instead, I believe a second explanation is more likely: The chroniclers are reporting elite ideology. This appears to be a common problem with the chronicles. Murra (1961:47), for example, reports that the European chroniclers often misunderstood the internal organization of the peasant community and relied too heavily on informants among the Inca elite. We would very quickly criticize a modern researcher who relied primarily on elite informants in describing contemporary land tenure arrangements and labor organization. Nonetheless, we have uncritically accepted the statements of the chroniclers. This is despite knowing that the Inca, like all states, had an ideology suitable for its political needs. For reasons of state, the Inca created a legal fiction in which llamas and alpacas and "all lands and other strategic resources were. . .defined as 'belonging' to the state. This [ideology] did not correspond to functional reality [Murra 1965:203]."

Indeed, the very existence of a division of lands into peasant holdings and those of the kings and religion may be too simple (Murra 1970:11). The agricultural work sequences, therefore, are probably statements of Imperial ideology. In this sense it is significant that the agricultural sequences in the chronicles are often found after a discussion of what happens to lands conquered by the Inca. The account could possibly be part of the myth perpetuated by the chroniclers (cf. Means 1925) that prior to the Inca all was disorder; that the Inca conquered territory and created an orderly administration in which the lands were divided into three parts and cultivated in sequence.

Conclusions

Data from contemporary Quinua demonstrate that the Inca agricultural sequences given by the chroniclers are improbable, for they would have ignored the realities of Andean agriculture. In so doing, they also indicate the general utility of contemporary ethnographic data for historical interpretation. Moreover, the methodology used here, which allows us to test general statements found in the chronicles with concrete data, is applicable to other problems and to other areas of the world. A people's economic organization is closely related to its ecological adaptation. If the ecological adaptation in the present is consistent with that of the past, then statements we make about economic relations from the ethnohistoric and archaeological record should be consistent with what can be proven as possible in the present. This is an additional and important—but, in fact, a little used standard (cf. Price 1974, Chapter 6 of this volume)—to test the validity of ethnohistoric data.

References

Acosta, El P. J. de
1962 *Historia natural y moral de las Indias* [1590]. Edicion preparada por Edmundo O'Gorman. Mexico: Fondo de Cultura Economica.

Arnold, D. E.
1975 Ceramic ecology of the Ayacucho basin, Peru: Implications for prehistory. *Current Anthropology 16*:183–205.

Arriaga, P. J. de
1968 Extirpación de la Idolatria del Pirú [1621]. *Biblioteca de Autores Españoles,* vol. 209. Madrid: Ediciones Atlas. Pp. 193–277.

Baudin, L.
1961a *A socialist empire: The Incas of Peru* (K. Woods, Trans., and A. Goodard, Ed.). New York: D. Van Nostrand Company.
1961b *Daily life in Peru* (W. Bradford, Trans.) London: George Allen and Unwin.

Bowman, I.
1916 *The Andes of southern Peru; Geographical reconnaissance along the seventy-third meridian.* New York: Greenwood Press. (Reprinted, 1968.)

Brush, S. B.
1976 Man's use of an Andean ecosystem. *Human Ecology 4*:147–166.

1977a The myth of the idle peasant: Employment in a subsistence economy. In *Peasant livelihood; Studies in economic anthropology and cultural ecology,* (R. Halperin and J. Dow, Eds.). New York: St. Martin's Press. Pp. 60–78.

1977b *Mountain, field, and family: The economy and human ecology of an Andean valley.* Philadelphia: University of Pennsylvania Press.

Cobo, B.

1964 Historia del nuevo mundo [1653]. *Obras del P. Bernabe Cobo,* vol. 2. Madrid: Biblioteca de Autores Españoles.

Custred, G.

1973 Puna zones of the south central Andes. Paper presented at the symposium "Cultural adaptations to mountain ecosystems," 72nd Annual Meeting of the American Anthropological Association, New Orleans, 28 November–2 December 1973.

Fonseca Martel, C.

1972 La Economía "vertical" y la economía de mercado en las comunidades Alteñas del Peru. In *Visita de la provincia de León De Huanuco en 1562,* Tomo 2:315–337. Huanuco: Universidad Nacional Hermilio Valdizan.

Freeman, L. G.

1968 A theoretical framework for interpreting archeological materials. In *Man the hunter* (R. B. Lee and I. DeVore, Eds.). Chicago: Aldine. Pp. 262–267.

Gade, D.

1975 Plants, man and the land in the Vilcanota valley of Peru. *Biogeographica,* vol. 6. The Hague: Dr. W. Junk B.V.

Garcilaso de la Vega, El Inca

1963 Comentarios reales de los Incas [1604]. *Obras completas del Inca Garcilaso de la Vega,* vol. 2. Madrid: Biblioteca de Autores Españoles.

Gibson, C.

1948 *The Inca concept of sovereignty and the spanish administration in Peru.* Austin: The University of Texas Press.

Gumerman, G. J., and D. A. Phillips, Jr.

1978 Archeology beyond anthropology. *American Antiquity 43*:184–191.

Harris, M.

1968a *The rise of anthropological theory.* New York: Thomas Y. Crowell.

1968b Comments. In *New perspectives in archeology* (S. R. Binford and L. R. Binford, Eds.). Chicago: Aldine. Pp. 359–361.

Holdridge, L. R.

1947 Determination of world plant formations from simple climatic data. *Science 105*:367–368.

Hunt, E., and R. C. Hunt

1974 Irrigation, conflict, and politics: A Mexican case. In *Irrigation's impact on society* (T. E. Downing and M. Gibson, Eds.). Anthropological Papers of the University of Arizona, No. 25. Pp. 129–157.

Josephy, A. M.

1968 *The Indian Heritage of America.* New York: Bantam Books.

Katz, F.

1972 *The ancient American civilizations* (K. M. L. Simpson, Trans.). New York: Praeger.

Lanning, E. P.

1967 *Peru before the Incas.* Englewood Cliffs, New Jersey: Prentice Hall.

Martin, L.

1974 *The kingdom of the sun; A short history of Peru.* New York: Charles Scribner's Sons.

Mason, J. A.

1968 *The ancient civilizations of Peru.* New York: Penguin Books.

Mayer, E.

1977 Tenencia y control comunal de la tierra: Caso de Laraos (Yauyos). *Cuadernos, no. 24–25*:59–72.

Mead, C. W.
1935 *Old civilizations of Inca land.* New York: Cooper Square Publishers. (Reprinted 1972).

Means, P. A.
1925 A study of ancient Andean social institutions. *Transactions of the Connecticut Academy of Arts and Sciences.* Vol. 27. Pp. 407–469.
1928 *Biblioteca Andina.* New Haven: Transactions of the Connecticut Academy of Arts and Sciences. Vol. 29. Pp. 271–525. (Reprinted in 1973 by Blaine Ethridge Books, Detroit.)

Metraux, A.
1969 *The history of the Incas* (G. Ordish, Trans.). New York: Random House.

Mitchell, W. P.
1974 *Status inconsistency and dimensions of rank in the central Peruvian highlands.* Paper presented at the symposium on "Social Stratification in the Andes." 41st International Congress of Americanists, Mexico City.
1976a Irrigation and community in the central Peruvian highlands. *American Anthropologist 78*:25–44.
1976b Social adaptation to the mountain environment of an Andean village. In *Hill Lands: Proceedings of an International Symposium* (J. Luchop, J. D. Cawthon, and M. Breslin, Eds.). Morgantown: West Virginia University Press.
1977 Irrigation farming in Peru: Evolutionary implications. In *Studies in peasant livelihood* (R. Halperin and J. Dow, Eds.). New York: St. Martin's Press.

Murra, J. V.
1960 Rite and crop in the Inca state. In *Culture in history* (S. Diamond, Ed.). New York: Columbia University Press. Pp. 393–407.
1961 Social structural and economic themes in Andean ethnohistory. *Anthropological Quarterly* 34:47–59.
1965 Herds and herders in the Inca state. In *Man, culture and animals: The role of animals in human ecological adjustments* (A. Leeds and A. P. Vayda, Eds.). Washington, D.C.: American Association for the Advancement of Science.
1968 An Aymara kingdom in 1567. *Ethnohistory 15*:115–151.
1970 Current research and prospects in Andean ethnohistory. *Latin American Research Review 5*:3–36.
1972 El 'control vertical' de un maximo de pisos ecológicos en la economía de las sociedades andinas. In *Visita de la Provincia de León de Huanuco en 1562; Iñigo Ortiz de Zuñiga, visitador* (John V. Murra, Ed.) Tomo 2:427–476. Huanuco (Peru): Universidad Nacional Hermilio Valdizan.

Murua, F. M. de
1946 Historia del origen y genealogía real de los Reyes Incas de Peru [1590] (C. Bayle, Ed.) Madrid: Biblioteca Missionalia Hispanica, Instituto Santo Toribio de Mogrovejo.

Orlove, B. S.
1977 *Alpacas, sheep, and men: The wool export economy and regional society in southern Peru.* New York: Academic Press.

Osborne, H.
1952 *Indians of the Andes; Aymaras and Quechuas.* New York: Cooper Square Publishers (Reprinted 1972).

Peattie, R.
1936 *Mountain geography: A critique and field study.* New York: Greenwood Press (reprinted).

Polo de Ondegardo, El Licenciado
1916 Informaciones acerca de la religion y gobierno de los Incas [1571] (H. H. Urteaga, Ed.) *Coleccion de libros y documentos referentes a la historia del Peru,* tomo 3. Lima: Imprenta y Libreria Sanmarti y Ca.

Prescott, W. H.
1874 *History of the conquest of Peru.* Philadelphia: J. B. Lippincott.

Price, B. J.
1974 The burden of the cargo: Ethnographical models and archeological inference. In *Mesoamerican archaeology; New approaches* (N. Hammond, Ed.). London: Duckworth.

Reid, J. J., M. B. Schiffer, and W. L. Rathie
1975 Behavioral archaeology: Four strategies. American Anthropologist 77:864–869.

Rhoades, R. E., and S. I. Thompson
1975 Adaptive strategies in Alpine environments: Beyond ecological particularism. *American Ethnologist* 2:535–551.

Rivera, J.
1967 *El clima de Ayacucho*. Universidad, Organo de Extensión Cultural de la Universidad Nacional de San Cristobal de Huamanga (Ayacucho), Año 3, No. 9.
1971 *Geografia General de Ayacucho*. Ayacucho: Universidad Nacional de San Cristobal de Huamanga, Direccion Universitaria de Investigación.

Rivero, M., and J. Von Tschudi
1854 *Peruvian antiquities* (F. L. Hawks, Trans.) New York: Kraus Reprint. (Reprinted 1971.)

Rowe, J. H.
1946 Inca culture at the time of the Spanish conquest. In *Handbook of South American Indians*. Vol. 2: *The Andean civilizations* (Julian H. Steward, Ed.). Washington, D.C.: Bureau of American Ethnology, Bulletin 143.

Schiffer, M. B.
1975 Archaeology as behavioral science. *American Anthropologist* 77:836–848.
1976 *Behavioral archeology*. New York: Academic Press.

Steward, J. H., and L. C. Faron
1959 *Native peoples of South America*. New York: McGraw Hill.

Thomas, R. B.
1973 Human adaptation to a high Andean energy flow system. *Occasional Papers in Anthropology*, No. 7. University Park: The Pennsylvania State University.

Tosi, J. A.
1960 Zonas de vida natural en el Perú. *Instituto Interamericano de Ciencias Agrícolas de la OEA Zona Andina, Boletin Técnico*, No. 5. Lima: Organización de Estados Americanos.

Vallee, L.
1971 La ecologia subjetiva como un elemento esencial de la Verticalidad. *Actas y Memorias del 39 Congreso Internacional de Americanistas*, Vol. 3:167–173.

Valcárcel, L. E.
1964 Historia del Peru Antiguo, vol. 2. *Economía, politica, derecho y moral*. Lima: Editorial Universitaria S.A.

Velasco, J. de
1841 *Historia del reino de Quito en la America meridional*. Tomo 2 y parte 2. Quito: Imprenta de Gobierno, por Juan Campuzano.

Von Hagen, V. W.
1961 *Realm of the Incas*. New York: The New American Library.

Webster, S. S.
1971 An indigenous Quechua community in exploitation of multiple ecological zones. *Actas y Memorias del 39 Congreso Internacional de Americanistas*, Vol. 3:174–183.

Wobst, H. M.
1978 The Archaeo-ethnology of hunter-gatherers or the tyranny of the ethnographic record in archaeology. *American Antiquity* 43:303–309.

6 The Truth Is Not in Accounts but in Account Books: On the Epistemological Status of History

BARBARA J. PRICE

Introduction

Contemporary anthropology has singularly failed to address a number of metatheoretical issues not, however, lacking potential significance for the field as a whole. Treatment of these problems has accordingly remained on an ad hoc basis, scattershot, empiricist, and inductive, unlikely therefore to lead to the establishment of broad and systematic canons of proof. There must be some way to determine that a statement—in the case of this chapter, a historical account—is "true," and in what ways and with what probability. The fact that these issues are raised at all is a function of the general intellectual framework that generates this discussion. One of its focal problems is that of the regularity of ideological phenomena, the extent to which they can be explained with reference to other aspects of the behavior stream, notably to the technoeconomic conditions of life. Another related focus, given a central diachronic example drawn from history, will necessarily entail the justification of analogical reasoning as a productive means of reconstructing certain behaviors no longer directly observable. This in turn opens questions of the nature of evidence in the social sciences, and of the role of paradigm in the logic of explanation.

Relations among the social sciences, particularly between history and anthropology and the bridge between them—ethnohistory—can be viewed from the standpoint of the processes used to verify or falsify statements generated in these various disciplines; such processes—functions rather of paradigm, not, in fact, of subject matter—act to differentiate them as fields of inquiry. Although this chapter treats a historical topic, its purpose is not the tradi-

BEYOND THE MYTHS OF CULTURE
Essays in Cultural Materialism

ISBN 0-12-598180-5

tional textual or structural analysis, which would call for methods distinctive to itself and lying beyond the scope of the present discussion. Its central example is admittedly a trivial one, selected on grounds of its general familiarity but used to make certain nontrivial epistemological points concerning the nature of proof of certain types of historical statement.

On Classes of Historical Evidence

Derived from a paradigm, a research strategy directs the search for information and determines the relevance of the answers to the questions. Contrary to much common usage, the term does not technically refer to the methodology of data collection, storage, or retrieval. A research strategy generates theory, the test of which is not primarily or exclusively against data, but against a hierarchical network of increasingly more general and inclusive theory to the level of the paradigm, the broadest and most general statement of problem and of investigative strategies and priorities. Underwriting this discussion is the paradigm of cultural materialism and cultural evolution, which holds that the central problem of anthropology—the explanation of the similarities and differences, of stability and change in human cultures—is most broadly and parsimoniously investigated by giving priority to the material conditions of life. Data in turn may be consistently evaluated with reference to concepts of adaptation, selection, and relative bioenergetic efficiency; causality is viewed as systemic, governed by the operation of positive and negative feedback loops. In the course of this discussion, this paradigm will be applied consistently and noneclectically to all classes of data treated.

Even the material conditions of life, however, are amenable to investigation from at least two contrasting, competing research strategies. In an emic strategy, verification or falsification of statements concerning such conditions (or anything else) is a function of the perception or point of view of the actors or participants in the system: Their judgments of correctness and of relative importance become the standards for assessing the truth of a statement or proposition. By contrast (Harris 1964, 1968), the test of an etic strategy and of the statements it generates is observer-oriented; as such, it is dependent upon the characteristics of the system, and not upon those characteristics as mediated through the perceptions of the actors. An etic strategy thus requires consistent operationalization of basic concepts to secure the intersubjective agreement upon which the canons of proof are based.

While themselves neither emic nor etic, some data lend themselves more easily to investigation by one strategy or the other. This leads to a number of ironies in American anthropology, and is not without implications for the relations among the subfields of the discipline. Much of the development of anthropology has emphasized an idealist paradigm (i.e., that human behavior is a function of ideas, values, beliefs, wills, etc., and is best explained by reference to such mental constructs), and an essentially emic research strategy, both of which may, but need not, be applied to ethnographic data (Harris 1968). Such a strategy applied for instance to archaeological data is, however, unproductive in that the informant concurrence necessary to falsify a statement is unavailable. It is unfortunate that such difficulty has not in practice acted as a significant deterrent. This problem may be reflected in numerous recent statements that archaeology requires its own "theory." The apparent weakness that its data cannot be used to test emic propositions is actually a source of strength for archaeology, which could then become thoroughly consonant with an etic ethnology carried out under a materialist paradigm. A major limitation in the emic strategy is revealed by such a contretemps: Because an etic strategy is capable of dealing with a wider range of phenomena, it fulfills one of the basic epistemological conditions wherein one may deem it more powerful than its competitor.

Archaeology, perhaps in part for the reasons just cited, seems impressionistically to heave a collective sigh of relief when ethnohistorically documented periods are encountered. The increased ethnographic richness of description is undeniable, but only a part of the situation; it is the advent of ethnohistoric materials that permits at last (but need not force) the employment of both the idealist paradigm and the emic research strategy that dominate American anthropology. One result in syntheses of sequences where the latest periods are known from written records is a peculiar eclecticism, where paradigms are tacitly switched in midstream. Comparability between parts of such sequences is lost, as is the consistent basis for retrodiction, or for any verifiable diachronic propositions. Thus one often encounters the retrodiction of essentially emic conclusions, including details of ideology and the meanings of symbols, into preceding periods where only etically-derived or -analyzable data are extant. This eclecticism precludes consistent means to verify or falsify—each member of the statement retains its own distinct canon, noncomparable with that of any other. On these grounds an analogy of this type is seen to be procedurally cross-paradigmatic, impossible of confirmation and therefore epistemologically illegitimate. A later section of this chapter will develop the point that analogical reasoning, like any means of generating testable lawlike propositions, cannot proceed in a paradigmatic vacuum.

Ethnohistory appears to occupy an intermediate epistemological position between anthropology on the one hand, and history on the other. A more awkward position is frankly difficult to imagine. Where anthropology is generalizing in principle, history must deal with the particular. Scientific statements of the changing properties of cultural systems are nomothetic, but historical events by their nature occur only once. This does not deny the presence of nomothetic elements in the context of historical events (even the idiosyncratic event, in all its particularity, is governed by the probabilities of human behavior)—only that it is philosophically optional to historians to look for them or analyze them, but incumbent upon anthropologists to do so. It follows that the tests for truth are different. Nomothetic statements, like all of science, are inherently probabilistic. We are dealing with correlations: The stronger the correlation generated by a theory, the stronger that theory vis-à-vis competing theories. Probabilism, however, means that we do not expect a correlation of 100%; differently phrased, it means that the single counter-example lacks the power to falsify. But probabilism is clearly inapplicable to the inherently unique event, and thus for a historical question it must first, minimally, be established that the event occurred. This form of verification differs sharply from the demonstration of a process that is in essence replicable and capable of reconstruction on the basis of the principle of uniformitarianism. And when idiosyncratic events are considered, a probabilistic reconstruction will be unsatisfactory in principle.

On the basis of differential reliability of evidence, the body of material termed "ethnohistoric" includes several classes. Reliability involves problems different from those involved in the assessment of authenticity or derivation of sources, determination of which requires techniques of historiography and bibliography not at present germane; instead it entails evaluation of the quality of evidence. Tey (1951) deals extensively with this question, noting that it is not always easy to distinguish an elicited statement from an eyewitness report, the description of ideal from that of actual behavior—what constitutes account books (records of the flow of energy within and between systems) from what are merely accounts. A Class I of ethnohistoric data—direct records of lawsuits, land and tax registrations, court proceedings, etc.—poses the fewest problems of reliability; unlike most documentary data they are almost entirely etic, reflecting their specific, restricted function in the system that produced them. They are account books, ongoing working records that never served per se as historical documents and that therefore involved little contemporary interpretation or deliberate manipulation.

Mitchell's example (Chapter 5 of this volume) is an instance of Class II, involving the description of native practices by foreign conquerors whose reports commingle, in unknown proportions, eyewitness observations with informant statements. Much of this documentation is a response to contemporary political, administrative, taxation, military, and directed-acculturative needs; on both the sides of informant and of recorder there are deliberate axes to grind. Use of such documents requires some valid techniques for sorting out emic from etic material, accounts from account books. Inconsistencies in what was ostensibly a description of Andean agriculture led to Mitchell's conclusion that this is the elicited account of an informant who may never have observed the practices in question, but who was well-grounded in the ideological system of his own culture. Within the corpus of documents itself there is no consistent control capable of making these distinctions except on an ad hoc basis: if analysis is restricted to the documents themselves without measurement against independent noninternal evidence (as has been

Mitchell's procedure), no internal differences in reliability of statements can emerge.

Class III, including the central example in this chapter, comprises a people's own record of its history, reduced to writing either by themselves or by conquerors. Considered strictly as a chronicle of events, this material constitutes the least reliable type of evidence. Entirely emic by nature, these data can be interpreted to yield etic conclusions in ways doubtless quite alien to the original "intentions" of the authors, once methods for doing so are developed. As previously suggested, and as Mitchell has done in his Andean agriculture example, that body of method involves regular competitive tests against non-internal evidence, and against a nonhistorical paradigm. The impression is that resistance to employing such a noninternal test may be somewhat less in the case of Class III than in that of other kinds of ethnohistoric data—perhaps more willingness to consider the material to be strictly accounts, "intended" among other purposes to make Our Side look good to a posterity very much in view. Many of these texts, moreover, served quite specific synchronic purposes as well, purposes of propaganda and of factional or individual glorification; these fall into a category we may call political myth. In such cases it is actually the synchronic function that explains their continued presence in the cultural system in question: But this function will not become apparent if documentary statements are "proved" only with reference to other documentary statements, without testing against external evidence of the state of that system.

Verification by testing against the nomothetic is a means of placing the burden of proof squarely upon the inherently particularist historical account. In this chapter the course taken is that falsification of such individual events is possible only indirectly, by demonstrating their membership in a class of events with internal inconsistencies such as to render their existence highly improbable. Mitchell does this in his demonstration that ecological constraints upon Andean agriculture render the system described by the chronicler impossible. It is not merely that these tasks are performed in a given way in the present (and might have been done differently in the past) but rather that a system of intensive agriculture with that mix of crops in that region can work only in some way comparable to what we observe today. Unless we suspend the uniformitarian concept of causality, these same constraints operated in the same ways in the past, producing the same effects: The chronicler's account is, must be, of the idealized prescription for investment of labor and payment of taxes—regardless of actual behavior upon which direct selection pressure operates. Underlying this falsification procedure is the hierarchical principle that the more specific statement cannot contradict the more generalized one, where both belong to the same universe. Thus the unique event must be contrasted against processes regularly explicable on a consistent uniformitarian, probabilistic basis. While this is not a direct test of historicity, it may lead to the conclusion that a passage contains no historicity whatever; paradoxically, as the following section will show, the procedure is capable of revealing considerable information on the state of the system—nomothetic generalizations, testable through other means.

The nature of evidence and the canons of proof to which it is subject will determine the quality of analogical (or any other) reasoning; reasoning from analogy, however, when used diachronically, evokes considerable ambivalence. Used synchronically it poses fewer logical problems and raises no doubts whatever: It is then called the comparative method, and constitutes one of the principal foundations of anthropological thinking. Partly the result of excesses, especially of the unfalsifiable procedurally cross-paradigm type, the skepticism attaching to this procedure is perhaps more generally a function of the eclecticism of American anthropology in general. No comparability can be established among statements analyzed from different premises; where the tests of right and wrong differ from each member of a statement there is no nonarbitrary way to establish a deductive link between them. Analogies drawn from history are not, however, without some popularity as a means of explaining prehistory on the one hand, contemporary phenomena on the other. Use of historical analogy is clearly legitimate, but only when appropriate procedures are designed for such use; a historical paradigm, oddly, does not accomplish this well.

This chapter will therefore treat a native historical account from the standpoint of the problems of type, quality, and quantity of evidence it provides concerning the events it purports to describe. As stated initially, the cultural materialist paradigm will be used to generate explanation at various hierarchic levels, and will serve as a consistent yardstick against which to measure competing explanations and interpretations. Reference to the material and technoeconomic conditions of life, and the application of the comparative method, permit some verifiable reconstruction of the system regardless of the veracity of the Aztecs' account of their own history—suggest in fact why this account reads as it does.

Consistent reference to the system assumes in effect an increased importance for the understanding of an account that formed part of the system, was perpetuated within it, and derived many of its characteristics as a result of that relationship to the larger whole, on the premise that a context governs the limits of probability of actual behaviors selected from a far wider range of what is hypothetically possible. Even once the obviously supernatural events of the story are discounted, the historicity of the residue is perhaps equally suspect as a chronicle of events in time (cf. Raglan 1956). Nomothetic data, information concerning system and process, are paradoxically as achronic and lacking in particularity as mythic data. The two versions of the story used are those of Duran (1964), which as the fuller and more detailed account has been relied upon more heavily—and of Sahagun (1961), a briefer version used primarily as a supplement. The following composite summary stresses those episodes considered most significant for the development of the subsequent arguments.

The Aztec Early Migrations: What Might Have Happened in History

THE MYTH OF AZTEC ORIGINS

The Aztecs, the last of seven tribes to leave Chicomoztoc in the Chichimeca, did so under the aegis of their god Huitzilopochtli in order to seek the Promised Land. The migration took many generations and resulted in the foundation of many settlements along the way, settlements at which temples were built and populations established. The Aztecs seem to have been, or to have become in the course of this trek, at least partly agricultural. On entering the Meseta Central they stopped briefly at Tula, then went on to Tequixquiac where they cultivated borrowed land. At Chapultepec they constructed a fortified camp in anticipation of attack from the armies of Azcapotzalco, Tacuba, Coyoacan, Xochimilco, Colhuacan, and Chalco. Subsequently the Aztecs petitioned the king of Colhuacan for the land on which to settle, and were granted Tizapan—"a wilderness occupied only by vipers and poisonous snakes"—in the king's hopes that the vermin would destroy the Aztecs. The king's emissaries were shocked to find that instead the Aztecs ate the vermin, and were also cultivating the fields and planning a temple. The Aztecs petitioned for rights of trade and intermarriage at Colhuacan.These were granted, and the king's daughter presented as a wife to the Aztec leader; whereupon she was promptly sacrificed and open war precipitated with Colhuacan. Driven from Tizapan, the Aztecs fled, still in search of their Promised Land, omens of which were communicated in the course of the retreat. But the site designated by the omen was an uninhabited tract at the boundaries—not clearly delimited—of the polities of Azcapotzalco, Texcoco, and Colhuacan. All had some degree of claim upon the territory; the Aztecs had none. Duran (1964:31) describes their trepidation in building their first small temple in what was effectively a squatter settlement. Sahagun claims that the Aztecs settled among reeds and rushes because the land belonged to another. In search of wood and stone not found on the island to build a proper temple, the Aztecs considered petitioning alliance with Azcapotzalco, Coyoacan, and Texcoco; Sahagun (1961:196) calls them in fact vassals and subjects of Azcapotzalco. Instead, however, the Aztecs hunted and fished, and sent their wives to sell in those towns on market days. The eventual completion of the temple, of course, marks the foundation of Tenochtitlan.

PRELIMINARY QUESTIONS OF HISTORICAL AUTHENTICITY

The myth of ultimate Northwest Mexican origins of the Aztecs (i.e., in the Chichimeca) has been buttressed somewhat by linguistic reconstruction of this area as the origin of the Uto-Aztecan language family, primarily on grounds that this is the area of contemporary maximal diversity of those languages. But linguistic diversity is a function of diversity of speech communities, and an absence of any overarching imperium to weld the area ever into a single polity (= speech community). In other words, no counterweighting centripetal tendencies were present; all conditions favored linguistic differentiation and diversification through time. Because linguistic reconstruction alone cannot be used to yield reliable geographic information, the Northwest Mexican and Southwestern U.S. Uto-Aztecan groups could equally well be viewed as outliers of a family centered more deeply into Mexico.

On the other hand, if we allow some 200 years (eight generations) for the presumed trek from Chicomoztoc, one would have to postulate a phenomenal rate of demographic growth during that period in order to found, populate, and then leave behind, those intermediate settlements. The traditional dating—that the Aztecs left Aztlan (Chicomoztoc) in A.D. 1090 and reached Tula in A.D. 1163 (73 years, not quite three generations)—posits a situation that is flatly impossible. Unless, of course, one assumes a large initial group of migrants; but the aridity of the Chichimeca precludes the formation of large demographic aggregates. Modes of production are, of necessity, either nomadic hunting-gathering, resembling a rather more productive Basin Shoshone pattern (Steward 1955)—or semisedentary to sedentary oasis agriculture that may be full-time or seasonal depending upon local ecological constraints, and may have resembled the contemporary Pima-Papago or Tarahumara patterns. Any of these possibilities involves considerable circumscription; none favors, nor can support, significant population growth.

It may be argued that it is futile to dispute the truth of this account of ultimate origins, that the origins of any people become lost in time and encrusted in legend. But unless some consistent method applicable equally to all parts of a narrative is developed, rejection of one part merely on the basis of its obvious mythic trappings would be procedurally arbitrary. Here the test against the nomothetic has been used. Even the linguistic evidence of Northwest Mexican origins has, for example, been noted as equivocal. Nor is it possible to make any sense of the demography implied in the account, in that a population would have had to be impossibly above the carrying capacity of its homeland, or reproduce at a rate not consonant with what is known of the biology of the human species. Neither alternative is acceptable. Despite an overtly apparent lack of historicity, it is worth considering even this part of the story; as shall be demonstrated, the question of origins has direct repercussions upon the evaluation of the narrative of the entry into the Basin of Mexico, the entire acculturative spectrum then presented, the changing socioeconomic institutions of the Aztecs, and their relation to the political economy of fourteenth- and fifteenth-century Central Mexico. Reconstruction of what might have happened in history cannot proceed without systemic consideration of all these parameters.

Given the mode of production characterizing the Chichimeca of Northwest Mexico (geographically specified because, significantly, the term occurs also as a pejorative, on the order of "boondocks" or "barbarian" in the Greek sense), one would expect the types of band organization that characterized the area at contact. From Duran's description the Aztecs were at least partly agricultural and semisedentary, politically egalitarian, as were other groups known to be comparable. Yet even in the early phases of their Long March, while they were presumably organized as egalitarian bands, they nonetheless used the foundation of a temple to establish a land claim. Bands, however, are not supposed to behave this way, and in fact do not do so. Such activity implies the production of a regular surplus above subsistence needs, sufficient to permit or warrant diversion of energy in this form; it implies the existence of at least an incipient level of ranking, a form of political organization presupposing some intensification of production and some degree of economic centralization—or, of course, tribalization, where such centralization is imposed. Neither alternative implied by the behavior—incipient ranking or tribalization—is consistent with what must have emigrated from Chicomoztoc; the inconsistency is of a magnitude to render untenable the migration hypothesis.

The foregoing argument builds the foundation for a far more powerful alternative hypothesis: There was no Long March because none was ever necessary. The Aztecs were already essentially there, a marginal group among others at the geographic fringes of the Basin of Mexico, probably from the region northwest of Tula. This is significant for two principal reasons. First, the zone is ecologically clinal, with aridity gradually increasing to the north and west. In wet years, or wet phases of climatic cycling, much of the area is potentially cultivable, particularly with irrigation to reduce the risk. Second, both the wet maximum and the irrigation technology obtained during the Toltec florescence, accounting in all likelihood for the florescence itself and for the location of its capital at Tula (Armillas 1969). Groups inhabiting the area would through time come under increased state impaction from the expanding Toltec and, following Fried (1967, 1975) the result should have been tribalization. The institutions described by Duran conform to Fried's tribal model, and thereby suggest a prolonged and intimate contact of the Aztec with state organizations. For this to have occurred they would have had to live at the margins of the Basin of Mexico itself, in a zone that is an interface between a long-standing heartland of complex stratified societies and the extensive desert that circumscribed their expansion. The West Mexican desert itself was never significantly penetrated by the Central Mexican states (the existence of some trading activity across it does not vitiate this statement), never was incorporated into their political orbits.

Tribes, in Fried's model (cf. also Price 1978a), are formed from the impact of states upon neighboring peoples who are normally egalitarian in organization; because states deal with such institutions only with difficulty, the states tend to impose forms of leadership and other controls with which they can effectively neutralize the population in question. This is consonant in turn with Lattimore's (1940) observation of the mutual acculturation that regularly occurs at frontiers, particularly when the latter are clinal; in some respects the Aztecs, from their account, could be interpreted as resembling the Mongols. But the comparison is overstated; the niche occupied by the Mongols was a pastoral one, absent in Mexico, one which could support larger populations than could the hunting–gathering–cultivation mix of the Chichimec economy. Further the Mongols, unlike the Aztec, were mounted, preadapted technologically for extremely efficient cavalry warfare. In other words, during some phases of China's history, Mongols and Chinese could meet as well-matched adversaries, as would not have been the case for an egalitarian tribal group entering the Basin of Mexico.

Any parallels in this comparison lie principally in the acculturative frontier situation, the fluctuating ecological boundaries, the waxings and wanings of state power in the nuclear area, and the common impacts of states to form tribes. The major differences—which ultimately torpedo this as an analogy—are in the comparative demography, and thus in the critical balance of power relationships deducible from it. In turn, the Aztecs' chances in the Basin of Mexico cannot be calculated in the same way as those of the Mongols in China; any model of a rise to power will have to differ with variations in demographic and technoeconomic conditions. Still bearing in mind the distinction between a historical statement and a statement concerning the nature of the system, we shall examine the acculturative process and the Aztec rise to political dominance.

A MATERIALIST VIEW OF AZTEC HISTORY

Adoption of the tribal model provides the basis for analyzing the evolving adaptation of the Aztec to the ecology and political economy of the Basin of Mexico. Once more the historical narrative will be systematically compared with uniformitarian processes demonstrable on the basis of independent evidence, in an attempt to determine what this "history" is really telling us. To anticipate the expanded discussion below, the Aztec, as a presumably tribal group, were acculturated by means of participation in a series of client relations under the patronage of the established polities on the Meseta Central. Under circumstances of intensification and shift of the mode of production in the fourteenth and fifteenth centuries, this process of "peasantizing" marginal groups seems to have been mutually profitable, especially in the short run and for the patrons. Documented shifts in balance of power relationships in the region are directly linked to shifts in the economy, particularly in its agricultural sector where demands for labor were chronic and increasing.

At Tequixquiac the Aztecs farmed "borrowed land," as they subsequently did at Colhuacan and at Azcapotzalco, where Sahagun flatly terms them "vassals and subjects." Further relationships of this sort were overtly considered on the occasion of the rebuilding of the temple which marks the foundation of Tenochtitlan, but were rejected in favor of more commercial methods of obtaining necessary materials. Clientage of this sort has received relatively little attention in the literature of the area, although Calnek (1977 and personal communication) has independently alluded to such an institution. Apparently some sort of rural proletariat (the specific rents or services owed are not spelled out), nor yet true serfs (clients evidently maintained geographic mobility), they cannot be identified with the later mayeque (serf) class whose origins and status stem at least in part from conquest and appropriation of their lands. In that the Aztecs petitioned Colhuacan for rights of trade and intermarriage, it is probably safe to assume that client groups regularly lacked these privileges as a matter of course. The Colhuacan account, the fullest description in the narrative, implies moreover that client populations were regularly settled in marginal lands; while no evidence is furnished concerning the Tequixquiac sojourn, the Azcapotzalco episode concurs. Given the known demographic and economic context, this point becomes critical in the explanation of the institution of clientage.

State organizations involving large populations, socioeconomic differentiation and stratification, high-energy modes of production, and well-developed urbanism characterized the Meseta Central during at least the entire millenium preceding the rise of Tenochtitlan. The probably pristine emergence of Teotihuacan was based on the shift in the mode of production involving increasing dependence upon a hydraulic agriculture of increasing scale: the Irrigation Revolution. Its capital, with a population of some 125,000, was virtually a primate city, with few if any potentially competing centers of population or of power. This fact implies, first that the overall regional population was small in contrast to that of later times; second, concomitantly, that zones of extremely intensive production were of restricted, oasis-like character and distribution, with most land still cultivated in relatively extensive fashion (cf. Boserup 1965, Price 1977). Post-Teotihuacan demographic and productive trends involved the interrelated processes of population growth and the associated spread of intensive agricultural regimes into all zones capable of supporting them: an intensification of the irrigated mode of production. Observed changes not only of size but of distribution of population provide clear material evidence of these developments, in fact permit their reliable reconstruction. It should be apparent that this "history" is of changing characteristics of the system, with no direct implication of particular idiosyncratic events.

In response, by the fourteenth and fifteenth centuries the settlement pattern had altered concomitantly from a primate city distribution to one involving a series of small competing city-states of some 10,000–30,000 population. The fact that a number of these now constitute districts of modern Mexico City (designations comparable to Greenwich Village, or Harlem, or Washington Heights—all presently neighborhoods of Manhattan but formerly separate communities) emphasizes how small the distances, and hence the states, actually were, and therefore helps to explain the intensity of competition: The civic centers of Tenochtitlan and Tlatelolco are 20 minutes' leisurely walk apart, with continuous settlement between.

While a shift in the mode of production provides an amelioration of an existing man/energy ratio, the intensification of that new mode inevitably leads once more to declining efficiency (Harris 1975, 1977). Niches favorable to the new regime are filled in; once filled in they neither expand nor replicate themselves. Either the system must stabilize demographically and economically at the limit set by this new carrying capacity, or, for expansion to continue, another shift in mode of production is ultimately "required." The endemic warfare among these small city-states, none of which could gain consistent military or economic advantage over the others during this period, is a response to these conditions, and provides part of the evidence from which we infer those conditions.

A further shift in the mode of production was in fact under way at the time of the Aztecs' presumed entry into the Basin of Mexico: the shift to chinampa cultivation (Armillas 1971). Analyzable initially as an aspect of the intensification of the existing hydraulic regime—a means of expanding cultivable land area by drainage and related reclamation operations—in those restricted areas permitting its practice, chinampa agriculture came to produce the bulk of the energy (calories) in those areas: a shift. The settlement of the Aztec clients on marginal lands, not once but repeatedly, makes sense in this context. Marginal lands are defined on the basis of the technological regime of the population exploiting them as those requiring maximal labor investment to create or assure productivity (lands that are marginal in one technological system may not, of course, be so in another).

Probably the most powerful inducement for the occupation of any such lands at all is population pressure—a condition that certainly obtained at this time in Central Mexico. At least twice the Aztecs were settled on land so barren that there was nothing to eat but snakes, lizards, water insects, etc. While Duran's narrative states that it was hoped that these vipers might eat the Aztecs, this was doubtless not the aim of the king of Colhuacan. If one may speak momentarily of motivation, it would be unlikely that he should wish the decimation of his labor force. After an unspecified time his emissary reported "with surprise" that he found the Aztecs cultivating the fields. This suggests the inference that the use of client groups to furnish the labor necessary in land-reclamation projects was probably widespread. Given the competitive pressures exerted by each small state upon the others, it would have been to the advantage of the Colhua king to bring as much of his territory into production as he could: Greater production meant greater population, which in turn meant more cannon fodder. Doubtless his neighbors adopted comparable policies.

Therefore the marriage/sacrifice of the king's daughter is hardly necessary to explain the outbreak of war. If we accept that the clients had successfully reclaimed the wastelands in the kingdom, and the assumption that this reclamation involved chinampa construction, then we must note that the clients were accordingly in de facto possession of the best, most productive, most risk-free agricultural land in Colhuacan. Furthermore, they were building a temple on it (a claim to title), and petitioning the king for, in effect, diplomatic recognition—the rights of trade and intermarriage. Trade in this context almost certainly refers to participation in state-sponsored redistributive exchanges (cf. Price 1978b), not to market trade in subsistence goods. Intermarriage probably implies access to the network of asymmetrical MBD marriages among ruling houses (Calnek 1966), used to reinforce political hierarchies and establish political alliances; this is the real significance of the episode of the king's daughter. Given the existing unstable military and political situation, the constant rises and falls of political fortunes and the fluctuations of local balances of power, the king of Colhuacan could hardly have failed to notice that his clients had become serious political competitors. Nor would he have been likely to countenance the situation, involving as it would have done the partition of his realm. Duran's account of these events manifests a self-pitying tone apparent elsewhere in this narrative of the Aztecs' early adventures. In view of the materially based realities of life, this hardly seems warranted.

The occupation of Tenochtitlan is itself the outgrowth of these general linked processes of intensification and competition. Duran describes the scale of pile driving and landfill operations necessary to create even sufficient dry land for permanent habitation. Unmodified, this island and its immediate vicinity lack any agricultural potential; the investments of capital and labor necessary to produce the modifications are extraordinarily expensive when compared to the problems posed by nearby areas, already inhabited. The title to the island upon which the city of Tenochtitlan was built seems to have been under a cloud; had the area produced anything of value it would probably have been in serious dispute among at least three polities.

This analysis, and no manifest historical destiny or brilliance or charisma of leadership, explains the ultimate hegemony of Tenochtitlan over the Basin of Mexico by the time of the arrival of the Spanish in the sixteenth century. Given the process of a developing shift in the mode of production, those communities having greatest access to the new technoeconomic regime, or more territory permitting its use, will tend to grow economically, demographically, and inevitably politically at the expense of their neighbors. The military and political power of Tenochtitlan was based on its control, direct and/or indirect, of probably the largest continuous expanse of chinampas in the Basin of Mexico. Although the system had, by the Conquest, already come to occupy those niches most easily reclaimed, there are suggestions that its expansion was continuing into more difficult and labor-demanding zones. Under other circumstances the system might have continued to expand to the limits of the swampy lacustrine, high-water-table ecological niche. A glance at a map underscores the locational advantages of Tenochtitlan in the control of the bulk of the existing system, an advantage over even such competing chinampa communities as Xochimilco and Chalco.

FURTHER CONSIDERATION OF AZTEC POLITICAL ECOLOGY

Additional aspects of political economy are documented in the narrative, if indirectly and somewhat casually, and even when the documentation contradicts the thrust of the specifics of the account. Given the preceding discussion, the analysis turns from agricultural system to the linked problems of food availability and local specialization of production. The incident of the vipers is telling, particularly in the king's ostensible hope that the vermin might eat the Aztecs. Duran mentions the horror of the Aztecs' neighbors to find the Aztecs eating the vipers. In conjunction with the argument developed thus far, this is highly suggestive.

Most calories consumed in the contemporary Basin of Mexico derive from the two co-staples, maize and beans, regularly available year-round via a market system which links relatively nearby localities of differentiated production. Both are storable; should either fail the result is widespread famine. Together these crops—consumed at each meal—also provide the bulk of dietary protein for the peasant sector, a protein that is reasonably complete, requiring only occasional supplementation with animal proteins. This section of the discussion will develop the position that the contemporary pattern constitutes an adequate analogue that can be used with some reliability to interpret and explain the relevant aspects of the Aztec system; the epistemological implications will subsequently be explored in greater detail.

One substantive difference between the fourteenth to sixteenth centuries on the one hand and the present system on the other—a difference with a visibility sufficiently great that its functional significance tends to be overly magnified—is the contemporary presence of domestic animals as sources of protein in contrast to their pre-Hispanic absence. In pre-Conquest times dogs and turkeys were the only domestic protein sources; since both ate maize, both competed directly with man and would have been correspondingly expensive to raise. Not that domestic animals are cheap now: Tax (1953) and McBryde (1947) comment for Highland Guatemala on how few communities keep large domesticates, note that only the better-off families have animals, and cite the cost as an explanation. Most contemporary peasants in Mexico and Guatemala raise chickens and turkeys, in spite of the fact that they do not pay for themselves; the practice is a form of insurance against emergency. Neither poultry nor eggs are regularly consumed; eggs are sold in the market for cash, to be converted into maize and beans. Because of this peasant dietary strategy of exchanging protein for calories, many peasant populations are etically vegetarian in diet.

The implication is that the observed presence or absence of a trait in a system does not provide sufficient basis for the untested, unexamined assumption that that trait makes a difference in behavioral terms (Price 1978b). If our reference is the peasant sector, the introduction of domestic quadrupeds has affected the diet very little, certainly not to an extent that would impugn the analogy. Other aspects of the total body of material evidence tend to support this conclusion: There has been little or no impact reflected in the settlement pattern. If a systemic change is fundamental, it should be manifested in changes in the numbers and distributions of populations: This *is* the test, its validity assured by deduction from the paradigm. By and large, however, areas heavily settled in the sixteenth century are still heavily settled; zones which today support few people supported few in Aztec times as well. Carrying capacity has not been significantly altered (industrialization has had far more profound an effect here); no new niches were opened up for settlement as a result of the introduction of European animal domesticates into the Basin of Mexico. Within the paleotechnic sphere, there is far more evidence for comparability of these two systems than there is for noncomparability. Again the analogy stands.

This description can accordingly be taken to hold for the ecosystem of the Basin of Mexico in the fourteenth and fifteenth centuries, a time period characterized by rapid population growth and increasing demographic pressure, by the progressive crystallization of this pattern. As implied above, the energy efficiency in production was probably deteriorating sharply. Kovar (1970) has moreover assembled evidence chronicling a series of more or less severe, uncomfortably frequent famines occurring during the period—an indication that population may have been approaching carrying capacity as determined by the availability of the basic sources of both calories and protein. In some years maize and beans were scarce and expensive; there were years when consumption had to be cut, years when famine and emigration may have acted as temporary Malthusian checks on a population tending ever upward. In this context we find the Aztecs, atop their barren island, with unimpeded access to a storehouse of aquatic protein in relatively efficient packages. All else being equal, those roasted and boiled snakes probably represented a potentially more regular intake of higher quality protein than would have been available to most of the Aztecs' neighbors.

However, the Aztecs seem to have practiced the customary peasant strategy of turning protein into calories; in any case, those supposedly fastidious neighbors were buying these selfsame items in the markets, with, one assumes, a regularity sufficient to keep meat-sellers and fishmongers in business. Sahagun (1961:Book 10) mentions most of these ostensible "vermin" among the wares of these vendors. And when the Aztecs wished to obtain wood and stone to rebuild their original adobe and thatch temple, they rejected a strategy of clientage; they hunted and fished, and sent their wives to sell the meat in the markets of nearby towns. At this point one cannot feel particularly sorry for the "outcaste Aztecs"; one can only become positively irritated with the whining and the crocodile tears. For the purpose of reconstructing an evolving political economy, however, inconsistencies of this sort become extremely significant.

It is an obvious inference that the Aztecs, far from being despised outcastes, were in fact regular participants in an intercommunity symbiotic network linking local populations with different extractive and/or craft specializations. Contemporary local economies whose fundamental material characteristics can be operationalized as comparable provide an analogy on the basis of which the institutional structure of Aztec can be reconstructed, and the probabilities governing the evolution of such phenomena be assessed. Under stated conditions this pattern of locally specialized production in subsistence goods, together with institutions of exchange, may act to raise regional carrying capacity; to the extent that it does so, it can be analyzed as adaptive behavior.

A geographically diverse area such as the Basin of Mexico, with its close juxtaposition of distinctive ecological zones and spotty distribution of resources, would tend to favor relatively early inception of this aspect of a technoeconomic system; owing to obvious environmentally conditioned differential returns on labor investment strategies, these processes should become evident, probably at a demographic level absolutely lower than that necessary to trigger comparable developments in a more uniform environment. Geographic serendipity of this sort can be predicted to assume a relatively greater significance the lower the efficiency and the higher the energy costs of transportation.

Elevation of carrying capacity may occur when a local group need not produce for itself all that it consumes. This means that (*a*) a population may adopt a maximizing strategy of production without having to set aside land or labor for less rewarding crops or pursuits. Elements that might once have acted as limiting factors in production at the household or community level need not therefore continue to do so. Moreover (*b*) populations are permitted to colonize areas unable to support the cultivation of staples but which produce other resources for which there is demand. The extent to which this exploitative pattern is efficient must be determined empirically, particularly with reference to parameters such as demand level and overall demographic conditions. Only if exchanges are regular and institutions organized to handle a relatively large volume of the range of subsistence staples can trade act to raise carrying capacity or to stimulate local economic development; long-distance trade in sumptuaries does not, by itself, function in this way. In causal terms this analysis relies upon the systemic positive feedback relations between population and the mode of production.

Development of institutions of symbiotic exchange at the local level, whatever factors permit it, should be more precocious and proceed more rapidly as population grows and demographic pressure increases. This complex of behavior is equally clearly both a response to and an exacerbation of declining man/resource ratios. Predictably, local specialization of production coupled with an intense local marketing pattern should accompany chronic local shortages of agricultural land. A system of this type in the Basin of Mexico, documented for the time of the Conquest (Sanders 1956) was probably maximally intensive at that time, when population too had reached a peak; during the fourteenth and fifteenth centuries this pattern would have been developing consistently in that direction.

SYMBIOTIC SYSTEMS: THE AZTECS AND CONTEMPORARY ANALOGIES

Contemporary Tzintzuntzan (Foster 1948, 1967), an internally stratified pottery-making and-exporting community, manifests a pattern in which most of the pottery manufacture is carried out by those who lack sufficient land to maintain a household economy at or above the break-even point. In ethnographic-present Panajachel (Tax 1953), the community specialty is an agricultural one—truck production of onions and garlic, involving tiny plots of land and staggering inputs of hand labor. Maize is grown on marginal land, in insufficient quantities to feed the community; most maize consumed is purchased. Panajachel is notably land-poor, as are most of the Lake Atitlan villages, all of which are engaged in some form of specialized production. There is no question that the craftsmen and crafts villages are comparatively poor, certainly poorer than those able to support themselves from agriculture. Part of this, of course, is definitional: In these modes of production *the* means of production is land. Those lacking access altogether, or to sufficient quantities to break even, are un- or under-capitalized. Whatever the emic components and the values associated with land and land tenure, this is the bottom line. Those in craft activities in effect have been forced there because of their comparative lack of capital; their relatively greater poverty is hardly surprising.

Probably the best regional analogue of the Aztec period system in Central Mexico is the Southwest Highlands zone of Guatemala (McBryde 1947), including the Atitlan villages. This is a region of diverse and broken terrain, in which a 2-hour drive takes one through an impressive sample of the world's environments. Although Guatemala City bounds the zone, and Quezaltenango—the country's second largest city—is situated within it, most of the region is entirely rural and constitutes the densest strip of settlement in the country. Between a topography that renders much land unarable, and an extremely inequitable system of land tenure, pressure on the land is chronic and increasing with population growth. Each community participating in a symbiotic network has one, perhaps two, specializations, agricultural or craft; because everyone with a specialty in a community generally has the same one, there is little internal exchange within the settlement—a sharp contrast with the urban economic pattern characterized by internal symbiosis among numbers of differentiated resident producers. In contemporary Guatemala the degree of specialization at the rural community level has reached a point of fractionation where a community such as Momostenango, which weaves wool, raises no sheep; wool, produced in areas above the growing line for grain, is purchased in the market. Following Adam Smith's observations on the relationship of market volume to degree of specialization in production, some communities produce professional middlemen who follow the market circuits, buying cheaper and selling dearer, if with a marginal point spread. Finally, at or near the socioeconomic bottom are those communities etically specialized in the provision of unskilled labor to coastal fincas (cf. Smith 1977).

One further caution in the analysis of such systems, past or present: It is far too easily overlooked that the limits of growth of such networks are determined—as are those of any population—by the food supply. Someone, within or adjacent to that system, must produce a regular surplus of food staples above local subsistence needs. The efficiency of transport is only one determinant of how distant that food reservoir can be. In contemporary Guatemala the Pacific Coast and Pacific Piedmont make up the very real bioenergetic deficits of the Highland communities; maize surpluses are produced here, and this zone is the principal market for the labor that translates into the requisite infusion of cash into the Highland villages. For the Aztec, much grain was locally grown, with more imported via taxation and tribute from the 200 km (125 mile) radius beyond which further imports of maize and beans became prohibitive given foot transport; evidence of the famines suggests pressure upon these supplies, which all the intensification of symbiotic exchange alone—without concomitant, necessary, intensification of the mode of production itself—could not have enhanced significantly.

It would seem that the initial Aztec contribution to the symbiotic market network of the Basin of Mexico, almost certainly on a regular rather than the occasional basis implied in Duran's account, was hunted-gathered aquatic proteins—more or less the inventory offered by Sahagun, commodities exploited and sold long after the explosive urbanization of Tenochtitlan. One would normally consider these to be relatively high-priced items, especially so in terms of the Central Mexican ecosystem. Unlike maize, beans, or craft products, these animal protein sources are highly perishable. Like any hunted-gathered resource the degree of human control of production is chancy and the risks high. Populations occupying prime maize or truck-crop lands were in fact better off. They still are. But the Aztecs would have been no worse off, no lower in status, than many comparable groups in the Basin who, with little agricultural potential and no other capital, exploited such commodities as lime, firewood, clay, salt, or engaged in various gathering or craft activities. The "despised, rejected, man-of-sorrows" tenor of Duran's account is excessive in view of the regularity, predictability, and in fourteenth- and fifteenth-century Central Mexico universality of the behavior in question.

History, Logic, and Explanation

Many of the most obvious epistemological difficulties inherent in the use of analogy to generate testable lawlike statements stem from the fact that one term in a statement postulating a relationship (such as $A \to B$) happens to be missing. This condition nearly always obtains in treatment of diachronic (historical or archaeological) examples, where we are dealing with a past system. In practice, and for reasons that are largely pragmatic, one member of an analogy is regularly drawn from ethnography, when both behavior and its results upon the system are directly observable. When, as in synchronic comparison, both are observable, problems of significance and relevance may remain; but the underlying logic is much less challenging, and the result, less controversial, is generally termed the comparative method.

An analogical statement customarily takes the form

If $A \to B$ (observed)
then $A_1 \to B_1$ (inferred).

For a past system the problem is the reconstruction of A_1, no longer visible, in a context where what does remain visible may not be relevant or significant in terms of the questions we are asking. Accordingly, we need first an operation to reconstruct the single missing term in nonarbitrary fashion, on the basis of the observable changes it has left (B_1) upon the system of which it formed a part. Second, any such procedures require consistent, noneclectic criteria of relevance and significance—merely one aspect of the more general problem of verification/falsification, and are therefore a function of paradigm. The role of paradigm throughout the entire process of analogical reasoning is but little acknowledged; at best it is confused with substantive information, as in Flannery's blithe aviso (1977) concerning such inference in archaeology, that the ones who know more ethnology and ethnohistory will do a better job. Unfortunately this happens not be be correct—knowledge of data cannot effectively understudy the role of the paradigm. One may control all the data in the world, yet lack the means to order them or put them to work.

The logical skeleton supporting analogical reasoning provides a basis for the use of this approach to problems of explanation and of causality. We may initially use the principle of uniformitarianism to establish the similarity of the cause–effect relationship itself in both past and present (basically a covering-law procedure): If under stated conditions $A \to B$ is observed in the present, then under those same conditions $A \to B$ can be safely asserted for the past as well. This argument is necessary but not per se sufficient for our problem; it does not directly address the $A_1 \to B_1$ problem, where the missing, not observable A_1 must first be reconstructed from its directly observed presumed consequences B_1. In order to use A and $A \to B$ to reconstruct A_1 and the $A_1 \to B_1$ relationship, an explicit statement of equivalences is required. In other words, the causal relationship of *A* to *B* must be substantiated as an "if and only if" proposition, that *B* can be caused only by *A*.

Given the fact that logic is universal but science probabilistic, difficulties are created in the establishment of the equivalence, and in the interpretation of its significance. In science, the equivalence must be taken not in the universal sense of logic, but with the probabilism of other statements characteristic of the scientific domain. Establishment of an equivalence is in practice only partly a task of logic—and partly one of paradigm. In the case of cultural materialism, we may deduce that when the material effects of behaviors resemble each other in two instances, then the behaviors responsible (even when one set of behaviors may no longer be directly observable) can to that extent be deemed similar with a high probability of correctness. Notably this statement is restricted to those behaviors that produce material effects upon their environments or contexts—a limitation that for this paradigm is far less severe than it might be for others. It follows that the correct way to strengthen an analogy is to demonstrate as many similarities as possible among parameters whose importance is deduced from the paradigm used in the analysis.

Data, as implied above, are hardly the exclusive property of any one paradigm, although they may be most productively investigated or generated by one research strategy or another (and in the case of data recovered through archaeology only etic statements are remotely falsifiable). In this chapter the longest single example treated involves the establishment of an equivalence between Aztec Mexico and 1930s Guatemala, with one member taken from history and the other from ethnography. Irrespective of their origins, both sets of data were treated noneclectically from the consistent standpoint of the materialist paradigm (comparability of data source would thus seem to have little bearing upon the strength or legitimacy of an analogy as long as the analysis is uniform, invoking common canons of proof, and insofar as the analytical paradigm presents no restrictions concerning this parameter). When, however, one member of the analogy is treated from one paradigm, and the other from some different one, the results are inevitably noncomparable: The analogy is procedurally cross-paradigm and therefore illegitimate. Since the determination of relative importance of factors, and of standards of verification/falsification are set by the paradigm, these may differ legitimately from one example to another: Competition among paradigms is legitimate where eclecticism is not.

Competition of this sort, characteristic within each level of the hierarchy of scientific thinking, can be illustrated by comparison of the present position with the so-called "genetic model" (Romney 1957, Vogt 1964). The latter is a historical paradigm that explains cultural similarities and differences on the basis of differential historical relations—a criterion cited as essentially irrelevant to the cultural materialist paradigm. Assuming the present arguments were to have been developed from the genetic model, the analogy between the Aztec and the Highland Guatemalan economies would have been seriously weakened by the lack of close linguistic and historical relations between the groups.

Both paradigms are operationalizable and capable of consistent application. But the genetic model does not consider critical the problem that a single language family, the Uto-Aztecan, manifests a spectrum of levels of sociocultural integration ranging from the Basin Shoshone to the Aztec—and conversely, that all of these levels of complexity, through parallelism or convergence, are found in other language families. Level of sociocultural integration is not a significant parameter here, as historical relationships are not to the materialist position. What constitutes a problem to be explained, the nature of that explanation, how satisfactory it is judged to be, will all differ between paradigms. This is why control of data alone is insufficient for the construction of an epistemologically powerful analogy: Data do not order themselves, or govern the intellectual operations performed on them. This is also why A, B, A_1, and B_1 must be treated comparably and consistently in analogical reasoning. If they are not, the result is not competitive but eclectic, and thus de facto totally aparadigmatic.

Given a competition of paradigms, it is possible to apply at this level the criteria of relative strength that are regularly used at lower levels of the hierarchy of scientific thinking: The more powerful theory is one that explains the greater number of observations, does so more parsimoniously, and has the greater ties through the reticular structure of general theory. If this procedure for judgment is adopted, it may become apparent that a historical paradigm may not be the most powerful tool for the explanation even of historical data. The genetic model implies a relatively passive transmission of institutions from ancestor to descendant; the explanation, as opposed to the simple documentation, of change is thus difficult.

Institutions, from the perspective of these arguments, perform work; how well or efficiently they do that work under stated conditions governs the probabilities of institutional stability or change. Because this analysis works equally well within or across historical lines, these latter become less relevant and less powerful in the organization of research. The materialist paradigm is stronger than its competitor because it explains all that the competitor does and far more. Finally, the evolutionary-materialist—but not the historical—paradigm is applicable universally in that its basic parameter of comparison, that of relative efficiency, is derived from a uniformitarian principle of causality.

Conclusions

To return at last to the Aztecs, we ask why a story so replete with improbabilities was so widely told. Told it must have been; some of the events to which it refers (regardless of whether they ever happened) begin more than

300 years before the Conquest and its latest form was recorded by the Spanish from informant statements. It is not, cannot have been, history in the sense of a chronicle of events; the overtly supernatural elements do not constitute a legitimately separable part of the narrative, removal of which would leave a residue that is in some sense "true." Rather, such elements confirm the entire story, including the more naturalistic episodes, as myth; it is all of a piece. Confirming the assertion of lack of historicity are two additional observations: first, the Aztecs burned their old books and rewrote their history in the reign of Itzcoatl when they rose to power (cf. Padden 1967:55); given the nature of this account, a tentative attribution to the postrewrite period would not seem amiss (Sahagun 1961:Chap. 29). Second, histories of other polities in the area, referring to the same time periods, recount different events and in different orders.

For a state-organized population, its history, its mythology, and its history-transmogrified-into-mythology tend to be used interchangeably and quite comparably for any number of political and ideological purposes. States quite regularly in fact rewrite history, for the latter is capable of being mobilized and sent into battle. Institutions, following the materialist paradigm, perform work, and their efficiency at performing it directly affects their persistence in the system. There is no reason to except ideology from this generalization, in spite of the widespread misconception that the paradigm is incapable of encompassing phenomena generally termed "ideological" (cf. Harris 1974, 1977). All it does is put such phenomena to work instead of contemplating them as isolated entities, explicable only in terms of each other. This in turn renders them subject, of course, to the same principles of explanation that govern the rest of the behavior stream.

Having examined the components of the narrative, we turn next to consideration of the whole, and of the system of which it is an element. Parallels elsewhere for the individual episodes and for the overall organization suggest the real function of the story; these parallels occur in comparable sociopolitical and economic contexts. The Quest for the Promised Land, including the early period of exile, persecution, and Wandering in the Desert is hardly unfamiliar. It is a political myth, establishing land claims and political legitimacy, two constantly recurrent themes. It is a demonstrable impossibility that the Aztecs actually founded all those settlements, but the claim to have established temples and thereby territorial claims in those areas is more than compatible with the expansionist career of the Aztec Empire. The clouded title of the island on which Tenochtitlan was built (the Promised Land)—a boundary so hazily drawn that it would have incited chronic war among three city-states had any of them seriously wanted it—substantiates the interpretation that the myth functioned as a title deed, legitimizing possession. In a context of severe and increasing demographic pressure and incessant warfare, the legitimation of land claims constituted a not insignificant political problem; this was one means of bolstering such a claim.

In terms of the political system, moreover, it is notable that the Long March of the Aztecs included a stop at Tula, mentioned without much elaboration (it would probably have needed little). Toltec ancestry, at least in later times, became the badge of legitimacy of all the ruling houses on the Meseta Central. As the Aztec empire grew and became increasingly centralized, Toltec ancestors (equivalent to noble status) became increasingly requisite to bureaucratic and political participation (Calnek 1977). In a fashion doubtless comparable to the common practice of Elizabethan England where newly created peers acquired pedigrees traced to the Norman Conquest, Toltec ancestry was probably fairly accessible at some times and in some quarters. The early stop at Tula seems in a small way to serve a similar end; a pilgrimage to the font of political legitimacy, it represents an early brush with Manifest Destiny.

The emphasis upon humble beginnings and early persecution (accompanied by the Uriah Heep flavor of the Duran account) is notable in view of the fact that the descriptions in question are of perfectly ordinary behaviors widespread throughout Central Mexico, and therefore evidence neither of persecution nor of outcaste status. Rather this seems the functional equivalent of Born in a Log Cabin or How the West Was Won. As in these last two, there is a strong association with highly successful imperial expansion; it is an aspect of a Manifest Destiny legend. Taken in conjunction with those conveniently founded settlements, all of this adds up to an ideology precisely consonant with what the Aztecs were in fact doing. If this was a story to be handed down to posterity, this does not seem to be its principal function in the system. Evolution, including cultural evolution, is opportunistic, with any long-run effects of institutions not significant in explaining their retention. Retention, modification, or loss depend far more heavily upon short-run functions immediately responsible. In terms of those short-run costs and benefits, the material conditions of Aztec life on a strictly synchronic basis manifest exactly the problems addressed in this narrative. Etically this is far less a historical account of origins than the charter, the justification of an existing social and political order.

This evaluation of one small part of the corpus of Aztec historical documents as political myth has been an etic one, tested against its postulated function within the total behavior stream of which it formed a part—not against its unknown and unknowable emic significance in the beliefs of the actors in that system, or against a network of symbols or other mythic elements, equally enigmatic. Myth may justify and help to maintain certain adaptive political and military behaviors on the part of states, may legitimize the positions of actors in that system. It does not explain the causes of either the behaviors or the positions, even where it can and must be analyzed as one mechanism by which they are perpetuated. Any information conveyed in this account is not historical, but nomothetic and systemic, testable against data from many sources and against general theory once valid strategies are operationalized for such testing. Unless such strategies, furthermore, are regularly applied to this class of data, any nomothetic content will remain latent and neglected, and the narratives themselves either swallowed whole as a literal record of events, or consigned to the class of *Just So Stories*.

Interpretation of textual materials must minimally be considered subject to general rules of logic and of reasoning. This chapter has attempted to begin the development of intersubjectively valid procedures that conform to broad scientific canons. It does not seem unduly radical to suggest, moreover, that the linkage of a given text with an overall behavior stream constitutes a critical component of its meaning. If that linkage is ignored in favor of exclusive concentration upon the statement of the text itself, whatever information that text conveys is in fact obscured, and we are left with no reliable way to decide among alternative or competing interpretations. Because this narrative of the Aztecs' "early history" is imbedded in a political context involving overt imperial expansion, this very fact irrevocably colors the significance of what is communicated in the manifest content, effectively turns that content into something quite different. An etic strategy applied to this body of data produces results distinct from the more customary use of an emic one—qualitatively different, broader and more generalized in scope, and serving epistemological ends not entirely comparable. Causal statements of the sort developed in this paper—or of any sort at all—neither inhere in data nor grow out of them. Explanation, rather, is imposed upon data, otherwise mute, as a function of theoretical operations performed on them—a function of paradigm and investigative strategy.

Acknowledgments

This was written at the urging of William Mitchell, whose work (Chapter 5 in this volume) revealed a gap in the theoretical literature—whereupon he proceeded to apply a certain pressure on me to write this. Accordingly, our two papers were written together and developed in tandem through various stages. I can say only that I hope this turned out to be the ammunition he wanted, and that I consider it fitting that the two are published together.

Additional thanks to Marvin Harris and Morton Fried; their influence is too pervasive to require specific documentation. In particular, however, I cheerfully acknowledge the obvious debt to *Cows, Pigs, Wars, and Witches*. Suggestions at various stages from Jane Bennett Ross, Eric Ross, Michael Billig, and William Sanders have modified or strengthened a number of the arguments. I am relieved that Patty Jo Watson located a major hole in the reasoning in an earlier draft, and appreciate the assistance of Peter Wolrich in enabling me to slither out with some semblance of grace.

The title is drawn from Josephine Tey's *The Daughter of Time,* a mystery novel about, among other things, the theory of history. Tey's opinion of accounts as manipulable to serve political ends, and of account books as direct records of what I have called the flow of energy, parallels comparable views expressed in the present paper, differing primarily in being more witty and better written.

References

Armillas, P.

1969 The arid frontier of Mexican civilization. *Transactions of the New York Academy of Sciences,* Series II, No. *31*: 697–704.

1971 Gardens on swamps. *Science 174*: 653–661.

Boserup, E.

1965 *The conditions of agricultural growth.* Chicago: Aldine.

Calnek, E.

1966 The Aztec imperial bureaucracy. Paper presented at 65th Annual Meeting, American Anthropological Association, Pittsburgh, Pa.

1977 Secondary state formation in late prehispanic Central Mexico. Paper presented at 76th Annual Meeting, American Anthropological Association, Houston, Texas.

Duran, Fray D.

1964 *The Aztecs* (D. Heyden and F. Horcasitas, Trans.). New York: Orion.

Flannery, K. V.

1977 Review of *Mesoamerican archaeology: New approaches* (N. Hammond, Ed.). *American Antiquity 42*:659–661.

Foster, G. M.

1948 *Empire's children: The people of Tzintzuntzan.* Smithsonian Institution, Institute of Social Anthropology, Publication No. 6.

1967 *Tzintzuntzan: Mexican peasants in a changing world.* Boston: Little, Brown.

Fried, M. H.

1967 *The evolution of political society.* New York: Random House.

1975 *The notion of tribe.* Menlo Park: Cummings.

Harris, M.

1964 *The nature of cultural things.* New York: Random House.

1968 *The rise of anthropological theory.* New York: Thomas Y. Crowell.

1974 *Cows, pigs, wars, and witches.* New York: Random House.

1975 *Culture, people, nature,* 2nd ed. New York: Random House.

1977 *Cannibals and kings.* New York: Random House.

Kovar, A.

1970 The physical and biological environment of the Basin of Mexico. In *The natural environment, contemporary occupation, and 16th century population of the valley.* Occasional Papers in Anthropology, No. 3:13–67. University Park: Pennsylvania State University, Department of Anthropology.

Lattimore, O.

1940/1962 *Inner Asian frontiers of China.* Boston: Beacon Press.

McBryde, F. W.

1947 *Cultural and historical geography of southwest Guatemala.* Institute of Social Anthropology, Publication No. 4. Washington D.C.: Smithsonian Institution.

Padden, R. C.

1967 *The hummingbird and the hawk: Conquest and sovereignty in the valley of Mexico, 1503–1541.* New York: Harper Colophon Books.

Price, B. J.

1977 Shifts of production and organization: A cluster-interaction model. *Current Anthropology. 18*: 209–233.

1978a Secondary state formation: An explanatory model. In *Origins of the state: The anthropology of political evolution* (R. Cohen, and E. R. Service, Eds.). Philadelphia: ISHI.

1978b Demystification, enriddlement, and Aztec cannibalism: A materialist rejoinder to Harner. American Ethnologist 5(1):98–115.

Lord Raglan
1956 *The hero: A study in tradition, myth, and drama*. New York: Vintage.
Romney, A. K.
1957 The genetic model and Uto-Aztecan time perspective. *Davidson Journal of Anthropology, 3*:35–41.
de Sahagun, Fray B.
1950–1969 *General history of the things of New Spain* (C. E. Dibble and A. J. O. Anderson, Trans.). Book 10, *The People* (1961). Santa Fe: School of American Research and University of Utah Press.
Sanders, W. T.
1956 The Central Mexican symbiotic region. In *Prehistoric settlement patterns in the New World* (G. R. Willey, Ed.). New York: Viking Fund Publications in Anthropology, No. *23*:115–127.
Smith, W. R.
1977 *The fiesta system and economic change*. New York: Columbia University Press.
Steward, J. H.
1955 *Theory of culture change*. Urbana: University of Illinois Press.
Tax, S.
1953 *Penny capitalism: A Guatemalan Indian economy*. Institute of Social Anthropology, Publication No. 16. Washington, D.C.: Smithsonian Institution.
Tey, J.
1951 *The daughter of time*. New York: Dell.
Vogt, E. Z.
1964 The genetic model and Maya cultural development. In *Desarrollo cultural de los Maya* (E. Z. Vogt, and A. Ruz L., Eds.). Mexico: Universidad Nacional Autonoma de Mexico. Pp. 9–48.

7 Patterns of Diet and Forces of Production: An Economic and Ecological History of the Ascendancy of Beef in the United States Diet[1]

ERIC B. ROSS

Introduction

Currently, there is intense debate over why some animals are considered edible or inedible or are simply differentially valued as food among various populations (cf. Harris 1974, 1977; Ross 1978; Harner 1977). Behind much of the controversy, however, lies a deeper level of disagreement over the nature and intelligibility of cultural phenomena—and, consequently, the question of the larger social-political relevance of anthropology.

Structuralists and symbolic anthropologists tend to regard dietary systems as they view culture itself, as primarily an ideological system which "assigns values to the system's physical components [Nutini 1971:537]"—in this case, animals—and thereby structures their use. Moreover, cultures are construed as intrinsically meaningful and this meaning is generally considered essentially arbitrary in its relation to the material world. In contrast, as developed here and elsewhere, the cultural materialist view regards dietary behaviors and values within a comparative, ecological-historical frame, with differences in dietary practices resulting from recurrent, rather than idiosyn-

[1] I want to thank Peter Bird, Norma Diamond, Penelope Eckert, Susan Harding, Conrad Kottak, Barbara Price, Jane Bennett Ross, and Karen Dennis for their helpful and encouraging reading of this chapter and David Massad for assistance in researching the connections between contemporary agribusiness and the meat industry. I also want to express special appreciation to Marvin Harris whose interest in the issues developed in this chapter made the writing more of a challenge than I initially envisaged. I am grateful as well to members of the Thursday "bag lunch" seminars of the University of Michigan Archaeologists, for their positive response to ideas to which few of their ethnological colleagues are sympathetic.

BEYOND THE MYTHS OF CULTURE
Essays in Cultural Materialism

ISBN 0-12-598180-5

cratic, causal processes and co-evolving with the human ecological systems in which they occur.

Pursuing the implications of this contrast for understanding dietary systems and their origins, I will discuss a structuralist model of United States meat consumption recently proposed by Marshall Sahlins (1976) and will describe an alternative (and, I believe, more compelling and legitimate) materialist analysis.

Sahlins suggests that Americans prefer beef because of a cultural logic that has no sensible correspondence to material circumstance and, indeed, seems, in his view, to transcend it as it transcends history. Thus, he writes that "the exploitation of the American environment . . . depends on the model of a meal that includes a central meat element" (in particular, beef) that is based on "a sexual code of food which must go back to the Indo-European identification of cattle or increasable wealth with virility" and which has "functional consequences [that] extend from agricultural 'adaptation' to international trade and world political relations [1976:171]." Arguing that "specific valuations of edibility and inedibility . . . [are] in no way justifiable by biological, ecological, or economic advantage [1976:171]," Sahlins describes dietary systems—including that of the United States—as permutations of an underlying, seemingly universal principle (or structure): "edibility is inversely related to humanity [1976:175]"; i.e., "taken as a whole [the food system] composes a sustained metaphor on cannibalism [1976:174]."

It is this, in Sahlins' view, that explains why cattle, being least like ourselves, are said to be most prized as food, while dogs, being like kin, are tabooed as food (1976:174–175) although "nutritionally they are not to be despised [1976:171]." But as to why then different preferences ought to ever arise cross-culturally—why or how, for example, Americans came to have a high regard for beef and the Chinese for pork—the implication of Sahlins' work is that, if material forces have little impact on cultural logic, such differences must be largely fortuitous (Sahlins 1979). Yet, on careful and systematic examination, they seem quite otherwise.

The main intention of this chapter is to demonstrate that the reasoning with which Sahlins addresses the issue of differential edibility in general and the relative use of beef and pork in the United States in particular is spurious on logical and empirical grounds. His attribution of an American beef preference to an ancient Indo-European sexual code immediately suggests the kinds of deficiencies in his general argument. Since the same vague Indo-European ideological heritage culminated in a *taboo,* rather than a preference, on beef in India, it is obvious that ideology alone cannot explain American beef consumption, that one must consider material and historical factors. In examining these factors, as I will do, it will become apparent that it was actually pork which dominated the American diet until comparatively recently and that the significance of beef is attributable to a shift in the material conditions of food production as American agriculture was integrated into a maturing capitalist system.

It is also clear that the shaping of the American pattern of meat consumption accords with associations of dietary customs and material factors of production—ecological, demographic, and technoeconomic conditions —observable elsewhere. This suggests that the differential status of animals such as cattle and swine cross-culturally is not, as Sahlins argues, evidence for "the autonomy of culture" (1976), but actually a compelling demonstration of the shaping of cultural habits in regular ways by factors that are not primarily cultural. In the following sections, these factors will be examined in various historical and "cultural" settings.

Why We Don't Eat Dogs: A Beef with Sahlins

First, briefly, let me return to some of Sahlins' points to which I referred at the outset of this chapter and which, in spite of the fact that he offers little evidence to support them, warrant commentary. Consider, for example, Sahlins' assertion that dietary systems are essentially systems of meaning that are, in their totality, variants on the theme of cannibalism. Applying this to American dietary habits, Sahlins argues that dogs and horses are not eaten because they "participate in American society in the capacity of subjects. They have proper personal names, and indeed we are in the habit of conversing with them as we do not talk to pigs and cattle." Dogs are more strictly tabooed than horses because they are "as kinsmen" while horses "are as servants and nonkin." In turn, cattle and swine are said to "have the status of objects to human subjects" and are therefore regarded as comestible; but, because pigs are "barnyard animals and scavengers of human food" and thus more "contiguous" with humans, pork must be less prestigious than beef (1976:174–175).

At best, this borders on tautology: Pets are generally not major food sources, and vice versa. Or, put another way, animals that are not raised to be eaten are unlikely to be eaten. And there is, of course, nothing startling about the observation that commonly eaten animals tend to be objectified. Sahlins, however, attributes degree of edibility to this status as object (or subject) and simply presumes that such status is itself fortuitous. But, the degree and the manner of association of animals with human society is *not* random; there is far more than symbolic reason why dogs (like most carnivores) are not—except in limited or unusual circumstances—an efficient food resource and why cattle are not household pets or hunting companions. Indeed, it is ridiculous to maintain that such animals are not intrinsically suited to certain productive roles, which are optimally enacted in certain environments and for which these animals are usually enhanced through selective breeding by humans.[2]

Those which become a major food source do, indeed, tend to be treated

[2] Jewell observes that "cattle, sheep, goats and pigs have an evolutionary adaptation to the enviroments in which they originated and a limited ability to adapt to new ones [1969:103]."

more "objectively" than others; but, there is nothing particularly ideological about this either. Thus, in the United States during the nineteenth century, the provisioning of meat (primarily pork) for a large and expanding population required an increasingly factory-like mode of production. The systematic slaughter and processing of hogs into food products did not merely reduce the likelihood of a subjective relationship with them; it deanimalized and commoditized them. Production on this scale promoted—indeed, seems to have been contingent on—an effective "neutrality toward death" which could help reduce the development of the pig "dis-assembly line" to a largely technical problem (Giedion 1948:246).

In contrast, we permit canine pets to sleep and eat with us and even to pollute our streets; and we do not eat them. Since edibility appears to be his primary criterion for gauging the utility of animals, Sahlins argues that dogs therefore constitute an essentially irrational feature of American culture. But, there are two fallacies in particular to call attention to in this reasoning. First, as I have already suggested, not relying on dogs instead of cattle to provide millions of people with a regular supply of meat is not actually a matter of culture at all. Ruminants, rather than carnivores, are the best way to exploit grassland unsuited for cultivation, and one-third of the continental United States would, in fact, be economically marginal if it were not used primarily for raising cattle (or sheep) (Fowler 1961:30). One of the fundamental reasons that we depend so much on beef is that forages constitute over 70% of beef cattle feed (Hodgson 1976:627–629).

The second fallacy is a confusion between system levels. Many behaviors that seem "irrational" on the individual or local level are only parts of systemic processes that evidence their "rationality" on a higher or broader order of analysis. Thus, in the case of America's "automania"—an apt parallel to our "petishism"—Paul Sweezy has cogently argued that its adverse effects such as traffic congestion and pollution, from an analytical viewpoint, "are essentially superficial phenomena"; that one can really only comprehend the role of the automobile in the contemporary United States in terms of the profound economic forces which shaped such industries as auto manufacture and affected the course of urban and industrial development in such a way that over 80% of American workers are dependent on a car for getting to work (Sweezy 1973:4, 14).

In a similar sense, the "contradictions" of unequal development that characterize capitalism in general also apply to the issue of canine pollution that so concerns Sahlins and which is just one of many unpleasant social costs of our system of production. The essential point here is that the vitality of dogs is not necessarily to be measured exclusively in terms of their value as food—but, in their role as consumers! When Sahlins regards our keeping of dogs as pets as a triumph of "cultural logic over material effectiveness [1976:169]," he fails to ask the important question: effective for whom? One of the most lucrative aspects of the modern meat industry is the intensive elaboration of animal by-products into marketable commodities, among which pet food is one of the most profitable, with annual sales of dog food alone amounting to over two billion dollars (SAMI 1978; George n.d.).

Thus, while it may initially seem clever, it is not especially edifying for Sahlins to promote the view of American culture as materially illogical simply by describing America as "the land of the sacred dog [1976:171]." For, as Alan Beck, the director of New York City's Bureau of Animal Affairs, has observed, "breeders and owners are responding to a demand for dogs and cats created by the huge pet food industry. . . . The dog has been *made* a sacred cow [1974:34, italics added]."

Dogs, of course, have other, more immediate uses for different sectors of the population. For example, as the United States has become more intensely urban and social life more atomistic, protection and companionship have become important functions. In a society where, as Jules Henry once noted, we have no "guarantee that we will never stand alone," dogs seem to fulfill vital psychological needs which other animals—especially cows—cannot, and which the pet industry is ready to exploit (cf. Pet Food Institute 1976). Moreover, with urban crime increasing, amidst urban decay and chronic unemployment, dogs are often an important form of security. This is reflected in demographic changes in the urban dog population, which "is becoming composed of larger dogs [Beck 1975:1316; 1973:57]."

Yet, Sahlins finds the dominance of a cultural logic over material conditions nowhere more evident than in the "fact" that pet dogs live "in calm assurance that they themselves will never be sacrificed to necessity or diety [1976:171]." If so (and surely canine testimony is emic data of an especially unreliable kind), this self-assurance is seriously misplaced, for evidence suggests quite clearly that material circumstance does indeed affect the status of pet dogs. Why else would it be the case, for example, that "pet owners are more likely to live in single family dwellings or larger apartments and have higher median income than non-owners [Beck 1975:1315]." Evidence that dog ownership is not simply the result of "correlations in a symbolic system," however, has been even more forcefully demonstrated in New York City where non-dog-owners (members of a distinct culture from that of dog-owners? Surely not!) successfully lobbied for strict regulation of canine defecation. The consequences—which are beyond comprehension by structuralist logic—suggest that many household pets actually had been living in a tenuous relationship with their owners: In the weeks following passage of the new law, there was a staggering increase in dog abandonment. Such are the hazards in contemporary America of being treated no better than kinsmen.[3]

This, then, returns us to a central problem with the general structuralist proposition that "edibility is inversely related to humanity." Evidence sug-

[3] Dog abandonment is actually a chronic problem. Stray dogs, which are a notable feature of urban areas, are not a self-perpetuating population, but are continually being replenished by stray or abandoned pets (Beck 1973:57).

gests that such formulas have really little logical immediacy in the face of actual cultural experience and, indeed, grossly distort it with disconcerting regularity, on the ideological level as well as on the behavioral. Thus, among the Kalapalo Indians of central Brazil, very few terrestrial or arboreal animals are considered edible, primarily as a result of the highly productive lacustrine environment which the Kalapalo inhabit (Ross 1978). A major exception are monkeys, which are eaten—according to Kalapalo logic—precisely "because they are like human beings [Basso 1973:17]." Or, consider the case of societies in which people practice endo-cannibalism, that is, where they regularly consume deceased kin (cf. Dornstreich and Morren 1974; Lindenbaum 1979). Such practices compel one to ask why the structuralist proposition that Americans do not eat dogs because they are like kin should be taken seriously, when close human kinship elsewhere is a guarantee of ending life as a meal. If food systems are "a metaphor on cannibalism," it is a mixed metaphor at best, and one which lacks the credibility or cogency that sensible explanation requires.[4]

Beef and Pork: A Comparison of Europe and China

Without denying that animals do acquire metaphorical and symbolic associations—although these vary considerably through time—a cross-cultural examination of differential use or valuation of beef, pork, or dairy products reveal that these sentiments or habits arise in conjunction with and, indeed, out of definite material conditions. Among them, human population density and degree of agricultural intensification are preeminent.

The principal beef-producing and beef-consuming areas of the world, for example, are in countries that possess considerable and sparsely inhabited grassland—characteristics, in general, of comparatively young countries (such as Uruguay, Paraguay, Argentina, New Zealand, and even the United States). With increasing population and accompanying rises in land values, extensive forms of production such as cattle grazing tend to yield to more intensive forms of agriculture—usually based on cereals—and more efficient forms of protein production such as raising swine or dairy cows (Corey 1950:31), which are also more consonant with smaller land holdings that emerge in areas of higher demographic concentration.

Stewart Fowler, an authority on animal husbandry, points out that,

[4] Sahlins pursues the cannibalism metaphor even further, arguing that Americans only refer frankly to inner parts of edible animals because they do not normally consume them—e.g., heart, tongue, and liver—but, for preferred cuts, "the organic nature of the flesh . . . is at once disguised and its preferability indicated by the general term 'meat,' and again by particular conventions such as 'roast,' 'steak,' 'chops,' or 'chuck' [1976:174]." Sahlins seems to have forgotten about other terms such as rump, rib, breast, ham, shoulder, leg, and loin, all of which are analogues of parts of the human body and belie his cannibalism metaphor.

"since the hog is an efficient user of concentrated feeds rather than a consumer of bulky roughages, the production of swine is closely associated with 'true' agriculture (crops and improved pastures) and not with the range like cattle and sheep [1961:66]." Thus, swine are characteristically associated with regions of demographic concentration far exceeding what is favorable for beef production—although hogs are also well suited to a variety of underdeveloped economies, even where human density is relatively low, for a related reason, that they make efficient use of a wide range of otherwise marginal resources, including garbage, agricultural waste, and wild nuts. Thus, in contrast to cattle they "can be easily raised by every farmer and require small capital [Corey 1950:104]," which makes them equally suitable to pioneering (woodland) conditions and situations of land pressure (including intra-urban environments). Dairying also tends to become rather prominent in more densely settled regions, both because of its high efficiency of land use and the perishability of its products which require a ready (virtually daily) market.[5]

European history usefully illustrates many of these associations. In the time of the great European temperate forests, through the Roman era to the twelfth century, extensive woodland favored swine as the principal domesticated animal (Darby 1956:185–191; Hemardinquer 1979:55–56). Thereafter, population growth and the clearing of forests brought about an increase in cereal production and cattle raising. By the fourteenth and fifteenth centuries, rural pig production had declined drastically, compounded by great increases in the price of salt with which pork was typically processed (Hemardinquer 1979:56). Beef actually became commonplace in some regions such as Paris by the sixteenth and seventeenth centuries, while the comparative scarcity and high price of pork advanced it to the status of a luxury food (Forster and Ranum 1976:xi). Fatback, in fact, was not infrequently included in dowry payments in France (Hemardinquer 1979:52), while, in London, roast pig "was a famous city dainty and was regularly sold at Bartholomew Fair, a 'Bartlemy pig' being considered the *ne plus ultra* of savoury morsels [Curtis-Bennett 1949:52]."

By the sixteenth century, however, continued population growth had forced a further shift in the general pattern of European food production. Ac-

[5] Thus, in the United States, as cattle raising, followed by hog production, gradually shifted west during the nineteenth century, dairying rose to prominence in the more densely populated northeastern states such as New York and Pennsylvania (Fowler 1960:54–55; U.S. Tariff Commission 1922:7). Today, it is actually Los Angeles, however, one of the country's most urbanized regions, that holds the lead in market milk production, despite an absence of pasturage and the average farm size of only 15 acres (Lantis 1963:205). Such regular relationships between dairying, mixed agriculture and livestock raising, and distance from urban markets were first systematically examined by Johann von Thunen in the early nineteenth century. Von Thunen's model of regional patterns of land use, while predicated on certain ideal conditions such as a homogeneous environment, has continued to represent and clarify certain cross-culturally observed relations between population and economy and has bearing on the evolution of the regionalization of U.S. hog, cattle and dairy production.

cording to Blum, "increased pressure on the land . . . combined with the retention of inefficient agricultural techniques, brought about a greater emphasis upon cereals and a deemphasis of animal husbandry [1978:187]." Further, as Braudel observes, "cereals were at a premium. Their prices rose to such unduly high levels that there was no money for buying extras. Meat consumption diminished in the long term until about 1850 [1967:130]." Where it continued, cattle raising shifted to the more intensive mode of dairying, so that, by the 1600s, "cheese, a source of cheap protein, was one of the great foods of the people of Europe [Braudel 1967:143; cf. Tannahill 1973:208]." By the following century, "in regions where animal husbandry was a major activity, dairy products figured importantly in rural cuisines [Blum 1978:184]."

In general, by then, meat was in short supply throughout Europe, especially in the peasant sector; but, when meat was eaten, it was likely to be pork—especially after the adoption of the potato in the eighteenth century, the spread of which precipitated a marked resurgence of hog raising in many parts of Europe (Morineau 1979:36; Hemardinquer 1979:55–56,58). When there was beef, as today in India, it "often came from sick or half-dead beasts who could no longer function as work animals [Blum 1978:186]." Meanwhile, there were interesting ideological developments: the religious doctrine of meatless days expanded until, in pre-Commonwealth England, "on about half the days of the year meat could not be eaten [Wilson 1973:31]"; while, by 1700, there were many doctors espousing the view that it was actually healthier to eat meat in moderation (Braudel 1967:132).

With the profound social and economic changes induced by the industrial revolution, the emergence of an urban, industrial proletariat meant an even graver problem of protein shortage and malnutrition, particularly in England. Pressures to import meat from the United States, Australia, and New Zealand were evident by the 1860s (Harrison 1963:21) and, as far as the contribution to the national diet made by domestic meat production, a significant percentage consisted of the flesh from diseased animals (Perren 1978).

Horse meat was incorporated into the European diet under just this pressure of meat scarcity. Thus, it is particularly instructive to report Sahlins' explanation of the phenomenon of "hippophagy" in France and its absence in the United States; he dismisses it with "the totemic sentiment that the French are to Americans as 'frogs' are to people [1976:172]," thus suggesting that eating horse meat is simply another bizarre habit indulged in by a nation known for other cultural eccentricities (among which one is tempted to include structuralism).[6] But, the fact is that "horsemeat is consumed *in much of Europe* with equanimity," not merely in France—having generally arisen to utilize aged farm animals as a cheap source of protein among the working class (Cade 1976:2,6).

[6] I want to thank Conrad Kottak for the information that structuralism tastes like chicken.

By today, demographic growth across Europe has produced an intensive agriculture characterized by a very low ruminant-to-hog ratio which reverses the pattern found in younger countries which still have considerable rangeland and dependence on cheap beef cattle. (Thus, in 1960, West Germany, with a population density of 559 persons per square mile, had a ruminant-to-hog ratio of 0.6; while Argentina, with a density of only 13, had a ratio of 11.2 [Fowler 1961:9].) This also represents a large part of the reason that beef consumption did not become negligible in countries such as England; for the emergence of a complex international capitalist division of labor by the late nineteenth century included among its features substantial investment by Britain in overseas grassland—in Australia, Argentina, and in the United States (Strickon 1965:235; Perren 1971; Smith 1969; Mulhall 1885:91). Thus, when the Great Plains opened up in the 1880s, British and Scottish capitalists invested as much as 45 million dollars in ranching companies; and, during the same decade, "pioneer efforts in Argentina's refrigerated meatpacking industry were made by the British [Smith 1969:33]." A marked improvement subsequently took place in the nutritional situation of the English working class (Frisch 1978:26) with increased beef (and pork) imports which, by World War I, represented 40% of total meat consumed in England (Perren 1971:434). (By 1938, 80% of all meat sold in London markets was imported [Harrison 1963:24].)

The ancient agricultural societies of Asia, in contrast, did not have a similar opportunity to appropriate distant grasslands to maintain beef in their own diets after demographic growth had cost them the luxury of leaving large amounts of land uncultivated in order to graze livestock (Buck 1956). In India, cattle are village scavengers (Harris 1977:227); in China, where they can be found, they have been important primarily as a source of traction and, as in India, their enormous strategic value in this regard developed into a religious respect for these animals and a distaste for their consumption. We can even trace the emergence of this valuation as the Chinese economic system intensified. In the Han dynasty (207 B.C.–A.D. 220), before China had experienced intensive population growth, "beef [was] especially prized because the ox was such a useful animal that the government occasionally prohibited its slaughter [Yü 1977:74]." By the time of the T'ang dynasty, however, in a remarkable parallel to Europe in the late Middle Ages, pharmacologists were asserting that eating beef was unhealthy (Schafer 1977:99). By the eleventh century, this view was more widespread; it has, in fact, been noted that "Buddhism's most important influence on . . . diet was the relative unpopularity of beef," though, significantly, this generally vegetarian religion had no effect on pork consumption (Freeman 1977:164). By the 1940s, it was reported that the Chinese considered it "insulting, or at least improper, to offer beef to a guest at an honorable dinner [Yang 1945:47]."

Cattle raising, as we would espect, was primarily a feature of frontier regions; at the opposite demographic extreme, around urban centers, some dairying was to be found (Sprague reports from contemporary China that "the number of dairy cattle is limited. Dairying is handled by production brigades usually located near the larger cities [1975:631].") But, through most of China, bovines, usually in short supply, were prized for "plowing, pulling vehicles, turning millstones, turning irrigation wheels, and the like [Buck 1956:246]." The prospects for animal husbandry were limited, however. The reason, as Buck observed in 1937, was that "The dense population in China necessitates the production of the greatest amount of food possible per unit of land . . . by growing crops for their seed or tuber products, rather than by devoting the land to pasture and crops for animals [1956:245]." Where beef was consumed, it was usually after an animal had died, and even then the meat was most likely to be sold in an urban market. As in eighteenth century Europe, the rural masses were more apt to depend on pork or poultry (Yü 1977:75; Mote 1977:201). Swine, of course, were admirably suited to the intense Chinese agricultural regime since they could be raised at little cost and also provide valuable fertilizer (Yang 1945:35). Pork was "clearly *the* flesh food [Anderson and Anderson 1977:336]"; and, in the 1940s, Yang reported that "on market day one can find hundreds of slaughtered pigs for sale but only one or two cows." Yet, he observed, "the price of beef is always lower than that of pork . . . a direct outcome of the aversion to slaughtering the cattle [Yang 1945:47]," which, as we have seen, arose out of material conditions of production.

The Development of Patterns of Meat Consumption in the United States

Until quite recently in the United States (see Table 7.1), pork usually was consumed at a rate equal to or greater than beef; there is certainly little doubt that beef was rarely a match for pork before the 1870s. It has, in fact, been noted that "up to 1850 [pork] formed a higher percentage of the American diet than any other 'article of provisions' except wheat [Towne and Wentworth 1950:181]." It is not enough, however, to present such an historical challenge to Sahlins' fantasy of beef; it is necessary as well to examine the changing relative importance of pork and beef in such a way as to leave few doubts about the factors responsible. That is the objective of the present section.

THE SIGNIFICANCE OF PORK IN THE COLONIAL DIET

By the time that English settlers began to colonize the eastern seaboard of North America, it was widely recognized in the Old World that "no animal was so easily fed, and no animal so easily put on flesh" as the hog (Bennett 1960:92). Eminently suited to early woodland conditions, swine, as Bidwell and Falconer observe in their monumental history of early American

TABLE 7.1
U.S. Per Capita Meat Consumption 1900–1977 (in pounds)[a]

Year	Beef	Pork
1977	125.9	61.5
1976	129.4	58.2
1975	120.1	54.8
1970	113.7	66.4
1960	85.1	64.9
1950	63.4	69.2
1940	54.9	73.5
1920	59.1	63.5
1900	67.1	71.9

Sources: Harris and Ross 1978:91; U.S. Senate Committee on Agriculture, Subcommittee on Livestock and Grains 1972:119

[a] Figures represent carcass weight, that is, include bone and fat and do not allow for cooking losses.

agriculture, "seem to have adapted themselves to their new environment with less difficulty than any other domestic animal [1925:31]." Especially with Indian corn to supplement nuts and other forage, pigs quickly achieved a strategic edge and pork a place in the diet which cattle and beef could not rival (Martin 1942).[7]

This is not to say that cattle or horses were not raised in significant numbers in many regions. Cattle, in particular, were important as draft animals and as a source of milk and hides, as well as meat; and, like hogs, they were frequently exported at a modest rate (Gray 1933:102, 140–47, 205–10). But, in fact, they rarely constituted more than a minor portion of total meat consumed domestically and rarely rivalled the more prolific hog in the subsistence economy. In eighteenth-century Pennsylvania, pork consumption appears to have been about double that of beef (Lemon 1972:165). In New England, where livestock production long before the Revolution had stimulated the development of an important meat-packing export industry, pork was not only "the catalyst of the great West Indian trade [Towne and Wentworth 1950:94]," but also the staple of the frontier family.

Cattle, more than swine, may have represented wealth, their ownership being in general a function of capital resources; but one also finds that, "cut into merchantable pieces and salted, barrelled pork was a local medium of exchange [Bidwell and Falconer 1925:154]." Moreover, cattle were not even primarily valued for their meat (Hilliard 1972:4), but rather for milk, butter and traction (Bidwell and Falconer 1925:166–67); while most often older oxen

[7] One reason that mutton achieved relatively little importance in colonial America was that wool was then a cornerstone of the British economy and America a major market for English wool exports (cf. Williams 1964:67–68). Thus, colonial sheep-raising was discouraged.

and dry milch cows were eventually sold to specialists who fattened them on corn for sale to urban markets (Bidwell and Falconer 1925:353–358). But, for the average New England family, beef was just an occasional treat (Bidwell and Falconer 1925:161). In contrast, "from the viewpoint of the family larder, the most necessary farm animal was the hog; few meals of this period anywhere were complete without some pork product [Russell 1976:286; see Cummings 1940:16]."

The same held for the southern colonies, where, even among southern whites, pork consumption exceeded that of beef by at least three to one (Hilliard 1972:9, 130; Gray 1933:207; Martin 1942:41–45). As Hilliard writes in *Hogmeat and Hoecakes:*

> Being inexpensive to produce and easily preserved, pork was the preferred meat of whites and was the flesh most commonly issued to slaves. During the nineteenth century, this preference for pork came to be a distinctive element of southern culture and as a food item, pork completely eclipsed all others [1972:9].

As we shall see, however, this persistent pork focus in the South must be understood within a complex system of interregional economic symbiosis that involves, among other factors, the eventual dominance of the southern economy by cotton production and the import of foodstuffs from such swine-producing regions as the Midwest.

THE EARLY PACKING INDUSTRY

The early preeminence of pork is closely associated with the technological means of preserving meat and the differential constraints on marketing beef and pork. Until the mid-nineteenth century, little fresh meat was available except what was locally slaughtered. When distances were relatively short—as in New England—hogs and cattle could both be driven to market and their meat available fresh. But, because hogs were generally harder to drive, had a higher mortality rate and were more susceptible to shrinkage in transit, they were more likely to be processed locally and shipped as smoked or cured pork products. But, another reason that pork was more often packed and so achieved wider distribution than beef was that, in terms of methods of preservation up to the 1870s—curing, pickling, salting—processed pork was more flavorsome than beef and was often to be trusted, especially in warmer regions, where fresh meat was not. As Cummings noted, the flavor of pork "actually improves [as] a result of preservative processes . . . . It is said that because of its flavor value a pound of bacon goes as far as three pounds of beef-steak [1940:405]."

Thus, it would not be until the advent of efficient methods of refrigeration after the Civil War, that fresh beef would even begin to be competitive with pork products among the general population. Until refrigeration and railroads combined late in the nineteenth century to effect reliable mass distribution of fresh beef, "consumer apathy towards salted beef supported a limited interest in beef packing [Walsh 1978:5n]."

In addition to hams and bacon, another impetus to hog production was the general utility of lard as a lubricant and illuminant. Indeed, as the corn-fattening of livestock to finish them for market became more common, improvement in the quality of lard provided an additional incentive for such supplementation in the case of the hog, since corn—which hogs metabolize with great efficiency—produced a better, firmer lard which was easier to pack (Towne and Wentworth 1955:164–165). By 1800, as a result, a strong symbiotic relationship was established between corn production and swine raising; and as corn became one of the major agricultural products of a rapidly expanding frontier, hogs came to be widely regarded as a form of condensed corn, and the most efficient way to market the grain (Cummings 1940:15; Towne and Wentworth 1955:181).

As population pushed west after the Revolution, hogs thrived in the sparsely settled, wooded countryside where they were permitted to range freely—usually needing only brief fattening on corn in autumn to ready them for market. In those days, "Every farmer had at least a few [hogs]. . . . As the region grew more prosperous, the number of hogs possessed by a farmer became one of the indices of his wealth [Clemen 1923:53]." And, in inns throughout the region, pork was the staple on the menu. As Yoder observes, "Many tavern keepers of the newer parts of the country considered a supply of bacon, along with a keg of whisky, to be the prime requirement for inn-keeping [1969:144]."

With gradual improvement of east–west roads, moreover, corn surpluses of the trans-Appalachian region—beyond what was made into hominy, home brew, and hog feed—began to produce enough hogs to drive overland to eastern cities (usually accompanying droves of cattle to feed on undigested corn from their droppings).

Although the mortality was apparently high, millions of hogs were eventually marketed live on the Atlantic seaboard (Towne and Wentworth 1955:115). But, even more, the widespread value of pork products locally, in the East and South, and abroad encouraged the development of numerous packing establishments throughout the Midwest to process hogs into pork products without the losses such arduous overland drives could incur (Clemen 1923:72–73; Hopkins 1928:9–13; Towne and Wentworth 1955:115).

"PORKOPOLIS" AND THE CORN-BELT

By 1850, Ohio alone accounted for about a third of all American meat packing (Clark 1916:484). Stimulated by ready access to surplus corn, proximitous to the food-importing cotton plantations of the lower Mississippi, strategically situated on the Ohio River, and infused with capital from Boston packinghouses, Cincinnati became the paramount hog-packing center of the

R|R

nation (Clark 1916:482–83).[8] Here, in the city that came to be known as "Porkopolis," American meat packing first transcended local markets under the impetus of new canal and railroad links to the East and, through the development of mass-production techniques to slaughter and disassemble hogs (Giedion 1948:214–218), "originated and perfected the system which packs 15 bushels of corn into a pig and packs that pig into a barrel, and sends him over the mountains and over the ocean to feed mankind [Clemen 1923:93]."

Contemporaneous with the development of the pork-packing industry and the rise of the corn-belt, the first decades of the nineteenth century also saw Ohio become a major cattle-producing region and the prototype of another American agricultural symbiosis, that between grassland and corn producers. The Ohio Valley was an area of considerable subregional variation in which a pattern of integrated specializations rapidly took shape. Northern Indiana, for example, was unsuited to corn farming and required substantial drainage for which most settlers lacked the capital resources. For the most part, a small group of enterpreneurs developed the area as pasture for cattle that were latter fattened elsewhere on corn (Henlein 1959:20; Gates 1973:176–177; Merk 1969:xv). Areas such as central Kentucky and the Miami Valley developed into important cattle-feeding regions. The complexity of the interaction among local adjustments of habitat and market is suggested by Henlein's description of "the Miami Valley [which] brought in stockers for feeding, exported yearling steers to the western-central Ohio grazers, and exported cow calves to the Western Reserve dairymen [1959:52]."

Such commercial specialization was encouraged by the development of transportation, by the construction of canals and turnpikes during the 1830s and the railroads in the 1840s and 1850s, which effectively tied the western states to the food-short cities of the Northeast and to the European market and thereby brought Cincinnati to worldwide prominence. But, improved transportation also brought more people. By 1830 settlers were venturing into Illinois and Indiana (Hopkins 1928:15; Bogue 1963:47–48). As Ohio itself became more densely inhabited, it assumed the role of fattening cattle that could be raised more cheaply on the prairies of Illinois and Iowa (Bogue 1963:47–48). Settlement moved even further west; by 1840 Iowa and Wisconsin were grazing cattle and Illinois was growing corn on which to fatten them (Hopkins 1928:17–18). Ohio's own role as cattle feeder began to decline thereafter and by the 1860s in some counties grain production was being displaced by dairying (Hopkins 1928:16).

As turnpikes and railroads spread and settlement increased, land values rose and open grassland gave way to more intensive uses such as cornfields

---

[8] It should also be noted that, from the beginning, hog-packing in Cincinnati also generated certain (though a limited number of) by-products; the most significant was lard for lamp-oil, of which Cincinnati alone produced 1.2 million gallons a year by the 1840s (Clark 1916:493).

and corn-based feeder operations. Large ranches were subdivided into tenant farms whose occupants were encouraged to grow corn—which was well suited to prairie climate and soil—and actively discouraged from raising cattle, since cheaper western grazing lands made a feeder industry more profitable (Gates 1973:138). The extension of the corn-belt also stimulated the increased production of hogs (Gates 1973:138, 198, 164–165; Clemen 1923:209), both because of the inherent efficiency of the hog as a converter of corn and because, as the cattle industry moved west, more eastern regions were developing better marketing facilities, which improved opportunities for the sale of pork and even corn directly. Thus, the eighth U.S. Bureau of the Census' Agricultural Report (in 1860) observed that "in localities favorably situated for the sale of corn, the business of feeding it to cattle became a comparatively unimportant one [quoted in Hopkins 1928:18]."

The successive transformations of midwestern production point out with great clarity the extent to which the raising of cattle was above all a commercial proposition. Their raising or feeding was rarely governed by sentiment and was as likely to decline in importance when economic conditions were unfavorable as they were to flourish when grass (or corn) was cheap. The evolution of the prairie economy testifies to the shaping of cultural dispositions by material circumstances, with "the commercial farmer . . . [trying] to find the combination of crops and livestock that would give him the greatest return on his investment of labor and capital [Bogue 1963:123]."

For reasons of economy, then, the livestock production in the Midwest after the passing of the open prairie was generally a mixture of cattle and hogs (Bogue 1963:97), and "the hog was as important on the farms of the prairie triangle as the steer or milk cow [Bogue 1963:103]." Even where cattle were dominant, the profits derived from them were often directly contingent on swine; thus, according to one report, "in a large number of cases in the Corn Belt, the profit from cattle feeding [was] largely the added profit procured from the hogs fattened more economically in conjunction with the cattle feeding operation [Croxton 1902:41]" as hogs salvaged undigested corn from cattle droppings just as they had earlier on eastern drives (Henlein 1959:72). Dairymen were also accustomed to raise hogs on waste products of buttermilk and on whey (Bogue 1963:103).

Since cattle tended to involve substantial capital investment and entailed considerable risk, hogs were the primary strategy for most small and marginal farmers to market their corn, apart from what they might sell to more affluent cattle producers or, later, to commission men and grain elevator operators. The low capital requirements and the high productivity of swine offered flexibility and greater security in an increasingly complex and problematic market where corn prices, in particular, were subject to great variation and when the monetary and banking structure in general was subject to tremendous strains that evidenced themselves in severe depressions, recessions, and financial panics throughout the first half of the nineteenth century (North 1966).

THE SHIFT FROM A SOUTHERN TO AN EASTERN MARKET

Although the prominence of pork packing in the Midwest resulted from conditions favoring corn production (and, thus, was also limited eventually by climatic and edaphic conditions which set certain constraints on corn), it was also enhanced by a pattern of regional specialization and by the articulation of the United States economy as a whole with Europe and, especially, England.

In particular, there was a vital linkage between the westward expansion of the cotton South and the extension of corn and hog production in the prairie states. Until the 1840s, the major outlet for midwestern produce was the Ohio–Mississippi River system, and the principal market was the South, where the dominance and rapid expansion of cotton production created great demand in the plantation regions for imported food-stuffs—most of which came from the Midwest and consisted of flour and pork products (Bidwell and Falconer 1925:173)—without which the rapid westward extension of the plantation system was impossible (Bidwell and Falconer 1925:171; North 1966:67–68). In particular, after the 1840s, rising cotton prices significantly displaced any serious agricultural diversification or subsistence production in much of the newer southern lands, with corn relegated to land that was unsuited to cotton (Smith 1958:76).

At the heart of the American pre–Civil War economy, then, was the production of cotton. As North and Thompson observe,

> American exports of cotton provided a major share of the world supply and contributed more than half of the value of the nation's total exports. Her external trade relations, the prosperity and expansion of the South, and the influence of the South upon other economic regions, all hinged on that one vital crop [1968:190].

Thus, as the florescence of cotton production turned the South into a food-deficit region, it caused corn and hog production to flourish in midwestern states such as Illinois, Ohio, and Indiana (Gates 1960:330).[9] The vitality of southern cotton production also enabled the South to obtain goods and services from the Northeast (the Liverpool–Southern commerce was mediated through northern ports [North 1966:126–28]), stimulating industrial and urban growth which eventuated in the usurpation of the western economy by the northern states.

Above all, however, the cotton system itself was sustained by northeastern and, especially, by British capital (North 1966:129). As a result, it is difficult to sustain the argument of a simple cultural-symbolic origin for American patterns of meat production; Porkopolis was, on the one hand, the

[9] Border states such as Tennessee were close enough to the cotton-producing states that they also could supply livestock, among which swine outnumbered cattle. A comparison of hogs and cattle in Tennessee counties in 1860 shows the former more prevalent than the latter by anywhere between 5 and 18 times (Clark 1942:178–190).

outcome of local ecological and demographic conditions and, on the other, a by-product of the textile mills of Manchester.

It is interesting to ask, however, why so little beef went south, while most prairie cattle were driven or shipped east. Part of the answer lies, first, in the fact that pork was processed and, in this manner, could easily be shipped both east and south—most dramatically to the South through the 1840s, but by the 1850s at increased rates to rapidly growing northeastern urban areas (Gates 1960:330). The shipments to the South of barrelled pork were certainly facilitated, moreover, by the fact that the cheapest river transport consisted of several thousand flatboats that plied the Ohio–Mississippi system, even during the heyday of the steamboat, and which were not especially conducive to shipments of live animals (Gates 1960:328–329).

Cattle, however, were still largely driven or shipped live to marketing centers, where they were then slaughtered. But, even more, the fact that most were destined for eastern cities—far from being a consequence of regional cultural dietary preferences—was a function of differential economic specialization. Cattle supplied not merely meat—for which northern urban areas, swelled by European immigration, certainly had a growing need—but also hides to provision an important leather industry which had originated in the early colonial era in New England. (Pigskin, however, was generally too thin or fragile for use in durable leather goods.) Thus, by the eve of the Civil War, when the major industrial use of leather was footwear, "the country's principal shoe-manufacturing center was in eastern Massachusetts [Clark 1928:33, 116]." In contrast, while there was some small-scale manufacturing in the South, after 1815 "the increasing cheapness of [northern] factory products . . . and the expansion of commercial cotton planting [Gray 1933:456]" reduced it greatly—so that leather goods, including shoes, saddles, etc., were obtained from the Northeast (Clark 1928:116), paralleling the importation of flour and pork from the Midwest.

By the 1850s, railroads had begun to shift western produce to eastern and European markets; the output of the packinghouses in Ohio began to extinguish most of what remained of an eastern livestock industry, reducing it to a dairy focus on the eve of the Civil War (Bidwell and Falconer 1925:450) and causing the abandonment of such farming areas as the northern hill country of New England (Ullman 1956:864) which also, by the turn of the century, would turn to dairy production (Wilson 1936:10). With the war itself, the southern market was almost entirely replaced by a demand for meat—largely pork—by the North, by the Union Army, and by Europe (the export of pork products rising from 50 to 218 thousand pounds between 1861 and 1864 [Rothstein 1969:391–392]).[10]

River traffic did not entirely cease during the 1850s, but it did decline rapidly as east–west rail connections undermined the strategic position of Cin-

[10] After the war, however, pork was once again marketed in great quantities to the South (see footnote 15).

cinnati. More conveniently situated river towns such as St. Louis acquired a larger share of the remaining riverine commerce (U.S. Congress in North and Thompson 1968:203), furthering Cincinnati's decline; but above all, westward settlement and the extension of the railroads shifted the center of the pork-packing industry to Chicago (Clemen 1923:137–144). There, a beef-packing trade was also beginning to take shape; for, just as it had been more economical to pack pork than drive hogs a long distance, so, as settlement moved west of Cincinnati, the economy of droving declined and beef-packing enterprises began to develop (Clemen 1923:79). Chicago, in particular, provided a convenient outlet for grass-fed cattle from northern Illinois and parts of Iowa, Indiana, and Michigan (Bidwell and Falconer 1925:393). Although hogs remained the basis of Chicago's meatpacking industry, the role of beef was destined to expand as the railroads and eastern and fôreign capital began to develop the nearby plains, a veritable "sea of grass."

Thus, at the heart of the imminent transformation of the American meat economy—much as it also rested on the emergence of monopoly capitalism in the post–Civil War period—was a fundamental ecological transition. As Clark observes, the westward movement onto the Great Plains "produced the steer as inevitably as the corn frontier had produced the hog [1928:506–507: 1916:484]."

THE DEVELOPMENT OF THE GREAT PLAINS

Until the 1870s, pork was not only the dominant meat in the domestic economy but the principal export meat as well (North and Thomas 1968:194; Mulhall 1885:91). Hogs were the basis of the midwestern packing industry, while most western beef cattle were still largely slaughtered to supply fresh meat for local consumption. Thus, in 1867–1868, almost 800,000 hogs were packed in Chicago, compared to 35,000 cattle (Shannon 1961:231).

Yet, certain convergent developments had begun to create conditions that would favor an intensive and national beef industry. During the decades preceding the Civil War, for example, cattle had been introduced onto the plains of northeastern Texas (Dale 1960). The principal market for these animals during this period was New Orleans (North and Thomas 1968:203–204), although herds were occasionally driven north into Ohio and to Chicago (Dale 1960:6–7), which encouraged the nascent beef-packing industry. During the Civil War, however, the Texas herds were isolated from an effective market; in a semiwild state, they simply multiplied, until, by the late 1860s, as railroads began to cross the Great Plains, they constituted an enormous reservoir of animals with which to begin to stock these vast public grasslands (Clark 1956:743).

Until the 1860s, however, the Plains were the treaty lands of Indians and the habitat of the buffalo on which they subsisted (Sandoz 1954:32). Hornaday, in his classic monograph on the North American bison, dates the era of the beginning of their systematic destruction from 1830 (1889:493), about the time that Texas cattle first began to spread northward (Clark 1956:743). By

1869, the Union Pacific Railroad had divided the Plains buffalo into two great herds and simultaneously provided the means for marketing buffalo products on a massive scale. Dodge City, which would soon become the largest cattle market in the world—from which Texas longhorns would be shipped east by rail—was transformed virtually overnight from a military post in Indian territory to a major center for buffalo hunting (Vestal 1952:1). "During the years 1871 to 1874 but little else was done in that country except buffalo killing [Hornaday 1889:493]" and by 1875 the southern herd was virtually gone (Hornaday 1889:501).

Up until 1870, as many as six million buffalo had occupied the Plains, and "even as late as 1875 the farmers of eastern Kansas were in the habit of making trips every fall into the western part of the state for wagon loads of buffalo meat as a supply for the succeeding winter [Hornaday 1889:486]." But, powerful interests were served by the extermination of the buffalo: It was an absolute prerequisite for the advance of cattle raising on the Great Plains; and it was widely considered necessary to end the resistance of the Plains Indian (Dale 1965:13; Vestal 1952:38). Thus, "soldiers of the tiny garrisons strung along the frontier heartily approved the destruction of the herds as the only means likely to keep the Indian on his reservation [Vestal 1952:38]."

This systematic program was not, however, without more direct economic motive as well. Between 1872 and 1874 alone, over 12 million pounds of buffalo meat and over 32 million pounds of bone, for the manufacture of bone china, were shipped out of Dodge City; and, largely as a result of the English demand for leather during the Crimean War, 1.3 million buffalo hides left there during the same brief period (Vestal 1952:41–44). The railroads themselves, which brought these demands, created a more local market with their own need for meat to supply construction crews.[11]

By 1875, the grass on which the great buffalo herd had grazed beckoned prospective cattle ranchers. The railroads, which had shipped out buffalo hides and bones, now turned eagerly to shipping cattle; army garrisons, the railroads, and mining towns provided ready local markets. But, above all there were the Indians who now depended on the federal government for food; "the Indian Department . . . became the purchaser of many millions of pounds of beef annually to feed the reservation Indians [and] a number of important cattlemen laid the foundations of their large enterprises by securing lucrative government contracts [Dale 1965:14; cf. Frink *et al.* 1956:13]."

The raising of cattle on the Plains was also quickly assimilated into the established interregional symbiosis with corn-producing states to the east with their constant need of cheap, grass-fed cattle to fatten on their surplus grain (Dale 1965:244). By 1860, Texas had already become the first ranked source of such feeder cattle (Bidwell and Falconer 1925:398) and, as the 1870s unfolded, the role of Plains cattle in this respect continued to grow. Where

[11] William Cody, one of the most famous buffalo hunters, contracted with the Kansas Pacific in 1867 to provision its workers with meat (Hornaday 1889:478).

branchlines of railroads such as the Union Pacific and the Atchison, Topeka, and Santa Fe crossed the major cattle trails, at places like Dodge and Abilene, important cattle markets developed (Clemen 1923:193). By 1871, before the slaughter of the buffalo had even begun to peak, over 700,000 head of range cattle were being shipped by rail to packinghouses in Chicago and elsewhere in neighboring corn-belt states (Harris and Ross 1978:92; Frink *et al.* 1956:13). Productivity on this scale was a critical stimulus to the general capital intensification of the meat industry—and thereby to the elaboration of the previously modest role that beef had played.[12]

THE RISE OF THE MODERN MEAT INDUSTRY

The structure of Western meat production up to the 1870s was still largely atomistic, although clear tendencies toward consolidation were in evidence since the 1840s. More than any other factor, perhaps, it was the railroads that expedited the trend toward greater centralization in the meat-packing industry and its emergence in this manner in Chicago a decade after the Civil War. Beginning in the late 1840s, they enabled the packing industry to transcend the spatial limitations of natural waterways and canals, which had made the South the principal market for the Ohio basin (U.S. Congress in North and Thomas 1968:196–205), and to overcome the seasonal constraints that had forced packers to suspend activity during the winter when rivers froze. By the late 1850s, the railroads had also exerted a profound influence on the spatial distribution of packing operations:

> The advantage of rails in terms of speed of movement, seasonal reliability and flexibility of route enabled both new packing centres to emerge and encouraged a greater degree of concentration within the industry. . . . The closure of the Mississippi River during the Civil War consolidated this trend as river towns were forced to turn to rails to reach outlets. This increasing dependence on railroads encouraged the centralization of processing at main termini [Walsh 1978:10].

In creating a transport system that enabled the industrial Northeast to appropriate much of midwestern production, which formerly had been marketed through New Orleans (North 1966:141–153), the railroads also signified the increasing penetration of eastern and foreign capital that played such a critical role in transforming meatpacking into a highly concentrated industry (Walsh 1978:17–22). By the time that the westward movement of the agricultural frontier and the expansion of the railroads had shifted the center of the pack-

---

[12] Of course, the period of the 1870s–1880s is one in which the image of the independent, heroic cowboy emerges in conjunction with that other American legend, the cattle drive up from Texas to such towns as Abilene and Dodge and Kansas City. Overlooked is the fact that *even* the business of driving cattle became, during this era, a highly organized affair which produced not a few millionaires. Skaggs observes that the cattle-trailing firm of Lytle, McDaniel, Schreiner, and Light Cattle Company alone "controlled no less than 15 percent of all the cattle trailed northward from Texas during the twenty-five years that followed the Civil War. Indeed, if ten years of that period in which the company did not even exist were also taken into account, the firm's real contribution to the movement of cattle would approach 30 percent [1973:26]."

ing industry to Chicago in the late 1850s, that industry was "in the hands of men of larger experience and with better eastern connections [Clemen 1923:144]." Many of these men amassed enormous capital through government contracts and speculation (largely in pork) during the Civil War[13] (Seligman 1971:173–174; Corey 1950:41–42) and were in an excellent position—financially as well as geographically—to develop the opportunities that arose with the opening of the Great Plains.

Thus, despite the fact that pork was the basis of an important export trade and the packing industry in 1870 "was ready to merge into a mature industrial economy [Walsh 1978:22]," the immediate conditions that propelled the meat-packing industry into a phase of intensive centralization favored the role of beef rather than that of pork. The Plains initiated an unprecedented era of cheap cattle raising that seemed so profitable that millions of dollars were invested by Scottish and English capitalists (Dale 1965:89; Clemen 1923:185; Frink 1956:27; Graham 1960).[14] Burgeoning livestock shipments stimulated a dramatic expansion in railroad milage—in fact, most of the 9000 miles (14,400 km) constructed between 1860 and 1888 were added after 1879 (Clemen 1923:191)—and, again, this was a profitable field for investment of foreign (as well as eastern) capital. (According to Kotz, "a substantial portion of the capital used to build and consolidate American railroads between the Civil War and the 1890s came from Europe, particularly England [1978:26].") This widespread rail network, in turn, proved critical in several respects for the development of a system of mass-produced beef.

But, what was especially decisive in the centralization of a high-volume system of beef production, however, was the development of new refrigeration technology which "made it possible to utilize to the fullest extent the supply of livestock and . . . made the distribution system of meats nation-wide and world-wide. It prevented decay of perishable products. As it lengthened the period of consumption it led to greatly increased demand [Clemen 1923:8]." While this gave a certain stimulus to the trade in fresh pork, it was principally beef that refrigeration advanced, since it made practicable the centralized slaughter and mass production of fresh (dressed) beef, a form in which beef could effectively compete with pork in taste and especially in price (cf. Perren 1978:72, on the limited appeal of American pickled beef in England.). Moreover, American swine were immediately placed at a severe disadvantage because they had never been bred to produce *fresh* meat, but rather to yield flesh which was ideally suited to salting and curing and which was fairly soft and fatty (Perren 1978:71). Thus, after the 1870s, meat packing—although still heavily involved in pork—shifted its focus, as it entered

[13] Gustavus Swift, P. D. Armour, and Nelson Morris all "entered the meat business before the Civil War in the capacity of small pork packers [Temporary National Economic Committee 1940:15]."

[14] Schlebecker reports that "now and then profits reached as high as 40% on the invested capital" in Plains cattle operations during the 1870s (1963:6).

the era of corporate capitalism; it became "in large part a beef business and national in its scheme of distribution [Clemen 1923:173]."

Initially, however, dressed beef met intense opposition from two interest groups: (*a*) the railroad owners, who found it more profitable to transport livestock, and who wanted to protect their substantial investments in terminals and stockyards along their routes and did not want to invest in expensive new refrigerated cars (Kojovich 1970:461–462); and (*b*) butchers, whose livelihood was based on the local slaughter of interstate shipments of livestock. The resistance of the railroads was weakened by the precariousness of the industry itself, paradoxically a direct consequence of redundant track built largely to profit from livestock shipments; "parallel building and overextension led to frequent rate-cutting. . . . Competition and disastrous price wars would break out. . . . These practices made the major American railroads financially insecure by the late 1880s [Kotz 1978:2]," and this insecurity undermined the industry's united front against dressed beef.

The situation of the butchers, on the other hand, echoed that of many other local commercial interests during the late nineteenth century that were fending off new industrial combinations. Refrigeration had enabled a handful of midwestern packers to mass-produce and distribute dressed beef at prices with which local butchers could not compete.

Butchers' associations sought to protect their interests through protectionist legislation on the state level, in particular, through laws that prohibited the sale of dressed meats unless "inspected by state officials twenty-four hours before slaughter [McCurdy 1978:644]." Such measures would have effectively curtailed the development of a centrally organized national dressed beef industry. In order to counter this, the packers waged an intensive legal campaign during the 1880s which culminated in a *federal* meat inspection law that, unlike state inspection regulations, did not militate against out-of-state, centralized slaughter operations. Thus, what has often been viewed as a victory for progressive, antitrust forces was, in fact, the consummation of a concentrated effort by the major meat packers themselves to establish a national market.

While refrigeration lay at the center of the wide-scale marketing of beef, it was also a major element in achieving the efficiency of operations which made dressed beef profitable and able to undersell local butchers. Outstanding was the fact that dressed beef saved the expense of shipping the 35–40% of a steer that was inedible (McCurdy 1978; Corey 1950:40), leaving that portion available for the packers to elaborate into a lucrative by-products industry. Thus, from the 1870s on, by-products became "the gold-mine of the [packing] industry [Clemen 1923:347]." Cattle, which had long been characteristic of more heavily capitalized agricultural operations, now offered greater opportunities for profit than did swine to a capital-intensive meat-packing industry, since "by-products, the handling of which required large capital outlays, made up a smaller portion per pound of live-weight of hogs than other animals being considered [Arnould 1971:20]." Thus, what had made the hog so economical for small farmers—the fact that 70–75% of the animal, compared to 50–55% for a steer, was edible (Thompson and Kilborun 1941:80)—now made swine less profitable for modern packers, for whom meat was not necessarily the primary determinant of production strategies. In the Twin Cities market area in 1912, for example, a 1000-pound steer generated over 15 dollars in by-products, compared to just under a third that value from an equal weight in hogs (Wild 1915:24–25).

At the same time, what had formerly been the major by-product of hogs, lard, was gradually being replaced as an illuminant and lubricant, by the increasing use of petroleum (Clark 1928:35), while, in contrast, a rising demand for hides by Eastern manufacturers meant a market for more and more cattle. By the 1880s, American cattle yielded 13–14 million cowhides annually; a decade later, after the entry of the major packers into the tanning business, leather manufacturing became more concentrated and the output of leather products, especially footwear, accelerated until, by 1905, "the United States exported more sole leather than all the other great leather-producing countries of the world combined [Clark 1928:765]." But, this productive capacity still exceeded the American cattle supply so that by 1914, over three-quarters of all hides converted into leather were, in fact, *imported.* Thus, the American leather industry could absorb whatever domestic cattle producers could supply (Clark 1928:463–468, 764–765). This critical difference in the profitability in cattle and hog by-products had evident effect on the development of monopoly control over the livestock markets; by 1916, when five firms (Armour, Swift, Wilson, Morris, and Cudahy) dominated the meat-packing industry, they slaughtered just over 82% of all federally inspected cattle killed, compared to only 61% of hogs (Federal Trade Commission 1920:33; Arnould 1971:20).

Yet, because of the importance of the export market, hog production did not immediately decline with the rise of the beef monopoly (Larmer 1926:37; Mulhall 1885:91; Williams 1969:218); indeed, between 1870 and 1880, U.S. hog production actually increased 96% (Towne and Wentworth 1950:209).[15]

[15] One measure of the continuing importance of swine is to be found in the pattern of meat processing in towns such as Kansas City, the prominence of whose stockyards was directly associated with its being a major terminus of Texas cattle trails. Nevertheless, one of its major meat-packing firms, George Fowler, Son and Company, which was established there in 1880, by 1886 was annually processing 10,000 cattle—but 425,000 hogs (Skaggs 1973:85). Moreover, in the aftermath of the Civil War, the South continued to depend heavily on pork imported from the corn-belt states; according to Hilliard, "while the remainder of the nation shifted away from a heavy consumption of pork, much of the South may have actually increased the proportion of pork in the diet [1972:66–67]." That is to say, that the Civil War did not fundamentally alter the Southern focus of production away from cotton toward greater agricultural diversification; while slavery came to an end, much of the agricultural population of the South became tenant farmers—by 1900, about 61% of farmers in South Carolina were tenants, while "as recently as 1935, three-fourths of the state's cultivated land was planted either in cotton or in corn [Landes 1970:107]." Corn, however, generally was produced in insufficient quantities and corn meal was imported in considerable quantities from the Midwest in the late nineteenth century. Simultaneously, "millions of pounds of [pork] were shipped south every month. Broad thick sides of Iowa, Illinois, Ohio and Indiana salt pork were sliced into five and ten-pound orders on Saturday for hungry families of cotton farmers [Clark 1944:157]."

But, in the long run, as, domestically, the expansion of hog production was ecologically constrained by limits on the extension of the corn-belt, foreign demand was limited by the crucial role played by swine in European agriculture. Thus, in 1877, when a pleuro-pneumonia epidemic among European cattle opened up the British market for U.S. beef (Bogue 1963:283), providing another important stimulus to the beef-orientation of the U.S. meat industry, it also increased the economic importance of continental swine production and led to a series of protectionist tariffs across Europe to exclude U.S. pork (which had been underselling native hog products) (Shannon 1961:194; Larmer 1926:37; Duncan 1959; Gignilliat 1961; Williams 1969:227–228). The result was a sharp fall in U.S. pork exports, while beef exports were on the rise (Mulhall 1885:91). Although U.S. pork was being exported to the continent again by the 1890s (Bogue 1963:282–283), the 1880s were a crucial decade in the development of the American meat industry; European tariffs had provided one more factor contributing toward the ascendancy of beef in the packing industry—and such protective tariffs would appear again, as in the 1920s (Shover 1965:11).

THE DECLINE OF BEEF

Even as the beef industry expanded, the ecological conditions which had underwritten its beginnings began to deteriorate. The bonanza of the Plains was extraordinarily brief and the period of cheap, fresh beef in the eastern cities, which had helped to establish the Chicago meat monopoly, gave way by the end of the nineteenth century to an era of rapidly rising prices.

Depression in 1884 ruined many of the cattle companies (Clemen 1923:189) and rising land prices and the contraction of grassland, both the result of a steady influx of homesteaders (accelerated by the advance of the railroads), and the degradation of the range from overstocking, all compelled more intensive strategies of beef production—especially expensive new breeds that could be moved off grass at ever younger ages to be finished on corn. Thus, as Trager notes, "before 1900, cattle generally matured five or six years before being marketed and were rarely fed much besides grass. After 1900, land in the West became too expensive to keep a steer even three or four years, much less five or six." (By the eve of World War II, animals were rarely kept on the range beyond 1–2 years [Thompson and Kilbourn 1941:69].)

While cheap grassland continued to be a cornerstone of beef production, corn began increasingly to influence the price of beef as the burden of productivity shifted to feed lots[16] which, in turn, "developed as part of a system to market feed grains," in particular, the corn surplus, (Ward *et al.* 1977:265)—for, "without the ruminant market, grain prices would decline

[16] By 1912, 74% of the total feed costs of beef cattle were represented by corn (U.S. Tariff Commission 1922:25).

sharply [Hodgson 1976:628].'' Corn-feeding of cattle was encouraged, moreover, by the eventual development of the U.S. Department of Agriculture's grading system, which designated as ''choice,'' meat that had intramuscular fat (i.e., was ''marbled''), which corn-fed cattle add more rapidly than forage-fed cattle do. As Ward has noted, ''because of the more favorable price, the choice grade is the predominant goal of feeders, and thus it is apparent that the existing grading system has imposed a structure on the industry which in turn has institutionalized consumer tastes and a demand for grain-fed cattle [1977:265].'' But, the point is that corn-fed beef is not intrinsically superior to grass-fed (Hess and Hess 1977:48; Hornaday 1889:447); although it has come to be regarded as a response to comsumer preference, in fact such ''taste'' was conditioned by the economic interests of corn-producers and persistent pressure to dispose of grain surpluses.

The increasing use of grains sustained the growth of the meat-packing industry but encouraged a tighter integration of the various phases of beef production. Larmer describes this period as one of rising costs and increasing complexity:

> Costs of production advanced. The investment required . . . increased many fold. Financial problems came and grew with the increasing complexities of the business. There were credit upheavals and disasters in the eighties, in the nineties, in 1908. The livestock producer found himself involved in a more and more complex national economic structure with its increasingly intricate workings [1926:2].

Western meat production evolved into a system of ''meat-packing plants, flour mills, grain-elevator companies and railroad corporations,'' (Rothstein 1969:401–402) in which the major meat-packing firms played a dominant role. Armour, for example, became important in the grain market, operating numerous elevators in the Midwest and accounting for almost one-quarter of all Chicago grain receipts by 1917 (U.S. Federal Trade Commission 1920:213–214).

Increasing monopoly and changes in the resource base of meat—especially beef—production made increasing prices a major cause of concern in eastern states by the turn of the century. By 1902, a report from the U.S. Department of Labor observed that ''during the last few months perhaps no subject has been more discussed by the press and the public than has the advance in the price of fresh beef [Croxton 1902:794].'' Between 1890 and 1902, for example, June fresh western beef prices in Boston had risen from $6.37 ½ per 100 pounds to $10 per 100 pounds (Croxton 1902:795–796). In Massachusetts, in general, between 1897 and 1910, the price of roast beef rose 37%—less than the price of pork, but enough to cause a severe decline in beef consumption (The Commission on the Cost of Living 1910:93).

According to Corey, ''production of beef cattle reached its peak around 1900, and then began a decline [1950:96–97].'' A rapidly expanding U.S. population (increasing some 40% between 1900 and 1920 [U.S. Tariff Commission 1922:2]) was easily able to absorb what had previously been sold abroad; exports consequently fell off and, by 1913, the only chilled beef received in England was from South America (Perren 1971:444; Strickon 1965:235), where U.S. firms such as Armour and Swift were also beginning to develop grassland for beef production (Smith 1969:33–34, 57).

Thus, after 1907, U.S. beef surpluses were quickly declining; while, in association with an increase in farming and urban growth, dairying and hog production were on the rise (U.S. Tariff Commission 1922:2–3). There was, in fact, an absolute decline in the number of beef cattle from 1900 to 1920 in most parts of the country (with just a brief revival during World War I) (U.S. Tariff Commission 1922a:13) which was attributable to two major factors: the continuing reduction in carrying capacity of rangeland, and the fact that, in the more developed parts of the central and midwestern states, "dairying, hog, and crop production to a considerable extent displaced cattle raising [U.S. Tariff Commission 1922:16]."[17] These changes were reflected in a constant rise in beef prices; total meat consumption declined 12% between 1909 and 1939, while per capita consumption of beans rose 37%, other vegetables, 26%, and dairy products, 19% (Corey 1950:154).

The upward trend in beef prices was aggravated by a decrease in income during the depression years and obviously compelled many consumers to find substitutes. But, annual per capita consumption of beef and veal was already dropping before 1929: It fell from 87 pounds in 1907 to 59 pounds by 1920 (U.S. Tariff Commission 1922:2; Corey 1950:96–97, 113) and, from the late 1920s on, pork, which was usually cheaper than beef, constituted the greater share of U.S. meat consumption—a situation that presisted until shortly after World War II (Engelman and Gaarder 1958:9; Corey 1950:96–97). At that time, corn surpluses produced by new hybrids, petrochemical fertilizers, and irrigation revitalized U.S. beef production (Corey 1950:97; Pimental *et al.* 1977).

This second era of plentiful and comparatively cheap beef has proved as short-lived as that at the end of the nineteenth century, but it has been limited more by the rising costs of petroleum imports that subsidize U.S. agriculture (including feed grains such as corn) than by the availability of grassland. This latter point merits qualification: It is still the presence of grassland that, more than anything else, maintains an important role for ruminants in the American food system, despite the fact that the carrying capacity of such land is naturally low and, in many instances, deteriorating (Ward *et al.* 1977:267, 270; The Rockefeller Foundation 1976:29). It is as a result of such declining grassland productivity, however, and rapid urban growth and recurrent corn

---

[17] From about 1915 to 1935, hog production increased some 45%, while that of beef changed little between the period 1910–1914 and 1928–1932. Evidence also suggests that the proportion of beef that came from dairy animals advanced between these two periods from 25 to 33% (Fitzgerald 1935:4,9).

surpluses that, by 1973, "about half of the 150 million metric tons of grain fed to livestock was consumed by ruminants [Hodgson 1976:628]."

While the productivity of U.S. corn acreage only increased 31% between 1909 and 1945,[18] the introduction of new (largely energy-intensive) techniques of production at the end of the World War II raised yields by 240% by 1970 (Pimental *et al.* 1977:42). Enormous new grain surpluses "made possible a livestock production system based on grain feeding and still providing relatively inexpensive meat to the American consumer [The Rockefeller Foundation 1976:11; cf. Hodgson 1976:627]." The number of cattle and calves in the United States increased from 80 million in 1950 to over 132 million in 1974, resulting in cheaper beef and a dramatic rise in its consumption from 49 pounds (carcass weight) per person in 1945 to 85 pounds in 1960 and to 126 pounds by 1977 (Harris and Ross 1978:91; U.S. Senate Committee on Agriculture 1972:119).

The cost of this "green revolution" was considerable, however. Intensive feed grain production entailed a sixteenfold increase in the use of nitrogen fertilizer and a massive commitment to energy-intensive mechanization, imposing huge new production costs which led to a dramatic rise in farm indebtedness and a resultant loss of about 3.1 million farms between 1950 and 1974, and facilitated the ascendancy of corporate farms (Pimental *et al.* 1977:42–43; Hightower 1975; U.S. Department of Commerce 1978:691; George n.d.:24). Increased use of a hybrid corn with reduced protein value also impelled cattle feeders to make greater use of protein concentrates, usually fishmeal from Peru, which, therefore, has been diverted from a third-world population which itself suffers from protein undernutrition (Lerza 1975:52; Borgstrom 1967:281–282). When the total energy costs of this new agricultural regime are fully assessed, moreover, there turns out to have been an actual decline in overall efficiency since World War II of about 24% (Pimental *et al.* 1977).

As petroleum prices have risen steadily during the 1970s, so have the costs of production of feed grains. While corn yields barely changed between 1971 and 1973, the price of nitrogen fertilizer almost tripled. As corn prices, in turn, rose—from $1.08 a bushel in 1971 to $3.65 in 1974 (Morgan 1975:111)—so did those for beef—often by as much as 25% a year (*Business Week* 1979a:87). And, since it has been, at times, more profitable for grain dealers to market part of the corn crop abroad[19] (or for it to be processed domestically as beer or corn oil), it was inevitable that cattle and calf herds would be cut back, which they soon were.

---

[18] In Ohio, for example, the average yield of corn per acre was about the same in the decade 1920–1929 as in the years 1870–1879, despite an average increase in fertilizer per acre of 340% (Corey 1950:120).

[19] Between 10–12% of the U.S. corn crop is exported (The Rockefeller Foundation 1976:93). Two companies, Cargill and Continental Grain, control 45% of U.S. grain exports (*Business Week* 1979c:68).

By the late 1970s, cattlemen and feedlot operators, at least, were expressing "considerable apprehension about the future of animal production [The Rockefeller Foundation 1976:28]" and American consumers—for whom beef had been democratized during the 1950s and 1960s—no longer viewed steak as either a status marker or a dietary aspiration, as they might have at the end of World War II. Rather, they began to react against a situation of mass availability at escalating prices and turn to cheaper alternatives, including pork and vegetarianism. Swine production, in fact, has begun to show a marked resurgence and seems likely to be consumed in the future at a rate that rivals that for beef (*Wall Street Journal* 1979:24). On the other hand, as we will see next, an economy of inflation has created seemingly endless opportunities for corporate merger, as the trend toward greater integration has benefited from conditions that have intensified the indebtedness of smaller operations. Thus, 1978, according to *Business Week,* was a year when profits for the giant food processors reached record levels (1979a:46). In the same year, Cargill Corporation, the nation's largest privately owned company and the biggest grain dealer in the world, bought up the country's second major meat packer, MBPXL Corporation (formerly, Missouri Beef Packers); however expensive beef might get, it will probably persist as a profitable way to market grain (*Business Week* 1979c:68, 75–76).

THE BEEF INDUSTRY AND MONOPOLY CAPITALISM

Under these circumstances, however, the rise in beef prices cannot be attributed to the increased costs of energy alone; it owes a great deal as well to the degree of oligopoly in the meat industry (a reflection of trends in the food-producing sector as a whole and, indeed, throughout the American economy).

This tendency toward concentration was visible, as I have shown, in the rise of the Chicago meatpackers in the 1870s. That initial movement toward vertical integration was itself so pronounced that by 1920 the Federal Trade Commission was expressing its concern that the five largest packers—Armour, Swift, Wilson, Morris, and Cudahy—would "control the whole-sale distribution of the Nation's food supply within a few years [1920:42]." It was this potential that led to an agreement between the U.S. Government and these five firms—known as the "Consent Decree"—that ostensibly required the packers to divest themselves of stockyards and terminal railroads, to withdraw from wholesale fruit and vegetable canning operations and to stay out of retail activities. Nevertheless, this arrangement hardly suspended the trend toward greater concentration. Within 3 short years, Armour had bought up Morris & Company (Temporary National Economic Committee 1940:21); by 1937, Swift's operations alone included not only acquiring and slaughtering livestock, but also processing by-products (such as soap, glycerine, gelatine, hides, etc.), extracting oils from cotton seeds, coconuts, and peanuts, manufacturing animal feeds and fertilizers, phosphate and rock salt mining, and vegetable canning (through its subsidiary, Libby, McNeil and Libby) (Moody's Investor's Service 1937:1371).

Even before the end of World War I, the large packers slaughtered 71% of all federally inspected animals and produced about one-fifth of domestic fertilizer, three-fourths of all hides, and one-third of all cotton seed oil (Temporary National Economic Committee 1940:16–17). During the 1920s, a certain decentralization of the meat industry occurred briefly when refrigerated trucking and highway construction permitted small packing plants to develop, largely in the Corn Belt, by-passing the central stockyards and dealing directly and less expensively with cattle and hog suppliers (Arnould 1971:27; Temporary National Economic Committee 1940:17). As a result, by 1929, the market share held by the four major packers of all federally inspected animals killed had declined to 59%. But, they soon began to buy up many of these scattered, small packers and to build new, decentralized plants of their own. By 1935, the combined sales of Armour and Swift alone amounted to 61% of the total value of all meats sold (Temporary National Economic Committee 1940:17, 19). By 1957, Congressional hearings indicated that "economic concentration in meat packing was as great as before the Consent Decree [Consumer's Report 1957:252]."

The degree of vertical integration characterizing not only the meat industry today but food processing in general is staggering. Swift and Armour are themselves now subsidiaries of highly diversified corporations—a reflection of the accelerating trend toward corporate concentration, the result of which is that "control of manufacturing assets is lodged in a relatively few hands today [Federal Trade Commission 1969:162]." In every specialized sector of food processing, for example, whether bread, cereal, canned goods, or meat, four or fewer companies control 55% or more of the market (George n.d.:27–28). Thus, farmers find themselves compelled to deal with a few conglomerates that control seed, fertilizer, farm machinery, and the marketing of grain and livestock. Two companies, for example, DeKalb AgResearch and Pioneer Hi-Bred International, dominate the seed industry; Deere and Company and International Harvester command some 57% of the U.S. tractor market; and Ralston Purina and Cargill, Inc., control the animal feed industry (George n.d.:25).

The degree of integration in the food industry is partly a matter of conglomerates that have branched out into the diverse phases of food production. Thus, Pillsbury and General Mills have entered the restaurant business (with Burger King and York Steak Houses, respectively). Cargill, still a relatively anonymous company, originated over a century ago as a grain elevator operation; since 1950—the beginning of the magic decade in U.S. agriculture—its expansion into soybeans, poultry, fertilizer, and, most recently, meat has made it the largest privately owned corporation in the United States (Tamarkin 1978). Beatrice Foods, another relatively little known conglomerate, which began as a Nebraska dairy company, has acquired 400 other companies since 1950—more than any other company listed in the Fortune 500—and, with subsidiaries such as Dannon yogurt, LaChoy Chinese foods, and Eckrich meats, was earning by 1976 "more money than any other food processor in the United States [Martin 1976:119]." If one considers that U.S. agricultural production actually begins at the wellhead, perhaps the most integrated—not merely diversified—company is Esmark. Its subsidiaries include Vickers Petroleum, TransOcean Oil, Unitech Chemical, STP Corporation, Swift Agricultural Chemicals Corporation, and Swift and Company (the latter, the largest meat-processing company in the country) (Moody's Investor's Service 1974:964–965; 1978a:753–754; Standard and Poors 1979:5049).

Another equally important, but less conspicuous aspect of increased concentration throughout American business is the degree of interlocking directorates of major corporations, a kind of interdependence which has "burgeoned as these conglomerates have grown [Federal Trade Commission 1969:202]." According to Krebs, "among just 21 corporations involved in agribusiness, there are 53 direct interlocks and 1,081 indirect interlocks through 801 intermediate corporations [1979:64; cf. Finger *et al.* 1974]." In the case of Esmark, for example, there are connections with IC Industries (which owns Midas and Pepsi Bottlers), Pet (which operates Hardee's and Stuckey's restaurant chains), International Harvester and, through its parent company, Interco, Florsheim shoes (which depends on leather supplies, which happen to be a major by-product of Swift's operations) (Moody's Investor's Service 1979).

The result of these interlocking interests is to ensure the noncompetitive nature of the market, a condition already promoted by intensive concentration. According to a Federal Trade Commission staff report, "after adjustment for other factors affecting company profit rates, net profits of large corporations are positively correlated with the average level of market concentration in the industries they occupy [1969:225]." Through interlocking relationships, moreover, such companies maintain important linkages "with their suppliers, customers, potential competitors, and the financial institutions from which they borrow funds" which "may prevent or discourage independent behavior in market decisions [Federal Trade Commission 1969:199]" and result in huge monopoly overcharges for the public in general and for specific groups such as farmers. According to the FTC, for example, such overcharges amount to 200 million dollars in the seed industry alone (George n.d.:25); and "two recent national studies, one by an economist with the FTC, another by one with the USDA, claim consumers pay up to $14 billion a year more for their groceries because of food industry monopolies [Krebs 1979:62,65]."

Thus, while fertilizer, gasoline, and machinery costs are sky-rocketing, while consumer retail prices (especially for beef) soar and most farmers make little if any profit, the food industry has nonetheless proven to be a lucrative field for investment by large corporations. In particular, meatpacking and processing, the country's biggest food industry (U.S. Senate Committee on

Agriculture 1972:318), has been so profitable that most major packers have been bought up by conglomerates whose interests are far wider than food alone: Thus, Swift is owned by Esmark, Armour by Greyhound, MBPXL by Cargill, Wilson by Ling-Temco-Vought (which also owns Braniff), Iowa Beef Processors—the number one meat packer (*Business Week* 1979c:68)—by General Electric, and John Morrell and Company by United Brands (which also includes Baskin–Robbins and Foster Grant among its subsidiaries (Krebs 1979:65; Moody's Investor's Service 1978a:753–754; Federal Trade Commission 1969:512).

A full account of the current structure of the meat industry in the evolving system of U.S. monopoly capitalism must necessarily go one additional step, for behind these conglomerates and their complex networks of associations and the proliferating brand names that obscure the trend toward integration, there lies a more profound and concentrated level of financial control by a relatively small number of institutions whose pivotal role in the American economy has been more or less continuous since the late nineteenth century (Kotz 1978).

Recent research documents the preeminent role played by such financial institutions as Morgan Guaranty Trust, Citibank, Chase Manhattan, Manufacturers Hanover and the Lehman–Goldman, Sachs group—banks whose degree of power is only truly grasped when it is recognized that they are even one another's principal stockholders (U.S. Senate Subcommittee on Governmental Affairs 1978:260). Among these banks, Morgan's influence is particularly noteworthy: Out of 122 major corporations surveyed—whose common stock collectively had a market value in 1976 equal to 41% of *all* common stock outstanding in the United States—Morgan was found to be among the top 5 stock-voters in 56 (U.S. Senate Subcommittee on Governmental Affairs 1978:7, 257). As far as it can be determined now, the meat-processing companies to which I have referred earlier are related to these financial groups in the manner described in Table 7.2.

Thus, it is clear that the development of meat production in the United States in this century cannot be comprehended apart from the pattern of in-

TABLE 7.2
Bank Influence in the Meat Industry

Meat company	Parent company	Controlling financial group
Swift	Esmark	Morgan
Armour	Greyhound	Lehman–Goldman, Sachs
John Morrell	United Brands	Morgan
Wilson	LTV	Morgan, Lehman–Goldman, Sachs
American Beef Packers	GE Credit Corp.	Morgan

Sources: Moody's Investor's Service 1974, 1977, 1978a, 1978b; Standard and Poors 1979; Kotz 1978.

TABLE 7.3
Changes in Number of U.S. Farms by Size, 1950–1969

Size of Farm: (acres)	1969	1950	Percent Change
1–259	1,944,224	4,606,497	−58%
260–499	419,421	478,170	−12
500–999	215,659	182,297	+18
1,000+	150,946	121,473	+24

Source: U.S. Bureau of the Census, Census of Agriculture 1973:59.

creasing concentration and centralization of capital throughout the American economy (cf. Sweezy 1972:42). This tendency, as I have noted, has been particularly conducive to beef production in several respects. One consequence of the increasing capitalization of agriculture, which bears somewhat closer consideration in this regard, is the decline of small farms since the turn of the century, and the concomitant rise both in land concentration and in farm tenancy (cf. U.S. Department of Agriculture 1928).

The decline of small farms (see Table 7.3) has generally tended to reduce opportunities for expansion of pork production until quite recently. As spiraling production costs have accelerated the evolution of highly integrated corporations and led to the takeover of major meat-processing firms by giant holding companies, the development of such conglomerates and the huge monopoly overcharges which they have generated have accelerated the loss of small farms with which hog raising has typically been associated (see Tables 7.4 and 7.5).[20] Thus, where, in 1935, about 13% of American farm gross income came from hogs and about 7% from beef cattle (Fitzgerald 1935:2) and,

TABLE 7.4
Distribution of U.S. Livestock by Size of Farms,[a] 1969

	Acreage			
	1–259	260–499	500–999	1,000+
Milk cows	52%[b]	29%	13%	4%
Swine	43	33	17	7
Bulls and steers (incl. calves)	25	20	19	37

Source: U.S. Bureau of the Census, Census of Agriculture 1973:125–129.

[a]Includes all farms earning $2,500 and up.

[b]Percentages sum to more than 100 because of rounding figures off to nearest integer.

[20] I have included figures for Iowa since it is the leading state in cash receipts from the marketing of meat-producing animals. The disparity between beef cattle and swine in terms of associated land holdings, while quite marked, is not as striking as the nationwide figures because the latter include states with rangeland.

TABLE 7.5
Distribution of Livestock by Size of Farms,[a] Iowa, 1969

	Acreage			
	1–259	260–499	500–999	1,000+
Milk cows	60%[b]	33%	7%	1%
Swine	47	39	14	2
Bulls and steers (incl. calves)	28	40	24	8

Source: U.S. Bureau of the Census, Census of Agriculture 1972:90–93.

[a]Includes all farms earning $2500 and up.

[b]Percentages sum to more than 100 because of rounding figures off to nearest integer.

by 1950, "three and one-half million swine breeders annually market[ed] at American abattoirs nearly three billion dollars' worth of hogs—more money than realized from the sale of cattle, sheep, and lambs combined [Towne and Wentworth 1950:184]," by 1973, beef cattle and calves represented 27% of the cash receipts of farmers, compared to only 9% for hogs (Hodgson 1976:628).

Several other, related factors must be noted which also contributed to the rise in beef consumption since the late 1950s and early 1960s. First, beef consumption was actively and profitably promoted by supermarket chains which were, in fact, often closely associated with beef producers. Thus, the Kern County Land Company of California, with 2 million acres of grazing land in Arizona, New Mexico, and California and its own feed lots in Kern County, was developed as a major beef producer in the 1950s by the former marketing vice president of Safeway, Inc.; in 1967, Kern was taken over by Tenneco Corporation (Moody's 1967:3116)[21] (see Figure 7.1).

Perhaps more important has been the role of hamburger as a major source of cheap meat whose spreading popularity was closely associated with post-war surburban growth, the expansion of the national highway system, and a dramatic rise in working women. From the 1950s on, while steak tended generally to exceed pork and ham in price, hamburger prices were surprisingly uniform and lower than any form of pork (U.S. Department of Labor 1959:4–6). Much of the post-war rise in beef consumption resulted from the mass availability of hamburger, which has developed to the point that at least 40% of all beef consumed in the U.S. at present is ground beef (*Wall Street Journal* 1977:January 13, 1). There are several reasons for this. First, U.S. meat producers were slow to develop an adequate meat-type hog (The Rockefeller Foundation 1976:55). Second, a significant proportion of ham-

[21] Since one of the principal financial groups behind Safeway and, hence, interconnected to Kern is Merrill Lynch, it is fair to say, regarding their television advertisements, that when Merrill Lynch says they're "bullish" on America, they really mean it.

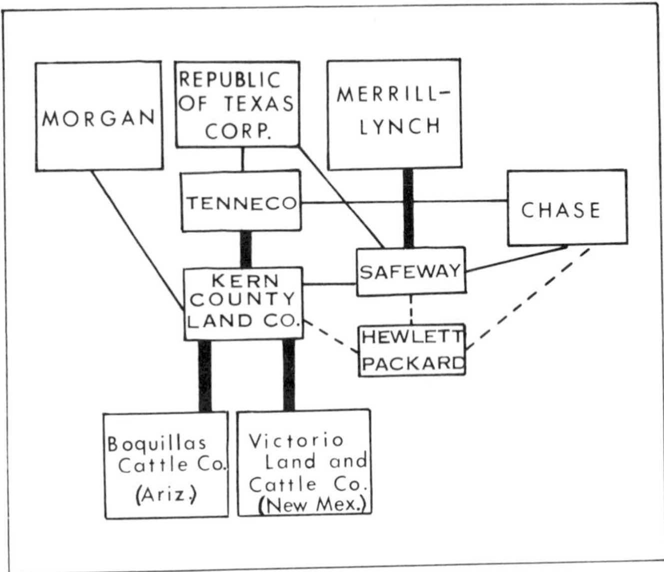

FIGURE 7.1. *The interconnections of meat producers, retailers, conglomerates, and financial groups. Ownership,* ——; *strong influence,* ——; *director interlock,* ---.

burger was a product of dairy cows, not specifically of beef cattle, and therefore reflected a general intensification of production in areas of population increase. Thirdly, while pork production was generally limited by corn production and, hence, by certain ecological constraints, beefburgers had much greater potential for market expansion since their producers could appropriate grassland in Latin America to modulate prices, while domestic pork and beef, based on increasingly expensive grain, became more costly.

Thus, the most dramatic rise in U.S. beef consumption since 1960 coincided not only with the proliferation of fast-food burger franchises, but also with "the rapid rise in United States beef imports [that began] in the early 1960s [Edelman 1979:10]"—amounting to 284 million pounds of beef from Central America alone in 1972 (Edelman 1979:10). Thus, American beef consumption continues to rest upon the availability of grassland—but, now, as part of a process of international capitalist underdevelopment in which arable land is actually being converted to cattle pasture (Edelman 1979; George n.d.:50) and being withdrawn from local subsistence production. Clearly, what has emerged is a direct descendant of the paradigmatic colonial relationship between England and Ireland, where Irish tenant farmers were reduced to marginal consumption while they produced wheat, hogs, and cattle for export to England (Kennedy 1973:26,28; Schumacher 1948:131). Just as clearly, it requires serious consideration of the ultimate social costs of what has become not only an expensive but also an unnecessarily high level of meat consumption in the United States, and consideration, as well, of more equitable and responsible alternatives. As observed earlier, it is apparent that such alternatives are already being elected by many Americans, though largely as a response to changing economic conditions.

Conclusions

I have reviewed at some length the evolution of the U.S. economy of meat production, within which framework an understanding of the relative and changing roles of beef and pork can ultimately be achieved. I have indicated the extent to which the respective significance of different animal sources of protein rests upon factors that are not primarily cultural—certain associations of land use and population pressure, for example—which also may explain the origins of dietary systems in other cultures, and the degree to which mundane economic and ecological factors time and again take priority over obscure, unconscious mental structures, with strategies of production being, at one and the same time, flexible yet constrained by objective conditions. Thus, on the local level, as Bidwell and Falconer note, "natural conditions of soil and climate, as well as economic conditions, such as the want of capital, scarcity of labor, and want of markets were influential in determining the choice of enterprises [1925:452; cf. Henlein 1959:66]." Thus, for every increase in the production of cattle, one can point to a decline elsewhere—associated with changes in the character of the local economy and its articulation with a wider economic system. Such trends are evidence that beef production (and that of pork, as well) was not driven by sentiment or an invariant cultural logic—but, was just one of a number of alternative strategies, one with definite advantages under specific economic, ecological, and historical conditions.

It has also been important to recognize the extent to which production strategies were affected, from the first moment of European settlement, by the place of the American economy within a larger mercantile system (Lemon 1972:27–29; Clark 1916:1; North 1956); and the degree to which patterns of U.S. production were influenced by "world-historical" developments that belie Sahlins' notion of culturally determined diet. Thus, the relatively negligible role of lamb in the American diet cannot initially be dissociated from Brithish mercantile policy which sought to develop a colonial market for English woolens (Clark 1916:11–12,22) (while the major stimulus to American sheep raising was the Civil War when wool replaced cotton that could no longer be readily obtained from the South [Clark 1928:26–30].) Similarly, as Bogue has observed,

> England's decision to lower tariffs during the 1840s . . . the later actions of a number of European countries in barring American pork . . . all had their effect upon the price level of pork, and this, in turn, influenced the decisions of prairie farmers [1963:112].

It is this wider system of interactions that, in combination with local and regional ecological conditions, has profoundly influenced the "design" of American life, that especially calls into question the legitimacy of any view of the autonomy of culture. Such a conception of "*a* culture as a self-perpetuating, structurally autonomous ordering of human life [Leeds 1971:229]"—the general view which informs Sahlins' discussion of the American diet, just as it did Lewis' model of the "culture of poverty"—is an anachronistic ideal at odds with the reality of a world economic system, existent at least since the fifteenth century (Wallerstein 1974; Schneider 1977; Frank 1978), or with the emergence of an international division of labor within which U.S. economic and cultural development has occurred. In view of this, the derivation of the contemporary U.S. sentiment toward beef from an ancient Indo-European symbolic order represents an idealization both of culture and of history, a detachment from time and space, which obscures both local and regional cultural ecological process and the world-economic context of cultures.

Thus, Sahlins contends that an ideological predilection for beef—for which no evidence can be adduced—determined the U.S. production of grains which, in turn, shaped our international trade and implies that everything would have been different if we ate dogs instead of cattle (since he emphasizes the common etymology of cattle and capitalism, I presume he does actually believe that American capitalism is a result of an ancient ideology of beef preference).[22] However, the causal sequence actually appears to be the opposite: The differential production of grains, such as corn or wheat, is literally rooted in local soil and climatic conditions. As Paul Gates observes, "superior soil, a long growing season, hot July and August days, combined with sufficient rainfall, created the modern corn belt in [the] prairie states [1960:326; cf. Diller 1941:12; Bogue 1963]"—not to mention the especially profound symbiotic relationship of corn, *not* with cattle, but with hog production. The production of corn surpluses has perenially affected national politics and international relations, in turn, through pressures exerted by farmers to dispose of that surplus (cf. Williams 1969). And cattle were *never* the first or the sole means for marketing corn—pork, bourbon, beer, and starch being among the others. Indeed, far from cattle production compelling the production of corn, it is generally the price of corn which is among the principal determinants of how the grain will be utilized; thus, "when foreign and domestic demands force prices upward . . . the amount of grain fed to beef and dairy cattle

---

[22] Sahlins has on several occasions called attention to the fact that the words "cattle" and "capitalism" have a common derivation (cf. 1979:53). What better evidence can one find of the semanticism that structuralists would substitute for history? It should also be pointed out, while on this etymological detour, that the term "cattle" only in recent times acquired a limited association with bovines; it formerly applied equally to swine, sheep, goats, and horses—that is, to domesticated quadrupeds in general (Neilson *et al.* 1961:425).

decreases [Hodgson 1976:627].'' All of this, of course, is of *critical* importance if we are to begin to comprehend why the U.S. produces beef (or pork) in the quantities and at the prices that it does.

Thus, a difference in the conception of culture, alluded to at the start of this chapter, involves more than the origin of dietary habits; it comes down to whether an anthropology is possible which is germane to contemporary social, political, and economic problems, including those of agribusiness domination and capitalist underdevelopment at home and abroad. From Sahlins, for whom ''the reason Americans deem dog inedible and cattle 'food' is no more perceptible to the senses than is the price of beef [1976:169],'' the most hope one can derive is in the misguided faith that things might be different if we just ate dogs instead of cattle (1976:171). While the eventual ascendancy of beef over pork coincided with the maturation of monopoly capitalism, agribusiness today is no more contingent on the nature of our diet than U.S. cattle production is on an ancient symbolic code; and American political economy will not be substantially altered if we all switch to pork or become vegetarians. For those of us who want not only to understand the world, but to change it, the answers are unfortunately *not* that simple. But, the beginning surely lies in isolating and confronting the important questions and in demonstrating that they are susceptible to systematic investigation and *serious* answers; in recognizing the reactionary implications of any ahistorical anthropology; and in recalling Marx and Engel's own advice on this point: ''That it is only possible to achieve real liberation in the real world and by employing real means . . . [that] 'liberation' is an historical and not a mental act [1970:61].''

References

Anderson, E. N., and M. Anderson

1977 Modern China: South. In *Food in Chinese culture: Anthropological and historical perspectives* (K. C. Chang, Ed.). New Haven: Yale University Press. Pp. 317–382.

Arnould, R.

1971 Changing patterns of concentration in American meat packing, 1880–1963. *Business History Review 45*(1):18–34.

Basso, E.

1973 *The Kalapalo Indians of central Brazil.* New York: Holt, Rinehart and Winston.

Beck, A.

1973 The ecology of urban dogs. In *Wildlife in an urbanizing environment.* Springfield: Massachusetts Cooperative Extension Service. Pp. 57–58.

1974 The dog: America's sacred cow? *Nation's Cities 12*(2):29–31, 34–35.

1975 The public health implications of urban dogs. *American Journal of Public Health 65*(12):1315–1318.

Bennett, H. S.

1960 *Life on the English manor: A study of peasant conditions, 1150–1400.* Cambridge: Cambridge University Press.

Bidwell, P., and J. Falconer
1925 *History of agriculture in the northern United States, 1620–1860.* Washington: Carnegie Institution.

Blum, J.
1978 *The end of the old order in rural Europe.* Princeton: Princeton University Press.

Bogue, A.
1963 *From prairie to corn belt: Farming on the Illinois and Iowa prairies in the nineteenth century.* Chicago: University of Chicago Press.

Borgstrom, G.
1967 *The hungry planet.* New York: Collier.

Braudel, F.
1967 *Capitalism and material life, 1400–1800.* New York: Harper and Row.

Buck, J.
1956 *Land utilization in China.* New York: The Council on Economic and Cultural Affairs.

Business Week
1979a Food: A move to higher-margin products. Jan. 8, No. 2567:46–50.
1979b Pillsbury's ambitious plans to use Green Giant. Feb. 5, No. 2571:87–88.
1979c Cargill: Preparing for the next boom—Worldwide grain trading. April 16, No. 2581:68–76.

Clark, A.
1956 The impact of exotic invasion on the remaining New World mid-latitude grasslands. In *Man's role in changing the face of the earth* (W. Thomas, Ed.) Chicago: University of Chicago Press. Pp. 737–762.

Clark, B.
1942 *The Tennessee yeoman, 1840–1860.* Nashville: Vanderbilt University Press.

Clark, T.
1944 *Pills, petticoats and plows: The southern country store.* New York: Bobbs-Merrill.

Clark, V.
1916 *History of manufactures in the United States, 1607–1860.* Washington: Carnegie Institution.
1928 *History of manufactures in the United States, 1860–1914.* Washington: Carnegie Institution.

Clemen, R.
1923 *The American livestock and meat industry.* New York: Ronald Press.

Commission on the Cost of Living, The
1910 *Report.* Boston: Wright and Potter.

Consumer's Report
1957 Meat: The big packers want a bigger bite. May:251ff.

Corey, L.
1950 *Meat and man: A study of monopoly, unionism, and food policy.* New York: Viking Press.

Croxton, F.
1902 Beef prices. Vol.7(41):794–806.

Cummings, R.
1940 *The American and his food: A history of food habits in the United States.* Chicago: The University of Chicago Press.

Curtis-Bennett, N.
1949 *The food of the people, being the history of industrial feeding.* London: Faber and Faber.

Dale, E.
1960 *The range cattle industry: Rancing on the Great Plains from 1865 to 1925.* Norman: University of Oklahoma.
1965 *Cow country.* Norman: University of Oklahoma.

Darby, H. C.
1956 The clearing of the woodland in Europe. In *Man's role in changing the face of the Earth* (W. L. Thomas, Ed.) Chicago: University of Chicago Press. Pp. 183–216.

Diller, R.
1941 *Farm ownership, tenancy, and land use in a Nebraska community.* Chicago: University of Chicago Press.

Dornstreich, M., and G. Morren
1974 Does New Guinea cannibalism have nutritional value? *Human Ecology 2*:1–12.

Duncan, B.
1959 Protectionism and pork: Whitelaw Reid as diplomat: 1889–1891. *Agricultural History 33*:190–195.

Engelman, G., and R. Gaarder
1958 Marketing meat-type hogs: Problems, practices and potentials in the United States and Canada. *U.S. Department of Agriculture, Marketing Research Report,* No. 227.

Ewen, S.
1976 *Captains of consciousness: Advertising and the social roots of the consumer culture.* New York: McGraw-Hill.

Finger, B. *et al.*
1974 Agribusiness gets the dollar. *Southern Exposure 2*(2,3):150–157.

Fitzgerald, D. A.
1935 *Livestock under the AAA.* Washington: The Brookings Institution.

Forster, R. and O. Ranum
1979 Introduction. In *Food and drink in history* (R. Forster and O. Ranum, Eds.) Baltimore: Johns Hopkins University Press. Pp. vii–xiii.

Fortune
1960 The new cattle business. *61*(4):222–228.

Fowler, S.
1961 *The marketing of livestock and meat.* Danville: The Interstate Printers and Publishers.

Frank, A. G.
1978 *World accumulation, 1492–1789.* New York: Monthly Review Press.

Freeman, M.
1977 Sung. In *Food in Chinese culture: Anthropological and historical perspectives* (K. C. Chang, Ed.). New Haven: Yale University Press. Pp. 141–176.

Frink, M. *et al.*
1956 *When grass was king: Contributions to the western range cattle industry study.* Boulder: University of Colorado Press.

Frisch, R.
1978 Population, food intake, and fertility. *Science 199*:22–30.

Gade, D.
1976 Horsemeat as human food in France. *Ecology of Food and Nutrition 5*(1):1–11.

Gates, P.
1966 The farmer's age, 1815–1860. In *Views of American economic growth: The agricultural era* (T. Cochran and T. Brewer, Eds.) New York: McGraw-Hill. Pp. 314–330.
1973 *Landlords and tenants on the prairie frontier: Studies in American land policy.* Ithaca: Cornell University Press.

George, S.
n.d. *Feeding the few: Corporate control of food.* Washington, D.C.: Institute for Policy Studies.

Giedion, S.
1948 *Mechanization takes command: A contribution to anonymous history.* New York: Norton.

Gignilliat, J.
1961 Pigs, politics, and protection: The European boycott of American pork, 1879–1891. *Agricultural History 35*:3–12.

Graham, R.
1960 The investment boom in British-Texan cattle companies, 1880–1885. *Business History Review 34*(4):421–445.
Gray, L.
1933 *History of agriculture in the southern United States to 1860.* Washington: Carnegie Institution.
Greenfield Popular Union
n.d. At the crossroads: Agriculture and agriculture labor in the Connecticut river valley. Turner's Falls.
Harner, M.
1977 The ecological basis of Aztec sacrifice. *American Ethnologist 4*(1):117–135.
Harris, M.
1974 *Cows, pigs, wars and witches: The riddles of culture.* New York: Random House.
1977 *Cannibals and kings: The origins of cultures.* New York: Random House.
Harris, M., and E. Ross
1978 How beef became king. *Psychology Today 12*(5):88–94.
Harrison, G.
1963 *Borthwicks: A century in the meat trade, 1863–1963.* London.
Hartley, D.
1954 *Food in England.* London: MacDonald.
Hemardinquer, J.
1979 The family pig of the ancien régime: Myth or fact? In *Food and drink in history* (R. Forster and O. Ranum, Eds.) Baltimore: Johns Hopkins University Press. Pp. 50–72.
Henlein, P.
1959 *Cattle kingdom in the Ohio valley,* 1783–1860. Lexington: University of Kentucky Press.
Hess, J., and K. Hess
1977 *The taste of America.* New York: Penguin Books.
Hidy, R., and M. Hidy
1960 Anglo-American merchant bankers and the railroads of the Old Northwest, 1848–1860. *Business History Review 34*(2):150–169.
Hightower, J.
1975 The industrialization of food. In *The people's land: A reader on land reform in the United States* (P. Barnes, Ed.) Emmaus: Rodale Press. Pp. 81–85.
Hilliard, S. B.
1972 *Hogmeat and hoecake: Food supply in the Old South, 1840–1860.* Carbondale: Southern Illinois University.
Hodgson, H.
1976 Forages, ruminant livestock, and food. *BioScience 26*(10):625–630.
Hopkins, J.
1928 *Economic history of the production of beef cattle in Iowa.* Iowa City: The State Historical Society of Iowa.
Hornaday, W.
1889 The extermination of the American bison, with a sketch of its discovery and life history. *Annual Report, Smithsonian Institution,* Part II. Washington, D.C.: U.S. Government Printing Office. Pp. 367–548.
Jewell, P. A.
1969 Wild mammals and their potential for new domestication. In *The domestication and exploitation of plants and animals* (P. Ucko and G. W. Dimbleby, Eds.). Chicago: Aldine-Atherton. Pp. 101–109.
Kennedy, R.
1973 *The Irish: Emigration, marriage, and fertility.* Berkeley: University of California Press.
Kojovich, M.
1970 The refrigerator car and the growth of the American dressed beef industry. *Business History Review 44*(4):460–482.

Kotz, D.
1978 *Bank contol of large corporations in the United States.* Berkeley: University of California Press.
Krebs, A. V.
1979 A galloping oligopoly in food. *Business and Society Review*:60–65.
Landes, E.
1970 *A history of South Carolina, 1865–1960.* Columbia: University of South Carolina Press.
Lantis, D. *et al.*
1963 *California: Land on contrast.* Belmont: Wadsworth.
Larmer, F.
1926 *Financing the livestock industry.* New York: Macmillan.
Leeds, A.
1971 The concept of the "culture of poverty": Conceptual, logical, and empirical problems, with perspectives from Brazil and Peru. In *The culture of poverty: A critique* (E. Leacock, Ed.). New York: Simon and Schuster. Pp. 226–284.
Lemon, J.
1972 *The best poor man's country: A geographical study of early southeastern Pennsylvania.* New York: Norton.
Lerza, C.
1975 Emptying the cornucopia. In *Food for people, not for profit: A sourcebook on the food crisis* (C. Lerza, and M. Jacobson, Eds.) New York: Ballantine. Pp. 45–57.
Lindenbaum, S.
1979 *Kuru sorcery: Disease and danger in the New Guinea highlands.* Palo Alto: Mayfield.
Margolis, M.
1977 Historical perspectives on frontier agriculture as an adaptive strategy. *American Ethnologist 4*(1):42–64.
Martin, E.
1942 *The standard of living in 1860.* Chicago: University of Chicago.
Martin, L.
1976 How Beatrice Foods sneaked up on $5 billion. *Fortune 93*:4:119–129.
Marx, K. and F. Engels
1970 *The German ideology.* New York: International Publishers.
McCurdy, C.
1978 American law and the marketing structure of the large corporation, 1875–1890. *The Journal of Economic History 38*(3):631–649.
Moody's Investor Service
1978a Moody's industrial manual. 1937–1978. New York.
1978b Moody's public utility manual. New York.
Morgan, D.
1975 Behind rising food prices. In *Food for people, not for profit* (C. Lerza and M. Jacobson, Eds.). New York: Ballantine. Pp. 109–114.
Morgan, E.
1975 *American slavery—American freedom.* New York: Knopf.
Morneau, M.
1979 The potato in the eighteenth century. In *Food and drink in history* (R. Forster and O. Ranum, Eds.) Baltimore: Johns Hopkins University Press. Pp. 17–36.
Mote, F.
1977 Yüan and Ming. In *Food in Chinese culture: Anthropological and historical perspectives* (K. C. Chang, Ed.). New Haven: Yale University Press. Pp. 193–257.
Mulhall, M.
1885 *History of prices since the year 1850.* London: Longmans, Green.
Muller, E.
1976 Selective urban growth in the middle Ohio Valley, 1800–1860. *Geographical Review 66*(2):178–199.

Neilson, W., *et al.*

1961 *Webster's new international dictionary of the English language.* Springfield: G. and C. Merriam.

New York Times, The

1978 The good news is cows eat grass; The bad news is they prefer grain. June 18, p. E7.

North, D.

1956 International capital flows and the development of the American West. *The Journal of Economic History 16*(4):493–505.

1966 *The economic growth of the United States, 1790–1860.* New York: W. W. Norton.

North, D., and R. Thomas (Eds.)

1968 *The growth of the American economy to 1860.* New York: Harper and Row.

Nutini, H.

1971 The ideological bases of Levi-Strauss' structuralism. *American Anthropologist 73*:537–544.

Perren, R.

1971 The North American beef and cattle trade with Great Britain, 1870–1914. *The Economic History Review* (2nd Ser.) *24*(3):430–444.

1978 *The meat trade in Britain, 1840–1914.* London: Routledge and Kegan Paul.

Pet Food Institute

1976 *Literature review of the psychological aspects of pet ownership.* Washington, D.C.: Pet Food Institute.

Pimental, D., L. E. Hurd, A. C. Bellotti, M. J. Forster, I. N. Oka, O. D. Sholes, and R. J. Whitman

1977 Food production and the energy crisis. In *Food: politics, economics, nutrition and research* (P. Abelson, Ed.) Washington, D.C.: American Association for the Advancement of Science. Pp. 121–127.

Robbins, W.

1975 Super prices in the supermarket. In *Food for people, not for profit* (C. Lerza and M. Jacobson, Eds.). New York: Ballantine. Pp. 122–129.

Ross, E.

1978 Food taboos, diet, and hunting strategies: The adaptation to animals in Amazon cultural ecology. *Current Anthropology 19*(1):1–36.

Rothstein, M.

1969 The American West and foreign markets, 1850–1900. In *The frontier in American development* (D. Ellis, Ed.) Ithaca: Cornell University Press. Pp. 381–406.

Russell, H.

1976 *A long, deep furrow: Three centuries of farming in New England.* Hanover: University Press of New England.

Sahlins, M.

1976 *Culture and practical reason.* Chicago: University of Chicago Press.

1979 Reply to Marvin Harris. *New York Review of Books,* June 28:52–53.

SAMI

1978 *Report for the Pet Food Institute.* New York.

Sandoz, M.

1954 *The buffalo hunters; the story of the hide men.* New York: Hastings House.

Schafer, E.

1977 T'ang. In *Food in Chinese culture: Anthropological and historical perspectives* (K. C. Chang, Ed.) New Haven: Yale University Press. Pp. 85–140.

Schlebecker, J.

1963 *Cattle raising on the Plains, 1900–1961.* Lincoln: University of Nebraska Press.

Schneider, J.

1977 Was there a pre-capitalist world system? *Peasant Studies 6*(1):20–29.

Schumacher, M.
1948 *The northern farmer and his markets during the late colonial period.* Ph.D. dissertation, UCLA.

Seligman, B.
1971 *The potentates: Business and businessmen in American history.* New York: Dial.

Shannon, F.
1961 *The farmer's last frontier: Agriculture, 1860–1897.* New York: Holt, Rinehart and Winston.

Sherrill, B.
1978 High on the hog; southern folkfood. *The New York Times,* Dec. 10. Section 10. Pp. 1,17.

Shover, J.
1965 *Cornbelt rebellion.* Urbana: University of Illinois Press.

Skaggs, J.
1973 *The cattle-trailing industry: Between supply and demand, 1866–1890.* Lawrence: University Press of Kansas.

Smith, A.
1958 *Economic readjustment of an old cotton state: South Carolina, 1820–1860.* Columbia: University of South Carolina Press.

Smith, P.
1969 *Politics and beef in Argentina: Patterns of conflict and change.* New York: Columbia University Press.

Sprague, G.
1975 Agriculture in China. In *Food: Politics, economics, nutrition and research* (P. Abelson, Ed.). Washington, D.C.: American Association for the Advancement of Science. Pp. 57–63.

Standard and Poors
1979 Register of corporations, directors, and executives, Vol. 2: *Directors and Executives.* New York: Standard and Poors Corporation.

Strickon, A.
1965 The Euro-American Ranching Complex. In *Culture and animals: The role of animals in human ecological adjustments* (A. Leeds and A. Vayda, Eds.) Washington D.C.: American Association for the Advancement of Science. Pp. 229–257.

Sweezy, P.
1972 *Modern capitalism and other essays.* New York: Monthly Review Press.
1973 Cars and cities. *Monthly Review 24*(11):1–8.

Tamarkin, B.
1978 What—and who—makes Cargill so powerful? *Forbes,* Sept. 18:150–156.

Tannahill, R.
1973 *Food in history.* London: Eyre Methuen.

Temporary National Economic Committee
1940 Investigation of concentration of economic power. Monograph No. 35, Large-scale organization in the food industries. Washington, D.C.: U.S. Government Printing Office.

The Rockefeller Foundation
1976 *The role of animals in the world food situation.* New York: The Rockefeller Foundation.

Thompson, R. W., and G. M. Kilbourn
1941 The meat packing industry. In *The development of American industries: Their economic significance* (J. Glover and W. Cornell, Eds.). New York: Prentice Hall. Pp. 63–83.

Towne, C., and E. Wentworth
1950 *Pigs: From cave to corn belt.* Norman: University of Oklahoma Press.

U.S. Bureau of the Census

1967 Census of agriculture, 1964. In *Statistics by Subjects,* Chapter 1, Farms and land in farms. Washington, D.C.: U.S. Government Printing Office.

1972 Census of agriculture, 1969. In Vol. I, *Area Reports.* Part 16, Iowa Section I, Summary data. Washington, D.C.: U.S. Government Printing Office.

1973 Census of agriculture, 1969. In Vol. II, General Report. Chapter 2, Farms: Numbers, use of land, size of farm. Washington, D.C.: U.S. Government Printing Office.

U.S. Department of Agriculture, Office of Information

1928 The ownership of tenant farms in the United States. *Department Bulletin 1432.* Washington, D.C.: U.S. Government Printing Office.

U.S. Department of Commerce

1978 Statistical Abstracts of the U.S. (99th edition). Washington, D.C.: U.S. Government Printing Office.

U.S. Federal Trade Commission

1920 The five larger packers in produce and grocery foods. *Report on the Meat-Packing Industry,* Part IV. Washington, D.C.: U.S. Government Printing Office.

1969 Staff report on corporate mergers, for the U.S. Senate committee on the judiciary, subcommittee on antitrust and monopoly. Washington, D.C.: U.S. Government Printing Office.

U.S. Senate Committee on Agriculture, Subcommittee on Livestock and Grains

1972 *Beef prices.* Washington, D.C.: U.S. Government Printing Office.

U.S. Senate Committee on Governmental Affairs, Subcommittee on Reports, Accounting and Management

1978 *Voting rights in major corporations.* Washington, D.C.: U.S. Government Printing Office.

U.S. Tariff Commission

1922a *Cattle and beef in the United States.* Washington, D.C.: U.S. Government Printing Office.

1922b Hides and skins. *Tariff Information Series,* No. 28. Washington, D.C.: U.S. Government Printing Office.

Vestal, S.

1952 *Queen of cowtowns, Dodge City.* New York: Harper and Brothers.

Wall Street Journal

1979 Strong pork demand, due to low prices, may indicate permanent shift from beef. Dec. 21, p. 24.

Wallerstein, I.

1974 *The modern world-system: Capitalist agriculture and the origins of the European world-economy in the sixteenth century.* New York: Academic Press.

Walsh, M.

1978 The spatial evolution of the mid-western pork industry, 1835–1875. *Journal of Historical Geography 4*(1):1–22.

Ward, G. M., *et al.*

1977 Beef production options and requirements for fossil fuel. *Science 198*:265–271.

Wild, L.

1915 *Studies in the marketing of farm products.* Minneapolis: University of Minnesota.

Williams, W. A.

1969 *The roots of the modern American empire: A study of the growth and shaping of social consciousness in a market-place society.* New York: Vintage.

Wilson, C. A.

1973 *Food and drink in Britain.* London: Constable.

Wilson, H.

1936 *The hill country of northern New England: Its social and economic history, 1790–1930.*

Yang, M.

1945 *A Chinese village.* New York: Columbia University Press.

Yoder, P.
1969 *Taverns and travelers: Inns of the early Midwest*. Bloomington: Indiana University Press.

Yü, Y.
1977 Han China. In *Food in Chinese culture: Anthropological and historical perspectives* (K. C. Chang, Ed.). New Haven: Yale University Press. Pp. 53–83.

III

IDEOLOGY, RITUAL, AND ECONOMY

8 The Material Conditions of Variation in Betsileo Ceremonial Life

CONRAD PHILLIP KOTTAK

Introduction

A major feature of biological evolution is its fortuitous character; from an array of available phenotypes natural forces select those fittest to survive and reproduce in a given environment. Given environmental perturbations or gradual shifts, adaptable varieties are not simply created but must be *chosen* from what the range of phenotypical differences has to offer. In the biological realm, then, natural selection can only depend on, and operate on, the variety at hand. Contemporary human populations also evolve, that is, adapt to changed circumstances, by—among other things—phenotypical modification.[1] However, behavior patterns can vary much more quickly and flexibly because they are less genetically restricted than among other animals. Culture, based on learning, can be set to work in adapting to change. Materialists see flexibility and adaptability as basic characteristics of the genus *Homo,* viewing such "uncommitted potentiality for change [Bateson 1972:497]" as a product itself of evolutionary selection. Variation is the stuff of which both biological and sociocultural evolution are made.

Nevertheless, the cultural evolution of specific human populations also has a conservative component: It proceeds in the fact of prior structures (a given sociocultural heritage) and is affected by the organizational material (sociocultural patterns) at hand when the change begins. Several anthropologists agree, and a few (e.g., Oliver 1962) have systematically demonstrated,

[1] Human populations continue to adapt to environmental change through genetic, physiological, and sociocultural adaptation. The last, however, is our most distinctive adaptive apparatus.

BEYOND THE MYTHS OF CULTURE
Essays in Cultural Materialism

ISBN 0-12-598180-5

that human populations and their cultural ways cannot be regarded as blank checks on which environment can freely and mechanically write.

This chapter's relationship to other materialist and evolutionary studies should be made clear at once. Many previous studies—Julian Steward's (1955) best known works, for example—have shown the role of *common* material conditions in generating sociocultural similarities among *unrelated* populations. This is also a frequent aim of Marvin Harris's cultural materialist determinism as revealed in the following quote: "By a deterministic relationship among cultural phenomena, I mean merely that similar variables under similar conditions tend to give rise to similar consequences [Harris 1977: xiii]."

These goals are perfectly appropriate, and such studies have increased our understanding of how similar forces generate similar sociocultural results. However, the aim of the present work is different. Focusing on the Betsileo of Madagascar, I will attempt to show how and why encounters between *identical* (or at least similar) cultural raw material and *dissimilar* material conditions tend to result in dissimilar consequences. This is simply an application to cultural data of the Darwinian model of branching evolution—descent with modification—through natural selection. Since cultural heritage can be held constant, the role of specific material conditions in effecting sociocultural change can be made particularly clear.

In this chapter I examine ways in which variable material conditions have historically determined—and still affect—variation in Betsileo ceremonial life. Material conditions are those that govern a group's access to valued and strategic resources. As such, they include the physical environment and biotic variables—rainfall, temperature, land forms, plants, and animals—that affect the formation of local ecosystems. They also include culturally available means of production and relations of production within such ecosystems and such regional forces as warfare, trade, and migration that join local systems into larger networks. However, most significant for understanding contemporary sociocultural variation among the Betsileo are *the material conditions that create and are created by systems of socioeconomic stratification*—artificial, human determinants of differential access—conditions not of nature but of a particular social form, the state.

The Betsileo, whose contemporary population nears one million people, are 1 of 20 *ethnies*—populations, "cultures," or ethnic units into which the Malagasy Republic divides its citizens. All these ethnic groups speak closely related languages and can generally be regarded as heirs to a common cultural heritage, that of the Proto-Malagasy (Vérin, Kottak, and Gorlin 1970). The Betsileo homeland spans perhaps 40,000 km^2 of central Madagascar's southern highlands (see Figure 8.1). Environmental and economic contrasts between the better watered, traditionally more populous and more agricultural eastern part of the Betsileo homeland and the more arid, more sparsely populated, more pastorally oriented south and west are historic material conditions. These conditions underlie much of the sociocultural variation en-

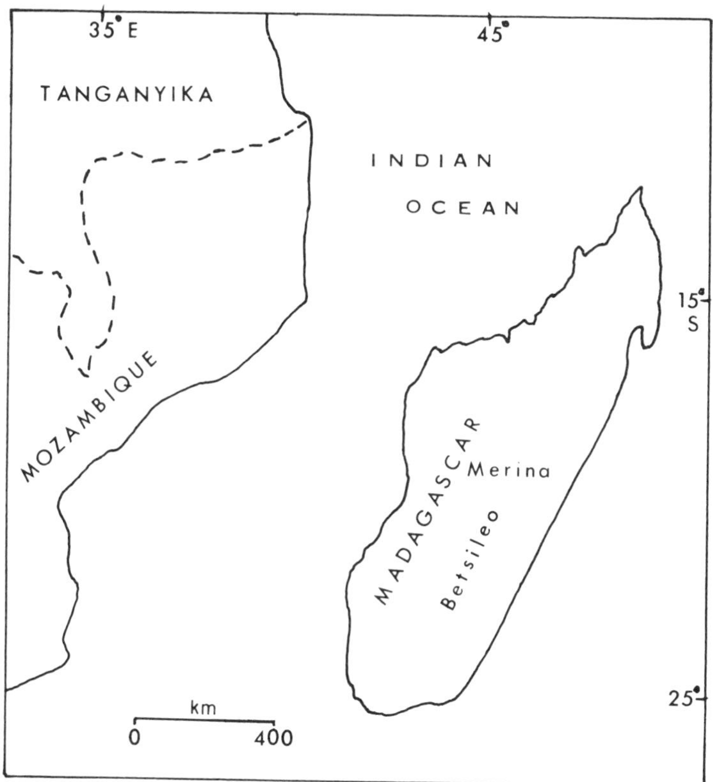

FIGURE 8.1 *Madagascar and the Betsileo.*

countered among the contemporary Betsileo—including the ceremonial forms and functions examined in this chapter.

State organization originated in the agricultural east during the eighteenth century (Kottak 1977, 1980). Although all Betsileo are recent (perhaps post-sixteenth century) offshoots of a common population and culture, central government and socioeconomic stratification never fully developed in the west and south. Continually attacked by their eastern (Tanala), southern (Bara), and western (Bara and Sakalava) neighbors, the Betsileo were conquered by their northern neighbors—the Merina, creators of Madagascar's major state—early in the nineteenth century. Since then the Betsileo have been ruled by foreigners: first Merina, subsequently (after 1896) French.

Prior Structure and Cultural Evolutionary Models

The continuing feedback between materialist, ecological, and evolutionary approaches in anthropology has considerably expanded our understanding of cultural evolutionary processes. Furthermore, I also believe that because of the growth of structuralism, materialists are paying more attention to relationships between prior structure and the material context of change. Although Lévi-Strauss' (cf. 1967:57–58) most characteristic and familiar use of the term *structure* is for universal attributes of the human mind or brain that he considers to be responsible for the cross-cultural recurrence of similar cultural forms or manifestations, he also occasionally uses *structure* to refer to the sociocultural manifestations and representations themselves. In this case, his structuralism can be used more easily within a materialist analysis. For example, when Lévi-Strauss tells us that the structure of the Dobuans is very different from the structure of the Trobrianders (1967:42), he is not talking about universal mental structures. Nor is he when he writes that "the great lesson of totemism is that the form of the structure can sometimes survive when the structure itself succumbs to events. [1966:232]." The interaction between prior structure (sociocultural heritage) and material conditions forms a framework for understanding a variety of types of evolutionary processes (Figure 8.2).

As noted, Julian Steward (1955) explicated sociocultural regularities or analogies involving form and function among widespread *unrelated* populations. He was demonstrating *convergent evolution;* he offered middle range generalizations intended to explain similarities attributable to common material conditions. Both flexibility—human populations are not so bound by their sociocultural heritage or prior structure that they may not change as material conditions change—and a certain inevitability—material conditions limit the variety of potential responses—are basic to Steward's formulations.

Materialist studies have also tried to explain similarities and differences among *related* populations, groups like the Malagasy that now are separate but that share a common sociocultural heritage (cf. Kottak 1971, 1972). It is in such cases, as well as in studies of specific evolution (Sahlins and Service 1960), that materialists must examine what Lévi-Strauss describes as "the structure which underlies the many manifestations and remains permanent throughout a succession of events [Lévi-Strauss 1967:22]." When related groups separate and encounter similar material conditions, not only are they likely to retain much of their common prior structure and cultural content,

Prior Structure (sociocultural heritage)	Natural Selective Forces (material conditions): Similar	Dissimilar
Same	parallel evolution	divergent evolution, adaptive radiation
Different	convergent evolution	"pure history"

FIGURE 8.2 *Interrelationship of prior structure and material conditions in types of sociocultural evolutionary processes.*

they can also be expected, to some extent, to change in parallel ways *(parallel evolution)*. Material conditions encountered in different places can, of course, never be identical; they must be evaluated as relatively similar or dissimilar by examining a combination of specified variables.

Like convergence, parallel evolution concerns the production or retention of *similarities*. If neither material conditions nor prior structure are common to the populations under consideration, there is little basis for materialist comparison of them. One is in the realm of "pure history." However, by holding prior structure constant, and viewing sociocultural variation among related groups against a background of variation in material conditions, a processual, materialistic explication of variation and transformations becomes possible. This will be my object here.

Although anthropological investigations of *divergent evolution*, which often culminates in an *adaptive radiation* of related populations, are not new, they are less common than studies of convergent evolution. Models essentially of adaptive radiation have been previously applied by Sahlins (1958) to Polynesia; by Gulliver (1955) to the Jie and Turkana of Uganda; and by Steward (1956) and his students to Puerto Rico. Such a model makes it possible to see sociocultural differences among related populations as so many variations on a common theme, and to link this variation—considered synchronically or diachronically—to differences in material conditions. Applied to the 20 or so "ethnic units" of Madagascar (Kottak 1971, 1972) or, as is done here (and more fully in Kottak [1980]), to 3 contrasting southern Betsileo villages, the model has enabled me to explore and elucidate certain relationships between form, content, structure, behavior, and change, on the one hand, and material factors on the other.

Maurice Bloch (1975) has also used the related populations of Madagascar to examine the structure or structures that underlie variant manifestations and remain permanent throughout a succession of events, and to explicate relationships between material variation and transformations of structural relations and cultural representations. His comparison of Zafimaniry (a swiddening Tanala offshoot) and Merina suggests a particular problem that confronts any anthropological analysis of Malagasy populations: Sociocultural forms are often so similar that perceiving variation demands that attention be diverted from the shared *forms* themselves toward (*a*) variable *behavior* motivated by interpretation of similar forms; (*b*) variable *meanings* of the same forms (in Victor Turner's [1975] words, different *signata* of the same *signans*); (*c*) variable *contexts* into which these forms and associated behavior enter; (*d*) variable *functions* of the same forms and associated behavior; and (*e*) variable *modes of articulation* of forms, behavior, and their contexts with other such forms, behavior, and contexts.

For example, Bloch (1975:216) finds only minor differences between Merina and Zafimaniry kinship terms as forms. Merina, but not Zafimaniry, use terms recognizing age distinctions among father's siblings. This probably reflects differential inheritance of permanent rice fields in the former but not in the latter. Bloch found, however, that a much more important difference between Merina and Zafimaniry involved variant use of the same terms. For example, Zafimaniry widely extended affinal terms (beyond such primary affinals as parents-in-law) and limited the term *havana* to kin. The endogamous Merina, however, used *havana* for both kin and affinal relations. Bloch relates these differences in "tactical meaning," to contrasts in rural social organization—themselves linked to varying material conditions.

The Basis of Variation in Betsileo Ceremonial Life

Consider now the form and scale, content and functions of Betsileo ceremonials. Several ceremonials are common to Betsileo, Merina, and other Malagasy. Some of them, and the ideology that orients participation, perhaps reflect Proto-Malagasy cultural heritage. Others have been spread by political conquest, emulation, and diffusion. However, we shall see that although ceremonial forms and orienting ideology are shared, considerable explicable variation is revealed when one considers who organizes and sponsors them, who attends, who gives what, when and where they occur, and their overall material context and effects. We shall see that the same ancestor-oriented ceremonial forms have acquired new and very different functions depending on context.

I will use three Betsileo villages—Ivato, Ambalabe, and Tanambao (the last two are neighboring villages in the canton of Mahazony)—to illustrate material contrasts that have produced variation in Betsileo ceremonial life. The Mahazony villages, on one hand, and Ivato on the other, sample the contrast between the drier, traditionally more pastoral, less populous south (and, by extension west) and the more agricultural east. (Although still less densely populated and more reliant on stockbreeding of zebu cattle than the east, the south and west have become progressively more agricultural as a result of the extension of irrigated systems of rice cultivation following conquest and pacification of the Betsileo by the Merina and of Madagascar by France.) These three villages also sample contrasts in socioeconomic *stratification* among the Betsileo, with Tanambao (a "junior commoner" village) near the bottom of the hierarchy of wealth, prestige, and power; Ambalabe intermediate; and Ivato (a "senior commoner" village) near the top. Reflecting historic economic and demographic shifts that have followed Merina and French conquest, the Mahazony villages now rely more on irrigation for rice cultivation, whereas more of Ivato's fields depend on its more reliable rainfall.

Of the three villages, Ivato's historical political importance has been greatest; today its senior commoner core, retaining differential and privileged access to rice land and other strategic resources, is more fortunate than most other Betsileo. The people of Tanambao, most recently settled and poorest of the three, represent the opposite end of the socioeconomic continuum among Betsileo villages. They suffer a land and labor shortage and must struggle to feed and house themselves. Now as in the past, economically, politically, and in most cases socially, Ambalabe is intermediate. Many aspects of contemporary life in the three villages including the scale, types, and functions of ceremonials reflect these contrasts.

CEREMONIALS AND THE SUPERNATURAL REALM

Ceremonials held for different reasons and of varying scale bring Betsileo from different villages together throughout the year. Some, like tomb-centered ceremonials—in which dead bodies are handled, wrapped in new shrouds, and/or transferred to new tombs—are confined to the winter ceremonial season, between June and September, whereas others, including funerals, can occur at any time. Ceremonials afford opportunities for kin, in-laws, and fictive kin ("blood siblings") to express their mutual obligations, for relatives and neighbors to socialize, and for regional status and prestige of individuals and groups to be demonstrated. In addition, certain Betsileo social groups, including the common descent group—uniting descendants of people buried in the same tomb—emerge only at ceremonials. Most important, however, in the consciousness of the natives who organize and take part in them, ceremonials allow Betsileo to recall, commemorate, and/or appease their dead ancestors. The persistence of Betsileo ceremonials is guaranteed by their overdetermination—the plethora of cultural values and meanings they express and functions they serve, but their functions and effects vary in the context of different material conditions.

Huntington's (1974:96) statement that "the conspicuous burial of the dead is the ultimate activity of Malagasy systems of religion, economics, and social prestige" is as true of the Betsileo as of the Bara or Merina. Ironically, for people whose ceremonial life pays so much attention to the dead, Betsileo, apparently like other Malagasy, have little to say—other than the stock informant's answer of "custom"—about why they do what they do. Students of the Malagasy have commented on vagueness and inconsistency in their religious beliefs (e.g., Bloch 1971:124, *et seq.;* Dez 1956:122). On death, for example, at least two spirits leave the body. One goes to a mountaintop, or, nowadays, to heaven or hell, and has no more to do with the living. The other stays nearby, wandering the hills, occasionally invading homes and dreams, assembling with other such spirits in the tomb to receive offerings from the living.

The Betsileo supernatural realm consists of beings, powers, and forces. Among the beings are gods, souls, several categories of ancestral spirits, ghosts of evil-doers, and legendary beings, spirits of nature and water. The major sacred force is *hasina,* a mana-like power that flows from the land through ancestors to living people and into the sociopolitical order, and thereby incorporates nature and culture, past and present, dead and living, acephaly and the state into a single conceptual order (cf. Bloch 1977; Delivré 1974).

Prior to the spread of Christianity among the Betsileo, missionary G. A. Shaw (1878:2) described their religion as more concerned with the wonder-working spirits of the dead than with a supreme being. To be sure, pre-Christian Betsileo recognized a creator–god, Andriananahary or Zanahary, as maker of earth and sky, but he had little to do with human affairs. Customarily Zanahary was invoked to initiate ceremonials, as cooked rice, pieces of beef, and vessels containing rum were laid out on banana leaves placed on shelves in the northeastern corner of the house of the patriarch–sponsor. Zanahary, whose offering was placed on the top shelf, was invited to come, partake, and leave. The ancestral spirits, whose offerings were placed on the next shelf down, were much more critical to the ceremonial's success. The Betsileo, like other Malagasy, terminologically preserve ancestors and dead kin in the human realm. Significant is the fact that when Malagasy talk of people in the abstract, they use a term translatable as "living people," rather than simply "people." The humanity of the dead is not forgotten; it is always necessary to distinguish living people from dead people.

Offerings and invocations to Andriananahary, to the ancestors of the hosts, and to the dead slaves that served them in the afterworld necessarily preceded any opening of the ancestral tomb for reasons other than burying someone. Another reason for such ancestor-worship sessions could be thanksgiving—for a successful harvest, an increasing herd of cattle, growing wealth or prosperity, fertility of self or descendants, recovery from illness, or return home from a long journey. Such ceremonies might also be held because a diviner had diagnosed ancestral displeasure (perhaps because a descent group taboo had been violated; that displeasure would be acknowledged in the session designed to overcome it), or because an ancestor had appeared in a dream. Problems that led to the diagnosis of ancestral ill will include illness, sterility, other misfortune, or someone's death. Other sessions called on the ancestors to intervene with other spiritual beings.

It would seem that Betsileo could always find an appropriate occasion for holding such a ceremony, although, as is indicated later, ceremonials clustered in the post-harvest season. Betsileo beliefs in ancestral ability to work good and evil seem much more similar to Bara (Huntington 1974:73–74) than to Merina, who, states Bloch (1971: 125, 162), believe that their ancestors have little power over the living and offer no direct benefit to them.

SEASONALITY AND SCALE OF BETSILEO CEREMONIALS

Seasonality governs most Betsileo ceremonials, particularly tomb-centered regional events like *famadihana,* the ceremonial inauguration of a new tomb, involving transfer of mortal remains from at least one old tomb to the new structure. A definite ceremonial season spans the Malagasy winter, from June through September. Table 8.1 analyzes Betsileo ceremonials according to scale

TABLE 8.1
Classification of Southern Betsileo Ceremonials According to Scale, Seasonality, and Frequency

Scale	Seasonality	
	Seasonal	Year-round
Familial	Circumcision	
Local (village)		Marriage ceremony *Saondrazana* (vow fulfillment) Curing sacrifice
Neighborhood	Rewrapping inside tomb Naming ceremony Rewrapping outside tomb	Infant's funeral
	LANONANA[a,b]	
Regional	*FAMADIHANA*	ADULT'S FUNERAL

[a] Most common ceremonials capitalized.
[b] An intermediate category, somewhere between seasonal and year-round.

and seasonality. My fourfold classification of scale perhaps masks a gradual increase in participation from familial through village, through neighborhood, through regional ceremonials. Circumcision attracts fewest people. Normally held in the boy's paternal village, circumcision unites maternal and paternal grandparents and siblings with the parents and their son, who is usually circumcised by a paid specialist between his first and second year.

Other seasonal ceremonials are tomb-centered, involving handling and rewrapping of the dead bodies within them. The scale of tomb-centered ceremonials varies with the status and wealth of the sponsor from primarily village affairs (in which bodies are simply wrapped in new shrouds inside the tomb), through events attracting an entire neighborhood, or, when a new tomb is inaugurated, a whole region.

Of events that are not seasonally confined, weddings, curing sacrifices, and vow fulfillment ceremonies (*saondrazana,* literally "thanking the ancestors") are of smallest scale. The marriage ceremony per se is a creation of state organization (government authorizaton must be obtained) and European contact (small-scale Christian ceremonies attracting close relatives of the bride and groom are sometimes held). Betsileo culture uses no major ceremonies to mark the several steps traditionally involved in the gradual establishment of a marriage: its arrangement by elders, trial marriage, negotiation of bridewealth, notification of the bride's relatives, childbirth, the paternal meal offered in the mother's village, and teknonymy.

Other ceremonies are addressed toward ancestors but do not involve opening tombs or handling remains. Of largest scale and closest to a party of any Betsileo ceremonial is the *lanonana* or thanksgiving ceremony, which ranges from a neighborhood to a regional affair but is of smaller scale than a tomb inaugural (*famadihana*) or adult's funeral. *Lanonana* are held for a variety of reasons but have as a common theme thanksgiving to ancestral spirits for some successful outcome—for example, a cure. Typically they are held following the instructions of a ritual specialist, though they may also be homecoming ceremonials. *Lanonana* occur throughout the year, but the larger ones are concentrated in the winter ceremonial season.

Similar to *lanonana,* but of only village scale, are curing sacrifices and vow-fulfillment ceremonies. Both involve sacrifices of one steer, in the first case at the direction of a curer who has diagnosed ancestral displeasure, transgression of a taboo, or, rarely, spirit possession or loss of soul as a cause of illness and has prescribed cattle sacrifice as a cure. The second type, vow fulfillment, is a personal ritual in which an individual sacrifices a steer to fulfill a vow made to ancestors, presumably—but Betsileo were vague about this—to repay general ancestral blessing or some instrumental action or intervention on the individual's behalf.

Of nonseasonal ceremonials an adult's funeral is the only event of regional scale. Funerals, as cases discussed later illustrate, vary in scale depending on age, social attributes, and political prominence of the deceased and his or her kin. Other things being equal, number of participants and the geographic range of their villages increase with the age of the deceased. The funerals of prominent senior commoners may attract more than 1000 people representing more than 100 villages, whereas an infant's funeral attracts mostly close kin, neighbors, and residents of the child's village. The typical crowd might number between 300 and 400.

FACTORS IN CEREMONIAL ATTENDANCE

Tables 8.2 and 8.3 provide more detailed information on the seasonal occurrence of Betsileo ceremonials. In Table 8.2, responses to an interview schedule on ceremonial attendance from informants in Ivato and the two Mahazony villages are arranged according to the different types of ceremonials they attended in specified months of 1966 and 1967. It shows how many respondents attended ceremonials (*ceremonial mentions*) rather than how many ceremonials actually took place. Table 8.3, in contrast, involves Ivato alone; its figures document the monthly occurrence of particular ceremonies between June 1966 and November 1967 rather than ceremonial mentions. The correspondence between the two tables probably largely reflects the fact that my inverview schedules were filled out at the end of winter, 1967, so that people remembered the funerals and other events they had attended from June through September 1967 more often than earlier events.[2]

[2] These interview schedules were filled out during the latter part of Malagasy winter, 1967, from July to September as part of research supported by a postdoctoral fellowship and field research grant from the Foreign Area Fellowship Program. I am indebted to Isabel Wagley Kottak and Joseph Rabe for assistance in that research. I intended to compose lists of all ceremonials

Despite the skewing introduced by the timing of my interviews, some significant patterns are demonstrated in Tables 8.2 and 8.3. As expected, funerals are most widely distributed throughout the year. Although, like tomb-centered ceremonials, *lanonana* cluster in the winter, they are more widely distributed than other winter ceremonials, occurring as early as March and as late as November (Table 8.2). Only one *famadihana* occurred outside of the winter, in April; all the others were held between July and October. Table 8.2 demonstrates that informants in all three villages attended ceremonials—whether funeral, *lanonana,* or *famadihana*—during every month of the year, but with a marked clustering between July and September. August was the modal month in all three villages. Statistics thus confirm that the ceremonial season that exists in Betsileo consciousness[3] is borne out in their actual ceremonial attendance.

Interview schedule results also demonstrate the regional nature of Betsileo ceremonials. Only 13% of the ceremonials attended by Ivatans had been held in that village; the figure was similar (15%) in the two Mahazony villages. However, ceremonials did draw most of their personnel from the canton where they were held. About three-fourths of the ceremonials mentioned by the villagers in Mahazony were in that canton, and 92% of the ceremonials mentioned by respondents in Ivato, which is located on the borders of two cantons, involved one of them.

Betsileo attend an average of about five ceremonials a year, and some participate in three times as many. Thus, in their lives Betsileo could attend hundreds of these events. Any Betsileo can be expected to make a major contribution to a *famadihana* involving transferal of the remains of any grandparent or greatgrandparent. Any Betsileo can be expected to attend a *lanonana* sponsored by a parent, sibling, child, and probably an uncle or an aunt. Any Betsileo can be expected to be a major participant in a funeral involving the village of any grandparent, and possibly great-grandparent; or of close affinals—either through one's own marriage or the marriages of children, siblings, or parent's siblings.

Although similar ties based on kinship, descent, affinity, and neighborhood provide entries to ceremonials in Ivato and the Mahazony villages, there is an important contrast between the two regions in types of ceremonials attended. Half of the ceremonials attended by Ivatans, in the agricultural east,

---

attended by these respondents during one year. However, informants in all three villages tended to concentrate on the ceremonials they had attended most recently, often forgetting earlier ones. To combat this tendency, I habitually asked Ivatans I interviewed, after they had completed their initial listing, whether they might have forgotten other ceremonials attended during the past year, particularly funerals, which are not confined to the ceremonial season. Since, however, I was often not present when Joseph Rabe, my field assistant, was conducting these interviews in the Mahazony villages, I have no way of knowing whether differences in interviewer's persistence may have accounted for certain differences in the number of ceremonials mentioned by respondents in the three villages.

[3] Bloch (1971:147) reports that the law limits Merina *famadihana* to the months of July through September inclusive.

TABLE 8.2
(Remembered) Ceremonial Attendance; Number of Individuals Attending Types of Ceremonials in Specified Months: Combines Ivato, Ambalabe and Tanambao

	Months												Totals	
Type of ceremonial	1	2	3	4	5	6	7	8	9	10	11	12	*N*	Percentage
Funeral	1	2	1		3	5	7	43	18	2	1	2	85	46.7
Lanonana			2		1	6	14	14	8	1	6		52	28.6
Famadihana				1		1		19	6	4			37	20.3
Marriage						1					3		4	2.2
Circumcision						1		2		1			4	2.2
Total by month	1	2	3	1	4	14	27	78	32	8	10	2	182	100.0

TABLE 8.3

Specific Ceremonials Attended and Mentioned by Ivatans, June, 1966–November, 1967

	Months																		Totals	
	1966							1967												
Type of ceremonial	6	7	8	9	10	11	12	1	2	3	4	5	6	7	8	9	10	11	*N*	Percentage
Funeral	2	1					1	1	1			1	1	3	6	3	2		22	66.7
Lanonana	1	1			1								1	2	1				7	21.2
Famadihana				1										1					2	6.1
Marriage																		1	1	3.0
Circumcision																	1		1	3.0
Total by month	3	1	1	1	0	1	1	1	1	0	0	1	2	6	7	3	3	1	33	100.0

TABLE 8.4
Types of Ceremonials Attended—Ivato Compared with the Two Mahazony Villages

Type of ceremony mentioned	Ivato (percentage of 209)	Mahazony (percentage of 90)
Funeral	51	17
Lanonana	30	44
Famadihana	12	33
Other	7	6
Total	100	100

were funerals, about a third were *lanonana,* and only 12% were *famadihana.* In contrast (Table 8.4) *lanonana* was the most common ceremonial mentioned in the Mahazony villages (44% of the responses), followed by *famadihana* (33%), and then funerals (17%). The smaller number of funerals attended by Mahazony villagers may reflect both lower population density in the south and the generally more restricted social networks of junior commoners, or it may be sample error or chance.[4]

However, one major difference does stand out. People in Mahazony attend a greater variety of traditional ceremonials than people in the agricultural east. Not only are *lanonana* more common in the south, the ceremony of largest scale—the *famadihana*—is commonplace in the south, but very rare in the east. Respondents in Ambalabe and Tanambao together mentioned 16 different *famadihana* held in 1966 or 1967, compared to only 2 cited by Ivatans (for these years). The greater frequency of tomb inaugurals in Mahazony is the most obvious expression of *greater ceremonial activity in the more sparsely populated south.* Some of the reasons for this difference—and for the very different functioning of exactly the same ceremonial forms in the context of demographic and socioeconomic variation—are examined after considering some actual Betsileo ceremonies.

Case Analysis of Betsileo Ceremonials

TOMB INAUGURALS (FAMADIHANA)

As noted, Betsileo *famadihana* are ceremonies that center on transfer of mortal remains from old to new tombs. When removed from a tomb or a temporary burial site, corpses or fragments are always wrapped in new shrouds (old, decaying shrouds are never removed). Most generally, the term *famadihana* applies to rewrapping of the dead (from roots that mean "to turn over the dead"). Among the Betsileo I studied, the term is used almost exclusively for the inaugural ceremony held in the post-harvest season following

[4] Only 23 informants responded to this interview schedule in the 2 Mahazony villages, compared to 27 adults in Ivato.

a new tomb's completion. Remains are transferred to the new sepulcher from one or more old burial sites. Consider this case.

From Wednesday, July 26 through Friday, July 28, 1967, I attended a *famadihana* near Little Ambalavao, a village in the canton of Mahazony, where tomb inaugurals are much more common than in the agricultural east. Samuel, a resident of Little Ambalavao, and Lawrence, who lives in the nearby village of Maso, organized and hosted the *famadihana,* involving the transfer of the bones of their grandfathers and other deceased from two old tombs (donor tombs). As the event got underway, visitors made their presence and contributions known at a reception hut. Following Betsileo custom, young men were designated as official welcomers. In the highly ritualized welcoming speech, the young man began by thanking (the Christian) God for the safe arrival of each party. He recalled the reason for constructing the new tomb: The old tomb was too crowded. He told of the manner in which 15 families (*fianakaviana*), representing descendants of ancestors in the tomb, had divided equally the cost—135,000 CFA ($540.00 U.S., 1967)—of the mason's fee and additional expenditures on cement and other building materials. He related that work on the tomb had begun in 1960 and had been completed in 1966. The young greeter also told the guests of the petition to the government and receipt of authorization for the *famadihana.*[5]

A representative of each guest party then responded to the greeting, thanking God and the ancestors for successful completion of the tomb and authorization for the *famadihana.* Following a practice witnessed at all major Betsileo (and Merina [Bloch 1971:154]) ceremonies, the guest then enumerated the gifts his party had brought, stating the number of baskets of white or cooked rice, pots and pans, shrouds for the dead—either Betsileo-manufactured traditional silk shrouds or factory-made textiles. The guest's speech was followed by a ritual acceptance speech delivered by the host. The offerings were carefully recorded in a notebook by members of the greeting party. They would eventually be reciprocated. The average village party consisted of about 17 people. In all, representatives of at least 78 villages—about 1300 people—attended.[6] In the main they came from Mahazony and adjacent cantons. However, people who had ancestors in the tombs came from as far as 115 km away.

The ceremony culminated on Friday, with the opening of the two old tombs and the transfer of their remains to the new sepulcher. Remains (a mound of dust—all that survived of nineteenth-century ancestors) were first gathered from the older tomb, located in the hills about a kilometer away. Next, the (more intact) remains of the people who had been buried in the old tomb in the valley, only a few meters distant from the new structure, were ex-

[5] Dez (1956:119) points out that, at least since the time of Merina Queen Ranavalona I (1825–1861), fees—sometimes exorbitant—have been paid to government officials to obtain authorization for ceremonials. For related points see Shaw (1877:84) and Bloch (1971:148).

[6] This ceremony was, therefore, more than twice as large as the largest (500 people) of the eight *famadihana* attended by Bloch (1971:148). Bloch suggests, however, that Merina *famadihana* can be much larger than those he observed.

humed. Most of them still recognizable, they were divided into three bundles, men, women, and children, respectively, and, after having been wrapped in shrouds, were interred in the new tomb. Older people accompanied the bundles into the tomb, where others were already actively preparing the new domicile, placing pots and other cooking and eating utensils, tobacco, and rum in the back of the tomb. The ceremony ended a few hours later.

THE COMMON DESCENT GROUP

Certain Betsileo social groups exist only in a ceremonial context. We may recognize, for example, major participants in a tomb-centered ceremonial like the one just described as members of the same *common descent group,* consisting of descendants of a given ancestor (or group of related ancestors interred together)—be the ancestor male or female, the descendants male or female, or the genealogical links connecting them male or female. The Betsileo common descent group differs from the smaller, localized descent branch, which is more patrilineal and which includes descendants who actually make their living off the ancestral estate. By bringing all descendants together, tomb-centered ceremonials remind people who cultivate the ancestral estate of the residual rights of the others. By contributing to the high cost of constructing a new tomb, and by participating in the organization of the ceremonial, common descent group members reinforce their potential rights in the ancestral estate. Alliances based on past marriages between descent groups of different villages are also recalled and may be reinforced through common ceremonial participation.

Major contributions were offered at the Mahazony tomb inaugural just described by people from several different villages who claimed to be members of the same common descent group. Other large offerings were made by affinals of the hosts. Nine steers and cash contributions totaling at least 18,000 francs (at 250 francs per $1.00, $72.00 U.S. in 1967) were received. A total of 36 shrouds were presented, including 12 traditional silk Malagasy textiles and 24 factory-made wrappings. About 350 baskets of white rice were presented. Six of the steers came from affinals,[7] the other three from people who had ancestors in the tombs. A gift's value depended on closeness of genealogical or affinal connection.

Certainly the 135,000 francs expended on the construction of the new tomb were not recouped from the 18,000 francs that the two hosts received as contributions. However, the personal financial burden of the *famadihana* does not appear to have been onerous for either of the two organizers, since the rice brought by village parties was sufficient to feed the guests, and the cash contributions were more than sufficient to provide rum. The mason's fee

[7] Of the six steers donated by affinals, one came from Lawrence's wife's brother, one from the father-in-law of a female native of Maso, and one from the village where Lawrence's daughter had married, two from relatives of husbands of Little Ambalavao native women, and one from Samuel's wife's father. Note the lack of a clearcut preponderance of either "wife-givers" or "wife-receivers" among the affinals, also true of my data on affinal prestations at other ceremonials.

was equivalent to about $550 U.S., and the contribution of each of the 15 "families" who equally divided the cost of the tomb (over several years) was the equivalent of the selling price of about 600 kg of paddy, representing about half the average annual production of the average rice field in this area. In addition to the mason's fee, each family was expected to purchase four or five bags of cement—increasing the contribution considerably. Including the cost of cement, each family expended the equivalent of about $50 U.S. for the tomb. The cash value of the tomb was certainly greater than that of any house in either host village and further expenses were incurred in contributions at the ceremony itself.

Although their contributions gave members of all 15 families the right to be buried in the new tomb, certainly not all expected to exercise this right. In accordance with a policy of maximizing rights to different local descent group estates and burial rights in different ancestral tombs, a Betsileo may contribute to the cost of several new tombs throughout his or her lifetime. The burdens can be onerous, and can lead to debt, as I will show.[8]

FUNERALS

In contrast to *famadihana,* which are limited to the months of June through October, and in contrast to other secondary funerary ceremonials, which also cluster in these months, are funerals, which can take place at any time of year. Note, however, that so great was the role that seasonality played in the Betsileo past in determining when ceremonies would be held that when kings, princes, chiefs, and even senior commoner governors died, their bodies were often dried out and preserved as long as eight months for interment in the winter, after the harvest.

In regional scale, the Betsileo funeral immediately follows the *famadihana*. The number of participants at a funeral and the geographical range of their villages vary with age, socioeconomic and ritual status, and other attributes of the deceased and his or her close kin. This can be illustrated by contrasting cases.

THE FUNERAL OF A SENIOR COMMONER

Consider the August 1967 funeral of a prominent native of Ivato, senior commoner Therese, a woman in her nineties. Attendance at Therese's funeral reflects several attributes of the deceased and her family. Her funeral was a

---

[8] In contrast to the Betsileo, Merina at least avoid expenses connected with the upkeep of multiple ancestral tombs. Bloch (1971:116) reports that a decision about a future burial place is made soon after marriage, since no one wants to pay for the upkeep of more than one tomb. Betsileo continue to reinforce multiple estate rights because, with ancestral land actually being cultivated by a greater proportion of the Betsileo population, there is a greater chance that they might eventually activate rights in landed estates associated with various tombs. Since land is abundant among the Merina colonists described by Bloch (1971), tomb affiliation is not a route to land use. For such people, as Bloch shows, the tomb is the linking symbol to the glory of a past society rather than a repository of demonstrated ancestral remains and potential or actual land-use rights.

tribute to an independent and active person and the oldest surviving member of her sibling group. Her husband had been a well-known local schoolteacher; her oldest son taught primary school in their canton seat; one of her grandsons was a bureaucrat in the national captial and another—an instructor at a Catholic secondary school—had earned a university degree. Furthermore, the deceased was the child, sister, and aunt of three major figures in regional politics. Moreover, along with her spouse's descent group, her own was one of the major senior commoner descent groups in the agricultural east.

For these reasons, among the several hundred people who came to her funeral were a number of government employees and elected officials. The guests were received in 16 houses in her own and nearby settlements, including that of the mayor of her canton seat, also a national assemblyman. The funeral also reflected the strong ties of Therese's family to Catholicism. When we arrived, Therese's attendants were singing Christian chants, rather than traditional Malagasy funeral songs, and the interment took place on Thursday, before dusk, both taboo for burials according to Betsileo cultural dicta.

The 16 households that had agreed to act as hosts supplied the rice, and 5 cattle were killed. Beef from some of the slaughtered steers was cooked and consumed at the ceremonial; in this case, it was sent for cooking to each of the 16 host households. As a funeral terminates, raw beef of at least one steer is given to representatives of each village, to be taken home and redistributed. Condolences and contributions, generally monetary, were presented to at least three different reception groups, and notebooks listing gifts were kept by all three.

I consulted two of the three notebooks listing contributions—that compiled in Ivato (her native village) and that kept by Therese's younger son (in the village where Therese had resided with her husband). He listed representatives of 71 villages; 16 others had offered condolences and contributions in Ivato. Probably well over 100 villages paid their respects to Therese and her kin. Her younger son and his wife seemed proud to proclaim to me that they had received a total of 25,000 francs—about $100 U.S.—in cash contributions. They said this allowed them to recoup their expenditure on the one sacrificial steer they had contributed; they even made a profit. One of the five slaughtered steers came from the herd of Therese and her husband. Her two sons gave one each, and her siblings' children in Ivato paid 10,000 francs ($40 U.S., 1967) for the steer they slaughtered, purchased in a village near Ivato. Its cost was divided into four equal shares, representing the children of her three brothers and one sister. A fifth steer was given by her closest relatives from her mother's village of origin. Steers were offered by others, general affinals, but were declined on the grounds that there was sufficient meat already. Money, generally 6000 francs ($24 U.S., 1967) was accepted instead.

Governing contributions to Betsileo funerals and other ceremonials is what Elman Service (1966) and Marshall Sahlins (1968) have called the principle of *balanced reciprocity,* the expectation that what is given, closely calculated, eventually will be received in kind. As at a *famadihana,* the value of a funerary contribution reflects closeness of genealogical and affinal ties, as well as geographical proximity where neighborliness is the only social tie. For example, other settlements in the valley shared more in the cost of Therese's funeral, not only by lodging guests, but also in their larger monetary contributions, than more distant villages.[9]

THE FUNERAL OF A JUNIOR COMMONER

The scale of a junior commoner's funeral is understandably smaller. Consider the August 1967 funeral of Joesfather, a 75-year-old man who was regarded as the head of a descent branch localized in the Mahazony village of Tanambao and its hamlet Amboangy, where Joesfather lived and died. The deceased's six closest male relatives in Amboangy and Tanambao received condolences and funerary offerings from Saturday until Monday. Betsileo term these men "judges," because they decide whether steers offered for slaughter at the funeral will be received. The decision to accept or reject is made according to the individual case, but generally it is refused if made by a fairly distant relative of the deceased or if the familial or pecuniary situation of the prospective donor is known to be precarious. Offers of close relatives of the deceased, or of his wife, are more often accepted. Furthermore, if the donor insists with sufficient fervor, the judges may ignore other considerations and accept the gift. Ten houses in Tanambao and four in Amboangy lodged and fed the guests. Household heads received a share of the beef each time a steer was killed, but from their own granaries supplied cooked rice for the guests.

The funeral of this man, the oldest male member and head of a junior commoner descent group localized in Tanambao and Amboangy, illustrates (though not necessarily typifies) funerals of men of similar age, status, and affiliation in the canton of Mahazony. (One difference is that the organization of the funeral and reception of the guests devolved on Joesfather's cousins, in the absence of siblings and sons. Joesfather's only son had predeceased him by several years.)

As a member of the reception committee, my field assistant Joseph Rabe had access to the notebook that listed the villages attending and the amounts of their contributions. Apparently not all of the parties from the 79 villages (52 of the villages were in Mahazony, though 5 other cantons were included) attending presented offerings, since a total of only 49 contributions—representing just 27 villages—were recorded. Contributions included money and shrouds (2 of Betsileo silk, 15 factory-made coverings). Fourteen steers were offered, of which seven were accepted and seven declined. The would-

[9] Despite the smaller scale of the contemporary Merina funeral, Bloch (1971:138, 142) also notes the active role of neighbors, who provide money and rice, and offer the deceased person's kin protection against witches on the night following death. The Merina emigrant community appears to be most clearly activated as a social unit by the funeral. To an extent this is also true of Betsileo villages, particularly when they include members of several descent groups or different strata.

be donors then gave money instead. Their average gift was only about 1700 francs ($6.80 U.S., 1967), considerably less than the 6000 francs accepted in lieu of a steer at Therese's funeral.

As noted, seven steers, given by contributors from six villages, were killed. One of them came from the herd of the deceased. Three were provided by close kin (cousins and nephews) representing other local descent groups. Significant lessons from this case—compared with the senior commoner's funeral—include its smaller scale, the role of the "judges" in accepting or rejecting offers of cattle, and the larger number of cattle *actually slaughtered.* These contrasts are discussed next in the analysis of variation in the functioning of Betsileo ceremonials in different socioeconomic and demographic contexts.

DETERMINANTS OF CEREMONIAL ATTENDANCE

Although all Betsileo take some part in ceremonial life, in the same region and even in the same village some people regularly attend more ceremonials than others; some of this variation reflects sex, age, and social and economic status. Data from Ivato demonstrate that the most significant distinction determining ceremonial participation is sex. Ivatan men annually attended between 3 and 15 ceremonials, women between 2 and 7. Men went to ceremonials about twice as often as women, a mean of 9.4 compared to 4.4.[10] There is a curvilinear relationship between age and ceremonial attendance. Among those who attend ceremonials most frequently are young, unmarried males, who use these occasions to meet and court young females. On the other hand, older, wealthier men—as figures of regional significance—are invariably asked to represent Ivato at ceremonials in its neighborhood and region. Depending on their health and energy—and their evaluation of the prestige of the ceremonial sponsor or deceased and of the importance of maintaining ties between Ivato and the ceremonial site—senior Ivatans may choose *either* to attend themselves or to designate a younger man as representative. Through their own or their representatives' participation, senior Ivatans preserve regional social and political alliances.

The Ivatan who attended the largest number of ceremonials in 1967 was Rakoto, one of Ivato's wealthiest and most respected peasants, who went to 15. Rakoto was 55 years old and still energetic enough to walk long distances to a variety of regional events. On the other hand, 28-year-old Pierre, who ranked sixteenth on a list of 25 Ivatans according to annual rice production, but who ranked second in ceremonial attendance (14), seemed to avail himself of virtually every opportunity to attend ceremonials, whether as a designate of an elder or as a distant kinsman or affinal. For Pierre, and other young household heads whose fields have not yet been augmented through inheritance from their fathers and/or grandfathers, ceremonials offer recreational, economic, nutritive, and sexual benefits. Especially during the lean

[10] Computing the correlation ratio, eta^2, 42% of the variation in frequency of ceremonial attendance was associated with sex.

season from December through February, before the harvest, Pierre is a veritable funeral hopper. At ceremonials he consumes nutritious meals of rice and beef, makes sexual liaisons, and obtains raw meat to bring back to his wife and young children. Any Betsileo can, if he wishes, use the ceremonial system to gain access to these benefits.

Betsileo Ceremonials: Function and Context

The rest of this chapter indicates why it would be foolhardy to attempt to explain Betsileo ceremonials with reference to a single function or effect that they accomplish. The functions and effects of Betsileo ceremonials are numerous: They help distribute food; they link local groups into regional systems; they provide opportunities to establish and reinforce alliances based on marriage; they give concrete form to common descent groups; and, at different times and places, they reduce, maintain, or increase differential access to strategic resources. Most significantly, the implications of Betsileo ceremonial life have varied historically and still vary from region to region and in the context of socioeconomic stratification.

REGIONAL DISTRIBUTION AND ADAPTATION

In addition to their manifest purposes—to bury the dead, transfer bones, fulfill kinship obligations, and honor the ancestors—Betsileo ceremonials are also feasts; cooked rice, meat, and rum are always available.[11] Frequent attendance at ceremonials by poorer Betsileo permits them to conserve the rice in their own granaries and to avoid spending cash that might otherwise go to (generally Merina) butchers in local markets. However, most Betsileo attend not because they are hungry but to honor the dead, the ancestors, and the living sponsors—and simply to enjoy themselves. Many people did, nevertheless, recognize the nutritional benefits of ceremonials. One informant told me that although the government officially discouraged ceremonial slaughter of cattle, it did not push the matter, since it recognized an important source of nutrition for peasants.

It is intriguing to note that one of the periods that Betsileo assert to be a common time of death—the December–February rainy season—coincides with the lean period just prior to harvest, when granary supplies are lowest.[12] I

[11] Huntington (1974:40) also notes that wide distribution of beef at rituals is an important addition to the Bara diet.

[12] Future research, including examination of medical and canton records of dates of death will be necessary before I can judge the Betsileo assertion that more people, especially the old, die during the winter months and during the rainy season (December through February) than at other times of year. What can be asserted, however, on the basis of my data, is that in 1967 more Ivatans did attend funerals during the winter, especially in August and September, than during other months.

It is surprising—and I find it hard to believe that it is not due to dimming of respondents' recollection or to chance—that no Ivatan attended funerals between August and November, 1966, nor in March or April, 1967.

lack sufficient data to test the possibility of an actual rainy-season clustering of deaths. However, should future data confirm it, such a clustering would ensure that the funerary distribution of rice, meat, and rum would automatically and homeostatically increase at precisely that time of year when Betsileo nutrition is poorest, when rice supplies, especially of poorer households, have been exhausted. It is between December and February that poorer Betsileo normally contract debts, borrowing paddy that they must repay twofold at harvest. It is also during these months that poorer Betsileo reluctantly turn from the rice they prefer to the protein-poor manioc that they tolerate as their daily staple.

Oral traditions suggest that funerary slaughter of cattle was customary among the Betsileo—as is generally true throughout Madagascar—prior to Merina conquest.[13] Ceremonial slaughter continued among an increasingly agricultural, decreasingly pastoral Betsileo population, whose settlement pattern emphasized small, dispersed hamlets located near rice fields. In the absence of markets then—and given such a settlement pattern—ceremonial slaughter necessitated regional distribution, since beef could be neither consumed nor stored in a single hamlet. Hamlets were linked by ties of common descent, membership in the same named descent group, affinal ties, fictive kinship, and other bases of association, so that representatives of several hamlets could be expected to attend any ceremonial.

Ceremonials still provide dramatic expression of social integration on a regional scale, while simultaneously distributing beef over wide areas, although over time, with denser population and agglomeration into villages, the geographic range of ceremonials has contracted. However, the possibility of activating multiple affiliative links remains. The point here is not so much what motivates individual Betsileo to attend ceremonials, but the fact that so many ways of gaining access to ceremonials exist. These potential linkups may be activated or not depending on the individual circumstances. Thus, ceremonial attendance may be seen not just as a mechanism of regional sociopolitical integration but also as part of individual adaptive strategies.

A biologically useful strategy might also be seen in another, less frequent, Betsileo ceremonial—the curing sacrifice. In this fairly rare ritual, a curer prescribes that the afflicted person sacrifice an ox and drink its blood. Illness—although diagnosed as brought on by ancestral displeasure, witchcraft, spirit possession, or soul loss[14]—may actually be malnutrition. As Rappaport

---

[13] The *famadihana* and other rewrapping ceremonials were, however, introduced by the Merina; see following.

[14] I suspect that such curing sacrifices may still be prescribed for spirit possession and soul desertion, two Betsileo maladies reported by nineteenth-century missionaries (Haile 1899; Moss 1900:476–477); I observed neither. Spirit possession is common among the Bara (Huntington 1974:199, *et seq.)*, Sakalava (Gardenier 1976:142–156) and the Malagasy-descended people of Mayotte Island in the Comoros (Lambek 1978). The possessions that Huntington describes are the work of nature spirits; they cluster in the springtime months just prior to the rainy season and occasion long-lasting (2 weeks) regional gatherings. The eventual cure follows protracted dancing

(1968) has argued for the Tsembaga Maring of New Guinea, if one individual in a household or village suffers from illness related to malnutrition, then it is likely that other members of the household or village are also suffering nutritionally. Ceremonial slaughter of an ox not only appeases the ancestors, but also eases hunger and provides high quality protein for other villagers. Since the curing sacrifice, unlike most other ceremonies, may occur at any time of year, nutritional crises may be met. The only such curing sacrifice I heard about during my fieldwork among the Betsileo involved a resident of a land-poor village of slave descendants near Ivato. I suspect that differential access shows up medically and that such sacrifices are correspondingly more frequent among slave descendants and junior commoners than among richer Betsileo.

Markets now offer an alternative to the nutritive function of ceremonials, given cash from such crops as tobacco, coffee, and surplus rice. Peasants with cash can, if they wish, go to market and buy beef every week. (Missionary John Haile [1899:328] reported in 1899, before the market had fully penetrated their homeland, that Betsileo *never* ate meat except at other people's tables—as guests—and at funerals.) Although ceremonials have served many functions in addition to regional food distribution, the contrast in frequency of tomb-centered ceremonials between the south (e.g., Mahazony) and east (e.g., Ivato), reflecting differential market penetration, must be significant. Within a radius of 10 km from Ivato, where winter ceremonials are fewer and smaller in scale, are three canton seats that hold weekly markets on different days. With more cash and easier access, Ivatans attend markets much more frequently than people from either of the two Mahazony villages, whose markets are less accessible.

CEREMONIAL AND STRATIFICATION

In several studies (e.g., Harris 1974; Rappaport 1968; Suttles 1974) anthropologists have examined the adaptive value of intercommunity feasting, which is often ceremonially organized. Several economic and ecosystemic functions have been attributed to ceremonials—for example, stimulating surplus production, redistributing human and animal populations with respect to strategic resources, and leveling out temporary resource imbalances between communities located in different microenvironments. By and large these studies have involved *tribal* populations and have focused on negative feedback effects of ceremonial in apparently stable human ecosystems. As the preceding section has shown, similar functional arguments can be made about

---

and special license by the possessed. As is generally true in Madagascar, Bara victims are usually women. I never observed an acknowledged case of Betsileo spirit possession; nor did I witness soul loss, described by nineteenth-century missionaries. People who have temporarily lost their soul (*ambiroa*) are lethargic and lose weight. Eventually a curer ritually conducts the ambiroa back into the afflicted person's body. Cattle sacrifice (including the Bara victim's drinking of blood as it gushes from the animal) is part of the treatment for all such maladies.

certain aspects of Betsileo ceremonial. Thus, by providing opportunities for impoverished-malnourished people to eat, and—in areas like Mahazony—by allowing the relatively poor to make smaller contributions than the relatively wealthy, Betsileo ceremonials can help to even out access to food and other strategic resources.

However, an interpretation of Betsileo ceremonials demands much more. The functions and effects of Betsileo ceremonials vary regionally today as they have varied historically. Rights and obligations connected to ceremonials have been among the positive feedback mechanisms that have contributed to the rise of socioeconomic stratification and state organization among the Betsileo. Furthermore, Betsileo history shows that ceremonial participation can assume new and very different functions in a stratified and state-organized society. Accordingly, Betsileo ceremonial life will now be approached from the viewpoint of variation and change. Specifically, in those parts of the Betsileo homeland where stratification and state organization are most developed, the contributions of ceremonial toward increasing—rather than evening out—differential access to strategic resources stand out and will be emphasized.

To see how this works, recall the cases discussed above. We have seen that the size and regional scale of a Betsileo ceremonial directly reflect the focal individual's reputation, which varies depending on his or her access to strategic resources, including power, wealth, and prestige. However, although the total value of guests' contributions also increases with the focal person's reputation and stratum, *ceremonial expenditures by his or her immediate family may not.* Thus, although several more people attended and were fed at the funeral of senior commoner Therese, more steers were actually killed at the funeral in Tanambao of Joesfather, a junior commoner. The monetary contributions to the senior commoner's funeral were larger, however, and her son and daughter-in-law boasted that their guests had provided more than enough money for them to recoup the cost of the steer they had sacrificed. No profit appears to have accrued to Joesfather's relatives. The junior commoner's relatives therefore collected less and personally gave up more than the senior commoners.

In the south and west, several customs keep wealth differentials from being widened through ceremonial contributions. Reception committees at funerals, for example, are expected to decide whether to accept or decline a steer by evaluating the donor's economic status. Furthermore, all steers must be slaughtered and their meat immediately consumed or given away. Since they are neither hoarded nor converted into their actual cash value, they cannot be used to increase the wealth of the dead person's close relatives. The burden of providing cooked rice and other food aside from beef is customarily distributed among several households.

Close calculation of the value of gifts and the obligation to return equivalent value would also seem to soften exacerbation of wealth differentials through ceremonial observances. However, if two groups participating in the same ceremonial system are of unequal socioeconomic status—as is commonly the case in the Ivato region—merely equivalent exchange cannot function to level, *but at best maintains the status quo,* and can even force those with marginal resources into debt.

I suggest that exactly the same cultural forms, in this case ceremonials, can function differently in different regions and in relation to socioeconomic attributes of organizers and participants. Here again, the longstanding contrast between the agricultural east and the more pastoral south (and west) is implicated. Thus, in less stratified, more pastoral Mahazony, the obligation to contribute to ceremonials increases with relative wealth. Richer people are expected to give more. This means that in the long run resources are balanced out; there is regional redistribution of rice, meat, and cash; and there is no progressive buildup of the wealth of certain minimal descent groups over others. Around Ivato, on the other hand, in a more densely populated region where nobles, senior commoners, junior commoners, and slave descendants live in neighboring settlements and participate in the same ceremonials, ceremonial prestations—guided by a more rigid standard of balanced reciprocity—contribute to socioeconomic differentiation.

In a subsistence-focused economy where cash is in short supply, an offering of 500 francs from a person whose granaries are loaded with rice and whose purse is filled with cash is obviously less of a burden than a poor person's gift of the same amount. The obligation of the relatively poor to return equivalent value to the relatively wealthy can lead to financial hardship and debt when there is no ready access to means of reciprocation. In areas where stratification is developed, therefore, the leveling, redistributive function of ceremonials is of reduced significance.

Senior commoners not only boast about their receipts but also excuse their own smaller expenditures and the smaller shares of beef that they offer at ceremonials by claiming that their Christianity and enlightened progressiveness force them to underplay customary ceremonial observances. Therese's relatives offered precisely these excuses for only killing five steers at her funeral. In Mahazony, the funeral of a person of her status would have demanded the slaughter of several more cattle.

CEREMONIAL AND THE STATE

With the growth of the state—and particularly after Merina conquest—Betsileo began to participate in new kinds of ceremonials. And, as has been indicated, the functions and implications of Betsileo ceremonies changed, from leveling to siphoning wealth, in the context of stratification and state organization. In several instances ceremonial obligations and observances began to hurt rather than help most of their Betsileo participants—particularly with the addition of Merina demands.

State administrations, whether Betsileo or Merina, have transformed ceremonials from redistributive and leveling devices into occasions for collecting state revenues and siphoning peasants' wealth; thus they further exacerbate differential access to strategic resources. Early in the evolution of the Betsileo state of Lalangina in the agricultural east, the "privilege" of sacrificing steers at funerals and other ceremonials was reserved for nobles and senior commoners. I suggest that such sacrifice, rather than being a privilege dear to the hearts of Betsileo elites, was actually a leveling device in which large numbers of subjects would avail themselves of meals hosted by wealthier people—free from the obligation of reciprocating. However, the "privilege" of slaughtering steers was gradually extended to junior commoners and by now has become a universal Betsileo custom. As the privilege of hosting such feasts and the canon of balanced reciprocity became culturally obligatory for junior commoners and, nowadays even slave descendants, the material effects of the ceremonial system gradually changed. Whereas formerly ceremonial participation had equalized access to strategic resources, it now accelerated socioeconomic differentiation by siphoning scarce resources from poor to rich.

Ceremonials also provided a formal context for collecting state revenues. In the ceremonial distribution of sacrificial beef among Betsileo and Merina alike, the rump became the state representative's due. It was traditionally presented to kings, princes, or their noble or senior commoner representatives; when several steers were sacrificed, "rump" might actually be presented as one or more whole animals for the official's herd.[15]

Furthermore, not only did their Merina conquerors modify Betsileo ceremonials, they introduced and fostered the diffusion of their own ceremonials and tomb architecture throughout the southern highlands. Continuing a fashion adopted by high-status Betsileo in Merina days, most Betsileo tombs constructed in this century have used the traditional Merina sepulcher as a model. Prior to Merina incorporation, few Betsileo tombs were imposing structures. However, construction of tombs after Merina models entailed much greater expense for the Betsileo than their traditional burial places. The gradual dissemination of the Merina tomb complex began as high-status Betsileo commissioned Merina structures. One such tomb was constructed in Ivato in Merina days by Merina masons, at a cost of 40 cattle and 2 slave women.

Betsileo commission new tombs for various reasons. The decision to construct the Mahazony tomb whose inaugural ceremony was described before appears to have been triggered by the utilitarian consideration that the old tomb was too full. On the other hand, new tombs may also be commissioned by economically ascendant individuals and groups as status symbols. Since successful individuals generally initiate construction, one might wonder

[15] Shaw (1877:84) reported that the senior commoner head of each village was entitled to half of the "sirloin" of every sacrificial animal, with the other half going to the native king. Merina overlords and their Betsileo representatives retained this ceremonial tribute.

whether tomb construction functions to divert their wealth from entrepreneurial use (and the corresponding magnification of their differential wealth) into a nonproductive status symbol, thus leveling socioeconomic contrasts. Apparently this is not totally true, since when a new structure is initiated by economically ascendant individuals, not just they, but other members of their common descent group who are unlikely themselves to be buried in the new tomb are also expected to contribute.

When people are poor, neither they nor their local descent segment is likely to commission a new tomb. Indeed, their obligations to contribute to the cost of several other tombs limit the amount they can spend on the tombs where they are most likely to be buried. However, if they are to fulfill culturally specified notions of a wide bilateral network of rights and obligations and to honor several ancestors, they cannot shirk such responsibilities, on pain of social ostracism and at the risk of ancestral displeasure. Obligations based on common desent, bilateral kinship, and marriage therefore reduce the potential leveling effect of the expense of tomb construction, and thus help to maintain wealth differentials in Betsileo society.

Siphoning of wealth from poor to rich can also be seen when Betsileo ceremonials are viewed in the context of their social, economic, and political relationships to outsiders. In several ways, tomb construction and associated *famadihana* and other Merina-derived tomb ceremonials have channeled strategic resources from Betsileo into Merina hands. Furthermore, not only Betsileo but Merina peasants as well have suffered as a result of their ceremonial obligations (cf. Haile [1892]—a British missionary, who described obligations associated with tomb and ceremonial in the Merina countryside late in the nineteenth century).

Though there is reason to doubt the total objectivity of a missionary's account of traditional Malagasy ceremonial, there must be some accuracy in Haile's characterization of tomb construction and *famadihana* as occasions on which the living were impoverished to aggrandize the dead—and, I add, the rich. Haile states that because of ceremonial expenses, many Merina were plunged into poverty or involved in debt from which they were never able to extricate themselves. He attributes the continuation of ceremonial outlays to pressure by kin to satisfy ancestral expectations. Bloch (1971:148, *et seq.*) makes similar comments about the causes and effects of rewrapping ceremonies among contemporary Merina, noting, for example, that for every *famadihana* he attended, the people directly involved (usually children and siblings of the focal corpse) had to sell cattle or land. Despite major expense and debt, Bloch (1971:162) notes that Merina continue to participate in these customs. People must, after all, be surrounded by their kin in the vaguely conceived Merina afterlife; the *famadihana* is a sacred obligation. A major factor is terror, in a world cognized through a kinship model, of being buried alone and spending eternity away from relatives.

Nineteenth-century Betsileo lived in a stratified society governed by

Merina and their agents, and in which Merina controlled commerce and such skilled trades as masonry. Even today, Merina are the major Malagasy commerical figures in Betsileo country, and Merina masons still build Betsileo tombs. Within the context of tomb construction and *famadihana,* Merina have reaped profits from the sale of rum,[16] silk shrouds, and other ceremonial items; bands of Merina musicians have availed themselves of Betsileo demand for their services; and masons have acquired cash by talking Betsileo into elaborate tombs.[17] As Haile reported for Imerina, the expectation of cash and labor contributions toward the construction of tombs from people with little cash has created debts, which Betsileo have been expected to repay with substantial interest to Merina creditors and their agents, local senior commoners. Contracting debts as a result of their participation in state-regulated ceremonials, peasants have been forced to sell rice, cattle, slaves, and even their rich fields, to meet demands conceived by their overlords. In Betsileo days, as under Merina rule, peasants could be reduced to slavery for inability to pay their debts.

It is apparent, therefore, that no single functional explanation of Betsileo ceremonials can be defended. Functions of ceremonials have varied according to region, stratum, other socioeconomic considerations, and the intervention of the state in the regulation of ceremonial and regional distribution. In some cases—for example, Mahazony—as may have been true generally prior to the evolution of stratification and state organization among the Betsileo, ceremonials can still function as adaptive mechanisms of regional redistribution, making food generally available on a fairly constant basis and leveling out differential access to strategic resources between communities.

However, as stratification developed and became more pronounced, rigid maintenance of the norm of balanced reciprocity—which was undoubtedly inherited from a similar, but more flexible, ideology of reciprocation in the more egalitarian past—meant that ceremonials could no longer function merely to redistribute wealth when they brought together members of different communities and different strata. Rather, since ceremonial attendance and prestations measured prestige, wealth differentials were actually magnified. The wealthier, the more prestigious the host, the greater the number of people in attendance and the greater the web of ceremonial debt relationships governed by balanced reciprocity.

Moss (1900:475) reported an even more startling change in Betsileo cere-

---

[16] Describing changing Betsileo funerary customs, Shaw (1877:81) comments on rum's intrusion into Betsileo funerals, and blames much of the change on the Merina. He notes that the amount of sugarcane grown—chiefly by the Merina, who also made most of the rum—had increased tenfold in a few years. He describes Betsileo exchanging funerary bullocks with Merina for pitchers of rum. Moss (1900:475–476) notes that heavy debts were incurred at Betsileo funerals, especially over the rum.

[17] For a discussion of similar hardships for some and benefits for others associated with participation in another ceremonial system, the *cargo–fiesta* complex in highland Latin America, see Harris (1964).

monial in the context of stratification, noting that although the number of oxen sacrificed increased with the wealth of the host family (cf. Haile 1899:332), the largest shares of the funerary meat were being given to the wealthiest and most influential people, while poorer Betsileo sometimes got no meat at all. Ceremonial's transformation from leveler to siphoner therefore seems well advanced by the turn of the twentieth century.

Furthermore, to the roster of ancestral Betsileo funerary practices, the Merina added, and promoted the spread of, a new type of tomb that was more expensive and more reliant on Merina skills than the traditional Betsileo structure. Transmitted with Merina tombs was the *famadihana* complex. Both tomb and *famadihana* stimulated Betsileo, like Merina peasants, to invest wealth in nonconvertible, nonproductive symbols of prestige, while providing a new market for Merina skills and products and abundant profitable opportunities for Merina artisans and business people.

As Bloch (1971) reports, the ideal Merina (homeland) peasant community (excluding slaves and their descendants) is modeled on kinship, cooperation, and a degree of egalitarianism. Although peasants hide their differential wealth in their ordinary lifestyle, they may appropriately spend as much as (or more than) they can afford on ceremonies and the ancestral tomb. Today's Merina emigrants still invest their differential wealth in the land of their ancestors, in a social fund built around ancestral tomb and house—both of which are visited rarely, for holidays and ceremonies. Bloch describes social pressure to continue to make such investments. He reports, for example, a shopkeeper's complaint that neighbors were pressuring him to sponsor a rewrapping ceremony in order to stop his accumulation of money. Another informant told Bloch "The neighbours will think us wicked to have money while the dead do not have new (shrouds) [1971:162]."

In these cases, as often in the *cargo–fiesta* system of highland Latin America (cf. Harris 1964), the distribution of wealth is being rearranged in two ways: (*a*) *Intra*community and *intra*stratum wealth differences are being leveled out, as those with a temporary advantage are forced to make larger contributions of time, food, and money to ceremonials; and (*b*) peasants, reliant on outsiders' skills and permissions for key aspects of ceremonials, are forced to participate in an extra-village market economy. Major contributors, mystified by their obligations to dead kin, pass their wealth on to outsiders and incur debts to wealthier people, rather than reinvesting it in their own community of living kin and neighbors.

In the context of stratification, ceremonial obligations have had many of these effects among the Betsileo. Finally, to various degrees, state officials have usurped all Betsileo ceremonials and used them as occasions for collecting revenues (cf. Dez 1956:119). In some instances, state demands were extremely onerous and led not only to exacerbation of wealth differences among Betsileo but also to debt slavery and the transfer to the Merina and their agents of Betsileo ancestral lands.

Thus we see, in this study of divergent cultural evolution among the Betsileo, that exactly the same cultural forms—in this case ceremonials and associated obligations—can acquire new and very different functions and effects in the context of different material conditions. In this case the accelerated development of socioeconomic stratification and state organization in the agricultural east as compared to the south and west—itself ultimately resting on environmental and economic contrasts—is the major material condition explaining variation in the nature and effects of Betsileo ceremonial life.

References

Bateson, G.

1972 *Steps to an ecology of mind.* New York: Ballantine.

Bloch, M.

1971 *Placing the dead.* London: Seminar Press.

1975 Property and the end of affinity. In *Marxist analyses and social anthropology* (Maurice Bloch, Ed.). London: Malaby. Pp. 203–228.

1977 The disconnection between power and rank as a process: An outline of the development of kingdoms in central Madagascar. In *The evolution of social systems* (J. Friedman and M. Rowlands, Eds.). London: Duckworth. Pp. 303–340.

Delivré, A.

1974 *L'histoire des rois d'Imerina: Interprétation d'une tradition orale.* Paris: Klincksieck.

Dez, J.

1956 Le retournement des morts chez les Betsileo. *Société d'Ethnographie de Paris.* Pp. 115–122.

Gardenier, W.

1976 *Witchcraft and sorcery in a pastoral society: The central Sakalava of West Madagascar.* Ann Arbor: University Microfilms International.

Gulliver, P. H.

1955 *The family herds: A study of two pastoral peoples in East Africa, the Jie and Turkana.* New York: Humanities Press.

Haile, J.

1892 *"Famadihana,"* a Malagasy burial custom. *Antananarivo Annual 16*: 406–416.

Haile, J.

1899 Betsileo home-life. *Antananarivo Annual 23*:326–337.

Harris, M.

1964 *Patterns of race in the Americas.* New York: Walker.

1974 *Cows, pigs, wars, and witches.* New York: Random House.

1977 *Cannibals and kings: The origins of cultures.* New York: Random House.

Huntington, W. R.

1974 *Religion and social organization of the Bara people of Madagascar.* Ann Arbor: University Microfilms International.

Kottak, C. P.

1971 Cultural adaptation, kinship, and descent in Madagascar. *Southwestern Journal of Anthropology 27*:129–147.

1972 A cultural adaptive approach to Malagasy political organization. In *Social exchange and interaction* (E. Wilmsen Ed.), Ann Arbor: Anthropological Papers of the Museum of Anthropology, University of Michigan, No. 46. Pp. 107–128.

1977 The process of state formation in Madagascar. *American Ethnologist 4*:136–155.

1980 *The past in the present: History, ecology, and cultural variation in highland Madagascar.* Ann Arbor: University of Michigan Press.

Lambek, M.

1978 *Human spirits: Possession and trance among the Malagasy speakers of Mayotte (Comoro Islands).* Ann Arbor: University Microfilms International.

Lévi-Strauss, C.

1966 *The savage mind.* Chicago: University of Chicago Press.

1967 *Structural anthropology* (C. Jacobson and B. G. Schoepf, Trans.). Garden City, N.Y.: Doubleday.

Moss, "Mrs."

1900 Betsileo funeral customs. Translated from a native account. *Antananarivo Annual 24:* 475–477.

Oliver, S. C.

1962 Ecology and cultural continuity as contributing factors in the social organization of the Plains Indians. *University of California Publications in American Archaeology and Ethnology 48*(1).

Rappaport, R. A.

1968 *Pigs for the ancestors: Ritual in the ecology of a New Guinea people.* New Haven: Yale University Press.

Sahlins, M. D.

1958 *Social stratification in Polynesia.* Seattle: University of Washington Press.

1968 *Tribesmen.* Englewood Cliffs, New Jersey: Prentice-Hall.

Sahlins, M. D., and E. R. Service

1960 *Evolution and culture.* Ann Arbor: University of Michigan Press.

Service, E. R.

1966 *The hunters.* Englewood Cliffs, New Jersey: Prentice-Hall.

Shaw, G. A.

1877 The Betsileo: Country and people. *Antanananarivo Annual 3:*73–85.

1878 The Betsileo: Religious and social customs. *Antanananarivo Annual 4:*2–11.

Steward, J. H.

1955 *Theory of culture change.* Urbana: University of Illinois Press.

1956 *People of Puerto Rico.* Urbana: University of Illinois Press.

Suttles, W.

1974 (orig. 1960) Variation in habitat and culture on the northwest coast. In *Man in adaptation: The cultural present* (2nd ed.) (Y. A. Cohen, Ed.). Chicago: Aldine. Pp. 128–141.

Turner, V.

1975 Symbolic studies. *Annual Review of Anthropology 4:*145–161.

Vérin, P., C. P. Kottak, and P. Gorlin

1970 The glottochronology of Malagasy speech communities. *Oceanic Linguistics 8:*26–83.

9 On Being an Untouchable in India: A Materialist Perspective

JOAN P. MENCHER

Introduction

It is rare to find a sociological description or a historical account of any highly stratified society written from the viewpoint of members of the lowest stratum. An account of Indian society written from this point of view might be useful not only in throwing light on the circumstances of life of a considerable portion of India's population, but also in providing a balance to a large body of sociological writings on India, which focus on relatively high-ranking groups, or individuals in high positions.

Though this has never been the main focus of my work, due to a chain of circumstances during my first period of fieldwork in Tamilnadu[1] I became personally involved with the Paraiyans (an untouchable caste).[2] From that

[1] The original work in Tamilnadu was supported by an NSF postdoctoral fellowship in 1962–1964. Subsequently, in 1967, while in India on a grant to Columbia from the NIMH, further work was done on the complex relationship between agriculture and social structure in Tamilnadu. The current comparative research, which focuses on problems of social structure and development, has been conducted as part of a joint Columbia University–Delhi School of Planning and Architecture project supported by an NSF grant to Columbia University. This chapter is based on field work in 1970–1971 and the summer of 1972; it is a revised version of an article that originally appeared in the *Research Abstracts Quarterly of the Indian Council of Social Science Research,* Vol. 3 (2 and 3), and is printed with their permission.

[2] It is difficult to decide which term to use. *Harijan* is often preferred by villagers; *untouchable* or *Scheduled Caste* by the educated. In order to differentiate some of the major groups, it is also sometimes useful to use specific caste names (Paraiyan, Chamar, etc.). I have taken the liberty in this chapter of using sometimes one, sometimes the other, because it seems to me truer to real life usage, and makes reading less repetitious. I hope that no one will be offended by my usage. I have not mentioned any of the small untouchable groups in Kerala or Madras by name, since they are not likely to be recognized by readers unfamiliar with the local scene.

BEYOND THE MYTHS OF CULTURE
Essays in Cultural Materialism

ISBN 0-12-598180-5

point on, while not losing sight of broader problems of development, I have tried to pay special attention to the Harijans,[3] and the roles in which they have been cast, and have cast themselves, in the present and in the future.

In this chapter, I want to focus on the question of identity as it relates to the untouchable landless laborer (though I will also mention briefly other landless laborers and educated untouchables). What does it mean to be an untouchable? What are the socioeconomic and political forces that dominate an untouchable's life? What does it mean to be considered polluting, and what are some of the forces maintaining and forces opposing untouchability? I will suggest that the untouchable today is caught in a circular situation: Without radical reform that elminates economic barriers, there can be no change in their position; yet without a change in the stigmatized aspect of their identity, it is exceedingly difficult for any radical economic change to take place.

Indian society is extremely stratified, with 42% of the population too poor to afford the minimum necessary calories for healthy living, let alone adequate shelter or health care, and 5% of the population enjoying 22% of the national income (Dandekar and Rath 1971:31, 36–38). According to the demographer, Chandrasekhar (1972:xxiii), about 14% of the Indian population consists of Scheduled Castes (85 million people), the majority of whom belong to a few of the major untouchable castes on the subcontinent.[4] More than 75% of this population is engaged in agriculture (Dubey and Mathur 1972:165). Close to 90% of this 85 million people belong to the segment of the population too poor to afford the minimum necessary calories.

[3] In 1963, when I started working for the first time in Tamilnadu (after having worked in Kerala in 1958–1960 and in 1962), the Harijans in the first village I worked in, Manjapalayalam, went out of their way to help me with my work. At that time, I was doing a collection for the Museum of Natural History in New York in addition to my main work, and they offered me all possible help with this also. They made me feel always welcome in the colony, especially after a long or trying day. It was the one place I could in some way relax and feel at home, and this helped to transform my time there into a deeply satisfying personal experience. When I left I promised to help find a way for some of the Harijan girls to go on with their studies and, largely through the help of friends in Madras, managed to secure scholarships for four of the girls. The oldest of these girls has now finished high school, and is studying to be a secretary. Because they knew the Harijans were my close friends, people in the village came to identify me with them, and when I returned to live in the village in 1967, there was a considerable amount of antagonism toward me, especially on the part of some of the wealthier Naickers. Perhaps this helped me to become more acutely aware of the position of Harijans and the quality of their life. Though I have since worked in two other Tamil villages, and have had student assistants working in many others, it was this initial experience that started me looking at problems of Indian society from the bottom up.

[4] The term *Scheduled Castes* has been called a bit of legal jargon developed by the British, for it was the British who drew up the list of castes so designated. The list obviously includes the main large untouchable castes of India, caste-clusters like the Paraiyans, Chamars, Mahars, etc. However, included in the category of Scheduled Castes are others that (at least according to some scholars) should not be classified with the untouchables. The Rajbhansis of Bengal constitute such a case. In any case, I have used data for Scheduled Castes, when referring to published census reports, because that is what is available. (For a good discussion, see Dushkin 1972.)

In another paper (Mencher 1974), I have discussed the question whether this segment of the poor ever had a better position in Indian society, and have shown from historical documents that it appears they rarely did. It is striking that in the 1961 census, although only 16.7% of the total population was counted as being solely agricultural laborers, 34.5% of Scheduled Caste members were in this category. In other words, one third of the agricultural workers in the country in 1961 belonged to Scheduled Castes (Dubey and Mathur 1972:165). (If anything, these 1961 figures are on the low side, since they tend to ignore people who were primarily laborers, but also owned small plots of land.) For the rest of the poor, those belonging to higher castes, their position in pre-British days was often somewhat better.

As a result of the breakup of many traditional industries during the first half of the nineteenth century, the concomitant suppression of the industrial revolution in India (by means of the forcible removal of capital resources and the stifling of the developing textile industry), and the rapid increase in population from 1860 onward, and without the availability of industrial jobs, we find today a large number of landless laborers coming from lower-ranking caste Hindu communities, and even from some of the higher castes. The relationship between untouchable landless labor and the rest of the rural poor is dealt with below.

Furthermore, it should be noted that: (*a*) From the point of view of the people at the bottom, the caste system has functioned and continues to function as a very effective method of economic exploitation; (*b*) both in the past and today, one of the latent functions of the caste system has clearly been to prevent the formation of social classes with any commonality of interest or unity of function (Mencher 1974). In present-day India, this function of the caste system has undoubtedly been one of the reasons for its persistence, and for the extent to which well-to-do Hindu leaders have avoided doing things that could substantially lessen the impact of caste, though officially they condemn caste. In other words, caste is still very useful. This point will be discussed in detail.

After a brief description of the present position of the untouchable landless laborer in India (based primarily on detailed data from Madras and Kerala, but drawing as well on the works of others and newspaper reports), a number of related problems are discussed. First of all, I raise the question of group identity, of what Berreman (1971) calls "stigmatized identity," and the extent to which people belonging to stigmatized groups accept or reject the definition of themselves held by others. Second, I want to briefly explore in what ways the position of the untouchable landless or semi-landed laborer differs from that of the caste Hindu.

To what extent and how have they been kept divided from one another, and under what circumstances are they now beginning to unite? A related question will be this: To what extent has class identity begun to override caste, and to what extent are the two compartmentalized into different arenas of life? Is there any correlation between the overriding of caste differences (or in some cases religious differences), and the development and incorporation of leftist ideology? Would it be possible for the strong sense of identification of the individual with the total society (which is reported for socialist states like Cuba or China) to develop, as long as there are so many barriers between people in South Asian society?

Some brief comments will also be necessary about the fate of individual members of untouchable castes when they gain in political power, when they get educated, or when they enter government service. Each of these topics could be an essay in its own right, just as this presentation must leave out much that would go into each such essay. The common factor in all these topics is the focus on aspects of identity that distinguish the man at the bottom from those above him, in spite of shared regional identity, religion, language, or other aspects of culture.

Characteristics of the Harijan Population

UNTOUCHABLE LANDLESS LABORERS

> The distribution of the untouchable castes in India is quite uneven. Some of the groups are quite small in number, and confined to specialized occupations. . . . Others . . . are very large in number. . . . Among the numerous untouchable castes, it is rare to find more than one sub-caste in any village, or often in any subregion. . . . Among the untouchable castes, only a small number account for the majority of the Harijan population in any given region and these tend to be concentrated in specific districts . . . the greatest concentration was and is to be found in the irrigated wheat and rice regions of the Indo-Gangetic plain, and the coastal belts of the south. For India as a whole, the percentage was 14.69 in 1961, whereas for Madras State it was 18% with only 3 States ranking higher, West Bengal, Punjab, and Uttar Pradesh [Mencher 1974].

For Kerala, the percentage of untouchable population is considerably lower, 8.49%, but part of the reason for this is that many untouchables in Malabar converted to Islam and (in the south) to Christianity. Furthermore, the figure for central Kerala and Kuttanad, the main rice-producing parts of the state, is higher than the general state average. For Tamilnadu, the highest percentage of the untouchable population is to be found in the main rice-producing districts of the state: Chingleput, South Arcot, North Arcot, and Tanjore. In Chingleput District, the Paraiyans constitute about 26% of the total population (Mencher 1974). By far the majority of these Paraiyans are agricultural laborers. A few also own or work as 50–50 sharecroppers on small plots of land; a few work as sharecroppers on somewhat large holdings of 2–3 acres; an even smaller number own enough to be self-sufficient or even to occasionally employ others (apart from the few women needed by everyone for transplanting). One rarely finds a man who is actually well-off; indeed, we did not encounter a single such case in any of the eight villages studied intensively in our project, or in any of the neighboring villages. The percentage of land owned by Harijans in the eight villages studied in our project varied from about .1% to about 6.0%. However, even those who own some land usually have a problem of getting water. In the eight villages, only one Harijan was able to get a government loan for a tube-well.

In some of the villages Harijans work as untied laborers, in some as tied laborers for particular landlords, and in some on what is called *alvaram,* whereby a man gets one measure of paddy for every six obtained by the landlord. This is most popular in villages that have many tube-wells, requiring constant supervision by the same man. On the whole, the bound or tied laborers are paid a lower wage than those who are free to pick and choose. In this area, the main way one gets to be a tied laborer or *padiyal* is by debt bondage: When a man is in debt, he is expected to work only for the man who has given him the loan, unless he has no need for workers on a particular day. The extent to which this occurs varies from village to village even within small areas. It relates to a number of factors, including the extent to which other non-Harijans form a significant part of the landless labor pool, the details of land tenure in the particular village, and other sources of income for the poor.

In a large number of villages in central Kerala there are tied laborers, not only among the large untouchable caste of Cheruman or Cherumakkal, but also among Muslims and some of the lower semi-untouchable castes. There, the main factor influencing the amount of tied labor is the possibility of alternative employment for even a small segment of the population. A related factor seems to be the extent of development of agricultural labor unions (cf. Mencher 1975).

While not all of the landless laborers are by any means untouchables, it is certainly clear that being an untouchable carries additional burdens along with it. In a sample of five villages in Chingleput District studied in 1967, 85% of the Paraiyans had less than 1 acre of land, and derived their main income from agricultural labor; whereas this was the case with only 56% of the Naickers (the other large agricultural community in this region) (Mencher 1978:136). In a larger sample of eight villages surveyed in 1971, 94% of the Paraiyans owned 1 acre or less; 54% of Naickers owned 1 acre or less; and 66% of the total population including Harijans and Naickers owned 1 acre or less of land.

In the village in Kerala where I was working in 1971, none of the Cherumakkal families owned over 1 acre of land, whereas among other castes that furnish agricultural laborers, there are a sizeable number of people having modest though adequate landholdings. In general many villages in Kerala have a few Harijans who own a little over 1 acre of land (and it must be noted here that the administrative unit called a village typically includes a very large geographic area, and often upwards of 10,000 people). Nonetheless, the vast majority of Harijans in Kerala are landless, apart from a few cents of land

(1 cent = .01 acre) around their house site. (P. Sivanandan, personal communication, based on doctoral dissertation in progress, Department of Economics, University of Kerala).

Thus it should be clear from the outset that a very high percentage of rural Harijans belong to the lowest social class in the economic system. Having established this, I should like to explore two related matters: (*a*) the concept of stigmatized identity as it relates to the Harijans in the areas I have studied; (*b*) the forces reinforcing these stigmatized identities; the forces pushing toward the maintenance of caste distinctions in the face of a growing proletarian consciousness; and on the other side, the forces leading to a breakdown of stigmatized identities, and ultimately toward the recognition of social classes.

The concept of sociological identity has been particularly elaborated upon in materials dealing with various ethnic groups in the United States, as well as in discussions of racial groups. It is not possible to go into a discussion of that vast literature here, but I would like to point to two aspects of the question: (*a*) How others see members of another group; (*b*) how members of a group see themselves. I am primarily concerned with the latter aspect. In a study of Puerto Rican Americans, Fitzpatrick has referred to identity as:

> those points of reference whereby persons (or a group) define themselves in relation to the world and to other people: an awareness of persons (or a group) of who they are and where they belong . . . the problem of identity has another dimension. It is related to the sense of group solidarity in the acceptance of certain values, goals, or meanings [1971:7,24].

What do we mean by stigmatized identity? Berreman, in an excellent discussion of stigmatized ethnic identity, points out:

> *First,* that stigmatized ethnic identity is experienced as oppression. It is a human day-to-day experience of degradation and exploitation, not simply an abstract concept.
>
> *Second,* that people resent that identity and that experience regardless of the rationalizations offered for it.
>
> *Third,* that people continually attempt to resist, escape, alleviate or change that identity and that experience . . .
>
> *Fourth,* how people respond to stigmatized ethnic identity depends upon their definitions of themselves, of others, and of the situations in which they interact [1971:10–11].

He then goes on to state:

> It is not consensus on the legitimacy of systems of oppression which enables them to continue, but agreement on who has the power, and when and under what circumstances and with what effect it is likely to be used . . . . People cease to get

along in stratified societies when *this* crucial agreement changes or is challenged . . . resistance to stigmatized ethnic identity . . . is an intrinsic and inescapable feature of systems incorporating such identity [1971:10–11].

How does this stigmatized ethnic identity function in Tamilnadu and Kerala villages today? In Tamilnadu, it is immediately obvious that the Paraiyans are singled out from others, because their houses are set apart in a different part of the village. The untouchable *cheri,* or colony (as it is often called), is anywhere from a short distance across a field or a road to 2.4 km (1.5 miles) from the main village site. Even where it is close geographically, it is clearly thought of as "separate" from the village. Untouchables themselves speak of going to the village, and use the term *ur* ("village") to refer to everyone else except themselves. Likewise, villagers refer to Harijans by a number of terms, the most polite and acceptable (to the Harijans themselves) being "colony people," or Harijans (see Southworth 1974). Being physically separated means that much of daily life is conducted apart. Once a man's work is finished, he returns to his dwelling area and spends most of the remaining part of the day there. When there is no work in the fields, most of a man's time in the village is spent in his dwelling area.

In Kerala, the situation is more complex. Usually the untouchables are located on hilly, dry land formerly owned by the high-caste landlord to whom they were attached.[5] Nowadays, each family has its own 10 cents of land (.1 acre) as a result of the new land legislation, though it is sometimes too rocky to be used for cultivation. Many of the Harijans do not have any water at all nearby, which means that even water for drinking or cooking must be carried a long distance, usually uphill. Untouchables are usually found in several distinct clusters, rather than in a single distinct area as in Tamil Nadu.

One also finds other families scattered among the Cherumakkal, and the Cherumakkal themselves might be scattered through the geographic area called a village. (This correlates with the pattern of dwellings, each in its own separate compound, commonly found in Kerala; see Mencher 1966:146.) In Kerala, one also finds a number of other untouchable castes, which are insignificant demographically speaking, though socially they have been used to keep people apart (see Mencher 1974). However, there is one other very large semi-untouchable group in Kerala, the Izhavas or Tiyyars. They are actually the largest Hindu group in the state, accounting for close to 27% of the total

[5] It is true that sometimes the untouchables were able to cultivate the land around their huts for their own family—to grow some vegetables, cut firewood, and the like. But it was also true that this depended on the fertility of the soil, the slope of the land, and availability of water (especially in summer). In addition, until quite recently, they did not have any security of tenure: even though rarely used, the threat of possible eviction always existed. This served to discourage making improvements in the tiny plot around the house. Traditionally, if a Harijan planted a coconut tree near his hut, the landlord could in theory (and sometimes in practice) claim its fruit when it started bearing.

population (Mencher 1966:158). It is this group that was the original spearhead of anti-caste agitation in Kerala in the 1930s.

Traditionally, there have been (and to some extent there continue to be) a large number of overt ways in which a man or his family's stigmatized identity is made evident, ways in which the untouchable landless laborer—and even the rare better-off untouchable—was singled out and made to be aware of how he was considered inferior to other poor of higher caste. They were not allowed to bathe in the same bathing pools as higher-caste people, to take their water from the same well or pond, or (in many cases) to walk down the street of the highest castes, or in some cases to even follow in the footsteps of a higher-caste person. They were clearly not allowed inside the houses of higher-caste people. In both Tamilnadu and Kerala, they were not allowed to cover the upper part of their body, nor to wear footgear.

LAND TENURE

In the Tamil villages we worked in, we found a very small percentage of land given on 50–50 sharecropping to Harijans, much less than the amount given to higher-caste landless families. A number of rationalizations are given for this. Perhaps the most common is the stereotyped view that Harijans are not as enterprising or as hard-working and devoted agriculturalists as higher-caste people. Yet we found in one village, where the landowners did not get along well with the poor-caste Hindu group (who elsewhere are the main tenant caste), that the landowners were full of praise for the Harijans as tenants. In other words, where the landowners need the Harijans to control other poor, they are considered excellent tenants. It is clear that their work habits are not the main reason why there are few Harijan tenants in Chingleput District.

Perhaps the main reason why Harijans seldom become tenants in this area is that the vast majority are too poor to have the necessary equipment. They do not have any bullocks or plows. In addition, some caste Hindus feel that having a Harijan tenant might bring them in too close contact with Harijans. This explanation is most commonly given by Brahmans, who traditionally never had direct contact with untouchables but always used intermediaries.

IN THE SCHOOLS

According to the Harijan Welfare Department, 28% of all pupils in the first three grades of school are Harijans, but as one goes higher the numbers drop appreciably. This fits well with our data. Harijans are often more eager to send their small children to school than some of the poor higher-caste people, since the Harijans see education as a way around the caste system. (I return to a discussion of educated Harijans later on.) Yet, in looking at the "failures" from the local school, it is easy to see how they are distributed (see Tables 9.1 and 9.2). It is immediately obvious that Harijans constitute most of

TABLE 9.1

Pachaiyur Union Higher Elementary School: Attendance and Failures (1969–1970)

Class	Total students		Harijans		Backward communities[a]		Forward communities[b]	
	Attending	Failing	Attending	Failing	Attending	Failing	Attending	Failing
I	51	11	20	8	27	2	4	1
II	58	24	22	16	32	6	4	2
III	49	22	22	17	25	5	2	–
IV	40	12	9	7	23	5	8	–
V	43	13	10	6	26	7	7	–
VI	42	15	6	4	32	9	4	2
VII	21	10	2	1	16	9	3	–
VIII	31	7	4	3	17	4	10	–
Total	335	114	95	62	198	47	42	5

[a] Backward communities include: Vanniyars (Naickers, Gounders, or Padiyachis), Thambirans, Yadavas, and a few other groups, which are entitled to certain privileges because they are considered to be backward in relation to others. (Formerly Chingleput Vanniyars were called Naickers, and those of North Arcot were called Gounders, while those of South Arcot were called Padiyachis. These groups moved around a great deal during the nineteenth century.)

[b] Forward communities include such castes as Brahmin, Mudaliar, Reddiar, etc.

TABLE 9.2

Percent of Failures up to End of Class VIII (Pachaiyur Elementary School)

Total students—34%	Harijans—65%	Backward community—24%	Forward community—12%

the failures. The headmaster gives the usual explanations, familiar to most Americans as the explanations offered for failures of ghetto children in the United States: lack of attendance, lack of parental interest, and lack of care and attention in studies. In one village high school, perhaps an extreme case, Harijan failures were common in all classes, but no Harijan student was ever allowed to pass the tenth standard (i.e., to enter the final year of high school) until 1971. Several students failed repeatedly in the 10th standard, until they gave up the attempt. It almost seemed as if the teachers did not want to give Harijans a chance at the Secondary School Leaving Certificate (SSLC) examination (which is under State Government control, and therefore outside the influence of local teachers). Though an extreme case, one does often find continual discouragement of Harijan students by caste Hindu teachers.

But this is no explanation for the failures in the early grades. In the early grades other factors seem to dominate. To begin with, children of 6 or 7 years of age may be expected to help look after younger siblings along with their studies. Since there is rarely a nursery attached to the school, this often means that at least some of the Harijan students will end up taking many days off from school. Furthermore, many of the parents find providing adequate clothes for small children an additional burden for the family. The students themselves rarely have any place to sit and study at home. If they were allowed to sit and study in the school building at night, the situation might be helped, but this would require electrifying the schools and paying someone to supervise study halls. And of course, it would only help those students who live near enough to come in the dark. Free lunches have sometimes helped to keep these students in the school, but have not helped with the problem of studying.

If a Harijan child does manage to complete his SSLC and wants to go for higher education, he still has several hurdles to get over. This is particularly true in Tamilnadu. Often village officers and local school officials make it difficult for a child to get the necessary certificates by saying that his family is poor and has less than the maximum amount of land allowed in order to qualify for a government scholarship to college. Indeed, many village officers advise Harijan parents that it is not good to send their children for higher education.

In the colleges, one often finds that all of the reserved seats are not filled. The facile explanation usually given by higher-caste officials was that there were no qualified candidates, but we have been told by people involved in Harijan welfare that this is not true. First of all, there are a number of ways in which colleges can manage to manipulate selections so that not all of the seats are filled. Second, the reservations of seats was originally meant to allow students who had slightly lower marks coming from Scheduled Castes to enter the college but, in actual fact, this is rarely done. Furthermore, because the vast majority of the Harijan students belong to the lowest socioeconomic group, many cannot afford college even if they get a scholarship. The scholarships at best only provide for free tuition and boarding and lodging. They do not give money for transportation from home to school, for clothes, for sundry items like toothpaste, or for postage to write an occasional letter home. Yet for a family living close to the survival level, it is hard enough to manage without an income from a teenaged son, and to have to provide him with even Rs. 15 a month is impossible.

Questions of Harijan Identity

OTHER WAYS OF INDICATING STIGMATIZED IDENTITY

There are numerous ways in which villagers make Harijans aware of their peculiar and stigmatized identity. Let me just list a few of the ways that have been observed by my assistants or myself in Tamilnadu and Kerala. (*a*) It is very common for people to object to Harijans appearing in public wearing clean clothes, sandals, or pressed shirts (and they often make their feelings known with disapproving looks, or comments such as "Who do they think they are?"). (*b*) Harijan laborers are commonly ordered to walk alongside a bullock cart, instead of riding on it, when passing through a village—even in the side streets. (*c*) Harijan messengers are often ordered to dismount from a bicycle when they go from one village to another, even when on panchayat business (the *panchayat* is an elected village council). (*d*) In one Kerala village, Harijan laborers were obliged to take their meals sitting on the road outside their employer's compound. (*e*) In Tamilnadu, high-caste people will not enter the *cheri,* but will stand outside and shout for a person to come, in order to avoid pollution. (*f*) In one Tamil village, when Harijans who lacked a decent source of water near their colony began to take water from a nearby pump-set, the high-caste owner of the pump-set put cow dung in the water to prevent this. (*g*) In central Kerala, Harijans (as well as other low-caste people) still use certain special forms of address, and special demeaning ways of referring to themselves (such as *adiyan* 'slave,' instead of *nyaan* 'I'), in talking with some of the older Nayars and Nambudiris. (*h*) Harijans are commonly excluded from entry into local temples (in spite of laws to the contrary), and in Kerala are excluded from private temples and bathing pools which are however open to all high-caste people.

Even though there exists legislation against these practices, the high-caste landowner has the weapon of economic sanctions to use against any offenders of traditional caste regulations: He simply does not hire the offending laborer. An example from one of our villages in Tamilnadu might make it clear how this operated:

> The bus stop at Pachaiyur gives an interesting picture. Many, belonging to various castes, might be waiting for the bus. But, excepting Mudaliars [the main high caste in the region] none can be found at the bus stop. As soon as the bus arrives, from

> nowhere a crowd arrives consisting of different lower-caste men. I found out that lower-caste men, instead of waiting at the bus stop, wait in nearby places unseen and when the bus comes, they make their appearance because they do not want to be seen with Mudaliars, or rather, because the Mudaliars do not want to be seen among lower-caste people at the bus stand. . . . Even in the bus they sit separately, and elder Harijans prefer to stand. . . . Even in the reading room and in the rice mill also, lower-caste men would be seen at one place and Mudaliars at another side. . . . There is a local prostitute in Pachaiyur. Naickers and Pillais see that no Mudaliar is there when they go [from field notes of a project assistant].

While this picture does not hold true for all villages, it certainly does apply to many, at least in Tamilnadu. In Kerala, it is somewhat different because of the strength of the Marxists. At least in public, Harijans will not avoid being seen close to higher-caste people, and even orthodox higher-caste people will normally hide any aversions they might have.

THE SELF-CONCEPT: ARE WE REALLY POLLUTING?

Do Harijans accept this picture of untouchables as "polluting," or as somehow deserving of being stigmatized? I have discussed this in greater detail elsewhere (Mencher 1974), but would like to reiterate some of the most important points. It is clear to me that those at the bottom have a more materialistic view of the system and of their role in it than those at the top. Indeed, many of them state this explicitly. Obviously, material and vested interests are a pivotal point for all, but people at the bottom do not need to rationalize its inequities. To a man at the top, it is comforting to view himself as privileged because of his deeds in a past existence, his *karma,* or because of his "caste duty" or *dharma,* and thus to feel free to continue to exploit the lower-caste people who serve him. However, this does not imply that the lower-caste people have internalized these values.

It is important to distinguish between the overt acceptance of such values and the holding of contrary covert opinions (which are often unexpressed to outsiders). When asked for reasons why things are the way they are, especially if no high-caste person from the village was around, I was invariably given explanations like: "They own all the land" or "even the poor Naickers have the support of the rich people of their own *jati,*" or as one Harijan girl put it: "We can't ask them to work for us, no! Instead of that, those people only take work out of us, so naturally they are supposed to be higher than we are." Others spoke explicitly of the power (Tamil *adikaram*) of the higher-caste people to coerce those of lower caste. Apart from the fact that literacy was very uncommon, one did not find records of complaints from untouchables in earlier times because it was simply too dangerous to express any but the "official" view outside of one's own community. In any case, who was there to listen or do anything?

When it came to food, there again was a clear dichotomy between the untouchables' private values and the "official" ones of the larger society. Many spoke to me about how much they preferred beef to any other kind of meat, and how much they could buy for half a rupee in the nearby market town. In one of the villages where I worked, there had been a Paraiyan who actually earned his living about 20 years back as a full-time butcher.

A personal incident told to me by one of my research assistants gives some idea of the attitudes of Paraiyans toward the eating of beef. He is a young man with a Master's degree in social work, who had not lived in his village apart from occasional holiday visits. His father was a railway employee, and they had lived in government quarters, where most of their neighbors were higher-caste people. As a result his immediate family had given up eating beef. His father's sister, who lived in their native place, was quite amused at his attitude toward beef eating, and at his breaking with traditional ways. One day when he was visiting their village, she gave him a curry that tasted slightly strange to him; she told him it was baby goat. A few days later, she revealed to him that he had eaten beef, and all of his relatives had a good laugh at his expense. The point of this incident is to indicate the difference in the attitude toward beef eating among Paraiyans in private, as opposed to the attitudes that they must pretend to have while dealing with higher-caste people. My assistant's father had given it up, not because he did not like beef, but because he was "passing" among higher-caste people, or at least was trying not to call attention to his untouchable status.

In relation to stigmatized identity, I am trying to say that while low-caste people are hurt badly and suffer from being stigmatized, that is not the same as saying that their own self-image, their own picture of their customs or habits, is a bad one. My assistant and I made a recording in one Madras village that illustrates this point very clearly. I was sitting on a stone at the edge of the village. A Mudaliar lady from the next village was also sitting there, because she had come to watch some laborers harvest her fields and thresh the paddy in the village where I was staying. One Paraiyan girl, Mallika, and her friends came by and stopped to chat. We asked her to sit down, but she refused, saying, "I am not supposed to sit with the person who is sitting there." I asked the Mudaliar lady why. The Mudaliar lady replied: "We don't object, they just have a feeling that we might object, but it is not that we actually object now." Mallika got incensed when the Mudaliar lady said this, and the instant she finished talking she replied: "Don't say that." Then turning to us, she said: "In front of you they wouldn't say anything if we sit, but afterwards, when they go back, she would say "I can't stay there, Harijans, they are very bold. They come and sit alongside, right next to us.' " (Mallika did a bright and saucy imitation of how the Mudaliar lady would talk to others if she [Mallika] were to actually sit down.) The Mudaliar lady blinked, and didn't say a single word after this.

Later, when we interviewed this same girl along with several other Harijans, she explained: "They don't eat meat, that is why they say we are not supposed to go near them. They say that if we touch them, then when they go back home, scorpions will bite them. I don't believe it, but they say like that. . . . They are always in the shade, they don't need meat for strength. They need only milk."

TOUCHABLE LANDLESS LABORERS

The previous examples give some indication of what stigmatized identity means to a Harijan in terms of his everyday existence. A question that needs to be answered in this context is, how different is the daily life of a *non*-Harijan landless laborer? That is, if we consider the person who is in the same economic position as the Harijan, how much better is his life by virtue of his identity being *un*-stigmatized? Does he derive tangible benefits from being "touchable," or is membership in a touchable caste largely of psychological value?

For the northern part of Tamilnadu, the majority of non-untouchable landless laborers belong to the Vanniyar (or in Chingleput District, the Naicker) caste. It is not clear what their position was earlier, but around 1871, when we have a fairly detailed caste census, more than two thirds of them were small farmers or peasant proprietors (Kumar 1965:59). Many were tenant farmers in addition. Between 1871 and the mid-twentieth century, with rapid population expansion, a tendency for the concentration of landholdings, and the development of capitalist farming, a considerable percentage became landless laborers (with either no land, or tiny plots unable to sustain their families). Another group became landless laborers in the 1950s when many landowners, fearful of tenancy laws giving permanent rights to tenants, took back their land and started farming it directly with hired labor.

There are also a number of other smaller castes in Chingleput that provide bodies for the agricultural labor market. This includes some former semi-migratory tribal groups like the Irula, a few members of former toddy-tapping communities (these are not numerous in the northern part of Tamilnadu), and impoverished higher-caste Mudaliars—though most of this latter group prefer doing manual labor away from their native villages if they have to do it, so as to maintain their family's prestige in the village.

There are certain economic advantages members of these other communities have over the poor Harijans. For example, poor Irula females often are employed a few hours a day in homes of Mudaliars as maidservants, or even more often, a poor Mudaliar woman might work for a rich Mudaliar family. Men from Vanniyar and Mudaliar families get taken on as temporary tenants more often than Harijan men. And a rich Mudaliar is far more likely to employ a landless Mudaliar as his overseer to supervise his agricultural operations, than a Harijan. Nonetheless, the majority of landless caste Hindu laborers are not able to take advantage of their higher caste. For this majority, there is a striking resemblance to poor white families in parts of the American south—for the most part as poor as the Harijan, clinging to the caste status or sense of superiority (in the American south based on their skin color), in a situation where in actual fact they might have more to gain in the long run from joining together on the basis of social class.

The Role of Stigmatized Identity in Inhibiting Class Consciousness

INTRODUCTION

In the 1970s, every untouchable landless laborer belongs to or identifies with a caste, and also (to a greater or lesser extent) with a social class. It is crucial, in examining the development of class consciousness or proletarianization in South India, to explore in depth the factors leading to the overriding of caste, and the factors leading to its perpetuation and maintenance. The cases to be presented next provide support for the hypothesis that well-to-do upper-caste leaders have behaved in such a way as to lead poorer members of their own castes to believe that the benefits of upper-caste status are greater than they really are. It would appear that it is to the benefit of such leaders to maintain caste as a going concern, and to keep the poorer members of their own group unaware of any benefits they might obtain from joining with Harijans on the basis of common class identity. Thus I am arguing that stigmatized identity plays a crucial role in inhibiting the development of class consciousness; it can be used to mask common class interests.

CASES: SOME TAMIL VILLAGES IN OUR SAMPLE

The first village to be discussed, Manjapalayalam, consists of approximately 9% Brahman, 67% Naicker, and 10% Paraiyan households. 23% of the land is owned by Brahmans, 61% by Naickers, .1% by Harijans, and the remainder by the village temple and absentee landlords. Among the Naickers, over half have 1 acre or less land, and an additional 23% have under 3 acres. Six Naicker households and one Brahman household own over 25 acres of land each. The Panchayat president, a Naicker, is the wealthiest man in the village, owning land considerably above the legal limit, and deriving income from various legal and illegal sources.

Clearly, it would not be in the interests of the president, or the other well-to-do Naickers or Brahmans, for the poor members of the Naicker caste to join with the Harijans (who are all poor) and agitate for higher wages or express any of their dissatisfactions with their "lot in life." In various ways the poor Naickers are prevented from seeing common interests with Harijans as advantageous to them. When convenient, they are flattered into thinking that they are somehow better people than the Harijans. This will be done by the well-placed comment by leaders, the shouting of abuse at a passing Harijan, or the occasional buying of alcoholic drinks for Naicker laborers. These and a number of other devices are used to keep landless Naickers from focusing attention on the rather striking discrepancies between themselves and the rich Naickers.

In recent years, there has been an elaboration of a Naicker festival associated with a particular goddess (Draupadi), involving ritual fire-walking —performed by Naicker men only—which among other functions provides *all* Naickers with a glorious past, thus emphasizing their separateness from all others. Financed by collections from all Naickers in the area—poor as well as rich—but managed by the Manjapalayalam President, the function gave the poorer Naickers a feeling of being "supported" by their wealthier caste fellows, without the latter really having to do anything to improve the circumstances of life for the laborers. (Indeed, according to rumor, the president, in 1967, managed to get almost an entire cartload of paddy for himself out of what was collected for the festival.)

In another village, Perumalpuram, until recently the Paraiyans had been used by the Reddiars to keep the more numerous Naickers down. By taking advantage of splits among the Naickers, and by giving preferences to Paraiyans over Naickers, they provided some help for the Paraiyans, but it was only short-term help. A Harijan might get land on a sharecropping basis from a Reddiar (though most did not), but the Reddiars were not helping them to gain in political power or to increase their wages. In August 1970 the Naickers, led by one rich caste fellow, managed to get together on the basis of their anti-Reddiar and anti-Harijan feeling, and capture the *panchayat* presidentship. Here, as in the first village, the landowners have very successfully managed to keep the laborers in different camps.

In yet another village, Kamallur, where the Harijans are large in number, they managed to run a candidate for the presidency. The wealthy higher-caste candidate managed to get the polling booths set up so that the Harijans voted in one area across the railway tracks, whereas all the villagers had to vote at one place in the center of the village. Thus, they were able to intimidate any villager who might have wanted to vote for the poor Harijan candidate and against the rich caste Hindu candidate. In this village, there are a large number of poor caste Hindus, and the landowning people are most concerned about keeping them from joining with the Harijans. Because these Harijans have a few educated people in their midst and are followers of the late Dr. Ambedkar, they are considered troublesome by the better-off villagers.

In Chinnavur, another Tamil Village, the Mudaliars make a point of always talking about how the Naickers are much better workers than the Paraiyans. (In this village, the Mudaliars account for 18% of the population, the Naickers for 27% and the Paraiyans for 36%). Recently, when there was a program to distribute government land to the poor, the Mudaliar president, in league with the Naickers, managed to see to it that none of the Harijans got any land, and that all went to a selected number of poor caste Hindus. We recorded a revealing conversation on the road one evening between the panchayat president and the leader of the Naickers (himself a middle-sized landowner), in which they were talking about how to keep the Harijans from obtaining some desperately needed house-site land, which had been promised to them by the government under an official policy of giving title to Harijans on *poromboke* (government) land. In this village, a big point is made to keep the poor Irulas (a semitribal group) separated from the Harijans by the Mudaliars, by allowing the Irula women to work inside Mudaliar houses as maid-servants. Traditionally these people were only allowed in houses to catch rats, snakes, or scorpions, and never worked for villagers.

The allotment of land has been one of the major programs for improving the economic status of Scheduled Castes. However, the rule in Tamilnadu State was adjusted to provide that anyone having under 2.5 acres of wet land or 5 acres of dry land (even if it was irrigated by a tube well and got three crops a year) was eligible for land allotment. In this way, the panchayat presidents in several of our sample villages managed to see to it that the majority of surplus government land went to caste Hindus, normally those who belonged to the president's caste. According to the Commission for Scheduled Castes and Tribes, 17,410 acres were distributed in Tamilnadu (Dubey and Mathur 1972:167), but from the information we have obtained, it seems unlikely that much of this land actually went to Harijans.

TWO EXAMPLES OF CHANGE

Perhaps my point might become clearer by looking at two situations in Tamilnadu where some changes have started to occur. One is that of a Harijan who managed to become a panchayat president in spite of opposition by the economically dominant Reddiars, with the support of poor Yadavas (shepherds) and poor Chettiar shopkeepers. The second is that of a Harijan converted to Christianity who is the president of a small-town agriculturalists' association, which embraces a number of nearby villages, including one in our sample. I think the words of the Harijan president himself are far more eloquent than any I could produce, so let me quote his own statements (translated into Indian English):

> My birthplace is Ceylon. My father worked as a gangman in the railway in Ceylon. He earned a good amount of money and saved it for the future. He retired when I was 15 and joined the army. He used to send money to the village and my mother saved. We worked in the fields and only used what we earned. My father managed to buy 7½ acres of land in the village and I earned 1½ by coolie work. I did not study much, only to fifth standard in Ceylon. I can read and write Tamil. We have 5 acres wet land and 4 dry all together. My younger brother works in a factory in Madras and sends some money. Thus, I and my family including my brothers do not depend much on others for our livelihood. We work on our land and also sometimes go for coolie work. But not depending on others much, that is why I was able to become the President. I have been connected with the village *panchayat* for a long time. I wanted to contest the election even in 1965. At that time, only *panchayat* membership votes for the president election. A Reddiar was able to buy votes and I could not contest. In 1970, I decided to become the president.

There was no risk or fear in standing for the election, since they changed and had direct voting for president. I have got enough Harijan votes to defeat anyone. If at least one Harijan from a *panchayat* is like me in economic status, I am sure that every *panchayat* will have a Harijan president, bringing all the colony votes which outnumber the village votes. . . .

Other caste people like Yadavas and Chettiars worked for me. Only some Mudaliars joined with Reddiars. I even expected a wider majority than I got. . . . They threatened some Harijans who were *padiyals* under them to vote against me. These Harijans, though they favor me, voted against me under intimidation. . . . For every small thing I do, I face stiff opposition from Reddiars and I do not get open support from some of my caste-people. Most of them are coolies and they have to depend upon Reddiars to live. . . . They hesitate to come out openly to my support lest they would be deprived of their livelihood.

Reddi community's cruelty towards my community has made me to rebel against them. In my village, there is very much discrimination against my community. Formerly Harijans should not even walk in the road. So, for the past 10 years I used to oppose everything done by Reddiars.

The Reddiars oppose me in every step. They try their level best to defeat my proposals, and unneccessarily drag my caste people into trouble and bring the police to arrest them for petty things . . . I have to spend out of my pocket to get Harijans out on bail. They mockingly say to Harijans, "You have voted for him! Let him help you come out from the police station."

I am not rich. I had to spend Rs. 200 for my election by mortgaging a piece of land.

Government officials show no discrimination to me. But I cannot entertain them as other panchayat presidents do. Since I am a Harijan they hesitate to enter my house and I have to choose a public place to talk with them, whenever the people such as the Grama Sevak, Revenue Inspector, A.E.O., etc. come. They avoid coming to my village, instead they ask me to meet them in their offices.

In 1958, a Reddiar gave away a portion of house-ground for a public road. They insisted Harijans should not use that road. I appealed in civil court. They went to High Court. At last a judgement came in my favor. When road-work started Reddiars did not allow workers to proceed. After I became president, in November 1970, I went to Collector and asked for help since he is also a Harijan. He was moved by my story and gave suitable orders. I brought a constable and the work was done. Now, one Reddi whose house adjoins the road has constructed a thatched shed to prevent my caste-men from walking through. Again it is in court.

When I walk in the road I am abused by the Reddiar women in filthy language. Since they are women, I am not able to say anything. When I have to visit some houses in connection with *panchayat* work, I am made to stand outside the house for a long time, and even when I talk with them they do not show any respect and their language is deplorable. But, I do not mind these things. . . . As long as I get support from my people, I will be president. When I filed my nomination for presidentship, I was asked to withdraw fom the contest. V. Reddiar asked me to become vice-president like before, but I rejected his suggestion. The Reddiar said that a Harijan should not be such a prominent person and that I will not get cooperation from the village people. When V. was the president he made a big fraud. A well was sanctioned for the Harijans but he had it dug in the village instead. When it was dug, I objected and asked my people to take water. Then I reported the matter to the Harijan welfare board and they sent one official to the village. I then asked one of the women to take water in front of the official, but she was afraid. Then I had to give a blow to one woman and make her to take water. Then every woman from the colony went and took water. After that, the villagers petitioned the police saying that I made trouble, but they didn't get anywhere. Later on, the villagers began to dirty the well water with cow dung and other dirty things. Finally they gave up. Now the well is used only by Harijans.

A second man, Appadurai, is the president of an association called the Agriculturalists' Association in a small town. This association is mainly concerned with helping the agricultural laborers and small farmers use the various things made available to the poor by the government. Durai is a Harijan converted to Christianity, and educated up to intermediate (second year at college) in a school at the Kolar Gold Fields, where his father was employed as a coolie. He was formerly a Marxist, but now works for the DMK (The Dravida Munnetra Kazhakam or "Dravidam Progressive Party," a major political party in Tamilnadu which was in power from 1967 until the imposition of President's Rule in 1976). He is financially independent, earning a small amount of money from the association; his wife is employed as a headmistress of a higher elementary school. When he visits villages, his expenses are met by the farmers and coolies. Let me quote my student assistant:

He will move closely with villagers, sleep on the floor, even to just take boiled groundnuts and a cup of tea as his night food. When he visits a *cheri,* he says "I am one among you," because he was a Harijan before. He is helped in Annur by one Mudaliar, T.M., who is vice-president of the association. He has a command among police personnel, and ignorant villagers who have trouble with rich landlords seek his help. If village big shots have a poor man arrested and remanded in the police station, he immediately brings them out on bail and helps in the court room. He especially helps poor Harijans or Vettaikarans. But, he is clever. One poor Reddiar farmer did not pay his dues on a government loan. He was a man who had not voted for the present panchayat president. So, the village *munsiff* [a local official] took away his one pair of cattle. Appadurai was informed and he sent a taxi and brought the poor Reddiar to the town. In front of the Tahsildar, he proved it as a case of enmity, and freed the man as well as his cattle. If a poor person is harassed, he sends a taxi from the town, even though he himself might have used a cycle or bus. Taxi-traveling is felt as a luxury by the poor villager, and in doing that he gets a feeling he is on a par with the rich.

He has formed a Harijan milk society. Seventy-five Harijan households joined. After they collected the money, the panchayat president and the *munsiff* did some mischief. They went and told the colony people that "there is no society like this, they are only cheating you." Then the concerned people met with Appadurai and T.M. Mudaliar and they arranged for a public meeting along with the Panchayat Union Chairman, one DMK party Chairman, and several other locally important people. One Mudaliar from another Agricultural Association assured the people that the society would come into being, and that they should not listen to the President's propaganda. The initiative to form the society had occurred before the *panchayat* elections, but after the elections they wanted to destroy it because they felt the Harijans were too insolent. After that, those two went to the record office

> and by bribing one clerk managed to get him to say that no application had been submitted. Then, T.M. Mudaliar was able to show that the application had been sent by registered post. Now Appadurai has again applied for an order to start the society, and it should be under way soon.

What are the forces working against stigmatized caste identities, and in favor of class? Clearly, stigmatized caste identity cannot be overridden unless there is some sort of conscious effort, either on the part of villagers or outsiders. In Kerala there have been a large number of forces operating in this direction, though perhaps the most important has been a tradition of 30 to 40 years of Communist ideology. Thus, in one Kerala village where I worked in 1971, we were told that Harijan youngsters had begun to attend the local school, and strict observance of pollution rules was challenged about 50 years ago, under the influence of a young Marxist (who later became a Member of Parliament). According to one of my assistants, a young man with a Master's degree in economics who comes from a Harijan family in Quilon District of Travancore:

> 20 years ago, the influence of Communism brought a new shape to the life of my village. Some of the high-caste Nairs became the spokesmen of this new ideology. My father and uncles also joined them. They, the leaders of all castes, conducted meetings in Pulaya houses, slept in Paraya houses, etc. This phenomenon actually swept away the caste feeling in my village, especially untouchability. I have gone to the homes of many high-caste friends, and they come to my house also and accept food. We have many Nair friends who come to my family house, take food and sleep overnight.

In Kerala, there is considerable difference between different regions in the extent to which importance is given to caste distinctions in daily life—or to put it another way, in the extent to which class identity overrides caste. This is not to say that caste has no function in areas where class considerations dominate, but rather that the sphere of caste identity is more limited. Thus, even where class tends to dominate, marriages are mostly arranged within the same caste, and each caste group tends to have its own specialities in cooking as well as a number of particular customs of its own. However, there is the kind of free mingling described above—at least among members of the same social class.

On the whole, the most conservative region is in central Kerala, the area of our project research, though even here one does not encounter the kind of political manipulation of stigmatized identity that is characteristic of politics in other parts of India. In part, this difference may be due to a more conscious commitment to socialism in Kerala, at least a verbal commitment, or at least to a greater sophistication among rural people. Many writers have attempted to equate political party membership in Kerala with caste, but on the basis of my own work there (from 1958 on), I believe that class has been the main determining factor—with the exception of two specific groups: Nairs of central Kerala and Christians. Members of both these groups have traditionally been associated predominantly with the Congress Party, regardless of their socioeconomic class. Even among the Nairs, class factors have probably been more dominant in Trichur District than in Palghat District. And C. Fuller, a British social anthropologist who worked among Christians in Travancore, reported (personal discussion) that in 1972 class was clearly dominant among Christians.

There have been many reasons for the persistence of caste distinctions in Central Kerala, including the following factors:

1. By the end of the nineteenth century Travancore had already become a region of peasant proprietorship, Cochin had developed a combined pattern of peasant proprietorship and absentee landlordism, whereas Malabar was primarily an absentee landlard tract. In Malabar until the late 1960s and to some extent in Cochin, land ownership was concentrated in the hands of superior caste households and Hindu temples (Varghese 1970:217–218).

2. Central Kerala has been a Namboodiri Brahman stronghold, with the result that caste feelings were exacerbated in the region. The Namboodiris and a few select, large Nayar households continued to be rich and powerful landlords until relatively recently. Even now, a Harijan living on land that [according to the 1970 land reform law] now belongs to him, will refer to himself as "K-de mana Cherumakkal," that is "Cherumakkal of K house," his very identity being tied up with that of his recent landlord and former (prior to the mid-nineteenth century) owner. The question of agrestic servitude in Kerala has been dealt with in two other papers (Mencher and Unni 1973; Mencher 1974). It is clear that it was most prominent in Central Kerala, the main rice region of the state apart from Kuttanad.

In Kerala, as changes have come about in the old landlord–tenant relationships, there has been a profound change in the practice of caste. For example, in the part of Travancore from which my assistant comes, along with profound changes in intercaste behavior, labor union activity is exceedingly important and productive, with each political party supporting its own agricultural laborers' union. In the central Kerala area where I have worked recently, the only political party to support such a union was the CPM (Communist Party [Marxist]), and it has not yet been effective. The main determinant of wages has been the extent to which alternative sources of employment exist—for example, if the village is near enough to a small town that has a match factory (see Mencher 1975).

One still finds in villages in the Trichur–Palghat area that low-caste people are not officially allowed to use tanks or bathing pools owned by high-caste families. In one village, some low-caste people described their courage to us in taking their baths in a tank owned by a high-caste Nayar late at night. In another village, my assistant recounts the following story:

> One Telugu Chettiar came from . . . (a distant town) to sell cloth. He went to take a bath in the tank. One man, realizing he wasn't a Nayar, asked who he was. He said that he is a Chettiar from . . . come for selling clothes. The old man said: "This tank is not for any Chettiar or Cherumakkal." His tone was not quite so rough as in the old days. The Chettiar asked if the clothes sold were acceptable or not, or would there not be any pollution in wearing clothes sold by a Chettiar. The Nayar blinked and went away.

According to several informants, along with the freedom struggle and communism, the teachings of Sree Narayana Guru helped to form a social opinion among the educated people against the evils of untouchability:

> The leftist social leaders who later were to become the spokesmen of Communist ideology condemned the evils of untouchability. They also tried to help laborers to come out of the clutches of their employers and go for work anywhere. Another reason why untouchability has gone down in Kerala, is that before it was based on the power of the big *taravads* [traditional Nair households]. Now they are partitioned and have lost their power, things are changing. No family managed to keep a large number of agricultural laborers.

According to one informant, this is perhaps the biggest factor leading to its maintenance still: "Because it is illegal to enter the house or compound of someone without permission, the control of the house is still preserved as before. So, employees may be served food in separate places in the house. This is especially true in central Kerala."

It is clear that the process of transition from a man's identifying primarily with his caste to his identifying primarily with a social class, that is, the development of class consciousness, is still going on in Kerala—more advanced in some areas, slowly emerging in others. Age is an important element here. Older impoverished high-caste people tend to cling to their caste. The younger people, especially the literate, tend to be more practical and to be less concerned about status. Between 1962, when I previously worked in Kerala, and 1971 when I again worked there, I was struck by a major change in this regard. In 1962 there was a tremendous sense of hopelessness. In 1971, even though things have been materially worse in some ways, there was a sense of excitement about the possibility of transforming the society.

The situation in Tamilnadu is somewhat different. In rural areas of Chingleput District, especially southern Chingleput, the DMK has made a concerted effort to appeal to landless laborers, especially untouchables, that is in many ways similar to that made by the communists in Kerala. In this part of Chingleput, the area where our project has been located, they have made considerable efforts to override caste and to present themselves as being the helpers of the poor. Thus, leaders will go personally to the *cheri,* take food there, and in general let it be known that they are on the Harijans' side. In Chinnavur, the DMK leader who lost in the panchayat elections allows Harijans everywhere in his house, pays them a higher wage than other Mudaliars, and moves freely with them. Likewise, in Manjapalayam, the Naicker who ran against the present president, a man whose father-in-law is a DMK legislator, has made a point of eating in Harijan homes. Their antireligion stance has also been of help in this regard. It is hard to predict whether or not they will be able to maintain this image. A year before the last panchayat elections, that is in the fall of 1969, another DMK MLA (Member of the Legislative Assembly, the state legislative body) did come to the support of a strike by agricultural laborers, mostly Harijans, in one subregion where the party was not completely sure of their success, since the area had previously supplied a well-known Congress Member of Parliament. In this strike the Harijans succeeded in raising the harvest wage. On the other hand, the DMK failed to help out in another strike by Harijans elsewhere in the district, where the wages were actually lower. (However, this was just after the assembly elections, and maybe the party workers were tired [Mencher 1975].)

THE EDUCATED UNTOUCHABLE

What happens to the identity of the educated, employed untouchable? Where does he stand, how can he work? Harold Isaacs has dealt with some aspects of this question in his well-known book (1965). What I want to look at very briefly here is the educated untouchable in government service, or working in villages where they are subject to the constraints of caste, and where they identify classwise with some segment of the middle class. A few concrete cases might help to clarify the questions being raised here.

It was quite striking to me how the two educated Harijan postgraduate students working on our project had to hide their caste most of the time while in strange villages. Let me quote some relevant comments from their own notes:

> When I was in Chinnavur, if anybody inquired about my caste I told them daringly that I belong to Harijan community, because there my work was to collect data only in the colony. Also I was not residing alone, renting a house in the village. I was staying with the American professors. My stay at Pachaiyur was in the temple officer's rest house. My colleague told me that the executive officer had specifically asked him not to give equal place to Harijans inside the rest house, since it will affect his post if other higher officials happen to see a Harijan sitting and talking inside the rest house. My colleague also asked me not to reveal my caste to anyone since I stay in that place. If I tell I belong to such and such a caste, I would not have been given a chance to get a rented house in the village. Hence hiding my caste became my practice. In Manjapalayalam, a Naicker maidservant asked my caste. I said I was an Arcot Mudaliar. After a couple of days the primary health center doctor said to me, "I thought you belonged to my caste, now I know." (He is a Mudaliar.) I kept mum. In most villages, I tried my best to avoid the persons asking about my caste just for the sake of my work. I felt much for the

> position of the persons who are somewhat educated and scattered in society. In Chinnavur, the village President knew about my caste. He said he was very happy to see educated persons from my community, but always he talked to me in English, never in Tamil. When there was a possibility I might have to stay on in the village after everyone else left, he did not come forward to arrange for my meals or anything. He never encouraged my entering his house.

In one critical situation, my Malayalee assistant was saved from a potentially difficult situation by his hesitancy:

> One day I was enterviewing an old Nair man. At first he welcomed me and answered all questions. I could understand that he is a pure orthodox Hindu. I felt strange. Suddenly, he asked: "What is your '*swajanmam*'?"—meaning "own caste" literally. I was perplexed, since it is not the usual word for caste. Usually we say "*jati.*" I just repeated "*swajanmam*?" But he thought I was saying "own caste," meaning his own caste. Immediately after this, he ordered a cup of coffee for me. I hesitated to have it, but he insisted, so I took it. Yet, in this same village, I was staying with a Nayar family. They knew my caste, yet they behaved towards me with no ill-feeling. They were actually sorry when I left. In V. Namboodiripad's house, they knew my caste, but they insisted that I visit there and come inside and be given coffee. I don't know if they would show such behaviour to an educated native. They do not want to create any ill-feeling among people who come from other villages, especially when an effort is being made to eradicate untouchability. In this village, one *Mannan* (a particular low-caste) is an M.A. holder. He is the only person among the low-caste so much educated. If he is invited by some high-caste person here, he will be given a chair and coffee and they will talk freely. But if he is invited for a marriage, then he would be expected to be treated like any other low-caste person. So they avoid such occasions even if they are invited.

What about government officers? Let us look at one case: Raghavan is the *gram sevak* (village level worker) in Pachaiyur. In fact, it is his main headquarters, but he is forced to stay in the nearby town of Kancheepuram, because if he lived in the village, people would find out his caste too easily. In a village one cannot move with the villagers without revealing one's caste. He argues that if his caste were known, even the present work he is doing could not be done; he would not be welcome in the village. A few influential people know his caste, but they have kept quiet. Raghavan said to my student assistant:

> Whoever he may be, a Harijan will be looked upon with contempt; even Jagjivan Ram, the Union Minister, would face the same insult in a village. . . . The higher-caste people with good enough economic position are having the opinion that family planning is not for them, and they point out colony people and ask me to give such propaganda to them. . . . I have to face my unfavorable situations when I approach the colony people for the use and necessity for family planning. (Will you say your caste?) No, if the colony people know about my community, it might spread. I do not want to hide my caste from anybody, only for my profession I have to hide my caste. . . . If a high Scheduled Caste official takes interest in the

welfare of the Harijans he is not given proper place in the society. . . . Each Scheduled Caste person has to take his own interest for the improvement of himself. He should have enough courage to fight with the society to make him one with the forward community. If such a person happens to reveal his community to them he will not be given equal place with them. . . . Untouchability cannot be wiped off completely. It will prevail in one shape or another. . . . If a Harijan is educated he can stand on his own leg and he won't feel guilty when he moves with other persons. If he is given proper education then naturally his economic background is increased and there is a chance for the improvement of his future generation. I am the only SSLC (high-school graduate) from my village colony.

Within government service an educated untouchable is limited in what he can do for his community, or even for individual members of his own community. As one man put it:

I am governed by government rules, so what to do? I can only talk to MLAs (Members of the Legislative Assembly). They say—what I say is good, but because of party discipline they haven't the courage to do anything. For everything else, members of one party are all one, but if it involves something for Harijans, then it is different. That is why Dr. Ambedkar fought for separate electorates. Ambedkar said that the Scheduled Caste man should be elected by his own people only, and not by the general public. Now, if a Scheduled Caste man wants to contest even for a reserved seat, if he is a militant man, fighting for his own community he can't succeed, because he has to be elected by the general public. Men who come up have always to depend on caste Hindu men, so they can't be too bold. At one point, I suggested that if you want to change things on the lower level, then at least one year in five, the *panchayat* president should be a Harijan, and one year in five the chairman of the *panchayat* union should be a Harijan. Even if he is a poor man, or even if he is a dummy, he can't do that much harm in one year, but knowing that he has the right to such power can make a difference in how he behaves, and also in how others think about him.

But, even then, there are limitations. In one region, at one time, I was in a position to make four *panchayat* unions, over which I had jurisdiction, hold Harijan days once a month. Officially, it was there in the law that it should be held regularly, but most people just fill in that it was done. But, when I was in that position, I decided that I would do what was allowed under the law for my own people. And I sent word that once a month, I would hold a Harijan day in such and such a place and that on this occasion, I would distribute land to needy Harijans, government land that was not being cultivated. And I organized several camps. Then, one time, I decided to have a big meeting, and I asked several MLAs to come, and many people came. And we had a celebration. Then I spoke. I said: "Suppose someone from India is in the UN, and he talks up about the way people are treated in South Africa, or racial treatment in the United States, where they treat their black people very badly. And suppose the man next to him turns and asks: 'And how do you treat your Harijan brothers?' What could he say? Should we not put an end to all this?" I was surrounded by village officers, *panchayat* presidents, and all sorts of people. And I got a good response. But, after I spoke and the crowd dispersed, one Scheduled Caste MLA rushed up to me and he said to me: "You should not have spoken like that. It might have made the village Harijans feel good to hear you, but you should have thought of what will happen to them. When they get back to their villages, the various village officers will only take it

> out on our brothers. It is good to speak up, but as long as they have the power in the village, it will not do much good." I had asked the crowd: "Are we not ashamed to fight for someone else, should we not eliminate untouchability here in India?" But he maintained that when these people get back to their village, they will only be laughed at and made to feel worse. So, I learned a lesson and after that I tried to do what I could, but didn't simply speak up boldly like that.

Very often, it is assumed by caste Hindus that any Harijan government officer must be stupid, that he would not have got his job if there were not reserved posts. This is not to argue against the reservation of positions, because it is quite clear that deserving Harijans in many instances would not have got their jobs unless there had been reserved posts. A former high officer in the Directorate of Harijan Welfare in Madras, himself a Harijan, has explained to me at great length how hard it is to get deserving Harijan students into reserved seats in colleges, even though they might have excellent marks. Although the reserved seats are made available by law, he has explained that there are serious faults in the enforcement mechanism, so that he often had to apply considerable pressure to get colleges to honor their commitments to accept Harijans, and even then they did not accept as many eligible ones as they were required to by law.

This officer also pointed out several other interesting and related facts. One, which is most significant, is that the reservation of seats at the PUC level (first year of college) does not state that 16% of the Harijan students be admitted to the science section, 16% to the humanities, and 16% to the social sciences. As a result it is extremely difficult to get Harijan students into the science line. Yet, without getting into the science line in the PUC, the student will not be eligible for admission to the agricultural college, medical school, dental school, or engineering school, etc. Thus, being stopped at the PUC level often means that there are not enough candidates applying later on for the professional schools.

The usual excuse given for not putting more Harijans into the science line is that their marks are not high enough. But this is often self-defeating. One of the purposes of reserved seats is to allow students with lower marks to enter a given course. In many instances, the reason for the poorer marks may be related to poor instruction at the high-school level, since many of the Harijan students come from corporation or public high schools, whereas many of the caste Hindu students come from private high schools that provide better teaching in smaller classes.

There are other problems later on, when it comes to recruitment. As one officer explained to me:

> There is this process of cyclic rotation. So, if an organization has 100 jobs, then when one becomes vacant, it might be reserved for a Harijan, then the next five positions must be filled by others, before it is again the turn to fill by a Harijan. So, if it is 1 in 6 (he said the ratio differed from place to place) and there are 100 jobs, and it takes time for jobs to become vacant, then it means it will take at least

> 100 years before you get 16% of the jobs held by Harijans. If they are really sincere about filling up 16% of the seats by Harijans, then they should declare a moratorium and for 3 years, hire only Harijans. Even if the man they hire is a dummy, it will not matter. Because if the remaining 84% is really intelligent and efficient, 16% inefficient will not make that much difference. I am not arguing that the 16% *would* be inefficient, but simply to answer their argument that all Harijans are inefficient. I think 84% efficiency is way beyond what any department has nowadays anyhow.

It was also explained that at times when there is massive hiring, there often are not enough candidates because of the problems in the colleges. Thus, one highly placed Harijan officer in the Agriculture Department explained to me in relation to an incident when his department was hiring a large number of young recent graduates:

> I could have hired Harijans up to the quota, but I wasn't able to because there weren't enough candidates. In the agriculture college, they reserve 18% of the seats for Harijans, but just like the caste Hindu students, out of say 18 admitted in a year, only 10 are there by the senior year. From all communities, so many either fail, or drop out for one reason or another. Actually, they should take the 18% from people below the average, and consider brilliant Harijan students as part of the general quota. That would increase the number of Harijans, but they do not do that. Anyhow, I was not able to hire as many Harijans as I wanted to. Now, that means that it will probably be 50 or 100 years before the Harijan quota is filled. It is not every day that we have so many openings.

If an educated Harijan has a government job, he cannot really become a rallying point or a leader for Harijan protest, because as a government servant he is subject to restraints on his participation in political or even quasi-political activities.[6] This has often served to erect a barrier between the educated, government-employed Harijans and the rest of the community.

Harijans rarely have much scope for entering business. With the rare exception of Jyoti Venkatachalam who, notably, started a most successful pickle business, one would have to search far and wide to find Harijan entrepreneurs. This is not surprising. First of all they have had, at least until very recently, no access to sources of finance or to the types of experience that

[6] Before independence the Government Servants' Conduct Rules stated that "no Government Servant shall take part in, subscribe in aid of, or assist in any way, any political movement in Indian affairs [1946:7]." This rule was intended by the British Raj to keep Indian civil servants from engaging in any activity connected with the independence movement. It is striking that today, even though there have been some minor modifications in the rules for civil servants, government servants are still not permitted to participate in any political activity, to write pamphlets or any propaganda materials for any political party, or to work for any party without permission of the government. It has been pointed out to me in this connection (T.N. Krishnan, personal communication) that the reservation of government positions for Scheduled Castes might have one negative side effect: namely, to deprive untouchable protest groups of educated leaders by the process of giving many of them jobs in government, which in effect means absorbing them into the establishment and forcing them to choose between keeping their mouths shut or being out of work.

provide training for would-be entrepreneurs. In a table on caste background of medium and small-scale entrepreneurs in Tamilnadu by Milton Singer (1972:300), it is striking that none belongs to Scheduled Castes, though there are a few from the Naicker caste (the other large laboring caste in the Chingleput District).

It is clear that an educated, middle-class untouchable can merge with the urban middle class in a number of ways. Yet this does definitely involve being divorced from his own community. Another quote from my Tamil assistant illustrates this:

> My father migrated to Madras after my birth and that of my two younger sisters. Since we could not get decent accommodation in a Hindu house, we stayed in a Muslim area as a tenant. Then, after some time we moved to a decent house where forward community people resided. But the owner of the house belonged to our community.
>
> I was sent to a good school. I have been told by my father that our community was Adi-Dravida. A few of my own community people were also studying in the school. They were not given a seat in the front row because they were not clean. When I talked with them, some of my other classmates, the caste Hindus, used to discourage me, saying that they are Paraiyans. I asked them why, what is wrong if they are Paraiyans. (I had not realized that I was also Paraiyan.) They said, the Paraiyan will eat *mattu kari* (beef) and they won't have a bath daily. I had been given a front seat in our class, thinking I was a Christian.
>
> On the same day I approached my father asking why the Paraiyans are unclean and eat beef. He was shocked and laughed at me for awhile. Then he cleared the fact [explained] that I am also from Paraiyan community. I asked him, "If that is so why I am daily taking bath and not taking beef?" He replied: "My grandfather used to take beef but when he was staying in a hostel he stopped taking." So, I am not taking it because they are not preparing it in our house. He said, "It is good to take bath daily."
>
> One day I got a call from the school office to fill in the school final record book. Then the clerk came to know that I am Adi-Dravida. He didn't believe it and sent for my father. Later on I found out that he didn't believe me because I am not residing in a *cheri*.

In the 1970s, it is clear that perhaps the most critical function of stigmatized identity lies in its power to prevent the formation of class consciousness, and as a consequence the formation of such things as active agricultural labor unions that would function on the basis of class interest. The material from Tamilnadu shows a very close link between the manipulative behavior of powerful higher-caste politicians and middle or well-to-do landowners, and the maintenance of maximal social isolation of different segments of the labor force. This also shows up in the correlation between the extent of labor union activity and the overriding of caste distinctions on the most intimate level in Kerala.

Beteille (1971a) notes that it has not only been difficult for labor unions to isolate the pure wage laborers from sharecroppers and small owners, but having isolated the 'exploited class' they have been bedeviled by the distinction within it between Harijans and caste Hindus. Beteille's description of the eastern part of the old delta of Tanjore is also relevant to my main point since, as he shows, this is the only part of Tanjore (and possibly one of the few areas in the whole state of Tamilnadu) where the Harijans constituted the *whole* labor force, and therefore the distinction between caste and class was irrelevant. It is worth noting, however, that the members of higher castes in this area, all of whom were middle or large landholders, were forced to unite among themselves, overriding caste distinctions on many levels, in order to protect their common property interests. Such alliances also exist (at least potentially) in other areas, though as long as the laborers do not unite, they remain dormant.

Conclusions

I have tried in this chapter to bring together a somewhat heterogeneous body of facts, all of which seem to me to bear on the question of the identity of Harijans, the bottom seventh of India's population. It is clear that as long as the stigmatized aspect of their identity remains, a truly socialist state will be difficult to achieve. As Dr. Ambedkar noted back in 1935:

> How can there be a revolution if the proletariat cannot present a united front? . . . the social order prevalent in India is a matter which a socialist must deal with. . . . unless he does so he cannot achieve his revolution . . . if he does achieve it as a result of good fortune he will have to grapple with it if he wishes to realize his ideal. . . . He will be compelled to take account of caste after revolution if he does not take account of it before revolution [1968:36–37].

It is striking that in the years since this chapter was first written, especially from the mid-1970s on, there has been a noticeable increase in the number of atrocities committed against untouchables. Some have argued that the increase is only in the number brought to public attention, and certainly more are being written about in newspapers today in India than 20 years ago. Even allowing for this, it is clear that there still has been a definite increase in the number and scope of actual atrocities as well. This has been especially striking in states such as Bihar, Madhya Pradesh, and Gujarat, but there have also been some incidents reported in southeastern India (Andhra Pradesh and Tamilnadu). In part, the reason for the increase has been the fact that there has been legislation passed by various governments (central and state) at different times over the past 6–7 years that the Harijans eventually came to know about. Demands for justice to which they considered themselves entitled have had the function of focusing the resentment and hatred on the local landlords, who often had the ear of the local police even though higher officials might not have concurred. In the majority of the incidents that I have read of in the papers, the perpetrators of the atrocities got off either with no punishment, or else fairly leniently (compared with the treatment expected for the crimes in question). Nonetheless, there has been a growing outcry on the part of many people that something must be done. Furthermore, there is increased awareness, on the part of many people, of the close connection between caste and class in the rural areas, at least at the bottom of the hierarchy.

It now seems fairly self-evident that any kind of meaningful transformation of the Indian social system cannot occur unless society comes to terms with caste, and with the close connections between caste and class. It is quite striking to me that the two states in India where there have not been consistent atrocities reported on Harijans have been Kerala and West Bengal, where class ideology is more overt, and where the better-off would have reason to fear protests by non-Harijans of their own social class if Harijans were singled out for anything. This is not to say that the conditions of life for Harijans in Kerala are particularly pleasant. By far the vast majority live under conditions of extreme poverty, and are personally conscious of their caste position. But the basis for their plight today is that the vast majority in rural areas are agricultural laborers and in urban areas common coolies, and not their caste per se. Statistically, they may appear to be materially worse off than other agricultural laborers, but that is mostly a heritage of the past. Most of the Harijans interviewed in Kerala in 1975–1976, and again in the summer of 1977, clearly saw their misery as part of their class position, and as shared with non-Harijans in the same situation. This growth of class consciousness is probably the result of the many years of hard grassroots work by the Communist party starting in the early 1940s, and enhanced in recent years by the massive increase in literacy among the agricultural laborers in Kerala.

What the future will bring is hard to predict, but at the moment, the main focus of the movement for change is in the north Indian Hindi-speaking belt. The fate of the untouchables there will largely influence the fate of those in other regions.

This chapter provides a direct and clear picture of untouchable identity which is at variance with traditional myths. The symbolic status of pollution has rated highly in anthropological discourse, and it is clear that there continues to be such a focus, both among observers and among many segments of the Indian upper castes. The question remains "why?" It would be beyond the scope of this paper to present a full analysis of the scholarly establishment in the United States and elsewhere, but the reasons appear to be rooted in part in elite attitudes about those at the bottom of the socioeconomic hierarchy, the same kind of elite attitudes that, in the United States, bred the "Culture of Poverty" concept and related ideology.

It would not be very difficult to find situations in which the very same informants who spoke to me so freely about their views of the system would oblige someone who appeared to have power by presenting the official view of the system. All of them knew it well, and had learned what to say in the same way that inferiors the world over learn the official line. However, there is no question that there are serious barriers between Harijans and others. I have noted elsewhere that while I was working on an article about Harijans, a Brahman friend asked my help in meeting some Harijans. As he put it: "One needs connections to meet these people." It is clear that one not only needs connections, but also needs to convince them that one is on their side completely. Unless that is done, they are not going to risk saying what they really feel.

It is striking to what extent even leftist social scientists, both Indian and foreign, have accepted the standard views of caste. They may criticize it and claim that it must be given up, but it is accepted by all. It is my impression that this is, at least in part, related to Marx's own writing on India. Marx never had the opportunity to visit India, and thus his views of the system were of necessity based on what he read. And there was nothing for him to read that challenged the system. By his time there were social reformers, but none of them was questioning that the caste system and pollution regulations were based on critical symbolic factors, or that the lowly accepted their position as being based on their previous misdeeds in another life. The reformers wanted to remove the disabilities of the poor and the untouchables, but never questioned the foundations of the system. They certainly never provided a milieu in which village untouchables could openly question the status quo. As a result, many distortions crept into Marx's writings, which have been accepted until today by many orthodox leftists (who, of course, come from elite groups).

What people so often fail to understand is the extent to which power relations dominate life in Indian villages. Fear of oppression and of the use of brute force has dominated people's minds and hearts much more than appears in traditional pictures of Indian village life. As noted above, even today many of the perpetrators of violence against Harijans rarely are punished, and, in fact, they often include the local police. If this is true now, one can easily imagine the situation of untouchables in the past, in a village dominated by one or two wealthy landlord families. Even where the landlord may appear cordial and sympathetic, village Harijans know how easily friendliness has turned to hate and oppression elsewhere, and carefully control their behavior. Thus, one could say that an additional reason why some social scientists continue to advance the myth of caste is that they so strongly expect to find what others have found, and do not allow for the possibility that their informants may have more than one level of awareness of power relations. This is, of course, not a total explanation, and I hope to be able to explore this question in greater detail in work now in preparation.

References

Aiyappan, A.

1965 *Social revolution in a Kerala village: A study in culture change.* New York: Asia Publishing House.

Alexander, K. C.
1968 Changing status of Pulaya Harijans of Kerala. *Economic and Political Weekly*, Special No.: 1071–1075.

Ambedkar, B. R.
1935/1968 *Annihilation of caste*. Jullundur City (Punjab): Bheem Patrika Publications.
1948 *The untouchables*. New Delhi: Amrit Book Company.

Berreman, G. O.
1960 Caste in India and the United States. *American Journal of Sociology 66*:120–127.
1967a Stratification, pluralism and interaction: A comparative analysis of caste. In *Caste and race: Comparative approaches* (A. de Reuck and J. Knight, Eds.) Boston: Little, Brown. Pp. 45–73.
1967b Caste as social process. *Southwestern Journal of Anthropology 23*:351–370.
1971 Self, situation and escape from stigmatized ethic identity. Paper presented at 70th Meeting of the American Anthropological Association.
1972a Race, caste and other invidious distinctions in social stratification. *Race*. Special Issue: *Race and Stratification* (W. G. Runciman, Ed.) *13*.
1972b A Brahmanical view of caste: Louis Dumont's homo hierarchicus. In *Contributions to Indian sociology*. In press.

Beteille, A.
1965a The future of the backward classes: The competing demands of status and power, *Perspectives. Supplement to the Indian Journal of Public Administration XI* (1):1–39.
1965b *Caste, class and power: Changing patterns of stratification in a Tanjore village*. Berkeley: University of California Press.
1969 (Ed.) *Social inequality, selected readings*. Harmondsworth.
1970 Inequality in practice and principle. Mimeo. University of Delhi.
1971a Agrarian relations in Tanjore district, South India. Manuscript. University of Delhi.
1971b Class structure in an agrarian society: The case of Jotadars. Mimeo. University of Delhi.

Beteille, A., and M. N. Srinivas
1969 The Harijans of India. In *Castes old and new* (A. Beteille, Ed.) New York: Asia Publishing House.

Chandrasekhar, S.
1972 Personal perspectives on untouchability. In *The untouchables in contemporary India* (J. M. Mahar, Ed.) Tucson: University of Arizona Press. Pp. xi–xxviii.

Chatterjee, B. B.
1971 *Inpact of social legislation on social change*. Calcutta: The Minerva Associates.

Dandekar, V. M., and N. Rath
1971 Poverty in India-I. *Economic and Political Weekly:* 25–48.

Dubey, S. N., and V. Mathur
1972 Welfare programmes for Scheduled Castes: Context and administration. *Economic and Political Weekly*. Pp. 165–176.

Dumont, L.
1970 *Homo hierarchicus*. London: Widenfeld and Nicolson.

Dupuis,
1960 Madras et le nord du Coromandel. Paris: Librairie D'Amerique et D'Orient, A. Maisonneuve.

Dushkin, L.
1972 Scheduled Caste politics. In *The untouchables in contemporary India* (J. M. Mahar, Ed.) Tucson: University of Arizona Press. Pp. 227–317.

Fitzpatrick, J.
1971 *Puerto Rican Americans*. Englewood Cliffs: Prentice Hall.

Government of India
1932 Census of India, 1931: Depressed Classes. Vol. XIV. New Delhi: Government Press.

1964–1965 Census of India, 1961: Madras. Vol. IX: Parts II-A (General Tables), II-C (i) (Cultural Tables, V-A (i & ii) (Scheduled Castes), and X–VI (District Census Handbook, Chingleput, Vols. I-II). Madras: Madras Government Press.

1965 Census of India, 1961: Vol. IX, Part V-A (ii). Madras: Government Press.

1969 Report of the committee on untouchability, economic and educational development of the Scheduled Castes, and connected documents (Elayaperumal Report). New Delhi.

Habib, I.

1963 *The agrarian system of Mughal India (1556–1707).* New York: Asia Publishing House.

Isaacs, H. R.

1965 *India's ex-untouchables.* New York: John Day.

Krishnan, T. N.

1972 Taxation of property and net wealth in India. *Economic and Political Weekly:* 21.

Kumar, D.

1965 *Land and caste in South India.* Cambridge: Cambridge University Press.

Mahar, J. M.

1972 *The untouchables in contemporary India.* Tucson: University of Arizona Press.

Mencher, J. P.

1966 Kerala and Madras: A comparative study of ecology and social structure. *Ethnology 5*:135–171.

1969 Comments on the economic Position of Untouchables in Chingleput District, Madras. COPEC VII. Boston.

1970a A Tamil village: Changing socioeconomic structure in Madras State. In *Aspects of continuity and change in India* (K. Iswaran, Ed.) New York: Columbia University Press. Pp. 197–218.

1970b Change agents and villagers: An analysis of their relationship and the role of class values. *Economic and Political Weekly of Bombay.* Vol. V. Pp. 1187–1197.

1972 Continuity and change in an ex-untouchable community of South India. In *The untouchables in contemporary India* (J. M. Mahar, Ed.) Tucson: University of Arizona Press. Pp. 37–56.

1974 The caste system upside down: Or the not-so-mysterious East. *Current Anthropology 15*(4):469–494.

1975 Agricultural labour movements in their socio-political and ecological context: Tamil Nadu and Kerala. In *Culture and society: A festschrift for Dr. Aiyappan* (B. S. Nair, Ed.) New Delhi: New Delhi Thomas Press. Pp. 240–266.

1978 *Agriculture and social structure in Tamil Nadu: Past origins, present transformations, and future prospects.* Durham: Carolina Academic Press.

Mencher, J. and K. Raman Unni

1973 Anthropological research in Kerala: Past achievements, and future needs. *Indian Council of Social Science Abstracts Quarterly 2*(3):143–168.

Moore, B., Jr.

1966 Social origins of dictatorship and democracy. Boston: Beacon Press.

Saberwal, S.

1972 The reserved constituency: Candidates and consequences. *Economic and Political Weekly:* 71–80.

Shivaraman, M.

1972 Thanjavur, rumblings of class struggle in Tamil Nadu. In *South Asia in turmoil. Bulletin of Concerned Asian Scholars,* Vol. 4(1), Winter.

Sachchidananda

Studies of Scheduled Castes with special reference to change. Paper presented at Indian Council of Social Science Research, Conference on the Present Status of Research in Social Sciences.

Singer, M.
1972 *When a great tradition modernizes.* New York: Praeger.
Sonachalam, K. S.
1970 *Land reforms in Tamil Nadu.* New Delhi: Oxford and IBH.
Southworth, F. C.
1974 Linguistic masks for power: Some relationships between semantic and social change. Anthropological Linguistics 16:177–191.
Srinivas, M. N.
1962 *Caste in modern India and other essays.* New York: Asia Publishing House.
1966 *Social change in modern India.* Berkeley: University of California Press.
Suresh, Chandra
1972 Harijans need assistance, not pity. *Times of India.*
Unni, K, R.
1959 Caste in South Malabar. Ph.D. dissertation, University of Baroda.
Varghese, T. C.
1970 *Agrarian change and economic consequences: Land tenures in Kerala, 1850–1960.* Bombay: Allied Publishers.

10 Population Pressure, Land Tenure, and Voodoo: The Economics of Haitian Peasant Ritual

GERALD F. MURRAY

Introduction

In the following pages I will present both descriptive and quantitative information, gathered in a Haitian village during 21 months of fieldwork.[1] This information reveals the somewhat unexpected but empirically convincing and critical role which Haitian-peasant Voodoo plays in the contemporary land tenure system; specifically, this cult was found to function as a partially camouflaged resource-circulating mechanism, a role that seems to have arisen in the context of recent population growth.

Methodologically, I hope to illustrate the manner in which simple quantitative data—gathered and analyzed in a theoretical perspective sensitive to the interactions between material lifespheres and other domains of social life—can expose the operation of systems whose very existence may escape the notice of traditional descriptive ethnography. Substantively, I will argue that the discovery of these internal systemic linkages between Voodoo and aspects of the agrarian resource regime permits us to comprehend many superficially enigmatic elements that have come to characterize peasant Voodoo in recent years. We can also come to understand the persistence of the cult in the face of

[1] The fieldwork on which this chapter is based was carried out with a research grant given me by the Overseas Population Intern program at the University of Michigan, with supervisory support from the International Institute for the Study of Human Reproduction at Columbia University and the Centre d'Hygiène Familiale in Port-au-Prince, Haiti. Helpful comments on earlier drafts were made by Maria Alvarez, Conrad Arensberg, Lambros Comitas, William Dalton, Marvin Harris, Ira Lowenthal, Ron McDonough, Barbara Price, Eric Ross, and Vera Rubin. Any errors contained here are, of course, my own responsibility.

BEYOND THE MYTHS OF CULTURE
Essays in Cultural Materialism

ISBN 0-12-598180-5

what, until the past two decades, was almost unremitting opposition from the forces of church and state.

Haiti is a land whose inhabitants are mainly descendants of slaves who successfully overthrew the French and brought to a total halt a flourishing Caribbean plantation economy. After the French were ejected in 1804, the earliest Haitian leaders, following the colonial models most familiar to them, attempted to reinstate an organizationally tight plantation-like economic and social order. Their efforts failed. The newly freed slave population eventually thwarted all attempts to reinstate even the semblance of the old order. Government plans had called for a society of plantation gang laborers—not slaves, it is true, but de facto serfs who would be bound to certain plantations, who would labor under the supervision of the Haitian military, and whose reward would be a share in the produce of the plantations. What emerged instead was a society of peasant cultivators.

While few have denied Haiti credit for a uniquely successful revolt, the success of the economic and social system that subsequently emerged has frequently been questioned. Throughout the nineteenth and early twentieth centuries European and American writers tended to caricature Haitian leaders as pretentious buffoons and to dismiss the Haitian peasant as a slothful savage addicted to a superstitious rural cult generally referred to as Voodoo. Earlier assessments of Haiti tended to be racial in nature; the cessation of export prosperity was taken as evidence of the incapacity of blacks to rule themselves. Such racist analyses, however, have only yielded to more recent caricatures that tend to depict Haiti as a country of macabre and fanatical rulers controlling a voodoo-infested hinterland, a sensationalistic view that has received more popular attention than competent anthropological work on rural Haitian economy and domestic organization.[2]

At the outset of fieldwork, I had personally resolved to resist the siren-song of Voodoo and dedicate my time to the study of local agrarian economic organization, particularly the organization of land tenure and domestic labor. Research was carried out in a lowland village on the Cul-de-Sac Plain (see Figure 10.1). This community, Kinanbwa,[3] located some 3.2 km (2 miles) from the town that served as its administrative head, was inhabited by some 1200 people whose basic livelihood came from cultivation of a variety of crops, many of them destined for sale in local markets. The majority of adult females in the village were market women, whose trading activities provided substantial increments to domestic income.

The Cul-de-Sac Plain, however, turned out to be among the least appropriate settings in which to attempt analysis of an agrarian community without

[2] Two older examples of this genre can be found in Franklin (1828) and Prichard (1900). In similar vein, for the twentieth century we have not only Graham Greene's famous novel *The Comedians,* but also Diederich and Burt's *Papa Doc* (1969), whose front cover shows a black hand holding a burning skull impaled on a wooden stake, across which is blazoned the chilling legend "Atrocities in the Realm of a Madman."

[3] Kinanbwa is a pseudonym.

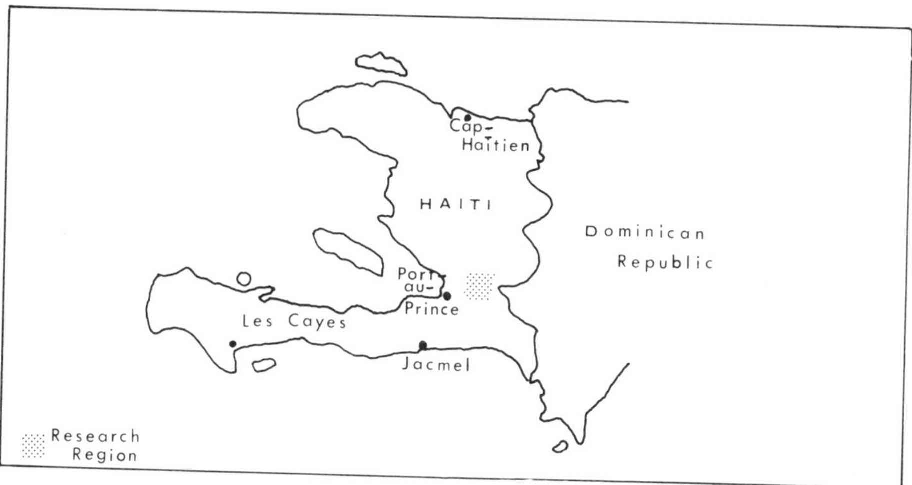

FIGURE 10.1. *Haiti and the Research Region.*

systematic attention to ritual concerns. While the vast majority of villagers among whom I lived were Catholics, more than 7 out of 10 of these Catholics openly admitted that they "served the loua," the local idiom that indicates participation in the folk cult to be described in these pages. The impressive amounts of money spent in the planning and execution of rituals gave credence to the Cul-de-Sac's popular reputation as one of the strongholds of Voodoo involvement. Capitulating to the inevitable, I adjusted my fieldwork accordingly, thus adding one more anthropologist to the long list of those who have chased after the secrets of Voodoo.

In the presentation that follows, I will first provide information on the cult itself, reserving discussion of the agrarian economy for later sections, where interactions between the two spheres will become clear.

An Overview of Voodoo

For most English speakers, the word "voodoo" elicits the image of a doll riddled with pins. This identification of Voodoo with illness- or death-inflicting sorcery has even made its way into the anthropological literature, in which discussions of Voodoo revolve around the question of magically induced sickness or death (Cannon 1942; Lester 1972; Lex 1974).

It is true that Haitian Voodoo offers sorcery as one of its ritual options, but by no means is the cult exclusively (or even principally) an outlet for ritual violence. The rather abundant literature on Haitian Voodoo (e.g., Deren 1970; Herskovits 1937; Rigaud 1953; Métraux 1959; Murray 1976; Price-Mars 1928; Simpson 1945; Lowenthal 1978) indicates clearly that we are dealing with a folk-religion or folk-cult[4]—that is, an activity complex involving *beliefs* in a pantheon of spirits, *rituals* performed to influence and interact with these spirits, and *specialists* who are resorted to for theological consultations and certain types of ritual leadership. The contexts in which interaction among believer, specialist, and spirit occur ordinarily have little or nothing to do with the black magic of the type symbolized by the pin-riddled doll.

GENERALIZED PATTERNS OF BELIEFS, RITUALS, AND SPECIALISTS

The rural Haitian pantheon is populated by an impressive variety of spirits, ghosts, vampires, ogres, and other preternatural creatures. But the undisputed protagonists of the Haitian peasant spirit world are a group of anthropomorphic spirits referred to generically as the *loua*. Though an unknown loua will occasionally make an appearance at a ceremony, the majority of loua are well known to their followers. That is, they have not only names (e.g., Legba, Dambala, Ogoun, Bosou) but also specific personality characteristics, food and drink preferences, color and clothing preferences, songs that are sung to them, and to some degree even specific drum rhythms whose summons they are more likely to obey.

But there are larger subdivisions of the loua that are made by believers. In the published literature, the most frequently found distinction is the one that is made between gentler spirits and more violent spirits. The gentler spirits, gener-

[4] Though Voodoo is frequently called the "folk religion of Haiti," the term "cult" might perhaps be technically more correct. As discussed elsewhere (Murray n.d.), participation in folk rituals, at least in Kinanbwa and apparently elsewhere in Haiti, entails simultaneous adherence to several theological and ceremonial tenets of institutionalized Roman Catholicism, including worship of the Christian God (Bon-Dieu) as the Supreme Being and mandatory baptism at the hands of a Catholic priest. That is, the practitioners remain Catholics and Voodoo is a complex that does not constitute a separate religion apart from Roman Catholicism.

ally called *loua rada* in the literature, are conceived of as being "older" than the more violent band of spirits, the *loua pétro.* (In fact the Rada loua were generally referred to as "Guinee loua" by the villagers among whom I worked). There are other groups of loua referred to, but the tendency among many believers appears to be that of dichotomizing the pantheon. Among my own informants, this was epitomized by the frequent use of the terms "sweet loua" and "bitter loua."

The dichotomizing principle crosscuts the previously mentioned identification practices. That is, the name of a given loua need not be irrevocably stationed in either the bitter or the sweet sides of the pantheon. Most in fact appear to straddle. The major female loua, Erzulie, for example, sometimes appears as Erzulie Freda Dahomey—a gentle, generally benevolent Guinee spirit. But at other times the Erzulie who appears is Erzulie Jé Rouj (red-eyed Erzulie, a violent Pétro loua who is believed to kill with great frequency). Some analysts (e.g., Métraux 1959; Deren 1970) handle this by calling these different "manifestations" of the same loua. In contrast, the villagers among whom I worked considered them to be separate spirits (*dé nam apa*). In either case, a central feature of rural Haitian theology appears to be a tendency to dichotomize the pantheon and to allow for appearances of most loua in both camps. The possible linkages between this phenomenon and other features of economic and social organization will become clearer.

In addition to the loua, there are other spirits and preternatural creatures. Competing for second place in importance would be "the dead" on the one hand and the vampire (*lougarou*) on the other.[5] When one's parents die, they are "owed" a number of rather costly ceremonies sometime during the life of their individual children. But in addition to making offerings of this sort, individuals in some parts of Haiti frequently interact with their parents, having them summoned back from the dead. The vampire, in contrast, though playing an active role, never converses directly with his or her victims while in the vampire state. These creatures are ordinary villagers during the day. It is at night that they turn into tiny bird-like creatures and fly from place to place sucking the blood—generally, of young (or even yet unborn) children. As will be discussed next, the importance of the dead and the lougarou appears to be increasing over time. As will be shown, their growing ascendancy, is closely related to structurally deeper economic and social organizational changes that have taken place. And it will be argued that the relation is more than one of simple symbolic mirroring; the dead and the lougarou, rather, become critical tools in the pursuit of an incalculably important community goal.

Turning to a second domain, that of ritual, it is clear that most rituals of Haitian Voodoo are oriented first and foremost toward interaction with the loua. These rituals have been described at length in the literature, and only some major themes will be mentioned here:

[5] The rural Haitian *lougarou,* though lexically derived from the French *loup-garou* (werewolf), is conceptualized as a human being that turns into a bird-like animal at night and sucks the blood of children. The term "vampire" is thus probably a more appropriate gloss.

1. *Animal sacrifice.* The loua may make their followers ill or may help protect them against illnesses originating elsewhere. In return for release or protection, they want their "children" to "serve" them. The major (and most expensive) form of service generally given is the slaughter of animals to feed the loua.

2. *Possession.* The loua manifest themselves generally by possessing their followers. The loua mounts the head of the individual; the individual becomes the horse, the loua the rider. The possessed person assumes the behavior and personality of the loua who is mounting him.

3. *Drumming, dancing, and singing.* Most possessions of ordinary devotees occur in the context of chanting and dancing, to the accompaniment of percussion instruments dominated by batteries of sacred drums. Each song (*chanté loua*) is directed toward a particular spirit. There are dance styles and drum rhythms characteristic of groups of spirits—for example, there is a distinctive Pétro rhythm for summoning the violent spirits and the dances to this rhythm are violent and jerky, as opposed to the more undulating movements characteristic of dances to the gentle Guinée loua.

4. *Calling the loua with the asson.* In the traditional Voodoo of the village, possession frequently used to be oracular. The loua would give instructions to the assembled followers via the lips of a possessed person. In certain parts of Haiti, especially in the vicinity of Port-au-Prince, it seems that possession has somewhat lost its oracular function. When instructions are sought from the loua, rather, a specialist trained in the use of a sacred gourd-rattle (*asson*) must now be called in. Working behind a closed door, the officiant summons the loua and has them talk directly from a clay jug (*govi*).

This practice underlines yet a third major feature which Haitian Voodoo shares with other folk cults: the use of various specialists. Though specialists who deal with the spirits are called by different names in different parts of Haiti, the term *houngan* is recognized in most parts of the country. (Female specialists are called *mambos.*) In the research area, the villagers tended to dichotomize specialists into two types. The defining criterion is the source of one's power. Charismatic specialists who rely only on what their own family spirits reveal to them are called houngan Guinée, or houngan makout. Another group of specialists have resorted to the purchase of secrets and of spirits. They go through a period of initiation at the hands of some well established houngan, at the end of which they receive the previously mentioned asson. The distinction between houngan asson and houngan Guinée only roughly parallels the theological distinction between Guinée loua and Pétro loua. Though the nonfamilial loua purchased by the houngan asson are viewed as Pétro loua, he can also diagnose problems caused by the Guinée loua of a client. Likewise, the houngan Guinée can deal with Pétro loua if the need arises.

EMPHASES OF PEASANT VOODOO

The generalized picture of Voodoo previously drawn emphasizes the elements that the cult as observed in the village shared with the cult as described in the literature. But the village cult took certain directions for which an examination of the literature had not prepared me. These can be briefly listed.

1. *Familialization of theology.* The spirits of the village pantheon were conceived of as family spirits. Each family, for example, inherits its own Erzulies, its own Dambalas, its own Ogouns. In the course of the evolution of peasant lifeways in Haiti and the "domestication" of this village economy into one of family based smallholdings, there has been a corresponding domestication or familialization of the pantheon (Murray and Alvarez 1973).

2. *Confinement of the loua.* If in fact theology molds itself mechanically to social organization and economy, in this village setting one would have expected a great emphasis on agricultural rituals. This in fact has not occurred. On the contrary, I found *less* involvement of the loua in agriculture than was reported even in the literature. It is God, not the loua, who makes land fertile, rain fall, crops grow. There were no rituals regularly performed on gardens, no offerings of first fruits, no invocations asking loua to help the crops grow in abundance. There was a belief that the ancestral spirits reside in the ground. But in the research community they inhabited residential ground, not the gardens. In short, the village loua have been partially banished from the domain of agriculture. This is most significant. But I will argue that their exclusion from the agricultural sector of the local economy may have occurred in the context of a critical alternative role which the loua now play in another sphere of that same economy.

3. *The cult of healing.* Though the loua are generally absent from the fields, they are quite active in the bodies (and minds) of human beings. Their principal activity at present appears to be causing different types of illness. Many rituals are oriented to the diagnosis of these problems, and healing ceremonies cost large sums of money. Even large week-long services, which are generally not staged for particular illness episodes but rather for more general reasons, nonetheless terminate with invocations to ensure good health. The principal request made to the loua is to remove "heat" and bring "coolness," concepts which the villagers themselves interpret in terms of physical illness and health. Because so many of the rituals are dominated by the theme of healing, because even those rituals in which healing may play no open part may have been financed by individuals dealing with family illness, and because the major source of income for houngans now is to be found in their healing role, it would not at all be metaphorical to call contemporary village Voodoo a variety of healing cult.

4. *The cult of the dead.* The literature refers to the existence of a cult of the dead—that is, rituals in which individuals interact with their dead parents and grandparents. I had not been prepared, however, for the particular form which that cult was found to take in the village. With great frequency sibling groups now speak to their dead parents in ceremonies in which a houngan asson is paid to call them back from the dead (*rélé mò*). What is most impressive, however, is the quality of the burial monuments. The tombs where many

peasants are buried literally cost more to construct than the wattle-daub cottages in which they spent their lives.

VILLAGE VOODOO IN MICROEVOLUTIONARY PERSPECTIVE

The brief description of the cult just presented reflects certain features that are important in contemporary village life. But the cult *today* is by no means an eternal feature of the rural Haitian landscape. Synchronic descriptions obscure the fact that the cult at a given moment is a compromise balance of elements that may individually be in a fairly rapid state of flux. The cult has been changing. Older informants agree about the more obvious changes; these changes can ultimately be linked to simultaneous changes which have been occurring in other lifespheres, thus imbuing these religious transformations with a systematic character amenable to analysis in an evolutionary framework. Summarizing the changes, older informants report that there has been:

1. With respect to ritual specialists: (*a*) a decrease in the role of older males in each family as vehicles of possession and recipients of healing instructions; (*b*) a concomitant increase in the use of extradomestic specialists as intermediaries between believers and their spirits; (*c*) a recent increase in dependency on formally initiated (and more expensive) specialists—the houngan asson—as being more powerful for certain rituals than the charismatic specialists—the houngan makout; (*d*) a redefining of the specialist career in such a way that the status of houngan makout is interpreted as merely the prelude to eventual initiation into the ritually more powerful status of houngan asson.

2. With respect to the belief system: (*a*) increases in the activity and general salience of the "bitter" spirits—Pétro loua—whom all families are believed to inherit but who rarely acted in the past; (*b*) a concomitant decrease in the relative importance of the "sweet" spirits—the more gentle Guinée loua; (*c*) an increase in the use of nonfamilial spirits—the "purchased loua"—to achieve personal and economic objectives; (*d*) an increase in the activity of preternatural creatures such as the lougarou, the villager who at night turns into a vampire-like destroyer of young children; (*e*) a general increase in the frequency of spirit-caused illness (*maladi loua*) as opposed to naturally caused illness (*maladi Bon-Dieu*); (*f*) a general increase in the severity of spirit-caused illness and in the occurrence of death as a result of such illnesses.

3. With respect to rituals and ritual expenditures: (*a*) a general increase in the use of "pétro" songs, drum rhythms, and dances, more violent in tone and content than songs, rhythms, and dances used to summon the gentler Guinée loua; (*b*) a restructuring of rituals in such a way that the final stages of ceremonies—be they lengthy "services" that last for several days or shorter subrituals within these services—are regularly dedicated to the invocation, entertainment, feeding, placation, and eventual dismissal of the violent Pétro loua; (*c*) an increasing involvement in rituals involving conversations with one's dead parents and grandparents, conversations that must be mediated by a formally initiated houngan asson; (*d*) dramatic increases in the number of animals that

must be slaughtered to placate the spirits; (*e*) visible and costly increases in the quality and style of burial monuments, with a growing insistence that it is shameful to be buried beneath the ground, that the dead prefer to be buried above ground in elaborate, expensive multichambered tombs.

This dynamic character and internal coherence of ethnographic minutiae such as the ones presented here are best exposed by a theoretical perspective attuned to the macrohistorical processes in which these minutiae unfold. The details of Haitian-peasant Voodoo take on unsuspected life and meaning when analytically juxtaposed to certain features of local economic and social life. Of particular interest are the recent ritual and theological shifts enumerated in the preceding paragraphs. These changes, I will argue, have been neither accidental nor random. They are systematically linked to other transformations that have been occurring in the social organization and agrarian economy of the village. It is to these domains that the analysis now turns.

Sharecropping, Land Purchase, and the Hidden Career

From the earliest days of fieldwork it was evident that the dynamics of land acquisition and the problems of growing land pressure were central themes in the economic life of this Haitian community. Virtually all males were gardeners, only a small minority of these gardeners supplemented their income with ancillary pursuits, and though most of the adult females in the village were heavily involved in marketing activities, the vast majority of households reported heavier reliance on the produce of the family gardens than on the profits of the woman's trading activities as the major source of domestic income. The economic destiny of each village household was, in short, closely tied to the family's holdings.

It was one thing to perceive the realistic importance of land, but quite another to develop reliable, step-by-step insights into the myriad subthemes of which the overall village land drama was ultimately composed. Both the literature and the more than two dozen village informants with whom I conducted open-ended interviews were helpful, however, in clarifying the outline of one of the major subplots, that of *inheritance*.

Summing up briefly, the traditional economic career of the Haitian peasant male—as generalized from accounts in the literature and from informants—begins with horticultural apprenticeship in parental gardens during boyhood and early teens. In the late teens, however, the father takes the young man to a family field and tells him that henceforth he can crop that field as though it were his own, bestowing in effect a preinheritance grant (cf. Herskovits 1937; Bastien 1951). Though it will not be fully his until the parent dies, he can use it as though it were his. This widely reported custom has been a traditional short-cut, eliminating parental death as a necessary prerequisite for access to family land and permitting young men to get a reasonably early start on their own economic careers.

But simple reflection will suggest the havoc that internal population growth could wreak on such a system, with its reliance on voluntary parental land grants. This custom of preinheritance grants, in fact, arose and flourished in the land abundant days of the nineteenth century. But, in the Haiti of the 1970s, with its population density of some 2000 persons per arable 2.6 km^2 (1 square mile), the system of preinheritance grants has been threatened and in some cases undermined, although parental generosity continues as a community ideal (and is occasionally reported as a fact by outside observers who treat such a collective norm as though it were an accurate representation of collective behavior).

The theme of inheritance, with its subplot of young adult preinheritance, continued to play a critical role in Kinanbwa, not only in the general descriptions that villagers gave of their way of life, but also in more specific case studies of individual economic careers. However, it was equally clear that something else was occurring at the same time. Important transformations had been working their way into the internal machinery of local land tenure, and things were not the same as before. Villagers were keenly aware of these changes; but no convenient, consistently agreed-on community theory emerged of what was in fact happening. Widespread visions of a past golden age, when parents gave land to their children as they were supposed to, had not yet been supplemented by equally widespread agreement on what was happening today or in what direction things were moving.

To go beyond reliance on informant generalizations, I collected specific economic information on each village household. To deal with the phenomenon of holding fragmentation and to maximize even further the specificity of the data, information on land tenure was gathered on a plot-by-plot basis, rather than asking villagers to generalize about their holdings as a unit. For each plot, information was elicited that included not only approximate size and crops planted, but also tenure and length of time the cultivator had been on the plot. As I will show, it is this plot-specific data that exposes some of the critical internal workings of the local land tenure system.[6]

THE RARITY OF LANDLESSNESS

Population growth had led to a clear diminution of the amount of land a household will have under cultivation at a given moment. The mean of approximately 1.5 carreaux of land (1 carreau = 1.4 hectares) under cultivation per household falls within the range found in other communities (Zuvekas 1978) but is substantially less than what the literature (and older villagers) report for times past. Even in the absence of hard data on the holdings of times past, the

[6] The methodological difficulty of eliciting reliable economic and demographic information in rural Haiti, and the strategies adopted to enhance the accuracy of the quantitative component of this research, are discussed at length in Murray (1977) and Chen and Murray (1976).

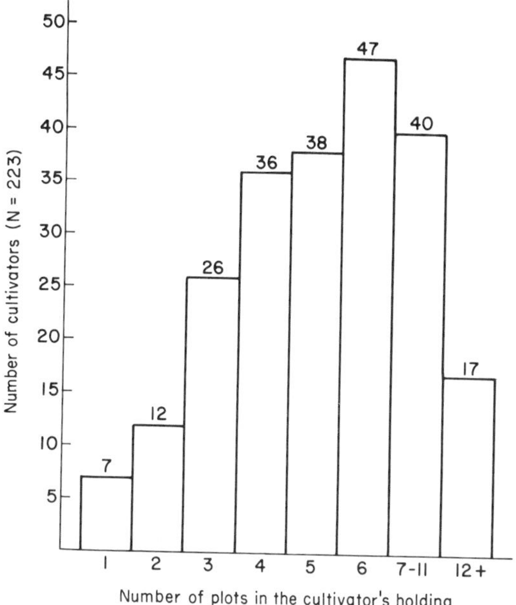

FIGURE 10.2. *Fragmentation of landholdings.*

phenomenon of average holding shrinkage leaps forth as a central theme in the dilemma of contemporary rural Haiti.

But if Kinanbwa had been losing ground in terms of average holding size, the community had nonetheless not experienced the emergence of a totally landless class of peasants relying solely on wage labor for their sustenance. All adult males in the village had access to at least some garden land, and though much of the land was being cropped under one or another of the sharecropping arrangements to be discussed, virtually every household had at least one plot that was being cropped under some form of proprietary tenure. Furthermore, as Figure 10.2 shows, the average cultivator was cropping several plots. The small size of the average plot (more than 80% of the plots are less than one-fifth of a hectare in size) maintains a small average quantity of cropped land, but the prevalence of multiplot holdings attests to a system whose protagonist continues to be the smallholding cultivator rather than the landless wage laborer.

THE ABSENCE OF DELAYED CAREERS

The rarity of absolute rural landlessness can be seen as a fairly direct product of Haiti's postcolonial history. But there is another contemporary pattern that is somewhat harder to account for, which exposes the operation of an otherwise elusive feature of the local agrarian economy. With the advent of land pressure, one would have expected a curtailment of the previously mentioned preinheritance grants. Statements from older villagers as well as data from Kinanbwa attest to the fact that dramatic curtailments have indeed taken

TABLE 10.1
Timetable for Entry into Independent Gardening

Dependent males residing with parents and cropping their own gardens	Crops own garden	Does not yet crop	Total
Under 18	6 16.7%	30 83.3%	36 100.0%
18–21	16 50.0%	16 50.0%	32 100.0%
22 +	27 81.8%	6 18.2%	33 100.0%
Total	49 48.5%	52 51.5%	101 100.0%

place, and that young men can rely much less on such preinheritance grants as the primary route to economic autonomy.

But one would then have predicted the phenomenon of disrupted or delayed careers, as young men would have to emigrate or wait for their parents to die for access to land. Young men from the village do in fact emigrate annually to the Dominican Republic to cut cane, but most come back. Emigration in Kinanbwa has not yet taken on the escape-valve dimensions so widely commented on in other parts of the Caribbean (cf. Roberts 1966; Lopez 1974)[7] But even more significantly, *the traditional life cycle goes on as before.* That is, young men continue to crop their first garden while still living as dependents in their parents' house; these first gardens tend to be cropped in the late teens and early twenties as before. The insistence of villagers that this continues to be the case is strongly borne out by quantitative data. There were 101 young men in the village who were old enough to have begun helping their fathers on their gardens and who were still living as dependents. For each of these young men, I ascertained whether, in addition to serving as assistants on parental gardens, they were also cropping gardens of their own. The data are tabulated by age in Table 10.1 and illustrate clearly the preservation of the basic outline of the traditional economic timetable. Whereas it is rare for a child under 17 to have his own garden, it is equally rare for a young man over 22 *not* to. This will turn out to be a most significant fact, significant not only statistically but also theoretically, as a manifestation of an adaptive systemic maneuver that preserves the

[7] Published information on rural Haitian emigration is hard to come by. There appear to be many areas where the rural exodus has taken on impressive dimensions. Informants in the Aux Cayes region of the Southern Peninsula informed me that as many as one out of three households in certain communities may be receiving regular remittances from the United States. Rawson and Berggren (1973) present data that indicate impressive emigration from the Artibonite to unspecified destinations. Rural communities in the Fond-des-Negres area are experiencing much emigration to Guyana (Ira Lowenthal, personal communication). More specific information on migration patterns has recently become available with the appearance of research by Uli Locher (1979) in Port-au-Prince and Theodore Ahlers (1979) in several parts of rural Haiti. See also the article by Buchanan (1979).

TABLE 10.2
Breakdown of Plots by Specific Tenure Arrangement

How cultivator gained access to the plot?	*N*	Percentage
Inherited	202	16.5
Purchased	177	14.4
Sharecrops	667	54.4
Wife's	57	4.6
Rents	78	6.4
Other	46	3.7
Total	1227	100.0

viability of one pattern by the introduction of strategic modifications in another.

THE ROLE OF SHARECROPPING

The most important modification comes in terms of the *source* of land for young gardeners. It is here that the Kinanbwa land tenure data expose a domain of internal patterning in which the actual behavior of community members appears to have made substantial departures from the traditional land tenure patterns embodied in the inheritance–preinheritance model discussed before.

The matter can best be phrased as a commonsense hypothesis. If land tenure operated as the traditional model envisions, then we would have a situation in which the vast majority of cultivators would be proprietors of the ground they are cropping. National census figures would at first glance appear to bear this out (Zuvekas 1978). Haiti's extremely low rate of landlessness makes it unique in Caribbean and Latin American context; more than 8 out of 10 cultivators describe themselves as proprietors.

General questioning had appeared to indicate that the same was true of the cultivators of Kinanbwa. In conversations villagers tended to say that they and their neighbors were proprietors. But given the multiplot nature of the typical holding, and the obvious existence of other tenure modes in the village as well, I was uneasy with the simple label of "smallholding peasant proprietor" as a characterization of the land tenure situation of the village.

To obtain somewhat more precise information, cultivators were asked to enumerate each of their currently cropped plots separately and to specify the manner in which they had gained access to the plot.[8] In view of the previously mentioned tendency of Haitian peasants to describe themselves as proprietors, it was expected that a heavy majority of plots would be plots cultivated by owners who had inherited them. But the rather astonishing breakdown given in Table 10.2 reveals how far this expectation was from the actual systemic reality.

[8] Information was also obtained about plots lying fallow and plots which cultivators were renting or sharing out to other cultivators. Analysis here, however, will concentrate on the "cropped holding," defined as the sum total of plots which individuals themselves are cultivating under whatever tenure arrangement.

The 1227 plots on which information is available constitutes over 95% of the plot inventory of the community. We see that more than half of these plots are being sharecropped.

This breakdown suggests the operation of a "system within a system," or—perhaps more accurately—the existence of a disparity between the model that emerges from an analysis based on simple self-labeling information and one that uses somewhat more refined breakdowns of the data. It must be pointed out: The self-labeling of the peasant as a proprietor is perfectly correct. In virtually every cropped holding, at least one plot is held under one or another proprietary mode. The labeling merely misses important aspects of the system. For though virtually every cultivator in the community is indeed an inheriting proprietor, we see that fewer than 2 out of 10 plots are being cropped by their inheritors. Rather, most of the plots are being cropped by individuals who stand in a tenancy relation to the plot. In Kinanbwa, these two apparently contradictory modes—proprietorship and tenancy—are joined here within the workings of a single complex land tenure system.

STRATUM-INTERNAL CHARACTER OF HAITIAN PEASANT SHARECROPPING

The question that immediately calls out for an answer is the identity of the owners of the 667 plots that are being cropped by tenants. Fortunately, some precise data were also gathered on each of the landlords as part of the same survey. It turns out that about 80% of the sharecropped plots have owners who live either in Kinanbwa or in nearby rural communities. Some 15% of the plots have owners listed as residing in the nearby town, but more than half of these are themselves cultivators residing in the periphery of the town. That is, the vast majority of landlords *are themselves peasant cultivators* who physically work their own plots of ground at the same time that they give land out to tenants.

Second, a substantial number of the sharecropped plots (more than 4 out of 10) are being given by one relative to another. That is, sharecropping tends not only to be intraclass, but to a large degree intrafamilial as well. The intraclass nature of Kinanbwa sharecropping is further emphasized by the fact that 110 of the sharecropped plots have tenants who are sons and owners who are their fathers.

Third, and most conclusive, the "landlords" and the "tenants" do not in fact constitute two discrete groups. That is, many individuals who have tenants on some of their own land will simultaneously *be* tenants on the plot of someone else. Among 109 landlords on whom complete data are available, 63 are simultaneously cropping at least one plot for another individual on a tenant basis. That is, nearly 60% of our "landlords" are themselves "tenants." And the remaining 40% may not be tenants themselves, but virtually all of them continue to crop their own plots of ground with their labor and that of their children. In short, the sharecropping that our data have revealed is a *stratum-internal sharecropping*. The stratificational frameworks used to analyze the interclass sharecropping of Latin America peasants, focusing on the maneuvers of an absentee landlord class to exact rent from totally landless tenants, would shed little light on the structural arrangements prevailing in Kinanbwa, and we are thus forced to turn to a fundamentally different type of conceptual strategy.

LAND PURCHASE AND THE TRANSFORMED CAREER

The plot-specific sharecropping data begin to fall into logical array once we begin to examine them through the lens of a "life-cycle" framework. Age-specific breakdowns of the village land tenure data expose a highly ordered internal sequencing of alternative land-development strategies used by the villagers, in a systematic fashion, at different points in their economic careers. The disaggregated data permit us to posit a modal career consisting of three distinct (but in many cases overlapping) phases.

The cultivators begin their careers now principally as sharecroppers. Though preinheritance grants from parent to child are still made, the tenure mode governing most plots cropped by males in their twenties and early thirties is that of the intracommunity sharecropping discussed above.[9] But by their mid-thirties most of the cultivators will begin to *purchase* plots of ground, entering thus into a new phase of their careers. Many continue even then to crop at least one plot on a sharecropping basis, but there is a statistically noticeable aggregate decrease in reliance on this tenure mode in the higher age groups. What is most impressive, however, is the systematic nature of the entry of older males into yet a third stage of the local agrarian career: the phase of landlord. As the cultivator acquires plots, largely through this purchase but also through inheritance at the eventual death of his parents, he will in the vast majority of cases turn over one or more of his plots to a younger person in the community to crop as a tenant. That is, age-specific breakdowns of the data expose the operation of a modal career whose final stage is the status of landlord.[10]

---

[9] Though preinheritance grants are still made to young men, these individuals now depend more heavily on sharecropping for the first phase of their carreer. Of the 78 gardeners under the age of 30, 59 (76%) were working at least one sharecropped plot, whereas only 53 (68%) were working at least one preinheritance plot. That is, the two land routes coexist (even in the same holding in several cases), but sharecropping by now appears to predominate. Looking at a differently defined "young" group, of the 47 dependent gardeners still living under their parents' roofs, 38 (81%) crop at least one of their plots on a sharecropping basis.

[10] In the over-35 age group ($N = 127$), 2 out of 3 cultivators have purchased at least one plot of ground. The subsequent percentage of peasant *landlords* rises steadily with age, even more regularly than the percentage of land purchasers, as older men come into at least some inheritance land on their parents' death. Whereas 2 out of 3 peasants in the 35–54 age group have at least one (generally younger) tenant, 8 out of 10 of the 55-or-over group are landlords. The smoothness of the rise into peasant landlordism is impressive.

The use of age-specific breakdowns to expose subtle internal patterning has been used effectively in the Caribbean by M. G. Smith, whose analysis revealed the operation of an orderly mating system in rural Jamaica (1962). Such cohort data may of course reflect not only the contemporary career but also changes across time in the modal career, and they must therefore be interpreted judiciously. Nonetheless, the strategy of disaggregating key variables by age provides a powerful tool for detecting internal life-cycle patterning that might otherwise pass unnoticed.

With regard to this patterning of economic careers, three observations are particularly important to draw attention to the larger system level. First, the individual behaviors that constitute a life cycle, in this case simultaneously, constitute a system for allocating resources. The life-blood of the community is its land, and the intermeshing of the economic careers of different individuals—the interactions among tenants, land purchasers, and/or landlords—results in a circulation of land.[11] The behaviors of tenants are systematically linked to the behaviors of landlords; the behaviors of land purchasers are likewise tied to the behaviors of land sellers. An individual's choice of behavior is also systematically linked to his age.

Second, this system is the product of recent change. Elsewhere specific evidence has been presented (Murray 1977) showing the manner in which, within the context of population growth, the incidence of sharecropping and landlordism has been increasing over time. This suggests that what we are now observing is the *transformed descendant* of the traditional inheritance–preinheritance system still reflected in community ideals. The transformation has not involved mysterious evolutionary "inventions," but rather the selection and emphasis of preexisting economic alternatives—tenancy and land transaction—until they have now become the statistically dominant themes in the economic careers of the peasants. Thus the young man who began life on parentally allocated land has slowly been replaced by a young sharecropper. And the image of the old patriarch, surrounded by sons laboring for him in his gardens, is being increasingly replaced by a different success model, that of the elderly landlord who, laying down his own hoe, dons a clean, longsleeved blue shirt, picks up his cane—symbol, not of weakness, but of authority—and calmly patrols his holdings, casting an approving eye on the work of his tenants. The actors are the same, but they are enacting a substantially revised script.

Third, it is also essential to point to the adaptive nature of the new arrangements. Where population growth had jeopardized the traditional intergenerational land flow by sabotaging preinheritance grants to dependent sons, the new arrangements constitute a systemic shift toward greater reliance on the options of tenancy and land purchase as alternatives to exclusive dependence on preinheritance grants. Because of this statistically interlinked sequencing of sharecropping, land purchasing, and landlordism, young men continue to acquire the plots they need to move into economic autonomy. Old men now have an alternative to filial labor on their holdings: They can turn part of their holding over to a tenant. These arrangements constitute in effect *alternative circuits for the flow of labor and land.* By avoiding the emergence of landless, economically dependent groups of young men, by making at least small quantities of land continually available to community members, this "rewired"

[11] To be more precise, it results in the circulation of *people* on to (and off of) different plots of ground. Cattle and money can literally circulate in a way that land cannot. Though I shall continue here to use the metaphor of "land circulation," the adaptive system being described here is in the last analysis basically a system of circulating human beings to and from plots of ground.

system has kept open the door to the vigorous economic maneuvering that has been a characteristic of rural Haiti, and has thus helped to preserve for at least a few generations more the viability (though certainly not the prosperity) of traditional agrarian life.[12]

The Ritual Mainspring

The model I have just presented leaves a number of unanswered questions; there is one in particular that would seem to threaten the credibility of the entire land circulating model. Recall: Land circulates to the young largely from the hands of landlords, but we have seen that these landlords rely on purchasing rather than simple inheritance as the source of the land which they share out. The entire system is made feasible by the emergence of a phase in the career of the typical cultivator, characterized by the purchase of one or more plots of ground. The entire resource-circulating system is kept moving, in other words, only because there is active movement in the local land market, movement characterized by energetic efforts on the part of peasants to save money for the eventual purchase of land.

The difficulty with the model is not that the Haitian peasant is poor—so poor as to be unable to raise money for land. Money is in fact raised. Every household in the village had some livestock, used almost entirely for purposes of rapid cash raising. And every household in the village dedicated impressively large parts of its holdings to the production of crops destined for sale.

The serious problem lies not in accounting for the cash, but rather in dealing with the embarrassing but critical question: Where does all this purchased land come from? The state is no longer selling land; there are no large landlords in the region selling off their holdings. Land is the centerpin of the economic destiny of peasant households, the critical resource whose acquisition is the central theme in the economic maneuvers of virtually all peasants. But if everybody is trying to buy land, who is doing all the selling?

As so often happens, the analytic importance of this question did not become apparent until late in fieldwork. But the data to answer the question had in fact, somewhat accidentally, been collected earlier in fieldwork. I had noticed the presence of an active land market, had been impressed at the number of people that seem to have been involved in land transactions, and had thus endeavoured to get basic and specific information on as many land trans-

[12] As shown elsewhere (Murray 1977), this system evolved in the context of population growth and, by alleviating at least one of the dilemmas created by this growth (i.e., the curtailment of preinheritance grants) the entire system can with some justification be termed an "adaptation to population growth." This by no means implies that it is a final solution to the problem of land pressure; it is merely a delaying action whose effect is that of at least ensuring that the decreasing land pool keeps circulating among the community at large. Cultural evolution takes the form, not of final solutions, but of precisely the type of interim waystage arrangement as that described here.

TABLE 10.3
Reasons for Selling a Plot of Land

	N	Percentage
Bury a parent	187	31.7
Healing of a sickness	138	23.4
Poverty: General cash needs	74	12.6
Bury a child	41	7.0
Pay off debts	38	6.5
Bury a sibling	23	3.9
Bury a spouse	19	3.2
Build a tomb	15	2.6
Anniversary service for dead	11	1.9
Wedding of son or daughter	10	1.7
Buy food	6	1.0
Raise capital for trade	6	1.0
Pay for child's schooling	5	0.8
Others	16	2.7
Total	589	100.0

actions as possible. The result was a corpus of data covering nearly 600 individual land transactions.

For each transaction a list of questions was posed eliciting information such as size of the plot, type of land, identity of seller and buyer, kin relation (if any) between the two, and some dozen other questions. It was revealing to learn that *virtually all of the land was being transacted among villagers themselves.* That is, not only is sharecropping a stratum–internal phenomenon; so is land transacting.

But the most revealing insight comes from examination of the responses to the question, why had the seller sold the plot of ground. Table 10.3 collapses the responses into 14 types of reasons that villagers gave for the sale of specific plots of ground. Figure 10.4 exposes the significant internal patterning of these responses more clearly by separating sales of land which cultivators made to finance some sort of ritual from those which were made for nonritual reasons, such as debts, schooling, food purchase, and the like. What immediately leaps out from these figures is the *dramatic importance of financing rituals as the major context for the sale of land.*

These tables furnish us, I believe, with the major element that was still missing from the blueprint we have attempted to draw for this Haitian peasant land tenure system. In so doing, the figures bring us face to face again with Haitian-peasant Voodoo. Why are the peasants themselves releasing those valuable plots of ground whose purchase by others provides the mainspring for the resource sharing system which we have discussed? The answer is this: The ritual system in which they participate, mediated by expensive ritual demands from the spirits, and buttressed by strong social pressure towards compliance

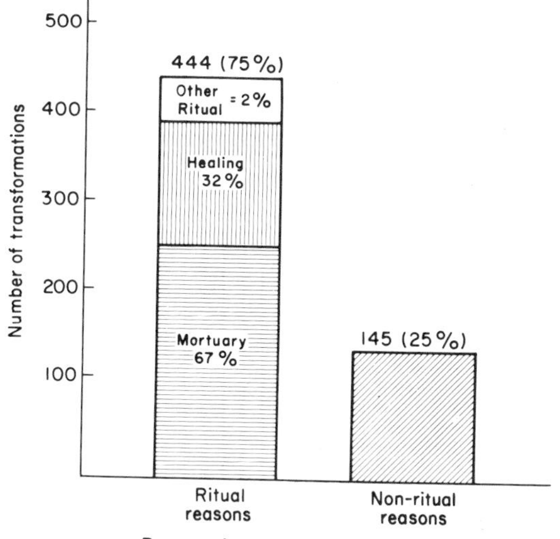

FIGURE 10.3. *The ritual context of land transactions*

with these demands by extremely interested neighbors, nudges peasants into periodically putting up part of their holding for sale. It is, in short, *the folk-religion of its members that keeps the community's land in circulation.* A heretofore hidden face of peasant Voodoo thus lies exposed. Underneath the colorful display of bizarre rituals and the clown-like shenanigans of spirit-possessed believers, a quiet and immensely serious land drama has been taking place. In colorful masquerade the spirits of the Voodoo pantheon have mesmerized both their followers and their observers with powerful drumming, colorful ritual, and a seemingly endless treasure chest of vivid folklore and secret charms. But the land tenure data presented here expose the presence of a very serious hidden agenda behind the functioning of this ritual system: the continued circulation of the peasant community's ultimate resource, its land.[13]

Discussion and Conclusions

The unexpected but empirically incontestable intrusion of ritual into the internal machinery of the land tenure system answers a number of questions but raises just as many others. Space permits discussion of only a few of the more important ones.

---

[13] I am grateful to George Bond, William Dalton, and Joan Vincent for pointing out analogies among the findings here and the findings of certain British social anthropologists, especially F. G. Bailey. Though analyzed from a different perspective, Bailey's *Caste and the Economic Frontier* (1957) also provides tabular data indicating the importance of funerals and other rituals as contexts for the sale of land.

IS THIS A TRUE SYSTEM?

Anthropologists have perhaps somewhat debased the currency of the term "system" by applying it loosely and metaphorically to virtually any type of complex social pattern. But I would argue that my use of the term "system" here is quite appropriate in a literal sense of the word. That is, the quantitative data reveal a chain of statistically interlocked behaviors. To the earlier discussed behaviors of tenancy, land purchase, and landlordism, we have now added an essential fourth element: land sale. But we see that a large majority of land sales are made in order to finance rituals. The villagers' ritual behaviors have thus been empirically linked to their land transacting behaviors and we are justified in considering these ritual behaviors central elements in a system.

WHAT KEEPS THE SYSTEM IN MOTION?

A system of the type discussed here is an abstraction from concrete human behaviors. There is nothing enigmatic about most features of the system described here. The behavior of tenants who agree to crop a plot on a share basis, of land purchasers who buy a plot, and of landlords who give out a plot to a tenant, are for the most part analyzable in terms of a cost–benefit calculus that would be intelligible to most outside observers. For an outside analyst the most enigmatic link in the chain is the behavior of the land seller who releases control of a valuable plot to finance a ritual. It is well and good that this behavior has useful collective results. But we must also account for the proximate mechanisms producing and sustaining this economically enigmatic behavior.

One is quickly impressed in the village by the clear manifestations of social pressure that surround crises. At an all-night wake, for example, if the family of the deceased fails to provide enough *klérin* (a local alcoholic beverage), some of those attending may begin openly complaining or singing mock songs against the *mèt véyé,* the family member who is in charge of the wake. On one occasion, shortly after a woman died and the wailing had begun in her compound, male relatives of the deceased woman approached the bereaved husband and began openly criticizing him because of his failure to have taken the necessary steps during her illness—one of which, in their opinion, entailed the calling in of the services of a houngan. At another wake, a woman who had lost her daughter began openly reciting, as part of her public wailing, a *gourde* by *gourde* account of the money she had spent in trying to get her daughter healed, of the time she had spent traveling back and forth between the village and Port-au-Prince in search of medicines, of the nights she had lost sitting up with the girl.

All of these events give testimony to the presence of incalculably strong social pressure to make substantial, visible expenditures during crises of sickness and death. Whereas such expectations exist in most cultures, in rural Haiti failure to comply meets with immediate, vigorous, open public criticism.

In the eyes of the community, there is generally no valid excuse for not spending the money. When all other resources fail, virtually every household has at least some land that it can sell, and villagers have strong, openly stated expectations concerning the importance of vigorous action when sickness or death strikes and the disgrace that attaches to the individual who clings to his land in order to deprive his sick child of that care that is his right, or his dead father of the honorable burial that is his due.

There is no strict rule that the money must be raised via the sale of land, however. The person who has enough animals, for example, can fulfill his obligations through their sale. But there are few households who have enough livestock to do this. But in addition, there appears to be a mechanism that renders it cheaper to finance a ritual via land sale than via animal or crop sales. The neighbors are well aware of the reluctance of people to part with their land. For a serious illness in the family, or for a death (especially of a parent), there will be expectant speculations about whether the stricken household will have to sell off any of its land. If the afflicted people sell off a plot, they have proven to their neighbors that they are not skimping on their obligations. But if they try to finance the ritual by other means, the resulting ceremony would have to be very elaborate to forestall gossip or open criticism. This is especially true in the case of parental funerals. Any sibling group that tried to bury its parents without selling some of the land that the parents left, would have to stage the funeral of the century to avoid criticisms. It is possible to do this. But in most cases it would probably be cheaper to sell off a plot of ground.

In short, *social pressure* appears to be the major proximate trigger for ritual expenditure. This social pressure operates, of course, in the context of a belief system. But I doubt that either cognitive belief in the spirits or emotional fear of their retribution would suffice to sustain land-selling behavior in the absence of the clear reinforcement supplied by the pressure that the community simultaneously applies.

WHAT IN TURN SUSTAINS COMMUNITY PRESSURE FOR EXPENSIVE RITUALS?

Social pressure may be an effective intervening mechanism, but the question still remains as to why certain societies exert pressure in a given direction whereas others do not. The pattern being discussed here strikes casual observers as particularly enigmatic. More than one visitor to our community commented in wonder on the fact that the peasants' tombs appeared more elaborate than the houses in which they had lived. It would indeed be strange if the community continued to exert pressure for expenditures whose prime beneficiaries appear to be the stonemasons who are paid from $200.00 to $400.00 U.S. to build the tombs.

I believe the information already provided gives at least a partial answer to this particular enigma. The question of *cui bono* remains valid; but in this particular system, the nature of the behavior-sustaining payoff is perceived by asking, not merely *what* is done with the money spent, but more importantly *how* is this money first raised. And we have seen that it is generally raised by releasing part of one's holding for sale. It is this land release that constitutes the major payoff for other members of the community and it is this land-circulating phenomenon that I believe helps place the otherwise enigmatic pressure for expensive rituals in an intelligible context.

HAS VOODOO ALWAYS PLAYED THIS RESOURCE-CIRCULATING ROLE?

Discussion up to now has been largely synchronic in thrust, focusing on the internal workings of a resource-circulating system that has been found operative at one point in time. But this particular system has by no means been an eternal feature of the rural Haitian landscape. The three-phase career culminating in landlordism is the result of a historical development away from an earlier nineteenth century system in which sharecropping and stratum–internal land purchase appeared to play much less important systemic roles. If these economic features of the system have been altered over time, is the same true of Voodoo belief and ritual?

The fragmentary nature of the evidence concerning Voodoo in the eighteenth and nineteenth centuries make any answer to this question tentative. But one thing is clear: It would be both theoretically and empirically unwarranted to seek the *origins* of Voodoo in terms of the twentieth-century land-circulating function. In terms of many of its constituent elements—including dancing, drumming, possession, animal sacrifices—the cult had begun to form as early as the second half of the eighteenth century, and perhaps earlier, when Haiti was still the French plantation colony of Saint-Domingue.

Furthermore, the functions of the cult—its linkages with nonritual life-spheres of its practitioners—appear to have varied over time, adapting themselves to the specific problems of a given generation of practitioners. During the colonial period, the cult was interpreted by many slave-owners as being largely recreational in purpose, though laws restricting nocturnal dances indicated an awareness that these events could easily take on other functions. During the early stages of the final insurrection that began in 1791, the cult played a revolutionary role, providing both the symbols and the leadership around which insurgent slave groups mobilized. But, as practiced by the children and grandchildren of these insurgents, the revolutionary features of the cult receded somewhat into the background, yielding center stage to those symbols and rites that were of greater relevance to smallholding peasants. The late nineteenth century thus saw the fullblown emergence of domestic Voodoo, or peasant Voodoo, a cult whose bilaterally inherited spirits bear such a strikingly close resemblance to the patterns of bilaterally inherited land and whose functions now focused on the organization of peasant life rather than the mobilization of insurrections.[14] Throughout all of these functional transformations, the constituent elements of the cult—possession, animal sacrifice, drumming and dancing, and others—remained, if not identical, at least clearly recognizable continuations of earlier cult elements. What has most changed has rather been the nature of the integration of these constituent elements into other nonritual lifespheres.

In short, the functions of Voodoo have changed as the society in which its practitioners have lived has itself changed. There is little evidence to support the view that Voodoo has had a perpetual resource-circulating function. My positing of that function for contemporary Voodoo is based on the evidence of the land tenure tables. In the absence of evidence for such a function in the nineteenth century, and in the presence of historical evidence that the cult's function changes over time, it is safer to assume that its current land-circulating function is the product of a recent microevolutionary shift.

HOW MIGHT THE SHIFT TO LAND CIRCULATING HAVE OCCURRED?

The following is a first approximation to a possible reconstruction of the course of events leading up to Voodoo's present function. There is solid statistical evidence (Murray 1977) that, as population pressure grew, the formerly marginal arrangements of stratum-internal tenancy and stratum-internal land transacting were gradually selected with increasing frequency and acquired over time their present status as the dominant land-circulating arrangements in the community.

But if this process were to unfold smoothly, there had to have been a simultaneous, instrumentally prerequisite selection of those community behaviors that resulted in a releasing of land for purchase, without which the other elements of the transformation would have been greatly encumbered. The major land sales in nineteenth century Haiti were those made by the government, or by military and civilian officials who received governmental land grants (Moral 1961). But by the end of the nineteenth century, such grants and interclass sales had virtually ceased.

But land pressure itself did not cease; in fact it increased, and with it the pressure to intensify the availability of land-acquisition options. Most of the land sold in the nineteenth century had been sold by the government, or by generals and officials. But, there is evidence that there were already occasional, sporadic land sales made by peasants themselves, and that these were

[14] The potentialities of Voodoo in the domain of politics are never far, however, from the surface. *Caco* leaders who resisted the American marines earlier this century were reported to be Voodoo adepts, which accounts for perhaps part of the animus that the occupation forces manifested against the cult. Furthermore recent governmental policy toward the cult has been one of undisguised acceptance, in contrast to previous public sector stances, to such a degree that in certain urban neighborhoods the status of governmental militiaman (*tonton makout*) is now reported to have become a prerequisite to being a successful houngan (Laguerre 1976).

to be the object of positive selection. Bastien (1951) gives evidence that such peasant land sales were taking place, and specifically mentions funerals as a source of major expenditure in times gone by.

But as land pressure grew, the community rewards and sanctions associated with such occasional land-financed rituals intensified and the frequency of such events increased. The present day outcome of this process is the situation described in this chapter: A system emerged in which ritually motivated land sales lost their sporadic, occasional character and instead became a central component of an elaborate stratum–internal land-sharing system. In the process of this evolution, nothing radically new was created. Rather, as is true with biological evolution, cultural evolution proceeded on the basis of the gradual selection of *preexisting* arrangements and alternatives, the transformation consisting of reemphasis and and rearrangement of these alternatives into a new systemic synthesis.

This evolutionary reconstruction is highly compatible with, and finds clear support from, the evidence of village ethnography. Recall: We earlier discussed the changes that older villagers recognize as having come over the cult. But if we reexamine these changes in the light of the land-circulating data, we notice immediately that the common theme underlying the changes is a shift toward *emphasis of those features that involve heavy expenditures:* the use of formally initiated rather than purely charismatic specialists; the sacrificing of larger numbers of animals; the construction of more elaborate burial monuments; and others. That is, the changes all veer in a direction that enhances the capacities of the ritual system to contribute to the escalating village land-circulating dynamic, thus indicating that the recent shifts in the former may in fact have occurred in conjunction with the evolution of the latter.

In all of these processes, we see clear analogies between biological and cultural evolution. When a structure begins to take on a new function, its subsequent development, while remaining faithful to the basic contours of the original design, will shift in directions that facilitate its new role. The domestic Voodoo of the mid-1970s is a clearly recognizable descendent of nineteenth-century peasant Voodoo. It is here being suggested that many of the features currently emphasized in the cult can be understood as products of a microevolutionary shift in community rewards and pressures toward those features of the cult which facilitate the unfolding of the now critical extradomestic land circulation.

IS THIS A "LATENT" SYSTEM?

One final matter is the question of whether villagers themselves are conscious of the operation of the system being discussed here—whether, in other words, they would agree with the thrust of this analysis. There are several features of the model for which I have no record of any supporting informant generalizations. Though villagers told me of changes that had come over the cult, these were viewed at least partially as a punishment from God for the decline of old virtues and the rise of selfishness. Not even the more reflective of my informants related the changes to demographic pressure: No informant ever praised the folk-religion of the village as a practical way of keeping land in circulation.

The validity of the "Voodoo-as-land-circulator" model, however, rests on the cogency of the land tenure tables, not on the presence or absence of informant agreement. But to say that villagers have not explicitly identified the systemic links between different spheres of the community's behavior is not to say that the entire complex unfolds in the absence of any awareness on their part. On the contrary, one of my informants was able to give me very good advice on how to go about purchasing land: You wait till a relative or neighbor of yours has a sickness or death in his family. You approach him; you tell him how sorry you are that he has this problem. You reach in your pocket, pull out a wad of bills, and say "look, brother, here's a couple of *gourdes* I can lend you to help see you through." You tell him, "I pray to God that you don't have to sell off any of your land. But listen, brother, if God forbid you should have to sell off a tiny piece, you'll keep me in mind, won't you?"

Would-be village land purchasers are, in short, quite clearly aware of the occasions on which their own life chances are likely to take a turn for the better. The justification for referring to this as a "hidden system" is perhaps more appropriately discussed in terms of the ability of the system to escape the notice of outside analysts. And it is this final observation which brings to light the methodological implications of this entire complex.

Both Haitian and foreign researchers have been intrigued by the mysteries of Voodoo; and many of them, in their search for its secrets, will make a beeline for the nearest houngan. Those so inclined should be encouraged; there are undoubtedly many spells, charms, and secret recipes yet to be written down.

But the complex analyzed in these pages points to the existence of other important secrets that not even the most cooperative sorcerer could possibly reveal. The researcher interested in those other mysteries—in those subterranean linkages, for example, which subtly bring religion into the service of forces emanating from other lifespheres—will have to search, not only in the temples of the specialists, but also in the homes and fields of the believers. And ethnographers who approach this task without the aid of at least some simple counting operations—the data presented in these pages, for example, have entailed nothing beyond simple counting—or without the aid of a general theoretical perspective that helps them decide what it is that they should count, run the risk of missing critical systems operating under their very noses. Competent, vivid descriptions of animal sacrifices, of drum rhythms, of the bizarre behavior of spirit-possessed believers, and of the secret formulas elicited from the lips of cooperative sorcerers, may continue to be the distinguishing feature of the discipline and the most avidly read chapters in the ethnographer's book. But by themselves they are no longer enough, at least not in the search for the even deeper Voodoo secrets of the type discussed in this chapter.

References

Ahlers, T.
1979 A microeconomic analysis of rural-urban migration in Haiti. Unpublished dissertation, Tufts University.

Bailey, F. G.
1957 *Caste and the economic frontier.* Manchester, England: Manchester University Press.

Bastien, R.
1951 *La familia rural haitiana.* Mexico: Libra.

Buchanan, S. H.
1979 Language and identity: Haitians in New York City. *International Migration Review 13*(2):298–313.

Cannon, W.
1942 Voodoo death. *American Anthropologist 44:*169–181.

Chen, K., and G. F. Murray
1976 Truths and untruths in village Haiti: An experiment in third world survey research. In *Culture, natality, and family planning* (J. Marshall and S. Polgar, Eds.). Chapel Hill: University of North Carolina Press. Pp. 241–262.

Deren, M.
1970 *Divine horsemen: Voodoo gods of Haiti.* New York: Chelsea House.

Diederich, B., and Al Burt
1969 *Papa Doc: The truth about Haiti today.* New York: Avon.

Franklin, J.
1970 *The present state of Hayti.* Westport, Conn.: Negro Universities Press. (Originally published, 1828.)

Herskovits, M. J.
1971 *Life in a Haitian valley.* New York: Anchor. (Originally published, 1937.)

Laguerre, M.
1976 The Black ghetto as an internal colony: Socio-economic adaptation of a Haitian urban community. Unpublished Dissertation, University of Illinois

Lester, D.
1972 Voodoo death: Some new thoughts on an old phenomenon. *American Anthropologist 74:*386–390.

Lex, B. W.
1974 Voodoo death: New thoughts on an old explanation. *American Anthropologist 76:*818–823.

Locher, U.
1979 The fate of migrants in urban Haiti: A survey of three Port-au-Prince neighborhoods. Unpublished dissertation, Yale University.

López, A.
1974 The Puerto Rican diaspora: A survey. In *Puerto Rico and Puerto Ricans: Studies in history and society* (A. López and J. Petras, Eds.), New York: Wiley. Pp. 316–346.

Lowenthal, I.
1978 Ritual performance and religious experience: A service for the gods in Southern Haiti. *Journal of Anthropological Research 34*(3):392–414.

Métraux, A.
1972 *Voodoo in Haiti.* New York: Schocken. (Originally published, 1959.)

Moral, P.
1961 *Le paysan Haitien.* Paris: G. P. Maisonneuve et Larose.
Murray, G. F.
1976 Women in perdition: Ritual fertility control in Haiti. In *Culture, natality, and family planning* (J. Marshall and S. Polgar Eds.). Chapel Hill: University of North Carolina Press. Pp. 59–78.
1977 The evolution of Haitian peasant land tenure: A case study in agrarian adaptation to population growth. Unpublished dissertation, Columbia University.
n.d. Bon-Dieu and the rites of passage in rural Haiti: Structural determinants of postcolonial religion. To be published in *The Catholic Church in Latin America* (T. Bruneau and U. Locher, Eds.) Montréal: McGill University, Center for Developing Area Studies.
Murray, G. F., and M. D. Alvarez
1973 Childbearing, sickness and healing in a Haitian village. Report submitted to the Division d'Hygiène Familiale, Port-au-Prince, Haiti.
Price-Mars, J.
1928 *Ainsi parla l'oncle.* Imprimerie de Compiegne.
Prichard, H.
1972 *Where black rules white: A journey across and about Hayti.* Shannon: Irish University Press. (Originally published, 1900.)
Rawson, I. G. and G. Berggren
1973 Family structure, child location and nutritional disease in rural Haiti. *Environmental Child Health 19:*288–298.
Rigaud, M.
1953 *La tradition Voudoo et le Voudoo Haitien.* Paris: Editions Niclaus.
Roberts, G. W.
1966 Populations of the non-Spanish-speaking Caribbean. In *Population dilemma in Latin America* (J. M. Stycos, and J. Arias, Eds.) Washington, D.C.: Potomac Books. Pp. 61–85.
Simpson, G. E.
1971 The belief system of Haitian Vodun. In *Peoples and cultures of the Caribbean* (M. Horowitz, Ed.) Garden City: Natural History Press. Pp. 491–521. (Originally published, 1945.)
Smith, M. G.
1962 *West Indian family structure.* Seattle: University of Washington Press.
Zuvekas, C.
1978 *Agricultural development in Haiti: An assessment of sector problems, policies, and prospects under conditions of severe soil erosion.* Washington, D.C.: Agency for International Development.

11 Trousseau as Treasure: Some Contradictions of Late Nineteenth-Century Change in Sicily

JANE SCHNEIDER

Introduction

On the eve of her wedding, a Sicilian bride displays her trousseau (called *corredo*), spreading its contents out on bed, chairs, and tables for invited guests to see. Today, the principal items of a trousseau are money plus commercially available household goods—tablewear and linens, furniture, and small appliances. Until two or three decades ago, however, ensembles known as "beds" (*letti*) predominated. A bed referred not to the piece of furniture, but to the bed coverings: two sheets, four pillowcases, a bedspread, and lingerie for the bride. Indeed, each bed was a cluster of whitewear (*biancheria*) that could include table cloths, napkins, towels, doilies, pillowcases, and intimate apparel, as well as sheets.

Most pieces of whitewear were hand embroidered or trimmed with handmade lace, each containing many women-hours of work. So great was women's commitment to trousseau preparation and to the needle arts in general, that other kinds of work in agriculture and industry were precluded, even when the opportunity for such work was there. Some observers of Mediterranean societies—most recently John Davis—suggest that cultural patterns making female labor unavailable for income-producing activities have impeded agrarian transformation and economic development in the area (Davis 1977:43–54). If this is a correct perception, then Sicily is a striking example.

Since the late nineteenth century, Sicily has specialized in the export of migrant workers, first to the Americas, subsequently to northern Europe. This exodus, constant except for a hiatus during and between the two world wars, and serious enough to have been called "Italy's hemorrhage," was a

BEYOND THE MYTHS OF CULTURE
Essays in Cultural Materialism

ISBN 0-12-598180-5

consequence of the island's failure to produce alternative exports for world markets. Perhaps contributions of female labor could have made a difference to the cost-competitiveness of agricultural or industrial commodities and thus stemmed the tide of out-migration. Historical evidence suggests, however, that embroidered beds became the staple of nonaristocratic trousseau in Sicily just as the mass migrations got underway.

This chapter poses the question: "What happened in the late nineteenth century which led ordinary women to take up needlework on a scale before unknown?" Data are from several sources. In a recent field trip, Peter Schneider and I obtained information from the vital registers of Villamaura, the pseudonym for a rural town of about 7500 population, where we also conducted research in the 1960s (Schneider and Schneider 1976).[1] This information provides the basis for a family reconstitution study which will compare the reproductive patterns of marriage cohorts (we sampled all marriages for 1850–1851, 1860–1861, 1870–1871, 1880–1881, 1890, 1899, 1910, and 1920) and by occupational group. (Villamaura, like most Sicilian settlements, is internally stratified; large landowners, professionals, merchants, shopkeepers, artisans, rich, middle, and proletarianized peasants have lived in close proximity for a long time.) Supplementing this demographic record are minutes of town council meetings beginning in 1860, house and land cadasters for the 1870s, lists of trousseau recorded by folklorists and in the archives of the notary public, oral histories, secondary sources, and a range of artifacts that we came upon by asking people to show us old houses, furniture, clothing, photographs, and products of local craftsmanship including embroidery.

In the following pages, I will first describe the marriage exchange system as it existed until a few years ago and then present evidence that embroidered whitewear was not a timeless part of it with roots in an unchanging past. The question "why embroidery" will be broached in three different contexts. The first has to do with class formation and the emulation of elite behavior; the second with symbolic links between embroidery and female purity, an important behavioral code in the Mediterranean. The third interprets evidence that embroidered sheets were wealth objects with significant liquidity in wide spheres of exchange. These three approaches are neither contradictory nor mutually exclusive; they complement and reinforce one another. I think,

---

[1] My analysis of trousseau grows out of a larger project that is concerned with class formation and demographic change in late nineteenth-century Sicily. Peter Schneider has been both a partner in this project and a key source of substantive and editorial criticisms of this chapter. I also received excellent criticisms and suggestions from Donna Gabaccia, Ashraf Ghani, and Patricia Torres; editorial assistance and encouragement from T. O. Beidelman. Joyce Reigelhaupt and Eric Wolf pointed out ways that I might tighten my argument, while Pamela Quagiotto and Pamela Wright helped me with linguistic evidence. Anthropology students and faculty at Yale University raised helpful questions after hearing my first draft in their Colloquium series. In addition to thanking these friends and colleagues, I wish to express my appreciation for many hours of conversation with Shirley Lindenbaum. Often touching on dowry systems as a problem for cross-cultural comparison, our talks were the inspiration for worrying about trousseau.

however, that the third, which conceives of trousseau as treasure, raises new and interesting questions about folk culture.

Trousseau and Social Reproduction

A trousseau of "beds," or sheets with whitewear in proportion, is hardly unique to Sicily. Brides all over southern Europe are, or were, similarly endowed at marriage. Ethnographies of this area, moreover, offer relatively consistent estimates of the number of beds or sheets that distinguish rich girls from poor girls. In Pitkin's south Italian study of the 1950s, 6 sheets (plus supporting whitewear) constituted a minimum *corredo*. The majority of brides brought 12; daughters of rich peasants and merchants married with 24; those of lesser landowners with 50; and women whose families owned large estates brought up to 100 sheets (Pitkin, 1960). This range is probably similar to that of Pisticci, where Davis (1973) found the minimum to be three "beds" and it matches closely the estimates given to me in Villamaura. In Silverman's Umbrian town, the poorest brides had 10 to 12 sheets, the richest 48 or more (Silverman 1975:198).

Trousseaux of whatever quantity represented a considerable expense for the bride's family. From the time she was born, her father and brothers labored to purchase the materials of which a respectable *corredo* was made, this responsibility being formalized in the saying, heard often in Villamaura, "swaddling clothes on the baby girl, whitewear in her hope chest" (*bambine nelle fascie, biancheria nella cascia*). To facilitate the preparation of trousseau brothers delayed their own marriages until their sisters were wed or, for those sisters who did not marry, until they were securely set up in careers of respectable celibacy as nuns, "house nuns," or servants of close kin.

While father and brothers put their earnings into basic *corredo* materials, mother and daughters invested labor in their elaboration, with mother serving as organizer and supervisor, and daughters doing most of the work. Before the age of 7 years, most daughters were skilled at sample stitching, and during their adolescence they became devotees of embroidery, sacrificing hours in the interest of perfection. Compared with other crafts, embroidery and lacework are not so much difficult as they are extremely tedious. Gömül, an expert on Turkish embroidery, says that like "digging a well with a needle," it requires the greatest effort, time, and patience of all the crafts (Gömül n.d.:7). Nor could the effort be spread throughout the year. Sicilian women rarely embroidered in the summer months, not because they had to work at the harvest but because the heat made their hands sweat: In the winter, days were short, and a craft that fatigued their eyes under the best of conditions became burdensome when done by candlelight or oil lamp. (Rural electrification came to the Sicilian interior in the 1920s.)

The preparation of trousseau was so costly, in terms of both money and time, that Sicilians used to say, during Chapman's fieldwork in the late 1920s, that they had "six children, two boys and four burdens," even though they loved their daughters and counted more on their affection than the affection of sons to sustain them in later life. People also told Chapman that the door through which a dead daughter passed is "blessed . . . and the older she is the greater the comfort; if she is single she relieves us from debt; if she is engaged she gives us life; and if she is married she fills the pot [quoted in Chapman 1971:30]." This expression refers to the legal and customary arrangement whereby a wife's property reverted to her natal family (her parents or brothers) if she died before having children of her own.

Of course, women's property could consist of many things, usually transferred to her as dowry at the time of her marriage. Trousseau is only one component of dowry along with land, houses, money, and education. Until the twentieth century, however, and probably until the 1930s, trousseau predominated in the dowries of nonaristocratic Sicilian girls. John Davis argues for Pisticci that this is a reasonable conclusion when the tax registers for land and houses show women owners to be in a small minority. A land cadaster for Villamaura drawn up in 1870 lists 3288 parcels of land of which 161 belonged to women. Of these, widows held 87 and 34 were in the land-owning class. Only 12 parcels of land, out of more than 3000, belonged to untitled women and all were extremely small, less than a hectare.

A house cadaster, prepared in 1877 for the 1881 census, suggests that houses sometimes entered dowry. Less than 2500 actual households (for a then population of 9682) appear in that census for Villamaura, but the tax register, making note of all rooms with a doorway to the street, has nearly 4000 entries.[2] Of these, 20 were attributed to women as members of groups of heirs; 250 to widows; and 395 to individual women, a few of whom were spinsters, the great majority married. In contrast to the land cadaster, untitled women were well represented in the latter group, but the group is far too small to conclude that, in the late 1870s, houses were transferred to daughters as a general rule.

Toward the end of the nineteenth century, an increasing number of nonaristocratic families went to the trouble of having their daughters' dowries registered with a notary public, which makes the notary's archive another source of information on dotal property. Of the 68 couples who married in Villamaura in 1880, the families of 20 (or 32%) visited the notary to register dowries, as did families of 18 (26%) of the 68 couples who married in 1890. They were rich peasants, storekeepers, an occasional carter and artisan, 10 peasants,[3] and 3 titled landowners. Most of them gave their daughters tiny

---

[2] A recent doctoral dissertation on the cultural history of Sicilian migrants to America explores the implications of this method of registering "houses" for taxation, and includes data from the 1877 cadaster in Villamaura (see Gabaccia 1979).

[3] As William Foote Whyte, summarizing the work of Pitrè, explained in some detail, the term "peasant" in Sicily referred to a range of occupations, minutely graded by status. In this context, it probably means better-off, or middle, peasant, bordering on rich peasant or *burgise*. As a rule,

parcels of land, which in all but 10 cases measured less than half a hectare, and in all but 2, less than a hectare. Slightly less than half gave small houses, usually of one or two rooms. As Davis indicates for Pisticci, the value of the *corredo* nearly equalled and in some cases surpassed the value of these token immovables. Similarly, 13 of the registered dowries included money, but in 10 of these, the amount was less than the trousseau's recorded value.

Given the likelihood that unregistered dowries contained no land, houses, or money, the situation for late nineteenth-century Villamaura appears to have approached Silverman's description of Umbria a few years ago: "For most girls the corredo and furniture are the total dowry, but a well-to-do family might also give a daughter money or property at her marriage, as an advance against her share of the family patrimony [1975:198–199]." How far into the twentieth century trousseau remained the central component of dowry in Sicily is hard to estimate on the basis of data available to me now. In Villamaura, as in Pisticci, landholdings began to fragment after about 1910 and gradually women acquired more of them, but the relationship between these developments is far from clear. It is possible that land divisions mandated by various reform programs increased the number of women owners by putting more of this resource into peasant hands. It is also possible, however, that fathers added more land (and houses) to the dowries of their daughters for reasons not directly related to land reform, with the consequence of accelerating land fragmentation.

There remains the further problem raised by Davis (1973) that in the underdeveloped regions of the Italian south and islands, land was losing its value as a source of agricultural productivity even before it was expropriated from large holders and redistributed, so much so that symbolic reasons for having it increased in proportion to reasons of economic security or gain, making women's ownership somewhat spurious. Perhaps this is why women whom I interviewed in 1977 claimed that, until very recently when education took over, trousseau remained the set-piece of a respectable dowry. One could always marry without land, houses or money, but never without trousseau, and several informants spontaneously recalled exemplary families who had recently sold off land to acquire their daughter's linens.

Further evidence that trousseau was central to marriage exchanges (the counterpart of a groom's promise to support his wife) are the institutions in Sicily (Southern Italy also) of the *minuta* and the *stima*. The *minuta,* no longer practiced, took place when the families of a newly engaged couple brought in a literate person, mutually agreed upon, to enumerate the goods that each was committing to the eventual new household. More important was the *stima (la vagghiata della robba,* or *vagghiu,* in dialect), which occurred on the eve of the wedding, when the bride's family hired a specialized *stimatrice*

---

the rich peasant either owned enough land to necessitate hiring day-laborers or sharecroppers to supplement his own work, or enough animals to necessitate leasing additional land. But even here there was marked gradation; not all *burgisi* were the same (Whyte 1944; also Chapman 1971).

(vagghiatura) to examine each article of assembled trousseau and price it. Usually a woman knowledgeable about textiles, the *stimatrice* assigned and recorded values in lire or onze, the currency of earlier regimes (see Salomone-Marino 1968:235–259; Pitrè 1939:27–39, 52–56; Whyte 1944:69–70).

Both the *minuta* and *stima* resulted in formal, written contracts, as they had for aristocratic families in earlier centuries (Leone 1978:81–83; Salomone-Marino 1876). Some of these contracts were notarized, but even when they were not, people kept the papers on which they were written, thereby protecting the claims of natal kin should they die without heirs. In a way the *stima* was the pivotal event of a Sicilian marriage. Attended by witnesses as well as the close relatives of the couple, it was an occasion not only for proud display, but sometimes for quarreling, as the bride's family pressed for high estimates, which the groom's family felt were a disadvantage to them, whether in balancing her wealth with land, or in the event it should have to be returned. Because the groom's family gained in status from a high valuation, however, this conflict of interests was usually overcome; then, in a joyous ritual, friends and relatives of the bride carried her handiwork, piece by piece, to the house where she would take up residence, one of them staying to act as guardian during the night (Salomone-Marino 1968; Pitrè 1939; Whyte 1944).

Status Emulation, Class Formation, and the Spread of Needlework

Trousseau was a central, and for many families the only, component of dowry throughout the ninteenth and well into the twentieth century, but its content seems to have changed in the course of this period. In 1808, Paolo Balsamo, a Sicilian propagandist for agrarian reform in the style of Arthur Young (whom he knew), wrote a memorandum urging his countrymen to cultivate linen despite the obstacles that an arid environment placed in the way of this endeavor. His argument was that "shirts, underwear, sheets, table cloths, napkins, towels and swaddling bands . . . bring to clothing and furniture that tidiness which enhances and adorns the civilized life [Balsamo 1845: 127–128]." The tone of his plea suggests that these articles were not yet in wide use among the peasants of his day, even though limited amounts of hemp (*canapa*) were cultivated, and hemp is a good, if coarse, substitute for linen.

In urging the acceptance of more "linens," Balsamo recognized that they were not necessities, but neither were they luxuries, he argued. He would have appreciated the term "decencies," which an English economic historian recently coined for just such things as sheets and underwear (see Eversely 1967:212; Harte 1973:108).[4] In contrast, the same memorandum claimed that

[4] Decencies "tor wear of the common people" proliferated in England nearly a century before Balsamo promoted their adoption in Sicily. In 1700, England imported just under 300,000

"lace and similar exquisite and fine work . . . serve to content the insatiable desire for appearances, pomp and luxury, among the rich and the great [Balsamo 1845:127]." From this we can assume that ornamented "decencies" were at that time largely enjoyed by Sicily's landowning aristocracy and court.

That ornamentation of whitewear in the form of embroidery and lace was a luxury that few could afford in the early nineteenth century is also documented by the content of the trousseaux. Salvatore Salmone-Marino, a folklorist of the late 1800s, collected a few contracts of *minuta* dating back to 1810 and in none of them is there any reference to embroidery, except for minimal decorations on handkerchiefs and swaddling cloths for infants (Salomone-Marino 1968:253–257). The same lack of attention to embroidery characterizes the notarized trousseaux which Pitrè found for 1847 and 1855, both for modest peasant families (Pitrè 1939:27–28). Nevertheless, Pitrè's examples, and Salomone-Marino's too, include several articles of bed-, table-, and underwear.

Working back from the present, oral histories collected in Villamaura in 1977, supplemented by a look at artifacts, give the impression that all but the poorest women married with richly embroidered "beds" from the turn of the century and probably a decade or two earlier. How to date the appearance of this custom is problematic, given that only a minority of families went to the trouble and expense of notarizing dowry before 1900. Nevertheless, many hints exist in the data on women's changing round of chores to be discussed in the following. For the moment, I think it is safe to assume that we are talking about a transition that occurred in the late 1800s, although at different rates for different occupational groups and different towns.

One way of characterizing, and perhaps understanding, the elaboration of embroidery in folk culture is to trace its diffusion through a process of status emulation similar to the one outlined in Veblen's study of the leisure class. An important reason why, in earlier centuries, only noble women were the owners of richly decorated linens is that they were freed by slaves, servants, and other dependents from many household tasks, leaving them with time to embroider. One is reminded that even in New England, "the possession of a good piece of old crewel work, done in the country, is as strong a proof of respectable ancestry as a patent of nobility, since no one in the busy early colonial days had time for such work save those whose abundant leisure was secured by ample means and liberal surroundings [Wheeler 1921:35]."

In addition to offering a marker of leisure status, embroideries and lacework conferred prestige by removing the materials to which they were applied several more steps from their natural state as fibers, and from the natural,

yards of Irish linen. By 1740, imports had reached 6.5 million yards. English linen industries grew rapidly in the same period, largely on the basis of imported Irish and Scottish thread. According to A. H. John, this is good evidence for expanded consumption of sheets and underwear among farmers, cottagers, and artisans, as well as the rich (John 1965).

bodily functions which they were intended to transform. Richard and Sally Price witnessed an extreme example of this in a small Spanish village in 1964 where the trousseau of a prosperous peasant girl included six monogrammed sanitary napkins (Price and Price 1966:312). Often embroidered whitewear was so totally separated from anything resembling nature that it was not even used. Indeed, in contrast to the textile labors of women in the lower classes, embroidery and lacework produced finery that was largely for entertainment, gift-giving and display, and for eventual transfer to daughters as heirlooms (e.g., Stapley 1924:56). Whether used or not, however, periodic laundering and sun-bleaching kept all whitewear white, and it is important to remember that the more intricate the stitches on any piece of cloth, the more difficult it is to iron. Leisure time and servants not only permitted upper class women to produce prodigious amounts of exquisitely decorated wear for bed, body, table, and frequently just for show; they also guaranteed that these luxuries could be maintained.

Between the Great Tradition of a courtly aristocracy in Renaissance Italy and Sicily, and the rising commitment to embroidery among Villamaura peasants and artisans in the late nineteenth and early twentieth centuries, was a process of class formation, which, as elsewhere in Europe, elevated a landed bourgeoisie, or gentry, into a mediational position between local, rural populations, and metropolitan centers of power and prestige. A brief summary of this process for Sicily best begins with the early 1800s, when European, especially English, capital combined with policies of the Neapolitan Bourbons, then rulers of the island, to create a capitalist market in land. For the next several decades, families of diverse but often humble origin began to accumulate land; they formed the core of the so-called *ceto civile*, the "civilized people" who were Sicily's version of a gentry class.

At first the rise of the *ceto civile* contradicted the interests of a preexisting aristocracy, but the contradiction was more apparent than real, for bourgeois landholdings were rarely gained at aristocratic expense so much as they were carved from other sources: from state expropriations of ecclesiastical and communal domain on the one hand; from peasant indebtedness on the other. As displaced peasant rebels increasingly threatened the *civili* from below, this rising group assimilated to the class above them, not only politically and through marriage alliances, but by emulating an aristocratic life style. From at least the late 1860s, the main difference between the new gentry and the old aristocracy was in the scale of this style and where it was lived. For the *ceto civile* carried out its version of elite behavior in the confines of the rural and interior towns whereas earlier holders of large properties usually resided for most of the year in cities, at the courts of kings and princes, and abroad.

Happily for the ambitions of the *civili*, the nineteenth century was a time of substantial agrarian transformation which was Sicily's version of the second agricultural revolution. Again foreign capital and government policy played key roles, in this case converting land once used for extensive, transhumant grazing into more intensively cultivated wheat fields and vineyards and, in south-central Sicily, into sulphur mines as well. Until the agricultural depression of the 1880s and 1890s, viable markets for grain, vineyards, and sulphur gave the rural bourgeoisie a generous financial base, if not for capitalizing their holdings, then at least for bringing civilization to the hinterland.

And this they did. The house cadaster of Villamaura shows that by the late 1870s, gentry families had already commissioned the construction of houses whose complex ground plans conformed to criteria recognized as *"civile"* throughout Italy and Europe. Articulated by Palladio, the great sixteenth-century architect of the Veneto, these criteria dictated that stables and storerooms should be totally separate from the residential quarters of the owners, even if in the same building, and that the architecture of the residential quarters should express the opposition of "nature" and "culture" wherever possible. Similar ideas were applied to the body, whose natural functions were camouflaged by fashionable clothes, chosen according to season, hour of the day, activity being pursued, and so on.[5] In dressing themselves, and their houses, no less than in the domain of architecture, the urbane *civili* insisted upon layers between layers, and here a proliferation of decencies was essential. Not only was the use of the handkerchief more hygienic than blowing one's nose in one's sleeve—to take a graphic example marvelously embroidered upon by Elias (1978:143–153)—but, as Balsamo had urged, linens of all kinds "enhance and adorn the civilized life." From the *civile* point of view, the more decorated these linens were, the more this was true.

Civile families in late nineteenth-century Villamaura had occasional live-in servants plus dependent women who came to their houses on a more or less regular basis to sew, wash floors, and nurse infants. Other women took sewing or children into their own homes while laundresses (*lavandai*) washed the linens of the rich in local streams. By the 1870s and 1880s, there were bakeries and pasta "factories," which produced daily allotments of bread and noodles for those who could afford them, so one imagines that *civile* women had abundant leisure time to embroider.

Women of other classes were different in this regard for, although according to oral histories taking us back to the turn of the century, wives of rich peasants hired poor girls for heavy housework and running errands, plus seamstresses to come into their houses and sew, these wives, and the wives of other peasants and artisans, made their own bread and pasta, nursed their own children, and did their own laundry (unless they were sick). How was it that so many of them, following the example of the *civili,* also became devotees of the needle arts? Part of the answer to this question appears later on, in a discussion of women's work. For the moment we need to follow the class

[5] For a more complete description of the *civile* house, its contents and how they were made in the late nineteenth century, and especially of the spatial segregation of "culture" and "nature," see Peter Schneider (1978).

formation process to the point where non-*civile* groups also experienced a rise in their standard of living.

A well-known corollary of rural bourgeois ascendance is peasant proletarianization; this occurred quite markedly in Sicily after the expropriation of the church and common lands in the 1860s. Yet peasant impoverishment was not the only consequence of the growing *civile* monopoly of local power. The expansion of this class both numerically, and as status-conscious consumers, brought in its wake a series of effects that improved the life conditions for middle groups, too. Artisans, for example, grew more numerous and more skilled in large part because, given the lack of roads and railroads, most of the things with which the *civili* adorned themselves and their houses were crafted locally. Better-off peasants, too, benefitted from *civile* expansion, among other ways by providing luxury foods and tobacco for tables of the gentry class.

These groups and others just below them on the ladder of wealth and status were, however, extremely vulnerable to the agricultural depression that engulfed Europe in the 1870s when American wheat, cheaply produced by mechanical means and transported by steamships, crossed the Atlantic, and to the economic dislocations of the 1880s and 1890s, which resulted from the transatlantic flow of Louisiana sulphur and the complete collapse of the wine grape market, due to diseased vines and French competition. In the long run, therefore, out-migration was the basis for upward mobility among non-*civile* groups.

Contrary to a common assumption that migrants from southern Italy and Sicily were overwhelmingly landless day laborers is the recent discovery by historians that artisans and better-off peasants participated too (see Gabaccia 1979). After all, the multiplier effects of *civile* expansion worked rapidly in reverse once the grain, sulphur, and vineyard economy was undermined. Another revision of once common assumptions stems from mounting evidence that perhaps a third of all migrants to America returned to their homeland, some of them several times. Finally, although migrants' remittances are impossible to follow with precison, it is clear that they played a decisive role in the Sicilian economy after 1900—above all as a cash reserve for peasants and artisians.

Reserve cash facilitated the purchase of land, so that gradually the number of small holdings increased vis-à-vis the number of vast estates. Especially impressive were the changes in peasant and artisan patterns of consumption made possible by remittance money. Even before World War I, members of these "middle sectors" began to build or add on to houses, and to acquire more diversified wardrobes and household furnishings. Interviews with survivors and descendants of that era portray the change as another aspect of civilization coming to the hinterland. That rich and middle peasants and artisans adopted the practice of embroidering trousseau was in this sense merely an extension of the modeling behavior that engaged them as a general rule.

Textile Arts and the Seclusion of Women

Even though a process of class formation and status emulation can tell us a great deal about the ever-wider distribution of embroidered decencies in Sicilian households after the mid-1800s, it does not fully explain why embroidery became central to trousseau. For one thing, history provides too many cases in which elite styles were reversed or rejected, ascetic movements nourished, counter cultures born, for emulation or modeling ever to be a sufficient cause of anything. Furthermore, to conclude that the downward circulation of embroidery and lacemaking was simply the consequence of upward mobility and "nouveau riche" excess is to overlook the labor requirements of needlework—requirements that once restricted such work to an elite domain. Posed as a problem of labor allocation, the ever-wider distribution of lace and embroidery in late nineteenth century Sicily becomes a corollary of the distribution of commercially manufactured cloth which in this period displaced an array of homespuns, and liberated nonelite mothers and daughters from the loom.

Let us return to the lists of peasant trousseaux which Salomone-Marino and Pitrè collected for the first few decades of the 1800s. By far the most numerous of the 35 to 40 items making up these lists were textiles and these ranged along a continuum from cloth intended for daily use to a special wedding dress. Purchased finery predominated in this dress: damasked silk from the famed Sicilian industries of the coastal cities, especially Messina, which was dyed with reliable dyestuffs (imported cochineal and indigo, or a domestic copper-sulphate derivative used with an alum mordant to produce a marvelous "peacock" blue-green). Portions of the costume, especially the bodice, were embellished with gold and silver thread, pieces of lace or macramé work in silk. Finally, a worked, sometimes inlaid, silver belt cinched it at the waist (Cocchiara 1957:42–48; Pitrè 1969:55–63).

In addition to the festival or wedding dress, purchased luxury fabrics such as silk or velvet (in one case Tibetan wool) figured in mantles and shawls, some of which were fringed, trimmed with gold thread or ribbon. Most of the other textiles—the necessities of daily use such as aprons, skirts, and whitewear for bed and table, were handloomed. Indeed, some trousseaux included lengths of cloth not as yet made up into particular articles (Cocchiara 1957:38). Descriptions of this cloth, as well as of skirts, sheets, and so on, mention the fibers of which they were made, the fineness of the weave, whether the weave was patterned in any way, and whether the cloth had been dipped in a home-prepared dye bath. From the evidence available, it appears that imported linen and cotton threads entered homewoven fabrics only to a very limited extent; domestic wool was also unusual except in shawls and for mattress stuffing. Domestic linen existed but was rare, due to problems of linen cultivation, and domestic cotton likewise. By far the most common cloths were of homegrown and homespun hemp, or hemp mixed with cotton to make fustians. When such cloth was woven without pattern or stripe, it was called *tela di casa ordinaria*—ordinary, homemade cloth (Bennetti-Ventura 1911).

Not only did trousseaux of the early nineteenth century emphasize hand-loomed textiles; they included looms and spinning equipment as a general rule. For in those days, a good wife was a good weaver, so much so that it was customary for prospective mothers-in-law to find pretexts for discovering the weaving skills of their son's betrothed before the wedding date was fixed. A proverb said that if, on a surprise visit, the girl were found relaxing, she would be a lazy wife. If she were found eating, one could expect her to ruin the groom with her gluttony. But if she were found weaving, then she would be exemplary, like the wife who is quoted in Bennetti-Ventura's study of Sicilian textiles: "From the time I was 14 to 50, I dressed myself, my brothers, my children and the children of those with cloth made by my own hands."[6] Peasant women who were ill-prepared for such work were little sought-after; another old proverb likened them to the white crow (*corvo bianco*) (Bennetti-Ventura 1911).

The shift from homespun to machine-made cloth for clothing, tablewear, and bedding was both rapid and thorough. The following observation makes this point:

> Were all weddings made in such a way? Yes, all, because in those days there was not a family which did not have so many looms in motion, so many daughters who were inside, and the youngest wound the spools. No one would have married a girl who did not know how to weave, no one.
>
> Today, this custom has fallen almost entirely into disuse; because the industry of weaving is no longer in the hands of our peasant women; the cloth of foreigners has been formidably competitive, and the houses where weaving still takes place are few [quoted in Pitrè 1939:20].

Nevertheless, the displacement of domestic weaving did not occur everywhere or in all sectors at the same time. For one thing, women continued to wear homespuns for quite a while after men adopted the *stilo inglese*—English style tailored suits which became fashionable in Sicily in the late nineteenth century. Men of the gentry class owned such suits earlier and in greater number than did peasants, although better-off peasants in Villamaura had tailored pants, jackets, and vests at least as far back as 1890. Towns also changed differentially. Those situated at lower altitudes and in close proximity to the transportation network—rudimentary as this was until the 1900s—experienced the "formidable competition" of commercially produced cloth considerably in advance of towns that were remote. Villamaura, at 300 m above sea level and on the road connecting Corleone with Sciacca, fell into

[6] For the proverb, see Pitrè 1939:21–22. It has other tantilizing equations, which I am unsure how to interpret; for example, if the girl were spinning, it meant she would give birth to many children.

this category, whereas a more isolated neighboring community that I visited several times did not.

The contrast between these two settlements is interesting. In the remote mountain town, there were still a few working looms in the 1960s and although by then women wove only rustic saddle bags, they could explain how linen and hemp were cultivated, soaked, and beaten into malleable fibers, how it took 15–20 days of dawn-to-dusk weaving for the mothers and daughters, rotating at the loom, to produce the three lengths of cloth that made one sheet when sewn together—more days if the weave were fine. In Villamaura, by contrast, no one had firsthand experience with the cultivation of fibers, except briefly during World War II and, although many women had spun wool for coarse wartime sock-knitting, none with whom I spoke knew how to weave. Older informants, attempting to date when looms were last used, envisioned their grandmothers at them, and not their mothers. In fact, there appear to be no surviving looms in Villamaura. People there characterize residents of the neighboring mountain town as "*meno evoluto,*" which means "less evolved" or backward. They say the best index of this is that the women there work outdoors rather than at the civilized indoor task of embroidery. Mountain women "*vanno in campagna*"—go out into the countryside—among other things to tend and process the locally produced fiber crops that Villamaura women gave up long ago.

These impressions, gathered during field work, of the differences between two communities, echo the conclusion of Cocchiara (1957:36) that ultimately weaving survived only in the mountainous zones of Messina and Trapani provinces in Sicily, Calabria, and Sardinia. Elsewhere the expression "tela di casa" became an unflattering nickname (an *injuria*). Vital statistics kept by municipal governments since 1820 in Sicily, include occupational information on men and women, and also permit tracing locally specific change. The data which I have for Villamaura reveal that a male weaver (a *telandaro*) who married in 1850 had become a cloth merchant by 1866 when his sixth child was born. Between then and 1881, four such merchants appeared in the sampled marriages (1850–1851, 1860–1861, 1870–1871, 1880–1881) alone. That these dealers were important is suggested by the fact that all married daughters of landed gentry or professionals, even though their fathers and mothers had been of artisan or (rich) peasant status. Since families generally attempted upward mobility through daughters, these cases of an opposite pattern must have attracted a great deal of attention, much as did the parallel example in Lampedusa's famous novel, *The Leopard.*

The Villamaura sample tells us that around 1866–1867, town clerks began recording the occupations of women married to peasants, shepherds, and artisans as "industrious" (*industriosa*); previously they had listed no occupations at all. In 1866, a woman who had married a stonecutter in 1850, appeared in the birth act of her fourth child as a seamstress (a *cucitrice*). This designation would be worth a detailed investigation. In the sample of families available to me now it reappeared in two birth acts in 1877 and then became general for the wives of virtually all artisans and better-off peasants (*agricoltori* or *burgisi*) in the mid-1880s—a decade when women in the neighboring mountain town were listed as *filatrici* or spinners. *Cucitrici* of the 1880s put seams in shirts and trousers. My informants thought that they did this as outworkers for local tailors, as well as for their own families, some perhaps with the aid of a sewing machine.[7]

The proliferation of *cucitrici* in Villamaura, beginning slowly in the late 1860s and expanding rapidly around 1883–1884, charts the penetration of commercial cloth. Significantly these dates correspond to important changes in policy at the level of the newly unified Italian state. For example, in the mid-1860s internal tariff barriers were dismantled to encourage a freer circulation of goods, including imports from abroad; in the 1880s, a national protective tariff nurtured the development of North Italian textile industries. Moreover, throughout these years, national policy directed both domestic and foreign capital into road and railroad construction—a transportation network being essential to the formation of a national market (see especially Sereni 1968:3–41). Villamaura had no accessible railhead until the twentieth century, but links by cart to Palermo and other coastal cities improved somewhat earlier. Cart drivers and retail merchants made up 1.1% of our 1850–1851 marriage cohort. By 1870–1871 their number had risen to 4.5% and by 1880–1881 to 8%.

What with cloth merchants and carters, the operations of the market and the policies of the state, commercially produced textiles were finding their way into the Sicilian interior in even more lengths and widths after, say, 1870. Among these textiles was sheeting, for the most part machine-made cotton, some of it mixtures of cotton and other fibers.[8] As spinning and weaving declined, women applied highly elaborate needlework to this factory produced and commercially distributed cloth (see Cole 1975:64 for a Bedouin parallel; also Hirschfield 1977).

In many respects, the transition is hardly remarkable. Embroidery had long existed in the upper class, as well as for the limited purpose of decorating the wedding dress. The skills that it requires are partially transferable from

[7] In 1866, a Palermo daily carried a brief article reporting damage to women's genitals from spending too many hours at an early model of the Singer. One operated this particular machine with an alternating, back and forth motion of the feet on a double treadle. We know from the history of later models that their worldwide distribution began in the late nineteenth century and it seems plausible that a few machines reached Villamaura to aid the *cucitrici* of the 1880s. I could not find any dates on the antique Singers which people still have, but they were said to be "in the family" for three generations.

[8] Not all of the new cloth was foreign, even though a great deal of it came from England. North Italian textile industries expanded with the unification of the national market during the 1860s, and especially under tariff protection 20 years later. Meanwhile, the Jacquard loom gave a few of Sicily's silk industries a new lease on life, one example being the Gulì works in Palermo. With this loom, Gulì could manufacture damasked cotton mattress covers that captured the *corredo* market in Southern Italy as well as Sicily, replacing the coarse, striped covers earlier woven at home (from an interview with descendants of the founder at the plant).

weaving; both necessitate an early acquaintance with the properties of different fibers and with sewing. According to women in Villamaura, learning to sew always precedes learning other textile arts. Yet the question remains why women, liberated from one kind of domestic chore should have taken up another one, especially one whose products were apparently less useful, and at a historical juncture when the Sicilian economy was losing its capacity to earn foreign exchange. If status emulation is not to bear the entire burden of explanation, what else was going on?

One might hypothesize that embroidery and lace-making evolved as a kind of make-work that ensured continuity in the division of labor by sex. Given its location and history, Sicily participated in the Mediterranean culture of honor and shame. As a set of structures and codes, this culture is familiar. Women brought status to their families in the degree that they were "pure": virgins at marriage, chaste as wives, continent as widows, and in general secluded from a public social life. If anything, hours spent at embroidery encouraged these virtues even more than spinning and weaving because when women worked on factory-made cloth, they no longer had anything to do with the cultivation and harvesting of fiber crops, tasks that had previously engaged them in cooperative endeavors with men outside the home.

I will argue that, like the status emulation hypothesis, the "make-work" hypothesis is not sufficient. Nevertheless, it has some real virtues which will be examined first in relation to married, or potentially married, women, then in relation to young girls before they marry. Regarding adult women, the disappearance of spinning and weaving added up to many hours of spare time, especially if one includes the hours of a growing number of women who could not marry because migration removed more males than females from the marriage market. By their very quantity, these hours were at least a theoretically serious threat to cultural continuity since they could have been allocated to work of the sort that men did, or to a search for pleasure outside the home. That these things did not happen on a significant scale may have a direct explanation: when the commodities which had been developed for export during the nineteenth century ceased to be viable, investors withdrew their capital and failed to encourage the production of anything else. Yet it is possible that this failure to consider alternatives was influenced by the perception that in Sicily, only the poorest women could be considered part of the labor pool. Other women were too committed to demonstrating their family's honor through the preparation of elaborate trousseau.

An interesting term to follow in the vital statistics records is *casalinga,* meaning housewife, a woman who lives at home without exercising another profession or occupation (Panzini 1956). During the 1890s and early 1900s, some Villamaura wives of better-off peasants and artisans continued to appear in the marriage and birth registers as *cucitrici* but an increasing number were called *casalinghe.* Furthermore, whereas the wives of middle to poor peasants and shepherds had previously appeared as "industrious" or "peasant,'' many of them also acquired the label *casalinga* after 1890. In the 1910 and 1920 marriage cohorts, almost all women received this designation, except for women in the gentry class who, like their husbands, were called *civile,* and a few women of the peasant class who were extremely poor.

The *Grande Dizionario Battaglia* clarifies the normative message conveyed by the term ''*casalinga*'': a housewife who ''loves to stay in the house, live in the bosom of her own family, occupying herself with domestic affairs, with the education of children, seeking refuge from rowdy entertainment.'' Literary citations assembled to illustrate this point include a few in which handwork or needlework symbolize a wife's resistance to the temptations of frivolity and vice. In the *Enciclopedia Italiana* (Vol. 9, p. 280), the term is equated with *casalina,* which means either a homewoven garment of unrefined cotton with a blue or black background or bottom, or a linen weaving frame. ''*Inga,*'' however, is a suffix meaning ''of the''—in this case of the house. If *casalinga* conveys a central idea, it is that being ''of the house'' is equivalent to having a serious occupation or profession, perhaps partly because of domestic textile production.

Turning now to nubile women, the link between textiles and restrained sexuality is even more explicit, as the English word ''spinster'' reminds us. This is because Christianity (other great religions, too) often equates industrious dedication to spinning, weaving, and embroidery with virginity. Already in the Middle Ages, cloistered nuns wove and decorated clerical vestments and altar cloths. As repositories of skill and design, convents ever since have taught girls both clothwork and morals even in such out-of-the-way places as Villamaura. There, before the suppression of religious orders in 1866, a Collegio of Santa Maria instructed ''respectable girls'' how to embroider in silk and gold as well as pursue ''domestic and manual labor, both necessary and ornamental, which a good mother of a family needed to know [Giacone 1932:128].'' In 1873, the state permitted the sisters of this Collegio to continue to train girls under the guise of an *opera pia* or charity; this training came to focus increasingly on embroidery.

According to Christian teaching, the production of beautiful and refined cloth is an act of religious devotion, no less than are vows of chastity. The two often go together as we see in the lives of ''house nuns''—devout women who, although they belong to no official religious community, never marry and spend their days embroidering for home and church. Other examples abound in the biographies of female saints such as Saint Agatha, the Christianized Penelope, whose following is considerable among Sicilian women. She continually put off her suitor, much to her father's dismay, on the grounds that she could not marry him until she had finished weaving a certain cloth. Agatha wove by night and day but ''her woman's work was never done,'' and instead of getting married she became the patron saint of spinners and weavers (see Pitrè 1969:143).

In the legend of Saint Agatha, devotion to weaving meant the postponement of marriage, but in the lives of women in Sicily, embroidery correlated with delayed marriage more closely than did weaving. This is because the expansion of embroidery at the end of the nineteenth century roughly coincided with the demographic transition from large to small families, a transition that depended in part on marriage age. According to our family-reconstitution study for Villamaura, women's age at marriage was relatively low in all classes until the 1890s. After that, it was low among the poorest peasants who married in their late teens, but averaged 25 years or more in other groups.

In the early decades of the nineteenth century, women entered marriage with spinning and weaving equipment, tested skills as weavers, and some cloth. It was expected that they would produce many more lengths of the same as wives and mothers. In contrast, the embroidery regime of the end of the century, which was associated with a later age at marriage, made a distinction between work done before and after marriage. Before, a young girl embroidered her entire trousseau, being careful to project an image of herself as both industrious and modest; after marriage she did little if any embroidery, except for the layettes and baptismal dresses of newborn children and, when time permitted, occasional pieces for gifts (Cocchiara 1957:49). After marriage, women's primary task was to manage their daughters' trousseaux. Thus embroidery was above all an activity and symbol of virgin girlhood, the more so as it was usually white on white.[9]

Trousseau as Treasure

Like our review of class formation and status emulation, this picture of women's work as an aspect of women's "value" illuminates the embroidery problem. It also complements, without detracting from, an explanation for this practice based on rivalry for status. Indeed, ethnographic data indicate that, in the status hierarchy for women, types of work and degrees of purity went hand in hand. Thus in Chapman's account, young girls "with status pretensions" substituted embroidery for knitting and weaving and assumed they would "never bake their own bread or do their own laundry." At the same time, status-conscious peasant and artisan women remained "in com-

[9] This is not to suggest, however, that the link between needlework and the demographic transition was universal. In Kutch and Saurashtra in India, where, incidentally, domestic embroidery also developed in the nineteenth century, it is the needles of older, married women that "throb with life" as they prepare embroidered trousseau for their soon to be child-bride daughters (Namavati 1966). And in Hungary, where "a girl of 14 is allowed to receive suitors" and one of 20 is "regarded as an old maid," the bride-to-be, young as she is, prepares her trousseau and an embroidered shirt for the bridegroom at the expense of learning how to bake bread, cook, and milk—skills crucial to her adult existence that she must then acquire from her mother-in-law. Her mother, however, "is expected to supply . . . an entire set of (handwoven) bed linen for everyday use," and an ornamental cover, if she can afford to make it (see Fél and Hofer 1969: 119–120, 130–133, 143). (Here too, dowry consisted largely of trousseau [Fél and Hofer 1969:25].)

plete isolation'' where they embroidered or supervised embroidery, and wore ''veils to Church in imitation of (the) wealthy.'' In all of these groups, women married late, sometimes later than 30 (Chapman 1971:31–32, 54–60, 98).

Interviews with elderly women from very poor families in Villamaura brought out a different complex of traits associated with the lower end of a female hierarchy: For these women, the most time-consuming activity was to save their children from starvation and this necessitated all kinds of low status work. They made brooms and cording for itinerant merchants and local mediators who put out the raw materials—the processed leaves and stalks of local plants. They gathered wild vegetables on what remained of public lands, followed the men on the fields at harvest time in order to pick up stray stalks of grain, and ground this grain on their own stones to avoid an onerous tax on machine-milled flour. The time employed in home-milling was to some extent compensated by time gained from cooking and baking, because the stone ground flour was too coarse for pasta or bread and tended to be eaten as a porridge, called *pitirru*.

Girls from very poor families often worked as maids to earn money for dowry and their mothers worked as laundresses to enhance the same fund. But sons' earnings went to the mother for food rather than sheeting; thus most families could manage at best a minimum trousseau for their daughters. Few hoped for upward mobility through female offspring; on the contrary, the sooner a daughter married and joined an independent household, the better. Sometimes—poignantly illustrating Pitrè's observation that ''marriages of the poor create new poor''—a mother was able to give the last of her own infants to a married daughter to nurse, that daughter having already begun to have children (see Pitrè 1969:34–36).

Early marriage and the pressure of poverty stood in the way of learning to sew—let alone embroider—and many women recall with bitterness that for them, clothes were made by piecing together the hand-me-downs of others whereas handwork consisted only in making brooms. In their view, having done no embroidery was worse than a social stigma; it confirmed the *civile* ideology that day laborers lived like animals, crowded into one or two rooms with their donkey and, as Malthus thought, breeding without control. Clearly, proletarian women had no honor, whereas women who embroidered did, and their embroidered trousseaux symbolized not only this crucial fact, but the layers between them and proletarianization.

By considering the cultural connection between certain kinds of handwork and sexual restraint, we have deepened our perspective on social status. The owner of embroidery and lace emitted more than a claim to participation in the Great Traditions of a civilization; there was also a message of assurance that her family would not sink, as it were, beyond the pale. One detects the familiar concerns of a ''petty bourgeoisie'': (*a*) how to distance themselves from those who, in an earlier generation, were their class equals; (*b*) how to cope with the unsettling reality that, were it not for a few lucky breaks, they could be proletarians, too; (*c*) how to find in their preoccupation with honor a justification for screening out the domestic tragedies associated with a neighbor's impoverishment.

But why, after all of this, was embroidery a central symbol of social position? Why not establish the same point with the wide range of consumer goods that factory production and improved transportation made ever more readily, and cheaply, available in the twentieth century? These goods conferred status, too. I raise this question because I am dissatisfied with the conclusion that embroidery was make-work, however much it distinguished the embroiderer. This seems to me to distort both women's commitment to it, and the central role that it played in marriage exchange.

As we have seen, bride and groom contributed different things to their new household. Against her status goods he brought productive resources—if not land, then at least the strength, social relations, and agricultural implements with which to earn a livelihood from the land or, if he were an artisan, the tools and skills of a trade. Yet there is no indication that her contribution, while different, was inferior to his. In writing about the Sarakatsani, Campbell suggests that the addition of sheep or gold sovereigns to a traditional dowry of household goods has improved women's chances to marry up, but this trend appeared only after 1945 (Campbell 1964:302). Pitkin's study and other accounts of Italy are quite explicit that in the past, *corredo* alone could attract a spouse of equal or superior status (see Pitkin 1960). Moreover, even though trousseau predominates over other goods in many Mediterranean dowry systems, ethnographers frequently comment that in the household, wife and husband enjoy matched status and use reciprocal terms of address (see Chapman 1971:36–41; Friedl 1967). In a Sicilian proverb, "The man is the soul of the house. A good wife is the primary wealth of the house [quoted in Chapman 1971:36]."

One kind of evidence that embroidered "beds" constituted a store of wealth lies in the ritual of the *stima*. The professional who examined assembled trousseau before a wedding used well established criteria to estimate value. Regarding the raw materials, linen outranked cotton, which outranked hemp; moreover, Belgian linen was superior to Irish linen, which was in turn superior to Italian. Silk thread had more value than cotton thread in embroidery. The *stimatrice* also examined workmanship, judging both the difficulty of the stitches and the precision of their execution. But most important, she looked at overall design, because different design sequences carried different values. These sequences were the heritage of Renaissance Italy and Sicily, also of eighteenth century France; they were kept and transmitted by cloistered nuns who, in Villamaura, sold them for a fee.

Designs were also available from local women who had received training as *disegnatrici* in Palermo, and from specialized journals and pattern booklets. Publications of this type have long contributed to the standardization of embroidery and lace-making in Europe, their existence dating back to the second quarter of the sixteenth century when wood-engraved printing came into its own. As a rule, pattern booklets instruct women not in creating or transferring designs, so much as in rigorously copying them by counting threads in the cloth or mesh ground (a process called embroidery *a fili contati* or *à points comptés*). Some of the designs to be copied were produced by men, but women authored many of the best known sequences. Such sequences usually originated in key centers of textile manufature such as Flanders and Venice in the sixteenth century; Milan since the late 1800s. These centers gave place names to particular patterns or stitches which the booklets then carried even to peasant households in far-away villages (Lefébure 1888:128, 188–192; Ricci 1958:35–46).

Some designs emphasized cut-work, done with sharp scissors but without an embroidery hoop, and relatively easy to execute. (Minimum "beds," if they were embroidered at all, were usually ornamented with cut-work.) More complicated and time consuming was drawn work (*sfilato*), transitional between embroidery and lace in that it involved removing threads from a woven ground. A Sicilian version of *sfilato* gained a continental reputation in the fourteenth century and is highly prized in *corredo* to this day (Fagone 1966: 122–125). Other *sfilato* patterns also had Renaissance roots, but in Northern Italy, not Sicily. Among the most prestigious and valued designs were those which incorporated the Venetian rose-point; open mesh cloth embroidered with palm, rose, peacock, or geometric motifs; and appliqués of Tuscan pillow lace. Significantly, there was little individual experimentation or artistic expression in trousseau preparation; most girls, guided by their mothers, adhered closely to the established designs (Chapman 1971:44).

The standardized criteria used by a *stimatrice* to estimate the value of trousseau in lire or onze obviously had some relation to a sphere of exchange, and the fact that designs with continental reputations weighed heavily in her calculus suggests that this sphere transcended not only a local arena, but ultimately, Sicily as well. One can question how much exchange value items of trousseau actually had—according to John Davis, not very much. *"Corredo,"* he writes, "is a poor sort of investment; it does not carry interest, nor does it have great liquidity; it is hard to sell it, and impossible to secure a loan with it [Davis 1973:36]."

Davis, however, is reporting a contemporary situation, and perhaps he has, as a reference, modern forms of saving against a rainy day: bank accounts, stocks and bonds, insurance policies, union benefits, and presumably fool-proof government programs covering crop damage, retirement, war injuries, earthquakes, and so on. In the period of concern to us here, these forms of long-run security were rudimentary at best; many of them have come into being for the Italian South and Sicily only with the considerable expansion of state institutions after World War II. Moreover, the period in question closely followed the breakup of a number of religious orders, which in earlier centuries had supplemented family strategies for "ultimate" survival.

What existed instead was a pyramid of patron–client relations whose ability to deliver protection and welfare depended heavily on personal criteria, and on the financial solvency of the *civile* class. Big spenders and poor investors, this class was shaken in times of trouble, too. In other words, in the late nineteenth and early twentieth centuries, most families were on their own to meet the crises of life—the loss of a work animal, an expensive litigation against encroachments on property, the untimely death of a breadwinner. Such were the events that raised their debt level and led them to the brink of the abyss where survival meant selling off productive resources and finding a daily, or hourly, wage. That people who reached this point often joined the migration stream is less significant than that they joined it as lumpen proletarians with no "monetary refuge" to ease the transition. Families that had such a refuge in some ways resembled states, which is perhaps why in wedding ceremonies bride and groom were the symbolic equivalents of a king and queen; their attendants the equivalent of a court.

In Villamaura, I was told that embroidered sheets and bed covers, especially the most valued and least used, saved a number of families from disaster. The point is not that "beds" were regularly exchanged; on the contrary, selling or pawning them was the last resort—a desperate, almost immoral, economic necessity. Yet oral histories reveal that sometimes women pawned whitewear at local grocery or yardgood stores to purchase food or sheeting for a daughter's trousseau. Itinerant merchants secretly negotiated with women who were eager for a "family allowance" but ashamed that anyone should know they would trade *corredo* to get it. Church sponsored pawn shops, the *Monte di Pieta,* dating back to the seventeenth century, made loans against whitewear, too. I also heard stories of creditors bursting in on troubled families and opening their linen chests, the contents of which had no legal protection against the claims of third parties—unlike other components of dowry that creditors could not touch (see Davis 1973:173–174; also Hughes 1978:282).

Most of the stories concerned families that had few resources to begin with; there were exceptions, however, reminiscent of those which a Philadelphia pawn broker reported in an interview with the *Literary Digest* in 1921. According to his account, "a reputable pawn broker can be described as a poor man's banker," but the rich who borrow from banks nevertheless sometimes ring the bell at night, carrying the family silver and other "ancient heirlooms" under their arms. Their purpose is to raise money to pay back debts which unlucky ventures have caused to become outstanding (Anonymous 1921). One should not imagine, in other words, that better-off families were immune to crises. Their vulnerability to disease was nearly as great as anyone's until the 1700s and after 1789, revolutions could do them in. Various accounts of upper-class dowries from earlier centuries suggest that as a rule of thumb, new households were formed with *corredo* that was commensurate with the value of immovable property, or a family was not worthy of its name (see Chojnacki 1975; Levi-Pisetzky 1969:942–946). Perhaps we should think of trousseau as a store of value that protected not only family members, but also family assets, providing the flexibility to meet crises by pawning or selling wealth instead of land.

The negotiability of whitewear ultimately depended on whether claimants, creditors, and pawnbrokers could resell their catch. Probable buyers in the stories told by Villamaura women were mothers engaged in trousseau preparation in distant communities, some in continental Italy. The size of trousseaux among the *civili* must have helped enlarge the sphere of exchange since no girl, however late she married, could embroider 50 or more beds by herself. A close study of the connections between landed families, the cloistered convents where nuns embroidered in part for wealthy clients, and the religious pawn shops, might further validate the hypothesis that, although *biancheria* was largely produced for use within the home, it was also potentially exchangeable for cash or food.[10]

To the extent that whitewear was a potentially liquid resource, it served as more than a symbolic layer between a peasant or an artisan family and proletarianization. It could constitute a real economic buffer when crises threatened, much like the wealth objects suitable for "emergency conversion" in Africa (see Herskovits 1962). In this context, the distinction between embroidered goods and consumer goods becomes clear, for although the latter also confer status, their time to depreciation is practically zero. It is important, in other words, to differentiate among *types* of prestige goods, or status symbols. Consumer goods may attract more attention and admiration than old lace because they are more fashionable, but it is among other things their fashion-bound quality that contributes to their rapid obsolescence. In contrast, old lace, especially if it conforms to well established patterns, keeps its value even as it appears out of date, and can be traded for "survival" in troubled times.

Lace, embroidery, and needlepoint fall into the range of prestige goods best characterized as wealth objects, or valuables. Significantly, in Sicily, the ideological complex that conflated virginity and delayed marriage with handwork of this sort, also cautioned women against "frivolity and vice." Many fashionable clothes and furnishings entered the marriage exchange system as gifts, which the spouses gave each other, or received from friends and relatives, but these goods were like the purchased cosmetics and perfumes which Salomone-Marino complained, already in 1879, were corrupting the "virginal fragrance" of the bride (Salomone-Marino 1968:245). They lacked the ageless value of precious things.[11]

---

[10] I am grateful to Ashraf Ghani for pointing out that the very large trousseaux of the *civile* class might have had an impact on the size of the market for embroidered whitewear.

[11] The same ideological complex constrained men against expensive temptations, too, the temptation of alcohol in particular. Wives were explicitly concerned that male earnings, earmarked for dowry, not be dissipated in local taverns.

But precious things are varied too, and a final step in this attempt to discover "why embroidery" is to contrast valuables among themselves. Recall that in the trousseau lists of the early nineteenth century there were a number of wealth objects—in particular silk, gold, and silver—associated with the wedding dress. Other items, not referred to as yet, included gold rings and earrings, a silver hair brush, and a rosary inlaid with pearl. The daughter of a carter from a Palermo suburb brought into her marriage several copper pots, plus a bronze mortar (Pitrè 1939:27–28), while better-off peasant girls had amber and coral (Pitrè 1969:45–63). Objects such as these did not disappear from trousseaux toward the end of the century, but it seems to me that their presence was less noticeable as time went on. The wedding belt, for example, gave way to a comparable, but much smaller, symbol—the wedding ring. Already in Palermo of the late nineteenth century, a white wedding dress worn with garlands of orange blossoms replaced the polychrome and damasked silk costume ornamented with gold buttons and gold thread (Pitrè 1939:63). (In the interior towns, however, this transition took longer [see Chapman 1971: 104].) The "traditional" costume of silk and gold depreciated much less rapidly than the "modern" one of machine made cloth and flowers, even though the latter became more fashionable and prestigious.

It appears that little is known of the processes by which peasants and artisans (as distinct from noblemen and gentry) came to own significant preciosities—especially articles of gold and silver, and the finely woven silks of urban craftshops.[12] We usually assume that sumptuary laws prevented the diffusion of these things. Nor do we have good accounts how such goods were removed from modest households. Regarding nineteenth-century Sicily, one wonders how nongentry families experienced a tax burden that not only increased steadily with Italian Unification, but was among the most regressive in Europe (Mack Smith 1968:406; Sonnino 1925:219–231); how a severe shortage of coin, coupled with a rising pace of circulation, affected them, particularly

[12] An important exception is the work of Jan de Vries (1975), which details a considerable expansion in the consumer behavior of Friesland peasants between 1550 and 1750—probably two critical centuries for Europe as a whole. Increased production for market underlay the change and new items included a range of clothes and decencies, the famous Dutch window curtains, household furnishings, farm equipment, and so on. Of special note was an increase in luxury goods. Large farmers owned an average of 2.6 silver-buttoned waistcoats in the first half of the eighteenth century; 4.3 in the second. And they increasingly ate from tin dishes and porcelain rather than wood. But most important for our purposes was a rise in silver and gold objects within the home for as de Vries says, these were "not just consumer goods but also a store of value . . . a reasonably liquid form of wealth with an extremely long depreciation period." In the sixteenth century there were few such things, only rings, buttons, chains, and buckles; by the seventeenth century, women had silver waistbands with key chains, knife sheaths, and purses, all partly of silver, attached; and in the early eighteenth century, prosperous peasants owned gold rings, silver spoons, silver and gold buttons, beakers, cups, and mustard pots. An object called an oorijser, which bound women's hair, was of iron in the Middle Ages, silver by the late seventeenth century, and gold by the eighteenth. It also grew in width until, by the second half of the 1700s, "it nearly covered the skull [p. 222–224]."

when the government issued decrees urging private citizens and ecclesiastical bodies to cash in plate for money and other concessions (e.g., Giuffrida 1978: 122); how they managed when the creation of a national debt out of several regional debts in the 1860s severely disrupted public finance, or when the depression of the last quarter of the nineteenth century triggered bankruptcies in agriculture and industry. These were events that would deplete the family coffers.

Regarding silk, Mack Smith has noted that rich Sicilians preferred French imports while poorer people "ceased to be able to afford it as their standard of living went down." This loss of a home market in turn weakened the Sicilian silk industry, despite the introduction of Jacquard looms in midcentury and, with the elimination of internal tariffs in the 1860s, manufacturing totally collapsed, making silk even less accessible to peasants and artisans (Mack Smith 1968:383, 454–456).

Although information pertaining to precious metals and silks in peasant households is lacking, I draw attention to them because they differ from embroidery in a fundamental way. As a group they required virtually no labor on the part of the family possessing them—ornamentation of the wedding dress being a partial exception (unless lace and macramé trim were also purchased, which they may have been). And while these objects did contain "embodied" labor (labor expended at an earlier time) they also derived value from certain properties intrinsic to their "nature"—their rareness, beauty, luster, durability, and so on. In the history of textiles, there is support for the idea that these different components of value—natural beauty and rarity on the one hand, a considerable investment of labor on the other—interacted in patterned ways.

For example, there are numerous cases where intensification of cloth production occurred to meet a crisis of gold or silver drain. Governments, such as the familiar regimes of mercantilist Europe, often took pains to mobilize labor for textile manufacture because labor-intensive cloth exports could earn bullion abroad. Also intriguing is the repeated tendency of precious cloths to take the place of metals as a medium of exchange and store of value—that is, to assume money functions. Thus, precisely when bullion was scarce, the imperial court of China periodically declared silk and brocade (also porcelain and lacquer wear) to be "money" (Yang 1952).

For a divergent, and yet similar, case, we can turn to Gambia (and other African countries) in the nineteenth century. There the Wolof wove cloth for exchange purposes when European contact made cowrie shells untenable by deflating their value, at the same time failing to introduce enough metal coins to fill the gap. According to Ames, the most beautiful of their cloths, pieces that were indigo-dyed with designs, did not circulate; their function was closer to treasure than to money (Ames 1955). Here a parallel can be found in the unique silks hoarded by the Chinese court, and in other famous textiles that filled the coffers of states, temples, monasteries, and churches everywhere. "The lily cannot hide in the garden," says a document of the Christian church called "Annals of the Virgin Saints,"

> for it is the flower of virgins (and) must deck the high altars. So with gold and silver and gems of the mine, they blaze in the chalice and . . . are curiously wrought in the mitre and the clasped cope, they glitter on the pastoral staff and processional cross; so with the work of the needle, the hanging, the frontal, the corporal, and the veil, all exercise the patient skill of the artist, all occupy the quiet hours of the convent [quoted in Dolby 1868:24–25].

Yet different types of cloth approximated gold and silver in different ways. Closest were the textiles that were woven with gold and silver thread (actually very fine wire) and silk to form rich damasks and brocades. In these fabrics—early specialties of Oriental civilizations as far west as Byzantium—exotic fibers, metals, and dye-stuffs were a major component of value; so also were the rare skills of the drawloom weaver, usually an urban (male) specialist whose lengthy apprenticeship taught him how to manipulate colors and textures as he wove complicated designs. Even in ancient and medieval history, embroidered cloth was different, the critical factor in its production being tedious, patient work—neither terribly skilled nor requiring rich materials. In the words of Pauline Johnston, "countries such as Byzantium, Persia and Japan which at various times have attained a very high degree of skill in the production of decorated textiles, have always regarded embroideries very much in the light of a poor relation [Johnston 1967:9–10]." (Also see Krsteva 1975; Wace 1935:37.)

Although embroidery and its close cousin, lace work, are potentially exquisite and highly reputed as fine arts, they developed as second bests to drawloom brocades that they were, at first, intended to imitate. Court-sponsored and urban embroidery industries (as distinct from household manufacture) came to perfection, in fact, in regions that were peripheral to the great civilizations, and also in those civilizations at the moment of their decline. Good examples of the former are England in the Middle Ages, and the Balkan peoples under Byzantine hegemony in the fourteenth and fifteenth centuries—especially the Balkan courts in Moldavia and Wallachia. In these regions, the conditions did not exist for silkworm cultivation and silk manufacture, but embroidery made it possible to elaborate indigenous cloths so that they looked like exquisite brocades. Indeed, "the ground material was often commonplace and embroidery covered it completely [Johnston 1967:65]." One is reminded of medieval convents in north Germany where white on white embroidery became "typical" because "of poverty, of lack of means . . . for the purchase of costly silk [Schuette and Müller-Christensen 1964:50]." (Also see Ricci 1958:30). Peasant household production was similar, too. According to A. J. B. Wace, "in peasant art, embroidery is often employed as a home craft substitute for the luxurious woven silks of the rich and upper classes, and especially used to decorate the draperies demanded by social custom for trousseaux and festivals [Wace 1948:51–52].''

With regard to declining civilizational centers, Johnston's study of Byzantine embroidery places great emphasis on *timing*. Almost unknown at the height of imperial development in the ninth and tenth centuries, when silk and brocade manufacture provided the foundation for an immense accumulation of bullion and slaves, embroidery industries developed in the wake of the Fourth Crusade (Johnston 1967:10–23, 77). At that juncture, the Venetians and Genoese extorted unfavorable trading agreements with Byzantium, which triggered the Empire's contraction. Imitative of drawloom weaving, embroiderers applied gold thread to lesser cloths through a method known as ''laying and couching'' and with time even the thread they used deteriorated in quality—becoming first gilded silver and then colored silk. Coincidentally, embroidery took on more intricate designs (Johnston 1967:65–71). In other words, the balance sheet of exotic materials and rare skilled labor, as against hours of tedious needle pushing, shifted a notch toward the latter, much as happened when orientalized togas of rich stuffs gave way to embroidered robes with the decline of Rome after Diocletian (Lefébure 1888:41).

The origin of lace provides a special example of intensive labor becoming a source of value in lieu of precious materials at a point where those materials became less accessible. Developing out of embroidery, lace differs from it in a fundamental way. One embroiders on a piece of cloth, although the mesh of the weave can be opened considerably by drawing threads. Lace, on the other hand, requires the construction of its own ground or scaffolding by techniques that resemble knitting, knotting, and weaving. In other words, lace is created from air. And where European embroidery traditions, initially imported from Asia, often relied on threads of precious metal or colored silk, dyed with exotic dyestuffs, the inspiration for lace came from white thread embroidery on a white linen ground. Its attraction consisting in a play on open spaces instead of color, it required a bare minimum of valued materials. Significantly, its development in the sixteenth century was accomplished by women in domestic settings rather than men in urban workshops, while the first centers to produce lace in abundance were Northern Italy and Flanders—regions that had enjoyed a precocious economic growth during the Middle Ages but that were then losing ground to the hub of the emerging capitalist system in England and Holland (Lefébure 1888:172; Ricci 1958:42–46).

Embroidered cloth was a second cousin to hand-loomed brocade as a wealth object (just as brocade, although it approximated precious metals, was a second cousin to gold); this is reflected in the behavior of appropriators and pillagers when confronted with a choice. In the eyes of a nineteenth century needleworker for the Catholic Church in England, Henry VIII will go down in history as the world's greatest enemy of embroidery. His agents, in their zeal to transfer monastic property to king and gentry, ripped the gold thread off vestments and melted it down for coin (Dolby 1868:13; also Undi n.d.)!

Greedier for the material than for the workmanship with which it was applied to the cloth, their preference has been echoed many times since, such as during Year Three of the French Revolution when 40 or 50 needlewomen at Angers were put to work picking gold and silver thread out of bed valances and canopies to be "sent to the smelting pots for the benefit of the nation . . . [Lefébure 1888:157]."

A recent demonstration of the preference for valued materials over labor can be found in twentieth century Sicily. According to my sources in Villamaura, when a family was wealthy enough to purchase Belgian linen for dowry, the daughter did not embroider it because it was precious enough by itself. This suggests to me that if ordinary Sicilian families had been able to hang on to gold and silk in the course of the nineteenth century, they would have felt less compelled to commit so much of their women's time to embroidery.

Conclusions

In attempting to understand the centrality of embroidered "beds" in Sicilian marriage exchanges, the first step isolated this practice in time, for in fact it is not an old tradition except in the upper class. Class differences with regard to embroidery then led to a consideration of social mobility and status emulation as fundamental processes in the diffusion of the needle arts. A brief review of Sicilian social history in the nineteenth century showed that this was indeed a period when large-scale changes in land use and tenure produced new wealth, new occupational groups, new levels of consumer and status behavior on the local level.

The nineteenth century generated another source of change in the form of machine-made, factory-produced cotton and fustian textiles. As these yard-goods penetrated the peripheries of Europe and the world, they unhinged local and regional relations of production. One must not assume that their impact was everywhere the same, however. Sicily, and perhaps the Mediterranean generally, was a place where, prior to industrial textiles, the standards of cloth consumption were relatively high, and even among peasants included a range of decencies as well as basic clothes. Domestically produced cloth met these standards, as women allocated time to the cultivation and refinement of fiber crops, spinning, weaving, and even dyeing. The exception was silk, which was largely the product of specialized urban manufacture in Sicily, and which provided the fabric for festive wear. Machine-made textiles not only undermined the Sicilian silk industry; they also displaced the industries of the home.

The precipitous decline of home spinning and weaving liberated the hours that made it possible for peasants and artisans to emulate elites; what had earlier maintained the needle arts as an upper class monopoly was leisure time gained from slaves and servants. However, so many liberated hours could not in themselves account for the transition to embroidery, because too many other conditions were also changing. The Europe-wide depression of the late nineteenth century brought about a crisis of development: How could the various regions of England and the continent continue to compete in foreign markets, or even in their own, once the vast American cornucopia, fertilized by European capital, began to spill its surplus overseas? In Sicily this crisis underlay a spreading revolt among artisans and peasants, followed by heavy out-migration. One wants to know why, in the midst of dislocations of such severity, women stayed at home embroidering. The question becomes even more difficult when it is recognized that the demographic transition, an aspect of the crisis, considerably reduced the average number of childbearing years, particularly among those groups most committed to trousseau preparation.

An initial answer to the question focused on the cultural complex of honor and shame. According to this line of reasoning, embroidery, although beautiful and a source of prestige, was also make-work, as good as, or better than weaving for keeping nubile girls and the women who supervised them, out of trouble. Ethnographic observation confirms a symbolic association between embroidery and sexual restraint. That its principle "function" and hence "cause" was to underwrite female purity in a tumultuous age of change is another matter, however. For this conclusion overlooks the considerable and fascinating evidence that, far from being make-work, "beds" were a form of stored wealth that families could fall back on in emergencies. Girls who produced them took great care to duplicate standardized design sequences, and to prepare several pieces that, although they might be displayed, were destined for linen chests and not for use.

We have noted that, until quite late in the twentieth century, the long-run viability of Sicilian families and their defense against proletarianization necessitated possession of mobile wealth as well as productive resources, so much so that the marriage exchange system gave equal weight to both. Moreover, gold, silver, and precious silk became less accessible to peasants and artisans in the course of the 1800s, while modern forms of insurance and security would not become a reality in Sicily until the 1950s and 1960s. Dedication to embroidery was, in the long sweep of things, an "interim arrangement." Not only did it evolve naturally out of the earlier domestic role of women, and descend with equal ease from the consumption styles of the rich, but its development also conformed to a pattern for which history has many parallels: the pattern of creating value through intensification of labor, when control over rare and desired things declines. If the wealth thus created (from whole cloth, as it were), was inferior to more liquid forms such as gold, this is somewhat beside the point. For how many choices were there within the means of Sicilian peasants and artisans in the late nineteenth century?

To focus on trousseau as treasure is not to abandon the understanding that embroidery was an important status symbol, nor does such an emphasis contradict its association with chastity and purity. It does, however, suggest that symbols which are also material goods may be multifunctional. Historically, the industrial revolution and the capitalist world system that so rapidly advanced and diffused it, drove a wedge between status goods and valuables—a wedge that was previously unrealized. For in the past, most of the "things" that people, regardless of class position, were pleased to own and display were also potentially convertible, whereas today it is a proportionally ever smaller elite that enjoys the security of ornamenting its domestic surroundings with negotiable treasures (actual houses being at best a partial exception). Yet social scientists, themselves products of an industrial age, attribute to past status goods the same one-dimensional quality that characterizes such goods today—the quality of communicating and celebrating social position. And this, I think, leads to other oversimplifications: exaggerating the distinctions between goods produced for use and goods produced for exhange, and between prestige goods and necessities. Much of today's vocabulary in the social sciences in fact represents these categories not only as mutually exclusive, but as opposites, just as it encourages us to oppose domestic and public spheres of economic activity as women's and men's work, respectively.

If we can generalize from this case study, until very recently items of trousseau were produced simultaneously for use and potential exchange; their content was at once ornamental and, when stored for emergency conversion, essential. The women who made and owned them, although they usually had little or no land, nevertheless contributed a critical resource to household viability; households as manufactories of cloth, which had exchange potential, were not wholly private domains. In each case, dichotomous categories are blurred and new kinds of relationship made apparent. We begin to see, for example, that the process of status emulation or filtering down of elite behavior was not just a matter of slavish imitation; it was at the same time a way for ordinary people to acquire goods that, should they ever have to be exchanged, would find ready takers because of their resemblance to elite goods whose spheres of exchange were worldwide.

In addition, we see that a cultural emphasis on sex segregation and female seclusion served both the symbolic end of demonstrating women's purity and the practical end of tying their labor down to looms and needles from which came treasures as well as decencies and clothes. Such observations prompt a reconsideration of persistent problems—for example, identifying the conditions that brought about the confinement of women to a domestic arena, and establishing the significance of dowry even when it contained no land.

They also influence the way we look at the present. In Sicily today, less cloth is embroidered and stored against a rainy day. Nor has *biancheria* retained its efficacy as a symbol of status, a prestigious gift, an object for display, having steadily lost ground to mass-produced consumer goods such as digital watches and ceramic wall tiles. Indeed, consumer goods now dominate wedding gifts and trousseaux. At first one wonders what role embroidery machines for home and factory have played in this transition. Early machines of this type appeared in Alsace before the end of the nineteenth century, but Lefébure, writing in the 1880s, argued that their impact on artistic handicrafts would only be temporary because "well-cared for handworks have . . . always been, and presumably always will be, wanted [Lefébure 1888:163]."

Today a few women in Villamaura produce embroideries for sale on home machines but I do not think hand-embroidering has declined because of this competition. Its decline seems related to a substantial reallocation of women's time away from the needle arts and towards education and wage-earning occupations. Local markets for machine embroideries have grown as a result, and one begins to see a new interest in the kinds of craft that fill American magazines for homemakers: "Use Embroidery's Laziest Stitch to Style Up Your Table Settings," "Big, Bold Stitches," and so on.

In 1951, half as many girls as boys attended middle school in Villamaura, while only 48 of the 125 students completing secondary school were girls. In 1971, girls accounted for 46% of the *scuola media* diplomas, 49% of high school diplomas; there were also 15 young women with college degrees. Although education is no more a guarantee of employability in Sicily than it is in the United States, it has clearly taken the place of embroidered trousseau: In the eyes of most parents, it makes their daughters more marriageable than a hundred beds. It also makes women's contribution to the establishment of new households less different from men's than was true in the past—which is symptomatic of an overall erosion of a once thoroughgoing division of labor by sex. Thus, although some women still embroider, they do so as outworkers for merchants who introduce their handwork into a world market for tourist and "ethnic" wares.[13] Many other women have entered into commerce as small shopkeepers, or into bureaucracies as secretaries, and a growing number work beside men in agriculture. Their income, small as it is in relation to men's, helps underwrite the purchase of consumer goods.

What seems remarkable about all these changes is that they have occurred without much ado, and in a period of relative calm. Yet they constitute a reorientation of established cultural patterns that is far more dramatic than the shift from weaving to embroidery, which occurred in the context of capitalist penetration, severe depression, failed revolution, and mass migration at the end of the nineteenth century. Clearly there are lessons here about folk cul-

[13] Recent accounts of this process suggest a continuum from situations where embroidery for the tourist market is occasional, and intended only to meet the most pressing needs for cash (Hirschfeld 1977), to situations where commercialization has transformed the activity into a cottage industry (Waterbury and Turkenic 1978). In Sicily today, needlework appears to fall closer to the latter than to the former condition.

Regarding the thorough-going sex segregation of the past, there were always exceptions. Chapman, for example, notes that "occasionally a man will boast proficiency in some feminine task. . . . The men who go to prison sometimes learn weaving and embroidery, and their handiwork is displayed with pride when they send it home [1971:33]."

ture. It would seem that, even though economic and demographic pressures shake little traditions loose from their moorings and bring about alterations in their content, people do not necessarily abandon them unless or until the externally supported institutional matrix undergoes considerable expansion. In this particular case, at least, a wide range of suprafamilial institutions—for the most part creatures of the postwar state—now gives Sicilians the security they need to relax their dedication to cultural codes previously associated with the accumulation of treasure in family treasure chests.

This is not to imply, however, that public institutions work better to cushion crises than items of trousseau. Obviously more efficient, and less humiliating as a last resort, they are also much farther from home. So today, in Sicily, we find adult women, wives, and mothers, coping with application forms, sitting in offices, and demonstrating in the streets. Ironically, the time available for these means of pressing a faceless bureaucracy to respond to personal need is time gained from supervising their daughters' handwork and keeping up embroideries of their own.

References

Ames, D. W.
1955 The use of a transitional cloth-money token among the Wolof. *American Anthropologist 57:*1016–1024.

Anonymous
1921 People and pledges that come to pawnbrokers. *Literary Digest 69:*48–50.

Balsamo, P.
1845 *Memorie inedite di pubblica economia ed agricoltura.* Vol. I. Palermo: Antonio Muratori.

Bennetti-Ventura, C.
1911 *Trine e donne siciliane.* Milano: Ulrico Hoepli.

Campbell, J. K.
1964 *Honour, family and patronage; a study of institutions and moral values in a Greek mountain community.* Oxford: Clarendon Press.

Chapman, C. G.
1971 *Milocca: A Sicilian village.* Cambridge: Schenkman.

Chojnacki, S.
1975 Dowries and kinsmen in early Venice. *Journal of Interdisciplinary History 4:*571–600.

Cocchiara, G.
1957 *Il folklore siciliano.* Vol. I. *La vita del popolo siciliano.* Palermo: S. F. Flaccovio.

Cole, D. P.
1975 *Nomads of the nomads; The Al Murrah bedouin of the empty quarter.* Chicago: Aldine.

Davis, J.
1973 *Land and family in Pisticci.* London: The Athlone Press.
1977 *People of the Mediterranean: An essay in comparative social anthropology.* London: Routledge and Kegan Paul.

de Vries, J.
1975 Peasant demand patterns and economic development, 1550–1750. In *European Peasants and Their Markets* (W. N. Parker and E. L. Jones, Eds.). Princeton: Princeton University Press.

Dolby, A.
1868 *Church vestments; their origin, use and ornament, practically illustrated.* London: Chapman and Hall.

Elias, N.
1978 *The civilizing process; the history of manners.* New York: Urizen Books. (Originally published, 1939.)

Enciclopedia Italiana di Scienze, Lettere ed Arti.
1949 Istituto della Enciclopedia Italiana (Istituto Poligrafico dello Stato).

Eversley, D. E. C.
1967 The home market and economic growth in England, 1750–80. In *Land, labour and population in the Industrial Revolution* (E. L. Jones and G. E. Mingay, Eds.). London: Edward Arnold.

Fagone, V., Ed.
1966 *Arte popolare e artigianato in Sicilia; repertorio dell'artigianato siciliano.* Caltanissetta/Roma: Salvatore Sciascia.

Fél, E., and T. Hofer
1969 *Proper peasants; traditional life in a Hungarian village.* Chicago: Aldine.

Friedl, E.
1967 The position of women: Appearance and reality. *Anthropological Quarterly 40:*97–109.

Gabaccia, D.
1979 Houses and people; Sicilians in Sicily and New York. Unpublished dissertation. Ann Arbor: University of Michigan.

Giacone, G.
1932 *Zabut; notizie storiche del Castello di Zabut e suo contiguo casale—oggi comune di Sicilia.* Sciacca: Guadagna.

Giuffrida, R.
1978 I problemi della circolazione monetaria siciliana dalla fine del settecento alla prima meta dell'ottocento. In *Storia della Sicilia.* Vol. VII. Societa Editrice Storia di Napoli e della Sicilia.

Gömül, M.
n.d. *Turkish embroideries, XVI–XIX centuries.* Istanbul: Touring and Automobile Club of Turkey.

Harte, N. B.
1973 The rise of protection and the English linen trade, 1690–1790. In *Textile history and economic history; essays in honour of Miss Julia de Lacy Mann* (N. B. Harte and K. G. Ponting, Eds.) Manchester, England: Manchester University Press.

Herskovits, M. J.
1962 Preface. In *Markets in Africa* (P. Bohannan and G. Dalton, Eds.). Evanston: Northwestern University Press.

Hirschfeld, L. A.
1977 Cuna aesthetics: A quantitative analysis. *Ethnology 16:*147–166.

Hughes, D. O.
1978 From bride price to dowry in Mediterranean Europe. *Journal of Family History 3:*262–297.

John, A. H.
1965 Agricultural productivity and economic growth in England, 1700–1760. *Journal of Economic History 25*:19–34.

Johnston, P.
1967 *The Byzantine tradition in church embroidery.* London: Alec Tiranti.

Krsteva, A.
1975 *Macedonian folk embroidery.* Skopje: Institute of Folklore.

Lefébure, E.
1888 *Embroidery and lace; their manufacture and history from the remotest antiquity.* London: H. Grevel.

Leone, S.
1978 Costumi e vita sociale. In *Storia della Sicilia.* Vol. VII. Società Editrice Storia di Napoli e della Sicilia.
Levi-Pisetzky, R.
1964–1969 *Storia del costume in Italia.* 5 Vols. Milano: Istituto Editoriale Italiano.
Mack Smith, D.
1968 *A history of Sicily; modern Sicily after 1715.* London: Chatto and Windus.
Namavati, J. N., M. P. Vora, and M. A. Dhaky
1966 *The embroidery and beadwork of Kutch and Saurashtra.* Baroda: Department of Archaeology, Gujurat State, India.
Panzini, A.
1956 *Dizionario moderno delle parole che non si trovano nei dizionari comuni* (9th ed.). Milano: Ulrico Hoepli.
Pitkin, D. S.
1960 Marital property considerations among peasants. *Anthropological Quarterly 33:*33–39.
Pitrè, G.
1969 *La famiglia, la casa, la vita del popolo siciliano.* Bologna: Forni.
1939 *Usi e costumi, credenze e pregiudizi del popolo siciliano.* Vol. II. Firenze: G. Barbera.
Price, R. and S. Price
1966 Noviazgo in an Andalusian Pueblo. *Southwestern Journal of Anthropology 22:*302–322.
Ricci, E.
1958 *Ricami Italiani, antichi e moderni.* Firenze: Felice le Monnier.
Salomone-Marino, S.
1879/1968 *Costumi e usanze dei contadini di sicilia, a cura di Aurelio Rigoli.* Palermo: Andò.
1876 Le pompe nuziali e il corredo delle donne siciliane ne'secoli XIV, XV e XVI. In *Archivio Storico Siciliano* 7. Pp. 209ff.
Schneider, P.
1978 Class formation and material culture in nineteenth century Sicily. Paper presented at the annual meeting of the American Anthropological Association, Los Angeles.
Schneider, P., and J. Schneider
1976 *Culture and political economy in Western Sicily.* New York: Academic Press.
Schuette, M. and S. Müller-Christensen
1964 German and Italian embroidery of the Middle Ages. *Craft Horizons 24*(6): 23–27, 50–51.
Sereni, E.
1968 *Il capitalismo nelle campagne (1860–1900).* Torino: Piccolo Biblioteca Einaudi.
Silverman, S.
1975 *Three bells of civilization; the life of an Italian hill town.* New York: Columbia University Press.
Sonnino, S.
1925 *I contadini in Sicilia.* Firenze: Vallecchi.
Stapley, M.
1924 *Popular weaving and embroidery in Spain.* New York: William Helburn.
Undi, M.
n.d. *Hungarian fancy needlework and weaving: the history of Hungarian decorative embroideries and weavings, from the time of the occupation of Hungary by the Magyars until today.* Budapest: Published by the Author.
Wace, A. J. B.
1935 *Mediterranean and Near Eastern embroideries,* from the collection of Mrs. F. H. Cook. Vol. I. (text). London: Halton.
1948 Weaving or embroidery? *American Journal of Archaeology 52:*51–55.
Waterbury, R. and C. Turkenic
1978 Embroidery for tourists: The spontaneous evolution of a putting-out system in a Mexican peasant community. Paper presented at the annual meeting of the American Anthropological Association, Los Angeles.

Wheeler, C
1921 *The development of embroidery in America.* New York: Harper and Brothers.
Whyte, W. F.
1944 Sicilian peasant society. *American Anthropologist* 46:65–74.
Yang, L.
1952 *Money and credit in China: a short history.* Cambridge: Harvard University Press.

IV

THEORY AND PRACTICAL REASON

12 Rethinking Leach's Structural Analysis of Color and Instructional Categories in Traffic Control Signals[1]

FREDERICK C. GAMST

Introduction

In this chapter I present a critique of Edmund Leach's (1970:15–32) structural analysis of color and related instructional categories in the domain of the English-speaking peoples' traffic-control devices for land (surface) transportation—that is, railway signals and the highway signals that have developed from them.[2] Briefly, Leach treats the use of the colors red–yellow–green in ordering the traffic control signal instructions stop–caution–go as an example of culture patterned after nature. The purpose of Leach's analysis is to clarify the sometimes obtuse and baroque methodology of Claude Lévi-Strauss, the noted French ethnologist, whose ideas are the subject of Leach's book. Although Leach succeeds in explaining Lévi-Strauss' method clearly and lucidly, without recourse to exotic and esoteric ethnographic data and arcane symbolism, his analysis is not supported by the facts of railway and highway color signals. In short, Leach "is insufficiently

[1] This chapter is reproduced with minor changes from the *American Ethnologist*, 1975, Vol. 2:271–296, with the permission of the author and of the American Anthropological Association.

[2] The principal ideas in this article were stimulated by experiences during 6½ years in railroad engine (locomotive) service and by conversations with "old timers." I am grateful to my former co-workers and to the National Science Foundation (for Grant GS 3040) and the National Institute of Mental Health (for Grant MH 21783) for their support of my current industrial ethnological fieldwork among railroaders. The financial support from the two agencies also enabled me to conduct documentary research, part of which is used in this chapter. I thank David A. Schum for useful discussion of psychological and engineering aspects of color and color coding, and I thank Stephen A. Tyler for helpful criticism of this chapter, although I am solely responsible for its contents.

BEYOND THE MYTHS OF CULTURE
Essays in Cultural Materialism

ISBN 0-12-598180-5

critical of his source material,'' which is a criticism he makes of Lévi-Strauss in his summary of the work of the French structuralist (1970:12).

Recently I have been making an ethnological study of modern American industry in order to test ethnological method and theory in our own readily accessible cultural setting. I especially wanted to test both structural–functionalist and structuralist models. This chapter is a result of my work with the latter and reflects my interest in the relationship between analysis and empirical data. I believe that if the general models generated by the practitioners of the science of man are valid, then they are valid for all men.

As Leach puts it, ''Thus, in investigating the elementary structures of cultural phenomena, we are also making discoveries about the nature of man—facts which are true of you and me as well as of naked savages of Central Brazil [1970:21].''

The railway and highway signals for traffic control considered by Leach are either *fixed,* permanently mounted, or *nonfixed,* handheld or vehicle mounted. Illuminated signals combine pigmented surfaces with other modes of coding. Therefore, it is necessary to consider the physical properties of color before discussing Leach's analysis of the signals. The sections which follow my summary of Leach's argument are concerned with the diachronic and synchronic development of railway signals and the historic relationship between them and highway signals. This evidence is then examined in structuralist terms (cf. Leach 1970:20).

The Continua of Color

The stimulus of color vision is electromagnetic waves known as visible light that occupy a small fraction of the continuum of electromagnetic radiation extending from cosmic rays, with a wavelength measurable in trillionths and billionths of an inch, through radio waves, with a length measurable in units ranging from feet to miles. The radiant energy of visible light has a wavelength varying from 16 to 32 millionths of an inch. This wavelength is customarily measured in millimicrons (mμ) or one-billionths of a meter. The visible spectrum of light has an approximate range from 380 mμ to 770 mμ (Judd 1952:24).

''Color'' exists only in the mind of the human viewer and is an apparent phenomenon. An interaction between radiant energy and the variable physiological processes of human visual sensation in the eye and the nervous system results in a reaction that is culturally patterned and differentiated. This reaction is the delimiting and, often, the naming of color categories for color space, that is, the fixing of coordinates for the color space resulting from stimulation of the retina by various parts of the spectrum of radiation. This radiation has three physical characteristics: (*a*) photometric magnitude or

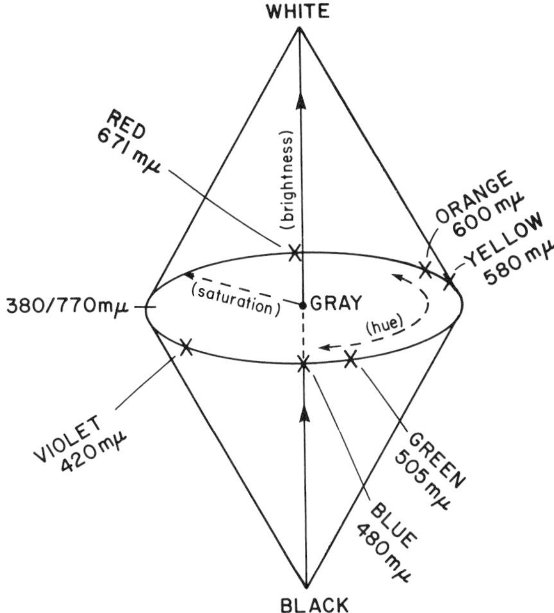

FIGURE 12.1 *A three-dimensional model of a double-color cone, depicting perception of all colors in their three attributions of brightness, hue, and saturation.*

luminance; (*b*) dominant wavelength; and (*c*) purity of wavelength. These characteristics correspond to three basic attributions (or color coordinates) of visual sensation: (*a*) brightness (or lightness or value); (*b*) hue (or shade); and (*c*) saturation (or chroma). (For additional information, see Munsell 1929; Davidson 1951; Conover 1958; Halsey 1959; Burnham *et al.* 1963; Billmeyer and Saltzman 1966:2–8, 15–17; Cornsweet 1970; Semple *et al.* 1971:103–146; Hickerson 1971; Reynolds *et al.* 1972; Bornstein 1973; Conklin 1973.) Within the three-dimensional color space delimited by the three color coordinates (see Figure 12.1) exist innumerable discriminable colors. Generally, people organize color experiences in accord with the three principal coordinates, even though they do not always label them.

Actually, the study of domains that include color is based upon variables more complex than those we have just outlined in this section. Colors have other modes of appearance besides the surface mode of the Munsell color chips and the color charts used by many investigators in their research into color perception and cognition. Since the now classic work of Katz (1935) in his *The World of Colour,* we have been made aware of the multiple "modes of color appearance." More recent work (Committee on Colorimetry of the Optical Society 1953) reduces Katz's 11 modes to 5. It has proved more useful to employ a small number of general modes for taxonomically describing color appearances (Beck 1972:17).

The five modes may be summarized as follows (cf. Beck 1972:16–32):

1. *Object mode* is subdivided into (*a*) *surface mode* and (*b*) *volume mode.* The former involves color as an attribute of a visually "hard" surface such as a highway stop sign illuminated in natural or artificial light. The latter involves perception of colors that fill a definite tridimensional illuminated space. For example, the color of red glass or a red liquid is perceived both in and behind the surface, as is the color of a signal smoke projecting into the air. Katz's mode of mirrored (*gespiegelte*) colors are collapsed into the volume of object mode.

2. *Illumination mode* is subdivided into (*a*) *illuminant mode* and (*b*) *illumination of empty space mode.* Both are perceived as properties of illumination. The former is the glow emanating from a light source, such as a signal lamp, with light coming from behind the surface. In the latter mode, colors are perceived as an attribute of empty space, for example the red empty space, illuminated by red lamps, of the control room of a warship. (The red light is used here for practical reasons.) Another example is the violet shafts of light projected into the night sky over the Hollywood Bowl in Los Angeles on performance nights to warn away aircraft.

3. *Film mode* is the fifth taxon. It occurs when all information concerning physical composition and location of an object has been eliminated. In this mode, a uniform luminance and chromaticity obtains.

All five modes have the three basic attributes or color coordinates of hue, brightness, and saturation. Each of the modes also has most of the following additional attributes: lightness, duration, size, shape, location, texture, glossiness (luster, transparency, fluctuation, insistence, pronouncedness, and fluorescence (see Beck 1972 for discussion of these). Research on color categories necessarily involves the question: which categories for which attributes of which modes? A subject may have different responses to the same hue

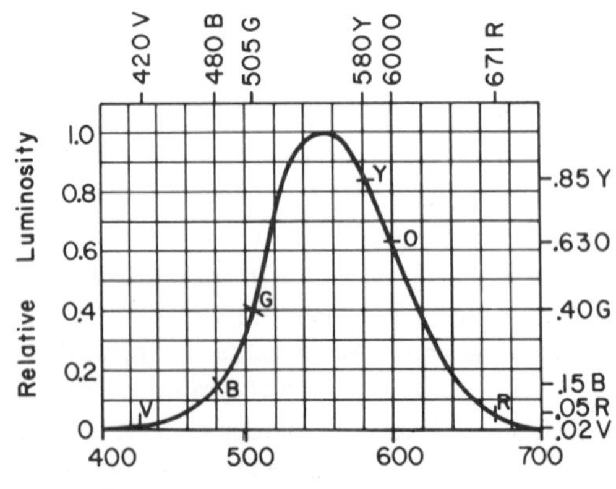

FIGURE 12.2. *Luminosity of colors on a scale from 0 to 1.0 (adapted from Judd 1952:9).*

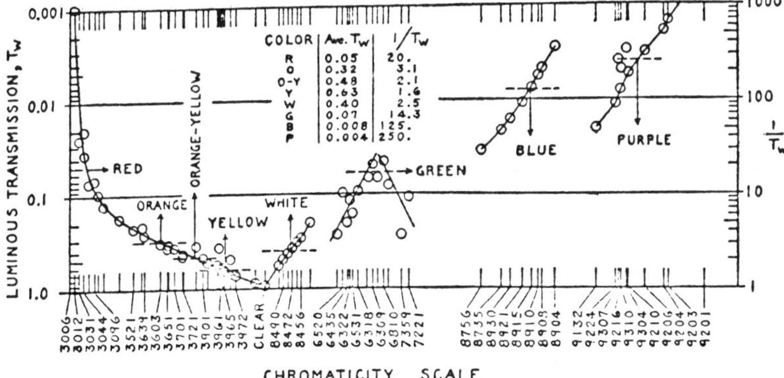

FIGURE 12.3. *Logarithmic scale representation of variation in luminous transmission of the signal lenses named in capital letters and noted by code number along the bottom of the figure (McNicholas 1936:965). (See also Gibson and Haupt 1939:644–646.) Full luminosity is 1.0. The color "W" refers to a LUNAR WHITE; the original WHITE of railroad signals is around 0.85 ± .10.*[6]

in different modes and be affected by various of the other 14 attributes of color.

In the model in Figure 12.1, grays range along the achromatic central axis from black through white. (Black is the absence or absorption of all light rays, and white is a combination of all colors.) Gray is perceived, and therefore represented here, as zero-saturation, having no hue. Brightness is depicted as varying, with distance above or below the circular central base plane of our model, between polar black and white. Saturation and hue are chromatic attributes. Saturation is represented by distance from the black–white axis, and hue to degree of removal from other wavelengths on the color circle.

Luminosity of pigmented surfaces is the brightness with which a color appears to the eye compared to a white surface illuminated at the same time by the same "white" light. Luminosity of colored lights is the brightness of a light compared to "natural white" light. The curve of the graph in Figure 12.2 shows ocular cone vision in daylight and refers only to the black-white attribute of vision. Figure 12.3 shows the luminosity of railroad signal lights.

Green Means Go and Red Means Stop?

In explaining French structuralism, Leach notes that in this manner of exposition, the continua of space and time are shown to be segmented by men into named classes and separate events. Furthermore, the behavior and artifacts produced by culture are segmented and ordered in the manner in which we suppose the products of nature to be so arranged (1970:15–16). Leach then gives a "very simple example" of what he means here (1970:16), an example that is never used by Lévi-Strauss (1970:19).

Leach notes that the color spectrum is a continuum rather than a number of physically discrete colors and that our recognition of colors is largely a result of variations in luminosity from dark to light and wavelength from long to short. The human brain discriminates between "different" colors. The brain's ordering mechanism allows anyone to be taught to regard red as the "opposite" of green (Leach 1970:16–17). "In our own [native English-speaking?] culture we have in fact been taught to make this discrimination, and because of it we find it appropriate to use red and green signals as if they corresponded to plus and minus [1970:17]." A number of such oppositions are made by native English-speakers, in which red is also contrasted with other colors, especially white, black, blue, and yellow. In such paired oppositions, "red is consistently given the same value . . . as a danger sign—hot taps, live electric wires, debit entries in account books, stop signs on roads and railways [1970:17]."[3] By referring to the stop signs, Leach shows he realizes that color coding for land traffic control is not confined solely to illuminants but also comprehends surface colors of objects. Leach next focuses upon the heart of his argument:

> Anyway in our case, with traffic lights on both railways and roads, green means go and red means stop. For many situations this is sufficient. However, if we want to devise a further signal with an intermediate meaning—*about to stop/about to go*—we choose the color yellow. We do this because, in the spectrum, it lies midway between green and red.
>
> In this example the ordering of the colors green–yellow–red is the same as the

---

[3] On the contrary, red may be a standarized signal for safety and rescue, as in air–sea rescue equipment, simply because "a small red area retains its hue at a greater distance than any other color when the background is black or blue-green" (Wulfeck *et al.* 1958:240). In industrial color coding orange as well as red is used to designate danger (Morgan *et al.* 1963:83). Purple is the standard industrial color used to designate danger from radiation. Blue is a standard color code (adapted from long-time railroad practice) warning of the danger of operating or moving equipment (e.g., elevators or boilers) under repair. Hot water taps are sometimes encoded with a red circular disk, not because of danger, but, together with the blue cold water disk, to represent the kind of water obtainable without using words or initials or words from a particular language. Railway stop signs in Anglo North America are not red, but are usually white with the word "STOP" in black, as are the familiar "X" shaped highway signs warning the motorist to "stop, look, and listen" for trains. Although the Highway Color Code in the United States adopted red as the color for stop signs in 1954 (Robinson 1967:27), this coding was not used originally or consistently. The earliest traffic control signs in the United States were blue with white lettering (Eno 1920:10), following the coloring convention on enameled street nameplates. The earliest proposed code, by William P. Eno, a pioneer in highway traffic control, used a black background with yellow lettering on stop, slow, and other traffic signs for the practical reason of providing greatest visibility (Eno 1920:11–13). A variety of this last color coding is still used: "Stop, eight-sided yellow sign with black letters or red with white letters [T.D.P.S. 1965:20]." Therefore, red, although signifying danger in many instances, is not *consistently* given the value of danger. However, my trait list does not invalidate Leach's contention any more than his list validates it. Such invalidation must come from our examination and rethinking of his structural analysis of color coding in signals for traffic control on land.

ordering of the instructions *go-caution-stop;* the color system and the signal system have the same "structure," the one is a transformation of the other [1970:17].

In a number of steps, Leach describes how one arrives at this transformation: (*a*) The color spectrum is a continuum in nature; (*b*) The brain cuts the continuum into segments; (*c*) The brain selects a representation of a binary opposition (plus/minus) and uses "green" and "red" as a binary pair; (*d*) The brain searches for an intermediate position (not plus/not minus) in order to end the discontinuity of the binary opposition. (*e*) It goes back to the continuum in nature and selects yellow as the intermediate signal, because this color is perceived as a segment lying between green and red in nature. (*f*) "Thus the final cultural product—the three-color traffic signal—is a simplified imitation of a phenomenon of nature—the color spectrum—as apprehended by the brain [1970:17–18]." According to Leach, the essence of his entire argument is shown by the diagram which is reproduced in Figure 12.4.

Figure 12.4 presents the so-called Hegelian dialectic of change in the scholastically ubiquitous triadic sequence, in this case of thesis–antithesis–synthesis. This sequence is one of self-transformation resulting from opposing forces in irreconcilable conflict. The transformation is effected through a combining (synthesis) that includes and overcomes the conflicting elements and that results from a particular level of intensity of the conflict.

Leach's diagram is of two superimposed triangles, the usual French structuralist model. The angles of the first triangle are the colors green, yellow, and red—differentiated along two axes: short through long wavelength and low through high luminosity. In the first triangle, the very basis of his analysis, it is clear that Leach is writing about both color stimuli and color categories. His presentation is, of course, not a purely structuralist argument based solely upon formal patterns of the ways in which symbolic elements logically inter-

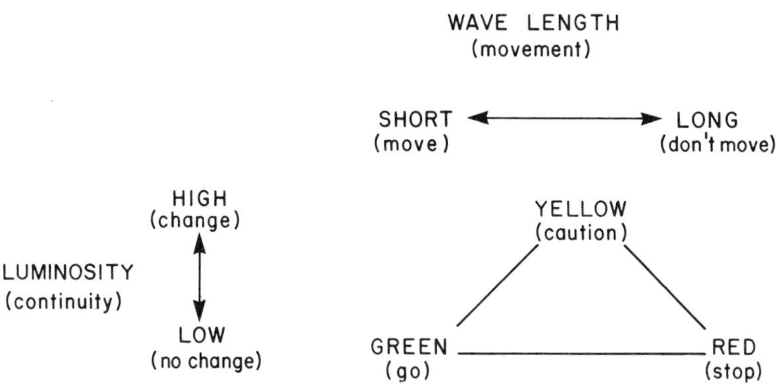

FIGURE 12.4. *Edmund Leach's "Traffic-Signal Color Triangle" (Leach 1970:19).*

relate in a system, without "any concession to naturalism" (cf. Lévi-Strauss 1967:49). Leach does work with phenomena in the physical world. Thus in this instance the structural model is "so phrased as to be open to empirical testing, and should be so tested [cf. Köbben *et al.* 1974:222]."

The angles of the second triangle are three instructions for movement: "*go*—continue in a state of movement; *caution*—prepare to change your state of movement; *stop*—continue in a state of non-movement [Leach 1970:18]." Differentiation in the second triangle is along the two axes of movement–no movement and of change–no change. In superimposing one triangle upon the other, the three colors become signals for the three underlying instructions. The "natural structure" of relations of colors is organized the same as the "logical structure" of relations of the instructions (Leach 1970:18). Here, there is a perspicacious depiction of a focal point of French structuralism, the seeking of examples of transformation of a natural structure perceived by the human brain into an elementary cultural structure, constituting a set of relationships paralleling those found in nature.

Leach concludes his analysis by saying, "the correlation between the members of the two triads are, in this case, more or less predetermined." The equivalences red–yellow–green and stop–caution–go are given, and there is no need to pay attention to possible alternative patterns (1970:19–20). However, he admonishes, "But in the general case, a structural analysis needs to start by setting out *all* the possible permutations and to proceed by examination of the empirical evidence on a comparative basis [1970:20]." I now proceed to examine the empirical evidence and the other extant permutations of colors in the domain of color signals for traffic control on land.

The thesis of the following sections is that no Anglo cultural pattern modeled upon nature exists or existed for a two-signal system in binary opposition of red ("stop") and green ("go"). And when a third color was added to any extant binary system, it was not yellow. By the time technological evolution allowed the addition of a yellow, almost a century had passed since the period of solely two-color systems (if a binary system ever existed at all). Two component red–green and three component red–yellow–green systems are extant only when certain components of the highly complex domain of color signals for traffic control on land are removed from their evolutionary (diachronic) *and* from their structural–functional (synchronic) settings. Furthermore, *even if* red meant only 'stop/danger' (and it does not), my contention that the traffic control signals are not manifestations of culture patterned after nature would still be valid. I will show that this is because in actual systems, the short wave blue and violet signals indicting "stop" negate the structure hypothesized with only one wavelength (long-red) indicating "stop." Actual signal systems are rather random in their structures, within the limits emanating from practical considerations in the material world especially technology. As used in signal communication for land (or maritime)[4] traffic control, color categories do not lend themselves to building a model based upon nature, which incorporates structuralist patterns of relationship.

In the following section I try to show that signal lights on roads do not constitute a domain separate from those used on railroads and that their color coding is not as restricted in its scope or as supportive of his hypothesis as Leach assumes in his writing. Highway traffic signals were not an independent invention in response to the necessity of controlling the burgeoning vehicular traffic on streets in the early 1920s. They were, instead, taken directly from the railroads at a time when railroads had completed the transition from what I call "Signal System III" (which contained, among other things, a red ["stop"], green ["caution"], and white ["go"]) to "Signal System IV" (which contained, among other things, a red ["stop"], yellow ["caution"], and green ["go"]). (See Table 12.1 for Systems I through IV.) Throughout most of the nineteenth and into the beginning of the twentieth century in North America, an actual signal system would include a red ("stop"), an absolute blue ("stop"), frequently a red ("caution"), often a violet ("stop"), sometimes a white or white and green ("stop"), a green ("caution"), and a white ("go"). During the same period in Great Britain, the red ("caution")

---

[4] Another domain not mentioned by Leach is that of visual signals for nautical traffic control. These provide scant support at best for a triad of red ("stop/danger"), yellow ("caution"), and green ("go/safety"), or a dyad of any two of these, and they provide no support for a consistent use of red for "danger/stop" (cf. Prunski 1968). The range of nautical day and night color coding includes the following signal aspects either singly or in myriad different combinations. Lights are red, green, white, yellow, blue, and orange, and pigmented surfaces are red, green, white, black, black and white, and orange and white. Coded shapes of pigmented signals vary from balls, to cones, to double cones, to double frustums of cones. This patterning of pigmented visual codes does not include the several complex codes of multi-colored nautical signal flags (where distress is indicated by a blue and white flag or by one blue and white plus a second blue and white flag having one red stripe [Prunski 1968:199]). A single red light may indicate danger, for a vessel loading or unloading dangerous cargo in inland waters, but a pair of masts each with three vertically arranged red lights may indicate "go/safety," in marking the boundaries of a navigable channel through a stringout (of obstacles) marked along its length by single yellow lights, in inland waters only (Prunski 1968:117). Green signal lights may indicate extreme danger. For example, a minesweeper at work on the high seas (sweeping or exploding armed mines) displays three green lights and a white one (Prunski 1968:112). A vessel trawling on inland seas displays a red and a white light, and on the high seas, a green and a white light (Prunski 1968:105, 107). Finally, the ever present green, starboard side light and red, port side light indicate neither safety nor danger (but, instead, right and left), and vessels may pass on either side of one another. To this we should add the U.S. wind and weather and naval signal flags and lights circa 1914: white (square) flag, "clear or fair"; blue flag, "rain or snow"; white pennant or white light and red light, "westerly winds"; red pennant or red light, "easterly winds"; black pennant over white and black flag, "warmer," and under, "colder weather"; red flag with black square, "storm"; flag with white and blue diagonal lines, "danger"; and red pennant, "reserve speed and meal" (*Webster's New International Dictionary* 1924).

TABLE 12.1
Color Coding in Railroad Signal Systems.[a]

Systems	Codes of operating indications and color aspects
I. Early (1820–1840)	Stop: blue, red, white (black?) Caution: black, red, green Go: white
II. Proliferating (1840–1890/1900)	Stop: red, blue, violet, white, green and white Caution: green, red Go: white
III. Transitional (1890/1900–1920/1925	Stop: red, blue, violet, white, green and white Caution: red, green, yellow (red and green) Go: white, green (violet)
IV. Present (1920/1925–1974)	Stop: red, blue, violet, white, green and white Caution: yellow, red, white-lunar, green-flashing Go: green, white

[a]Major color-indications listed in estimated order of importance and use. Minor color-indications shown in parentheses. A particular signal system actually in operation did not necessarily have all of the major color-indications, especially the less important ones. The above does not include the survivals in train signals noted in a following section.

was about as common as the red ("stop"), and the green ("caution") was very much rarer than in North America.

Highway Signals for Traffic Control

Apparently the first signal lights for control of highway traffic were installed in Detroit and located in the first of the numerous "traffic towers" constructed in cities across the United States, beginning in 1917 with the one in the automotive center (Anonymous 1968:40). In accord with the railroad practice of the period, the tower employed *day signals* in the form of semaphore arms (movable wooden blades, in this case with either the words "stop" or "go" on their faces). As on railroads after sunset, *night signals* were used in addition, in this case red, green, and amber-yellow lights (Anonymous 1968:41–42). The first semiautomatic traffic light mounted on a mast was installed in Houston in 1921 with red and green lenses adapted from railway signals (Stark 1968a:58). In 1922 these traffic lights in Houston were extended to control a series of intersections by means of devices manufactured by a company producing railway equipment.

The first of New York City's traffic light towers was installed in 1919 and was "similar to signal towers on the railroads" (Eno 1920:43). "Ignoring . . . railroad practice as to colors [Signal System IV], amber (yellow) meant 'Go' for Fifth Avenue traffic and 'Stop' for 42nd Street; red stopped all traffic; green meant 'Go' for 42nd Street; 'Stop' for Fifth Avenue [Stark

1968b:48]." Originally, the *red meant traffic goes* on the main route, Fifth Avenue, and *stops* on cross streets (Eno 1920:43). Since the present railroad System IV of color sequence had only recently been introduced at that time, it is not surprising to find experimental highway variations of the System, which, I will show, was itself the result of decades of experimentation, practical consideration, and heated debate. With the genesis of highway signal lights in railroad signaling, it is not surprising that a pioneer American inventor of highway and, later, airway signals was a Baltimore and Ohio Railroad signal engineer, Charles Adler, Jr. (Malcolm 1966).

Highway traffic signal lights, then, do not provide a second independent domain of color and instructional sequences as posited by Leach, but are a development of railway signals, which together with the former comprise one domain of signals for control of land traffic. Before I turn to the first century of the development of this domain, I will make one last examination of highway signals. I will show that color codes of railway signals are more complex than any sequence of just three colors, as are those of highway signals. Actually, color codes of these kinds are arbitrarily created for traffic control devices which may have either colored lights, or pigmented surfaces, or both. Color coding is sometimes reinforced with other visual codes such as brightness, shape, angular inclination, flash rate, size, letters and numbers, and geometric and stylized pictorial symbols (Meister and Sullivan 1969:70–89; Grether and Baker 1972:69–77). More saturated colors can be obtained with lights than with surface pigments, but a greater number of readily distinguishable colors are gained in coding with surface pigments than with lights.

The original United States Highway Sign Code established four colors for traffic devices. Today twelve colors are so established, but not all are in actual use as yet, for example, "brilliant yellow-green" and "buff." The Safety Color Code of the American Standards Association (ASA) overlaps in many areas with the Highway Color Code, for example, ASA orange as well as red means 'danger.' Because we now read the literature of others in order to obtain ideas, it is not surprising that in 1948, the year the Highway Code recognized red for stop signs, orange was recognized as a similar signal color. The red stop sign was not officially adopted until 1954 (still not standard), and the orange pedestrian "WAIT" (equals "STOP") signal light was not adopted until 1961 (Robinson 1967). White (only coincidentally with railroad Systems II and III) is concurrently used as the pedestrian "WALK" (equals "GO") signal light. Flashing blue lights on emergency vehicles mean pull over to the side of the road and *stop,* in a manner similar to and perhaps derived from the very old railway blue "stop/danger" signal. Of course, contradictions exist. In Washington, D.C., for example, the "WALK" signal light may be either white or red.

Carlton Robinson sums up his review of color coding in highway traffic devices in 1967 by saying, "in the course of 40 years we have arrived at the present . . . not entirely consistent, use of seven colors in traffic control [1967:27]." Consistency is something we find even less of in the much older, more differentially specialized traffic control devices on railways; however, the point just made is that codes of highway signal lights, whether inconsistent or not, are far more complex than just red–yellow–green. As with railway signals, a cognitive structural code for highway signals is readily apparent only when we dismiss this complexity—and when we dismiss the antecedents of highway signals, a subject to which I now turn.

Railway Signals for Traffic Control

THE BACKGROUND TO RAILWAY COLOR SIGNALS

Safe and efficient railroad operations depend upon a large number of interrelated signal systems in which symbols of different kinds are used to communicate information, sometimes of a highly complex nature. Briefly, among the interrelated signal systems are overlapping *hand, lantern,* and *flag* signals in which these devices are used to trace combinations of points, arcs, and straight lines in the air to transmit innumerable pieces of information. *Locomotive whistle* and *communicating* (air whistle inside of locomotive cab) *signals* use many combinations of long and short whistles. The *locomotive bell* and explosive rail-mounted caps known as *torpedoes* each give only one signal. Verbal signals are invariably in the terse argot and technical terminology of "rails" (railroaders) (cf. Kemnitzer 1973). *Fusees* are flares; they are the technically most primitive of the color light signals we shall discuss. *Train signals* are colored lights, flags, or reflectors on engines and the rear of trains. *Cab signals* are colored or positioned lights in the locomotive cab governing movement of a train and used in conjunction with fixed block or interlocking signals. *Fixed signals* are the largest and most diverse class of railway signals. These, to which I will devote much attention, include: *switch* attached colored lights and colored metal targets, indicating the position of a track switch; *train order* colored lights with or without targets or semaphore arms, indicating any need to slow or to stop for taking delivery of written train orders governing progress of the train; *block* and *interlocking* signals using colored lights, semaphore arms, positions of lights, or combination of these to time–space and to control the speed of rail traffic in following and opposing movements along blocks (sections of track) or to control movement at crossings and junctions of two or more tracks with signals interlocked to prevent colliding movements; and *"boards,"* colored, lettered, and numbered signs used to control traffic: for example, "STOP," "YARD LIMIT," "JUNCTION," "DRAWBRIDGE," "RAILROAD CROSSING," and so forth. Railway colored light symbols used in the signals noted above are saturated spectral hues produced by light sources (electric incandescent filament or oil flame) behind glass filters (lenses).

BEGINNINGS OF RAILWAY COLOR SIGNALS WITH EARLY SYSTEM I

An argument could be made that black was the original, natural stop color on railways. In the 1820s the private Middleton Colliery Railway had a "telegraph," that is, a common eighteenth-century signaling device consisting of a wooden armed semaphore on a mast. This telegraph "is probably the first railway [fixed] signal in the world [Marshall 1971:38]." The railway was on an incline, and its strings of coal cars were raised and lowered to and from the mine at the apex and the coal ships moored along the shore at the bottom terminal by means of a *stationary steam engine* (precursor to the *locomotive steam engine*). The telegraph aided in the traffic control on this line. Its signal indicator was a "Black board" (Marshall 1971:39), perhaps because this color is strongly associated with danger in Anglo cognition.[5] Or, perhaps black was used because a dark arm contrasted with the daytime horizon, or, most likely, because equipment not already blackened with coal grime at a colliery is painted black, a practice that continues to this very day.

Formed in 1824, the first common carrier (British: public) railway opened in 1830 as the Liverpool and Manchester, an event which marked the advent of modern railroading. Its block and train signals were described in the *Railway Companion* in 1833 (Blythe 1951:26–27) as follows. Hand signals of the station agent indicated whether the block of track ahead was clear or occupied. To stop a train to pick up passengers, the agent hoisted a red flag by day and displayed a swinging (white) lamp at night. Train signals displayed at the rear of a train at night were either a blue or a red light. The red light was

[5] The reader may well ask: "Is red not associated with danger and violence in the English language?" The question, if answered fully, would be the subject of a paper different from the present one. Briefly, using the *Oxford English Dictionary* (1971), the most thorough reference on the English lexicon with examples even drawn from Anglo-Saxon, a survey of the entries under red, yellow, green, blue, violet, purple, black, and white reveals the following: (*a*) Red, which in English grades into the browns and yellows (brick red, chestnut bay), has associations of blood, fire, flowers (poppy, rose), ripe fruits (from which come the frequent similies of these four), lightning, sky, sun, earth, soil, natural healthy color of people (lips, cheeks), gold, shame (to blush with), anger, and a flag or sign of battle or defiance. To which we might add, the British maritime white ensign is the flag of warships and the red ensign of merchantmen. (Before 1864 these warships had white, or blue, or red ensigns according to the color of their squadron.) Red is also the banner of socialist change, but black is the banner and general color of deadly and destructive, socially chaotic anarchy (e.g., black hand societies). For these "cognitive" reasons a firm marketing insecticide in Anglo North America uses "Black Flag" for its trade name. Black also is a banner of Anglo piracy and of executions aboard a ship. Yellow has long been the flag of infectious disease and quarantine. It is difficult to imagine anything more deadly or dangerous than an area marked by a yellow flag in the time before modern scientific medicine developed. White, of course, is the flag of truce and safety. We should also note the following from the first edition of *Webster's New International Dictionary* (1924): red-letter day, a holy day marked in the calendar with red letters, "hence, a day that is fortunate, specially happy, or memorable"; red flag "also commonly used as the sign of an auction sale"; red-handed, caught in a crime with bloody hands; red land, "arable land"; red lane, the throat; red message, "A telegraphic message to be sent at night. It is copied on a blank printed in red ink." (*b*) Yellow is associated with cowar-

shown when a train was in motion, thus cautioning, but not stopping, a following train. When a train stopped, a blue light was displayed, thereby warning a following train of potential danger and causing it to stop. Thus the ubiquitous blue ("stop-danger") light of railroading and other industries was present from the beginning. Furthermore, red meant 'caution' as it does on many North American railroads to this very day and as it indicated in British distant (pointed blade) semaphore signals until it was abolished by statute, for practical reasons, in 1925 (Blythe 1951:111). I shall deal with the red flag at greater length next. White flags and lights have been used to indicate "stop" to pick up passengers until the present time (C. & O. 1958:23; C. M. St. P. & P. and others 1959:38).

By 1839, the Liverpool and Manchester had officially designated red flags and lights to mean "stop," but it also had a blue stop flag. A stationary white light meant "all is right," and an infrequently used green light meant slow and cautious movement, as did a black flag (Whishaw 1842:207). The black flag, which was in common use to slow trains over track under repair or in need of repair, would seem a "natural" color to indicate potential danger to Anglos. However, practical material considerations precluded its wider adoption and continuation in signal codes. A black flag or pigmented surface used during the day could not be transformed after dark into a night signal—a black light.

PROLIFERATION OF RAILWAY COLOR SIGNALING IN SIGNAL SYSTEM II

Devices for fixed block and interlocking signals were developed into their present forms on the pioneering British railways of the early 1840s. These were day signals, without lights, usually employing semaphore arms or disks,

---

dice, meanness, unworthiness (Yellow dog), and jealousy. (*c*) Green is also associated with jealousy and further signifies gullible, unripe, immature, and untrained. (*d*) Blue, like red, is highly varied in its associations: an omen of death, indicating the presence of devils or ghosts, constancy ("true blue"), sterling, genuine, affected with fear or discomfort or anxiety, dismayed, dismal, depressed, the color of servants' and paupers' clothing—the symbol of ignominy (Blue-gown), in the case of imprisioned whores but it also refers to learned women (Blue-stocking), the color of plagues and things hurtful (Blue devil), and what is indecent and obscene. (*e*) The early purple was a crimson and the color of royalty, but also for mourning and penitence, and often denoted bloody or blood stained. (*f*) Violet (the color of the flower) has no rich associations (perhaps because it may have been lumped with blue). (*g*) Black has entirely negative associations: somber, gloomy, dirty, foul, horrible, wicked, or a sign of disgrace, censure, or liability to punishment. (*h*) White has various associations: pure, spotless, innocent, free of evil, favorable, precious, beloved, but it is also a sign of mourning and of being a dastard or coward (White-livered).

What can be concluded from all this and Note 4? The answer for red, blue, and white is "almost anything one likes," although it could be said that multi-wavelength white—rather than green—would be "naturally" selected for the safety-go signal, as was, in fact, the case. Finally, a recent study indicates "that the emotional associations usually found with 'color' do not seem to be due primarily to the actual hue, or light wavelength involved, but to the degree of saturation and brightness [D'Andrade and Egan 1974:62]."

both painted vermillion-red, or red flags stretched upon a rectangular frame. According to an editorial (Anonymous 1878:477–479) in *The Railroad Gazette,* the technical journal of North American railroading, the semaphore arm at first had only one *signal aspect* (appearance, such as color or position). At right angles (90°) to the vertical trackside signal mast, the *signal indication* (meaning of a signal aspect) was "stop." This positioning of the semaphore "seems to conform to the natural gestures which we employ in trying to arrest attention or to induce anyone to stop" (Anonymous 1878:477–478). The natural impulse is simply to extend one's arm from the body and thus make a gesture resembling the semaphore raised to the stop position. The "proceed" (railroad term approximating "go") indication was given by dropping the semaphore (to 180°) so that the arm was hidden by the mast. This was simply the absence of the signal. As rail traffic and signaling developed, at times, a lower quadrant diagonal aspect (135°) was used as an "approach" (railroad: "caution") signal (Anonymous 1878:477–478). Similarly, the disk or framed flag was displayed full face for a stop indication and tilted until parallel to the ground or turned until parallel to the track and thereby made "absent" for 'proceed.'

Over the years, the 90° horizontal semaphore *usually* meant "stop," but, at times, could mean "proceed with caution" (C.C.C. & St. L. 1901:92; D.L. & W. 1900:10). After the turn of the century, 'approach' only rarely remained at its lower diagonal (135°) position (U.P. 1954:98–99, 100–101; N.Y., N.H. & H. 1956:120; A.T.S.F. 1948:110) and more commonly took the upper diagonal (45°) position. 'Proceed' aspects with a lower 135° or else a totally vertical and parallel to the mast 0° position both became common, sometimes on the same railroad (N.Y., N.H. & H. 1956:119–120). Thus even the archetype block and interlocking signal, the semaphore, does not display any discernible underlying cognitive structure but is merely the result, after its quite simple beginnings, of experimentation, often to avert the problems of falling and jamming arms. *No matter which of its aspects were displayed, the arm's color was, of course, always red.*

The reason for the red hue of the semaphore arm, according to Henry Johnson, a signal specialist of the nineteenth century, was the following: "The early color selected for semaphore blades was vermillion, because it was considered to contrast best with objects adjacent to signals, and had a more startling effect on the eye than any other color [1894:879]." This is the same reason given by present day experimental researchers for the use of a red as the standardized signal for safety in air–sea rescue (cf. Note 3). (Of interest, but outside of the scope of our discussion, is the fact that the German railroads also painted semaphore and other signals in many combinations of red and white, or in plain red; "the color used for them being chosen with sole reference to making the signals clearly visible over reasonably long distances [Anonymous 1893:285–286].") The old Army signaling flags employed for sending coded messages—the kind used in Boy and Girl Scouts—are red with a central white square, not to indicate danger, but for visibility. The same may be said for the red and white identification flags of the hierarchically related units of the United States Army. As noted by Rudolf Andres, a specialist in the study of color contrasts, "Red is one of the few colors which occurs extremely seldom as a background in nature [1973]." The distinctiveness of red, then, is as reasonable a cause for its *sometime* use to indicate "stop" as is an invoking of psychically deeply rooted associations with danger–violence–blood.

Just as the face of a semaphore arm is red for its visibility, the back of the arm is white for the stated purpose of making it invisible to a train coming from the opposite direction. In the past, it was recognized that red was *ordinarily* the most visible and the best color for semaphore arms; however, should a signal's background be a red brick building, then "a black signal arm . . . would be in order [Anonymous 1893:185–186]." Even more interesting for our investigation, Henry Johnson continues, "For the same reasons the red light was selected to indicate 'stop, possible danger ahead' [1894:879]." Finally, in a leading book on human engineering and equipment design, four "good pairs" of contrasting colors are noted: white and red, yellow and black, yellow and blue, and green and red (Morgan *et al.* 1963:66). Thus, parts of Signal Systems II and IV are quite simply explainable as a practical application of both (green or white) of the limited possibilities of good color contrasts with the red signal, rather than as systems patterned after color sequences from nature. (For similar reasons pioneering highway stop signs were—and, often, still are—yellow and black, cf. Note 3.)

The growth of industrialization in Britain fostered an increase in railway business, and night traffic became necessary for profitable railroad investment of capital. Night traffic in turn necessitated more and improved night signals; thus a movable red lens was connected to the semaphore arm, and an oil lantern radiating a clear "white" was mounted on the signal mast. (A whitish color[6] is the normal color of the light of such a lantern. [See Figure

[6] There are two kinds of railroad white signal lights: (*a*) the original, and still used, "whites" and (*b*) the more recent and now predominant "lunar whites." The original white varied considerably and was created by using a colorless or clear lens illuminated by various oil flames which had a highly luminous and slightly yellowish hue (Gibson, Haupt, and Keegan 1946:4). In Figure 12.5, this falls somewhere between the "Spectrum locus" of 580 to 590 mμ and the X mark at the "Planckian locus" of 2360° on the "equal energy" line of lunar whites, because the X mark represents the yellowist of the lunar whites (Gibson, Haupt, and Keegan 1946:13, 15; cf. also McNicholas 1936:961 and Breckenridge 1964:4–6). The original (yellowish) whites approach a bright ordinary yellow of high luminosity (Gibson, Haupt, and Keegan 1946:27) rather than one of the railroad signal yellows. These whites also approach the clear (colorless) yellow–white filter of near full luminosity, .920, tested by McNicholas (1936:961, 963, 965) and approximate the variable-source and beacon whites which have a colorless filter (Breckenridge 1964:14, 1967:54–55).

The lunar white is a slightly bluish or grayish white. Like the original white, it still has a mixture of all wavelengths of visible light, but it has a maximum absorption for yellow, so that it contrasts with this hue (see Figure 12.5). Lunar white not only has much less yellow light than railroad signal yellow, but it is also less luminous (Gibson and Haupt 1939:644–646); the original whites were more luminous than railroad signal yellow.

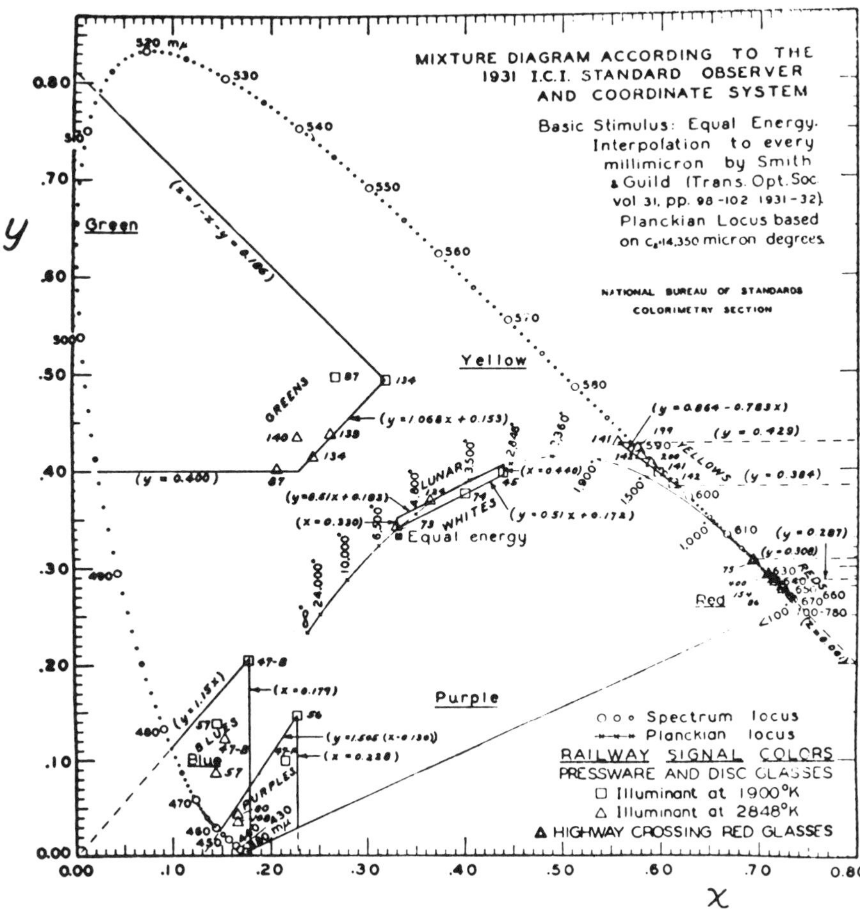

FIGURE 12.5. *A standard chromaticity diagram for railroad signal lights which are named with capital letters (*ordinary color loci are designated by underlined names* [*Gibson, Haupt, and Keegan 1946:16*]*).*

12.5.]) When the arm was raised to the 90° stop position on *home* (or close by the controlling point/station) semaphores, the red lens was simultaneously positioned in front of the lantern, giving a red night aspect (Anonymous 1878:477). Likewise, when the arm was moved to its 45° or 135° caution position on *distant* (from the control point) semaphores, the red lens was simultaneously positioned in front of the lamp, again giving a red night aspect (Johnson 1894:798; Wilson 1907:568; Blythe 1951:111). Commenting upon this ubiquitous red caution signal, a British railway official said that although it presented "many theoretical points of weakness, [it] has, like the English method of handling baggage, apparently worked satisfactorily enough in practice [Wilson 1907:568]." This is because of unverbalized locational as well as verbalized color characteristics of the signal codes (to be discussed below). When the semaphore arm was dropped to its (180°) "absent" or "off" position, the red lens and its signal were also absent and replaced by a white aspect (Anonymous 1878:477). The dichotomy here is the simple use of one distinct color, red, for whatever reason, and its absence, white.

THE FLORESCENCE OF SIGNAL SYSTEM II

By the 1880s Signal System II had spread over Continental Europe, over much of the British Empire in Asia and Africa, and over Anglo North America. A common element of System II, a so-called "purple," but actually a blue-violet having a very short dominant wavelength and very low luminosity,[7] at times replaces red in the color sequence as the stop aspect. When used, it is customarily relegated to traffic control on "slow tracks"—sidings, yard, and spur tracks but usually not the main lines (cf. Anonymous 1895:480). These kinds of replacement of red by violet persist into the present Signal System IV (P.R. 1925:14, 75; N.Y.C. 1937:20, 100–106). Another variation is that instead of violet, blue—also a very short wavelength—replaces red as the stop aspect (D.L. & W. 1900:21). Supplementing the night Signal System II by day or night were red fusees, whose flare indicated "stop," and green fusees, for "caution" (cf. S.P. 1903:10; G.R. 1912:18), just as the green block and interlocking signal meant "caution" and "go slowly" (C.C. & I. and I. & St. L. 1888:17).

In 1877, for practical reasons to be discussed below for North American railroads, one British railroad changed from white to green for the "go" indication. This was a harbinger of transitional System III. In this system, which was more widely used in Britain after 1890, red was used for 'stop,' but often violet was used on nonmain tracks. Violet was also used for "go," however (Anonymous 1895:480; Wilson 1907:568), and was suggested as a caution signal (Anonymous 1892:283). By 1905 regulations required green ("go") for all British railroads. Invariably, "red lights were exhibited at night on distant signals in the caution position," a practice forbidden by statute in 1925 (Blythe 1951:111). Red ('caution') signals were used in North America in

[7] Any consideration of railroad and signal purple is necessarily an involved one. In order to obtain an easily distinguishable sixth color light beyond red, green, white, yellow, and blue, it is necessary to use dichroic purple light. On railroads it usually appears as a hazy reddish and somewhat whitish light surrounded by a deep blue light. This is because the red and blue-violet components of the purple light are separated by the eye, which cannot focus on both colors at the same time. Specifications for railroad purple glass filters are such that the proportion of red light is low enough so that the signal will not be mistaken under some atmospheric conditions for a red light, in the same kind of signal device. The effect of the dichroic ocular aberration makes the purple distinct from the closely hued blue signal. In other words, in contrast to ordinary purple (italicized in Figure 12.5), railroad purples (not italicized) are violets and blue-violets with the addition of just enough red to make them dichromatically distinguishable from railroad blues, which coincide with ordinary blues and violets (cf. Gibson, Haupt, and Keegan 1946:16, 27). The loci of railroad purples in relation to other color lights are shown in Figure 12.5. Because railroad purple has the very low luminosity of violet and has its predominant wavelength in the blue-violet range of the spectrum, it is called "violet" in Table 12.1 and elsewhere in this chapter.

the past and, as explained below, are common today. The prohibition of white ("proceed") signals in Britain after 1905 standardized the use of a white ('danger–stop') signal on some railways to mean nothing but that very old use of white, "this being possible as white no longer signifies anything but danger [Wilson 1907:568]." For the sake of shortening my exposition, I shall focus upon North American rather than British railroads for the remainder of this chapter.

Blue and violet signals, which have been employed as vital parts of railway signal systems since before the middle of the nineteenth century, have two uses for stop indications, in addition to those already mentioned. A violet light, and sometimes a violet metal target, indicates 'stop' to prevent equipment from running onto the ground through an open derailing switch (cf. C.M. St. P. & P. and other R.R.s 1959:2). A crucial blue signal light or flag constitutes the strongest stop signal in railroading! Because of its great importance, its description is only rarely overtly reduced to the one word "stop," (as it is on the Southern Railroad 1956:15). It is usually rather lengthy, to emphasize its great importance, for example: "A blue signal displayed at one or both ends of an engine, car or train, or suspended from a mast placed in the center of track, or extended from ball of rail, indicates that workmen are under the engine, car or train. When so displayed, the engine, car or train must not be coupled to or moved (A.T.S.F. 1966:29–30)." An engine governed by such a blue signal always stops; the rule is never broken. This is an instance in which the railroad operating rule is not simply an ideal pattern of culture, but is also consistent with the actual behavioral pattern.

TRANSITIONAL SIGNAL SYSTEM III

The earliest standard code of railroad signals for the United States formally recommended in 1892 the by then long used System II for night color aspects and indications (Johnson 1893:42–43). By 1896, System II was still the practice in North America, and the American Railway Association had not yet even endorsed the use of green for a proceed signal, although one small railroad used green in this way (Anonymous 1896:229). Two major American railroads had adopted green for "proceed" by 1899 (Anonymous 1899:373). A great and wide ranging debate over the so-called "night signal question" in the two decades both before and after 1900 epitomized the difficulties of departing from System II, and the difficulties were clearly practical and not one of cognitive structure.

As a considerable part of the world industrialized and prospered in the late nineteenth century, rail transport of raw materials and finished products mushroomed. Such vastly increased rail traffic could not be handled and controlled without intensive application of signaling (by means of System II), in which a large amount of money had been invested. The greatly proliferated System II included numerous nonsystemic exceptions of color and shape to the operating rules. As one observer noted in 1878, the striking thing about signals then in use was "their remarkable indefiniteness" and their "diversity and even contradictory characteristics." Furthermore, one found that:

> Semaphores in great variety of shape and action are used . . . flags and banners of various colors are used, so that there is about as much confusion in this important language of railroad pantomime as there was among the bricklayers of Babel after the confusion of tongues [Anonymous 1878:477].

It is not surprising that arguments were made for the rationalization of railway signaling in the last several decades of the nineteenth century—arguments not only for standardization but also for simplification, efficiency, and safety. This debate usually centered on the night signal question: What is the best pattern of colors and indications for signal lights? As late as 1904–1905, the debate that filled the pages of *The Railroad Gazette* for many decades still raged hotly over the respective merits of a sequence of green ("caution"), and white ("go") and of yellow ("caution"), green ("go") (E.C.B. 1904:201; Anonymous 1905); uses of red, blue, and violet for purposes already described were relatively undebated inclusions for both sequences.

Among the arguments frequently advanced were that the kerosene-flame–white proceed signal could be confused with the new street and house lights then being fueled with illuminating gas in the industrial urban centers (cf. Anonymous 1878:479; Anonymous 1891:11). Wrecks did result from such confusion (cf. Anonymous 1905:593). Another common argument was the danger of wrecks occurring when the red lens of a signal in stop position was broken by accident or design, and the night signal thereby falsely showed white ("go") (Anonymous 1891:11; Johnson 1891:37). As early as 1878, one American observer said white should not be used for a night signal, but should be replaced by "blue or green glass" (Anonymous 1878:479). However, it was also argued that compared to white light, green could not be seen far enough at night (Anonymous 1905:592). Other strong practical arguments included the high cost of any change from the greatly proliferated System II. Some arguments touched upon what might be considered to be patterns of cognition, which made System II seem immutable: "To use white for caution and green for all-clear would . . . be the most radical change imaginable [Anonymous 1894:248]."

Argument in many instances was supplemented with experimentation, as when some experienced signal man worked with violet for 'caution' and also tried orange and amber glass (Anonymous 1894:248). Yellow was also proposed to replace white for "go" (Anonymous 1905:592). One signal man proposed green for "proceed" and white as the general stop signal, thus conforming, with regard to white, to past practice and to practice continuing into the present on certain railroads. Acting in an "unnatural," but understandable political fashion, the prestigious committee on signals of the American Railway Association (ARA) recommended not amber-yellow but a compromise combination of red and green lights set 9 inches apart for a mediating caution signal (Johnson 1894:879). This combination caution signal was used by several American railroads and was subsequently adopted by the Belgian State railroad (Anonymous 1905:593, 626; Anonymous 1907:309). (Here we should note that railroads outside of the English-speaking realm, and therefore beyond our discussion, use color signals which show their origins in the diffusion of rail technology from this realm. For example, Vietnam uses a red or purple for "stop," a yellow for "caution," and a green for "go" [United Nations 1954:22–23], thereby reflecting a French practice derived from Britain.)

Besides committing structurally "unnatural" and "illogical" acts, the signal committee of the ARA decided that glass lenses of uniform colors and standard hues were needed (Johnson 1894:879). In the period 1906–1908 the ARA in association with the Corning Glass Works engaged in intensive research to this end. Thus a certain level of technological advancement was necessary for the adoption of a yellow light in any signal system. This experimentation and practical investigation

> led to distinctive, closely specified standard-color lenses, including a yellow for the *approach* aspect which was neither greenish nor reddish. This paved the way for the adoption of green, previously used most often for caution, as the *proceed* aspect. By the end of World War I white was out, and its use is now prohibited [as a proceed indication] by I.C.C. order [Armstrong 1957:1, 52].

Once the lenses were perfected, not only the adoption of yellow, but the nonadoption of orange was done for practical and material rather than for cognitive reasons. Very rarely, the sun may cause a dangerous "phantom signal." A certain angle of the sun at certain times and locations will cause one standard aspect, for example red, to appear as another, yellow. A yellow signal light when backlighted by a strong sun commonly appears orange, as does a red when thus frontlighted. Therefore, any use of orange as a signal light would make the very rare phantom signal a common occurrence, with regard to red and yellow.

Structural Analysis of the Present Signal System IV

The transition from the structurally unnatural System II to the equally unnatural present System IV (from which highway signals were derived) was not a result of any underlying structural process but, among other things of: the balancing of practical and rational considerations; experimentation in the material world; scientific advances in color technology, glass, and electric illumination; traffic demands of an evolving industrial civilization; and the advent of large-scale illumination with white lights of streets and houses. Completion of the transition included retaining the uses of the white, green and white, violet, and blue stop signals already noted. It also included the addition of a common yellow ("caution") and a less common flashing-green ("caution"), as well as an increasingly more common lunar white ("caution").

The present multiple aspect Signal System IV in all of its complexity confounds still further any comparisons with natural structure. As was true with previous systems, red does not completely or always indicate "stop." A signal mast displaying a red signal and having affixed to it a plate with the letter "A" (absolute) or having no plate indicates "stop"—period. With a numbered plate affixed, red indicates 'stop and proceed' (at restricted or cautious speed). And with a number plate or with a plate bearing the letters "P" or "G" red indicates "permissive/grade" ('proceed at restricted speed without stopping' [C.M. St. P. & P. 1959:104–105; S.R. 1956:95]).

Today, in some railroad districts an engineer might run his train for hours against a succession of permissive red signals without being required to stop even once, in the same way that the pioneer British engineers followed the red signal at the rear of a moving train. As with the pioneers, our present day engineer would react reflexively to stop for a short wavelength blue (or violet) signal. On past and present railroads with red ("stop"), red ("stop-and-go"), and red ("caution"), the railroaders distinguish between them not by verbalizations (all are called "red" on the job), but by memorization of the location of the three kinds along the right of way. Number and letter plates are usually not discernible soon enough to act upon by day and are far less distinguishable at night. Thus indications, not only for red but for all other fixed signals as well, are perceived in part in terms of location in addition to the other signal aspects previously mentioned. When running fast, even a simple fixed signal, for example a "board" reading "SLOW, TRESTLE" located at the approach to a trestle over a deep gorge, is useless as a signal unless the railroaders know it is there long before first sighting it. (A heavy fast freight train could take up to 2 miles to brake to a stop.) As railroaders put it, "You've got to know the railroad [right of way] or you're in trouble."[8] The locational aspect of railway signals makes Leach's natural model less useful, even if it did not have the problems already mentioned.

The single yellow-approach aspect is followed by a double or flashing yellow advance-approach indicating "proceed; approach next signal not exceeding medium speed," and the single green aspect may follow a flashing green approach-limited indicating "proceed; approach next signal not exceeding limited speed" (A.T.S.F. 1966:104–105). Modern multiple-aspect

[8] A very well known example of the fact that, in most cases, the lack of a locational aspect means the effective lack of a fixed rail signal is as follows (Anonymous 1970). Engineer Joseph A. "Steve" Broady was from another railroad and had only a month's experience on the Southern's mountain line from Monroe via Danville, Virginia to Spencer, North Carolina. Consequently, he did not yet know the railroad and its vital signal locations. On September 27, 1903, he received fast mail train number "old" 97 almost an hour late and tried to make up most of the time on the "tight" 166 mile, 4¼-hour run. A trestle spanned a deep gorge outside Danville at the base of a

signal systems may have more than 15 sets of aspects and indications (B. & O. 1953:105–121; N.Y.C. 1956:86–99; P.C. 1968:64–79). Some railroads use all kinds of combinations of reds, yellows, and greens to provide multiple-aspect systems, with no discernible pattern of one color *always* being more restrictive than another. For example, in the 18-aspect Atlantic Coast Line system, red over yellow over green in "medium-approach slow" and yellow over red over green is the slightly more restrictive "approach slow" (ACL 1926:111–131).

Widespread use of white (often a lunar white) has been reintroduced, as an additional color in System IV, to indicate "restricting" (a *caution,* that is, "proceed on route indicated at restricted speed" [U.P. 1954:100–101]) or to indicate varieties of "caution" (B. & O. 1953:112; N.Y.C. 1937:20). White frequently still indicates "stop" (A.T.S.F. 1948:16; C.M. St. P. & P. and other R.R.s 1959:20), sometimes when flashing (P.C. 1968:25). The white ("stop") combined with green ("caution"), which was a widely used stop signal during the nineteenth century, continues to be used today (C.C.C. & I. and I. & St. L. 1888:17; C. & O. 1958:15). At times the addition of a white signal to a red signal makes the red more restrictive. On the Canadian National and other railroads, Rule 451a and b says that a single or double red is a "stop and proceed signal" and a red with a lunar white is a "stop signal" period (C.N. 1951:130). The use of white for "stop" in Britain had a widespread application late in the last century (Wilson 1907:568), and, as has been shown, it was part of the very beginning of railway signaling.

Finally, as one would suspect in the evolution of any cultural system, System IV is internally contradicted by numerous "survivals" from System II.

---

curving grade. The approach to the trestle had a "board" reading "SLOW UP, TRESTLE." The rest is the kind of history that legends are made of in Appalachia:

Well they gave him his orders at Munroe, Virginia
Sayin', "Steve you're a way behind time,
This is not 38 but its old 97
You must put 'er into Danville/Spencer on time."
He turned and said to his black greasy fireman,
"Just shovel on a little more coal,
And when we cross that White Oak Mountain
You can watch old 97 roll."
It's a mighty rough road from Lynchburg to Danville,
On a line on a three mile grade,
It was on this grade that he lost his average,
You can see what a jump he made.
He was goin' down the grade makin' 90 miles an hour,
When his whistle broke into a scream
They found him in the wreck
With his hand on the throttle, and a-scalded to death by the steam.

When the flanges of the train's wheels left the rails on the trestle, the train hurtled forward a full 100 feet on its way down to the bottom (see also Hubbard 1945:246, 251–261).

Applications of white for its old 'proceed' indication, in opposition to red ("stop"), remain in use for switch signal lights and pigmented metal targets to indicate that the switch is "lined for straight track" as opposed to red, or "switch lined for diverging track" (A.C.L. 1926:19; N.Y.C. 1937:20, 106; S.R. 1956:80–82; and cf. Anonymous 1891:11 for such a practice in System II). Furthermore, the train signals used on most railroads in North America are also survivals. Green *classification signals* on a locomotive indicate that another *section* of the same numbered *regularly scheduled* (by timetable) *train* is following; therefore, any other locomotive should remain stopped and in the clear of the main line for the following section. (The fact that this use of green "really means danger, though its color is caution' [Anonymous 1892:283]" did not go unnoticed in the era of System II.) White classification signals on a locomotive indicate that the train is an *extra train* (not authorized by a timetable schedule), and that it is safe to regard it as not being in danger of a following section. Similarly, *marker* lamps with lenses of two colors, whose display at the rear of a movement of railroad rolling stock formally designates it as a *train,* display red ("stop") to the rear when the train is on the main line and are turned to display green ("caution") to the rear when the train is waiting in the clear, to be passed, on a siding alongside the main line (C. M. St. P. & P. 1959:33–35). Some railroads have substituted in their markers System IV yellow ("caution") lenses for the System II aspect and indication (A.T.S.F. 1948:27–45). A few railroads use both System IV yellow and System II green, but in different operating districts (U.P. 1954:35–37; 1962:3).

Conclusions

Clearly, diachronic and synchronic investigation of all of Signal Systems I, II, III, and IV does not support the existence of any underlying structure patterned after nature, that is, the spectral continuum of wavelengths. With the evolution of industrial urban civilization, including its railway technology, and the development of its energy base of fossil fuels, a steady increase in rail traffic resulted, and rail operations became more complex in organization and differentiated in function. With increasing operational differentiation in the regulation of the rail traffic, a related and necessary differentiation was effected in the coding of visual signals for traffic control. Color coding in railway (and related highway) signaling, then, is the result through time of numerous reactions to practical considerations of interrelated material elements and is *not* the result of the dialectical process hypothesized by Leach. The result inconsistently incorporates various old but "unstructured" Anglo symbolic associations with colors; for example, white with purity and safety and black or blue with danger.

It is difficult to support the idea of an inherent assocation of a "stop" indication with a red aspect in the genesis of railway signaling. On the other hand, it is Leach's strongest point in support of his hypothesis that color-indication sequences are patterned after nature. However, whether red was selected as a railroad color indicating "stop" because of a sometime association of red with danger for English-speakers or for practical reasons, in railway signaling other colors also mean "stop," and red sometimes does not mean "stop." And, most important of all, even if red were (for whatever reason) exlusively the stop color, the interrelations found between red ("stop") and other colors and indications in railway signals are not those cognitively patterned after nature!

One might reason that Leach's structuralist arguments are properly phrased in terms of relationships and that therefore, it does not matter whether red means "stop" or "go" just as long as it contrasts with colors for "stop" or "go," thereby lending itself to a model incorporating structural oppositons. However, as I have shown, red may have several meanings in the same signal system, such as "stop" and "caution." Of course, the blue ("stop") is always contrastive (a reversal of Leach's long wave equals stop), but greatly differing stop wavelengths (red, white) may be in the same operative system. In any event, the use of white as a "proceed" in Systems I–IV and in current highway practice *alone* destroys any hypothesis of signal systems modeled upon the spectral continuum, because white is the presence of all visible color wavelengths. For just this reason, then, no structuralist model alternative to Leach's can be supported. Apart from the two points just made, the rest of the empirical data on coded colors and their interrelations bury the hypothesis in an avalanche of arbitrary "unnatural" practice, considered either synchronically or diachronically.

In the periods 1820–1890 and 1890–1920, the cognitive maps of most Anglos were in accord with the arbitray and unnatural railroad signal system. Not just railroad personnel and members of their families and friends who talked about their work knew the railroad code, but also those who had some contact with railroads. Between 1820 and 1920, this was true of most people, because the railroad was the only way to travel (and ship goods). When waiting for a train, people passed the time by observing the signals to note the approach or passing of trains: "The signal is white; that means the train is not coming, and the track is clear." Popular and technical books and periodicals of the time necessarily used the rail color code is any discussion of rail signaling. This was especially apparent in the newspapers in which wrecks dominated the front page during those days of unperfected rail technology before the advent of fuel energized highway and airway vehicles: "The engineer swears the signal was white just before he ran into the other train"; "The red [or blue, or purple] lens had fallen from the signal thereby displaying a white indication and the train ran on into a wreck."

By the 1930s, urban landscapes were dominated by highway traffic control signals evolved from limited aspects of the railway code. Most Anglos became *more* cognizant of the red ("stop"), yellow ("caution"), green ("go"), once it was standardized on highways, although exceptions, such as the ubiquitous American yellow stop sign, did not make the highway triad a closed system. By the 1950s, the automobile was the predominant mode of transport, at least in Anglo North America. And, as rail passenger transport declined, the vast majority of Anglos were no longer cognizant of the underlying railway part of the color code for land traffic control but were now aware of the highway code. Since 1970 in North America, the highway traffic code has become more complex. Because of the overwhelming growth of highway traffic (including its effect on pedestrian crosswalks on streets), the red–yellow–green traffic lights had to be augmented with additional colors. Thus the two or three decades in which the vast majority of Anglos were no longer cognizant of the underlying component of coding in land traffic control is now changing into a period in which they must reflect upon a more complex highway color code. If the passenger train has a renaissance in the United States and Canada for material reasons, such as the rising costs of energy, more people will be returning to the rails and again noticing and reflecting upon the myriad kinds of signals associated with that mode of transport.

In other words, the triad red ("stop"), yellow ("caution"), and green ("go") existed only in certain, but very common, highway signal devices between two point in time, namely, the early 1920s, when highway traffic signal lights became popular, and when the use of orange ("stop") and white ("go") became common on highways. The average person may not yet be accustomed to the last two color conventions. Today, fire engines are being painted white rather than red, and police cars use blue warning/stop lights. The average person is certainly not yet accustomed to these two changes. He still thinks and responds in terms of "fire engines are red," and "the cop was flashing his red light at me." After a period of reinforcement, these uses of white and blue will seem "natural." So, too, will the uses of orange and white described above. In the future, the rhyme used to teach young children pedestrian safety ("Hippity hop, hippity hop. Green means go, and red means stop.") will have no empirical referents. It will instead "be" and "seem natural" that "White means go, and orange means stop" as well. Thus, as technological systems evolve, systems of cognition gradually adjust to their changes.

The research presented in this chapter implies that the limitations of the French structuralist model used by Leach in his analysis of signals is not readily apparent to the reader of his work. This is because he inadvertently omits some of the color indications and their interrelations in the field, thereby creating a spurious validation of the hypothesis of the natural model. Some ethnologists see underlying patterns, relationships, and symmetrical arrangements in culture where the uninitiated skeptic does not. The credibility of ethnology in the social sciences depends on its ability to allay such skepticism (cf. Pelto 1970:19, 26, 36–41). The corroboration of structural models by empirical data readily verifiable and close at hand in Anglo society is one resolution of the ethnological credibility gap. As Robbins Burling has demonstrated (1970), our application of the ethnology of kinship to Yankee kin terms has not helped to close this gap.

Structuralists are frequently concerned with relatively changeless domains among preindustrial peoples. Such domains lend themselves to a timeless, logical analysis of the kind that has been used so successfully in linguistics, which is necessarily the most exacting of the social sciences. The cultural stasis of French structuralism may be as inappropriate to the study of a natural world in constant flux as is the static equilibrium of classic Anglo–American structural–functionalism. In the technological and economic systems of industrial society, time and change stand still for no analyst. This is not an argument against structuralism failing as history, but one against structuralism taking no account of history (and, in this chapter, of the present as well). The difficulties with colored signals patterned after nature constitute another example of what Stanley Diamond has referred to as where "the structuralist finds himself haunted by history on a rather elementary level [1974:311]." Color signal categories are not a closed cognitive domain. They relate functionally to other domains of culture as they change through time. The domain which is the subject of this paper can only be understood in the temporal context of its structural–functional variation, that is, in its evolutionary context.

If French structural analysis is to be a stronger method in our ethnological bag of tools, we must apply it to domains within our own Anglo sub-cultures, so that it may be honed to the keenest possible edge and its usefulness may be ascertained in a manner not clouded by exotic data. Otherwise, we can never be sure whether or not, "The name of the game is 'double-talk' or 'the emperor's new clothes.' [Marvin Harris 1974:178]." To date, structural analysis is frequently applied to descriptive data about ethnic groups that are knowable to scholars only in solitary or numerically limited ethnographies that are, in turn, factually limited or knowable only through very narrowly focusing corpora of the mythology of temporally distant agrarian civilizations. Analysis of this kind raises a question: Would the customary tightly knit structural analyses of domains from such limited bodies of data be considered valid if rich synchronic and diachronic data, of the variety available in the domain of traffic control signals in land transportation, were suddenly to become accessible? Of course, little or no probability of such accessibility exists in the respective cases of the ethnographies and the corpora. However, given the methodological insight provided by our analysis of these signals, one cannot but wonder about the nurturing of French structuralism in such exotic soil.

This chapter constitutes what Lévi-Strauss might call a "concession to naturalism" and a "sterile empiricism, devoid of inspiration [1967:49–50]." Of course, the question underlying that of the merits of structuralist arguments is not one of what is right but of what is useful. Utility depends upon one's viewpoint, hence metatheoretical and theoretical enculturation (for example, balancing the enthusiasm of its proponents, Harris says of structuralism: "An anthropology that substitutes models for data is a disease, not a science [1974:178]"). Despite the relativity of utility, a cavalier armchair detachment from the empirical world should not pervade French structuralism if it is to be broadly useful in the science of man. As noted by André Köbben and others: "We have to make sure that our models are not just playthings in the anthropological kindergarten, but are, somehow, statements based on reality (symbolic or behavioral) [1974:222]." Consequently, full field and documentary verification is needed to augment the desk analysis; otherwise, structuralism may characteristically produce a sterile formalism useful largely to the initiates of a particular band of ethnologists. Such formalism is a luxury of a scholarly elite. Increasingly, luxuries of this kind are something that society cannot afford in its restricted and more and more inadequate energy budget, from which all scholarship is supported.

Because of our customary exotic and esoteric sources of data, in formulating any body of ethnological method or theory, all of us must guard doubly against a common scholarly failing recognized by a member of the old agrarian and scholarly elite, Lord Francis Bacon, in his *New Method of Scientific Investigation* (1960:50–51):

> The human understanding when it has once adopted an opinion (either as being the received opinion or as being agreeable to itself) draws all things else to support and agree with it. And though there be a greater number and weight of instances to be found on the other side, yet these it either neglects and despises, or else by some distinction sets aside and rejects, in order that by this great and pernicious predetermination the authority of its former conclusions may remain inviolate. . . . But with far more subtlety does this mischief insinuate itself into philosophy and the sciences; in which the first conclusion colors and brings into conformity with itself all that come after, though far sounder and better. Besides, independently of that delight and vanity which I have described, it is the peculiar and perpetual error of the human intellect to be more moved and excited by affirmatives than by negatives; whereas it ought properly to hold itself indifferently disposed toward both alike.

References

A.C.L. (Atlantic Coast Line Railroad Company)
1926 *Rules of the operating department.*
Andres, Rudolf
1973 Auffälligskeitsgrad der fahrzeuglackierung. Industrie-Lackier-Betrieb Nr. 9.
Anonymous
1878 Semaphore signals. *Railroad Gazette 10*:477–479.
Anonymous
1891 Colored vs. "white" lights for all-clear signals. *Railroad Gazette 23*:11.
Anonymous
1892 White lights dangerous for signals. *Rainroad Gazette 24*:283–284.

Anonymous
1893 Color for signal posts and signals. *Railroad Gazette 25*:285–286.

Anonymous
1894 [Editorial]. *Railroad Gazette 26*:248

Anonymous
1895 International congress report on signals. *Railroad Gazette 27*:479–480.

Anonymous
1896 Colors for night signals. *Railroad Gazette 28*:229.

Anonymous
1899 [News Report from the Journal of the German Railroad Union]. *Railroad Gazette 31*:373.

Anonymous
1905 Colors for signal indications. *Railway Age 40*:592–593, 626–627, 686.

Anonymous
1907 The colors for signal lamps. *Railway Age 44*:309–310.

Anonymous
1968 Detroit: Pioneer user of "traffic tower." *Traffic Engineering 38*(9):40–42.

Anonymous
1970 Famous rail wrecks: The disaster at Stillhouse trestle. *The Train Dispatcher 52*:312–315.

Armstrong, J. S.
1957 All about signals—I, II. *Trains 17*(8):44–57; *17*(9):44–54.

A.T.S.F. (Atchison, Topeka and Sante Fe Railway System)
1948 *Rules,* Operating Department: Revised.
1966 *Rules,* Operating Department: Revised.

B. & O. (Baltimore and Ohio Railroad Company)
1953 Rules and regulations of the operating department.

Bacon, F.
1960 The new organon (F. H. Anderson, Ed.). New York: Liberal Arts Press. (First published in Latin in 1620.)

Beck, J.
1972 *Surface color perception.* Ithaca: Cornell University Press.

Billmeyer, F. W., Jr., and M. Saltzman
1966 *Principles of color technology.* New York: Interscience Publishers.

Blythe, R.
1951 *Danger ahead: The dramatic story of railway signalling.* London: Newman Neame.

Bornstein, M. H.
1973 Color vision and color naming: A psychophysiological hypothesis of cultural difference. *Psychological Bulletin 80*:257–285.

Breckenridge, F. C.
1964 United States standard for the colors of signal lights. National Bureau of Standards, Handbook 95.
1967 Colors of signal lights. *National Bureau of Standards, Monograph 75.*

Burling, R.
1970 American kinship terms once more. *Southwestern Journal of Anthropology 26*:15–24.

Burnham, R. W., R. Hanes, and C. J. Bartleson
1963 Color: A guide to basic facts and concepts. New York: Wiley.

C.C.C. & St. L. (Cleveland, Cincinnati, Chicago and St. Louis Railway Company)
1901 Rules governing employes.

C.C.C. & I. and I. & St. L. (Cleveland, Columbus, Cincinnati and Indianapolis Railway, and Indianapolis and St. Louis Railway)
1888 Rules and regulations for the running of trains and for the guidance of the officers and employes therein referred to.

C.M. St. P. & P. (Chicago, Milwaukee, St. Paul and Pacific Railroad Company [and 12 other Railroads])
1959 The consolidated code of operating rules.
C.N. (Canadian National Railways, Grand Trunk Western Railroad, Central Vermont Railway, Duluth, Winnipeg and Pacific Railway)
1951 Uniform code of operating rules.
C. & O. (Chesapeake and Ohio Railway Company)
1958 Rules and regulations . . . for the government of the operating department.
Committee on Colorimetry of the Optical Society
1953 *The science of color.* New York: Crowell.
Conklin, H. C.
1973 Color categorization. *American Anthropologist 75*:931–942.
Conover, D. W., and C. L. Kraft
1958 The use of color in coding displays [Wright Air Development Center Technical Report 55-471]. *Armed Services Technical Information Agency Document No. AD 204214.* Arlington, Virginia.
Cornsweet, T. N.
1970 *Visual perception.* New York: Academic Press.
D.L. & W. (Delaware, Lackawanna and Western Railroad Company)
1900 Instructions governing the use of automatic block and interlocking signals.
D'Andrade, R., and M. Egan
1974 The colors of emotion. *American Ethnologist 1*:49–63.
Davidson, H. R.
1951 Visual sensitivity to surface colors. *Journal of the Optical Society of America 41*:104–111.
Diamond, S.
1974 *In search of the primitive: A critique of civilization.* New Brunswick, N.J.: Transaction Books.
E. C. B.
1904 Simplifying night signals and shortening block sections. *Railroad Gazette 36*(11):201.
Eno, W. P.
1920 *The science of highway traffic regulation 1899–1920.* Washington, D.C.: Brentano's.
G. R. (Georgia Railroad)
1912 Rules for the government of the operating department.
Gamst, Frederick C.
n.d. Toward a method of industrial ethnology. Manuscript.
Gibson, K. S., and G. W. Haupt
1939 Standardization of luminous-transmission scale used in the specification of railroad signal glasses. *Journal of Research of the National Bureau of Standards 22*:627–649.
Gibson, K. S., G. W. Haupt, and H. J. Keegan
1946 Specification of railroad signal colors and glasses. *Journal of Research of the National Bureau of Standards* 36:1–30.
Grether, W. F., and C. A. Baker
1972 Visual presentation of information. In *Human engineering guide to equipment design* (revised ed.) (H. P. Van Cott and R. G. Kinkade, Eds.). Washington: U.S. Government Printing Office. Pp. 41–121.
Halsey, R. M.
1959 Identification of signal lights. I, blue, green, white, and purple. *Journal of the Optical Society of America 49*:45–55.
Harris, M.
1974 The emperor's clothing store. *Reviews in Anthropology 1*:170–184.
Hickerson, Nancy P.
1971 Review of Brent Berlin and Paul Kay, basic color terms. *International Journal of American Linguistics 37*:257–270.

Hubbard, F. H.
1945 *Railroad avenue: Great stories and legends of american railroading.* New York: McGraw-Hill.

Johnson, A. H.
1891 The use of white signal lights. *Railroad Gazette 23*:37.
1893 The proposed standard code for interlocking and block signaling. *Railroad Gazette 25*:42–43.

Johnson, H.
1894 Colors for signal lights. *Railroad Gazette 26*:879.

Judd, D. B.
1952 *Color in business, science and industry.* New York: Wiley.

Katz, D.
1935 *The world of color* (R. B. MacLeod and C. W. Fox, Trans.). London: Kegan Paul, Trench, Trubner.

Kemnitzer, L. S.
1973 Language learning and socialization on the railroad. *Urban Life and Culture 1*:363–378.

Köbben, A. J. F., J. Verrips, and L. N. J. Brunt
1974 Lévi-Strauss and empirical inquiry. *Ethnology 13*:215–223.

Leach, E.
1970 *Claude Lévi-Strauss.* New York: Viking.

Lévi-Strauss, C.
1967 *Structural anthropology* (C. Jacobson and B. G. Schoep, Trans.). Garden City, N.Y.: Anchor Books.

McNicholas, H. J.
1936 Selection of colors for signal lights. *Journal of Research of the National Bureau of Standards 17*:955–980.

Malcolm, R.
1966 Charles Adler, Jr. *Traffic Engineering 37*(2):46–47.

Marshall, C. F. D.
1971 *A history of British railways down to the year 1830.* London: Oxford University Press. (First published in 1938.)

Meister, D., and D. J. Sullivan
1969 Guide to human engineering design for visual displays. Canoga Park, California: Bunker-Ramo Corporation.

Morgan, C. T., A. Chapanis, J. S. Cook, and M. W. Lund (Eds.)
1963 *Human engineering guide to equipment design.* New York: McGraw-Hill.

Munsell Color Company
1929 *Munsell book of color.* Baltimore: Munsell Color Company.

N.Y.C. (New York Central System)
1937 Rules for the government of the operating department.
1956 Rules for the operating department.

N.Y., N.H. & H. (New York, New Haven and Hartford Railroad Company)
1956 Rules for the government of the operating department.

Oxford English Dictionary, The
1971 Compact Edition of, 2 vols. in microprint. London: Oxford University Press.

P.C. (Penn Central)
1968 Rules for conducting transportation.

P.R. (Pennsylvania Railroad System)
1925 Operating department rules for conducting transportation.

Pelto, P. J.
1970 *Anthropological research.* New York: Harper and Row.

Prunski, A.
1968 *Farwell's rules of the nautical road* (4th ed.). Annapolis: United States Naval Institute.

Reynolds, R. E., R. M. White, Jr., and R. L. Hilgendorf
1972 Detection and recognition of colored signal lights. *Human Factors 14*:227–236.
Robinson, Carlton C.
1967 Color in traffic control. *Traffic Engineering 37*(8):25–29.
S.P. (Southern Pacific Company)
1903 Rules and regulations: Operating department.
S.R. (Southern Railway System)
1956 Operating rules.
Semple, C. A., Jr., K. T. Burnette, E. J. Conway, and R. J. Heapy
1971 Analysis of human factors data for electronic flight display systems. *Air Force Flight Dynamics Laboratory Technical Report* 70–174.
Stark, C. W.
1968a Houston's coordinated traffic signals. *Traffic Engineering 38*(7):58–59.
1968b New York's early traffic signal towers. *Traffic Engineering 39*(2):48–49.
Texas Department of Public Safety
1965 Texas drivers handbook.
U.P. (Union Pacific Railroad Company)
1954 Operating rules.
1962 California division, Special Rules No. 16.
United Nations
1954 Railway operating and signalling techniques in Europe, Japan and the United States of America. *United Nations Publication ST/TAA/Ser.C/6.*
Webster's New International Dictionary
1924 Springfield, MA: G. & C. Merriam. First ed.
Whishaw, F.
1842 *The railways of Great Britian and Ireland practically discribed as illustrated* (2nd ed.). London: J. Weale.
Wilson, H. R.
1907 Colors for signal lamps. *Railway Age 44*:568.
Wulfeck. J. W., A. Weisz, and M. Raben
1958 Vision in military aviation. *Armed Services Technical Information Agency Document No. AD 207780.* Arlington, Virginia.

13

History and Ideological Significance of the Separation of Social and Cultural Anthropology

MARVIN HARRIS

Introduction

The separation of cultural from social anthropology is associated with the restriction of the concept of culture to ideational or cognitive entities. According to Goodenough "Culture consists of an inventory of percepts and concepts—of ideational forms—and a set of principles for ordering them [1969:330]." Cultural anthropology studies such forms. In contrast, "social anthropology . . . is concerned not with people's concepts, standards, criteria, and principles for acting and responding, but with events and their statistical patterns [Goodenough 1969:331]." Many anthropologists remain uninformed concerning the professional context in which the distinction between "social" and "cultural" arose. Confusion over the meaning of "social" and "cultural" runs so deep and has endured so long that one is forced to conclude that the lack of clarity serves a vital ideological function.

In this chapter, I show that the terms "social" and "cultural" first acquired anthropological usage in the nineteenth century. But from the 1870s to the 1920s, the option between "social" and "cultural" was devoid of epistemological, methodological, or theoretical significance. In the 1930s, two convergent influences—Radcliffe-Brownian structural–functionalism and Parsonian sociology—created a professional clientage that had use for a concept of culture restricted to ideational forms. However, neither the anthropological structural–functionalists nor the Parsonian sociologists can be described as "concerned not with people's concepts, standards, criteria and principles for acting, but with events and their statistical patterns [Goodenough 1969:331]."

BEYOND THE MYTHS OF CULTURE
Essays in Cultural Materialism

ISBN 0-12-598180-5

The social anthroplogy to which Goodenough refers is an imaginary creation of the ethnolinguistic movement (alias ethnosemantics, formal analysis, ethnoscience, etc.). This imaginary social anthropology has been created to avoid the onus of professional irrelevance implicit in an anthropology that cannot deal with the material, concrete, historical, behavioral and "etic," regularities of sociocultural life.

Social and Cultural ca. 1870–1930

During this period, the label *cultural anthropology* was adopted as conventional nomenclature throughout the United States while *social anthropology* won out as the standard in Great Britain. But the distinctive component in the meaning of social anthropology was precisely the same as the distinctive component in the meaning of cultural anthropology: *Social* and *cultural* merely meant *nonphysical anthropology*.

The holder of the first chair in social anthropology in Great Britain was Sir James Frazer at the University of Liverpool, 1907–1908 (Lienhardt 1964:20). Needless to say, Frazer's concern with the global evolution of magic, religion, and ritual bears no resemblance to Goodenough's "events and their statistical pattern." The meaning of Frazer's "social anthropology" and of the social anthropology of all anthropologists in Great Britian prior to 1930 is perfectly clear. Social anthropology was comparative sociology. Thus, in the Index of the *Journal of the Royal Anthropological Institute, Anthropology* is exclusively physical anthropology—anthropometry, blood groups, small-headed types of female Australian, etc.—while *Sociology* embraces every aspect of sociocultural life treated in American journals under the rubric *cultural anthropology:* chieftanship, couvade, economic stages of development in Africa, immolation of widows in New Guinea, pigs, Papuans, police courts, etc. In the *JRAI,* entries indexed under *culture* were rare and in most volumes there were none at all, during the period 1870–1930.

The reason for this preference is quite banal. "Culture," as Kroeber and Kluckhohn (1952) have shown, was the term given to sociocultural phenomena in late eighteenth-century to mid-nineteenth-century German social science. On the other hand, *society, sociology,* and *social* were the hallmarks of French social science starting from the time of Saint Simon and Auguste Comte. In 1871, Tylor, under the influence of Gustav Klemm and Theodor Waitz entitled his magnum opus, *Primitive Culture.* Although Tylor was also somewhat influenced by Comte, he refrained from using the French terminology. With the publication of Herbert Spencer's *The Study of Sociology* (1873) and *Principles of Sociology* (1876), the French terminology received the advocacy of the most influential British social scientist of the nineteenth century. "Social," "sociology," and "society," however, did not win a total victory; "culture" was preferred, for example, at the University of

London (see following). Elsewhere, the term *ethnology* provided a third alternative.

In the United States, "culture," "cultural," and "cultural anthropology" were strongly favored among anthropologists. Two sets of factors seem to be relevant for the explanation of this difference. First, Boas, Lowie, and Kroeber, the founders of twentieth-century American cultural anthropology, were German Americans. Adoption of the Germanic terminology was quite natural for them, especially since the reputation of German science was at its zenith and was held in greater esteem than French or British science by a large portion of the American scientific community. Second, the institutionalization of cultural anthropology in the United States occurred in a university setting where sociology had gained a prior foothold and where cultural anthropology was obliged to play second fiddle in staff and enrollment.

From 1889 to 1892, formal instruction in sociology was begun in 18 colleges and universities in the United States. While sociology courses were not given within departments of sociology until 1893, their impact can be gauged by the following: "During the period up to 1900, at least seven American university presidents were themselves the first to offer formal course work in sociology at their universities [Reiss 1968:13]." The institutionalization of American cultural anthropology proceeded at a much slower pace than the institutionalization of American sociology. For example, only one cultural anthropologist has ever been president of an American university (at Cornell). Several college textbooks on sociology were already in use before 1900 while the first American textbook in cultural anthropology appeared two decades later (Goldenweiser 1922).

The situation in Great Britain and in Europe generally was quite different. The British university system was relatively ossified and neither anthropology nor sociology underwent rapid expansion until the 1920s and even later. Of the two, however, anthropology had the head start academically and played the dominant role (Reiss 1968). In 1907, L.T. Hobhouse and Edward Westermark shared the only chairs of sociology in the United Kingdom at the University of London (Shils 1970:768–769). Both of these men were cast in the Tylorean–Spencerian mold and were destined to exert a greater influence over anthropologists than sociologists. Indeed, Malinowski, one of the earliest to possess a readership in social anthropology (at the London School of Economics), was Westermark's student. Paradoxically, however, Hobhouse, the "sociologist," was a devotee of the term culture as was another of Westermark's students, Charles Seligman. Thus, when Malinowski was offered (and declined) a readership at the University of London in 1923, it was for cultural anthropology (see Firth 1970:5)!

Similar abortive penetrations of culture and cultural into American sociology occurred during the same period (cf. Casey 1924; Gray 1924). As in the case of British social anthropology, there have been occasional lapses by Americans into deviant terminology. Lowie (1920) called his most important book *Primitive Society* (to distinguish it from Tylor's *Primitive Culture* and to align it with Morgan's *Ancient Society*?) while Radin (1932) called his introductory text *Social Anthropology*. When Lowie used society rather than culture, he may have wished to indicate an interest in social organization (social structure) as opposed to technology or ideology. This was certainly not the case with Radin, however, who relates his use of social to the omission of physical anthropology, archaeology, and linguistics. A similar distinction gradually developed among anthropologists in Great Britain who were trained in departments that omitted or slighted archaeology, linguistics, and physical anthropology. For some anthropologists on both sides of the Atlantic, therefore, cultural anthropology came to be associated with the Boasian "four-field" approach. This aspect of the meaning of culture had nothing to do with any serious epistemological issue concerning the difference between social and cultural.

The banal quintessence of the situation described thus far is set forth in a letter written in 1923 by Bronislaw Malinowski to the Director of the London School of Economics on the occasion of Malinowski's acceptance of a readership at that institution. Asked what he would like to call his readership, Malinowski replied:

> I suggest the title Social Anthropology, so that we are distinct from the U.C. [University College, University of London] people, who no doubt will insist on being *Cultural,* for Cultural is their *mot d'ordre.* Social will also indicate that our interest is mainly sociological, the School [i.e., L.S.E.] being the centre for sociology and all that pertains to it. Social Anthropology has also its good English tradition by now—I think this was the title under which Edward Tylor lectured in Oxford [Wrong. Tylor's chair was in Anthropology], Frazer in Liverpool and this is the way the science of primitive culture is usually distinguished from Physical Anthropology. Cultural is really borrowed from German, where Kultur means civilization with its fine shade of meaning not implied in the English Culture [quoted in Firth 1970:5].

One gains the impression from Malinowski's reference to the Germanic origin of *Culture* that national jingoism is another factor to be considered in the rejection of culture by British anthropologists. (Malinowski's foes at University College were the diffusionists under Elliot G. Smith who were the British counterparts of the German "museum moles" responsible for the Kulturkreise school.)

Among many contemporary British anthropologists, the preference for social often remains a matter of insignificant intellectual habit. How else explain the fact that the American cultural anthropologists are consistently referred to in British textbooks as social anthropologists? Geoffry Lienhardt (1964:30) even refers to Boas as a social anthropologist whereas Raymond Firth (1964:4) identifies Ruth Benedict as a social anthropologist responsible for "one of the more successful interpretations of Japanese attitudes."

Political Ideology of Durkheim, Radcliffe-Brown, and Parsons

The formation of a distinctive epistemological status for British social anthropology followed upon the further development of French bourgeois (non-Marxist and anti-Marxist) sociology. Durkheim explicitly addressed himself to problems raised by Spencer and Comte. He carried forward the analysis of what Spencer had called the *super-organic* through the medium of the established Comtean vocabulary and gave the name "social facts" to the basic units of sociocultural discourse. I shall return to a consideration of the epistemology of Durkheim's social facts in a moment.

As Radcliffe-Brown has indicated, Durkheim's influence was essential to the development of British structural-functionalism (cf. Goody 1973:198). This influence is relevant to the formation of an epistemologically significant penumbra around the preference of some British scholars for social and social anthropology. Durkheim's main ideological contribution was the development of a "scientific," state-supported system of morals, based on the notion of *collective conscience* and *organic solidarity* (cf. Turner 1977). The institutionalization of Durkheim's sociology followed upon the electoral success of the so-called Radical Party, a centrist liberal party whose political philosophy was known as *solidarism*. Durkheim's work was regarded by Leon Bourgeois [sic!], the leading solidarist and premier of France (from 1895 to 1896), as proof of the evitability of the Marxist polarization of class conflict. In Durkheim's analysis, class strugle was a temporary pathology, and organic solidarity, not revolution, was the predictable outcome of industrialization.

Why did British social anthropology reject its Tylorean and Spencerian antecedents in favor of French "solidarism?" After the First World War, the biological and racist components in nineteenth-century evolutionist anthropology were an embarrassment and an encumbrance in Britain's attempt to stabilize its overseas empire. Durkheim's ideas about organic solidarity were much more useful in the postwar colonial context. Applied to "tribal" peoples, solidarism sanctioned a timeless ("synchronic"), homeostatic, explicitly organismic view of exploited colonial populations. All social facts were analyzed from the point of view of their contribution to the maintenance of the solidary relations of the existing social structure. Neither conflict nor change were completely ignored; what was ignored was the system-destroying effects of change and conflict.[1] This mode of analysis survived the contradictory evidence of historical events until the end of the colonial period.

The international influence of Durkheim's solidarism was not confined

[1] As Goody (1973:208) acknowledges, "Harris himself realizes the statement that British anthropologists were uninterested in history is bunk." I not only realized it; I stressed it (Harris 1968:540). However, I also stressed the idiographic nature of their interest (Harris 1968:540).

to British social anthropology. Synchronic solidarist–structuralism was celebrated during precisely the same period and on a bigger scale in the United States. However, its dominion lay not within American anthropology, but within American sociology. Its chief exponent was Talcott Parsons, the institutionally most influential of all twentieth-century American sociologists.

Distinguishing his position with respect to Marx and Weber on the issue of the nature of modern societies, Parsons writes, "The principal point of reference for a different view in my case has been the work of Durkheim, notably his conception of organic solidarity [1970:855]." The British anthropological solidarists and the American sociological solidarists soon discovered each other, acknowledged their mutual significance and even adopted the same scholastic emblem:

> The physiological conception (of homeostasis) articulated . . . directly with the functional perspective then prevalent in the thinking of social anthropologists, especially A. R. Radcliffe-Brown and his followers. . . . Radcliffe-Brown was much influenced by Durkheim and came into my orbit by that route. For a considerable time, Merton and I came to be known as the leaders of a structural–functional school among American sociologists [Parsons 1970:849].

Structural–Functionalist Epistemology of Social

Anyone seeking to justify the separation of social from cultural along the lines proposed by Goodenough will find Durkheim's legacy among both British social anthropologists and American Parsonians a source of supreme intellectual vertigo. Durkheim's social facts are expressions of a postulated collective conscience. This conscience is the essence of all that is technically social—a combination of superorganic consciousness and moral imperative:

> In short, social life is nothing but the moral milieu that surrounds the individual . . . or to be more accurate, it is the sum of the moral milieus that surround the individual. By calling them moral, we mean to say that they are made up of ideas [1900:367, quoted in Turner 1977].

Durkheim's *Rules of the Sociological Method* is a consistent epistemology of emic sociocultural phenomena in which collective moral ideas, exterior to the individual, are assumed to determine thought and behavior. In other words, social for Durkheim is precisely what Goodenough means by cultural: the rules or "grammar" of social life!

At no point during the transmission of Durkheim's solidarist theories through Radcliffe-Brown and Parsons was there the slightest deviation from Durkheim's epistemology; the essence of social was never "events and their statistical patterns." For Radcliffe-Brown (1952), social structure is an arrangement of institutions and institutions do not exist without "jural norms."

In Radcliffe-Brown's paradigm of social life, actual behavior not oriented by appropriate values and rules is not part of social structure. This position is stated and restated by every modern British social anthropologist. As Nadel expressed it: "Sociologically relevant behavior is always purposive [1957:24]."

According to Lucy Mair, the orderliness in social arrangements "consists in relationships between persons that are regulated by a common body of recognized rights and obligations [1965:9]." This emphasis upon social structure as goals, norms, rights and oblilgations, and moral codes has been criticized by Raymond Firth precisely for its lack of correspondence to events and their statistical patterning:

> The introduction to *African Political Systems* (Fortes and Evans-Pritchard, eds., 1940)—a book which has had, very rightly, a powerful influence in British social anthropology—stresses how Africans could not carry on their collective life if they could not think and feel about the interests which actuate them, their institutions and their group structure; how they feel their unity and see their common interests in symbols, in the form of myths, ritual, sacred places and persons; how it is their attachment to these symbols more than anything else which gives their society cohesion and persistence; how the values expressed in these symbols are common to the whole society. The whole treatment is shot through with statements of such a psychological kind. Moreover, statements about social solidarity, social integration, and the like, seem often to involve concealed assumptions about the ends of human action which are psychological at bottom. I do not think such statements should be avoided. But I think they need validation by evidence of speech and action [1964:49].

It was to remedy this widely acknowledged defect in the structural–functionalist program that Firth developed his concept of "social organization." The latter is intended to refer to "concrete social activity" in acknowledgement of the fact that actual behavior is often at variance with social structure. But Firth merely succeeded in reducing the scale of acceptable emic and mental generalization. The essence of social order in social organization remains bound to Durkheim's super-organic moral milieu:

> Such ordering implies not simply chance patterns but reference to socially defined ends. By such coordinated, orientated activity, a society is kept in being—its members kept in relation with one another. One may describe social organization, then as the working arrangements of society. It is the processes of ordering of action and of relations in reference to given social ends, in terms of adjustments resulting from the exercise of choices by members of the society [Firth 1964].

Milton Singer (1968:531–532) has effectively disposed of the myth that Radcliffe-Brown's interest in "the concrete reality . . . of actually existing social relations" referred to a domain of inquiry epistemologically separate from that appropriate to idealist and emic cultural studies. Radcliffe-Brown states that "structured forms . . . can only be described . . . by the pattern of behavior to which individuals and groups conform. . . . These patterns are partially formulated in rules which, in our own society, we distinguish as rules of etiquette, of morals and of law [1952:198].'' Singer correctly concludes,

> At the very heart of the theory of social structure we find the concept of culture as a set of rules, implicit or explicit, of standardized modes of behavior and thought . . . the theory of social structure deals with social relations not simply as concrete actually existing objects of observation but as institutionalized and standardized modes of behavior and thought whose normal forms are socially recognized in the explicit or implicit rules to which the members of a given society tend to conform [Singer 1968:532].

The importance of rules, that is, of the ambient moral milieu, to British social anthropology, is confirmed by Edmund Leach, himself a leading British social anthropologist. Referring to Radcliffe-Brown and the British school of ''structuralists,'' Leach notes that the members of this school tended to

> concern themselves with only one formal aspect of society at a time—political structure, kinship structure, ritual organization, as the case may be. They display this system as a set of rules (jural obligations); they discuss the mutual interdependence of the rules and the fit between the society and its environment (ecology). But there is a tendency to play down any discrepancy between rule and practice [1968:484].''

The solution proposed by Leach is not to get closer to actual behavioral and etic events and conditions but to refine the logical form in which the rules are stated, specifically ''to start thinking of such rules as being of the generative kind [Leach 1968:488].'' By generative rules, Leach means the grammarian's notion of structure. This suggestion again obliterates any intelligent distinction between social and cultural.

In the case of certain ''social anthropologists'' based at Oxford, the convergence toward more thoroughly emic, idealist, linguistic, and cultural models (in Goodenough's sense) has produced a perfect unity in everything but terminology. Consider, for example, this excerpt from Pocock's *Social Anthropology:*

> The anthropologist is concerned with a systematic understanding of what he sees going on around him. He learns the culture, as he learns the language of the people. . . . The first step is to find out by participation and identification the meaning which people themselves attach to what they do. . . . In short the work of the social anthropologist may be regarded as a highly complex act of translation in which author and translator collaborate [1961:85–88].

Fortunately, there are counter-currents in British social anthropology concerned with developing methodologies appropriate to the study of personal networks and specific cases (cf. Epstein 1967). Even these efforts, however, cannot be described as being concerned primarily with etic behavioral events and their statistical pattern.

Concept of Culture Prior to 1950

Given the absence of a social anthropology concerned with behavioral events and their statistical patterns as opposed to rules and principles, how shall we account for a cultural anthropology that concerns itself exclusively with emic and mental phenomena? It is true that idealist and emic strategies dominate the history of social science in bourgeois and capitalist institutional settings (Harris 1968). But a consistent epistemological statement aimed at restricting culture to idea has developed only in the last few decades. If we seek historical precedent for culture as pure idea, we shall not find it in the work of Tylor, Boas, or the majority of American cultural anthropologists. Bock's (1968:17) attempt to use Tylor as precedent for a textbook concerned exclusively with ideational principles must be an example of what Bock calls the "freedom to believe." Bock claims that Tylor's definition shows "emphasis upon ideas and ideals." In point of fact, however, Tylor explicitly states that "culture is a subject apt for the study of laws of human thought and action [1871:1]." Moreover, like most cultural anthropologists, Tylor regarded material objects as an essential part of culture.

Indeed, the largest set of chapters in Tylor's *Anthropology* is concerned with technology, subsistence, and material items. It is difficult to suppose that Tylor intended us to view his beloved hand shuttles, crossbows, blowguns, drills, screws, water wheels, and other instruments, tools, and weapons merely as manifestations of percepts and concepts. This concern with culture as an actual tangible object was the essential ingredient in anthropology's successful institutionalization in museums of natural history and science (in which sociology departments are conspicuous by their absence). The interest in material objects was formalized in Clark Wissler's (1923) "universal cultural pattern." Culture in this scheme, consists of three main divisions: "material traits," "social activities," and "ideas." It might be possible for a logician to demonstrate the compatibility of Wissler's implicit epistemological assumptions with Bock and Goodenough's uncompromising idealism. But a more realistic view is that Wissler had no rigorous epistemological position and lacked any sense of the emic and etic alternatives and of the importance of the distinction between thought and behavior.

An additional precedent for *not* treating culture as pure idea is to be found in Ralph Linton's widely accepted distinction between ideal culture and actual culture, the difference between what people say they ought to do and what they actually are observed doing. A similar concern is evident in the work of psychologically oriented anthropologists such as Ruth Benedict and

Margaret Mead, for whom the study of deviants constitutes an important part of ethnography. Turning to Alfred Kroeber, after Boas, the greatest father figure in American anthropology, we find that as late as 1948, culture is emphatically and explicitly *not* a realm of pure idea: "The mass of learned and transmitted motor reactions, habits, techniques, ideas, and values—and the behavior they induce—is what constitutes *culture* [Kroeber 1948:8]." I conclude, therefore, that until about 1950, a majority of American cultural anthropologists favored emic operations and idealist strategies but preserved an eclectic interest in actual behavior and biophysical contexts. The concept of culture as pure idea lacked a significant clientage among anthropologists prior to that date.

Anthropology Surrenders to Talcott Parsons

Parsons' understanding of social systems involves the reduction of social life to a scheme of exclusively emic and mental actor types and emic behavior patterns. All of the data-language units of structural–functionalism are premised on the ontological saliency of rules, values, and expectations in the maintenance of given social systems. Four kinds of emic and idealist entities purportedly provide the information necessary for a description of the structure of social systems: (*a*) expectations of role-performance; (*b*) organization of plural role-units into collectivities; (*c*) patterning of rights and obligations among role and collectivity units; (*d*) the patterning of commitment to value (Parsons 1967). The last of these corresponds to what Parsons means by culture, elsewhere described as "standards of selective orientation and ordering [Parsons 1951:327]." Note that this definition of culture is indistinguishable from Goodenough's.

During the long Parsonian night, United States sociologists achieved the consensus that cultural anthropologists study a realm of pure ideas. Among sociologists this misapprehension will undoubtedly survive the destruction of the Parsonian paradigm (under equally emic and idealist auspices). For institutional and professional reasons, even Parsons' radical critics are unlikely to reject this convenient explanation of the autonomy of anthropological specialties.

Parsons, not Radcliffe-Brown, was responsible for placing the structural–functionalist restrictions on culture in the United States. While some British structural–functionalists eventually accepted the notion of culture as pure idea, Radcliffe-Brown himself maintained an ambiguous position. According to Radcliffe-Brown, social systems are composed of three parts: social structure or "the arrangements by which an orderly social life is maintained; ecology or "the way the system is adapted to the physical environment"; and culture, the "habits and mental characteristics that 'fit' the individual to social life [Radcliffe-Brown 1952:193]." In attempting to assess whether "habits" are meant to be pure idea or a combination of idea and behavior, we must remember that the definition of culture was of little interest to most British social anthropologists and that Radcliffe-Brown's epistemological pronouncements are not noted for their logical coherence.

Parsons, however, was the paramount epistemologist of the century. In 1950, he stood astride American sociology

> a motor force of great power, his continuous and pervasive productivity spread his influence into the . . . numerous subcenters with highly institutionalized training provision for postgraduate students. The enhancement of the prestige of Harvard University as a whole coincided chronologically with the prestige of the Department of Social Relations, which was largely the prestige of Talcott Parsons . . . (Shils 1970:796).

But Parsons' influence was not confined to sociology. The Department of Social Relations aimed at "integrating the theories of social structure, culture, and personality [Shils 1970:795]." Clyde Kluckhohn, one of the co-founders of the Department, upheld the anthropological interest in culture, converting it, however, to a purely emic and mental concept conforming to Parsons' scheme of social action. The most important link between Parsons and anthropology was forged by the very close intellectual and personal relationship between Kluckhohn and Kroeber during the late 1940s and 1950s. Kroeber and Kluckhohn collaborated in producing the influenctial *Culture: A Critical Review of Concepts and Definitions.*

One can only conclude that it was Parsons' influence that forced Kroeber to compromise the previously quoted position stated in 1948. Kroeber now assented to culture as consisting essentially of values:

> Patterns, explicit and implicit of and for behavior acquired and transmitted by symbols, constituting the distinctive achievement of human groups, including their embodiments in artifacts; the essential core of culture consists of traditional (i.e., historically derived and selected) ideas and especially their attached values; culture systems may, on the one hand, be considered a product of action, on the other as conditioning elements of further action [Kroeber and Kluckhohn 1952:181].

Whether culture is still to be regarded as including "motor reactions" and the behavior induced by values, is left, it would seem, deliberately ambiguous.

Somewhat later, however, Kroeber and Parsons (1958) jointly acknowledge total surrender of culture to Parsons' scheme. Parsons and Kroeber agreed that "Comte and Spencer, and Weber and Durkheim spoke of society as meaning essentially the same thing that Tylor meant by culture." The time had come, however, to end "this condensed concept of culture-and-society because . . . we believe that knowledge and interests have become sufficiently differentiated so that further distinctions need to be made and stabilized in the routine usage of the relevant professional groups." The reigning academic popes of sociology and anthropology proceeded virtually by incantation to exorcize the last devils of behavior from the culture concept:

> We suggest that it is useful to define the concept culture for most usages more narrowly than has been generally the case in the American anthropological tradition, restricting its reference to transmitted and created content and patterns of values, ideas, and other symbolic-meaningful systems as factors in the shaping of human behavior and the artifacts produced through behavior [Kroeber and Parsons 1958:583].

Because of the nature of Parsons' "social system," Kroeber's surrender went even further than conversion to culture-as-pure-idea. It was to be ideas exclusive of what Parsons meant by social system, namely, "the specifically relational system of interaction among individuals and collectivities [Kroeber and Parsons 1958:583]." This "system of interaction" as we have seen, is also pure idea. Never has there been an intellectual program more calculated to obscure and confuse students and laymen about the nature of sociocultural processes.

It should also be noted that some of Parsons' students in the Department of Social Relations were anthropologists who journeyed to England to learn more about British social anthropology. It is this sequence that accounts for David Schneider's inflated confidence in a book about kinship ideology in the United States, subtitled "A Cultural Account." The occurrence of actual cases, Schneider declares, "is quite irrelevant to the question of whether there is or is not a cultural entity [1968:7]." Parsons (1970:859) in commending this book refers to Schneider as "my old student and friend."

Influence of Linguistics

The spread of the Parsonian idealist epistemology of culture converged with the development of more or less sophisticated anthropological methodologies appropriate for cognitive analysis. Linguistics furnished the main stimulus for this development both in the United States and France. In the United States, concepts useful for the establishment of phonological contrasts and phonemic systems provide the basis for componential analysis. The term "componential analysis," itself introduced into cultural anthropology by Ward Goodenough, derives from Zelig Harris who used it to denote distinctive categories of sound and meaning (cf. Goodenough 1968:186). Somewhat later, Chomsky's tranformational–generative treatment of grammar served as the model for transformational analyses of kinship. Chomsky's influence has also been effective in removing neo-Bloomfieldian and behaviorist taboos about trying "to get inside the people's heads." Chomsky's concept of "deep structure" in grammatical analysis has inspired members of the formalist school to view culture as a set of rules or a code for generating behavior judged appropriate by natives possessing "competence" in the culture (cf. Hymes 1968).

Influence of French Structuralism

Converging with Parsons, Chomsky, Goodenough, Schneider, and others to drive behavior out of anthropology comes Claude Lévi-Strauss. For the world's most famous male anthropologist, "the final aim of anthropology is to contribute to a better knowledge of objectified thought [1969:13]." Far from studying behavior, Lévi-Strauss and his epigones are convinced that the empirical substance of social life in its entirety should remain beyond concern: "Social structure . . . has nothing to do with empirical reality . . . [Lévi-Strauss 1963:279]" Structuralism disposes of the problem of prediction, verifiability, and intersubjectivity as well as the problem of behavior by confining itself to "mechanical models" as opposed to "statistical models" (Lévi-Strauss 1963:283).

However Lévi-Strauss has associated mechanical models with social structure rather than with culture since the social of Comte and Durkheim still prevails in France. The American cognitive formalists and grammarians have not failed to benefit from the immense prestige associated with Lévi-Strauss' literary and philosophical fame and they have recognized the affinity between mechanical models and their own nonstatistical grammarian approach to culture. I am at a loss, therefore, to explain how Goodenough (1969:329) can offer Lévi-Strauss's work as an example of social as opposed to cultural anthropology!

Conclusions: Durkheim, Structuralism, and Cognitivism

Despite the fact that structuralists, cognitivists, and structural–functionalists are often critical of each other's research strategies and theories, they all have common roots in Durkheim. I have already described the continuity between Durkheim and the structural–functionalists (Radcliffe-Brown and Parsons). The connection between Durkheim and Lévi-Strauss is just as strong and acknowledged by Lévi-Strauss himself (Harris 1968:484) although he gives greater credit to Mauss, Durkheim's prize student. But the basic idea of Lévi-Strauss' structures can readily be found in Durkheim's later work. For example, in the *Elementary Forms of Religious Life,* Durkheim wrote:

> The collective conscience is the highest form of psychic life, since it is the consciousness of consciousness. Being placed outside and above individual and local contingencies, it sees things only in their permanent and essential aspects, which it crystallizes into communicable ideas. At . . . every moment of time it embraces all

> known reality; that is why it alone can furnish the mind with the moulds which are applicable to the totality of things and which make it possible to think of them [1914:444].

Like Durkheim, Lévi-Strauss believes that the mind has molds and that these molds make it possible to think about the totality of things. Indeed structuralist "structures" are nothing but the most fundamental molds which govern thought cast in the form of binary oppositions because of the way the human brain is allegedly "wired."

The connection between Lévi-Strauss's notion of structure and Durkheim's collective consciousness is better known than the connection between the latter and the American cognitivist notion of a grammar of culture. Yet Lévi-Strauss himself has always acknowledged a large debt to linguistics, especially to Ferdinand de Saussure, founder of the structural school of linguistics, and the followers of Saussure, such as Trubetskoy and Jakobson (Lévi-Strauss 1963). A contemporary of Durkheim, Saussure is best remembered for his distinction between *langue* and *parole;* language in its collective essence as distinct from language in its spoken manifestations—a distinction that has evolved in Chomsky's poststructuralist grammarian vocabulary into native "competence" versus "performance."

For Saussure and his followers up through Chomsky, it has been the study of *langue* and competence rather than *parole* and performance that has been seen as the true linguistic calling, just as for Lévi-Strauss it is the mechanical rather than the statistical model that deserves emphasis. But what was Saussure trying to do in making his famous distinction? According to Dell Hymes (1968:355), Saussure was greatly impressed with Durkheim's success in identifying social facts and wanted to do the same for linguistics—wanted to identify the collective unconscious rules and molds, the structure of *langue.* So out of Durkheim's anti-Marxist vision of a solidary moral realm of social facts there arose not only the British and American structural–functionalists and the French structuralists as well, but the entire tribe of American grammarians, cultural and linguistic, all equally ill-disposed toward the etic actuality of flesh and blood human behavior.

The idealist expropriation of culture is thus not a matter of whim or taste (who cares what you call it), but an emergent product of definite structural and infrastructural conditions. It fulfills the conservative bias inherent in university-sponsored American social science. The fact that individual anthropologists may engage in left-liberal or radical politics whereas their professional activities are yoked to a grammarian's paradigm does not alter the politico-ideological thrust of emicized and mentalistic cultural anthropology (cf. Hymes 1972). (What this paradox confirms is the lack of theory in the practice of radical and left-liberal politics.) It does not alleviate the massive ideological occlusion associated with solidarist structural–functionalist, structuralist, and grammarian principles.

The American grammarians belong to an intellectual tradition unrelated in a narrowly conventional historical sense to Parsons, Radcliffe-Brown, or

Durkheim (except through Saussure), but formal analysis and structural–functionalism are nomothetically convergent and functionally equivalent expressions of the same conservative thrust. Like the structuralists and structural-functionalists, the American grammarians accept the system as given and seek to account for its stability. This synchronic bias protects them from the obligation of predicting or retrodicting sociocultural transformations. Indeed, because of the epistemological clarity of the linguistic model, the American grammarians go even further than the structuralists or structural–functionalists in avoiding contact with etic behavioral events. They not only renounce prediction but by assigning etic and behavioral phenomena to a nonexistent subfield, they even relieve themselves of having to say what is happening in the present (cf. Fisher and Werner 1978).

Again, like the structural–functionalists, the grammarians offer a consensus theory of social structure. Their linguistic paradigm reaffirms Durkheim's collective conscience. Organic solidarity gives way to a homogeneous mental field possessing deep structures that organize the consensus of all "competent natives." All sociocultural phenomena are to be "accounted for" in terms of this society-wide consensus; dissensus and incompetent natives are epiphenomenal. Never has there been a sociocultural paradigm better calculated to avoid the study of conflict and political–economic process. The subjects prohibited to "modern cultural anthropology" are the guts of contemporary life. The grammarian's "competent natives" rules and codes cannot account for phenomena such as poverty, underdevelopment, imperialism, the population explosion, ethnic and class conflict, pollution and depletion of the environment, exploitation, unemployment, inflation, political repression, crime, urban blight, and war. These phenomena are the consequence of intersecting and contradictory vectors of belief, wills, and power. Hence, they cannot be scientifically understood as manifestations of codes, rules, or "structures."

One can only conclude therefore, that the emergence of the distinction between social and cultural anthropology and of the concept of culture as pure idea has a significance that would not have eluded Durkheim, however much those he most influenced seem to remain oblivious to it. By deflecting anthropological inquiry away from the actonic core of social life, all these wonderfully convergent strategies of consensus, competence, and mental structures, bid one join Durkheim in his mystical awe of the coercive strength of collective consciousness. Provided of course, that one understands with Marx that this unconscious systemic conspiracy does not serve the solidary needs of the entire social body but only certain previleged sectors thereof.

References

Bock, P.
1968 *Modern cultural anthropology*. New York: Random House.

Casey, C.
1924 The culture concept in social science. *Journal of Applied Sociology* 8:146–155.

Durkheim, E.
1914 *The elementary forms of religious life.* London: Allen and Unwin.
Epstein, A. L. (Ed.)
1967 *The craft of social anthropology.* London: Tavistock Publication.
Firth, R.
1964 *Essays on social organization and values.* London: Athlone.
1970 *A brief history (1913–1963).* Department of Anthropology 1970–1971, The London School of Economics and Political Science: 3–10.
Fisher, L., and O. Werner
1978 Explaining explanation: Tension in American anthropology. *Journal of Anthropological Research 34*(2):194–218.
Goldenweiser, A.
1922 *Early civilization: An introduction to anthropology.* New York: Alfred Knopf.
Goodenough, W.
1968 Componential analysis. *Encyclopedia of the Social Sciences 3*:186–192.
1969 Frontiers of cultural anthropology: Social organization. *Proceedings of the American Philosophical Society 113*:329–335.
Goody, J.
1973 British functionalism. In *Main currents in cultural anthropology* (R. Naroll and F. Naroll, Eds.). New York: Appleton-Century-Crofts. Pp. 185–215.
Gray, D.
1924 The developing study of culture In *Trends in American Sociology* (G. Lundberg *et al.*, Eds.). New York: Harper and Row: Pp. 177–220.
Harris, M.
1968 *The rise of anthropological theory.* New York: Thomas Y. Crowell.
Hymes, D.
1968 Linguistics: The field. *Encyclopedia of the Social Sciences 9*:351–369.
Kroeber, A.
1948 *Anthropology.* New York: Harcourt, Brace.
Kroeber, A. and C. Kluckholn
1952 *Culture: A critical review of concepts and definitions.* Harvard University, Papers of the Peabody Museum of American Archaeology and Ethnology: 47.
Kroeber, A. and T. Parsons
1958 The concept of culture and of social system. *American Sociological Review 23*:582–583.
Leach, E.
1968 Social structure, *International Encyclopedia of the Social Sciences 14*:482–489.
Lévi-Strauss, C.
1963 *Structural anthropology.* New York: Doubleday.
1969 *The raw and the cooked.* New York: Harper and Row.
Leinhardt, G.
1964 *Social Anthropology.* London: Oxford University Press.
Lowie, R.
1920 *Primitive society.* New York: Boni and Liveright.
Mair, L.
1965 *An introduction to social anthropology.* Oxford: Clarendon Press.
Nadel, S. F.
1957 *The theory of social structure.* London: Cohen and Ward.
Parsons, T.
1951 *The social system.* Glencoe: The Free Press.
1967 Sociological theory. *Encyclopedia Britannica 20*:799–802.
1970 On building social system theory: A personal history. *Daedalus,* Fall:826–831.
Pocock, D. F.
1961 *Social anthropology.* London: Sheed and Ward.

Radcliffe-Brown, A. R.
1952 *Structure and function in primitive society.* New York: The Free Press.

Radin, P.
1932 *Social anthropology.* New York: McGraw-Hill.

Reiss, A.
1968 Sociology: The field, *International Encyclopedia of the Social Sciences 15*:1–23.

Schneider, D.
1968 *American kinship: A cultural account.* Englewood Cliffs: Prentice-Hall.

Shils, E.
1970 Tradition, ecology, and institution in the history of sociology. *Daedalus 99*:760–825.

Singer, M.
1968 The concept of culture. *International Encyclopedia of Social Sciences 3*:527–543.

Spencer, H.
1896 *Principles of sociology.* New York: D. Appleton. (Originally published, 1876.)
1873 *The study of sociology.* New York: D. Appleton.

Turner, B.
1977 *The social origins of academic sociology: Durkheim.* Ph.D. dissertation, Columbia University.

Tylor, E. B.
1871 *Primitive culture: researches into the development of mythology, religion, language, art and custom.* London. J. Murray.

Wissler, C.
1923 *Man and culture.* New York: Thomas Y. Crowell.

Subject Index

E

F

R

S

T

U

STUDIES IN ANTHROPOLOGY

Under the Consulting Editorship of E. A. Hammel,
UNIVERSITY OF CALIFORNIA, BERKELEY

Andrei Simić, THE PEASANT URBANITES: A Study of Rural-Urban Mobility in Serbia

John U. Ogbu, THE NEXT GENERATION: An Ethnography of Education in an Urban Neighborhood

Bennett Dyke and Jean Walters MacCluer (Eds.), COMPUTER SIMULATION IN HUMAN POPULATION STUDIES

Robbins Burling, THE PASSAGE OF POWER: Studies in Political Succession

Piotr Sztompka, SYSTEM AND FUNCTION: Toward a Theory of Society

William G. Lockwood, EUROPEAN MOSLEMS: Economy and Ethnicity in Western Bosnia

Günter Golde, CATHOLICS AND PROTESTANTS: Agricultural Modernization in Two German Villages

Peggy Reeves Sanday (Ed.), ANTHROPOLOGY AND THE PUBLIC INTEREST: Fieldwork and Theory

Carol A. Smith (Ed.), REGIONAL ANALYSIS, Volume I: Economic Systems, and Volume II: Social Systems

Raymond D. Fogelson and Richard N. Adams (Eds.), THE ANTHROPOLOGY OF POWER: Ethnographic Studies from Asia, Oceania, and the New World

Frank Henderson Stewart, FUNDAMENTALS OF AGE-GROUP SYSTEMS

Larissa Adler Lomnitz, NETWORKS AND MARGINALITY: Life in a Mexican Shantytown

Benjamin S. Orlove, ALPACAS, SHEEP, AND MEN: The Wool Export Economy and Regional Society in Southern Peru

Harriet Ngubane, BODY AND MIND IN ZULU MEDICINE: An Ethnography of Health and Disease in Nyuswa-Zulu Thought and Practice

George M. Foster, Thayer Scudder, Elizabeth Colson, and Robert Van Kemper (Eds.), LONG-TERM FIELD RESEARCH IN SOCIAL ANTHROPOLOGY

R. H. Hook (Ed.), FANTASY AND SYMBOL: Studies in Anthropological Interpretation

Richard Tapper, PASTURE AND POLITICS: Economics, Conflict and Ritual Among Shahsevan Nomads of Northwestern Iran

George Bond, Walton Johnson, and Sheila S. Walker (Eds.), AFRICAN CHRISTIANITY: Patterns of Religious Continuity

John Comaroff (Ed.), THE MEANING OF MARRIAGE PAYMENTS

Michael H. Agar, THE PROFESSIONAL STRANGER: An Informal Introduction to Ethnography

Robert J. Thornton, SPACE, TIME, AND CULTURE AMONG THE IRAQW OF TANZANIA

Linda S. Cordell and Stephen Beckerman (Eds.), THE VERSATILITY OF KINSHIP

Peggy F. Barlett (Ed.), AGRICULTURAL DECISION MAKING: Anthropological Contributions to Rural Development

Thayer Scudder and Elizabeth Colson, SECONDARY EDUCATION AND THE FORMATION OF AN ELITE: The Impact of Education on Gwembe District, Zambia

Eric B. Ross (Ed.), BEYOND THE MYTHS OF CULTURE: Essays in Cultural Materialism

in preparation

Gerald D. Berreman (Ed.), SOCIAL INEQUALITY: Comparative and Developmental Approaches